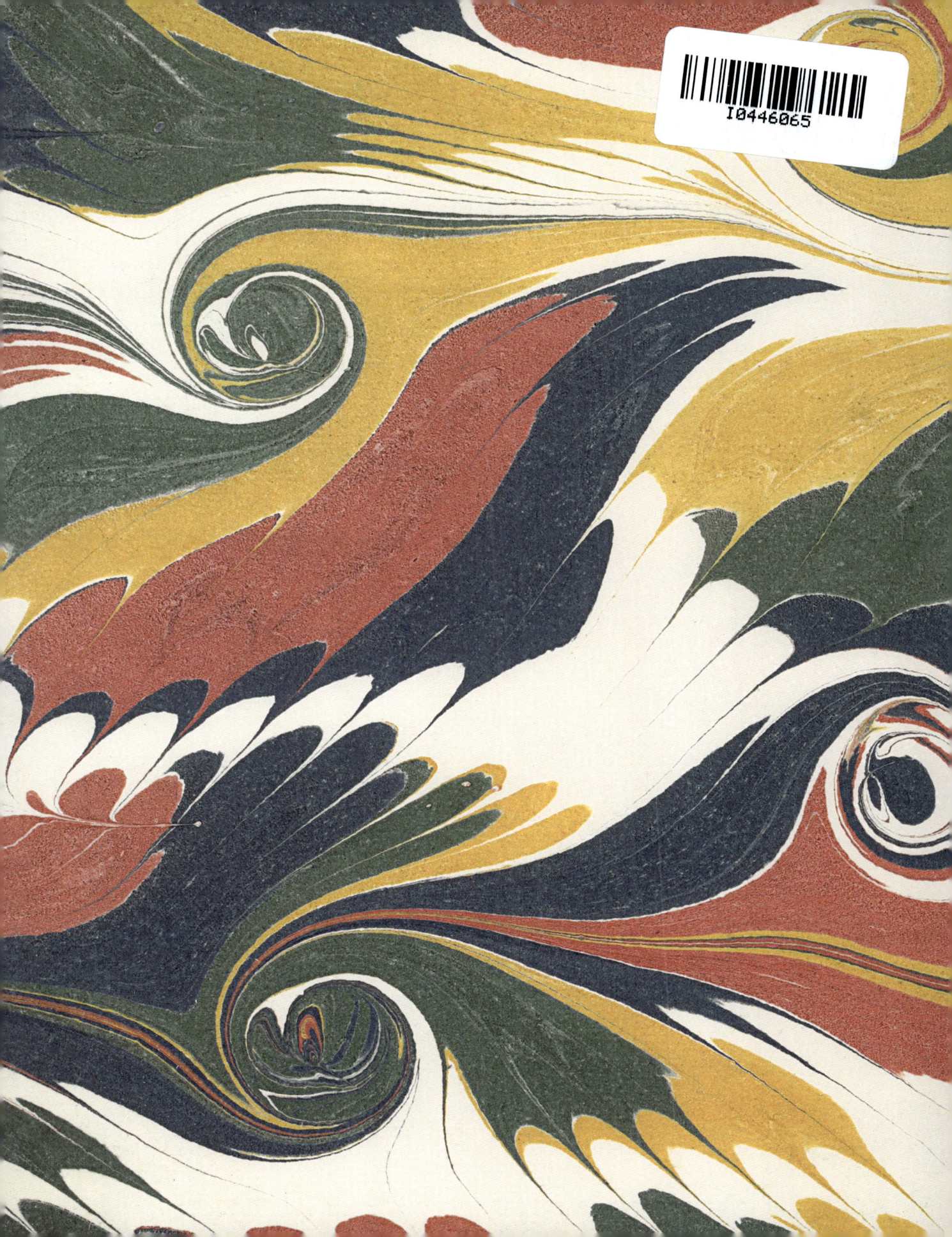

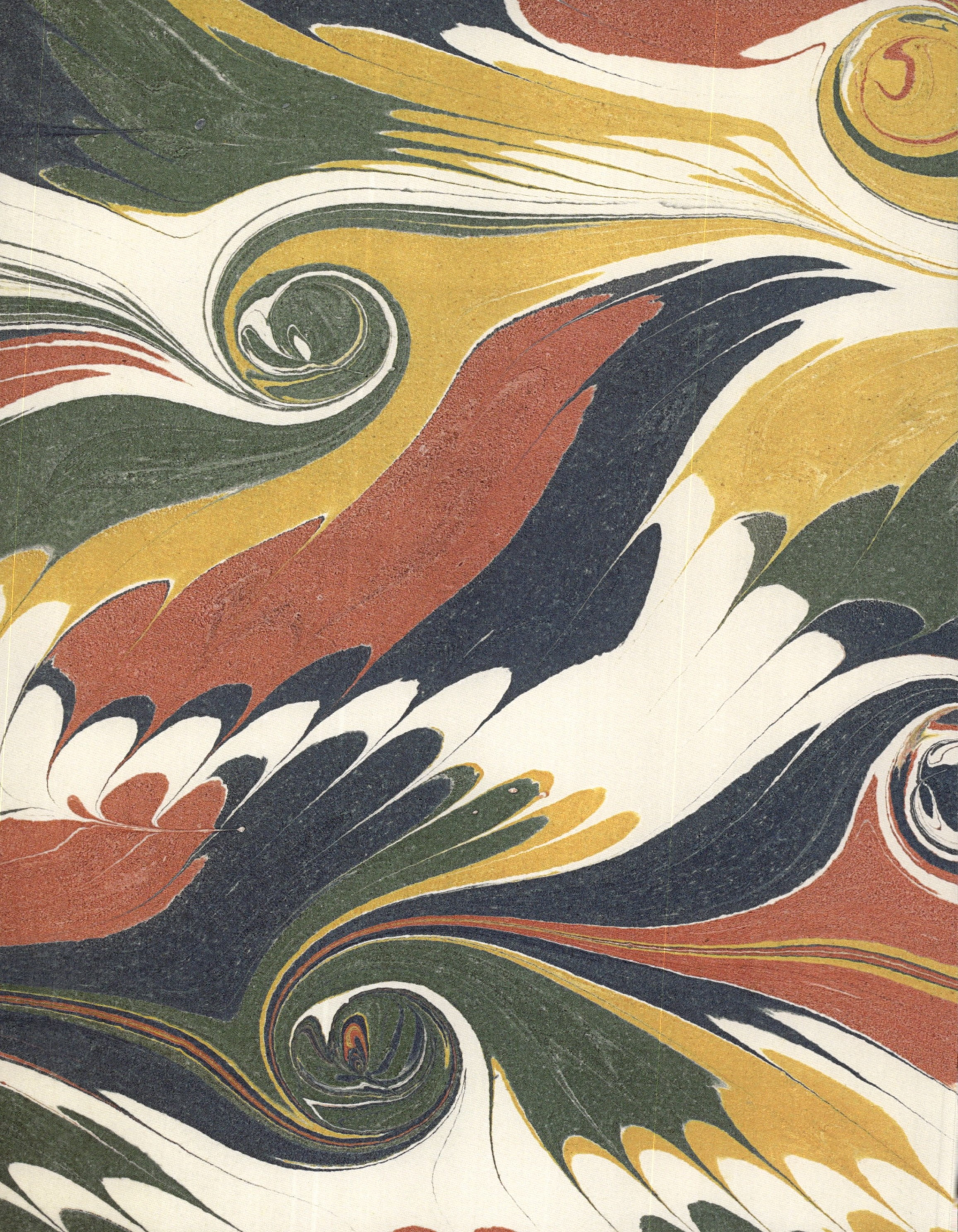

NATURE'S PALETTE.

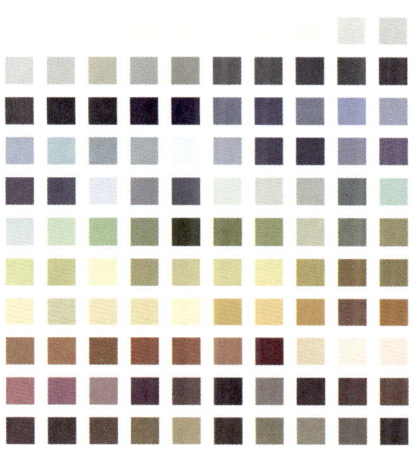

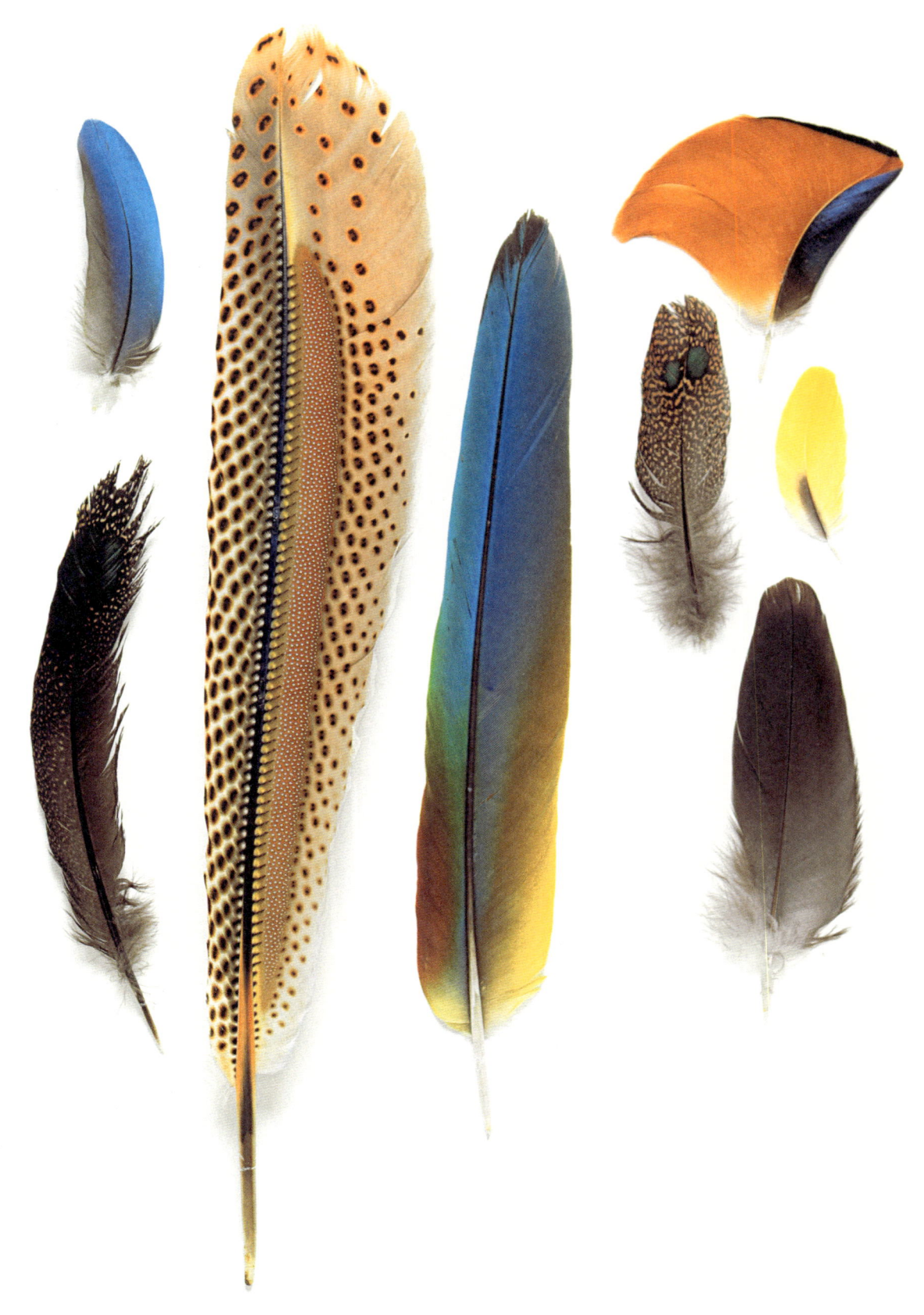

NATURE'S PALETTE.

**A COLOR REFERENCE SYSTEM
FROM THE NATURAL WORLD.**

WITH 1,000 ILLUSTRATIONS.

Princeton University Press
Princeton and Oxford

COLOURS.

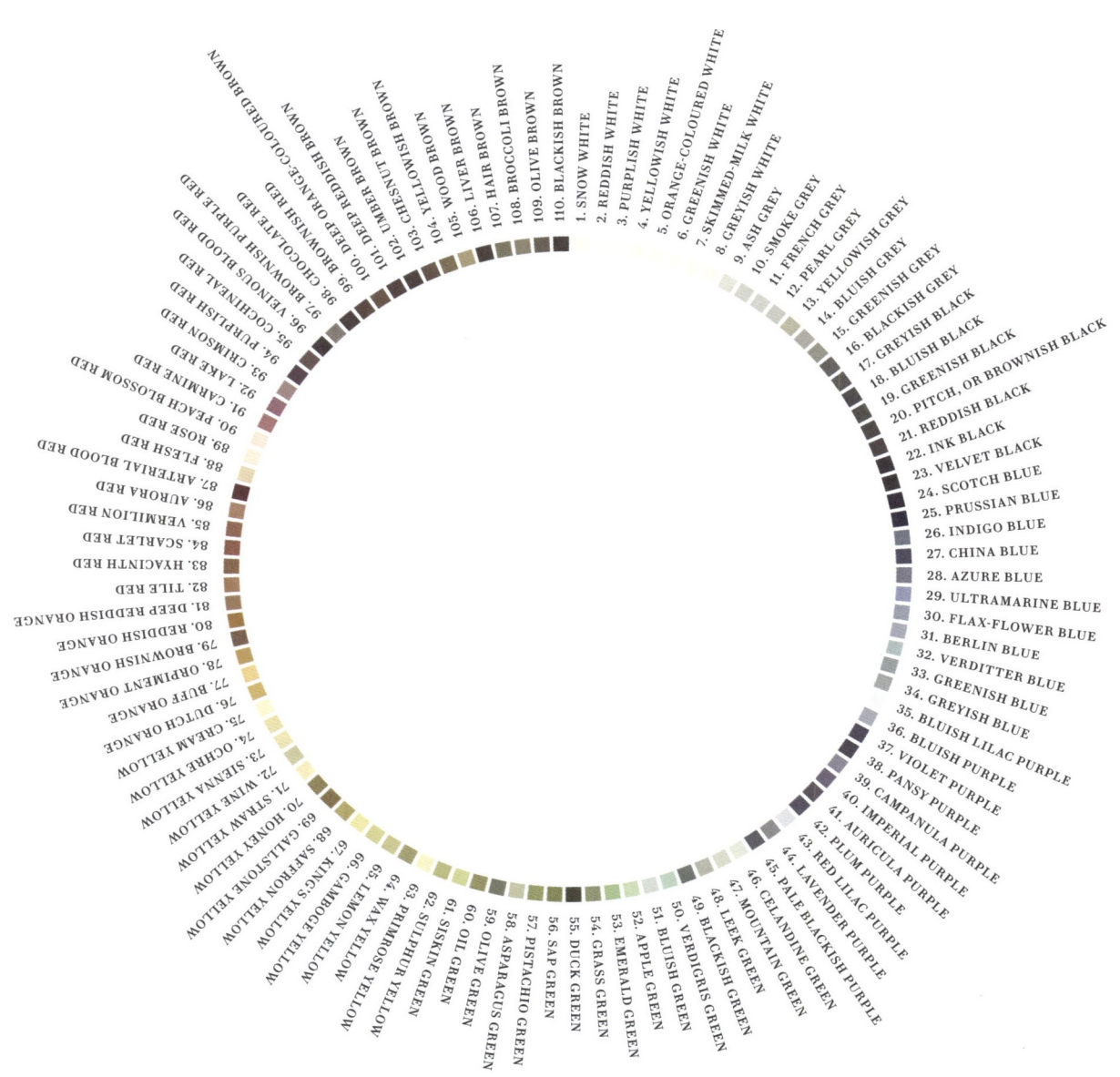

1. SNOW WHITE
2. REDDISH WHITE
3. PURPLISH WHITE
4. YELLOWISH WHITE
5. ORANGE-COLOURED WHITE
6. GREENISH WHITE
7. SKIMMED-MILK WHITE
8. GREYISH WHITE
9. ASH GREY
10. SMOKE GREY
11. FRENCH GREY
12. PEARL GREY
13. YELLOWISH GREY
14. BLUISH GREY
15. GREENISH GREY
16. BLACKISH GREY
17. GREYISH BLACK
18. BLUISH BLACK
19. GREENISH BLACK
20. PITCH, OR BROWNISH BLACK
21. REDDISH BLACK
22. INK BLACK
23. VELVET BLACK
24. SCOTCH BLUE
25. PRUSSIAN BLUE
26. INDIGO BLUE
27. CHINA BLUE
28. AZURE BLUE
29. ULTRAMARINE BLUE
30. FLAX-FLOWER BLUE
31. BERLIN BLUE
32. VERDITTER BLUE
33. GREENISH BLUE
34. GREYISH BLUE
35. BLUISH LILAC PURPLE
36. BLUISH PURPLE
37. VIOLET PURPLE
38. PANSY PURPLE
39. CAMPANULA PURPLE
40. IMPERIAL PURPLE
41. AURICULA PURPLE
42. PLUM PURPLE
43. RED LILAC PURPLE
44. LAVENDER PURPLE
45. PALE BLACKISH PURPLE
46. CELANDINE GREEN
47. MOUNTAIN GREEN
48. LEEK GREEN
49. BLACKISH GREEN
50. VERDIGRIS GREEN
51. BLUISH GREEN
52. APPLE GREEN
53. EMERALD GREEN
54. GRASS GREEN
55. DUCK GREEN
56. SAP GREEN
57. PISTACHIO GREEN
58. ASPARAGUS GREEN
59. OLIVE GREEN
60. OIL GREEN
61. SISKIN GREEN
62. SULPHUR GREEN
63. PRIMROSE YELLOW
64. WAX YELLOW
65. LEMON YELLOW
66. CAMBOGE YELLOW
67. KING'S YELLOW
68. SAFFRON YELLOW
69. GALLSTONE YELLOW
70. HONEY YELLOW
71. STRAW YELLOW
72. WINE YELLOW
73. SIENNA YELLOW
74. OCHRE YELLOW
75. CREAM YELLOW
76. DUTCH ORANGE
77. BUFF ORANGE
78. ORPIMENT ORANGE
79. BROWNISH ORANGE
80. REDDISH ORANGE
81. DEEP REDDISH ORANGE
82. TILE RED
83. HYACINTH RED
84. SCARLET RED
85. VERMILION RED
86. AURORA RED
87. ARTERIAL BLOOD RED
88. FLESH RED
89. ROSE RED
90. PEACH BLOSSOM RED
91. CARMINE RED
92. LAKE RED
93. CRIMSON RED
94. PURPLISH RED
95. COCHINEAL RED
96. VEINOUS BLOOD RED
97. BROWNISH PURPLE RED
98. CHOCOLATE RED
99. BROWNISH RED
100. DEEP REDDISH BROWN
101. DEEP ORANGE-COLOURED BROWN
102. CHESTNUT BROWN
103. YELLOWISH BROWN
104. WOOD BROWN
105. LIVER BROWN
106. HAIR BROWN
107. BROCCOLI BROWN
108. OLIVE BROWN
109. BLACKISH BROWN
110.

CONTENTS.

A COLOUR REFERENCE SYSTEM FROM THE NATURAL WORLD.

In 1774, in order to help identify and describe minerals, German geologist Abraham Gottlob Werner devised a classification system based on the external properties of minerals. He considered colour to be one of the key characteristics for mineral identification and devised a nomenclature of 54 colours for that purpose, assembling a collection of minerals as physical examples of each. Werner revised and expanded his nomenclature during the next 40 or so years, and periodically gave updated lists to his students, who used and added to them in their own works. In 1814 Scottish artist Patrick Syme expanded Werner's nomenclature to 108 colour terms and then in 1821 to 110. He supplemented Werner's references to mineral examples with references to animal and vegetable species, and added a painted swatch for each of the colour standards named.

On these pages are displayed the 13 colour plates from Syme's second edition of *Werner's Nomenclature of Colours* (1821), which presents each of Syme's 110 colour standard terms alongside a painted swatch, and, in most cases, reference to an animal, vegetable and mineral example that exhibits that colour. The colour standards are organized into ten groups: whites, greys, blacks, blues, purples, greens, yellows, orange, red and browns. On pages 8–9, Werner's complete mineral collection is displayed, each mineral accompanied by a colour swatch and name taken from Syme's second edition.

In *Nature's Palette* Syme's work has been fully realized and enhanced. An individual page is devoted to each colour standard and contemporary illustrations of every animal, vegetable and mineral referenced by Syme presented. In cases where he did not suggest an example, this volume provides one (indicated by *), completing Syme's colour reference system. Syme's colour swatch, original references and colour description appear at the top of each entry; he added a [W] to indicate that the colour name could be found in Werner's original or subsequent lists. Please note that over time, the colours in Syme's swatches and in the illustration plates have become more muted. Supplementing these pages are displays of 19th-century naturalists' collections in which each specimen has been paired with one of Syme's standard colours to demonstrate how the system might be used by naturalists and artists.

WHITES, GREYS AND BLACKS. *(pages 36 to 73).*

BLUES AND PURPLES. *(pages 88 to 121).*

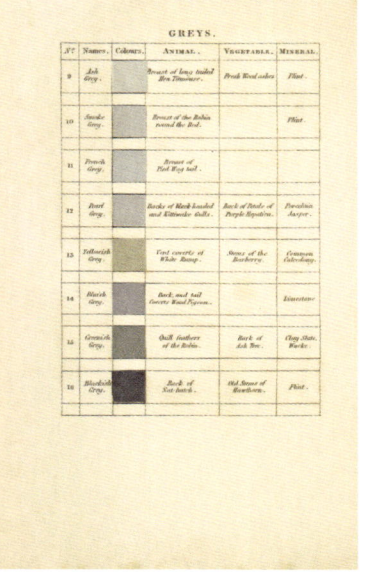

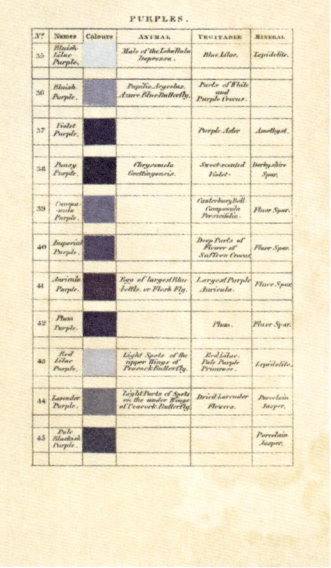

NOTES
Throughout the book we have retained Syme's idiosyncratic spellings of 'Verditter' and 'Chesnut' when referring to colour numbers 32 and 103.

Although Syme listed colour number 109 as 'Clove Brown' in plate 13 (far right), he referred to the same colour as 'Olive Brown' in the accompanying description on the adjacent page and when referring to the colour elsewhere. He regarded the two names as interchangeable. We have used the name 'Olive Brown' when referring to this colour throughout the book as that is the name he used most often.

GREENS.

Nº	Names	Colours	ANIMAL	VEGETABLE	MINERAL
46	Celandine Green.		Phalœna Margaritaria.	Back of Tussilago Leaves.	Beryl.
47	Mountain Green.		Phalœna Viridaria.	Thick-leaved Cudweed. Silver-leaved Almond.	Actynolite Beryl.
48	Leek Green.			Sea Kale. Leaves of Leeks in Winter.	Actynolite Prase.
49	Blackish Green.		Elytra of Melœ Violaceus.	Dark Streaks on Leaves of Cayenne Pepper.	Serpentine.
50	Verdigris Green.		Tail of small Long-tailed Green Parrot.		Copper Green.
51	Bluish Green.		Eggs of Thrush.	Under Disk of Wild Rose leaves.	Beryl.
52	Apple Green.		Under Side of Wings of Green Broom Moth.		Chrysoprase.
53	Emerald Green.		Beauty Spot on Wing of Teal Drake.		Emerald.

GREENS.

Nº	Names	Colours	ANIMAL	VEGETABLE	MINERAL
54	Grass Green.		Scarabœus Nobilis.	General Appearance of Grass Fields. Sweet Sugar Pear.	Uran Mica.
55	Duck Green.		Neck of Mallard.	Upper Disk or Yew Leaves.	Cryphodite.
56	Sap Green.		Under Side of lower Wings of Orange tip Butterfly.	Upper Disk of Leaves of woody Nightshade.	
57	Pistachio Green.		Neck of Eider Drake.	Ripe Pound Pear. Hypnum like Saxifrage.	Chrysolite.
58	Asparagus Green.		Brimstone Butterfly.	Variegated Horse-Shoe Geranium.	Beryl.
59	Olive Green.			Foliage of Lignum vitæ.	Epidote Olivine Ore.
60	Oil Green.		Animal and Shell of common Water Snail.	Nonpareil Apple from the Wall.	Beryl.
61	Siskin Green.		Siskin.	Ripe Colmar Pear. Irish Pitcher Apple.	Uran Mica.

YELLOWS.

Nº	Names	Colours	ANIMAL	VEGETABLE	MINERAL
62	Sulphur Yellow.		Yellow Parts of large Dragon Fly.	Various Coloured Snap-dragons.	Sulphur.
63	Primrose Yellow.		Pale Canary Bird.	Wild Primrose.	Pale coloured Sulphur.
64	Wax Yellow.		Larvæ of large Water Beetle.	Greenish Parts of Nonpareil Apple.	Semi-Opal.
65	Lemon Yellow.		Large Wasp or Hornet.	Shrubby Goldilocks.	Yellow Orpiment.
66	Gamboge Yellow.		Wings of Goldfinch. Canary Bird.	Yellow Jasmine.	High coloured Sulphur.
67	King's Yellow.		Head of Golden Pheasant.	Yellow Tulip. Cinque Foil.	
68	Saffron Yellow.		Tail Coverts of Golden Pheasant.	Anthers of Saffron Crocus.	

YELLOWS.

Nº	Names	Colours	ANIMAL	VEGETABLE	MINERAL
69	Gallstone Yellow.		Gallstone.	Marigold Apple.	
70	Honey Yellow.		Lower Parts of Neck of Bird of Paradise.		Fluor Spar.
71	Straw Yellow.		Polar Bear.	Oat Straw.	Nakerlite. Calamine.
72	Wine Yellow.		Body of Silk Moth.	White Currants.	Saxon Topaz.
73	Sienna Yellow.		Foot Parts of Tail of Bird of Paradise.	Stamina of Honey-suckle.	Pale Brown Spanish Topaz.
74	Ochre Yellow.		Foot Coverts of Red Start.		Porcelain Jasper.
75	Cream Yellow.		Breast of Teal Drake.		Porcelain Jasper.

ORANGE.

Nº	Names	Colours	ANIMAL	VEGETABLE	MINERAL
76	Dutch Orange.		Crest of Golden crested Wren.	Common Marigold. Seed-pod of Spindle tree.	Streak of Red Orpiment.
77	Buff Orange.		Streak from the Eye of the King Fisher.	Stamina of the large White Cistus.	Natrolite.
78	Orpiment Orange.		The Neck Ruff of the Golden Pheasant, in 3 or the Forty Nine.	Indian Cress.	
79	Brownish Orange.		Eyes of the largest Flesh-Fly.	Style of the Orange Lily.	Dark Brazilian Topaz.
80	Reddish Orange.		Lower Wings of Tiger Moth.	Hemimeris. Buff Hibiscus.	
81	Deep Reddish Orange.		Gold Fish lustre abstracted.	Scarlet Lewdington Apple.	

RED.

Nº	Names	Colours	ANIMAL	VEGETABLE	MINERAL
82	Tile Red.		Breast of the Cock Bullfinch.	Shrubby Pimpernel.	Porcelain Jasper.
83	Hyacinth Red.		Red Spots of the Lygœus Apterus Fly.	Red on the golden Rennette Apple.	Hyacinth.
84	Scarlet Red.		Scarlet Ibis, or Curlew. Mark on Head of Red Grouse.	Large Oriental Poppy. Red Parts of red and black Indian Pea.	Light red Cinnabar.
85	Vermillion Red.		Red Coral.	Love Apple.	Cinnabar.
86	Aurora Red.		Vent coverts of Pied Wood Pecker.	Red on the Naked Apple.	Red Orpiment.
87	Arterial Blood Red.		Head of the Cock Gold Finch.	Corn Poppy. Cherry.	
88	Flesh Red.		Human Skin.	Larkspur.	Heavy Spar. Limestone.
89	Rose Red.			Common Garden Rose.	Figure Stone.
90	Peach Blossom Red.			Peach Blossom.	Red Cobalt Ore.

RED.

Nº	Names	Colours	ANIMAL	VEGETABLE	MINERAL
91	Carmine Red.			Raspberry. Cocks Comb. Carnation Pink.	Oriental Ruby.
92	Lake Red.			Red Tulip. Rose Officinalis.	Spinel.
93	Crimson Red.				Precious Garnet.
94	Purplish Red.		Outside of Quills of Tail Feathers of Grou.	Dark Crimson Officinal Garden Rose.	Precious Garnet.
95	Cochineal Red.			Under Side of decayed leaves of Rose-pretty.	Dark Columbine.
96	Veinous Blood Red.		Veinous Blood.	Black Flower or dark Purple Anthemis.	Pyrope.
97	Brownish Purple Red.			Flower of deadly Nightshade.	Red Antimony Ore.
98	Chocolate Red.		Breast of Bird of Paradise.	Brown Disk of common Marigold.	
99	Brownish Red.		Neck on Throat of Red-throated Diver.		Iron Flint.

BROWNS.

Nº	Names	Colours	ANIMAL	VEGETABLE	MINERAL
100	Deep Orange-coloured Brown.		Head of Pochard, Wing coverts of Sholdrake.	Female Spike of Cattail Reed.	
101	Deep Reddish Brown.		Breast of Pochard, and Neck of Teal Drake.	Dead Leaves of green Panic Grass.	Brown Blende.
102	Umber Brown.		Moor Buzzard.	Disk of Rudvetia.	
103	Chesnut Brown.		Neck and Breast of Red Grouse.	Chesnuts.	Egyptian Jasper.
104	Yellowish Brown.		Light Brown Spots on Guinea-Pig. Breast of Snipe.		Iron Flint and common Jasper.
105	Wood Brown.		Common Weasel. Light parts of Feathers on the Back of the Teder.	Hazel Nuts.	Mountain Wood.
106	Liver Brown.		Middle Parts of Feathers of Hen Pheasant, and Wing coverts of Sheldrake.		Semi-Opal.
107	Hair Brown.		Breast of Pintail Duck.		Wood Tin.
108	Broccoli Brown.		Back of Black headed Gull.		Zircon.
109	Clove Brown.		Head and Neck of Male Kestrel.	Stems of black Currant Bush.	Axinite. Rock Crystal.
110	Blackish Brown.		Stormy Petrel. Wing Coverts of black Cock. Forehead of Fernwort.		Mineral Pitch.

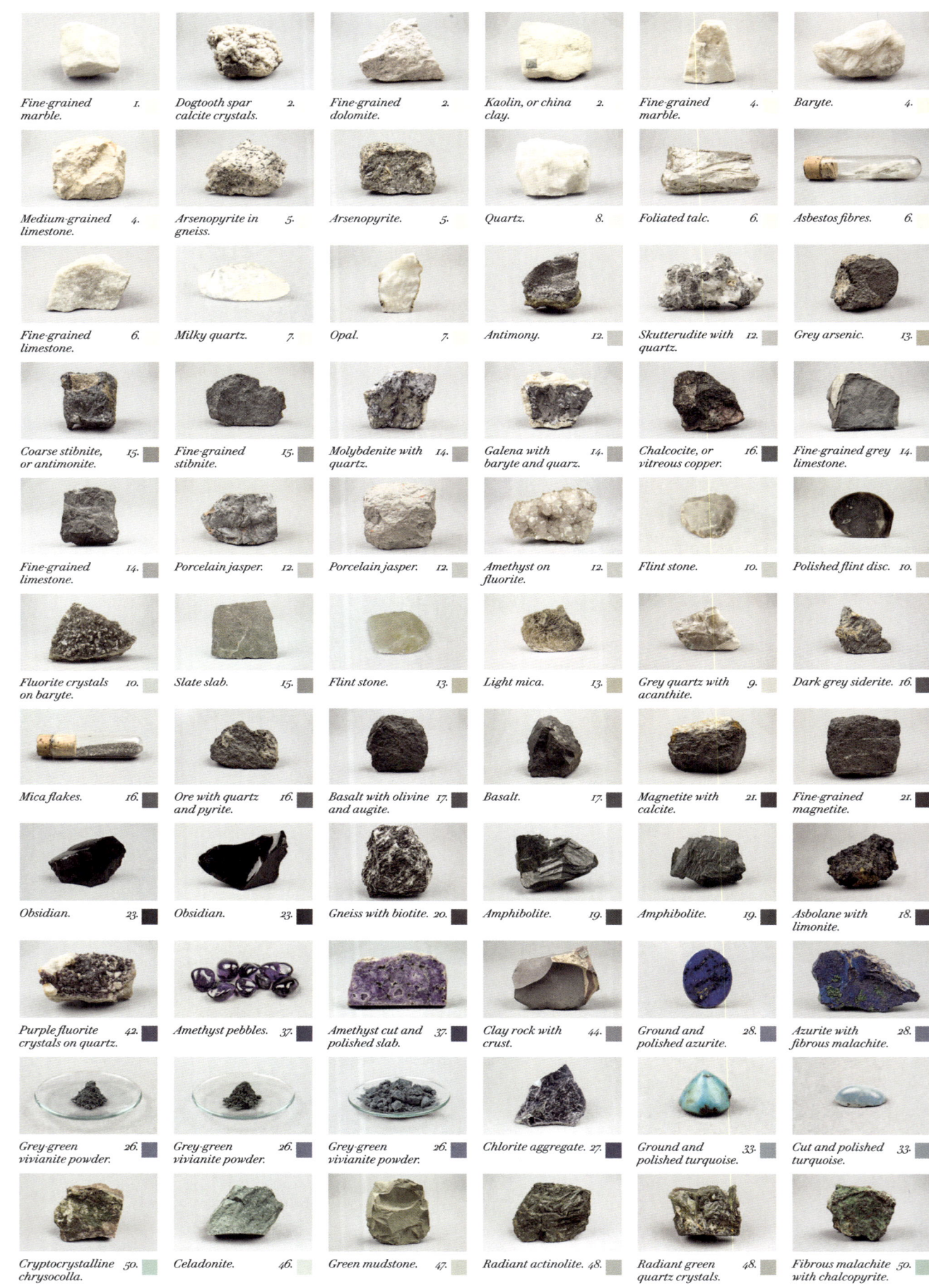

Fine-grained marble. *1.*

Dogtooth spar calcite crystals. *2.*

Fine-grained dolomite. *2.*

Kaolin, or china clay. *2.*

Fine-grained marble. *4.*

Baryte. *4.*

Medium-grained limestone. *4.*

Arsenopyrite in gneiss. *5.*

Arsenopyrite. *5.*

Quartz. *8.*

Foliated talc. *6.*

Asbestos fibres. *6.*

Fine-grained limestone. *6.*

Milky quartz. *7.*

Opal. *7.*

Antimony. *12.*

Skutterudite with quartz. *12.*

Grey arsenic. *13.*

Coarse stibnite, or antimonite. *15.*

Fine-grained stibnite. *15.*

Molybdenite with quartz. *14.*

Galena with baryte and quarz. *14.*

Chalcocite, or vitreous copper. *16.*

Fine-grained grey limestone. *14.*

Fine-grained limestone. *14.*

Porcelain jasper. *12.*

Porcelain jasper. *12.*

Amethyst on fluorite. *12.*

Flint stone. *10.*

Polished flint disc. *10.*

Fluorite crystals on baryte. *10.*

Slate slab. *15.*

Flint stone. *13.*

Light mica. *13.*

Grey quartz with acanthite. *9.*

Dark grey siderite. *16.*

Mica flakes. *16.*

Ore with quartz and pyrite. *16.*

Basalt with olivine and augite. *17.*

Basalt. *17.*

Magnetite with calcite. *21.*

Fine-grained magnetite. *21.*

Obsidian. *23.*

Obsidian. *23.*

Gneiss with biotite. *20.*

Amphibolite. *19.*

Amphibolite. *19.*

Asbolane with limonite. *18.*

Purple fluorite crystals on quartz. *42.*

Amethyst pebbles. *37.*

Amethyst cut and polished slab. *37.*

Clay rock with crust. *44.*

Ground and polished azurite. *28.*

Azurite with fibrous malachite. *28.*

Grey-green vivianite powder. *26.*

Grey-green vivianite powder. *26.*

Grey-green vivianite powder. *26.*

Chlorite aggregate. *27.*

Ground and polished turquoise. *33.*

Cut and polished turquoise. *33.*

Cryptocrystalline chrysocolla. *50.*

Celadonite. *46.*

Green mudstone. *47.*

Radiant actinolite. *48.*

Radiant green quartz crystals. *48.*

Fibrous malachite with chalcopyrite. *50.*

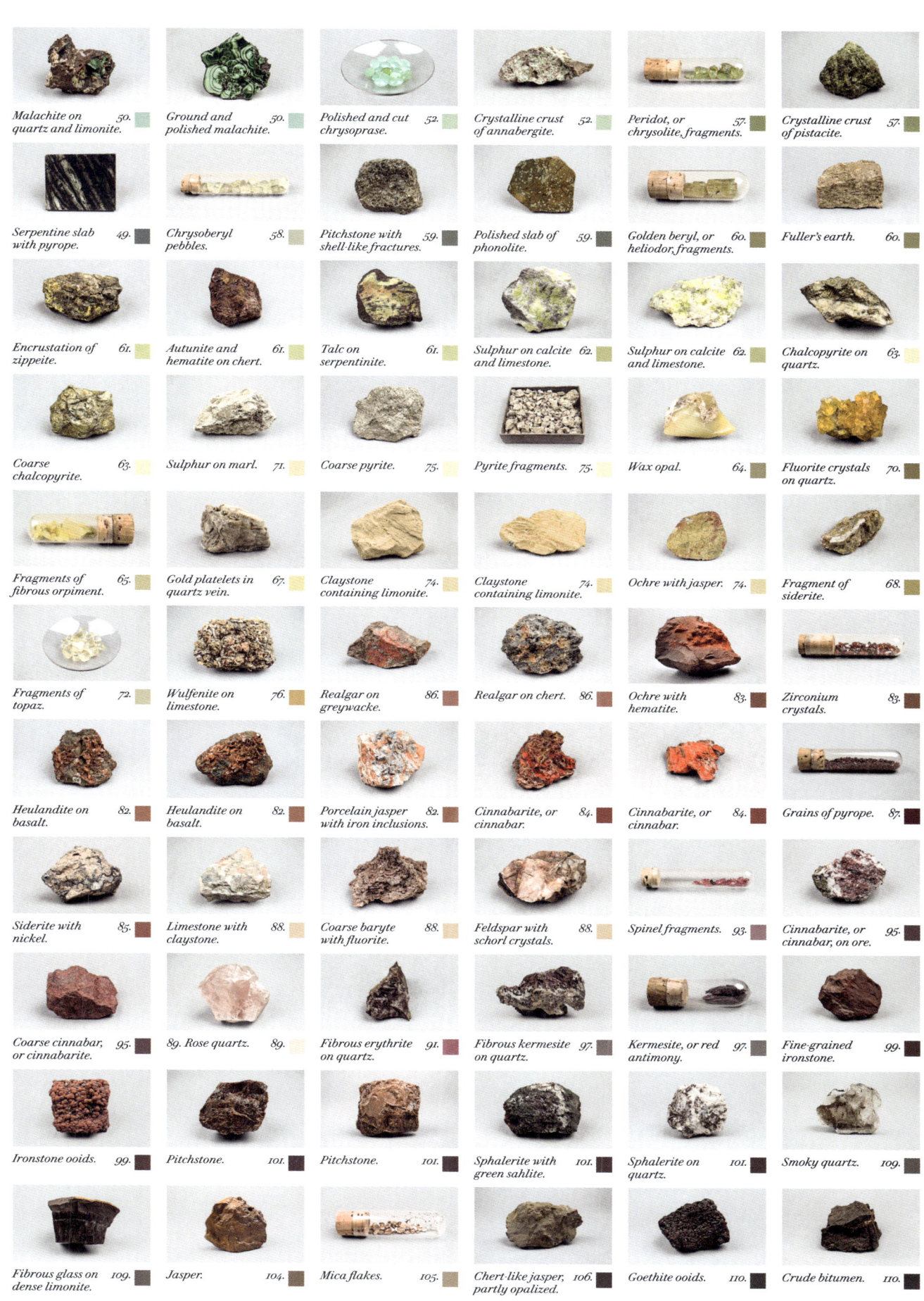

Malachite on quartz and limonite. 50.

Ground and polished malachite. 50.

Polished and cut chrysoprase. 52.

Crystalline crust of annabergite. 52.

Peridot, or chrysolite, fragments. 57.

Crystalline crust of pistacite. 57.

Serpentine slab with pyrope. 49.

Chrysoberyl pebbles. 58.

Pitchstone with shell-like fractures. 59.

Polished slab of phonolite. 59.

Golden beryl, or heliodor, fragments. 60.

Fuller's earth. 60.

Encrustation of zippeite. 61.

Autunite and hematite on chert. 61.

Talc on serpentinite. 61.

Sulphur on calcite and limestone. 62.

Sulphur on calcite and limestone. 62.

Chalcopyrite on quartz. 63.

Coarse chalcopyrite. 63.

Sulphur on marl. 71.

Coarse pyrite. 75.

Pyrite fragments. 75.

Wax opal. 64.

Fluorite crystals on quartz. 70.

Fragments of fibrous orpiment. 65.

Gold platelets in quartz vein. 67.

Claystone containing limonite. 74.

Claystone containing limonite. 74.

Ochre with jasper. 74.

Fragment of siderite. 68.

Fragments of topaz. 72.

Wulfenite on limestone. 76.

Realgar on greywacke. 86.

Realgar on chert. 86.

Ochre with hematite. 83.

Zirconium crystals. 83.

Heulandite on basalt. 82.

Heulandite on basalt. 82.

Porcelain jasper with iron inclusions. 82.

Cinnabarite, or cinnabar. 84.

Cinnabarite, or cinnabar. 84.

Grains of pyrope. 87.

Siderite with nickel. 85.

Limestone with claystone. 88.

Coarse baryte with fluorite. 88.

Feldspar with schorl crystals. 88.

Spinel fragments. 93.

Cinnabarite, or cinnabar, on ore. 95.

Coarse cinnabar, or cinnabarite. 95.

89. Rose quartz. 89.

Fibrous erythrite on quartz. 91.

Fibrous kermesite on quartz. 97.

Kermesite, or red antimony. 97.

Fine-grained ironstone. 99.

Ironstone ooids. 99.

Pitchstone. 101.

Pitchstone. 101.

Sphalerite with green sahlite. 101.

Sphalerite on quartz. 101.

Smoky quartz. 109.

Fibrous glass on dense limonite. 109.

Jasper. 104.

Mica flakes. 105.

Chert-like jasper, partly opalized. 106.

Goethite ooids. 110.

Crude bitumen. 110.

9. A COLOUR REFERENCE SYSTEM FROM THE NATURAL WORLD.

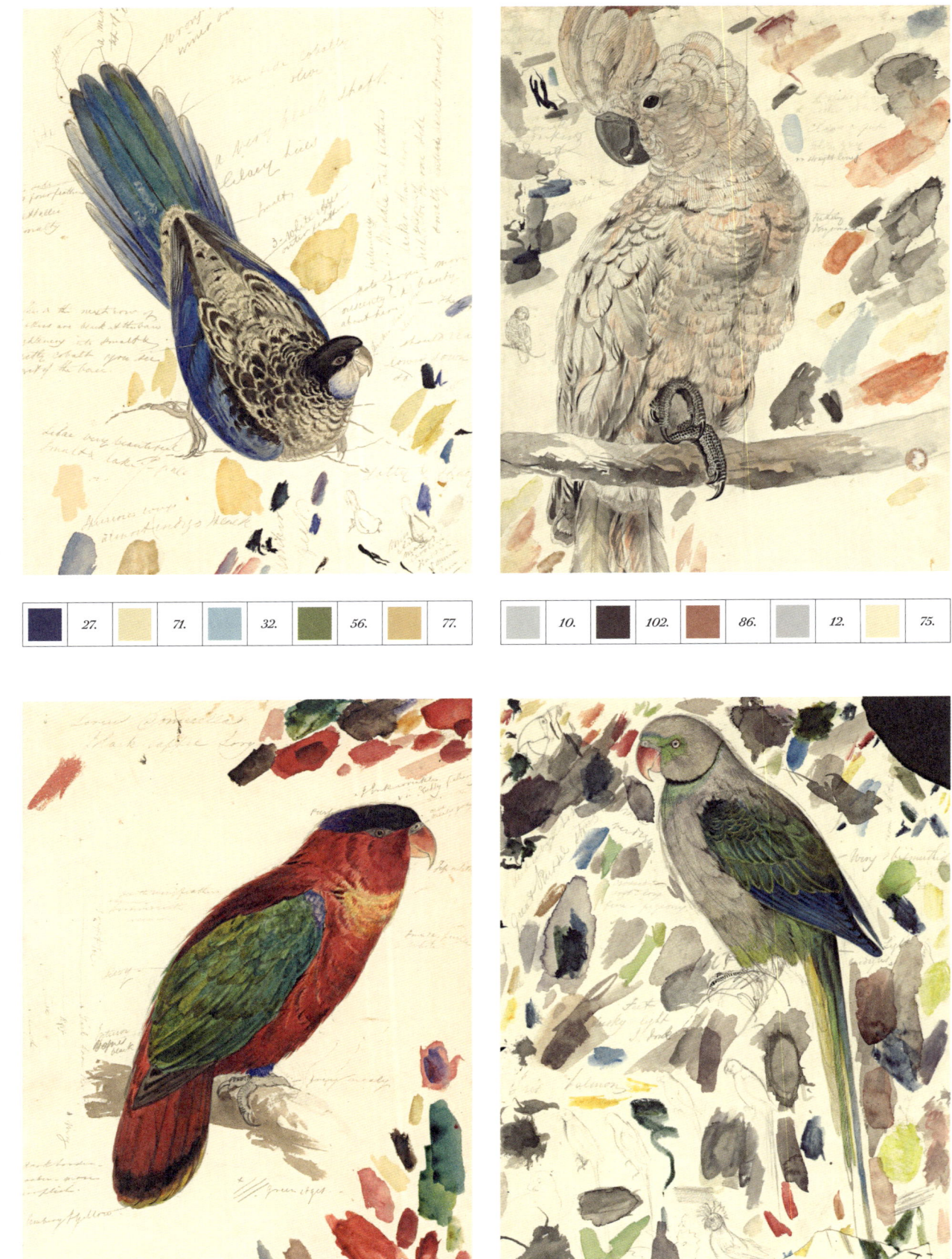

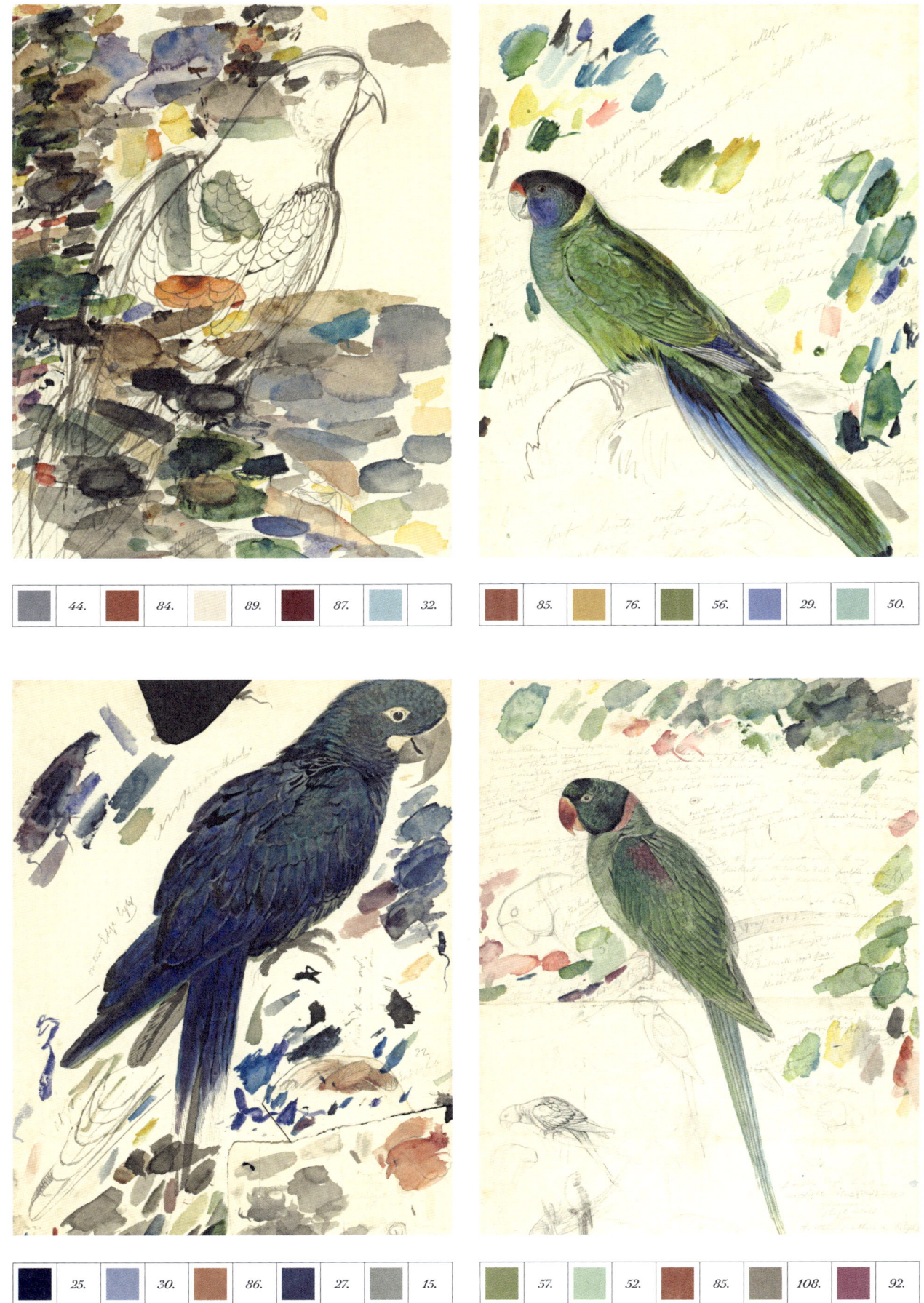

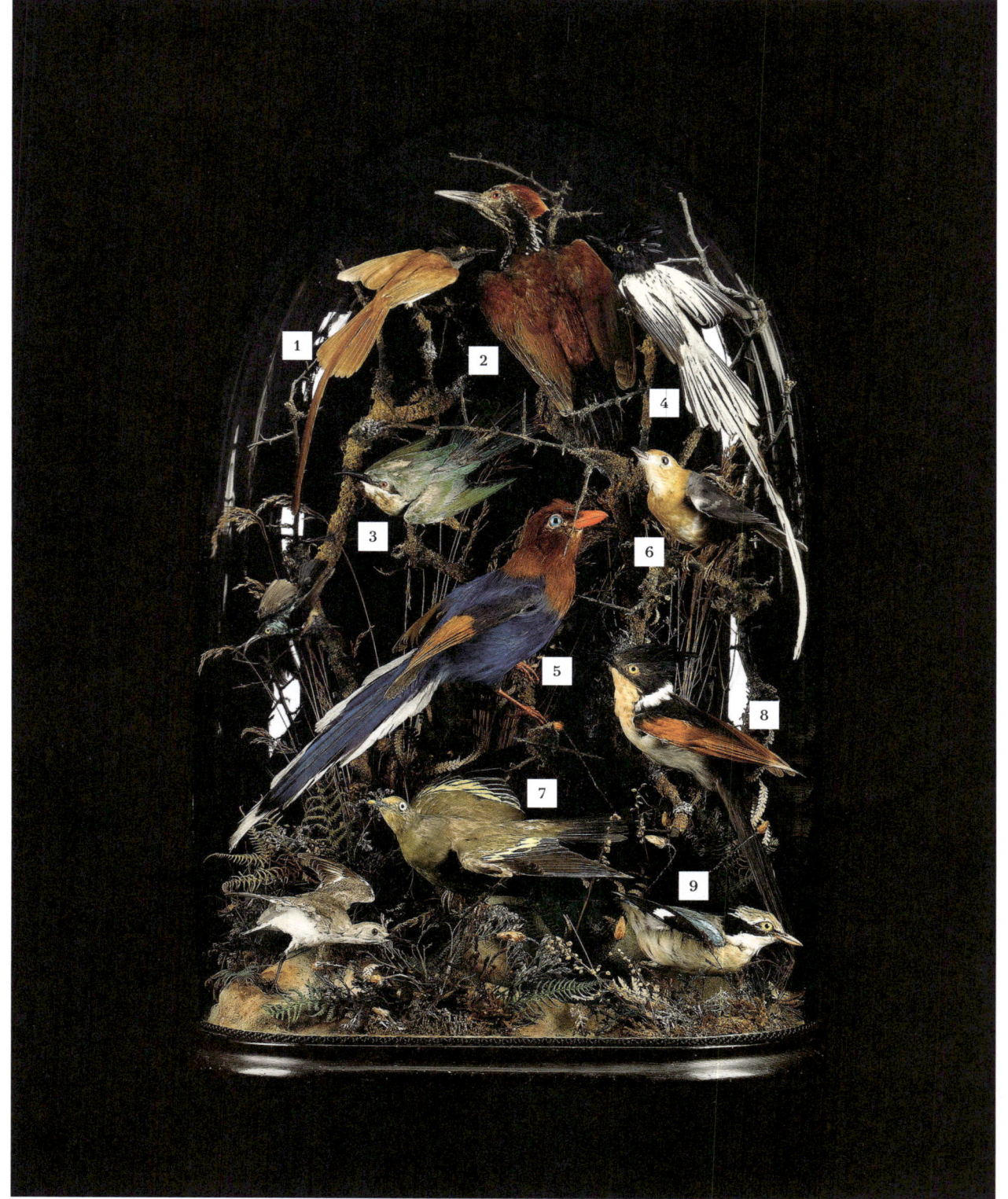

1		78. Orpiment Orange.	2		85. Vermilion Red.	3		53. Emerald Green.
4		1. Snow White.	5		28. Azure Blue.	6		77. Buff Orange.
7		64. Wax Yellow.	8		81. Deep Reddish Orange.	9		32. Verditter Blue.

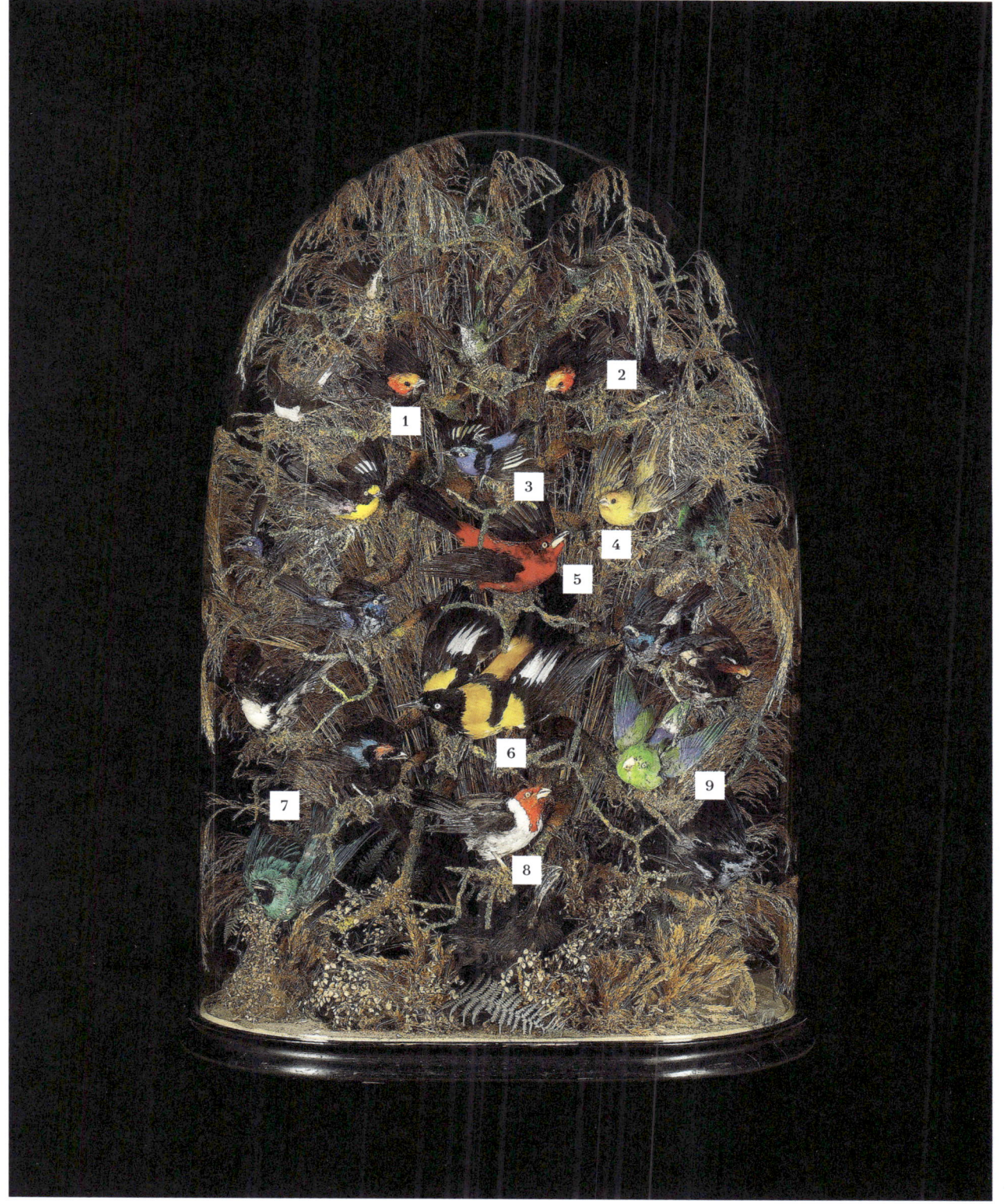

1		76. Dutch Orange.	2		98. Chocolate Red.	3		29. Ultramarine Blue.
4		67. King's Yellow.	5		84. Scarlet Red.	6		78. Orpiment Orange.
7		50. Verdigris Green.	8		8. Greyish White.	9		33. Greenish Blue.

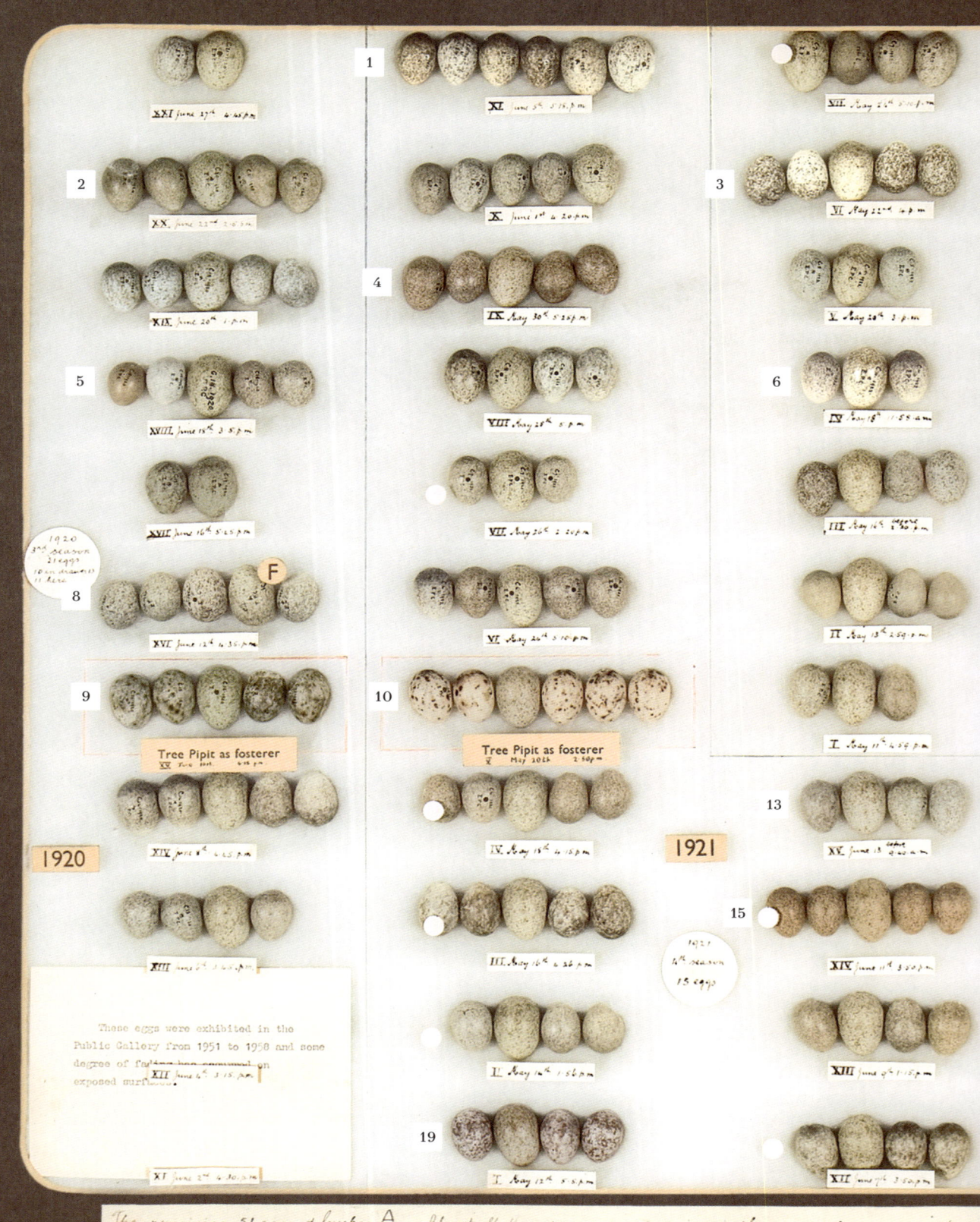

Tree Pipit as fosterer

Tree Pipit as fosterer

1920

1921

These eggs were exhibited in the
Public Gallery from 1951 to 1958 and some
degree of fading has occurred on
exposed surfaces.

The remaining 51 eggs of Cuckoo A. Almost all these eggs were seen deposited in the presence of many eminent orn

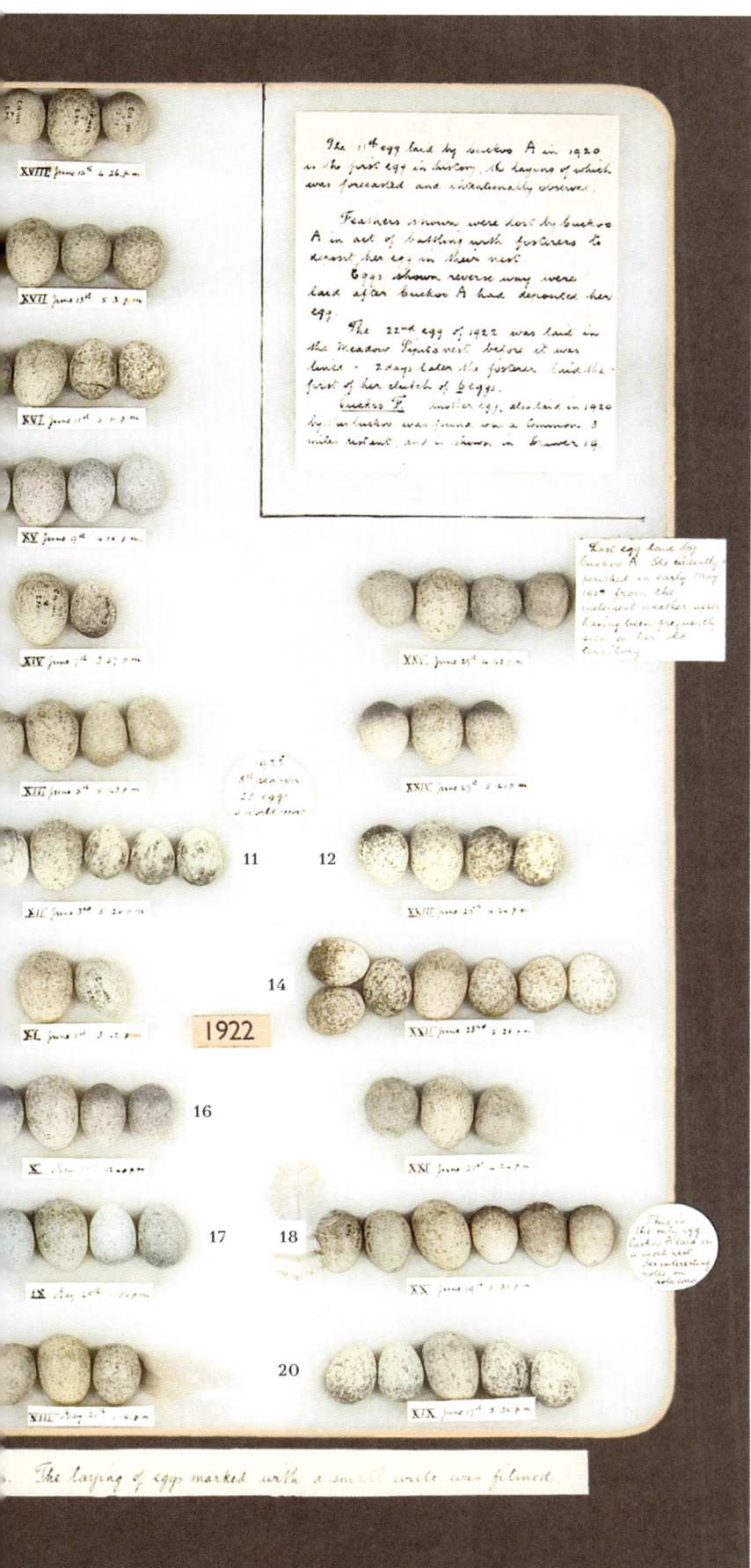

1		4. *Yellowish White.*
2		108. *Broccoli Brown.*
3		5. *Orange-coloured White.*
4		103. *Chesnut Brown.*
5		35. *Bluish Lilac Purple.*
6		2. *Reddish White.*
7		46. *Celandine Green.*
8		13. *Yellowish Grey.*
9		107. *Hair Brown.*
10		90. *Peach Blossom Red.*
11		7. *Skimmed-milk White.*
12		6. *Greenish White.*
13		8. *Greyish White.*
14		104. *Yellowish Brown.*
15		88. *Flesh Red.*
16		43. *Red Lilac Purple.*
17		51. *Bluish Green.*
18		102. *Umber Brown.*
19		79. *Brownish Orange.*
20		3. *Purplish White.*

left   Syme's colours matched to
        cuckoo eggs collected by Edgar
        Percival Chance, 1920–22.

pp. 10–11   Syme's colours matched to
        parrots illustrated by Edward
        Lear as preliminary drawings
        for *Illustrations of the Family
        of Psittacidæ, or Parrots*, 1832.

pp. 12–13   Syme's colours matched to tropical
        taxidermy birds displayed in
        glass domes, c. 1880.

INTRODUCTION.

*The Origins, Development and Influence
of Werner's Nomenclature of Colours.*

BY PATRICK BATY.

In his *Systema naturae*, of 1735, the Swedish botanist and zoologist Carl Linnaeus (1707–1778) outlined his ideas for the hierarchical classification of the natural world. He divided it into three kingdoms, namely the *regnum animale*, *regnum vegetabile* and *regnum lapideum* – the Animal, Vegetable and Mineral Kingdoms.

By 1753, in his *Species plantarum*, he had listed every species of plant then known, using binomial nomenclature – the two-term naming system by which every organism is given its distinct label, the genus and species. With the publication of the tenth edition of the *Systema naturae*, in 1758–59, he introduced the same system for animals, which he broke down into six classes – *Mammalia, Aves, Amphibia, Pisces, Insecta* and *Vermes*. However, he was less successful with minerals, as he lacked both the technology to identify their chemical composition and also a knowledge of crystals.

Before the late 18th century, mineralogy could hardly be called a science as it lacked precise definitions. The same substance was often given different names, while different substances were sometimes called by the same name. Its descriptive language was arbitrary, vague and ambiguous. It was generally acknowledged that a standardized set of terms relating to characteristics including form and colour would make identification and communication easier. Fortunately, as the Irish geologist Richard Kirwan (1733–1812) stated in the Preface to the second edition of his *Elements of Mineralogy*:

> After many ineffectual attempts to obviate these difficulties, by Linnaeus, Peithner,[1] and others, descriptive language was at last reduced to as much precision as it was capable of receiving by Mr Werner in 1774.[2]

THE WORK OF ABRAHAM GOTTLOB WERNER

Abraham Gottlob Werner (1749–1817) came from a family with a long association with the mining industry, including his father, who was inspector of the ironworks of the Count of Solms-Baruth in Wehrau and Lorenzdorf (now in Poland). After a short time working in the ironworks in Wehrau, by 1769 Werner had been invited to enrol in the recently founded Freiberg School of Mining. He soon realized, however, that he would be unable to progress far without a law degree, so studied for three years at the University of Leipzig.

Although he devoted himself to his legal education, Werner also continued his mineralogical pursuits, and in 1774, while still a student, he published the first modern textbook of descriptive mineralogy. The book was titled *Von den äusserlichen Kennzeichen der Fossilien* (later published in English as *A Treatise on the External Characters of Fossils* – at that time fossils meant rocks and minerals),[3] and it very quickly brought him to the attention of the mineralogists of the day, being described as 'the first example of the true method of describing mineral species'.[4]

Werner presented a method of identifying rocks and minerals by their external characteristics as perceived by the five senses – sight, touch, smell, hearing and even taste. Since he believed that a mineral's (visible) colour made the first impression, he produced a list of 54 colours under eight principal headings – white, grey, black, blue, green, yellow, red and brown. These generic colours (his *Hauptfarben*) were each modified by a descriptive word that tended to be based on either a mixture, such as reddish-white or

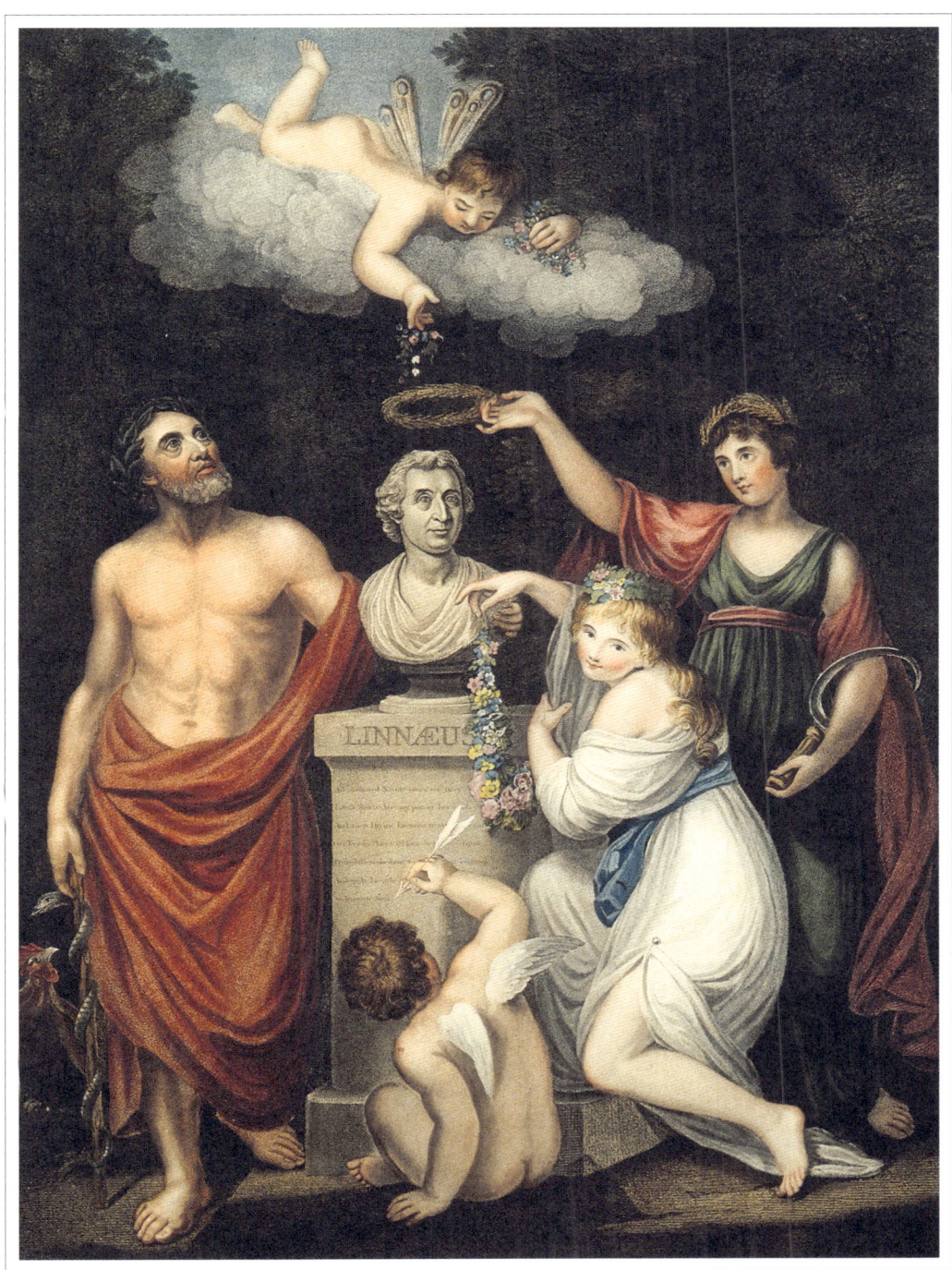

i.

(i).   James Caldwall after John Russell and John Opie, *Carolus Linnaeus*
         Receives Honour from Aesculapius, Flora, Ceres and Cupid, coloured
         stipple engraving, 1806. Carl Linnaeus is known as the 'father of modern
         taxonomy' for his work formalizing the modern system for naming
         organisms during the eighteenth century.

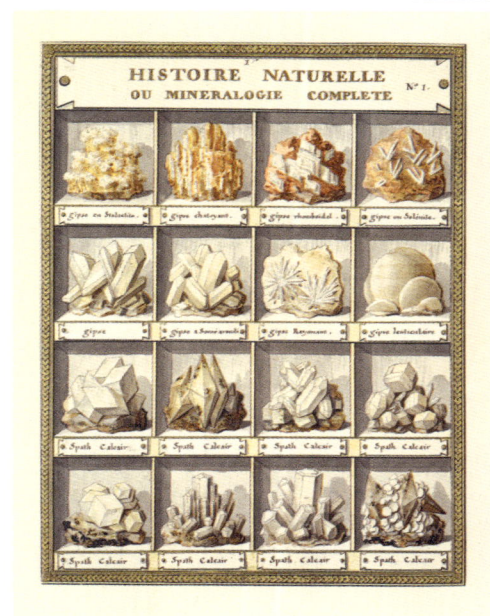

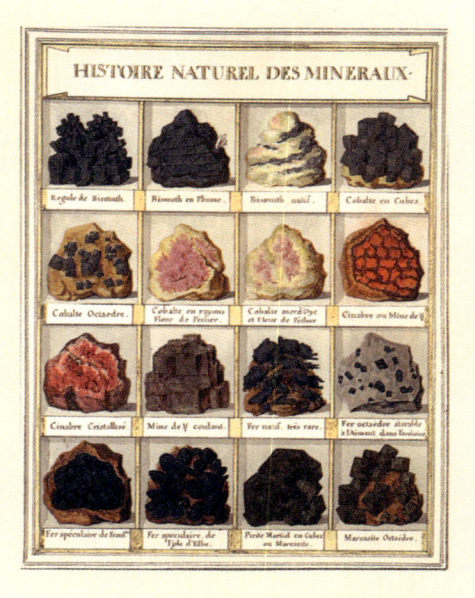

i.

ii.

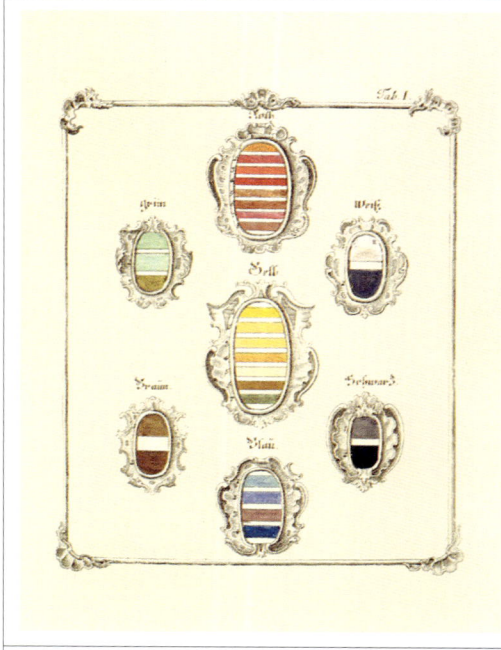

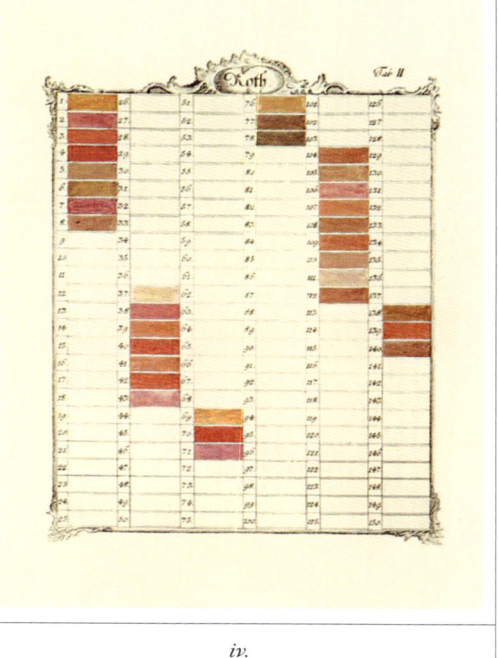

iii.

iv.

(i).   Plate 1 of minerals, Swebach-Desfontaines, *Histoire naturelle*, 1789.
(ii).   Plate 6a of minerals, Swebach-Desfontaines, *Histoire naturelle*, 1789.
(iii). Colour samples of the seven simple and natural principal colours, Jacob Christian Schäffer,
         Entwurf einer allgemeinen Farbenverein, 1769.
(iv).   Table II, chart of reds, Jacob Christian Schäffer, *Entwurf einer allgemeinen Farbenverein*, 1769.

bluish-black, or a pigment, for instance ochre-yellow or carmine-red, or a familiar object, thus sky-blue, apple-green, milk-white. Each colour was further divided into dark, clear, light or pale versions, which, in theory, increased the total to 216 colours.

Werner's system was designed to be of practical application to natural philosophers (scientists) as well as geologists. However, while all the colour names were reasonably self-explanatory and required no specialist knowledge, no actual colour samples were provided in the book, and subjectivity could lead to different interpretations. The serious mineralogist might have his own collection of rocks and minerals to refer to, stored in a special cabinet, such as that of Johann Wolfgang von Goethe (1749–1832) in his garden pavilion in Weimar.[5] Robert Jameson (1774–1854), the Scottish natural historian who studied under Werner (see below), had his own 'Colour-suite of Minerals',[6] made under Werner's supervision. Collections in academic institutions might also be available for students, but the amateur would have found it difficult to be absolutely certain of the colours described.

To improve accuracy for a few of the colours, Werner described how they could be mixed. For example, he said that for 'Morning, or aurora-red' (*Morgenroth, oder Auror*) the painter would use minium (red lead) and that the colour could be seen in examples of red lead ore from Siberia, from realgar and in some spots in red blende from Scharfenberg.

It is perhaps surprising that while Werner made a number of references to an earlier work of 1769 by naturalist Jacob Christian Schäffer (1718–1790), the title of which can be translated as *Plan for a Universal Relationship of Colours; or Research and Model for Determining and Naming Colours in a Way that is Useful to the General Public*,[7] he failed to follow its example by including colour samples. Schäffer came up with his plan after experiencing difficulties when producing a work of hand-coloured illustrations of insects. This early attempt at standardizing colours would ultimately fail due to practical issues. Having identified seven principal colours – white, black, blue, green, yellow, red and brown – Schäffer then detailed the pigments that should be used to produce them. So, for example, the pigments for red were given as minium, cochineal, cinnabar, carmine, *kugellack*,[8] Brazil red, Florentine lake and English red (or brown red). These pigments were also used to colour a red shield-like device in Table I at the end of the work, and were shown in the same order in compartments 1–8 of the red chart of Schäffer's Table II.

Table II was divided into 150 numbered compartments, of which only 33 were coloured. The others were left blank for the student to paint with mixtures of two or three of the principal colours. Compartments 69–71 contained a few of the colours relating to plants, for example number 71, rose red, was a mixture of cochineal and lead white. Compartments 76–78 were filled with some mineral colours – number 76, brick red, was produced by mixing minium, lead white, orpiment and English red. Compartments 104–12 were a random collection of colours: number 105, for example, was *kugellack* and Florentine lake mixed together.

However, this list of pigments already illustrates one of the problems Schäffer was faced with, because *kugellack* and Florentine lake were themselves variants of carmine, which was produced from the kermes insect. More than an understanding of the nature of pigments, what was required was confidence in the honesty and accuracy of the colourman, the supplier of the pigments. Early pigments were frequently adulterated and produced using a variety of processes, resulting in different versions, often with the same name. The problem was further compounded by the recipes for mixing the colours. As no proportions were given, the number of permutations was countless – all producing different results.

Werner borrowed from Schäffer but added grey to the principal colours, which he observed occurs frequently in the mineral kingdom, and also disagreed with the latter's use of numbers to identify colours as he thought they were not sufficiently memorable. That Werner found Schäffer's colour samples useful is shown by the fact that he related eight of his own ten examples of red to coloured strips in Schäffer's table. It seems likely that he would have done the same for the other principal colours, had Schäffer provided them.

THE DEVELOPMENT OF
WERNER'S COLOUR SYSTEM

The first foreign translation of Werner's book was into Hungarian, by Ferentz Benkö (1745–1816), a Calvinist minister. He had studied Werner's work while attending the mineralogical lectures of the German naturalist J. F. Gmelin (1748–1804) at Göttingen in the 1770s and published his translation when he returned to Hungary in 1784.[9] It subsequently became known as *Magyar Werner*. Benkö enlarged the original by adding his own notes, as well as Hungarian locations and examples, all of which are clearly marked as additions.

A translation into French by Claudine Picardet (1735–1820) was published in 1790 as *Traité des caractères extérieurs des fossiles*. She had already translated a number of key scientific works from English, Swedish and German, and later married Louis-Bernard Guyton de Morveau (1737–1816), the eminent chemist, politician and aeronaut who is credited with producing the first systematic method of chemical nomenclature. In her translation, Picardet added 17 colours to Werner's list.

While Richard Kirwan refers to Werner in the Preface of the first edition of his *Elements of Mineralogy* of 1784, he seems unconvinced by the importance of colour-naming, saying that it 'is difficult, if not impossible, to render the various shades of colour intelligible by any description'.[10] Ten years later, in 1794, when the second edition appeared, 'with considerable improvements and additions', he seems to have relented. On his pages listing colour terms, Kirwan cites 52 colours,[11] slightly fewer than Werner, and it is clear that he is using Picardet's translation. However, in his descriptions of the various minerals he also employs a number of the more general categories of colours based on mixtures found in both Werner and later

works. There are such vague terms as reddish, yellowish and greyish white, as well as new ones like purplish red and reddish purple.

In the list itself he only cites a generic black and has few whites or greys, but he does introduce two new colours – sparrow grass green and copper yellow. It is debatable whether the former was the same as grass green, or whether that was what he implied by meadow green. Further confusion arises when he uses the term grass green in his description of chlorite.[12] Kirwan includes about 20 of the colour terms in his description of agates, which 'as Mr Werner justly remarks, do not form a distinct species of stone, but consist of quartz, crystal, hornstone, flint, calcedony [*sic*], amethyst, jasper, carnelian, heliotropium, jade'.[13]

Werner's colour nomenclature was also applied by others, including Johann Georg Lenz (1748–1832), professor of mining and mineralogy at the University of Jena in Germany. He initially studied as a philosopher but having encountered Werner's system was sufficiently inspired to switch to mineralogy. In 1791 Lenz published his *Mineralogisches Handbuch durch weitere Ausführung des Wernerschen Systems*, which, as the title stated, was a development of Werner's book and used identical terminology. For example, his description of common flint (*Feurstein*) can be translated as 'sometimes it appears smoke-yellowish-dark grey and greyish black, sometimes brownish red, ochre yellow, reddish- and yellowish brown'.[14] Seven of these eight terms were used by Werner, and dark grey would have been a standard term pre-dating him.

Lenz's work was a great success and was expanded in later editions. By the time of the fifth edition, in 1796, 150 pages had been added, along with many more Werner-like descriptions. Among these additions, columbine red, hair- and wood brown (*kolombinroth*, *haarbraun* and *holzbraun*) proved to be very popular and were used by others later when describing minerals.

In 1796 Lenz also founded *Die Sozietät für die gesamte Mineralogie zu Jena* (The Society for the Entire Mineralogy of Jena), the first

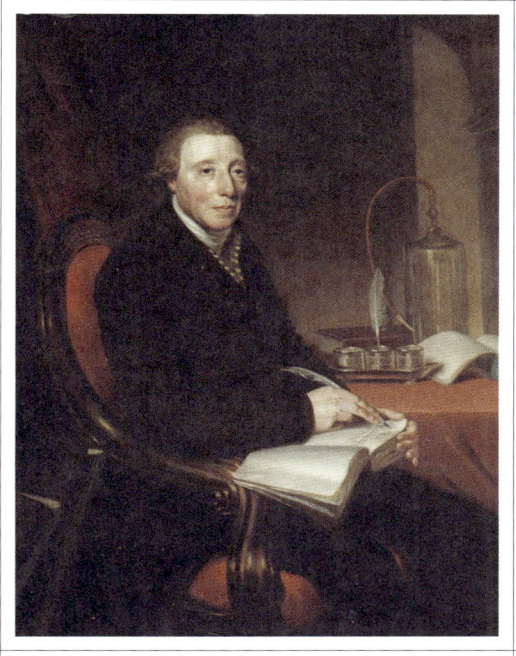

i.

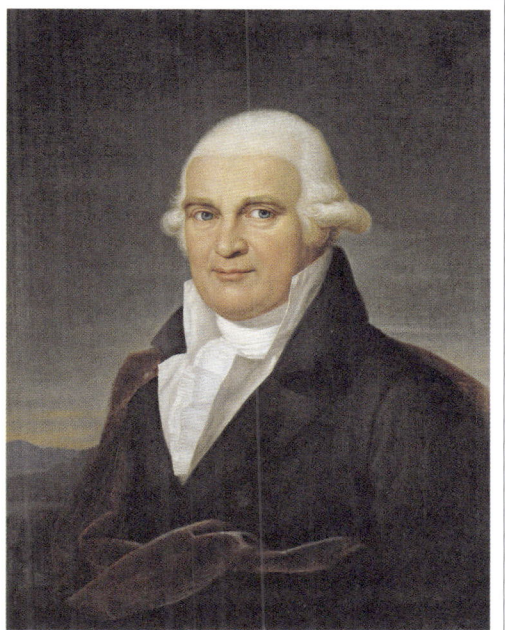

ii.

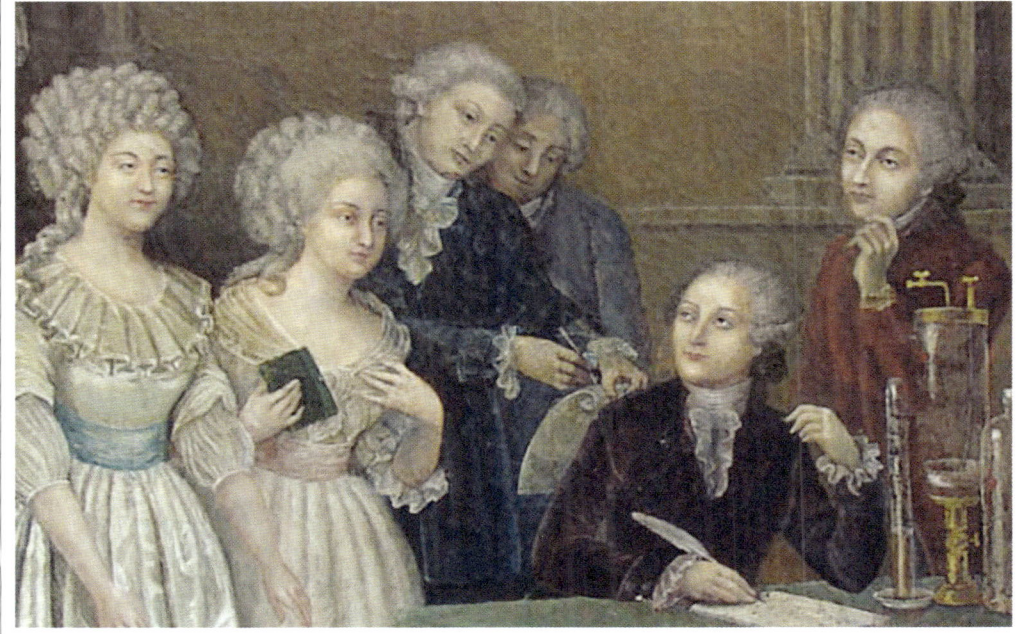

iii.

(i).   Portrait of the Irish geologist Richard Kirwan by an unknown artist.
(ii).   Portrait of German geologist Abraham Gottlob Werner by an unknown artist.
(iii). Group portrait of the French chemists (from left to right) Marie-Anne Paulze Lavoisier,
        Claudine Picardet, Claude Louis Berthollet, Antoine François Fourcroy, Antoine
        Lavoisier and Louis-Bernard Guyton de Morveau by an unknown artist.

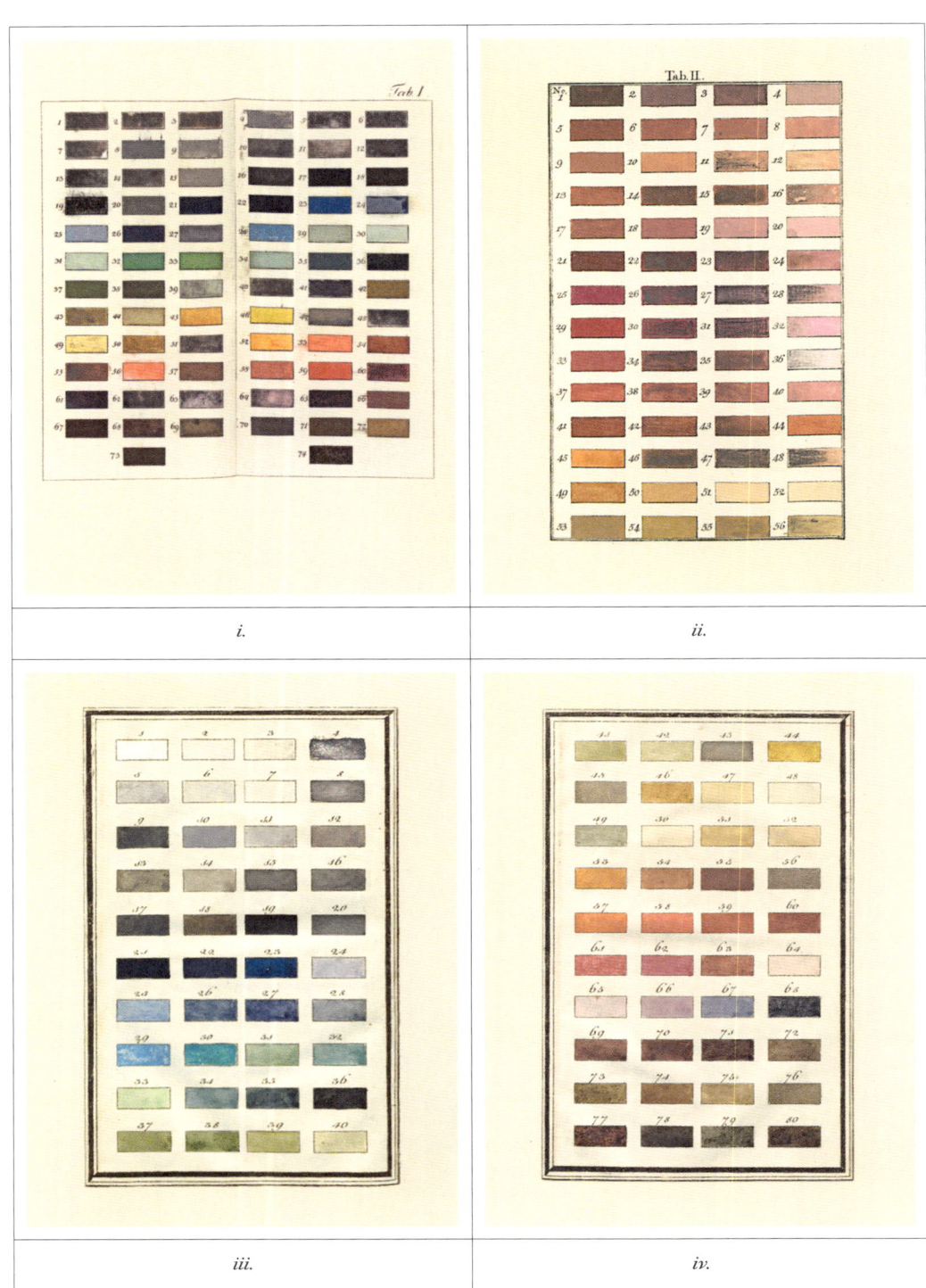

(i).   Colour chart, Johann Friedrich Wilhelm Widenmann, *Handbuch des oryktognostischen Theils der Mineralogie*, 1794.
(ii).   Colour chart, Franz Joseph Anton Estner, *Versuch einer Mineralogie*, 1794.
(iii).   Colours 1–40, Henri Struve, *Méthode analytique des fossiles*, 1797.
(iv).   Colours 41–80, Henri Struve, *Méthode analytique des fossiles*, 1797.

academic society devoted to mineralogical studies. Its members included Goethe and the great natural historian Alexander von Humboldt (1769–1859). Goethe was also one of the 26 subscribers to what is probably the rarest coloured mineralogy – Lenz's *Mustertafeln* ('Specimen Tables') – of 1794 (see p. 82). This consisted of tables divided into columns, which included a hand-coloured drawing of the minerals, their external form, break or fracture, transparency and lustre, hardness and name.

While Lenz's publications were highly significant and influenced others with their expanded range of colour terms, it was one of Werner's students at the Freiberg School of Mining, Johann Friedrich Wilhelm Widenmann (1764–1798) who added what had been missing so far – a colour chart. In fact, his *Handbuch des oryktognostischen Theils der Mineralogie*[15] of 1794, was based on the translated and expanded version of Werner by Picardet. Widenmann added a further three colours to Picardet's expanded list, greyish white and two browns, which appear to have been taken from Lenz, bringing the total to 74. The colours are illustrated in Table I at the end of the book, although in surviving copies a number have darkened or altered considerably with age.

It was also in 1794 that Franz Joseph Anton Estner (1730–1801), a German clergyman, published another expansion of Werner's book, *Versuch einer Mineralogie*, this time with 79 colour terms and drawing heavily on both Picardet and Lenz.[16] Estner's work is especially useful as he produced colour samples in four separate tables and, for the first time, showed some of the four variants that Werner said could be applied to the colours, so, for example, on the page of red samples there are four versions of *Blutroth* (blood red) from dark to pale.

Henri Struve (1751–1826) was a Swiss chemist who had turned to mineralogy from medicine, and in 1797, while honorary professor at the Lausanne academy, he had written *Méthode analytique des fossiles, fondée sur leurs caractères extérieurs*. This was available in two versions – one with two pages containing 80 colour samples and a cheaper version without.

Struve appears to have based his work largely on Widenmann and Lenz and also refers to Kirwan.[17] He introduced a few highly specific colour terms, such as *Rouge de kinorodon*, which he described as the red of the fruit of the shrub (*Rosa eglanteria*) or sweet briar[18] and also *Bleu d'évêque* (bishop's blue).

The mining inspector Ludwig August Emmerling (1765–1841) had also studied with Werner at Freiberg in 1786, and between 1793 and 1797 he published a three-volume textbook of mineralogy, *Lehrbuch der Mineralogie*. He refers to Lenz, Estner and 'Widemann' [*sic*] and employs at least 83 colour descriptions expanded from Werner. His work was perhaps most useful, however, in being one of the means of passing on more of his teacher's knowledge as Werner published relatively little on his ideas.

In charting the influence of Werner on colour terminology in the natural sciences, it might be expected that the French zoologist Pierre André Latreille (1762–1833) would make an appearance. In volume I of his 14-volume *Histoire naturelle, générale et particulière des crustacés et des insectes* he has a lengthy chapter on colour and examines several systems. He mentions that of the Austrian Jesuit entomologist Nikolaus Poda von Neuhaus (1723–1798), as outlined by the naturalist Giovanni Antonio Scopoli (1723–1788), but discounts it for its small range of colours. He also explains the colour wheel of the English entomologist Moses Harris (1730–*c*. 1788) and provides names for 72 of the colours (see also pp. 138–39), almost none of which are used by Werner and his followers. Although he does go on to mention Werner, he is clearly working from Struve's book, as he lists his extended range of 80 colours. Without passing comment on Werner's terms, Latreille moves on to what he describes as 'the most rational system that has yet been published on colour nomenclature' that of the French naturalist Jean-Baptiste Lamarck (1744–1829).[19]

Werner's influence can be seen again in a work by Joseph Maria Redemtus Zappe (1751–1826), an Austrian Carmelite monk. In his *Mineralogisches Handlexicon* (1804) he lists Werner's eight principal colours, but the total number of colour terms increased to 82. It is clear he was working largely from Picardet, Lenz and Emmerling. The same year, 1804, saw yet another work on mineralogy influenced by Werner. This was the second volume of *Handbuch der Mineralogie nach A. G. Werner* ('Handbook of Mineralogy According to A. G. Werner') by the German naturalist Christian Friedrich Ludwig (1757–1823). Throughout, he employed Werner's nomenclature as disseminated by Lenz and Emmerling.

The first English translation of Werner's key text appeared in 1805. This was by another former student at Freiburg, the English geologist and mining consultant Thomas Weaver (1773–1855). On his return to England from Germany he was appointed by the government to work at the gold mine at Croghan Moira in County Wicklow, in Ireland. He remained there until 1811, accounting for the fact that his translation was published in Dublin. In a letter to the Dublin Society, Sir Humphry Davy (1778–1829), the chemist and inventor, described the translation as being 'accurate and profound'.[20]

Entitled *A Treatise on the External Characters of Fossils*, the book was dedicated to Richard Kirwan. Weaver took the opportunity of expanding and updating Werner's original. The 77 colour terms included suggests that it was heavily based on the works of Widenmann and Emmerling, as Weaver himself acknowledges in the foreword, as well as that of Lenz. He explains that numerous other activities had prevented Werner from acceding to the many requests for an updated edition of his book, hence the need in the translation to refer to and include other sources of information:

These are principally copies of Mr. Werner's manuscript corrections and additions as circulated among his pupils, notes taken during his lectures in 1791–1792, and the Mineralogies of his disciples Wiedenmann [*sic*] and Emmerling.[21]

Werner's influence can also be seen in the work of English mineralogist John Mawe (1764–1829). While this is not obvious in Mawe's earliest work of 1802, by 1813 there are recognizable terms dotted throughout his *A Treatise on Diamonds and Precious Stones*. Numerous examples can be found, such as hyacinth red, yellowish- and reddish-brown, crimson red, indigo blue, sky blue and violet under 'Tourmaline', and blood red, cherry red, crimson red and fire red in the 'Garnet' and 'Opal' sections.[22]

In the following year, the English chemist and mineralogist Arthur Aikin (1773–1854) published his *A Manual of Mineralogy*. The first American edition came out soon after, in 1815, and again signs of Werner's terminology are evident, with examples such as wax- and honey yellow, blood red and smoke grey in his description of flinty chert.[23] Another early American work was published in 1816 by Parker Cleaveland (1780–1858), a geologist and mineralogist, entitled *An Elementary Treatise on Mineralogy and Geology*. He refers to Werner, Kirwan and Jameson, among others. His eight 'fundamental colours' and list of 80 colours is almost identical to that in Jameson's book of 1805, itself based on Werner's work.

THE DISSEMINATION OF WERNER'S THEORY BY JAMESON

Robert Jameson (1774–1854) had enrolled as a student at the mining academy in Freiberg in 1800, where he studied for two years under Werner. It was to prove a formative experience, and he went on to become the prime British exponent of the Wernerian geological system. In 1804, the same year he became Regius Professor of Natural History at the University of Edinburgh, he published a *Tabular View of the External Characters of Minerals for the Use of Students of Oryctognosy*, which, he tells us, he 'received from WERNER'. This was a translation in English of a list of 80 colour names. Then in 1805 the same list, albeit now extended by four names and with the corresponding terms in German, French and Latin, appeared as part of Jameson's *A Treatise on the External Characters of Minerals*.[24]

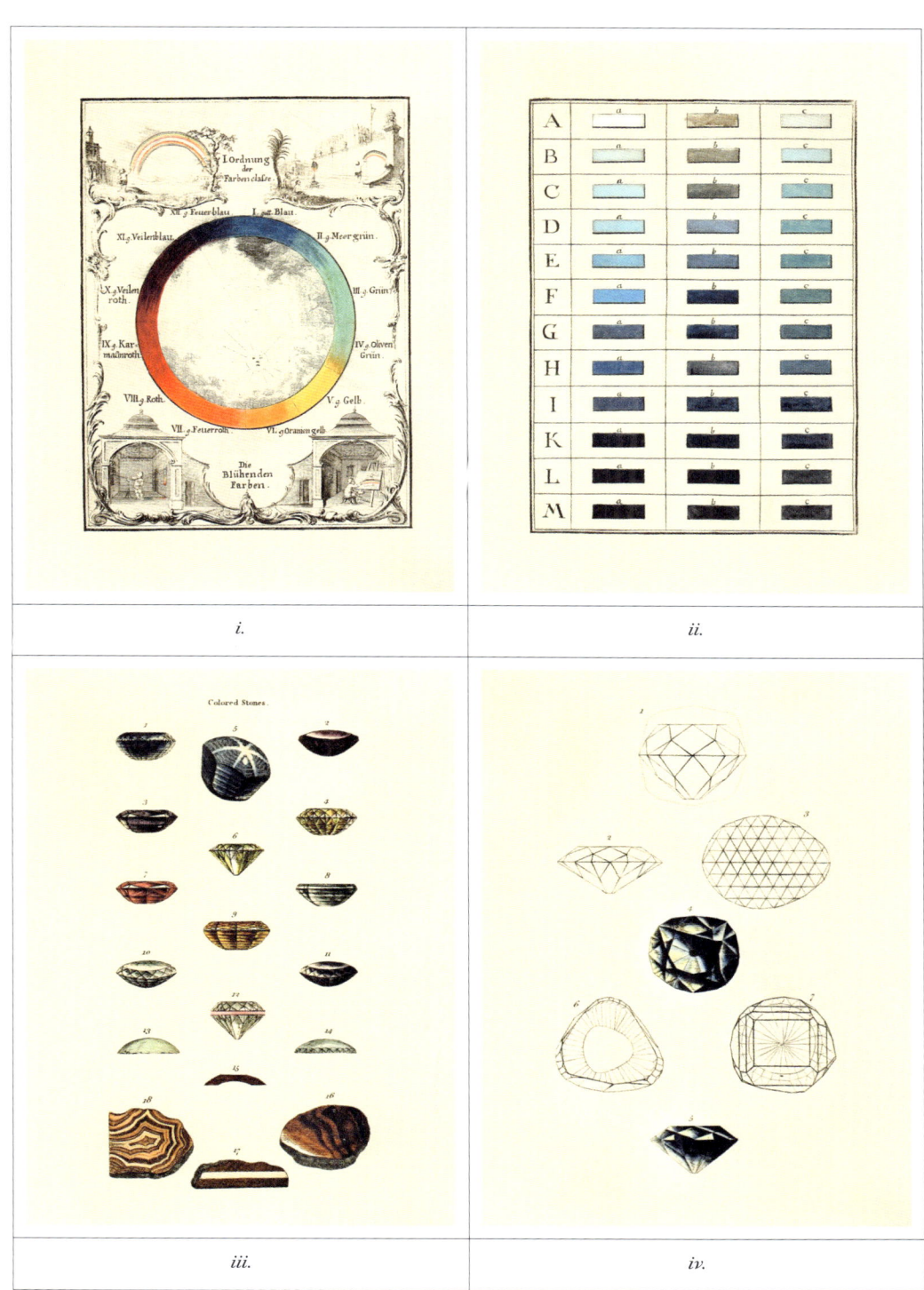

(i).   Colour wheel, Ignaz Schiffermüller, *Versuch eines Farbensystems*, 1772.
(ii).   Chart of blues, Ignaz Schiffermüller, *Versuch eines Farbensystems*, 1772.
(iii).   Coloured stones, John Mawe, *A Treatise on Diamonds*, 1823.
(iv).   Peculiar diamonds, John Mawe, *A Treatise on Diamonds*, 1823.

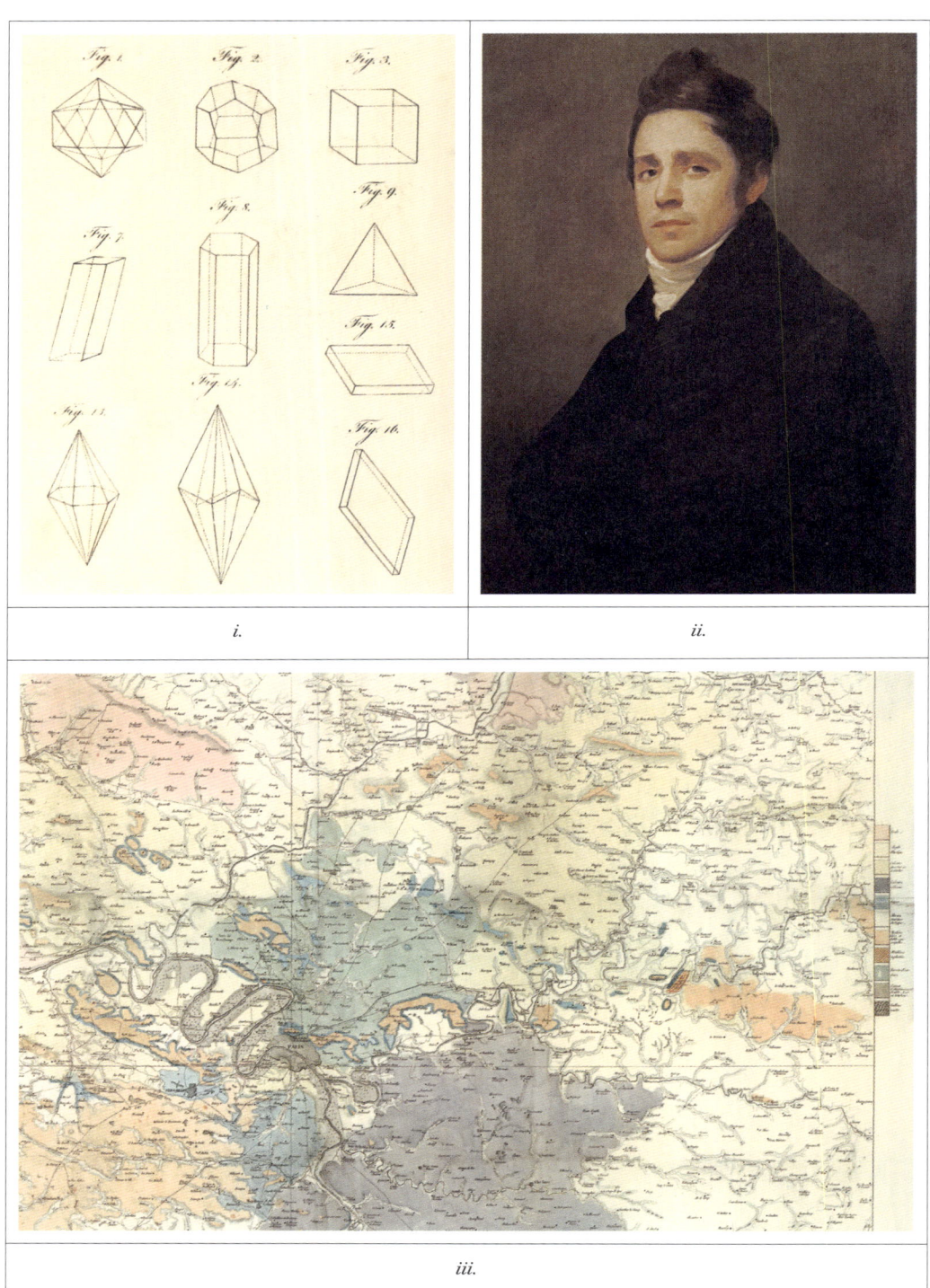

i.

ii.

iii.

(i).   Plate 1, Robert Jameson, *A Treatise on the External Characters of Minerals*, 1805.
(ii).   George Watson's portrait of mineralogist Robert Jameson, *c.* 1800.
(iii).   Georges Cuvier and Alexandre Brongniart, *Carte géognostique des environs de Paris*, 1810.

Rather than offering just one lead grey, Jameson introduced four variants – common lead grey, fresh lead grey, blackish lead grey and whitish lead grey. He also modified a few of the colours that had been in use for 30 years – in the green section he changed canary green to siskin green, in the red section brick red became tile red and in the brown section coal brown became broccoli brown. Jameson's list included 84 colour terms; by the time of the third edition of his book, in 1817,[25] he had added three more colours first introduced by Lenz: two blues – blackish-blue and duck-blue – and pea-yellow.

In 1808 Jameson founded the Wernerian Natural History Society, which he was to preside over until the early 1850s. At one of the first meetings of the Society, he read a paper on the colouring of 'geognostical' maps.[26] Geognosy or 'earth knowledge' was a term that Werner had used to describe the study of rocks and minerals and the formation of the Earth. In his paper, Jameson stated that in colouring maps: 'The colours must agree as nearly as possible with nature, that is, they must correspond with the most common colour of the rock.'

He listed some 30 colours to distinguish different rocks, which he states 'have been recommended by Werner', the majority being those that he had included in his *Treatise* of 1805. Charles Darwin (1809–1882) probably read Jameson's paper, since the *Memoirs of the Wernerian Natural History Society* was among the list of books marked as 'read' in his reading notebook, which he began in 1839.[27] As a student in Edinburgh Darwin had attended Jameson's lectures on natural history, but found them 'incredibly dull', saying that the 'sole effect they produced on me was the determination never as long as I lived to read a book on Geology or in any way study the science'.[28] One lecture, however, was entitled *On the Origins of the Animal Species*, and it is interesting to speculate what impact that might have had on Darwin. He may not have agreed with all that Jameson was teaching, but he came away with much that was to prove useful to him. Not the least was Jameson's *Manual of Mineralogy* (1821), Darwin's copy of

which was heavily annotated.[29] It is also highly likely Charles Darwin encountered *Werner's Nomenclature of Colours* while studying in Edinburgh, which he would use when on his famous voyage on HMS *Beagle* (see p. 131).

During his 50 years at Edinburgh University, Jameson increased the museum's collection of mineralogical and geological specimens, so that in 1852 it contained over 74,000 specimens, making it the second largest collection in the country. Access was limited, but he met his students there three times a week for exercises in the accurate description of the objects that it contained using the Wernerian system.[30]

SYME TAKES UP THE MANTLE

Jameson, it seems, also played a role in the small volume published in Edinburgh in 1814 entitled *Werner's Nomenclature of Colours, with Additions, Arranged so as to Render it Highly Useful to the Arts and Sciences, Particularly Zoology, Botany, Chemistry, Mineralogy, and Morbid Anatomy. Annexed to which are Examples Selected from Well-Known Objects in the Animal, Vegetable, and Mineral Kingdoms*. Its author was Patrick Syme (1774–1845), 'flower-painter', of Edinburgh.

Syme was a student of botany and entomology, as well as an artist, who painted for both the Caledonian Horticultural and Wernerian Natural History societies. As a member of the former and founder and President of the latter, Jameson would have known Syme. Syme in fact acknowledges 'Professor Jamieson' for his help both in laying out specimens of the minerals mentioned by Werner to work from, and also for the accuracy of Werner's terminology in describing the colours. The work contained 108 examples grouped in Werner's eight principal colours – white, grey, black, blue, green, yellow, red and brown. To these Syme added purple and orange, saying that they were equally entitled to be included.

Despite crediting Werner with establishing such a nomenclature, and explaining his system at some length, Syme draws attention to the limitations of his colour range. It was adequate for the description of most minerals but lacking when applied to general science. Syme intended his book to be a practical reference for a wider audience, as set out in his subtitle and the book's introduction. In order to help the user he provided examples, as far as he was able, from the animal, vegetable and mineral kingdoms of where the exact colour could be found in nature, arranged in columns after the colour swatches painted on strips of paper. Separate text provided the 'recipe' for each colour.

To expand its usefulness, Syme added a number of new colours, and to avoid confusion he tells his readers that Werner's original colours are indicated with the letter *W*. However, there are a few inconsistencies. For instance, scarlet red and liver brown were original Werner colours, but are not marked as such by Syme. On the other hand, cochineal red was a colour introduced by Claudine Picardet in 1790, and hair brown first appears in the writings of Lenz, yet both were marked as being Werner's colours.

A clue as to which source Syme may have been working from is given by the number of 'original' colours – 79. A close examination of the many works in various languages that appeared between 1790 and 1805 reveals only one that lists 79 colours – Estner's *Versuch einer Mineralogie*. However, Estner listed seven whites not eight, and the greyish white that Syme adds first appeared in Lenz's book of 1791. In the grey section Estner listed ten colours, but Syme only eight. The same is found in all the other colour groups – each one is different.

The lists produced by Struve and Latreille both contain 80 colours, but neither is identical to Syme in terms of colour groups or colour names. Closest in terms of colour names is Jameson's *Tabular View of the External Characters of Minerals* (1804), which also contained 80 colours, and which Jameson claimed to have received from Werner. However, there is no simple correlation. The influence of several authors can be detected – Lenz, Zappe, Picardet and Jameson .

It is interesting that when the third edition of Jameson's *Treatise* was published in 1817 (three years after Syme) his list of colour names was largely unchanged. This might suggest that he was not sufficiently convinced by some of Syme's new names to include them. Conversely, when Syme's second edition appeared in 1821, it did not include Jameson's additions. Syme did add one blue (Scotch blue) and one red (purplish red) to his second edition of 1821. Rather confusingly, the 1821 recipe for Scotch blue was the same as that for indigo blue in the earlier edition; he also retained the name indigo blue, but with an amended recipe; purplish red was a name that had already been used by Kirwan in his book of 1794; and raven black seems to have been renamed ink black in the second edition.

Although there were many different antecedents, Syme's book was quite different from anything of its type that had been published before. It was compact, almost pocket-sized, and laid out in a logical and practical fashion – ideal for field work. The colours were arranged by family groups and all the key information was placed beside the colour samples, they were also generally brighter than the ones published in those few earlier mineralogical works that included colour samples.

CONTINUING INFLUENCE

In 1858 the Egyptologist Sir John Gardner Wilkinson (1797–1875) published a curious work entitled *On Colour and on the Necessity for a General Diffusion of Taste Among All Classes*. He begins by saying how the English usually prefer 'quiet colours', but for those who are capable of understanding, it only requires proper instruction to develop an appreciation of the harmonious use of bright colours. He refers to *Werner's Nomenclature of Colours* and includes a table of the 'principal colours' in English, Arabic, French, German, Greek, Latin and Italian. Among these are 37 colour terms that have been taken from Werner.[31]

Towards the end of the century, in 1894, a most unusual nomenclature of colours was published, ostensibly for botanists and zoologists, but primarily for mycologists, by Pier Andrea Saccardo (1845–1920), called *Chromotaxia*.[32] A small book, printed in Latin,

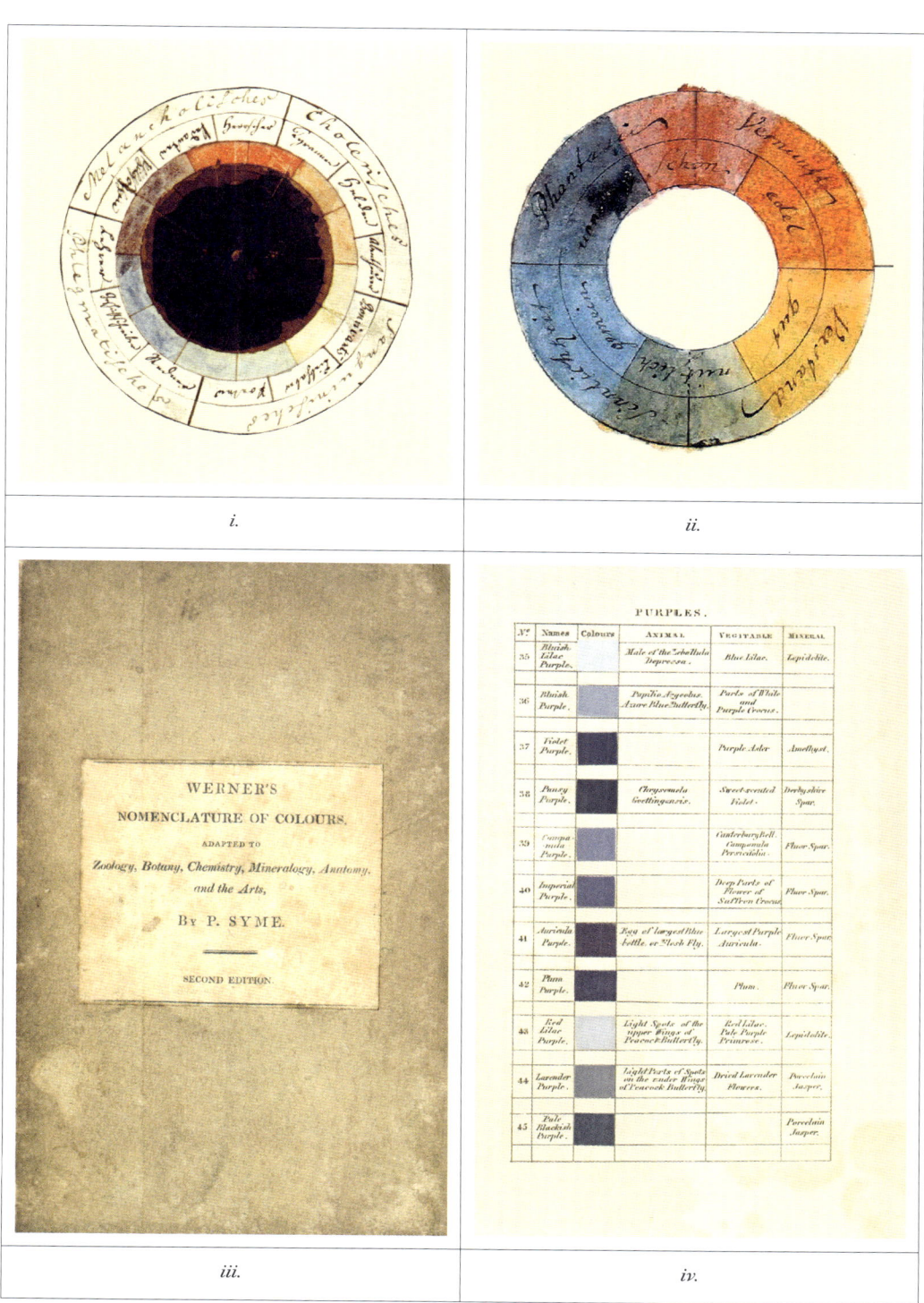

i.

ii.

iii.

iv.

(i).   The rose of temperaments, Johann Wolfgang von Goethe and
        Friedrich Schiller, 1798/99. It matches twelve colours to character traits.
(ii).   Colour wheel, Johann Wolfgang von Goethe, *Zur Farbenlehre,* 1810.
(iii). Cover, Patrick Syme, *Werner's Nomenclature of Colours*, 1821.
(iv).   Chart of purples, Patrick Syme, *Werner's Nomenclature of Colours*, 1821.

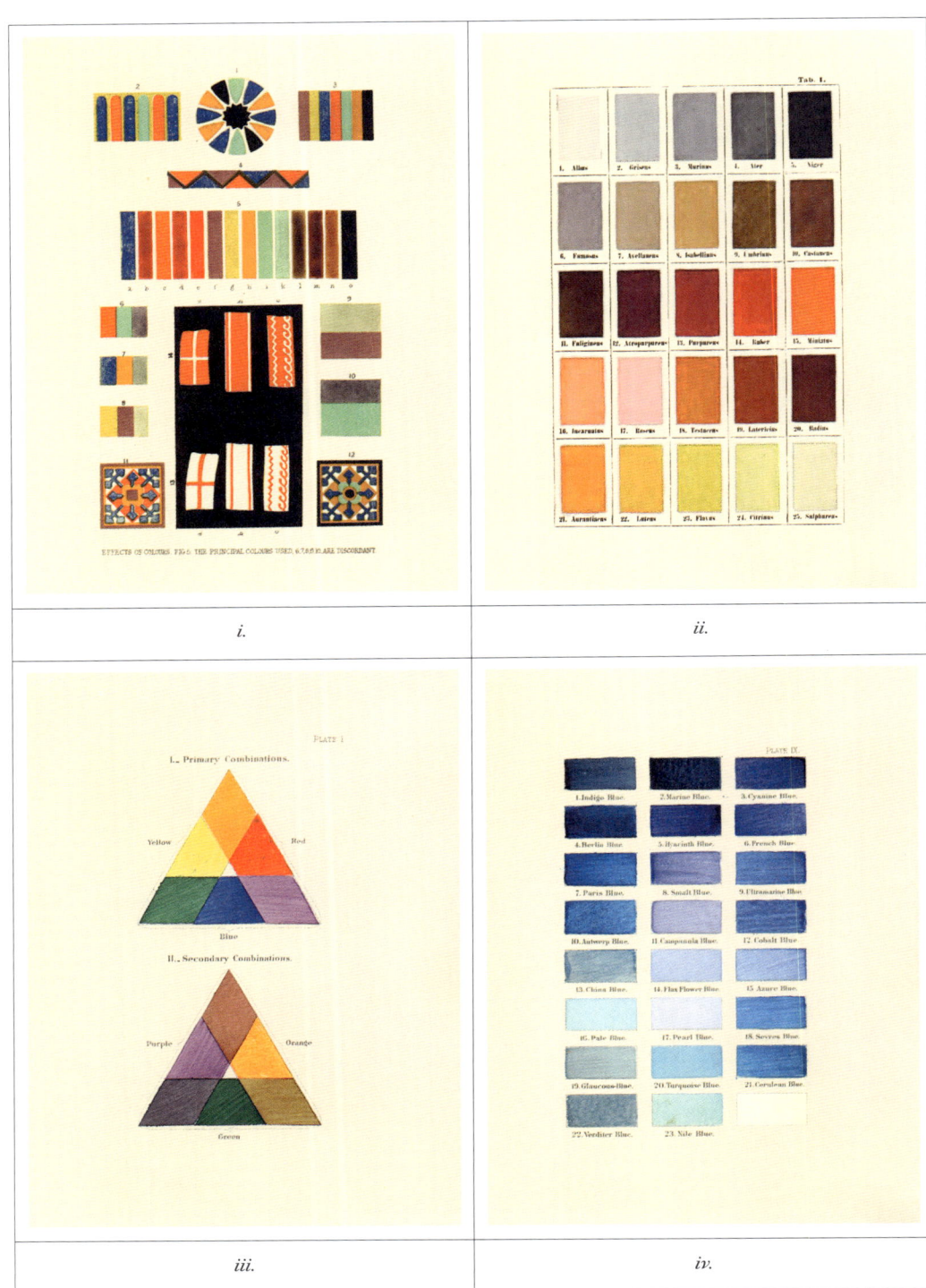

i.

ii.

iii.

iv.

(i).   Effects of colours, John Gardner Wilkinson, *On Colour*, 1858.
(ii).   Plate 1, Pier Andrea Saccardo, *Chromotaxia seu Nomenclator colorum*, 1894.
(iii).   Primary and secondary combinations, Robert Ridgway, *A Nomenclature of Colors for Naturalists*, 1886.
(iv).   Chart of blues, Robert Ridgway, *A Nomenclature of Colors for Naturalists*, 1886.

it contains a chart of colour names (*Tabella colori*) with translations in Italian, French, English and German. Although Werner received no credit, some very familiar terms can be found in various languages, for example flesh-coloured, peach-blossom colour, brick-coloured, Berlin blue.[33] The author also helpfully included 50 colour samples at the end (see also pp. 188–89).

The next significant influence is found in the work of an American ornithologist, Robert Ridgway (1850–1929). In addition to being the first full-time curator of birds at the United States National Museum (now the Smithsonian) and author of the eight volumes of *The Birds of North and Middle America* (1901–19), he also wrote two books in which he set out to standardize the colour names that ornithologists used to describe birds (see also p. 138 and pp. 142–43).

The first appeared in 1886 entitled *A Nomenclature of Colors for Naturalists*. It was a relatively modest work and included 186 colour samples. At least 19 of Syme's colour terms were included in Ridgway's book, including primrose yellow, wax yellow, saffron yellow, auricula purple and wood brown. In 1912 Ridgway self-published *Color Standards and Color Nomenclature*, which included 1,115 colours illustrated with painted samples reproduced on 53 plates. Once again, he

mentions *Werner's Nomenclature of Colours* (second edition, 1821) among the works that he drew names from.[34] On this occasion at least 25 colour names are recognizable from Syme's book, though it could be argued that many were not exclusive to Syme or Werner. The work became a standard reference used by ornithologists for decades after Ridgway's death in 1929, as well as by specialists in fields as wide-ranging as mycology, philately and food colouring.[35]

Whatever sources Syme borrowed and built on, his great achievement was to develop and broaden the basic, and very limited, colour range that had been first published by Werner and refined by successive mineralogists to produce a set of standardized colour terms for scientific descriptions. In spite of its small size and scope, *Werner's Nomenclature of Colours* is important for being the first of a series of colour reference systems that led to much greater things in the two centuries after its first publication. It progressed via a convoluted route that included sets of colours designed for French carnation and chrysanthemum growers (see p. 189) and British horticulturalists, and that included three British Standard colour ranges, while also taking in more specialized collections for camouflage purposes and children's education.

NOTES — (1). Johann Thaddäus Anton Peithner (1727-1792) Czech mining expert. (2). Kirwan 1794, p. xii, referring to the publication of Werner's *Von den äusserlichen Kennzeichen der Fossilien*. (3). There is a distinction, while all rocks are made up of minerals, not all minerals are rocks. There were two English translations of Werner's book, Thomas Weaver's *A Treatise on the External Characters of Fossils* in 1805, and Charles Moxon's *A Treatise on the External Characters of Minerals* in 1849. (4). Jameson quoted in Rees 1819 Vol. 38, s.v. Werner. (5). Hamm 2001, passim. (6). Jameson 1816, pp. 85-6. (7). By Professor Kärin Nickelsen: Simonini 2018, p.17; its original title in German is *Entwurf einer allgemeinen Farbenverein, oder Versuch und Muster einer gemeinnützlichen Bestimmung und Benennung der Farben*. (8). A red lake pigment also called columbinroth or kolombinroth; Eyssvogel 1756, p. 166. The latter name was introduced as a colour term by Lenz. (9). *A köveknek és értzeknek külsömegesmértetöjegyeikröl*. (10). Kirwan 1784, p. viii. (11). Kirwan 1794, pp. 27-30. (12). There are several other examples of possible confusion with the naming of terms. In theory, Prussian blue and Berlin blue are interchangeable, yet Patrick Syme uses both. (13). Kirwan 1794, pp. 330-1. (14). In the original: '...bald kommt er rauch - gelblich - dunkelgrau und gräulichschwarz, bald bräunlichroth, ocher-gelb, röthlich - und gelblichbraun vor', 1796, p. 14. (15). 'Handbook of the oryctognostic part of mineralogy'. (16). *Versuch einer Mineralogie für Anfänger und Liebhaber nach des Herrn Bergcommissionsraths Werners Methode: An attempt at mineralogy for beginners and enthusiasts according to Berg Commissioner Werner's method*. 3 volumes. Vienna 1794-1804. (17). Indeed, Henri Struve indicated that the new (second) edition of Kirwan's book was very different to the first and that he had now adopted Werner's methods. (18). Struve 1797, p. 8. Although it is worth pointing out that most would regard the red of the fruit of the dog rose (*Rosa canina*) as resembling *Rouge de kinorodon* more closely than the fruit of the sweet briar. Perhaps there was confusion with *Cynorhodon* (rose hip), *Dictionnaire languedocien-françois* by Pierre Augustin Boissier de Sauvages de la Croix, 2nd ed., 1821, p. 22. (19). Latreille 1803-4, p. 331. (20). Curry 1834, p. 167. (21). Weaver 1805, pp. viii-ix. (22). Mawe 1813, pp. 116, 137 and 141. From the dates, it seems that the influence came via either Jameson or Weaver's books of 1805. (23). Aikin 1815, p. 198. (24). Jameson 1805 pp. 5-15 (25). Now called *A Treatise on the External, Chemical, and Physical Characters of Minerals*. (26). Jameson 1811, pp. 149-61. (27). https://www.darwinproject.ac.uk/people/about-darwin/what-darwin-read/darwin-s-reading-notebooks (28). Hartley 2001, p. 61. (29). Secord 1991(b), p. 135. (30). Morrell 1972, p. 49. (31). Wilkinson 1858, pp. 81-90. (32). Full title *Chromotaxia seu Nomenclator colorum polyglottus additis speciminibus coloratis ad usum botanicorum et zoologorum* (33). Saccardo passim. (34). Ridgway 1912, p. 11. (35). Lewis 2012, p. 235.

THE EVOLUTION OF KEY
COLOUR STANDARD NOMENCLATURES
FROM WERNER TO SYME, 1774–1821.

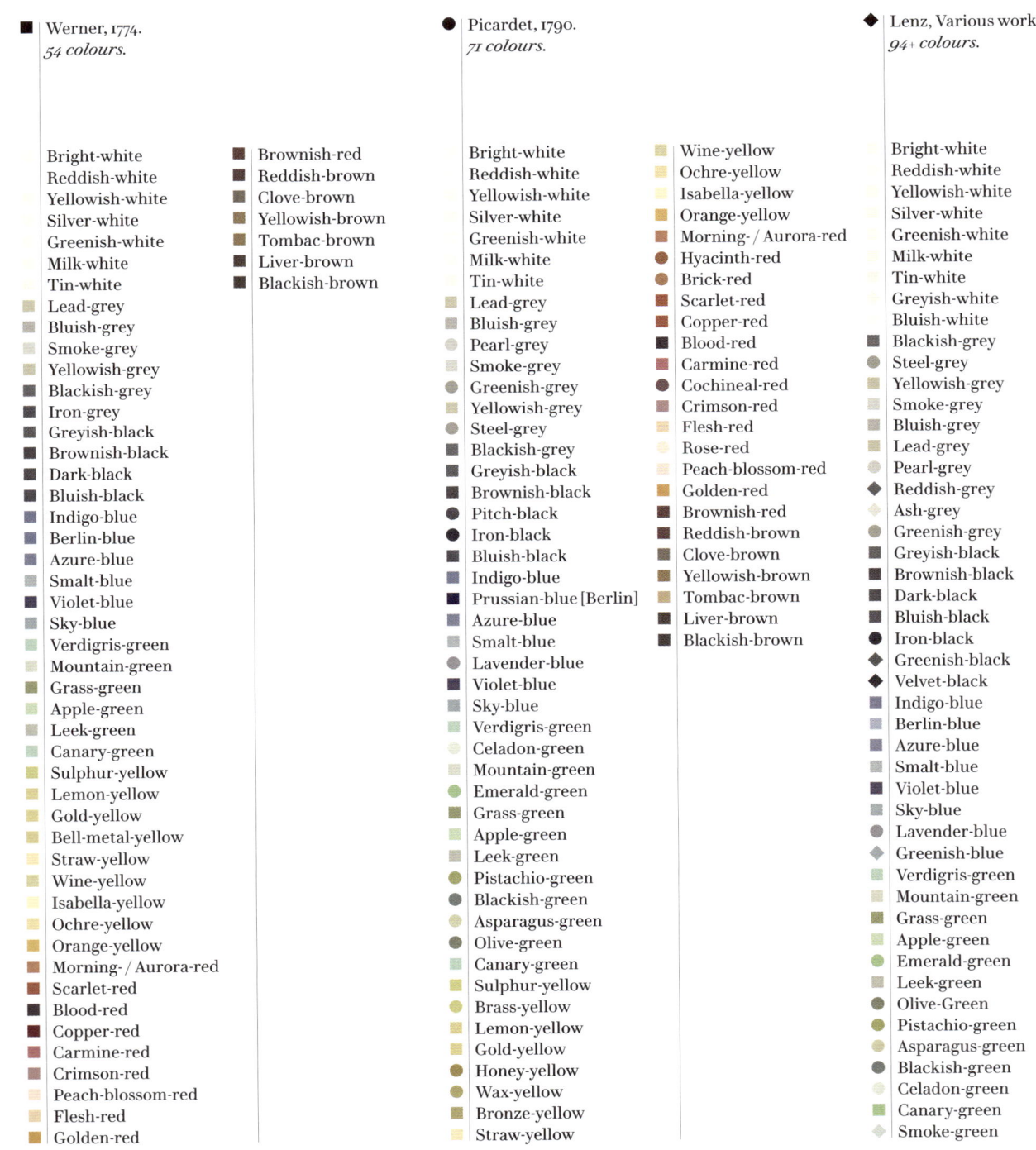

Werner, 1774.
54 colours.

Picardet, 1790.
71 colours.

Lenz, Various works.
94+ colours.

Werner, 1774:

Bright-white
Reddish-white
Yellowish-white
Silver-white
Greenish-white
Milk-white
Tin-white
Lead-grey
Bluish-grey
Smoke-grey
Yellowish-grey
Blackish-grey
Iron-grey
Greyish-black
Brownish-black
Dark-black
Bluish-black
Indigo-blue
Berlin-blue
Azure-blue
Smalt-blue
Violet-blue
Sky-blue
Verdigris-green
Mountain-green
Grass-green
Apple-green
Leek-green
Canary-green
Sulphur-yellow
Lemon-yellow
Gold-yellow
Bell-metal-yellow
Straw-yellow
Wine-yellow
Isabella-yellow
Ochre-yellow
Orange-yellow
Morning- / Aurora-red
Scarlet-red
Blood-red
Copper-red
Carmine-red
Crimson-red
Peach-blossom-red
Flesh-red
Golden-red

Brownish-red
Reddish-brown
Clove-brown
Yellowish-brown
Tombac-brown
Liver-brown
Blackish-brown

Picardet, 1790:

Bright-white
Reddish-white
Yellowish-white
Silver-white
Greenish-white
Milk-white
Tin-white
Lead-grey
Bluish-grey
Pearl-grey
Smoke-grey
Greenish-grey
Yellowish-grey
Steel-grey
Blackish-grey
Greyish-black
Brownish-black
Pitch-black
Iron-black
Bluish-black
Indigo-blue
Prussian-blue [Berlin]
Azure-blue
Smalt-blue
Lavender-blue
Violet-blue
Sky-blue
Verdigris-green
Celadon-green
Mountain-green
Emerald-green
Grass-green
Apple-green
Leek-green
Pistachio-green
Blackish-green
Asparagus-green
Olive-green
Canary-green
Sulphur-yellow
Brass-yellow
Lemon-yellow
Gold-yellow
Honey-yellow
Wax-yellow
Bronze-yellow
Straw-yellow

Wine-yellow
Ochre-yellow
Isabella-yellow
Orange-yellow
Morning- / Aurora-red
Hyacinth-red
Brick-red
Scarlet-red
Copper-red
Blood-red
Carmine-red
Cochineal-red
Crimson-red
Flesh-red
Rose-red
Peach-blossom-red
Golden-red
Brownish-red
Reddish-brown
Clove-brown
Yellowish-brown
Tombac-brown
Liver-brown
Blackish-brown

Lenz, Various works:

Bright-white
Reddish-white
Yellowish-white
Silver-white
Greenish-white
Milk-white
Tin-white
Greyish-white
Bluish-white
Blackish-grey
Steel-grey
Yellowish-grey
Smoke-grey
Bluish-grey
Lead-grey
Pearl-grey
Reddish-grey
Ash-grey
Greenish-grey
Greyish-black
Brownish-black
Dark-black
Bluish-black
Iron-black
Greenish-black
Velvet-black
Indigo-blue
Berlin-blue
Azure-blue
Smalt-blue
Violet-blue
Sky-blue
Lavender-blue
Greenish-blue
Verdigris-green
Mountain-green
Grass-green
Apple-green
Emerald-green
Leek-green
Olive-Green
Pistachio-green
Asparagus-green
Blackish-green
Celadon-green
Canary-green
Smoke-green

The need for the establishment of a universal standard colour system became important to natural scientists in the late 18th and early 19th centuries for the identification of species in the field and for taxonomic purposes. In addition, artists needed recourse to a standard set of colours in order to depict animals, vegetables and minerals accurately. Werner's original colour standard nomenclature, published in his mineralogy textbook *Of the External Characteristics of Fossils* (1774), featured 54 colour standards and was designed to be used in conjunction with his colour suite of minerals. Over the next 40 years or so he compiled revised and expanded lists and sent some to his students, including Widenmann and Jameson, and one to Picardet, who, in 1790, was the first to translate Werner's textbook into French. Mineralogists and naturalists followed in Werner's wake, creating their own lists of colour standards, each drawing to varying extents upon previous nomenclatures, including Werner's unpublished lists, at different stages, and adding new hues of their own. On these pages we show the development of published colour standard nomenclatures of particular relevance to Werner and Syme; we have necessarily had to be selective. Lenz wrote many works that included colour nomenclatures and we have chosen only those that pertain to the Werner–Syme development of lists of colour standards. The shape used to denote each colour name indicates the name of the scientist who introduced it in a published work within this context. Where the colour name was altered slightly but the hue remained the same, we have indicated the original name in square brackets.

⬟ Widenmann, 1794.
74 colours.

◼ Kirwan, 1794.
83 colours.

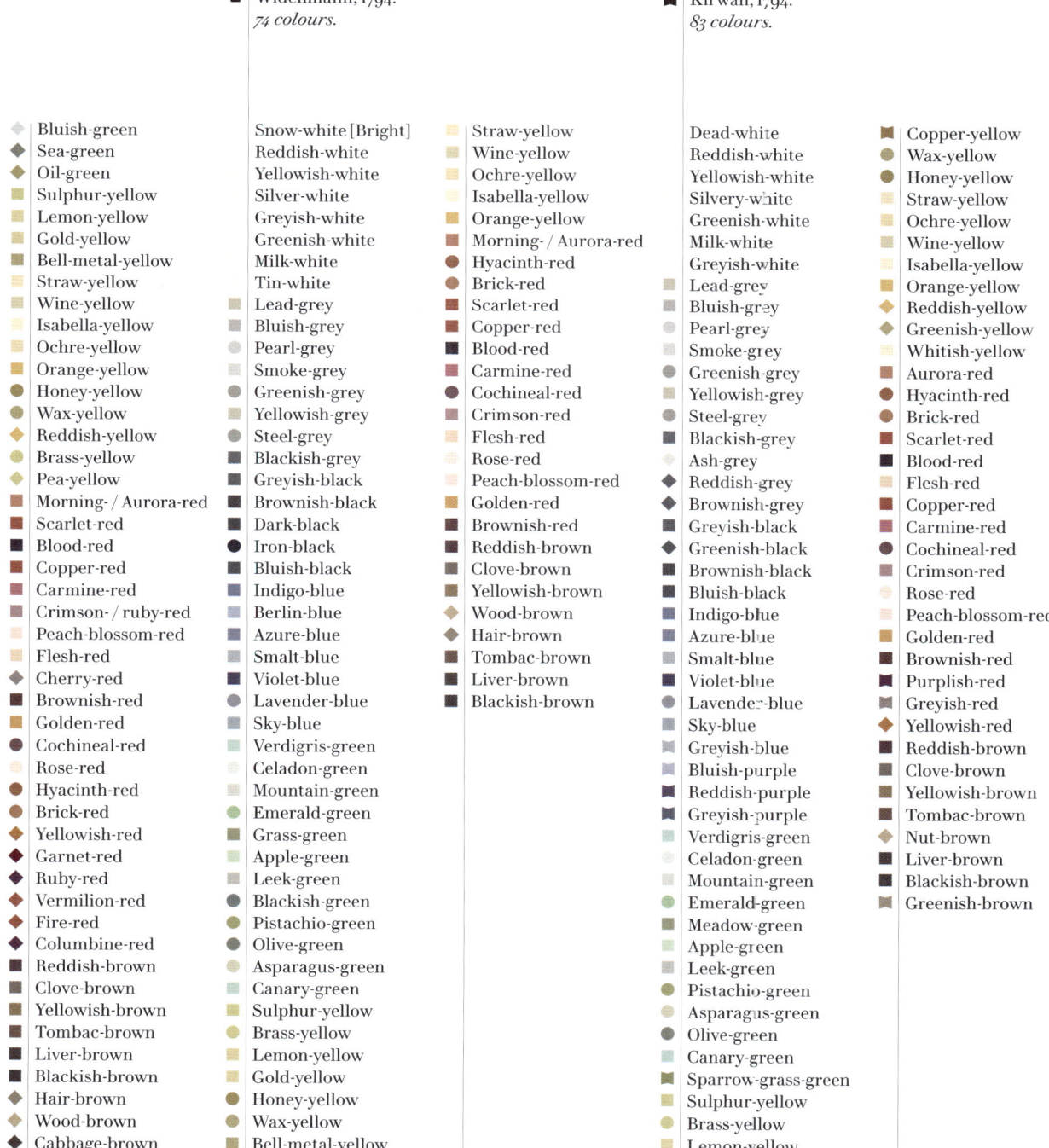

Bluish-green
Sea-green
Oil-green
Sulphur-yellow
Lemon-yellow
Gold-yellow
Bell-metal-yellow
Straw-yellow
Wine-yellow
Isabella-yellow
Ochre-yellow
Orange-yellow
Honey-yellow
Wax-yellow
Reddish-yellow
Brass-yellow
Pea-yellow
Morning- / Aurora-red
Scarlet-red
Blood-red
Copper-red
Carmine-red
Crimson- / ruby-red
Peach-blossom-red
Flesh-red
Cherry-red
Brownish-red
Golden-red
Cochineal-red
Rose-red
Hyacinth-red
Brick-red
Yellowish-red
Garnet-red
Ruby-red
Vermilion-red
Fire-red
Columbine-red
Reddish-brown
Clove-brown
Yellowish-brown
Tombac-brown
Liver-brown
Blackish-brown
Hair-brown
Wood-brown
Cabbage-brown

Snow-white [Bright]
Reddish-white
Yellowish-white
Silver-white
Greyish-white
Greenish-white
Milk-white
Tin-white
Lead-grey
Bluish-grey
Pearl-grey
Smoke-grey
Greenish-grey
Yellowish-grey
Steel-grey
Blackish-grey
Greyish-black
Brownish-black
Dark-black
Iron-black
Bluish-black
Indigo-blue
Berlin-blue
Azure-blue
Smalt-blue
Violet-blue
Lavender-blue
Sky-blue
Verdigris-green
Celadon-green
Mountain-green
Emerald-green
Grass-green
Apple-green
Leek-green
Blackish-green
Pistachio-green
Olive-green
Asparagus-green
Canary-green
Sulphur-yellow
Brass-yellow
Lemon-yellow
Gold-yellow
Honey-yellow
Wax-yellow
Bell-metal-yellow

Straw-yellow
Wine-yellow
Ochre-yellow
Isabella-yellow
Orange-yellow
Morning- / Aurora-red
Hyacinth-red
Brick-red
Scarlet-red
Copper-red
Blood-red
Carmine-red
Cochineal-red
Crimson-red
Flesh-red
Rose-red
Peach-blossom-red
Golden-red
Brownish-red
Reddish-brown
Clove-brown
Yellowish-brown
Wood-brown
Hair-brown
Tombac-brown
Liver-brown
Blackish-brown

Dead-white
Reddish-white
Yellowish-white
Silvery-white
Greenish-white
Milk-white
Greyish-white
Lead-grey
Bluish-grey
Pearl-grey
Smoke-grey
Greenish-grey
Yellowish-grey
Steel-grey
Blackish-grey
Ash-grey
Reddish-grey
Brownish-grey
Greyish-black
Greenish-black
Brownish-black
Bluish-black
Indigo-blue
Azure-blue
Smalt-blue
Violet-blue
Lavender-blue
Sky-blue
Greyish-blue
Bluish-purple
Reddish-purple
Greyish-purple
Verdigris-green
Celadon-green
Mountain-green
Emerald-green
Meadow-green
Apple-green
Leek-green
Pistachio-green
Asparagus-green
Olive-green
Canary-green
Sparrow-grass-green
Sulphur-yellow
Brass-yellow
Lemon-yellow

Copper-yellow
Wax-yellow
Honey-yellow
Straw-yellow
Ochre-yellow
Wine-yellow
Isabella-yellow
Orange-yellow
Reddish-yellow
Greenish-yellow
Whitish-yellow
Aurora-red
Hyacinth-red
Brick-red
Scarlet-red
Blood-red
Flesh-red
Copper-red
Carmine-red
Cochineal-red
Crimson-red
Rose-red
Peach-blossom-red
Golden-red
Brownish-red
Purplish-red
Greyish-red
Yellowish-red
Reddish-brown
Clove-brown
Yellowish-brown
Tombac-brown
Nut-brown
Liver-brown
Blackish-brown
Greenish-brown

INTRODUCTION.

Emmerling, 1799.
78 colours.

Snow-white [Bright]
Reddish-white
Yellowish-white
Silver-white
Greyish-white
Greenish-white
Milk-white
Tin-white
Lead-grey
Bluish-grey
Pearl-grey
Reddish-grey
Smoke-grey
Greenish-grey
Yellowish-grey
Steel-grey
Ash-grey
Blackish-Grey
Greyish-black
Dark-black
Iron-black
Brownish-black
Greenish-black
Bluish-black
Indigo-blue
Berlin-blue
Azure-blue
Violet-blue
Lavender-blue
Smalt-blue
Sky-blue
Verdigris-green
Celadon-green
Mountain-green
Emerald-green
Grass-green
Apple-green
Leek-green
Blackish-green
Pistachio-green
Olive-green
Asparagus-green
Canary-green
Sulphur-yellow
Brass-yellow
Straw-yellow
Honey-yellow
Wax-yellow
Bell-metal-yellow
Lemon-yellow
Gold-yellow
Wine-yellow
Ochre-yellow
Isabella-yellow
Orange-yellow
Morning- / Aurora-red
Hyacinth-red
Brick-red
Flesh-red
Scarlet-red
Copper-red
Blood-red

Carmine-red
Cochineal-red
Rose-red
Crimson-red
Columbine-red
Cherry-red
Peach-blossom-red
Brownish-red
Reddish-brown
Clove-brown
Hair-brown
Yellowish-brown
Tombac-brown
Wood-brown
Liver-brown
Blackish-brown

Jameson, 1805.
84 colours.

Snow-white [Bright]
Reddish-white
Yellowish-white
Silver-white
Greyish-white
Greenish-white
Milk-white
Tin-white
Lead-grey
Common lead-grey
Fresh lead-grey
Blackish lead-grey
Whitish lead-grey
Bluish-grey
Smoke-grey
Pearl-grey
Greenish-grey
Yellowish-grey
Ash-grey
Steel-grey
Greyish-black
Iron-black
Velvet-black
Pitch-black, or
brownish-black
Greenish-black,
or raven-black
Bluish-black
Indigo-blue
Berlin-blue
Azure-blue
Violet-blue
Plum-blue
Lavender-blue
Smalt-blue
Sky-blue
Verdigris-green
Celadon-green
Mountain-green
Leek-green
Emerald-green
Apple-green
Grass-green
Blackish-green
Pistachio-green
Asparagus-green
Olive-green
Oil-green
Siskin-green
Sulphur-yellow
Brass-yellow
Straw-yellow
Bronze-yellow
Wax-yellow
Honey-yellow
Lemon-yellow
Gold-yellow
Ochre-yellow
Wine-yellow
Cream-yellow, or
Isabella-yellow
Orange-yellow

Aurora- /
Morning-red
Hyacinth-red
Tile-red
Scarlet-red
Blood-red
Flesh-red
Copper-red
Carmine-red
Cochineal-red
Crimson-red
Columbine-red
Rose-red
Peach-blossom-red
Cherry-red
Brownish-red
Reddish-brown
Clove-brown
Hair-brown
Broccoli-brown
Chesnut-brown [*sic*]
Yellowish-brown
Pinchbeck-brown
[Tombac]
Wood-brown
Liver-brown
Blackish-brown

Syme, 1814.
108 colours.

Snow White [Bright]
Reddish White
Purplish White
Yellowish White
Orange-coloured
White
Greenish White
Skimmed-milk White
[Milk]
Greyish White
Ash Grey
Smoke Grey
French Grey
Pearl Grey
Yellowish Grey
Bluish Grey
Greenish Grey
Blackish Grey
Greyish Black
Bluish Black
Greenish Black
Pitch, or Brownish
Black
Reddish Black
Raven Black
Velvet Black
Indigo Blue
Prussian Blue
China Blue
Azure Blue
Ultramarine Blue
Flax-flower Blue
Berlin Blue
Verditter [*sic*] Blue
Greenish Blue [Sky]
Greyish Blue [Smalt]
Bluish Lilac Purple
Bluish Purple
Violet Purple [Blue]
Pansy Purple
Campanula Purple
Imperial Purple
Auricula Purple
Plum Purple [Blue]
Red Lilac Purple
Lavender Purple
[Blue]
Pale Blackish Purple
Celandine Green
[Celadon]
Mountain Green
Leek Green
Blackish Green
Verdigris Green
Bluish Green
Apple Green
Emerald Green
Grass Green
Duck Green
Sap Green
Pistachio Green
Asparagus Green

- Olive Green
- Oil Green
- Siskin Green
- Sulphur Yellow
- Primrose Yellow
- Wax Yellow
- Lemon Yellow
- Gamboge Yellow
- King's Yellow
- Saffron Yellow
- Gallstone Yellow
- Honey Yellow
- Straw Yellow
- Wine Yellow
- Sienna Yellow
- Ochre Yellow
- Cream Yellow [Isabella]
- Dutch Orange [Orange-yellow]
- Buff Orange
- Orpiment Orange
- Brownish Orange
- Reddish Orange
- Deep Reddish Orange
- Tile Red
- Hyacinth Red
- Scarlet Red
- Vermilion Red
- Aurora Red
- Arterial Blood Red
- Flesh Red
- Rose Red
- Peach Blossom Red
- Carmine Red
- Lake Red
- Crimson Red
- Cochineal Red
- Veinous Blood Red [Blood]
- Brownish Purple Red [Cherry]
- Chocolate Red
- Brownish Red
- Deep Orange-coloured Brown
- Deep Reddish Brown
- Umber Brown
- Chesnut [sic] brown
- Yellowish Brown
- Wood Brown
- Liver Brown
- Hair Brown
- Broccoli Brown
- Olive / Clove Brown
- Blackish Brown

Cleaveland, 1816.
80 colours.

- Snow-white [Bright]
- Reddish-white
- Yellowish-white
- Silver-white
- Greyish-white
- Greenish-white
- Milk-white
- Tin-white
- Lead-grey
- Bluish-grey
- Smoke-grey
- Pearl-grey
- Greenish-grey
- Yellowish-grey
- Ash-grey
- Steel-grey
- Greyish-black
- Iron-black
- Velvet-black
- Pitch-black
- Raven-black
- Bluish-black
- Indigo-blue
- Berlin-blue
- Azure-blue
- Violet-blue
- Plum-blue
- Lavender-blue
- Smalt-blue
- Sky-blue
- Verdigris-green
- Sea-green
- Mountain-green
- Emerald-green
- Apple-green
- Grass-green
- Blackish-green
- Leek-green
- Pistachio-green
- Asparagus-green
- Olive-green
- Oil-green
- Siskin-green
- Sulphur-yellow
- Brass-yellow
- Straw-yellow
- Bronze-yellow
- Wax-yellow
- Honey-yellow
- Lemon-yellow
- Gold-yellow
- Ochre-yellow
- Wine-yellow
- Isabella-yellow
- Orange-yellow
- Aurora-red
- Hyacinth-red
- Brick-red
- Scarlet-red
- Blood-red
- Flesh-red
- Copper-red

- Carmine-red
- Cochineal-red
- Crimson-red
- Columbine-red
- Rose-red
- Peach-blossom-red
- Cherry-red
- Brownish-red
- Reddish-brown
- Clove-brown
- Hair-brown
- Broccoli-brown
- Chesnut-brown [sic]
- Yellowish-brown
- Pinchbeck-brown [Tombac]
- Wood-brown
- Liver-brown
- Blackish-brown

Syme, 1821.
110 colours.

- Snow White [Bright]
- Reddish White
- Purplish White
- Yellowish White
- Orange-coloured White
- Greenish White
- Skimmed-milk White [Milk]
- Greyish White
- Ash Grey
- Smoke Grey
- French Grey
- Pearl Grey
- Yellowish Grey
- Bluish Grey
- Greenish Grey
- Blackish Grey
- Greyish Black
- Bluish Black
- Greenish Black
- Pitch, or Brownish Black
- Reddish Black
- Ink Black
- Velvet Black
- Scotch Blue
- Prussian Blue
- Indigo Blue
- China Blue
- Azure Blue
- Ultramarine Blue
- Flax-flower Blue
- Berlin Blue
- Verditter [sic] Blue
- Greenish Blue [Sky]
- Greyish Blue [Smalt]
- Bluish Lilac Purple
- Bluish Purple
- Violet Purple [Blue]
- Pansy Purple
- Campanula Purple
- Imperial Purple
- Auricula Purple
- Plum Purple [Blue]
- Red Lilac Purple
- Lavender Purple [Blue]
- Pale Blackish Purple
- Celandine Green [Celadon]
- Mountain Green
- Leek Green
- Blackish Green
- Verdigris Green
- Bluish Green
- Apple Green
- Emerald Green
- Grass Green
- Duck Green
- Sap Green
- Pistachio Green

- Asparagus Green
- Olive Green
- Oil Green
- Siskin Green
- Sulphur Yellow
- Primrose Yellow
- Wax Yellow
- Lemon Yellow
- Gamboge Yellow
- King's Yellow
- Saffron Yellow
- Gallstone Yellow
- Honey Yellow
- Straw Yellow
- Wine Yellow
- Sienna Yellow
- Ochre Yellow
- Cream Yellow [Isabella]
- Dutch Orange [Orange-yellow]
- Buff Orange
- Orpiment Orange
- Brownish Orange
- Reddish Orange
- Deep Reddish Orange
- Tile Red
- Hyacinth Red
- Scarlet Red
- Vermilion Red
- Aurora Red
- Arterial Blood Red
- Flesh Red
- Rose Red
- Peach Blossom Red
- Carmine Red
- Lake Red
- Crimson Red
- Purplish Red [Columbine]
- Cochineal Red
- Veinous Blood Red [Blood]
- Brownish Purple Red [Cherry]
- Chocolate Red
- Brownish Red
- Deep Orange-coloured Brown
- Deep Reddish Brown
- Umber Brown
- Chesnut [sic] brown
- Yellowish Brown
- Wood Brown
- Liver Brown
- Hair Brown
- Broccoli Brown
- Olive / Clove Brown
- Blackish Brown

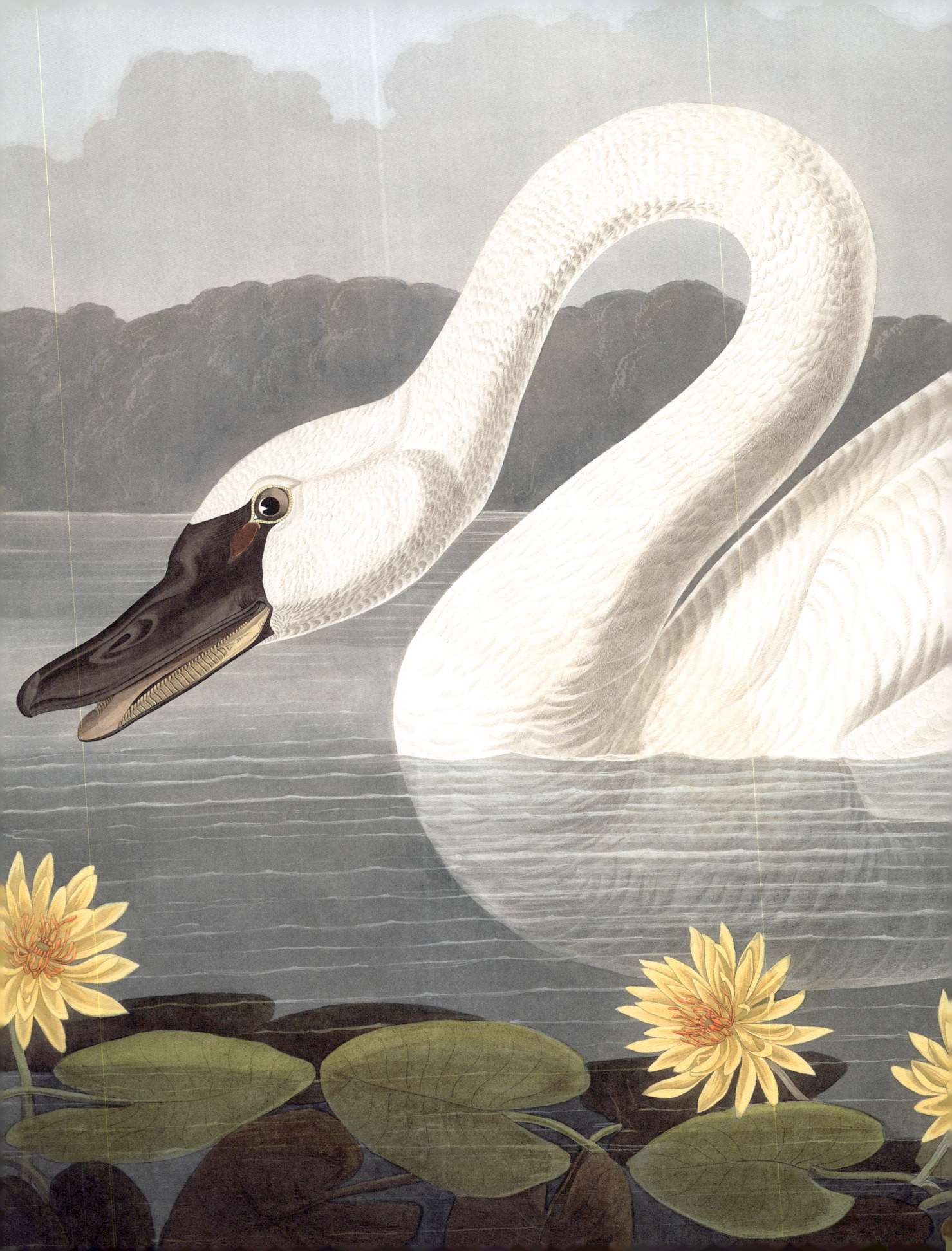

i.

WHITES, GREYS AND BLACKS.

WHITES.

No.	Names.	Colours.	ANIMAL.	VEGETABLE.	MINERAL.
1	Snow White.		Breast of the black headed Gull.	Snow-Drop.	Carara Marble and Calc Sinter.
2	Reddish White.		Egg of Grey Linnet.	Back of the Christmas Rose.	Porcelain Earth.
3	Purplish White.		Junction of the Neck and Back of the Kittiwake Gull.	White Geranium or Storks Bill.	Arragonite.
4	Yellowish White.		Egret.	Hawthorn Blossom.	Chalk and Tripoli.
5	Orange coloured White.		Breast of White or Screech Owl.	Large Wild Convolvulus.	French Porcelain Clay.
6	Greenish White.		Vent Coverts of Golden crested Wren.	Polyanthus Narcissus.	Calc Sinter.
7	Skimmed milk White.		White of the Human Eyeballs.	Back of the Petals of Blue Hepatica.	Common Opal.
8	Greyish White.		Inside Quill-feathers of the Kittiwake.	White Hamburgh Grapes.	Granular Limestone.

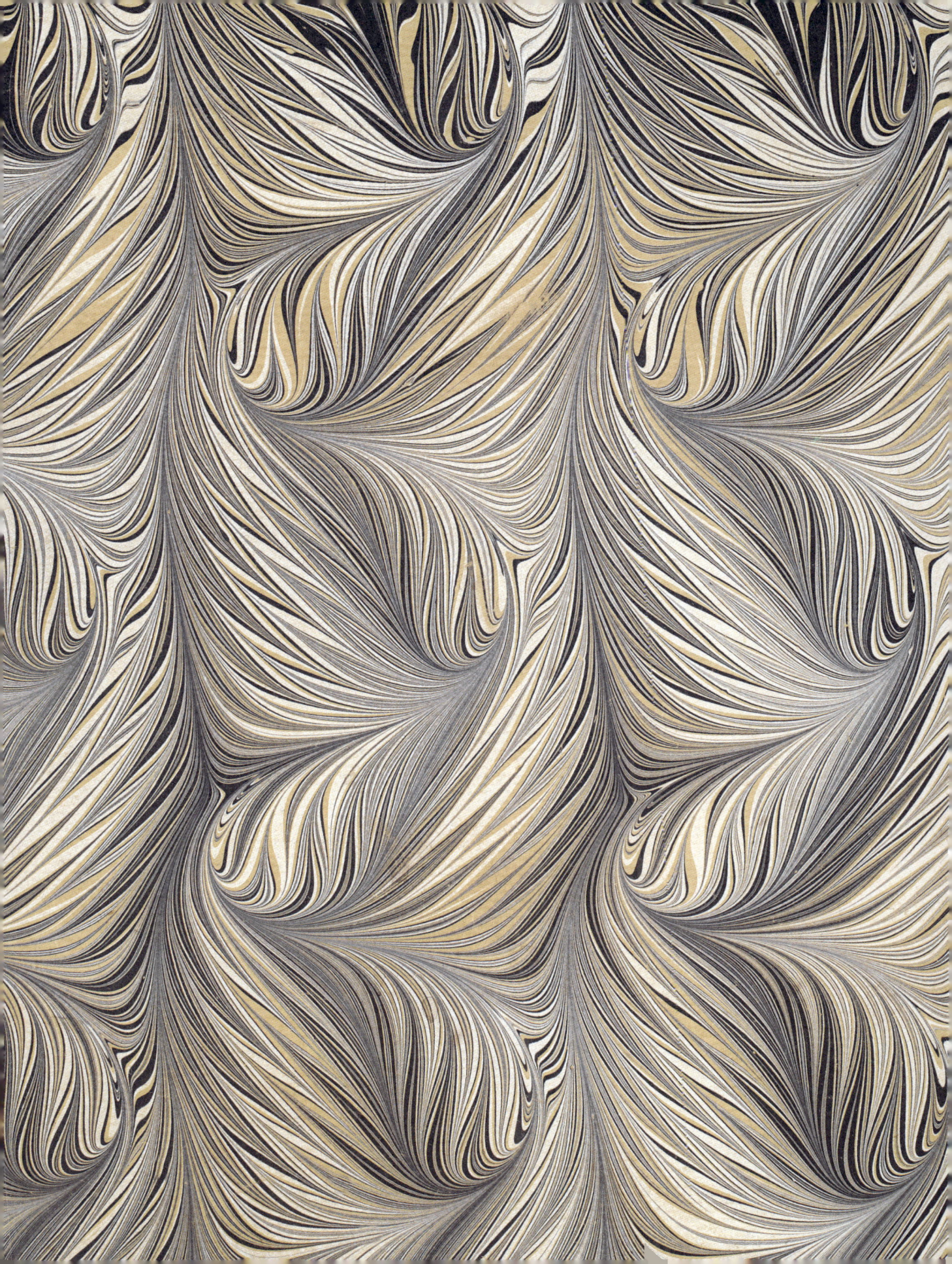

BLACKS.

BLACKS

No	Names	Colours	ANIMAL	VEGETABLE	MINERAL
17	Greyish Black		Water Ousel. Breast and upper Part of Back of Water Hen.		Basalt.
18	Bluish Black		Largest Black Slug	Crowberry.	Black Cobalt Ochre.
19	Greenish Black		Breast of Lapwing		Hornblende
20	Pitch or Brownish Black		Guillemot. Wing Coverts of Black Cock.		Yenite Mica
21	Reddish Black		Spots on Large Wings of Tyger Moth. Breast of Pochard Duck.	Berry of Fuchsia Coccinea	Oliven Ore
22	Ink Black			Berry of Deadly Night Shade	Oliven Ore
23	Velvet Black		Mole. Tail Feathers of Black Cock.	Black of Red and Black West Indian Peas.	Obsidian

GREYS.

GREYS.

Nº	Names.	Colours.	ANIMAL.	VEGETABLE.	MINERAL.
9	Ash Grey.		Breast of long tailed Hen Titmouse.	Fresh Wood ashes	Flint.
10	Smoke Grey.		Breast of the Robin round the Red.		Flint.
11	French Grey.		Breast of Pied Wag tail.		
12	Pearl Grey.		Backs of black headed and Kittiwake Gulls.	Back of Petals of Purple Hepatica.	Porcelain Jasper.
13	Yellowish Grey.		Vent coverts of White Rump.	Stems of the Barberry.	Common Calcedony.
14	Bluish Grey.		Back, and tail Coverts Wood Pigeon.		Limestone
15	Greenish Grey.		Quill feathers of the Robin.	Bark of Ash Tree.	Clay Slate, Wacke.
16	Blackish Grey.		Back of Nut-hatch.	Old Stems of Hawthorn.	Flint.

WHITES.

No.	Names.	Colours.	ANIMAL.		
1	Snow White.		Breast of the black headed Gull.		
2	Reddish White.		Egg of Grey Linnet.		
3	Purplish White.		Junction of the Neck and Back of the Kittiwake Gull.		
4	Yellowish White.		Egret.		
5	Orange-coloured White.		Breast of White or Screech Owl.		
6	Greenish White.		Vent Coverts of Golden crested Wren.		
7	Skimmed-milk White.		White of the Human Eyeballs.		
8	Greyish White.		Inside Quill-feathers of the Kittiwake.		

Syme's 1821 edition included five of Werner's original whites (numbers 1, 2, 4, 6 and 7), though he has renamed Bright White 'Snow White' and Milk White 'Skimmed-milk White'. One white is from the Lenz system (number 8) and two whites from his own 1814 edition (numbers 3 and 5).

WHITES.

	VEGETABLE.		MINERAL.	
	Snow-Drop.		Carara Marble and Calc Sinter.	
	Back of the Christmas Rose.		Porcelain Earth.	
	White Geranium or Stork's Bill.		Arragonite.	
	Hawthorn Blossom.		Chalk and Tripoli.	
	Large Wild Convolvulus.		French Porcelain Clay.	
	Polyanthus Narcissus.		Calc Sinter.	
	Back of the Petals of Blue Hepatica.		Common Opal.	
	White Hamburgh Grapes.		Granular Limestone.	

1.   SNOW WHITE.

(i).   *Breast of the black headed Gull.*
       [Chroicocephalus ridibundus]
(ii). *Snow-Drop.* [*Snowdrop*, Galanthus]
(iii). *Carara Marble.* [*Carrara marble*; *Metamorphic rock*]
       Calc Sinter. [*Calcite*; *Carbonate mineral*]

Snow White, is the characteristic colour of the whites; it is the purest white colour; being free of all intermixture, it resembles new-fallen snow. [W] †

† *Snow White is Syme's name for Werner's Bright White.*

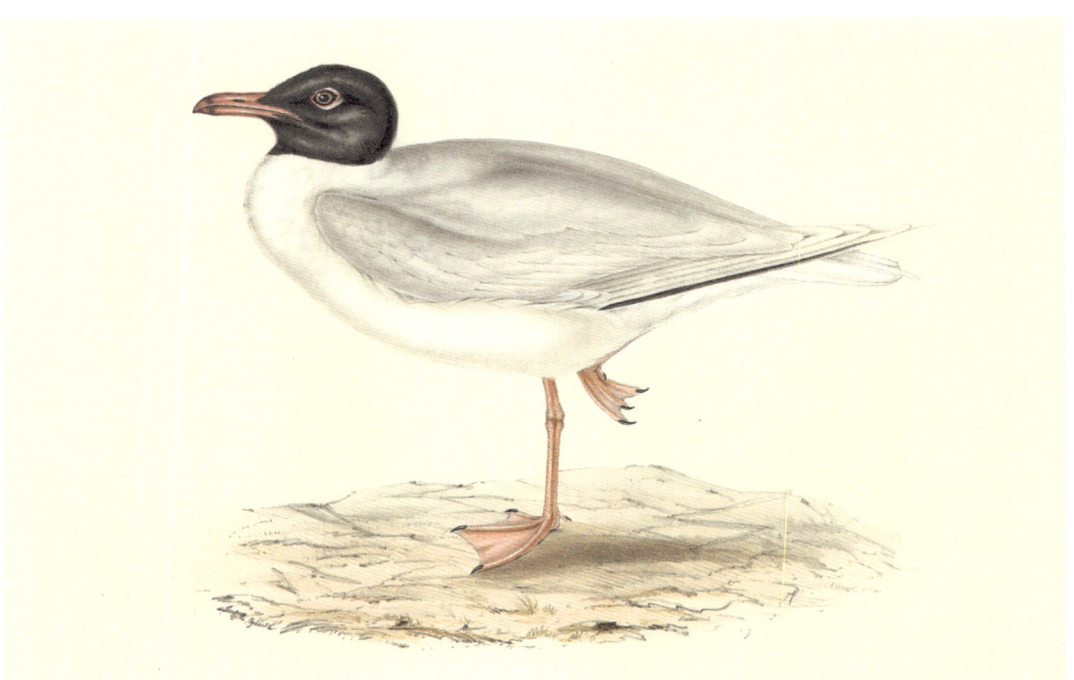

ANIMAL.

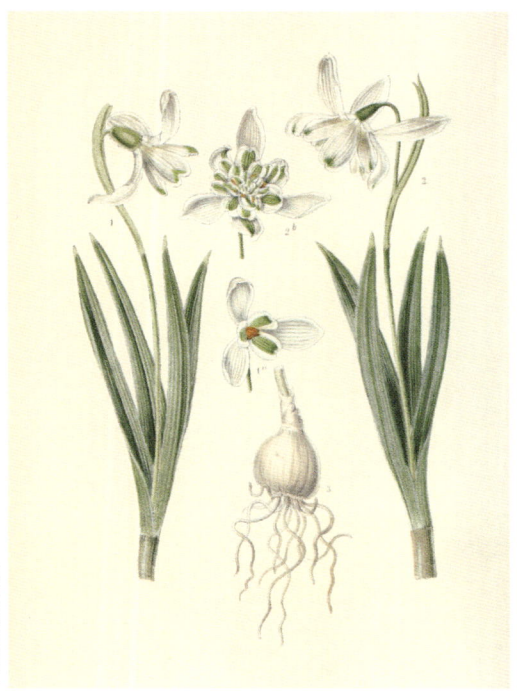

VEGETABLE.

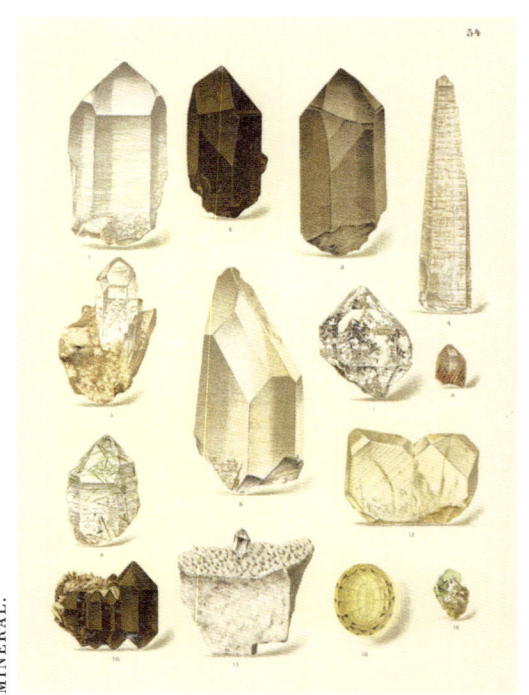

MINERAL.

ANIMAL.
John Gould, *Birds of Europe*, Vol. 5, 1832–37. Snow White is visible on the breast feathers of the black-headed gull.

VEGETABLE.
Cornelis Antoon Jan Abraham Oudemans, *Neerland's Plantentuin*, 1865. Snow White is visible on the petal of the snowdrop.

MINERAL.
Reinhard Brauns, *The Mineral Kingdom*, Vol. 2, 1912. Snow White is visible on the Carrara marble (bottom row, centre left). A piece of quartz is embedded within it.

2.　REDDISH WHITE.

(i).　*Egg of Grey Linnet.* [*Common linnet*; Linaria cannabina]
(ii).　*Back of the Christmas Rose.* [Helleborus niger]
(iii).　*Porcelain Earth.* [*Kaolinite*; *Clay mineral*]

Reddish White, is composed of snow white, with a very minute portion of crimson red and ash grey. [W]

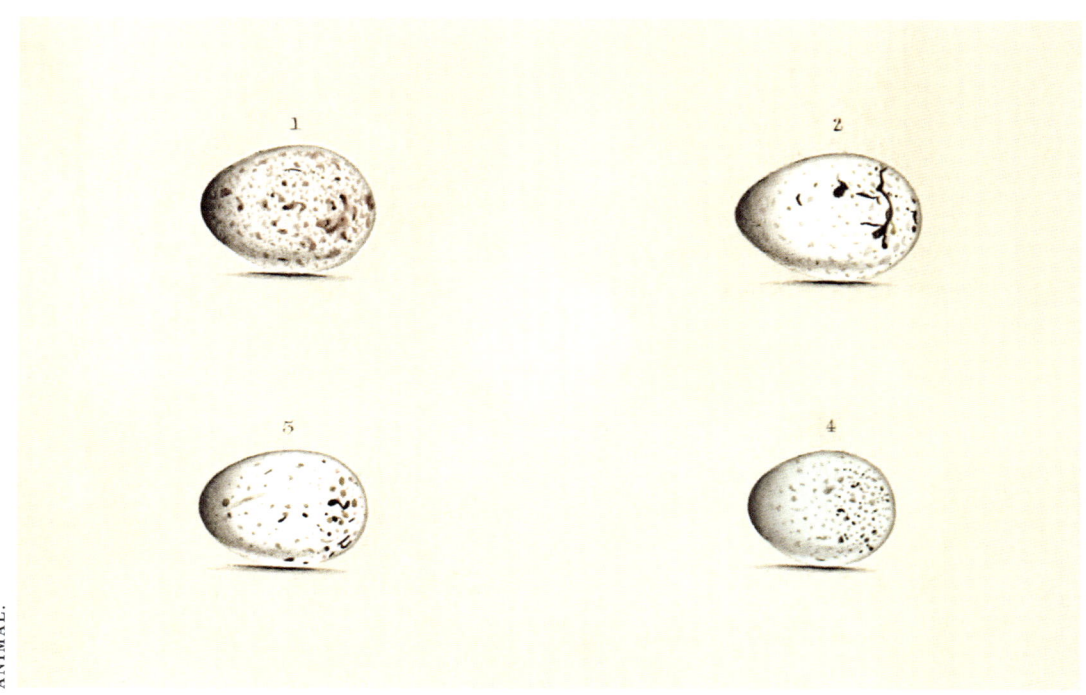

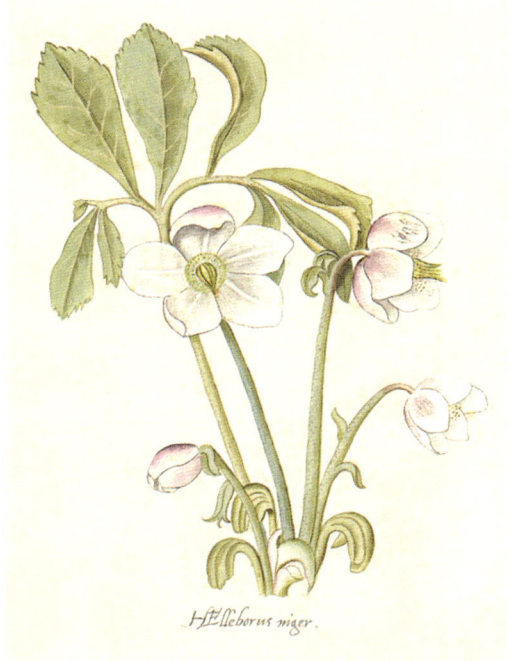

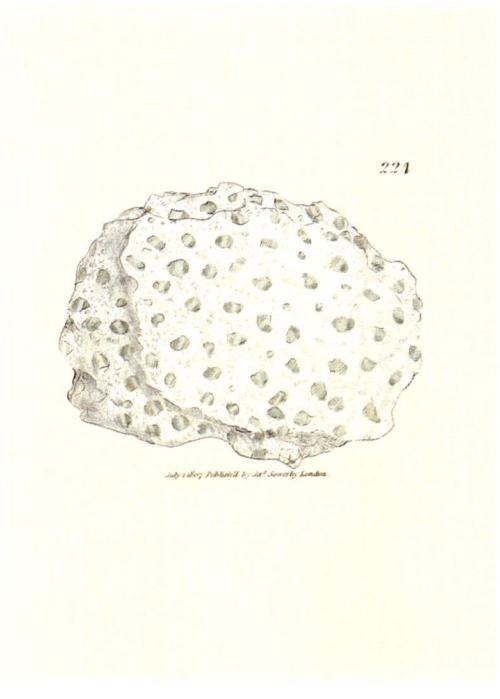

ANIMAL.
William Chapman Hewitson, *British Oology*, Vol. 1, 1833. Reddish White is visible on the egg of the common linnet (top row, left).

VEGETABLE.
John White, *Helleborus niger*, watercolour, *c.* 1600. Reddish White is visible on the back of the petals of the Christmas rose.

MINERAL.
James Sowerby, *British Mineralogy*, Vol. 3, 1802–17. Reddish White is visible on the kaolinite.

3. PURPLISH WHITE.

(i). *Junction of the Neck and Back of the Kittiwake Gull.* [Rissa]
(ii). *White Geranium.* [Geranium]
Stork's Bill. [Erodium cicutarium]
(iii). *Arragonite.* [*Aragonite; Carbonate mineral*]

Purplish White, is snow white, with the slightest tinge of crimson red and Berlin blue, with a very minute portion of ash grey.

ANIMAL.

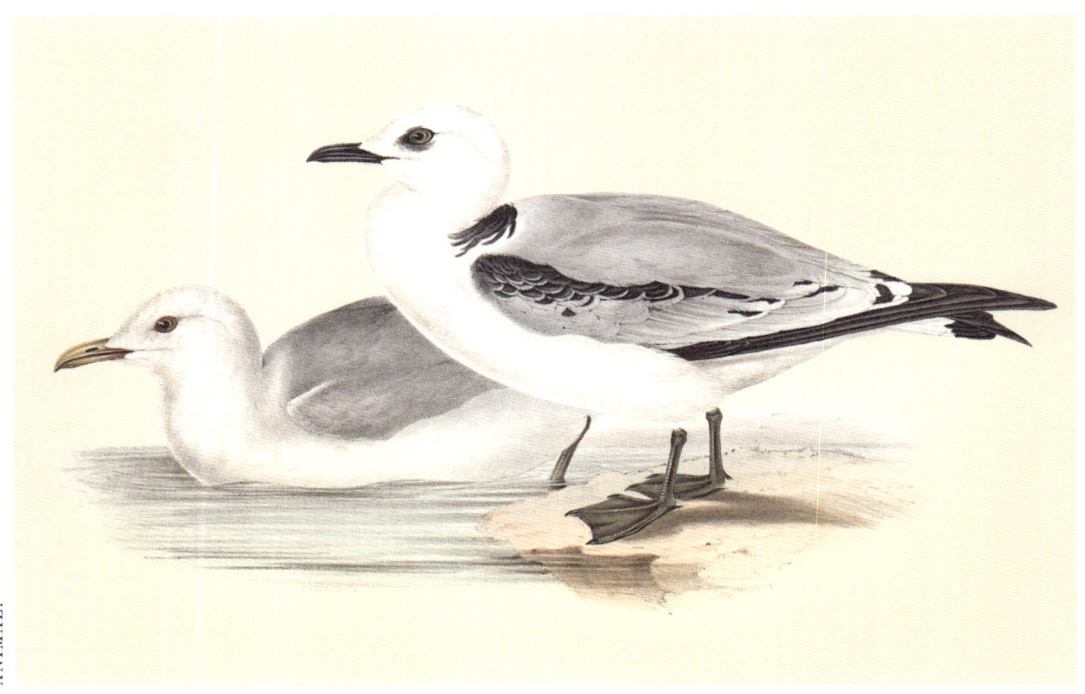

ANIMAL.
John Gould, *Birds of Europe*, Vol. 5, 1832–37. Purplish White is visible where the neck meets the back of the kittiwake gull (left).

VEGETABLE.
A. Mentz and C. H. Ostenfeld, *Billeder af Nordens Flora*, Vol. 1, 1917. Purplish White is visible on the petal of the stork's-bill.

MINERAL.
Gotthilf Heinrich von Schubert, *Naturgeschichte des Tier-, Pflanzen- und Mineralreichs*, 1886. Purplish White is visible on the aragonite (top row, centre left).

VEGETABLE.

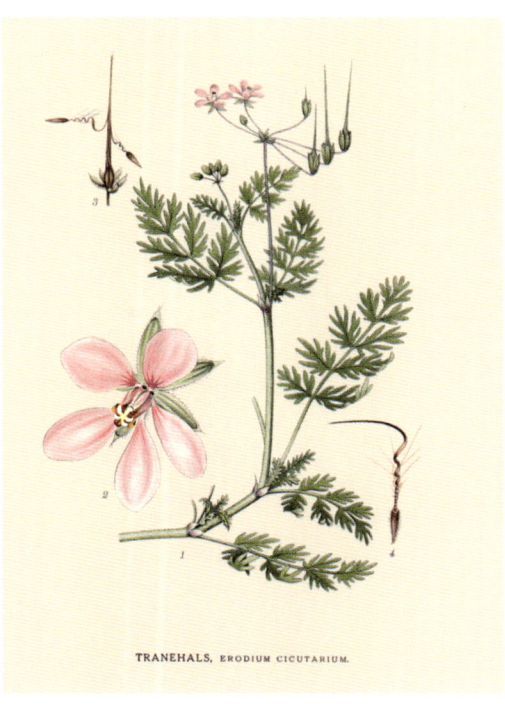

TRANEHALS, ERODIUM CICUTARIUM.

MINERAL.

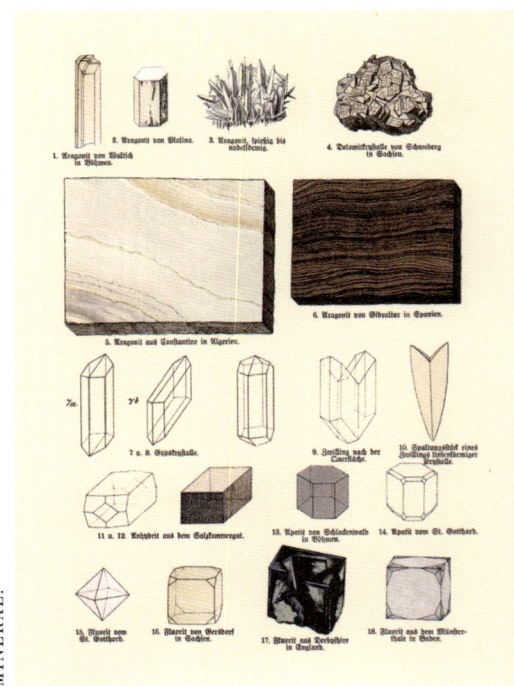

4. YELLOWISH WHITE.

(i).   *Egret*. [Ardeidae]
(ii).   *Hawthorn Blossom*. [Crataegus]
(iii).   *Chalk*. [*Carbonate mineral*]
         Tripoli. [*Rottenstone*; *Siliceous rock*]

Yellowish White, is composed of snow white, with a very little lemon yellow and ash grey. [W]

ANIMAL.

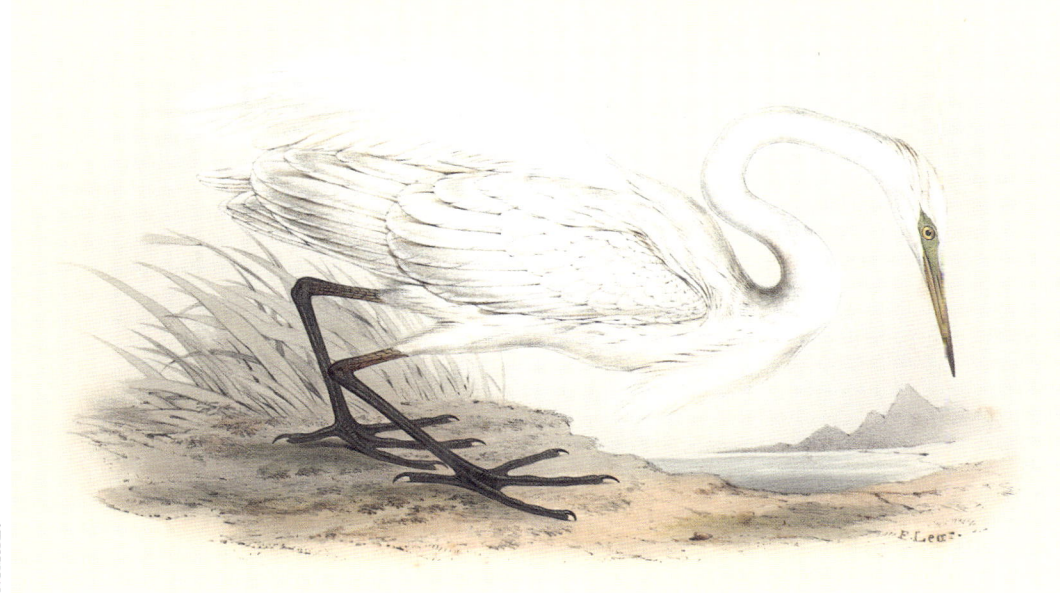

VEGETABLE.

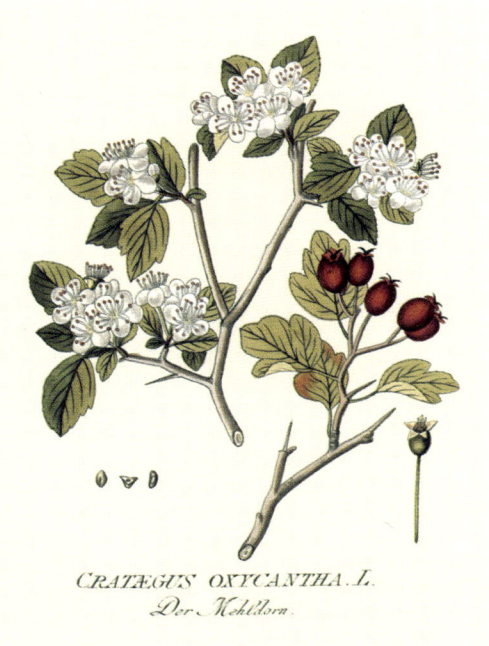

CRATÆGUS OXYCANTHA L.
Der Mehldorn.

MINERAL.

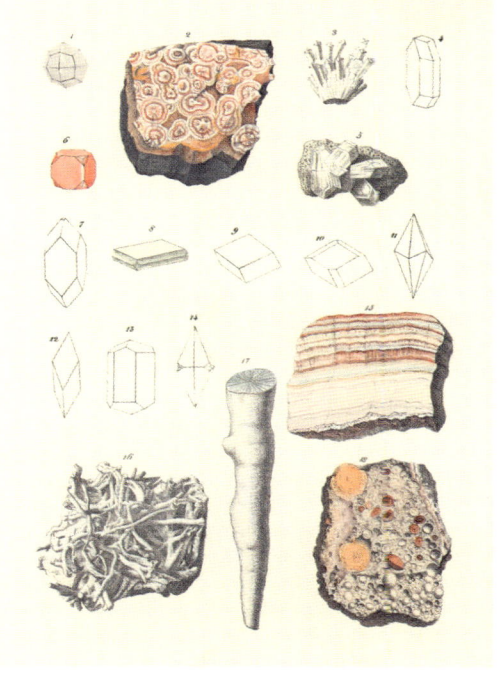

ANIMAL.
John Gould, *Birds of Europe*, Vol. 4, 1832–37. Yellowish White is visible on the feathers of the egret.

VEGETABLE.
Crataegus oxycantha, watercolour, date unknown. Yellowish White is visible on the petals of the hawthorn blossom.

MINERAL.
Johann Gottlob Kurr, *The Mineral Kingdom*, 1859. Yellowish White is visible on the chalk (bottom row, centre).

(i).   *Breast of a White Owl* [*Snowy owl*; Bubo scandiacus] *or Screech Owl.* [Megascops]
(ii). *Large Wild Convolvulus.* [*Bindweed*; Convolvulus]
(iii). *French Porcelain Clay.* [*Kaolinite*; pâte dure; *Clay mineral*]

Orange-coloured White, is snow white, with a very small portion of tile red and king's yellow, and a minute portion of ash grey.

ANIMAL.

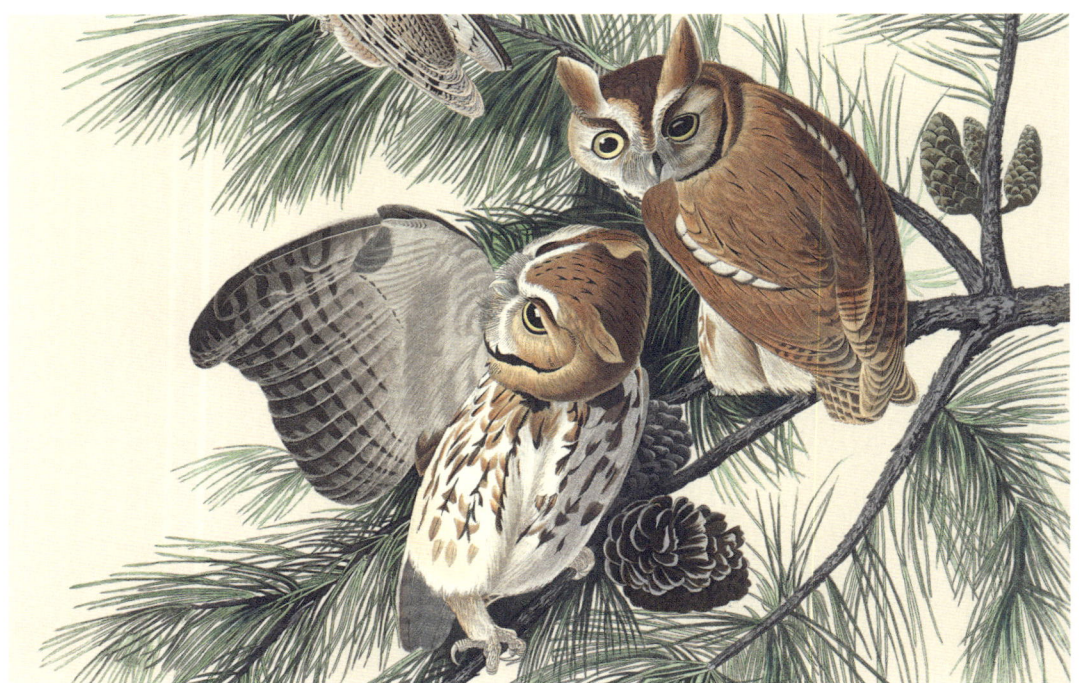

ANIMAL.
John Gould, *Birds of America*, 1827–38. Orange-coloured White is visible on the breast feathers of the screech owl.

VEGETABLE.
A. Mentz and C. H. Ostenfeld, *Billeder af Nordens Flora*, Vol. I, 1917. Orange-coloured White is visible on the petals of the bindweed.

MINERAL.
Alexandre Brongniart, *Premier mémoire sur les kaolins ou argiles à porcelaine*, 1839. Orange-coloured White is visible on the kaolinite. A piece of feldspar is embedded within it.

VEGETABLE.

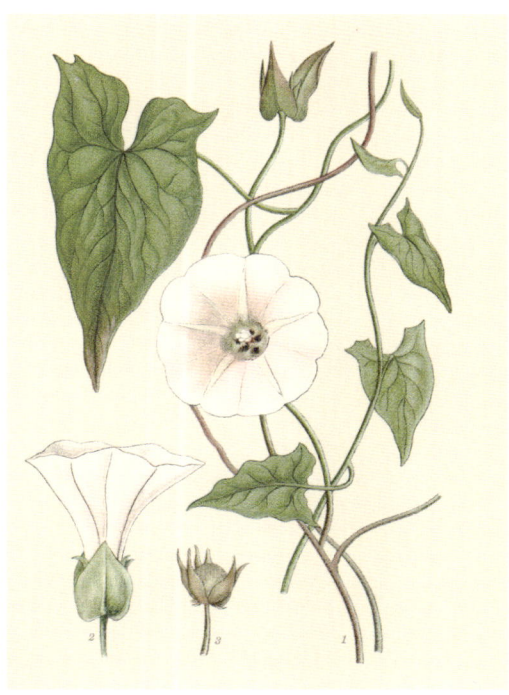

MINERAL.

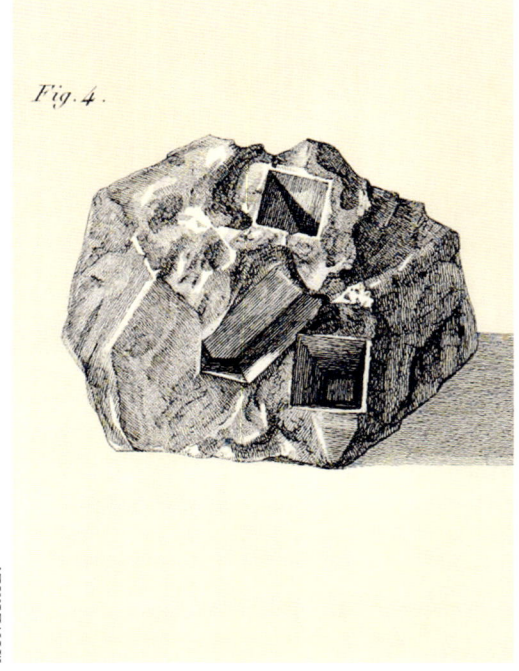

6. GREENISH WHITE.

(i).   *Vent Coverts of Golden crested Wren.* [*Goldcrest*; Regulus regulus]
(ii).   *Polyanthus Narcissus.* [*Daffodil*; Narcissus tazetta]
(iii). *Calc Sinter* [*Calcite*; *Carbonate mineral*]

Greenish White, is snow white, mixed with a very little emerald green and ash grey. [W]

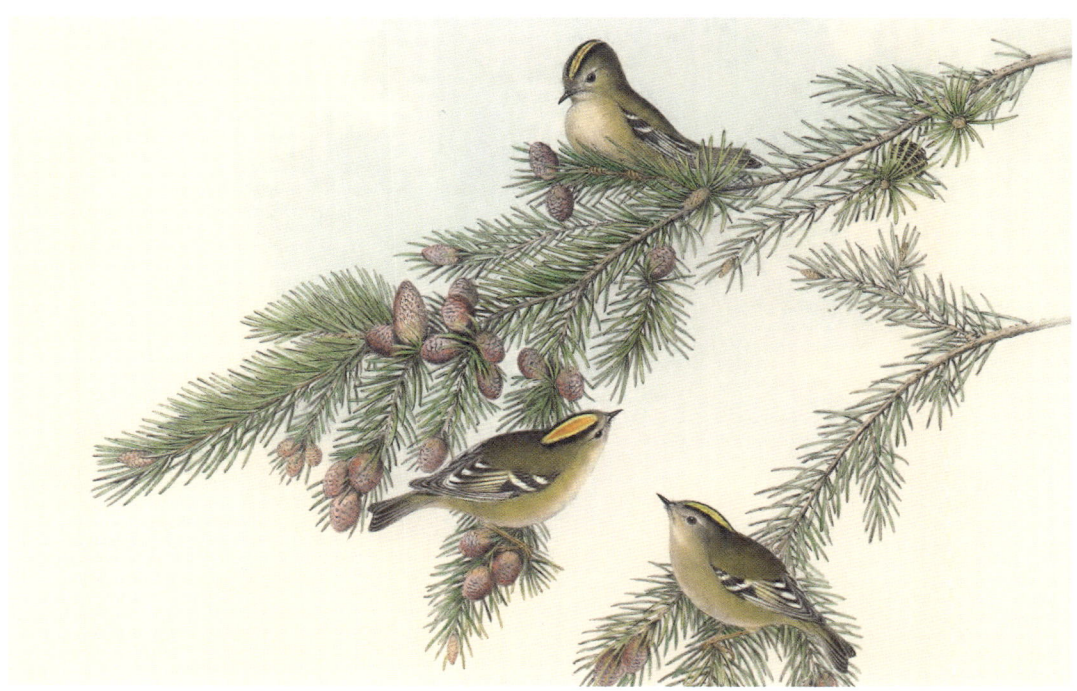

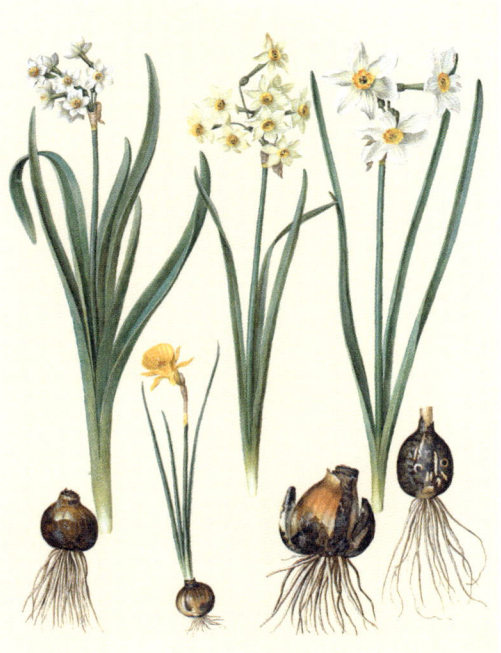

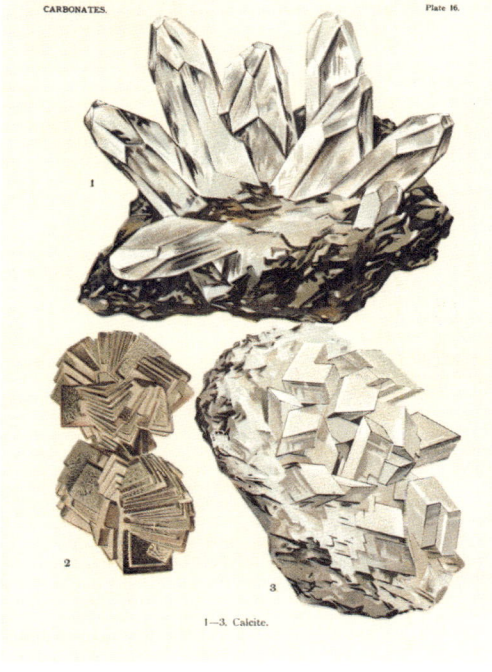

ANIMAL.
John Gould, *Birds of Great Britain*, Vol. 2, 1862–73. Greenish White is visible on the vent coverts, i.e. the feathers around the cloaca, of the goldcrest.

VEGETABLE.
Narcissus tazetta; Narcissus orientalis; Corbularia bulbocodium, watercolour, date unknown. Greenish White is visible on the outer petals of the daffodil (left).

MINERAL.
Leonard Spencer, *The World's Minerals*, 1916. Greenish White is visible on the calcite (top and bottom, right).

(i).   *White of the Human Eyeballs.* [Sclera]
(ii).   *Back of the Petals of Blue Hepatica.*
         [*Liverwort*; Anemone hepatica]
(iii).   *Common Opal.* [*Silica*]

*Skimmed-milk White,
is snow white, mixed with
a little Berlin blue and
ash grey. [W]* †

† *Skimmed-milk White is Syme's name for
Werner's Milk White.*

ANIMAL.

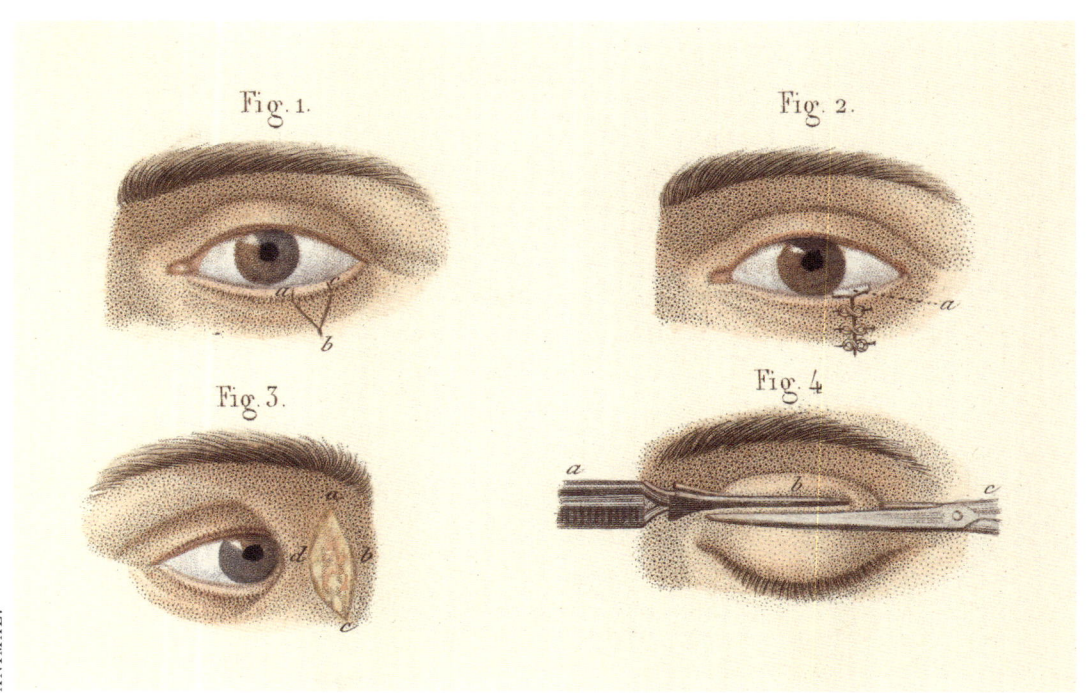

VEGETABLE.

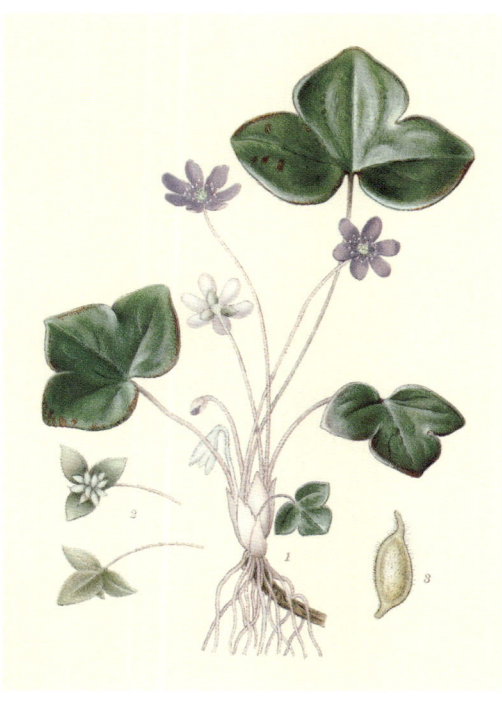

MINERAL.

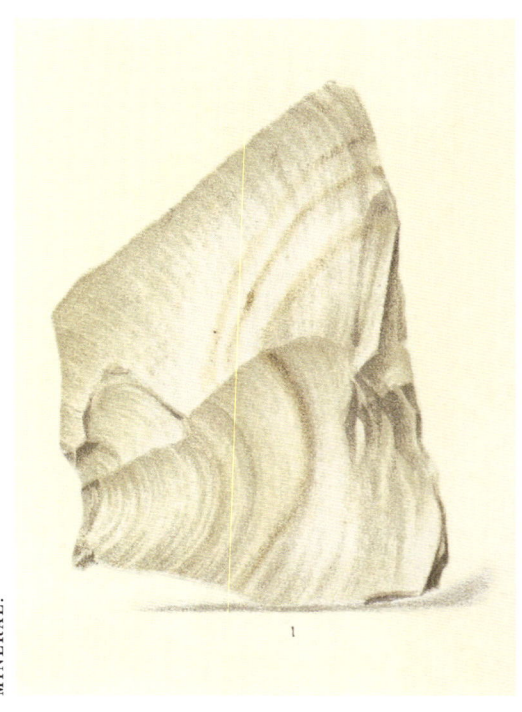

ANIMAL.
Claude Bernard
and Charles Huette,
*Précis iconographique
de médecine opératoire
et d'anatomie
chirurgicale*, 1848.
Skimmed-milk White
is visible on the white
of the human eyeball.

VEGETABLE.
A. Mentz and C. H.
Ostenfeld, *Billeder
af Nordens Flora*,
Vol. 1, 1917.
Skimmed-milk
White is visible on
the reverse side of
the liverwort petal.

MINERAL.
Reinhard Brauns,
*The Mineral
Kingdom*, Vol. 2, 1912.
Skimmed-milk
White is visible on
the common opal.

8. GREYISH WHITE.

(i).   *Inside Quill-feathers of the Kittiwake.* [Rissa]
(ii).   *White Hamburgh Grapes.* [Vitis]
(iii). *Granular Limestone.* [*Carbonate sedimentary rock*]

Greyish White, is snow white, mixed with a little ash grey. [W]

ANIMAL.

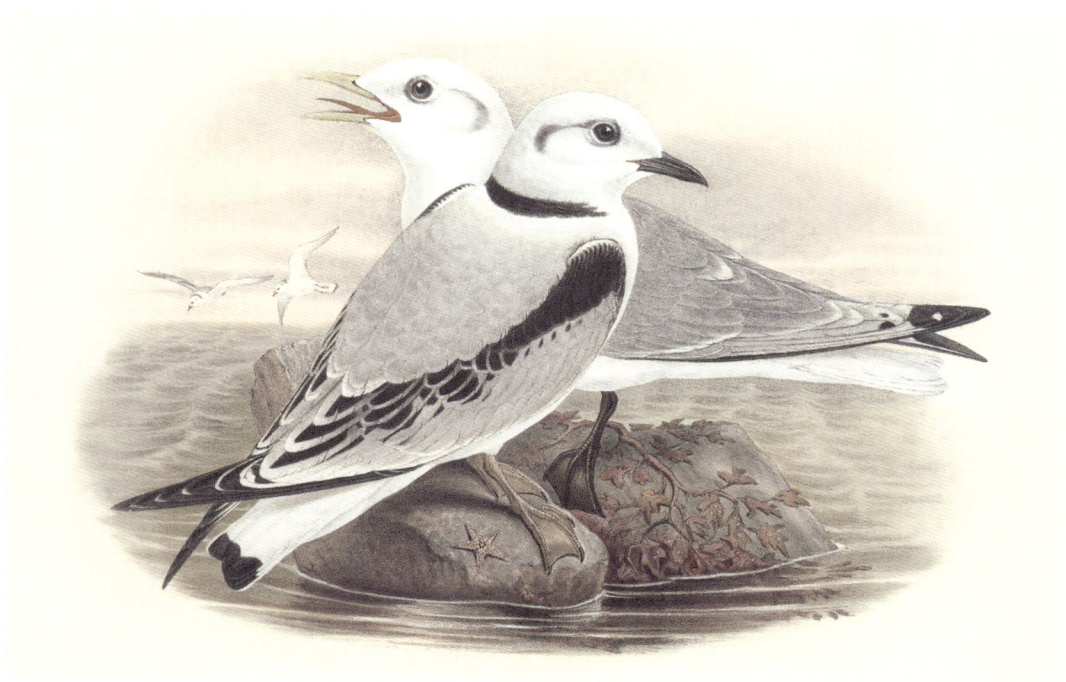

VEGETABLE.

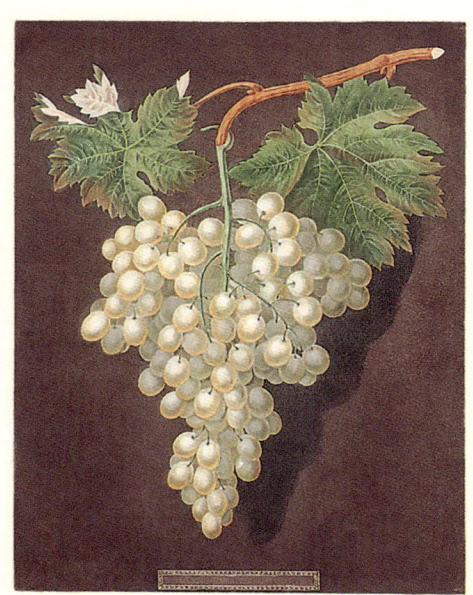

MINERAL.

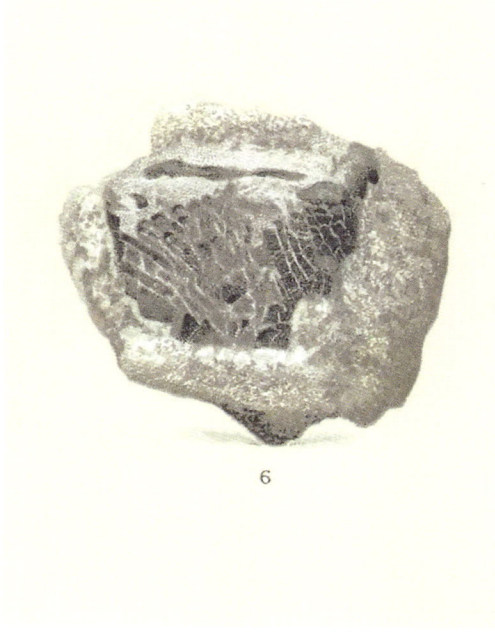

6

ANIMAL.
John Gould, *Birds of Great Britain*, Vol. 5, 1862–73. Greyish White is visible on the feathers of the kittiwake gull.

VEGETABLE.
George Brookshaw, *Grapes – White Hamburg*, watercolour, 1812. Greyish White is visible on the White Hamburg grapes.

MINERAL.
Reinhard Brauns, *The Mineral Kingdom*, Vol. 2, 1912. Greyish White is visible on the limestone.

GREYS.

No.	Names.	Colours.	ANIMAL.	
9	Ash Grey.		Breast of long tailed Hen Titmouse.	
10	Smoke Grey.		Breast of the Robin round the Red.	
11	French Grey.		Breast of Pied Wag tail.	
12	Pearl Grey.		Backs of black headed and Kittiwake Gulls.	
13	Yellowish Grey.		Vent coverts of White Rump.	
14	Bluish Grey.		Back, and tail Coverts Wood Pigeon.	
15	Greenish Grey.		Quill feathers of the Robin.	
16	Blackish Grey.		Back of Nut-hatch.	

Syme's 1821 edition included four of Werner's original greys (numbers 10, 13, 14 and 16), two greys from the Picardet system (numbers 12 and 15) one grey from the Lenz system (number 9) and one grey from his own 1814 edition (number 11).

GREYS.

	VEGETABLE.		MINERAL.	
	Fresh Wood Ashes.		Flint.	
			Flint.	
	Back of Petals of Purple Hepatica.		Porcelain Jasper.	
	Stems of the Barberry.		Common Calcedony.	
			Limestone.	
	Bark of Ash Tree.		Clay Slate, Wacke.	
	Old Stems of Hawthorn.		Flint.	

9. ASH GREY.

(i). *Breast of long tailed Hen Titmouse.*
[*Long-tailed tit*; Aegithalos caudatus]
(ii). *Fresh Wood ashes.* [Cinis]
(iii). *Flint.* [Quartz]

Ash Grey, is the characteristic colour of Werner's greys; he gives no description of its component parts; it is composed of snow white, with portions of smoke and French grey, and a very little yellowish grey and carmine red. [W]

ANIMAL.

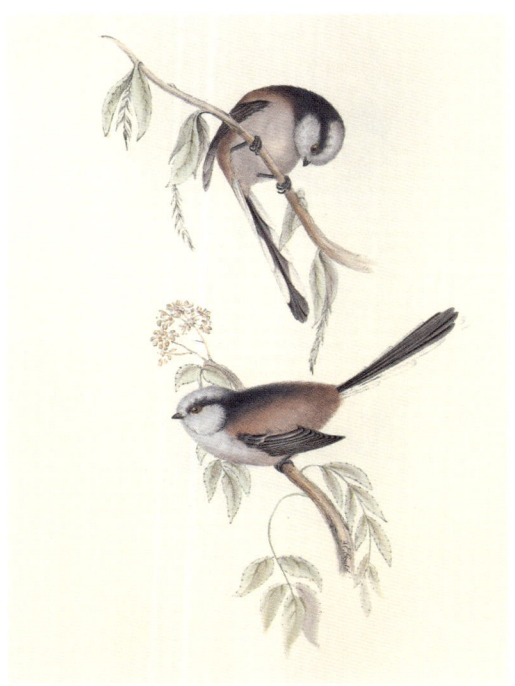

MINERAL.

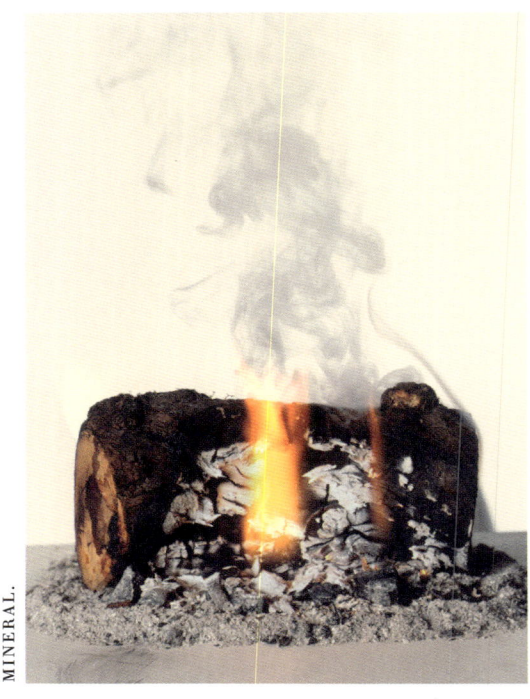

ANIMAL.
John Gould, *Birds of Europe*, Vol. 3, 1832–37. Ash Grey is visible on the breast feathers of the long-tailed tit.

VEGETABLE.
Burning log, date unknown. Ash Grey is visible in the ashes of burning fresh wood.

MINERAL.
Philip Rashleigh, *Specimens of British Minerals*, 1797. Ash Grey is visible on the flint.

VEGETABLE.

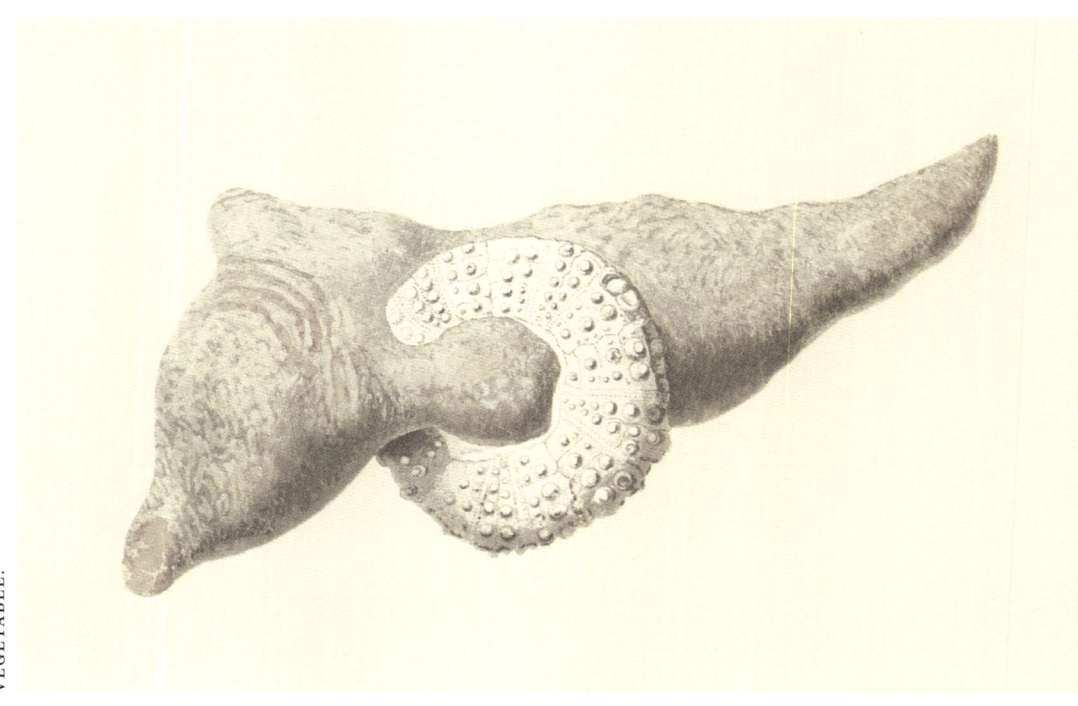

10. SMOKE GREY.

(i).   *Breast of the Robin round the Red.* [Erithacus rubecula]
(ii).   ——————
(iii).   *Flint.* [*Quartz*]

Smoke Grey, is ash grey mixed with a little brown. [W]

ANIMAL.

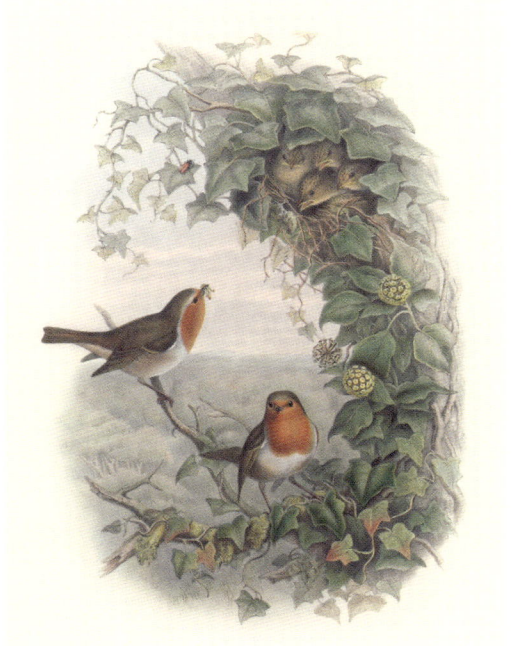

VEGETABLE.

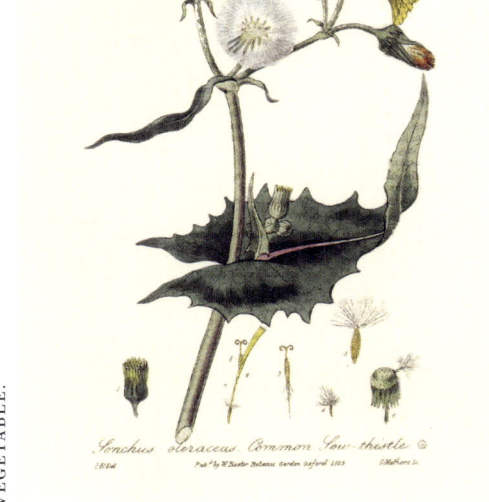

Sonchus oleraceus, Common Sow-thistle.

MINERAL.

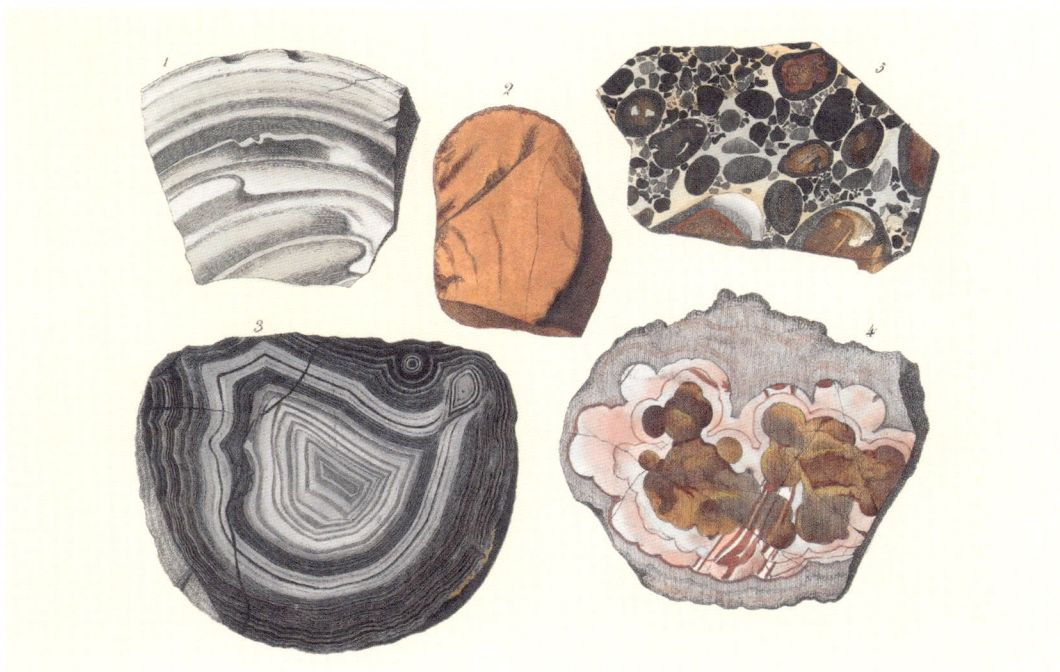

ANIMAL.
John Gould, *Birds of Great Britain*, Vol. 2, 1862–73. Smoke Grey is visible on the breast feathers of the robin, at the edge of the red.

VEGETABLE.
William Baxter, *British Phaenogamous Botany*, 1832–43. Smoke Grey is visible on the seed puff of the common sowthistle.*

MINERAL.
Johann Gottlob Kurr, *The Mineral Kingdom*, 1859. Smoke Grey is visible on the flint (top row, left).

(i).   *Breast of Pied Wag tail.* [*Pied wagtail*; Motacilla alba]
(ii).   ————————
(iii).   ————————

French Grey, nearly the steel grey of Werner, without the lustre, is greyish white, with a slight tinge of black and carmine red.

ANIMAL.

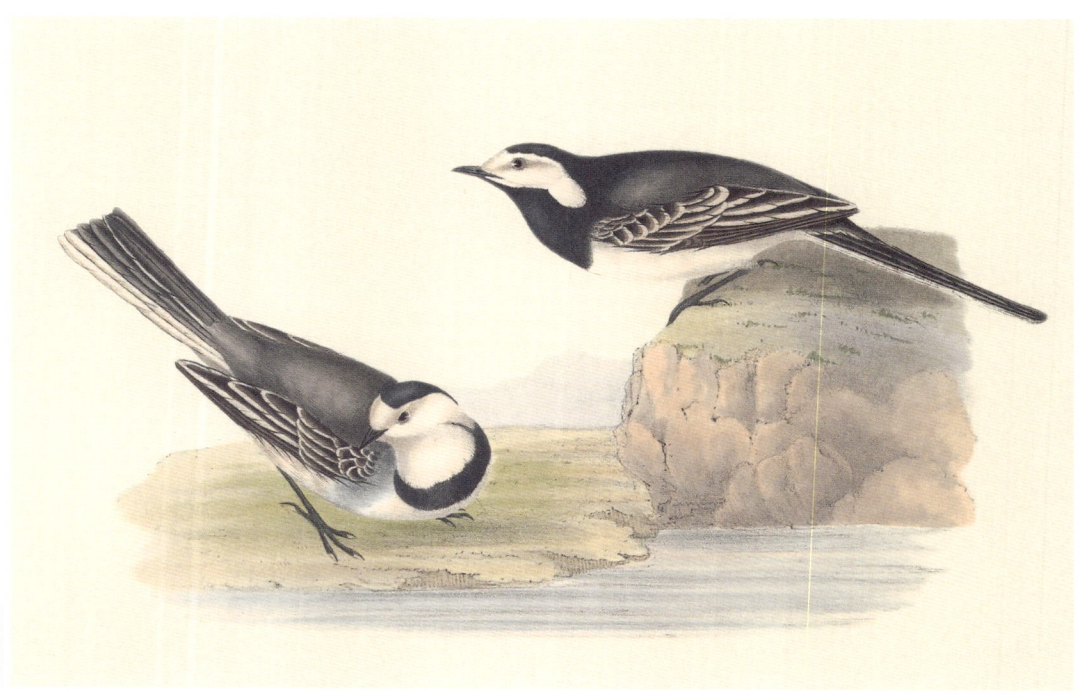

VEGETABLE.

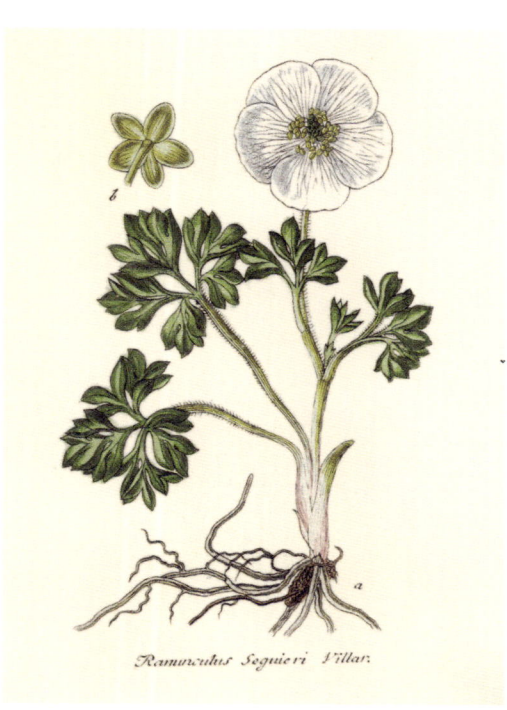

Ranunculus Seguieri Villar.

MINERAL.

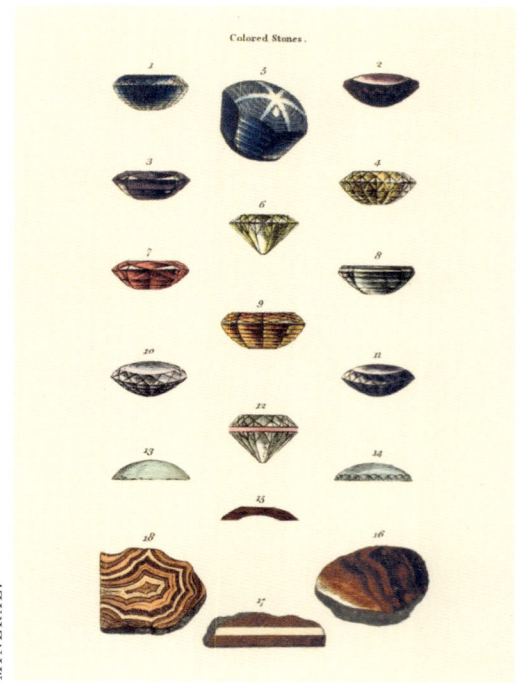

Colored Stones.

ANIMAL.
John Gould, *Birds of Europe*, Vol. 2, 1832–37. French Grey is visible on the breast feathers of the pied wagtail.

VEGETABLE.
Jacob Sturm, *Deutschlands Flora in Abbildungen nach der Natur mit Beschreibungen*, 1798. French Grey is visible on the petals of the *Ranunculus*.*

MINERAL.
John Mawe, *A Treatise on Diamonds*, 1823. French Grey is visible on the doublet gemstone (fourth row, centre).*

12. PEARL GREY.

(i).   *Backs of black headed* [Chroicocephalus ridibundus]
       and Kittiwake Gulls. [Rissa]
(ii). *Back of Petals of Purple Hepatica.*
       [*Liverwort*; Anemone hepatica]
(iii). *Porcelain Jasper.* [*Silica*]

*Pearl Grey, is ash grey
mixed with a little crimson
red and blue, or bluish
grey with a little red. [W]*

ANIMAL.

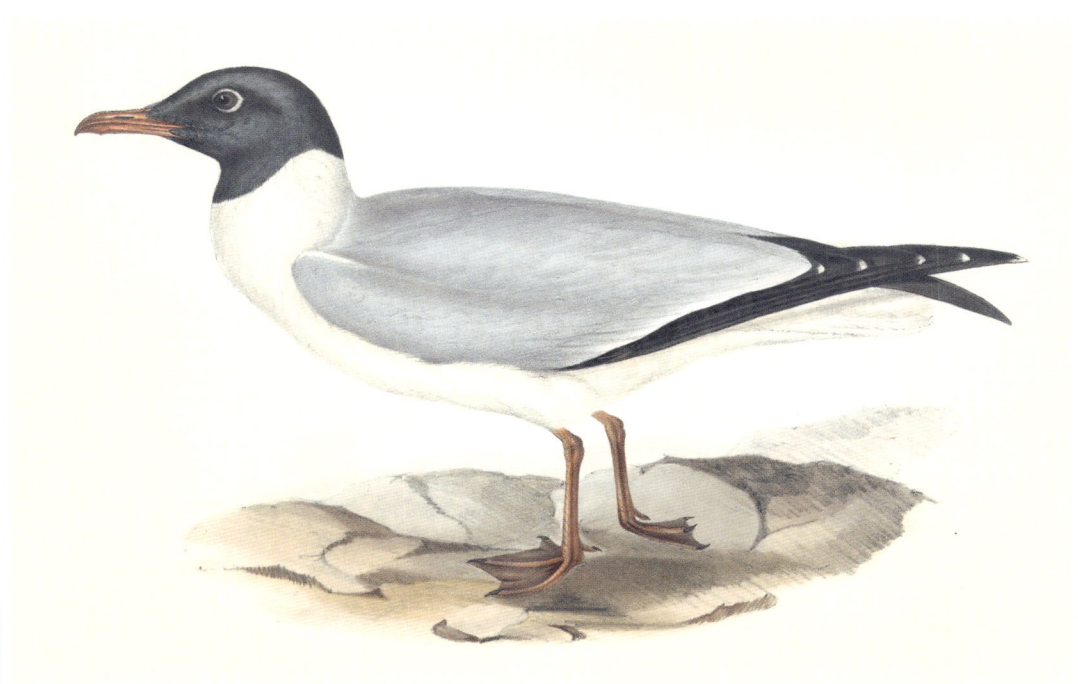

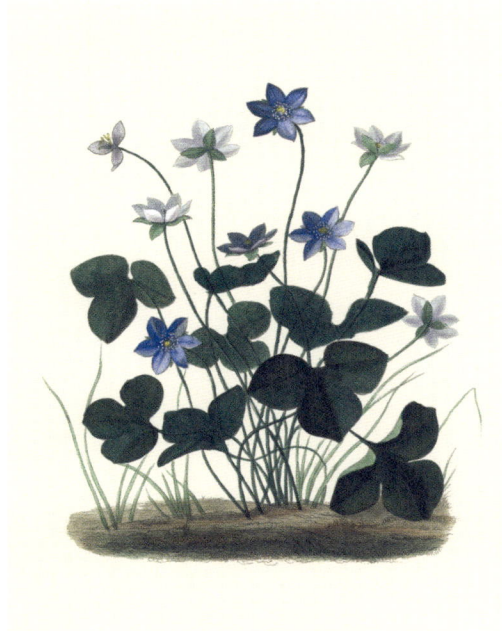

VEGETABLE.

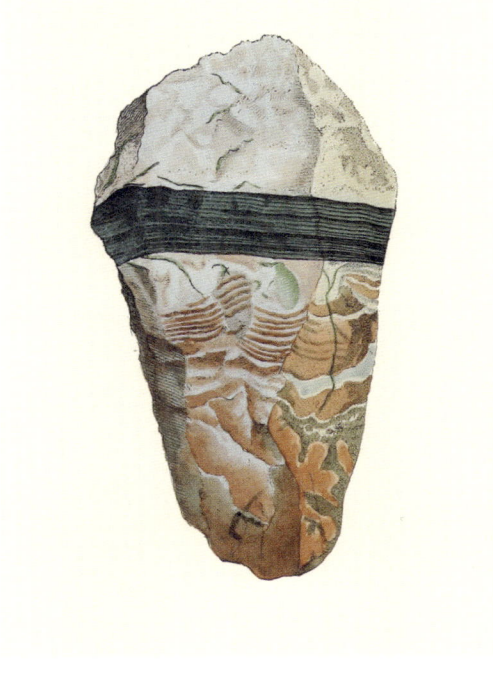

MINERAL.

ANIMAL.
John Gould,
Birds of Europe,
Vol. 5, 1832–37.
Pearl Grey is visible
on the back feathers of
the black-headed gull.

VEGETABLE.
O. Reveil, A. Dupuis,
Fr. Gerard and F. H.
Herincq, *Le Règne
végétal*, 1864–71.
Pearl Grey is visible
on the back of the
liverwort petals.

MINERAL.
James Sowerby,
British Mineralogy,
Vol. 2, 1802–17.
Pearl Grey is visible
on the upper part of
the porcelain jasper.

(i).   *Vent coverts of White Rump.* [*Hen harrier*; Circus cyaneus]
(ii).   *Stems of the Barberry.* [Berberis vulgaris]
(iii).   *Common Calcedony.* [*Chalcedony*; *Silicate mineral*]

Yellowish Grey, is ash grey mixed with lemon yellow and a minute portion of brown. [W]

ANIMAL.

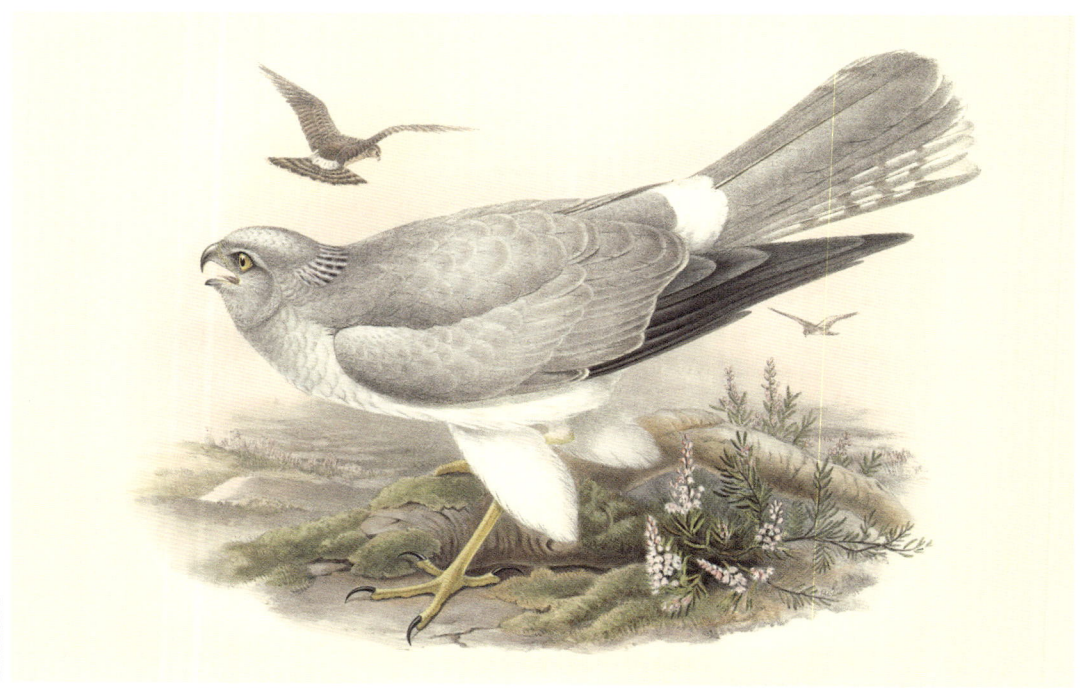

ANIMAL.
John Gould, *Birds of Great Britain*, Vol. I, 1862–73. Yellowish Grey is visible on the vent coverts, i.e. the feathers around the cloaca, of the white rump.

VEGETABLE.
Francesco Peyrolery, *Berberidaceae*, watercolour, 1765. Yellowish Grey is visible on the stem of the barberry.

MINERAL.
Philip Rashleigh, *Specimens of British Minerals*, 1797. Yellowish Grey is visible on the chalcedony (all specimens).

VEGETABLE.

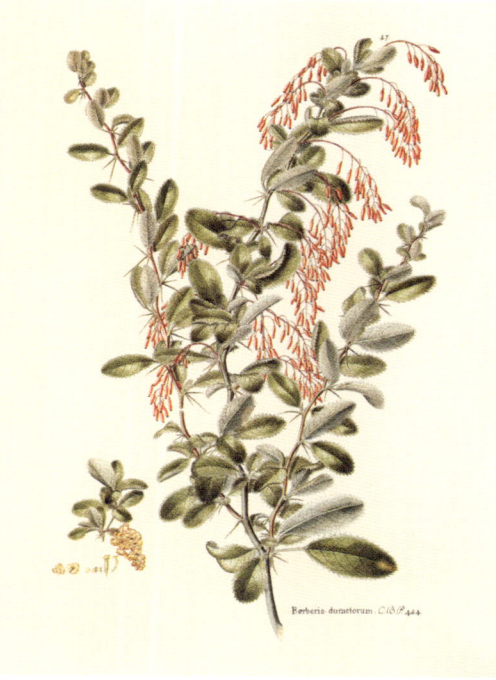

MINERAL.

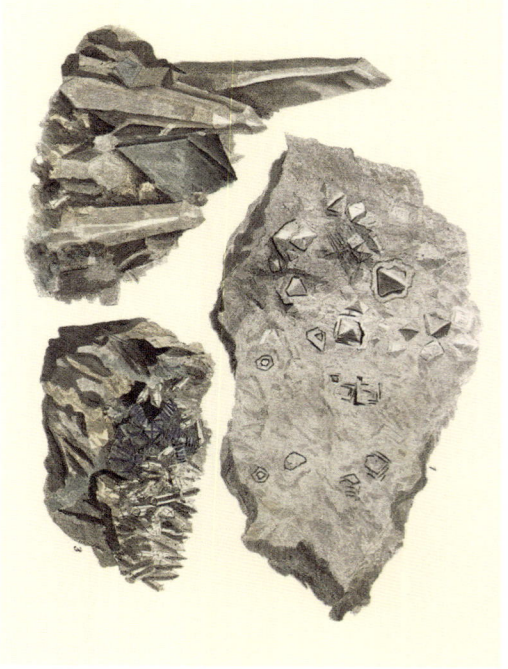

14. BLUISH GREY.

(i). *Back, and tail Coverts Wood Pigeon.* [Columba palumbus]
(ii). ———————
(iii). *Limestone.* [*Carbonate sedimentary rock*]

Bluish Grey, is ash grey mixed with a little blue. [W]

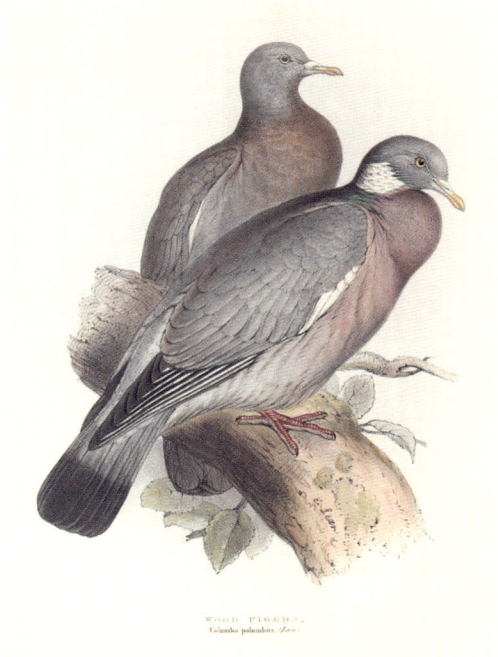

ANIMAL.

WOOD PIGEON.
Columba palumbus Linn.

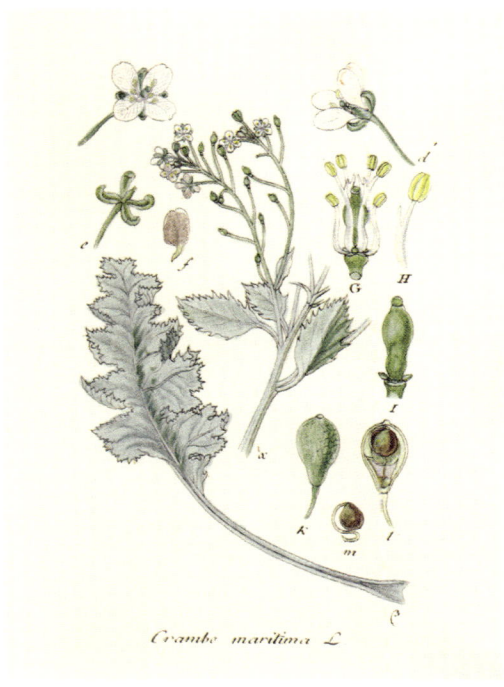

VEGETABLE.

Crambe maritima L.

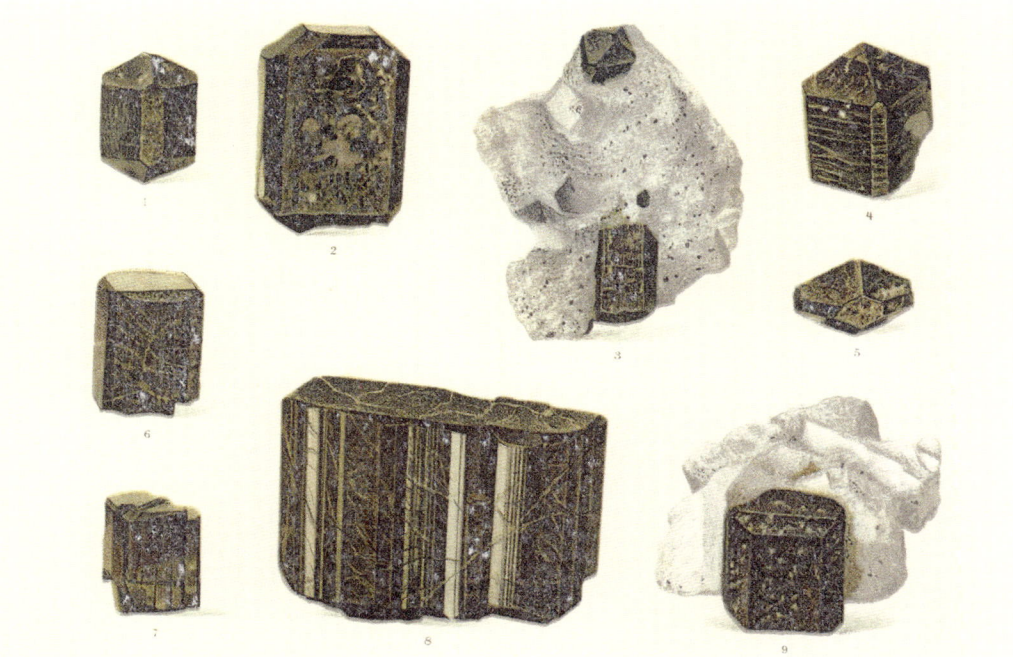

MINERAL.

ANIMAL.
John Gould, *Birds of Europe*, Vol. 4, 1832–37. Bluish Grey is visible on the back and tail coverts of the wood pigeon.

VEGETABLE.
Jacob Sturm, *Deutschlands Flora in Abbildungen nach der Natur mit Beschreibungen*, 1798. Bluish Grey is visible on the leaves of the sea kale.*

MINERAL.
Reinhard Brauns, *The Mineral Kingdom*, Vol. 2, 1912. Bluish Grey is visible on the limestone (top row, centre right). Two pieces of vesuvianite are embedded within it.

15. GREENISH GREY.

(i).   *Quill Feathers of the Robin.* [Erithacus rubecula]
(ii).   *Bark of Ash Tree.* [Fraxinus excelsior]
(iii). *Clay Slate.* [*Metamorphic rock*]
        Wacke. [*Greywacke*; *Sandstone*]

Greenish Grey, is ash grey mixed with a little emerald green, a small portion of black, and a little lemon yellow. [W]

ANIMAL.

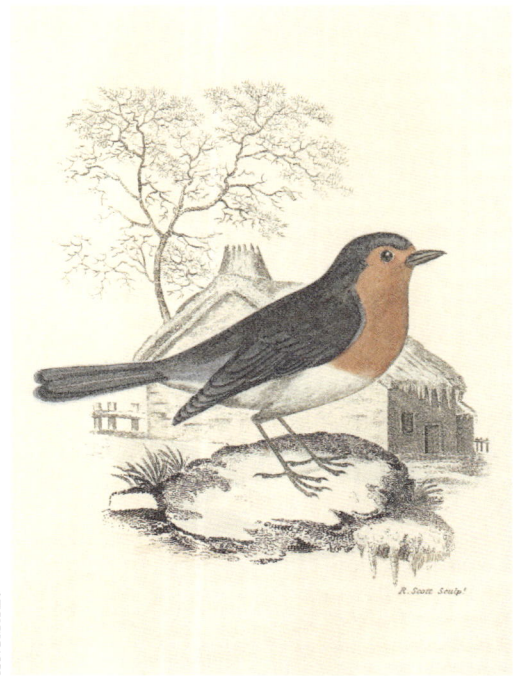

VEGETABLE.

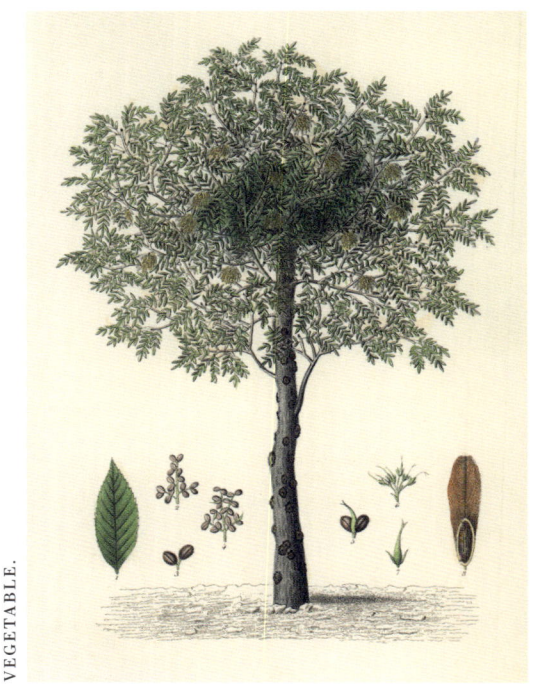

ANIMAL.
Patrick Syme,
A Treatise on British Songbirds, 1823.
Greenish Grey is visible on the wing and back feathers of the robin.

VEGETABLE.
O. Reveil, A. Dupuis, Fr. Gerard and F. H. Herincq, *Le Règne végétal*, 1864–71. Greenish Grey is visible on the bark of the ash tree.

MINERAL.
Reinhard Brauns, *The Mineral Kingdom*, Vol. I, 1912. Greenish Grey is visible on the clay slate (bottom row, left). Crystals are embedded within it.

MINERAL.

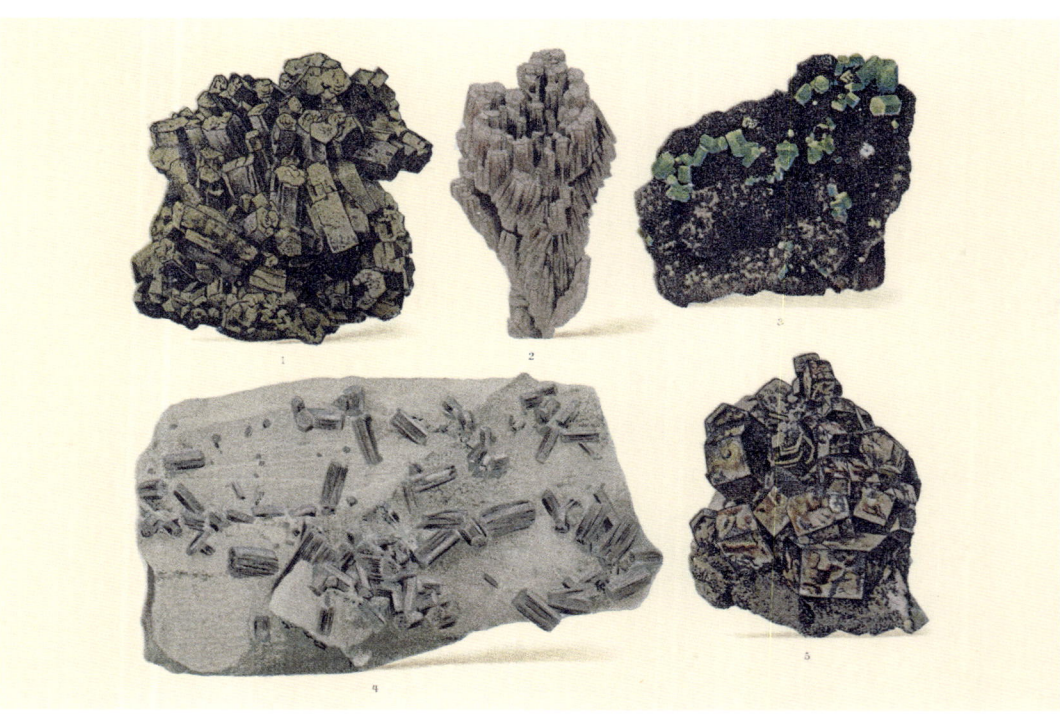

16. BLACKISH GREY.

(i). *Back of Nut-hatch.* [*Nuthatch*; Sitta]
(ii). *Old Stems of Hawthorn.* [Crataegus]
(iii). *Flint.* [*Quartz*]

Blackish Grey, blackish lead grey of Werner without the lustre, is ash grey, with a little blue and a portion of black.

ANIMAL.

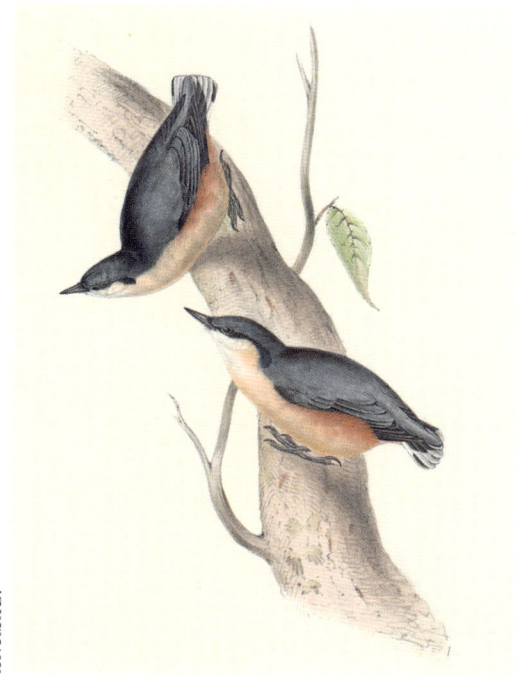

MINERAL.

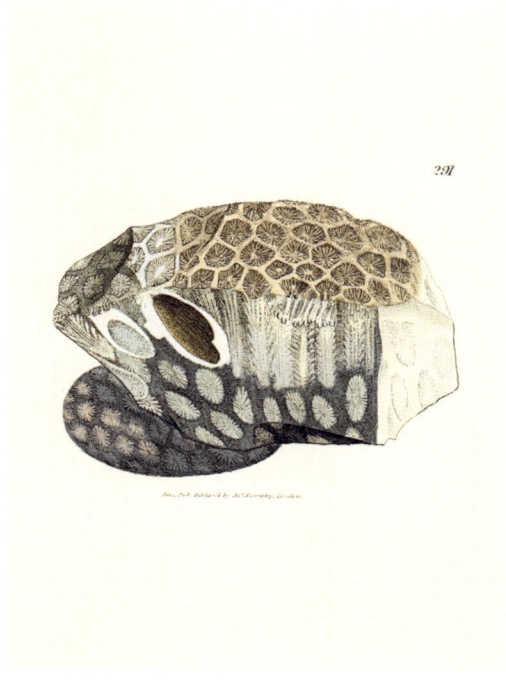

VEGETABLE.

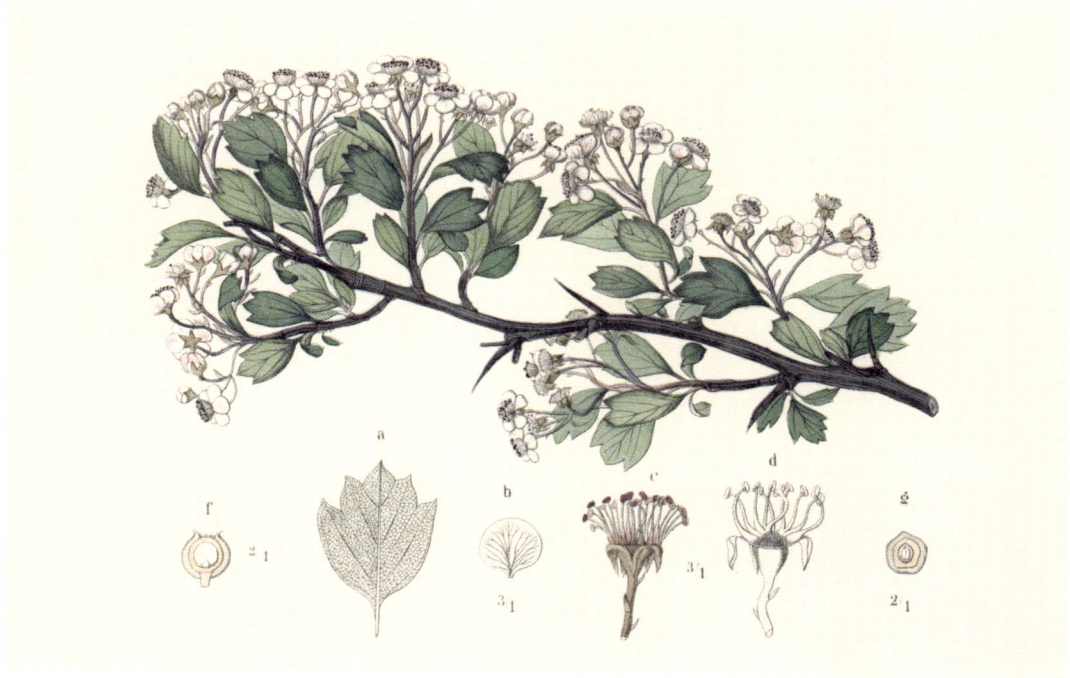

ANIMAL.
John Gould, *Birds of Europe*, Vol. 3, 1832–37. Blackish Grey is visible on the back feathers of the nuthatch.

VEGETABLE.
Heinrich Moritz Willkomm, *Illustrationes florae Hispaniae insularumque Balearium*, 1886–92. Blackish Grey is visible on the stem of the hawthorn.

MINERAL.
James Sowerby, *British Mineralogy*, Vol. 3, 1802–17. Blackish Grey is visible on the bottom of the flint.

No.	Names.	Colours.	ANIMAL.	
17	Greyish Black.		Water Ousel. Breast and upper part of Back of Water Hen.	
18	Bluish Black.		Largest Black Slug.	
19	Greenish Black.		Breast of Lapwing.	
20	Pitch, or Brownish Black.		Guillemot. Wing Coverts of Black Cock.	
21	Reddish Black.		Spots on Largs Wings of Tyger Moth. Breast of Pochard Duck.	
22	Ink Black.			
23	Velvet Black.		Mole. Tail Feathers of Black Cock.	

Syme's 1821 edition included three of Werner's original blacks (numbers 17, 18 and 20), two blacks from the Lenz system (numbers 19 and 23), one black from his own 1814 edition (number 21) and introduced one new black (number 22).

BLACKS.

VEGETABLE.		MINERAL.	
		Basalt.	
Crowberry.		Black Cobalt Ochre.	
		Hornblende.	
		Yenite Mica.	
Berry of Fuchsia Coccinea.		Oliven Ore.	
Berry of Deadly Night Shade.		Oliven Ore.	
Black of Red and Black West-Indian Peas.		Obsidian.	

17. GREYISH BLACK.

(i).   *Water Ousel.* [*American dipper*; Cinclus mexicanus]
        Breast and upper Part of Back of Water Hen. [*Waterhen*; Amaurornis phoenicurus]

(ii).   ———————

(iii).   *Basalt.* [*Igneous rock*]

Greyish Black, is composed of velvet black, with a portion of ash grey. [W]

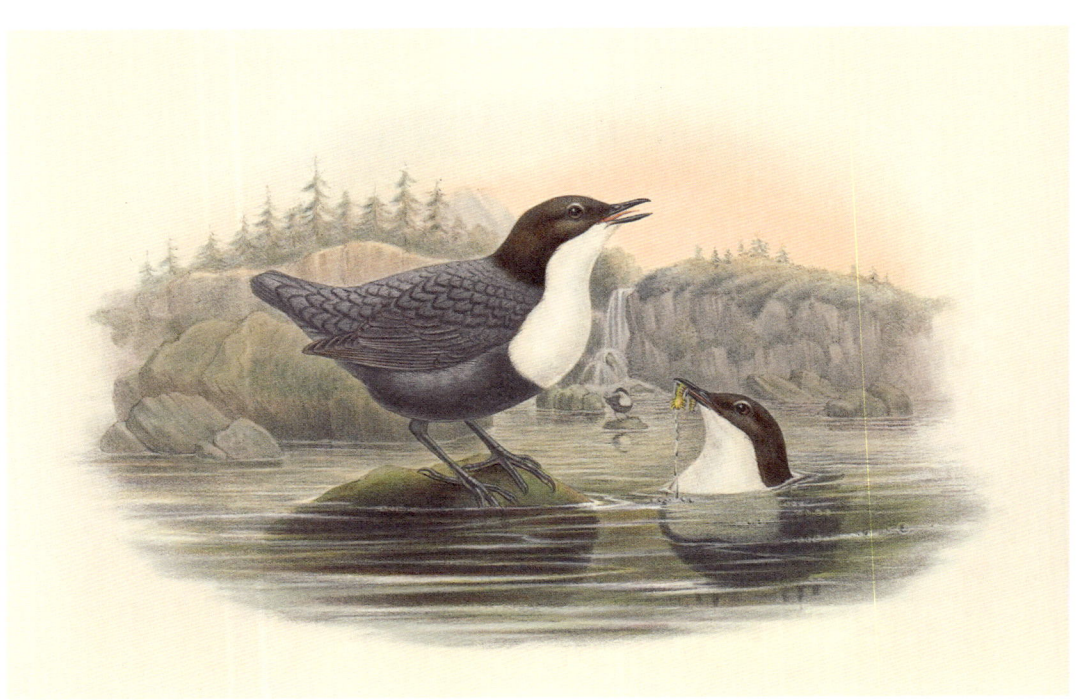

ANIMAL.

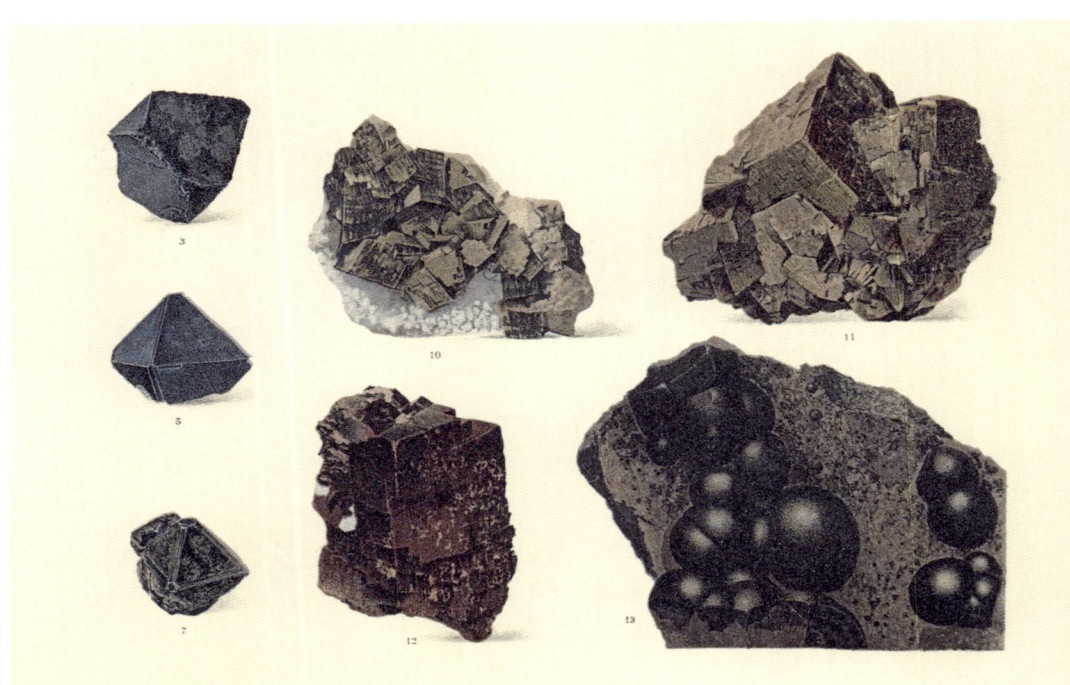

MINERAL.

64.   I. WHITES, GREYS AND BLACKS.

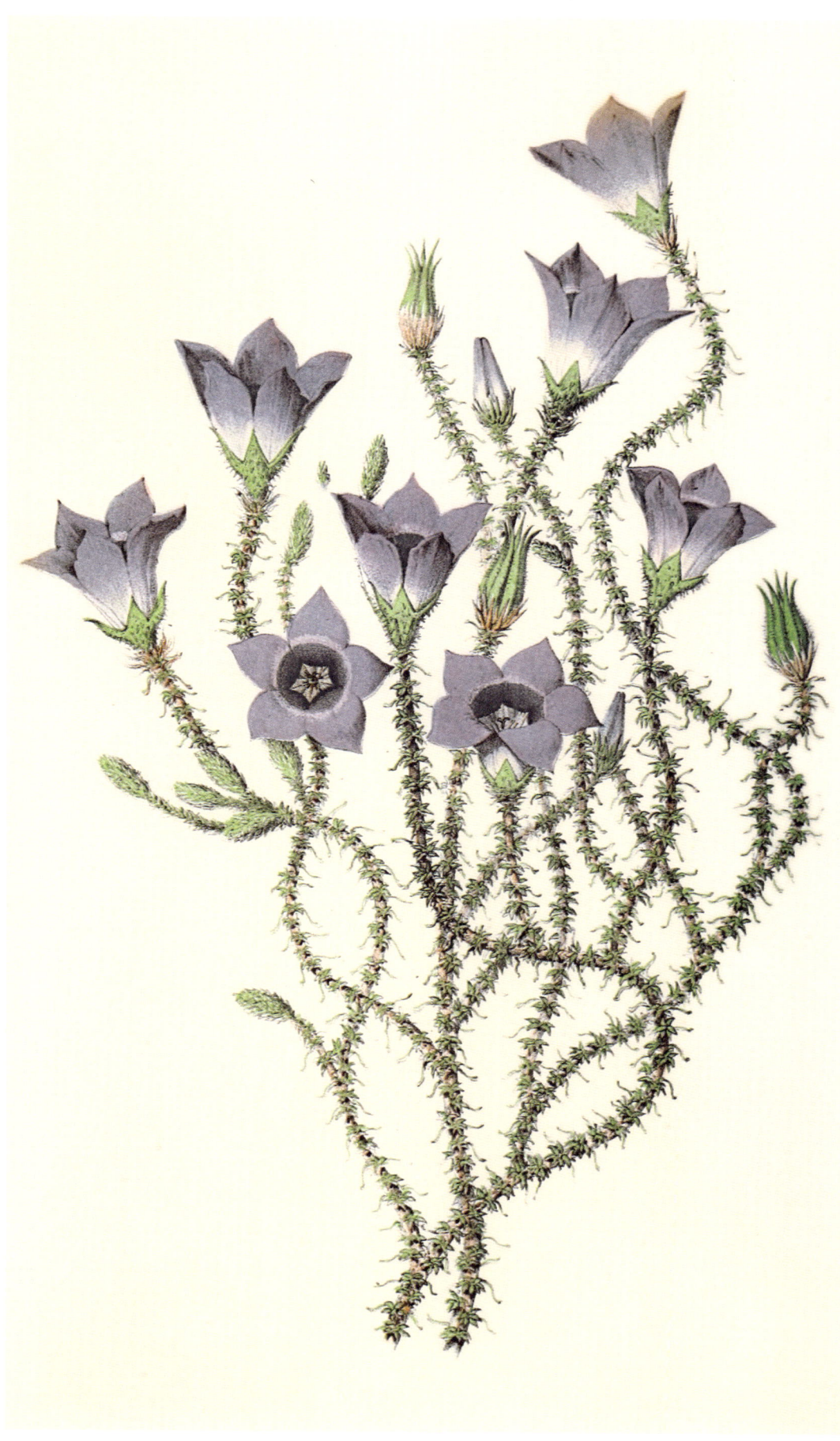

VEGETABLE.

ANIMAL.
John Gould, *Birds
of Great Britain*,
Vol. 2, 1862–73.
Greyish Black is
visible on the back
feathers of the
American dipper.

VEGETABLE.
Cornelis Antoon
Jan Abraham
Oudemans, *Neerland's
Plantentuin*, 1865.
Greyish Black is
visible on the centre
of the petals of the
Roella ciliata.*

MINERAL.
Reinhard Brauns,
*The Mineral
Kingdom*, Vol. 1, 1912.
Greyish Black is
visible on the basalt
(bottom row, right).
It has chalybite
embedded within it.

18. BLUISH BLACK.

(i).   *Largest Black Slug.* [Arion ater]
(ii).   *Crowberry.* [Empetrum nigrum]
(iii). *Black Cobalt Ochre.* [*Cobaltian Wad*;
        Manganese oxide or hydroxide]

*Bluish Black, is velvet black,
mixed with a little blue
and blackish grey. [W]*

ANIMAL.

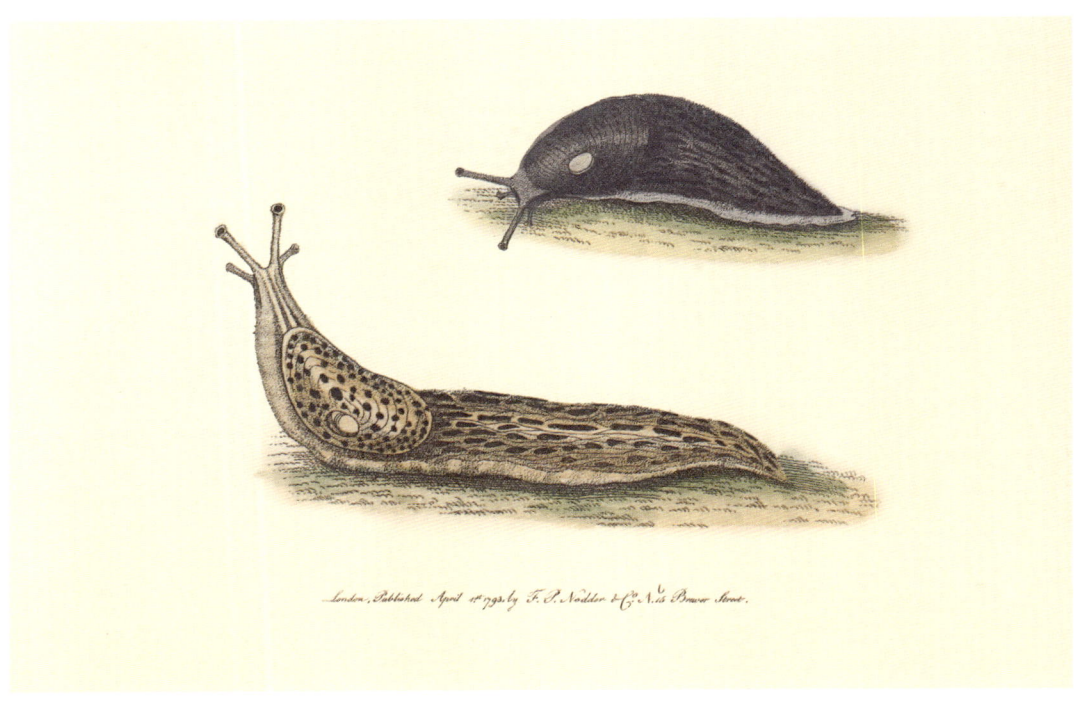

London, Published April 1st 1792 by F. P. Nodder & Co. N. 15 Brewer Street.

ANIMAL.
George Shaw and
Frederick P. Nodder,
*The Naturalist's
Miscellany*, 1789–1813.
Bluish Black is visible
on the black slug
(above).

VEGETABLE.
Black crow-berry,
watercolour,
date unknown.
Bluish black is
visible on the berries
of the crowberry.

MINERAL.
Reinhard Brauns,
*The Mineral
Kingdom*, Vol. 1, 1912.
Bluish Black is
visible on the cobalt
ore (all specimens
on the top two rows).

VEGETABLE.

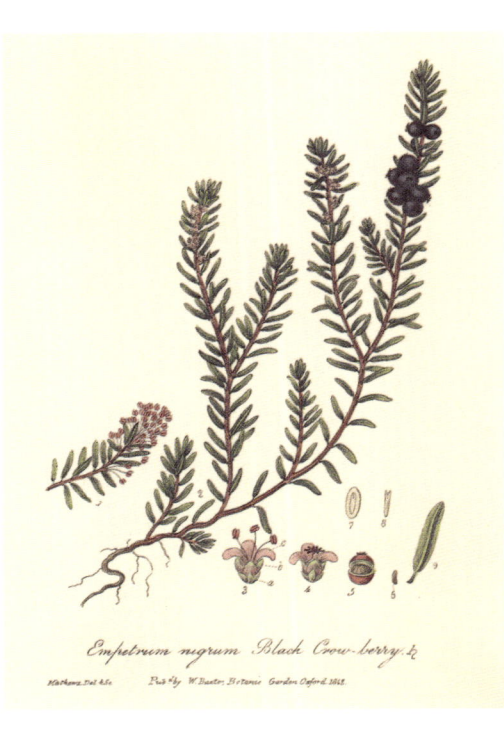

Empetrum nigrum Black Crow-berry.

MINERAL.

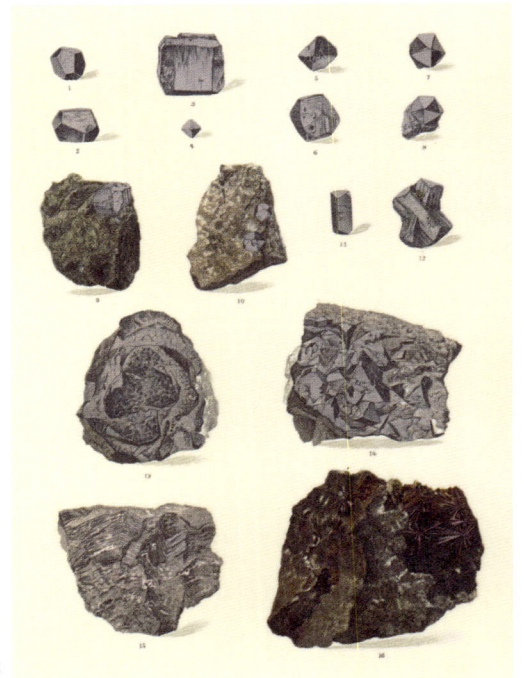

19. GREENISH BLACK.

(i).   *Breast of Lapwing.* [Vanellinae]
(ii). —————————————
(iii). *Hornblende.* [*Silicate mineral*]

Greenish Black, is velvet black, mixed with a little brown, yellow and green. [W]

ANIMAL.

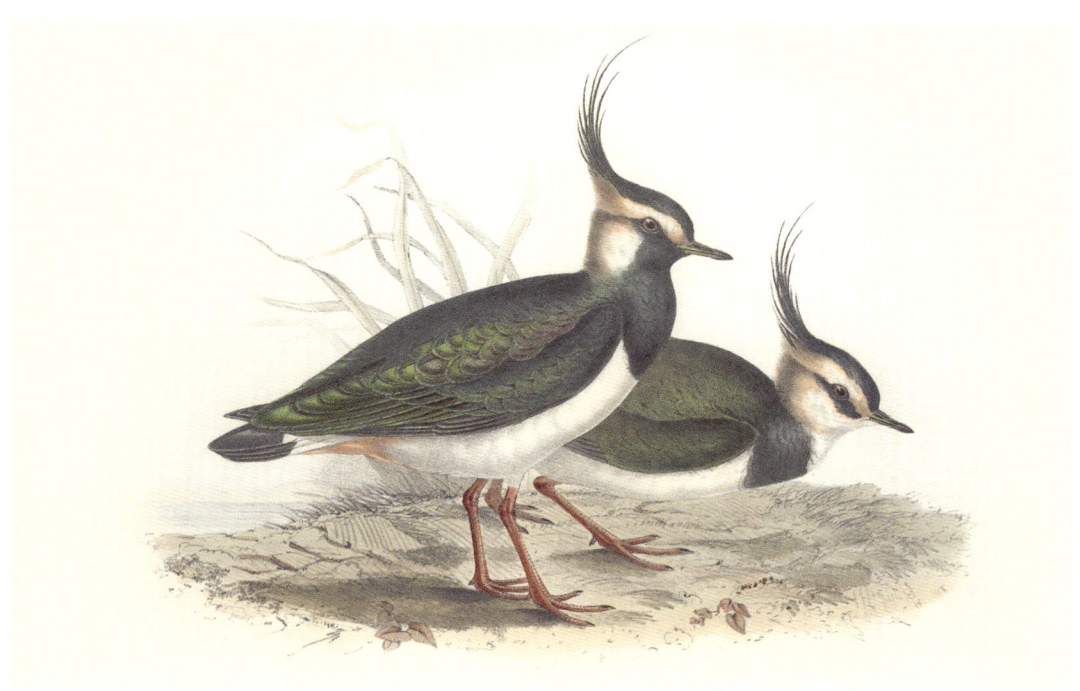

VEGETABLE.

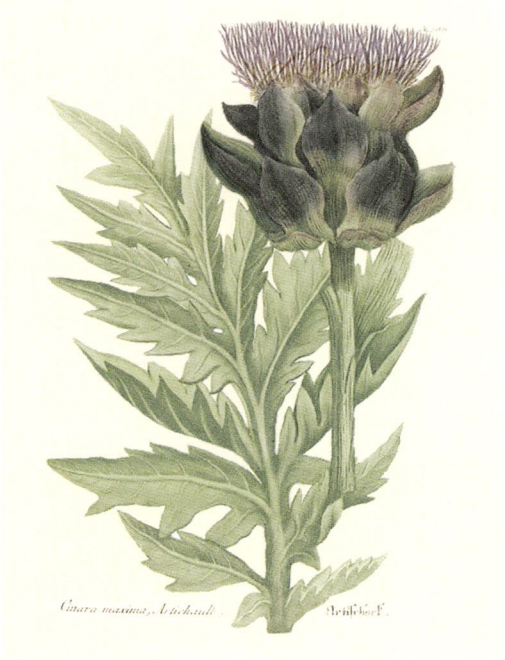

Cinara maxima, Artichault.   *Artichoke F.*

MINERAL.

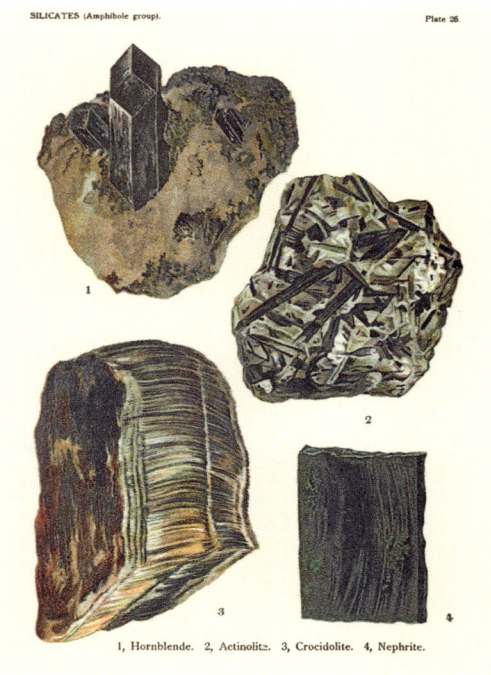

SILICATES (Amphibole group).   Plate 26.

1, Hornblende.   2, Actinolite.   3, Crocidolite.   4, Nephrite.

ANIMAL.
John Gould, *Birds of Europe*, Vol. 4, 1832–37. Greenish Black is visible on the upper breast feathers of the lapwing.

VEGETABLE.
Johann Wilhelm Weinmann, *Phytanthoza iconographia*, 1737. Greenish Black is visible on the bracts of the artichoke.*

MINERAL.
Leonard Spencer, *The World's Minerals*, 1916. Greenish Black is visible on the hornblende (top row, left).

20. PITCH, OR BROWNISH BLACK.

(i).   *Guillemot.* [*Common guillemot*; Uria aalge]
          Wing Coverts of Black Cock. [*Black grouse*; Lyrurus tetrix]
(ii).   ——————————
(iii).   *Yenite Mica.* [*Ilvaite*; *Silicate mineral*]

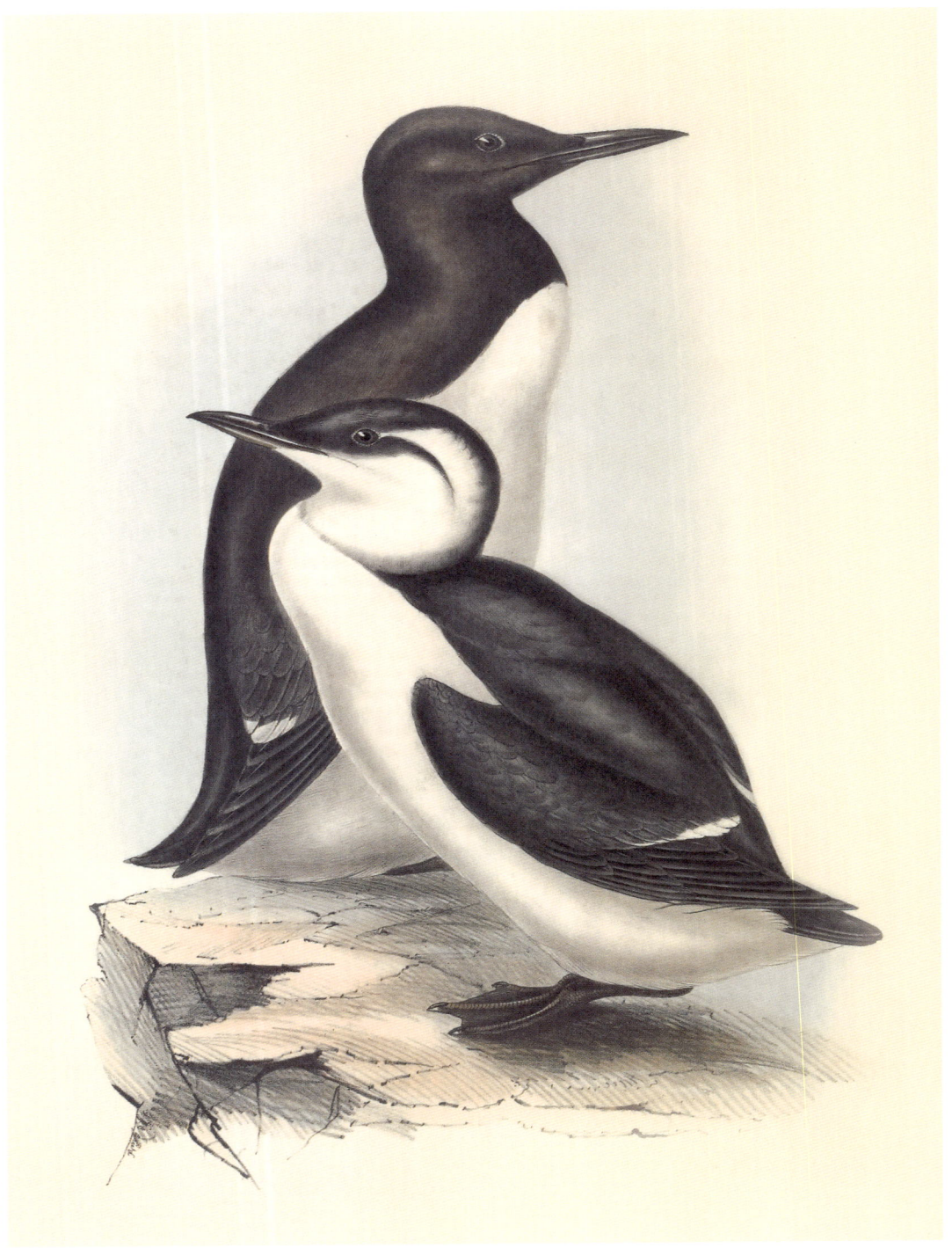

*Pitch, or Brownish Black,
is velvet black, mixed with a
little brown and yellow. [W]*

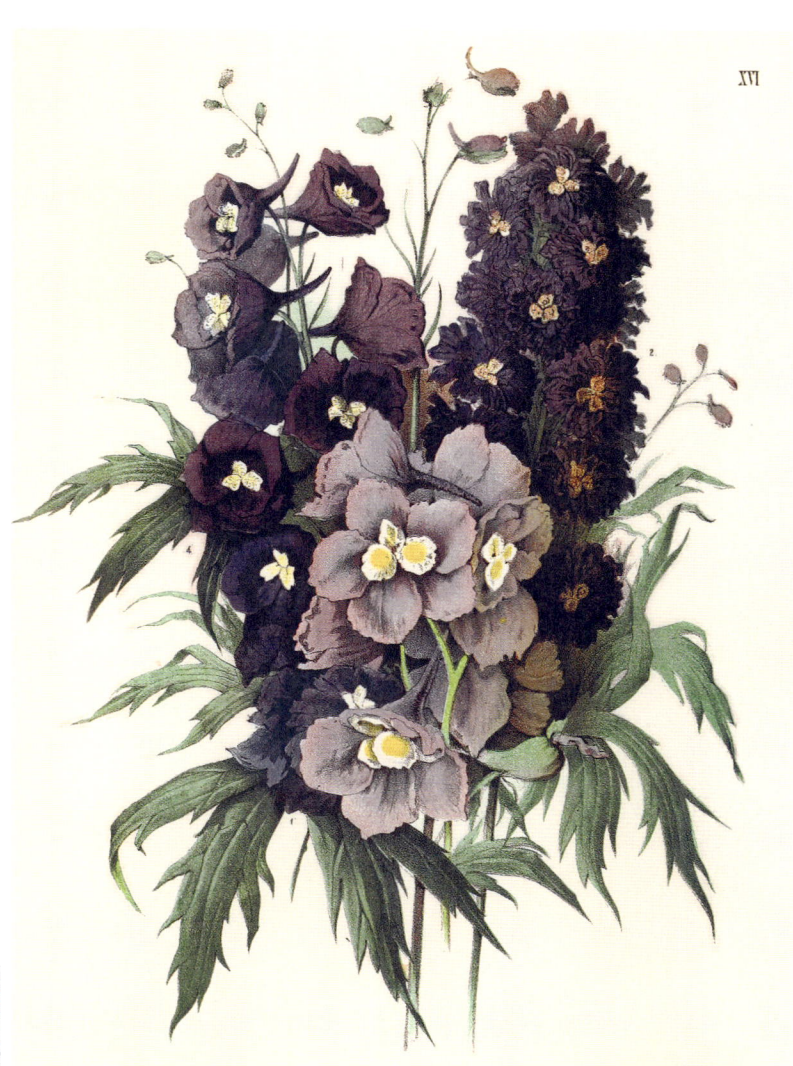

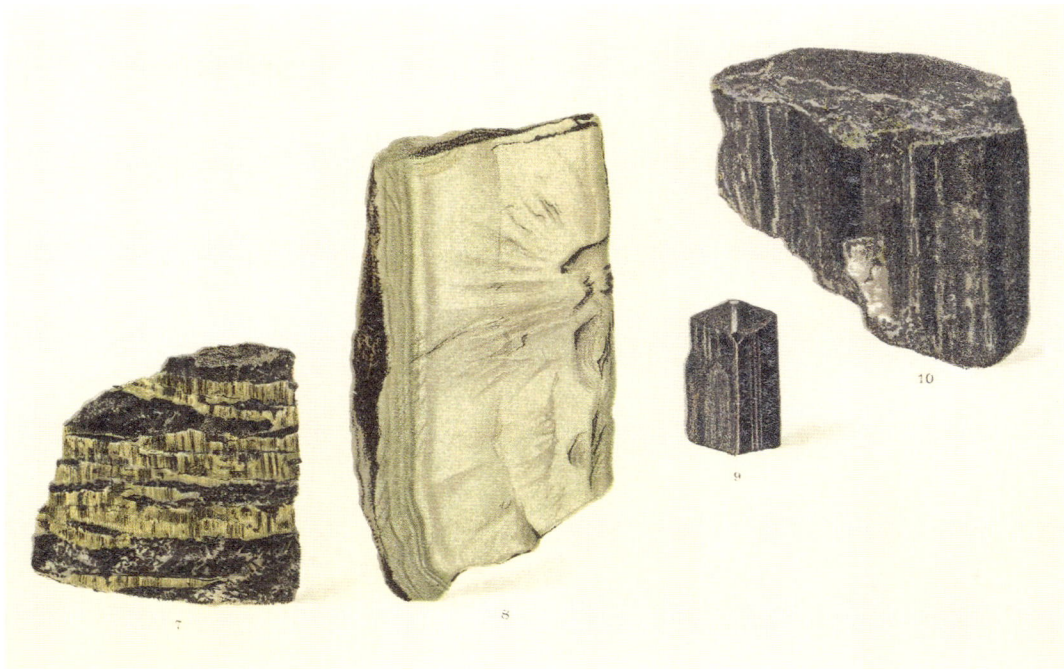

ANIMAL.
John Gould, *Birds of
Europe*, Vol. 5, 1832–37.
Pitch, or Brownish
Black is visible on
the wing feathers of
the common guillemot.

VEGETABLE.
Cornelis Antoon Jan
Abraham Oudemans,
Neerland's Plantentuin,
1865.
Pitch, or Brownish Black
is visible on the petals
of the delphinium.*

MINERAL.
Reinhard Brauns,
*The Mineral
Kingdom*, Vol. 2, 1912.
Pitch, or Brownish Black
is visible on the ilvaite
(second from right).

21. REDDISH BLACK.

(i). *Spots on Large Wings of Tyger Moth.* [*Tiger moth*; Arctia caja]
Breast of Pochard Duck. [*Common pochard*; Aythya ferina]
(ii). *Berry of Fuchsia Coccinea.* [*Scarlet Fuchsia*; Fuchsia coccinea]
(iii). *Oliven Ore.* [*Olivenite*; Copper arsenate mineral*]

Reddish Black, is velvet black, mixed with a very little carmine red, and a small portion of chesnut brown.

ANIMAL.

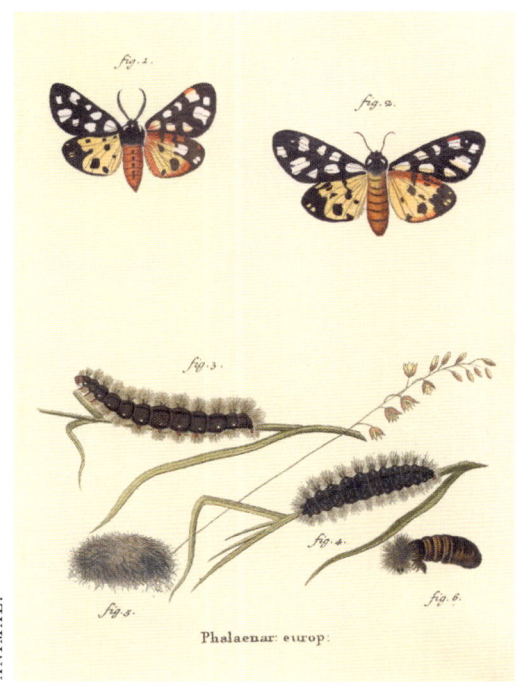

VEGETABLE.

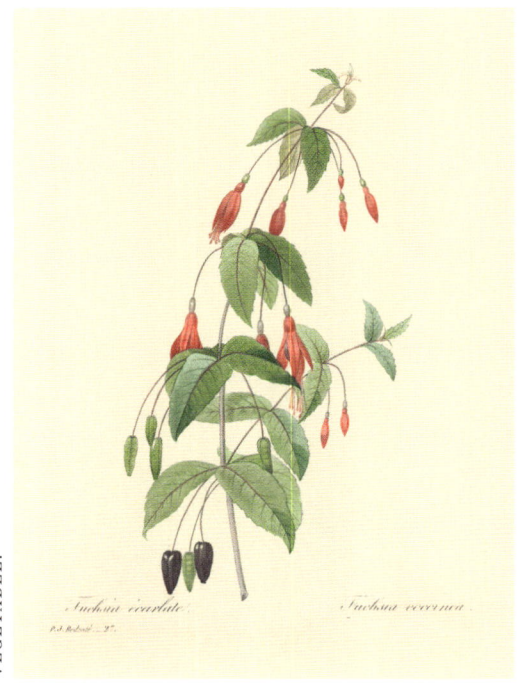

ANIMAL.
Thomas Brown,
The Book of Butterflies, Sphinxes and Moths, 1832.
Reddish Black is visible on the wings of the adult tiger moth (top row).

VEGETABLE.
Pierre-Joseph Redouté, *Choix des plus belles fleurs*, 1833. Reddish Black is visible on the berries of the scarlet fuchsia.

MINERAL.
Philip Rashleigh, *Specimens of British Minerals*, 1797. Reddish Black is visible on the olivenite (top row, left and right, and bottom row, left and right).

MINERAL.

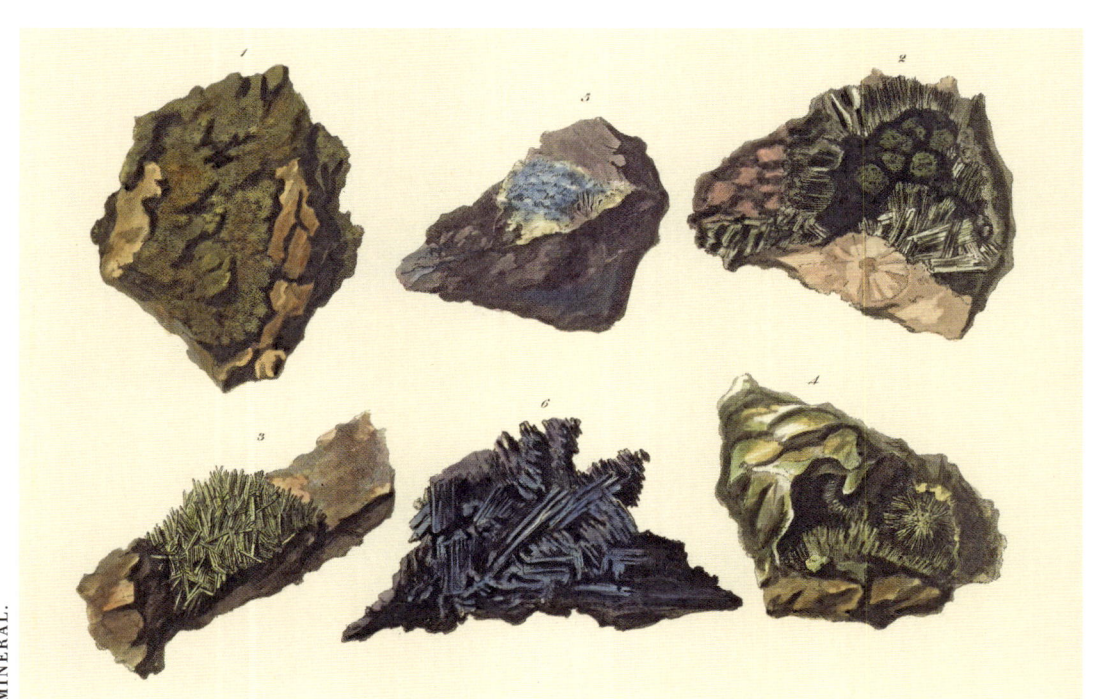

(i).

(ii). *Berry on Deadly Night Shade.* [*Deadly nightshade*; *Belladonna*; Atropa belladonna]

(iii). *Oliven Ore.* [*Olivenite*; *Copper arsenate mineral*]

Ink Black, is velvet black, with a little indigo blue in it.

ANIMAL.

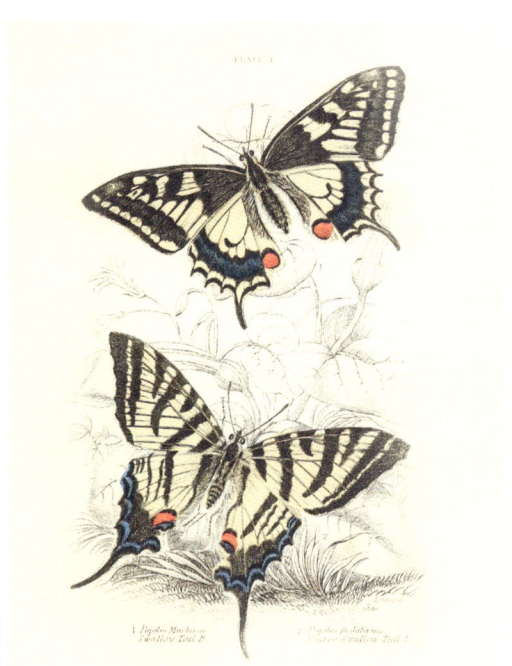

VEGETABLE.

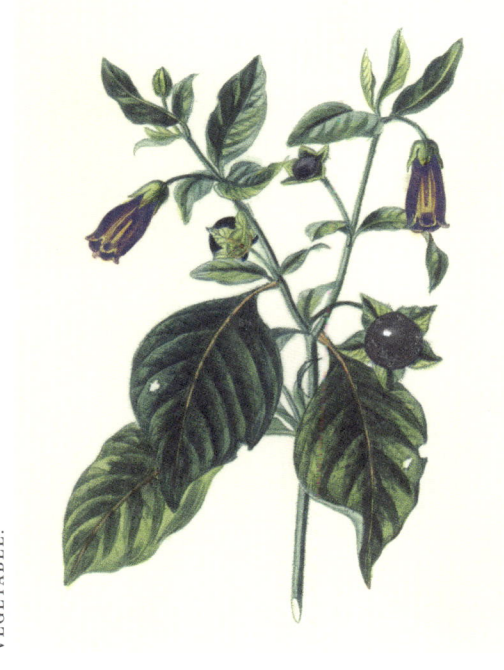

MINERAL.

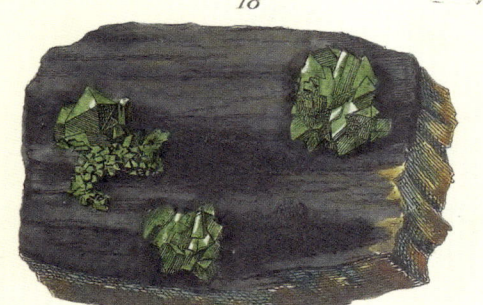

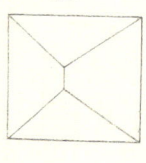

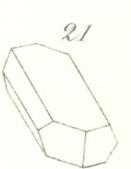

ANIMAL.
James Duncan, *British Butterflies*, 1840.
Ink Black is visible on the wings of the swallowtail (above) and scarce swallowtail (below).*

VEGETABLE.
Belladonna, watercolour, date unknown.
Ink Black is visible on the berries of the deadly nightshade.

MINERAL.
Johann Gottlob Kurr, *The Mineral Kingdom*, 1859.
Ink Black is visible on the olivenite (bottom row, left).

23. VELVET BLACK.

(i).   *Mole.* [Talpidae]
       Tail Feathers of Black Cock. [*Black grouse*; Lyrurus tetrix]
(ii).   *Black of Red and Black West Indian Peas.*
       [*Cowpea*; Vigna unguiculata]
(iii).   *Obsidian.* [*Volcanic glass*]

Velvet Black, is the characteristic colour of the blacks; it is the colour of black velvet. [W]

ANIMAL.

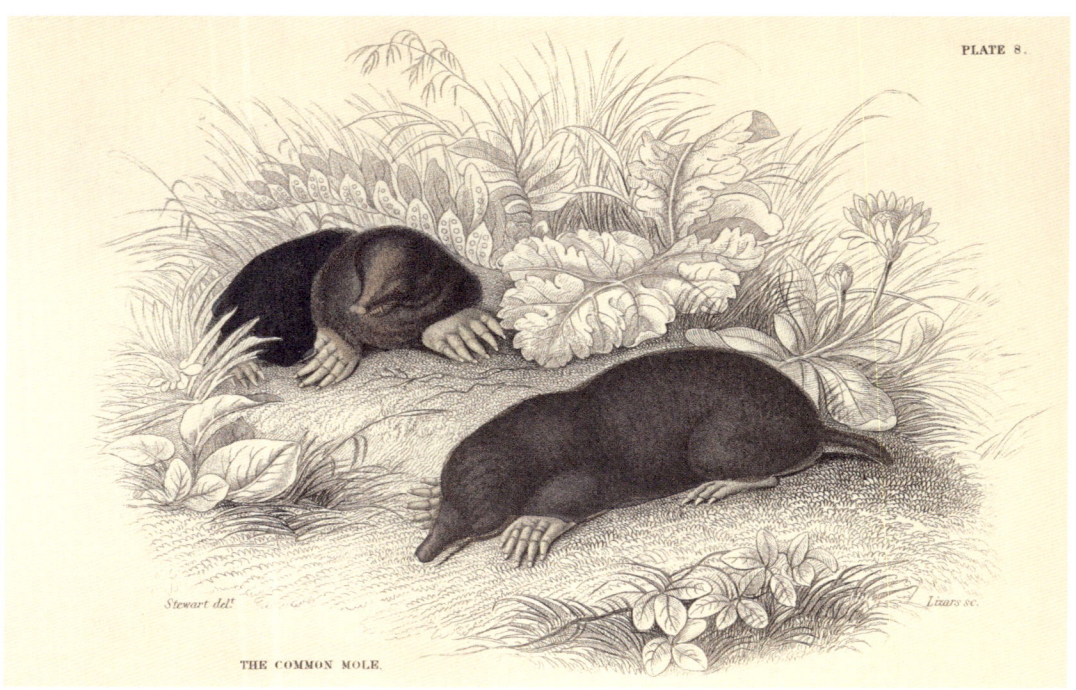

PLATE 8.

Stewart del.   Lizars sc.

THE COMMON MOLE.

MINERAL.

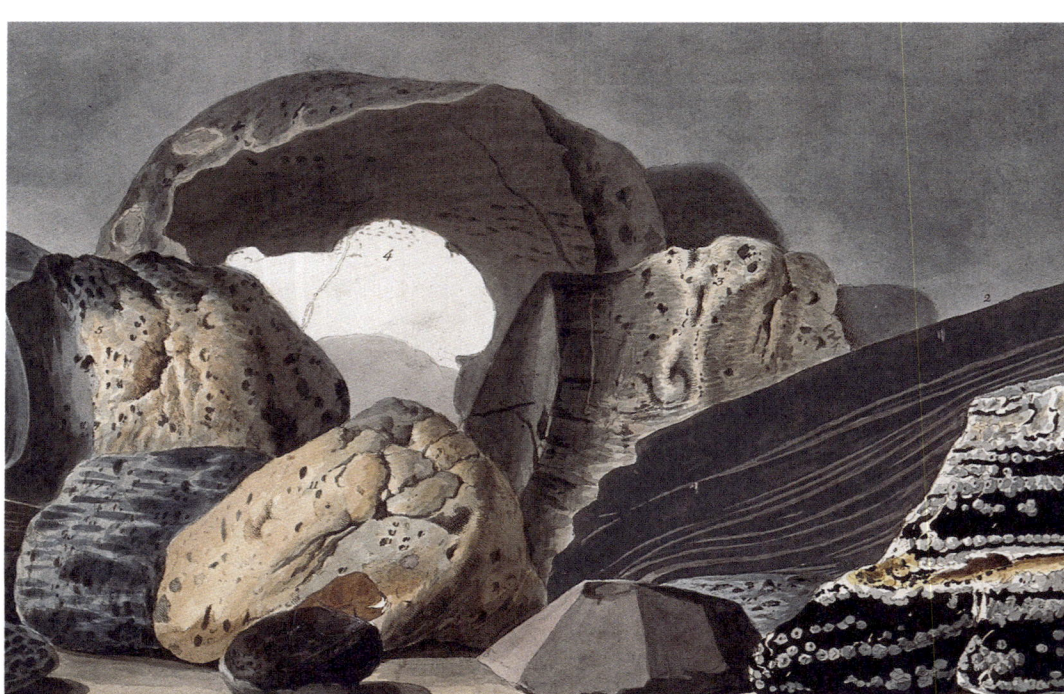

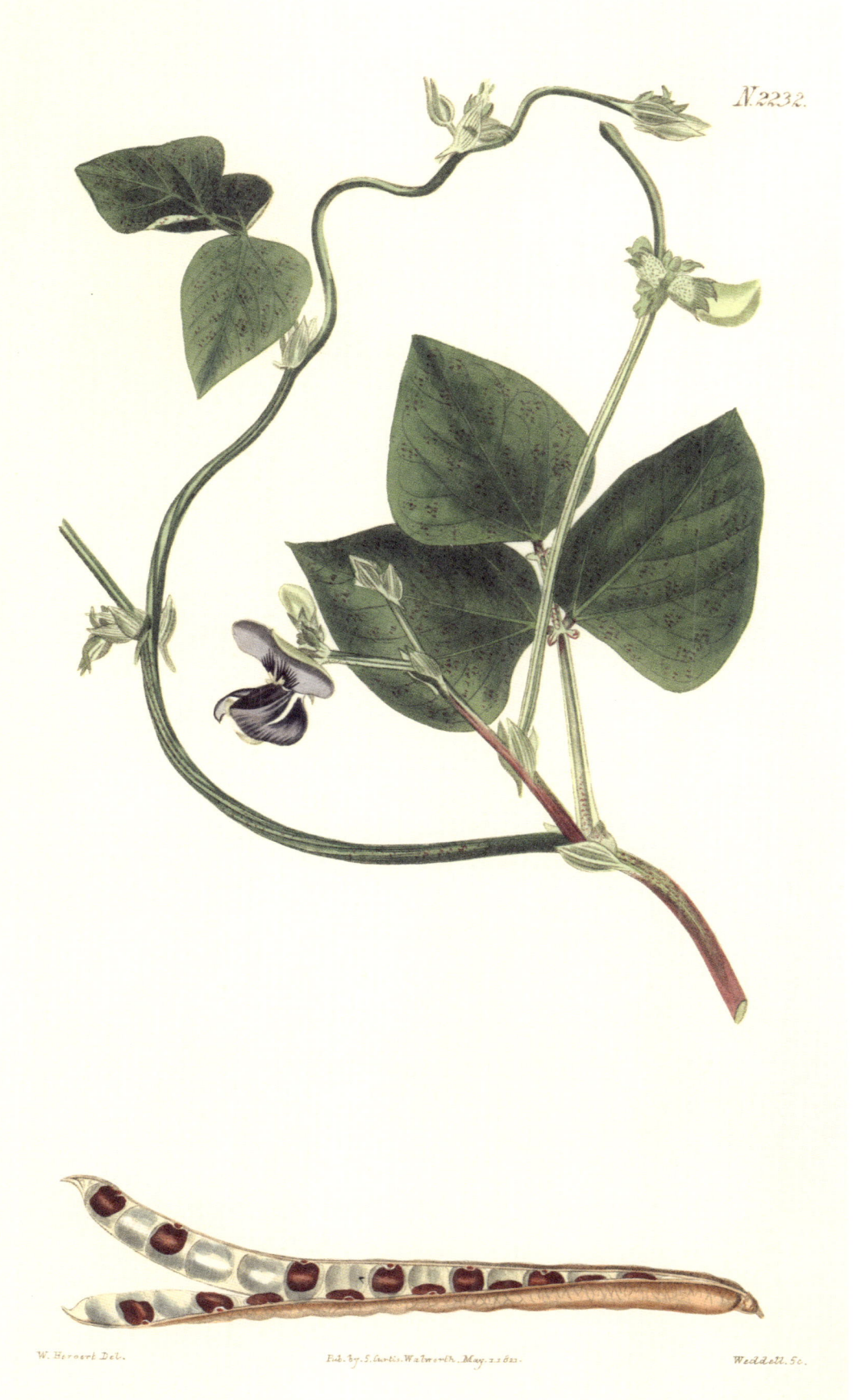

VEGETABLE.

W. Herbert Del.

Pub. by S. Curtis. Walworth. May. 1.1822.

Weddell. Sc.

73. I. WHITES, GREYS AND BLACKS.

ANIMAL.
William MacGillivray,
British Quadrupeds,
1849.
Velvet black is visible
on the fur of the mole.

VEGETABLE.
Weddell after William
Herbert, 'Cowpea',
*Curtis's Botanical
Magazine*, 1822.
Velvet Black is
visible on the peas
of the cowpea.

MINERAL.
William Hamilton,
Campi phlegraei, 1776.
Velvet black is visible
on the obsidian (right).

1. WERNER'S MINERALOGICAL SYSTEM AND HOW HIS NOMENCLATURE OF COLOURS BECAME SYME'S COLOUR STANDARD.

Colour suites of minerals and the Scottish Enlightenment.

BY PETER DAVIDSON, NATIONAL MUSEUMS SCOTLAND.

In 1814 the Edinburgh artist Patrick Syme (1774–1845) published the first edition of his book entitled *Werner's Nomenclature of Colours*. Already well known as a flower painter and teacher, Syme had begun to make a name for himself in the city as a skilled and meticulous practitioner in the field of natural history drawing.[1] He had also recognized the need for a 'general standard' of colour description and naming which he set out to provide.

As Syme acknowledged in his introduction and the book's title, the idea of a standardized system of colour reference and the style of colour terms were adapted and extended from the work of the German mineralogist Abraham Gottlob Werner (1749–1817). In his seminal publication of 1774, *Von den äusserlichen Kennzeichen der Fossilien* ('Of the External Characteristics of Fossils', that is, minerals), Werner had set out a guide for the identification of minerals by their external features, including colour, and had provided a table of colour terms that could be used as a standard reference. Werner's book was widely translated and adopted around the world, along with his system, which was disseminated by many of the pupils who had studied under him at the famous Freiberg School of Mining.[2] It was probably through one of these pupils, Robert Jameson (1774–1854), who was appointed Regius Professor of Natural History at the University of Edinburgh in 1804, that Syme became familiar with Werner's work.

In 1808 Jameson founded the Wernerian Natural History Society and Syme was appointed its official artist of natural history objects in 1811. In the preparation of his book, Syme was assisted by Jameson, who laid out a 'Colour-suite of Minerals' based on the Wernerian system, using the collections of the university museum. While acknowledging Werner's nomenclature, as well as Jameson's help, Syme also expanded on it, especially as he wanted his book to be of use to artists and other scientists beyond mineralogy, the field in which Werner was such a pioneer.

WERNER'S INTEREST IN MINERALS

Born in 1749 at Wehrau in Upper Lusatia in what was then Prussian Silesia (now in Poland), Abraham Gottlob Werner showed an early interest in rocks and minerals. A bright, energetic child, his favourite books were the 'New Mining Lexicon'[3] by Minerophilus (or Minerophilo Freibergensis; Johann Caspar Zeisig, fl. mid-1700s) and a reference work on rocks and nature by Johann Hübner (1668–1731).[4] He would wander the countryside collecting minerals, which he ground into powders to learn about their properties. His father, an inspector at the ironworks in Wehrau, would also bring him mineral samples from the ironworks.[5]

At the age of 15 in 1764 Werner began work in the ironworks as a clerk (*Hüttenschreiber*). However, his health suffered, and he travelled

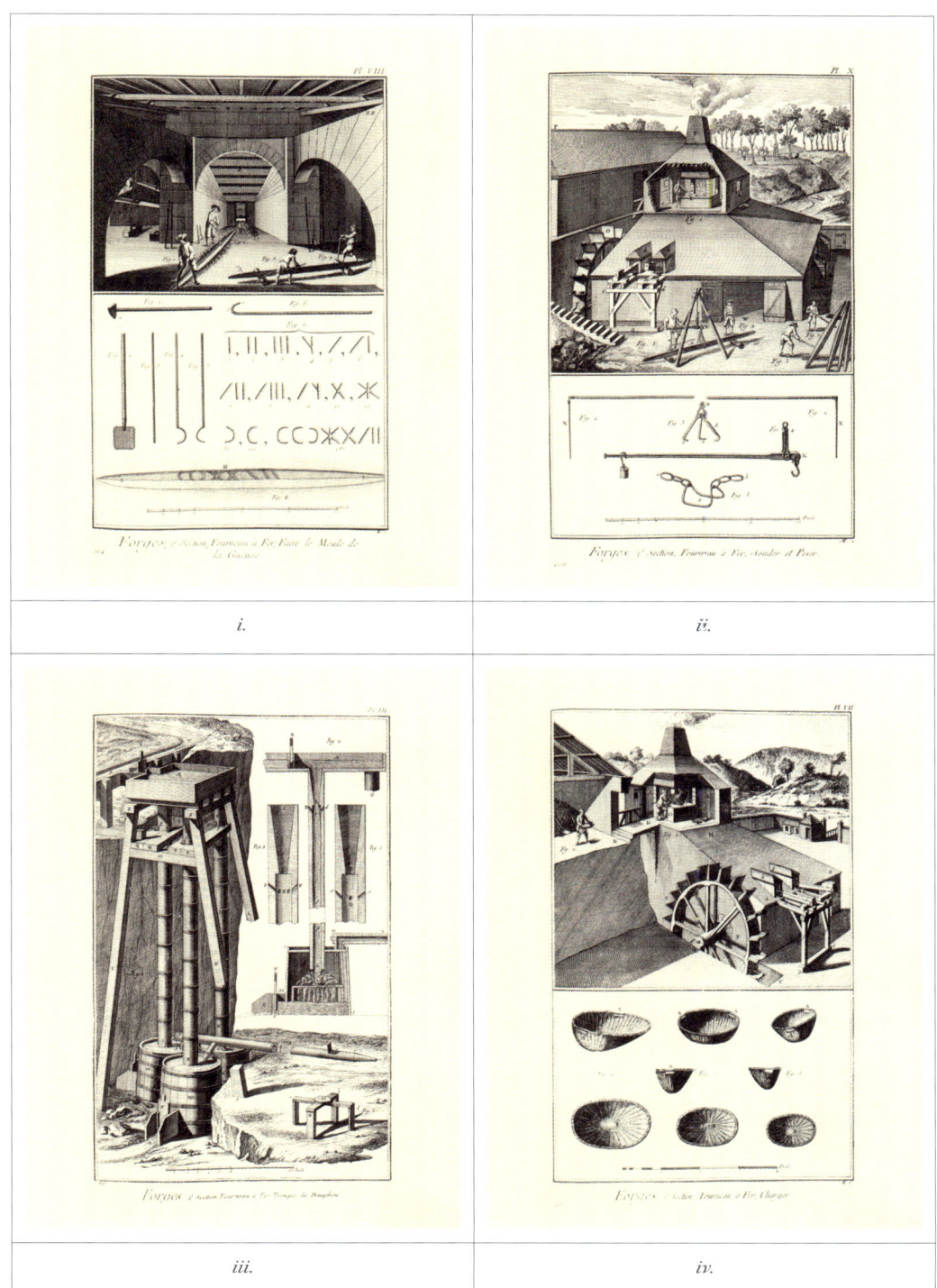

i.

ii.

iii.

iv.

(i–iv).   Illustrations from 'Forges, or the art of making iron', *Encyclopédie,* Vol. 4, 1765, edited by Denis
            Diderot and Jean le Rond d'Alembert. Plate (i) shows the blasting furnace and casting the mould for
            the pig iron, (ii) shows the process of surveying and weighing the iron, (iii) shows smelting apparatus
            and (iv) shows loading the ore into the furnace, and the baskets used to carry the ore and charcoal.

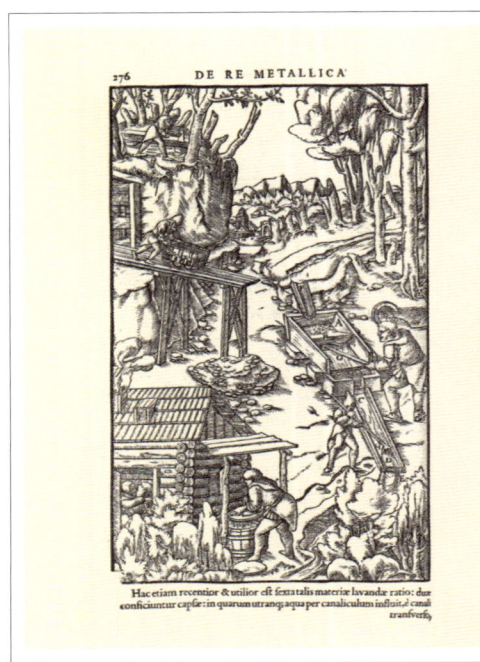

i.

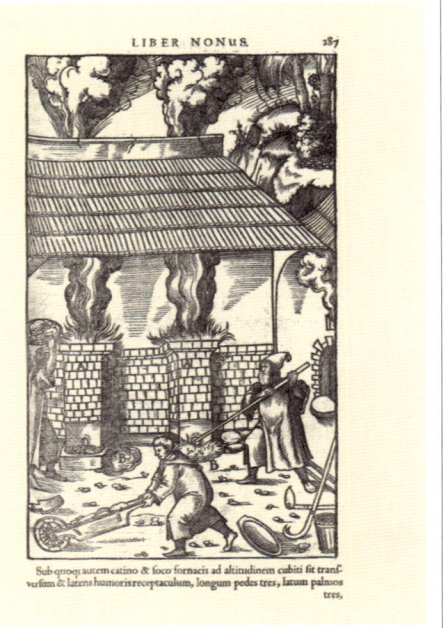

ii.

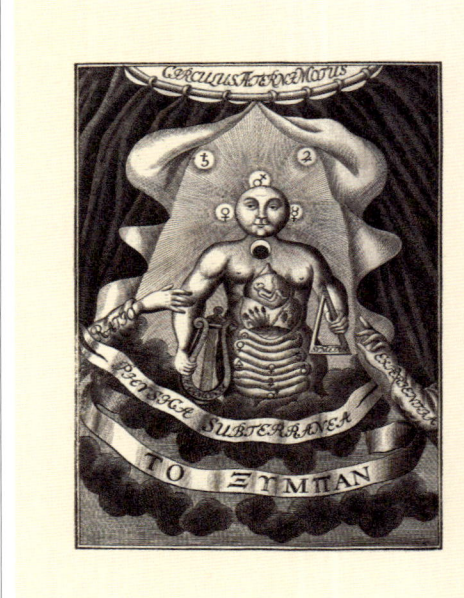

iii.

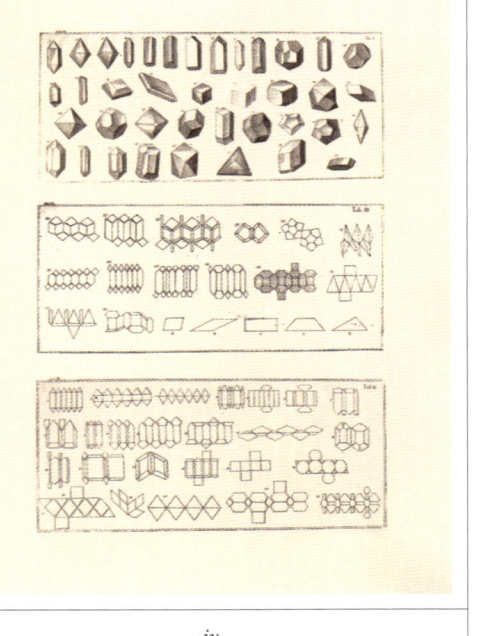

iv.

(i–ii).   Illustrations of the process of mining, refining and smelting metals,
           Georgius Agricola, *De re metallica*, 1621.
(iii).   Allegorical frontispiece showing the creation of terrestrial and
           subterranean life, Johann Joachim Becher, *Physica subterranea*, 1669.
(iv).   Mineral illustrations, Carl Linnaeus, *Systema naturae*, 1735.

to Karlsbad in Bohemia to take the cure. On the way he stopped in Freiberg, and was given a tour of the mines and mine workings at the recently opened Bergakademie, the School of Mining. Young Werner so impressed the staff that he was invited to attend the school and in 1769 enrolled as student number 52.

Werner was a diligent student and was fortunate to come under the wing of Karl Eugen Pabst von Ohain (1718–1784), chief mine inspector. Pabst was among the foremost mineralogists of his day and possessed an extensive collection of minerals and a large library. Werner later compiled a catalogue of the collection,[6] and noted in the introduction that Pabst believed the identification of minerals required a combination of observation of their external characteristics and their chemical composition. On completing his studies Werner was offered a post at the School, but realized that to further his career he would need university training, specifically in law. He therefore enrolled at the University of Leipzig in 1771.[7]

WORKS INFORMING WERNER'S IDEAS

In the centuries before Werner studied at Leipzig several important books on mineralogy had been published. These were now standard works and he would undoubtedly have encountered them, either at the mining school, the university or in Pabst's library. Among them were *De re metallica* and *De natura fossilium* by the German mineralogist Georgius Agricola (Georg Bauer; 1491–1555). Often regarded as the origin of modern mineralogy and geology, these books incorporated a systematic arrangement of minerals, with notes on external characteristics.

Then in 1669, the German physician and alchemist Johann Joachim Becher (1635–1682) set out an arrangement of minerals based on chemistry in his *Physica subterranea*. A highly significant milestone came in 1735 with the publication of *Systema naturae* by Carl Linnaeus (1707–1778). While Linnaeus is normally associated with biology and zoology, he also included his Third Kingdom of Nature – Minerals. The chemistry of minerals was also used as the basis of the classification system of Johann Heinrich Pott (1692–1777) in his *Chymische Untersuchungen ... Lithogeognosia* in 1757, the forerunner of many later systems.

Another prominent researcher in mineralogy was Johan Gottschalk Wallerius (1709–1785). He was a contemporary of Linnaeus and Professor of Mineralogy at Uppsala University. In his 1747 *Mineralogia* and then in his 1772 *Systematibus mineralogicum*, Wallerius set out his own classification system based on chemistry, but combined this with external characteristics to a greater degree than before. Wallerius's system defined his major classes (Earths, Stones and Minerals) as Linnaeus had done, then further subdivided them into a number of orders, then genus and finally species. While the classes and orders were set out according to compositional criteria, at genus and species level external characteristics were used. Colour was a major characteristic for differentiating species and genus, though other factors also came into play, such as crystal shape and hardness.

In addition to Agricola and Linnaeus, Werner was also influenced by another Swede, Axel Fredrik Cronstedt (1722–1765). Werner later translated into German Cronstedt's book on mineralogy of 1758,[8] and he looked to Cronstedt in an early version of his own system of mineralogy. For instance, he adopted Cronstedt's division of the mineral kingdom into earths, salts, inflammables and metals almost without significant change. Cronstedt's use of external characteristics to distinguish between minerals was similar to Wallerius's categories of colour, hardness, transparency, etc, but he did not create a list of their external characteristics. In Cronstedt's descriptions, minerals had colours assigned to them, but he made no attempt to create a standard reference system, and the descriptions themselves are quite vague.

It was a book published in 1756 that would prove to be an influential source for Werner's fundamental ideas. This was *Versuch einer Geschichte von Flötz-Gebürgen* by the German mineralogist Johann Gottlob Lehmann

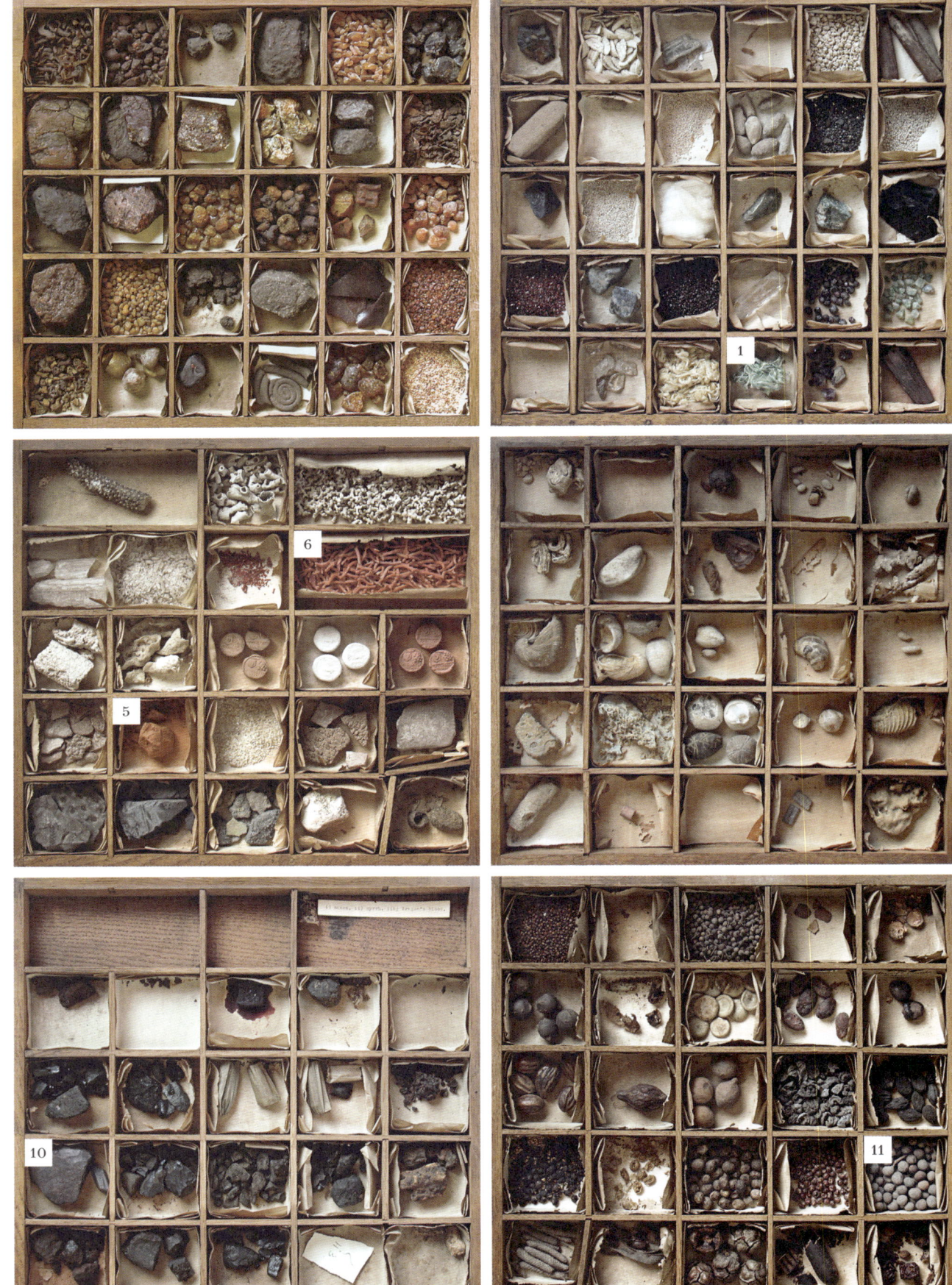

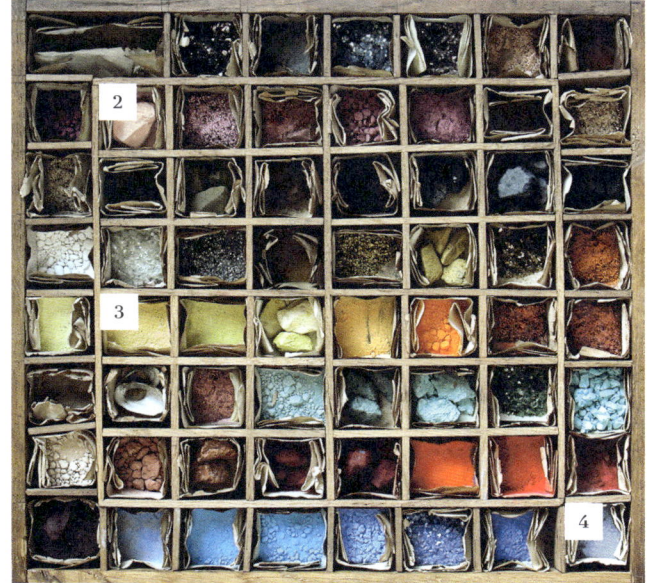

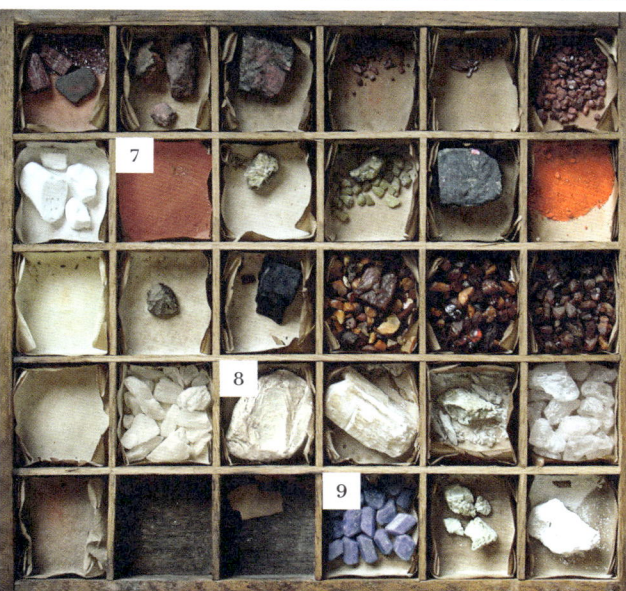

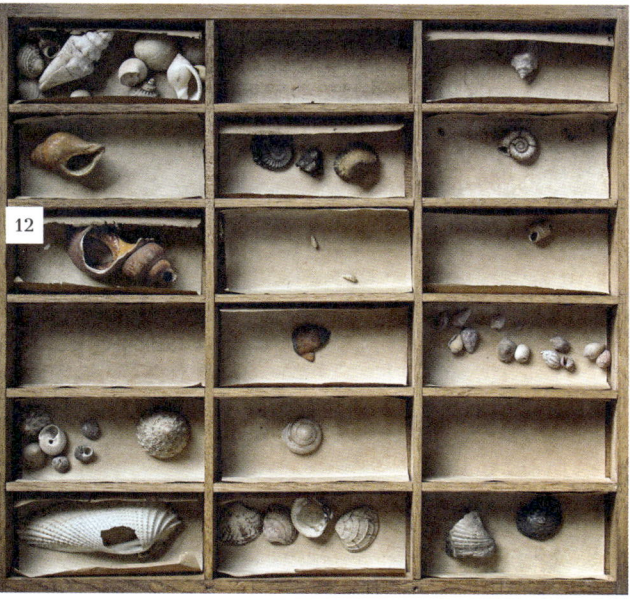

VIGANI'S CABINET.

An explosion of interest in medicine and the natural world during the Early Modern period in Europe led to a vogue for natural collections. The quantity and diversity of specimens assembled inside these 'cabinets of curiosities' became a symbol of status for their owners. These drawers of minerals, shells, fossils and fruits are taken from the cabinet of the Italian chemist John Francis Vigani (*c.* 1650–1712). They are part of his collection of nearly 700 samples of *materia medica* (medical materials), assembled in Cambridge, England, in 1703–04.

COLOUR REFERENCES.

1		BEZOAR ORIENTALIS.
		50. Verdigris Green.
2		RED OCHRE.
		90. Peach Blossom Red.
3		ORPIMENT.
		67. King's Yellow.
4		DEEP SMALT.
		31. Berlin Blue.
5		ARMENIAN BOLE.
		82. Tile red.
6		RED CORAL.
		85. Vermilion Red.
7		MINIUM.
		84. Scarlet Red.
8		TALCUM VENETUM.
		8. Greyish White.
9		ROMAN VITRIOL.
		28. Azure Blue.
10		HEPATIC ALOE RESIN.
		20. Pitch, or Brownish Black.
11		COCCULUS INDICUS BERRY.
		14. Bluish Grey.
12		TURBINIDAE SHELL.
		103. Chesnut Brown.

(1719-1767) in which he set out his theory of the formation of the Earth. Lehmann proposed that rocks were deposited from a primeval ocean (either by precipitation or erosion) to form the layers observed at the surface, with the oldest at the bottom. He also stated that other rocks could appear at the surface through accidental causes such as floods, earthquakes and volcanic eruptions.

EXTERNAL CHARACTERISTICS AND THE IDENTIFICATION OF MINERALS

One of Werner's lecturers at Leipzig was Dr Johann Karl Gehler (1732-1796). In 1757 Gehler had written and published a small book entitled *De characteribus fossilium externis* - on the external characteristics of fossils. Werner had begun a translation of Gehler's book into German, but on the advice of his friend, Christian Erhard Kapp (1739-1824), he added his own text to expand the original idea into his most famous book, *Von den äusserlichen Kennzeichen der Fossilien* (Of the External Characteristics of Fossils), published in 1774.

Werner's book was not an explanation of his mineralogical system - this was not published until 1789 - it was instead a straightforward guide to identifying minerals in the laboratory and classroom or in the field. It was also an attempt to create a standardized vocabulary so that anyone using his system when describing a mineral species would be understood by others. Werner's chief aim was to address a gap, as he saw it, in using external characteristics as a tool to identify minerals. He itemized these external characteristics as colour, cohesion, external crystal form (if present), size, lustre, fracture and hardness as well as taste and smell. Of these, however, he regarded colour as the most important, describing it as 'the first to strike the senses', and listed the colours that were relevant to minerals. Werner did admit, however, that it was not possible to distinguish minerals by colour alone, but rather a combination of all the characteristics was needed.

Werner based his colour scheme not on the spectrum of light but on a consideration of the colours found naturally in mineralogy, thus he included both white and black. He also argued that the colour of a mineral could reveal something of its chemical composition. For instance, copper minerals are largely green or blue, manganese minerals can be pink, iron can be indicated by red, and so on. In his system Werner listed eight principal colours: white, grey, black, blue, green, yellow, red and brown. These he then further subdivided and qualified either by modifiers such as bluish black or greenish yellow, or with descriptive names, such as milk white, canary green or sky blue. These in turn could have what he called shades - pale, light, clear and dark. In this way Werner's list of 54 individual colours could become 216 when all the variants were included.

The publication of his book in 1774, the year he left Leipzig, marked a turning point in Werner's life. It came to the attention of his old mentor, Pabst, who immediately made representations to the School of Mining to offer Werner a post as a teacher and as curator of its collections.

AN INFLUENTIAL TEACHER

Werner accepted the offer and at Easter 1775, six years after he had enrolled as a student, he became a teacher at the school, where he remained until his death in 1817. He began by teaching only mineralogy, but as his experience grew, so did his dissatisfaction with the old curriculum and he began to make changes. When the academy was first established, courses were offered in metallurgical chemistry, mine assaying, mine surveying, mathematics and physics, with an additional course in mining using models in the academy and mine visits. Mineralogy was available as an extra-curricular activity and was open to both students and the public. Werner introduced new teaching methods, improved the co-ordination between courses and expanded the curriculum as well as the mineral collections and library.[9] His fame as a teacher

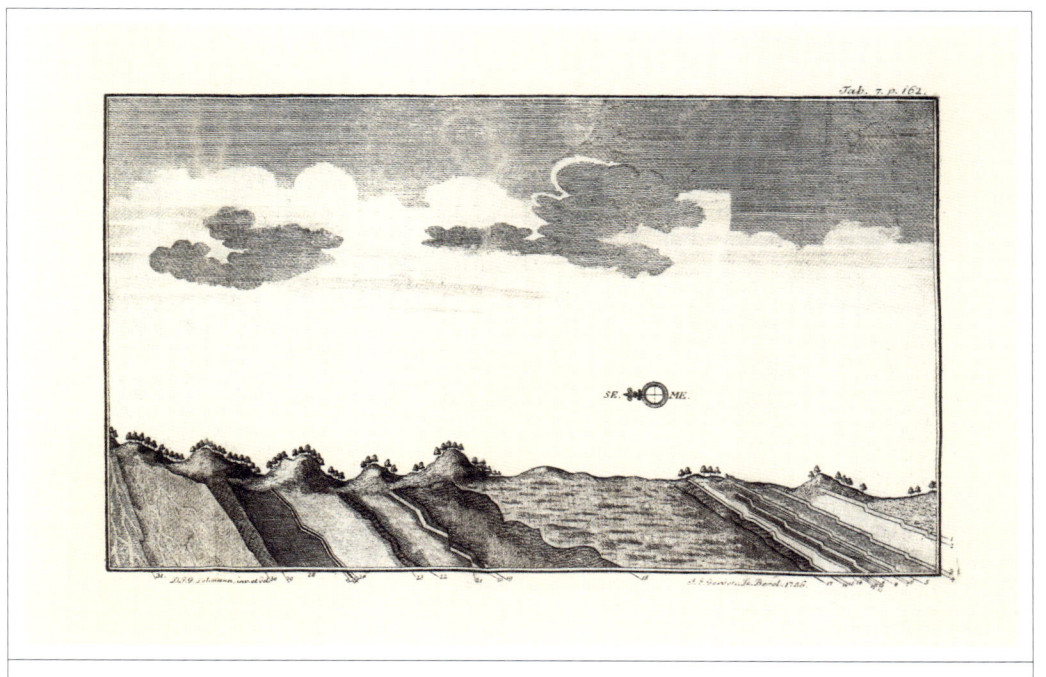

i.

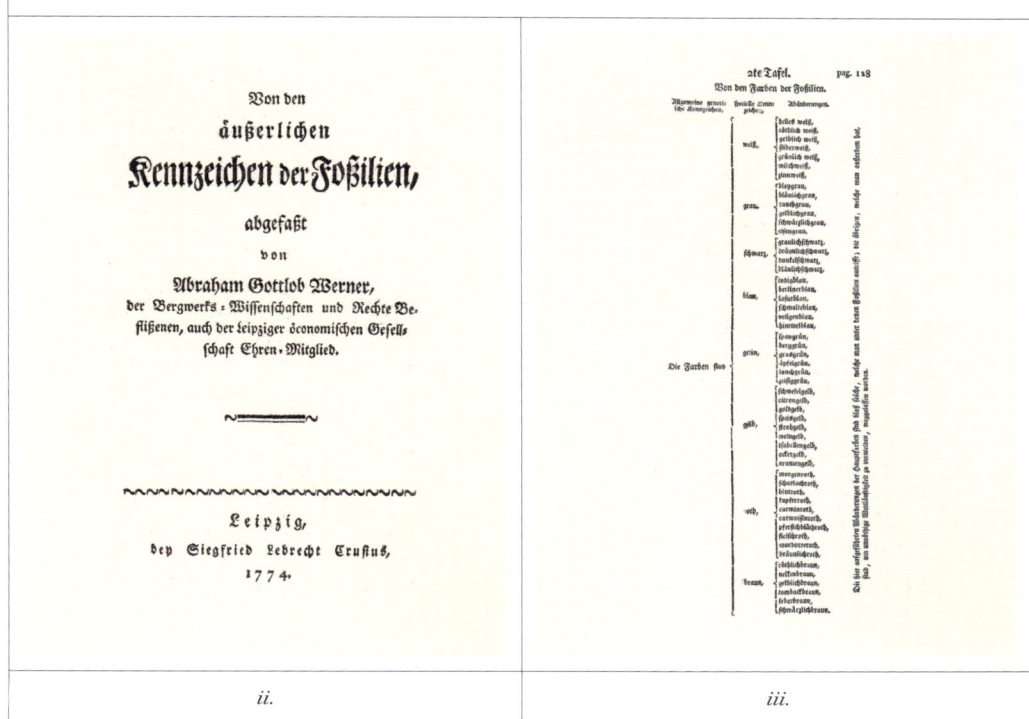

| *ii.* | *iii.* |

(i).   Illustration of strata, Johann Gottlob Lehmann, *Versuch einer Geschichte von Flötz-Gebürgen*, 1756.
(ii).   Title page, Abraham Gottlob Werner, *Von den äusserlichen Kennzeichen der Fossilien*, 1774.
(iii). List of 54 colours, white to brown, Abraham Gottlob Werner, *Von den äusserlichen Kennzeichen der Fossilien*, 1774.

i. (page 74)

No.	Die grüne Farbe mit ihren Abänderungen.	Aeussere Gestalten.	Bruch.
265.		Derb. S. no. 240. 250. 259. 267.	Fasrig.
266.		Derb. S. no. 236. 242. 255. 275.	Dicht, splittrig.
267.		Derb. S. no. 29. 240. 250. 259. 265.	Fasrig.
268.		Derb.	Blättrig.
269.		Sechsseitige, mit sechs Flächen zugespitzte Säulen.	Vollkommen muschlich.
270.		Derb. S. no. 32 a. 108. 146. 212. 215. 217 a. 282. 291.	Uneben.
271.		Derb. S. no. 275.	Krummschiefrig.

ii. (page 80)

No.	Die gelbe Farbe mit ihren Abänderungen.	Aeussere Gestalten.	Bruch.
285.		Derb, als Schiefer.	Schiefrig.
286.		Derb. S. no. 2. 42. 65. 85. 204. 281. 361.	Feinerdig.
287.		Derb. S. no. 354.	Dicht, splittrig.
288.		Derb.	Im Großen schiefrig, im Kleinen splittrig.
289.		Derb, eingesprengt. S. no. 260. 289.	
290.		Derb. no. 27. 40. 46. 77. 148. 220. 252. 290.	Fasrig.
291.		Derb. S. no. 108. 212. 215. 217 a. 222. 304.	Uneben.
292.		Derb, in mächtigen Lagern. S. no. 160. 171. 282. 300.	Dicht, splittrig.

iii. (page 100)

No.	Die rothe Farbe mit ihren Abänderungen.	Aeussere Gestalten.	Bruch.
359.		Derb. S. no. 6. 200.	Blättrig.
360.		Derb. S. no. 297.	Splittrig.
361.		Derb. S. no. 20. 42. 65. 85. 204. 281. 286.	Feinerdig.
362.		Derb.	Blättrig.
363.		Derb. S. no. 171. 186. 282. 292. 300. 380.	Dicht, splittrig.
364.		Derb, auch in Rhomben. S. no. 55. 375.	Blättrig.
365.		Tafelform. S. no. 284.	Blättrig.

iv. (page 106)

No.	Die rothe Farbe mit ihren Abänderungen.	Aeussere Gestalten.	Bruch.
383.		Derb. S. no. 237. 246. 302. 358. 379. 396.	Uneben, erdig.
384.		Derb. S. no. 324. 325. 370. 380. 386. 387. 389.	Dicht, splittrig.
385.		Derb. S. no. 237. 246. 302. 333. 379. 395.	Muschlich.
386		Derb. S. no. 324. 325. 370. 380. 333. 387. 389. 394.	Splittrig.
387.		Derb. —	—
388		Derb. S. no. 106. 127. 133. 152. 320. 332. 333. 335.	Muschlich.
389.		Derb. S. no. 324. 325. —	Dicht, splittrig.

(i–iv). Mineral charts from Johann Georg Lenz's *Mustertafeln der bis Jetzt Bekannten Einfachen Mineralien*, 1794. Based on Werner's principles, Lenz supplied a watercolour illustration of each of the 400 minerals charted in this field guide for mineral identification in order to show their colour.

soon spread and his new curriculum began to attract students from around Germany and much further afield, including Russia, Sweden, Norway, Denmark, Brazil, Spain, France, Mexico, Scotland and England.

Perhaps Werner's most important change was a new course on mineralogy, which was divided into two parts. The first dealt with the identification of minerals using his book on external characteristics, the *Kennzeichen*. To illustrate his nomenclature of colour Werner established a special collection, with carefully chosen minerals to provide an example for each colour. This was the principal reason why colour samples were not included in his original publication, as the 'Colour-suite of Minerals' served this purpose. The second part of the course involved the systematic arrangement of minerals based on the work of Cronstedt, but increasingly using Werner's own system. He also introduced lectures and courses on what he called *geognosy*, which dealt with, at least in part, the history of the Earth's surface. This is where Werner introduced his students to the tenets of Neptunism, with which he became inextricably linked.[10]

Neptunism was a theory of the origin of the Earth's crust influenced by Lehmann's notion that all rocks were deposited from seawater or eroded from older rocks.[11] It postulated that the Earth was originally covered by a primeval ocean into which the oldest rocks such as granite were deposited to considerable depth. Later these rocks were uplifted, exposed and eroded to form sedimentary rocks which formed the layers found at the Earth's surface. Werner taught this in his geognosy lessons and it became widely known as the Wernerian System. Through Werner's teaching or by way of his publications, and through his students and their work, his influence extended worldwide and has been described as the 'Wernerian Radiation'. One such student, Robert Jameson, played a key role in the dissemination of Werner's ideas, in particular his nomenclature of colours. It is said that Jameson produced more Wernerians than Werner himself.

ROBERT JAMESON AND WERNER'S NOMENCLATURE OF COLOURS

Robert Jameson was destined for a career in medicine and was apprenticed to a surgeon.[12] It was possibly through a fellow apprentice, Charles Anderson, that he first came into contact with the work of Werner. Anderson had translated and published (in *Encyclopedia Britannica*, 1809) one of Werner's books. He also translated the work of Leopold von Buch (1774–1853), a pupil and staunch supporter of Werner. Anderson would later become a founder member of the Wernerian Natural History Society. In pursuit of his training, Jameson also attended medical lectures at the University of Edinburgh, and it was here that he met the Reverend John Walker (1731–1803), Professor of Natural History. Walker had been a pupil of the great chemist William Cullen (1710–1790), and much of his early mineralogical work was founded on Cullen's teachings.[13] He had also been developing his own system of mineral classification influenced by Wallerius, the French naturalist Jacques-Christoph Valmont de Bomare (1731–1837), whose mineral system was heavily slanted towards external characteristics,[14] and, in particular, Axel Cronstedt.

By 1792/3, Jameson had already read several papers on Natural Sciences to the Royal Medical Society of Edinburgh, in which he seemed to embrace the Wernerian view. In 1797 he visited Dublin to study the mineral collection of Nathanael Gottfried Leske (1751–1786),[15] a geologist and close friend of Werner. The collection had been rearranged according to Werner's system by Dietrich Ludwig Gustav Karsten (1768–1810), one of his pupils, who then published a two-volume catalogue. Richard Kirwan (1733–1812), the Irish geologist, was instrumental in the purchase of the collection by the Royal Irish Academy and it was brought to Dublin in 1792, where it was arranged by Dr George Mitchell (1752–1803), who also translated the catalogue. In the catalogue and display of the collection, the first section is given over to external characteristics, particularly colour.

Inspired by what he read and saw in Dublin, Jameson travelled to Freiberg in 1800, where he immersed himself for two years in Werner's teachings and methods. Among the many students studying under Werner in Freiberg at that time was Karl Friedrich Mohs (1773–1839).[16] After Werner's death, Mohs succeeded his former teacher. His own *Treatise of Mineralogy*[17] proposed a system based on crystallography, but also contained a section on external characteristics, including Werner's colour scheme.

Jameson's appointment in 1804 as Regius Professor of Natural History at the University of Edinburgh placed him in an important position in the world of natural history. In 1808, he formed the Wernerian Natural History Society, named in honour of his former teacher, to provide a forum for the reading and discussion of natural history papers. Edinburgh at that time was experiencing the ferment that became known as the 'Scottish' or 'Edinburgh' Enlightenment,[18] part of the Age of Enlightenment that was sweeping through Europe. It was a period of intense philosophical, intellectual, medical and scientific study and research – especially in Natural Sciences. Jameson's prominent academic role afforded him the opportunity to promote the teachings of Werner to a wider audience, but it was the dispersal of those ideas through the Scottish diaspora which took Scottish Enlightenment ideas around the world.

In the same year that Jameson began his tenure as Professor he published his first major book, *A System of Mineralogy* (volume 1), which was followed in 1805 with the publication of *A Treatise on the External Characters of Minerals* – both of which were based on the work of Werner. While the *System* explicitly defines the colours of the individual mineral species according to the Wernerian system, it is the *Treatise* that provides an explanation and a table of Werner's scheme of nomenclature.[19]

A comparison between Werner's original list and Jameson's in his 1805 *Treatise* reveals that Jameson expanded Werner's 54 colour terms to 84, with the addition of some new greys

and other modifications (see p. 34). However, to a large degree he retained the names that Werner used, and, like Werner, Jameson did not include colour samples or swatches. A second, updated and expanded edition of the *Treatise* was published in 1816, and even though this appeared two years after the publication of Patrick Syme's *Werner's Nomenclature of Colours* in 1814, Jameson did not use the opportunity to add colour samples and his colour nomenclature remains largely unchanged.

While Syme probably based his system on the work of Werner and Jameson, he took his own approach.[20] He retained a high proportion of Werner's names, but introduced some of his own. Some of these are the result of his two new principal colours – purple and orange, which meant that colours such as violet blue and plum blue (as in Werner and Jameson) became violet purple and plum purple. Syme also used his background as an artist to introduce names such as Sienna yellow, and his knowledge of flowers showed in his pansy purple and auricula purple. In all Syme increased the number of colour references to 108, and then 110 in the second edition of his book, published in 1821.

Syme knew Jameson through his position as painter to the Wernerian Natural History Society and it is probable therefore that Syme became familiar with the work of Werner through him. Once the connection was established, Syme visited the museum to examine the mineral collection Jameson had arranged according to Werner's colour system. Syme undoubtedly recognized the simplicity and straightforwardness of Werner's combination of a principal colour, such as red, with a familiar or easily identifiable descriptor, such as blood, to derive his own, similar system for his colour references and the examples he gives of objects found in nature. Syme's choice of using hand-painted swatches as opposed to printing the colours directly on to the page may have given him a greater degree of control over the final colour, as it appears in the book. Colour printing was still very much in its infancy (see p. 235) and despite the progress that had been made by the end of the 18th century, reliable,

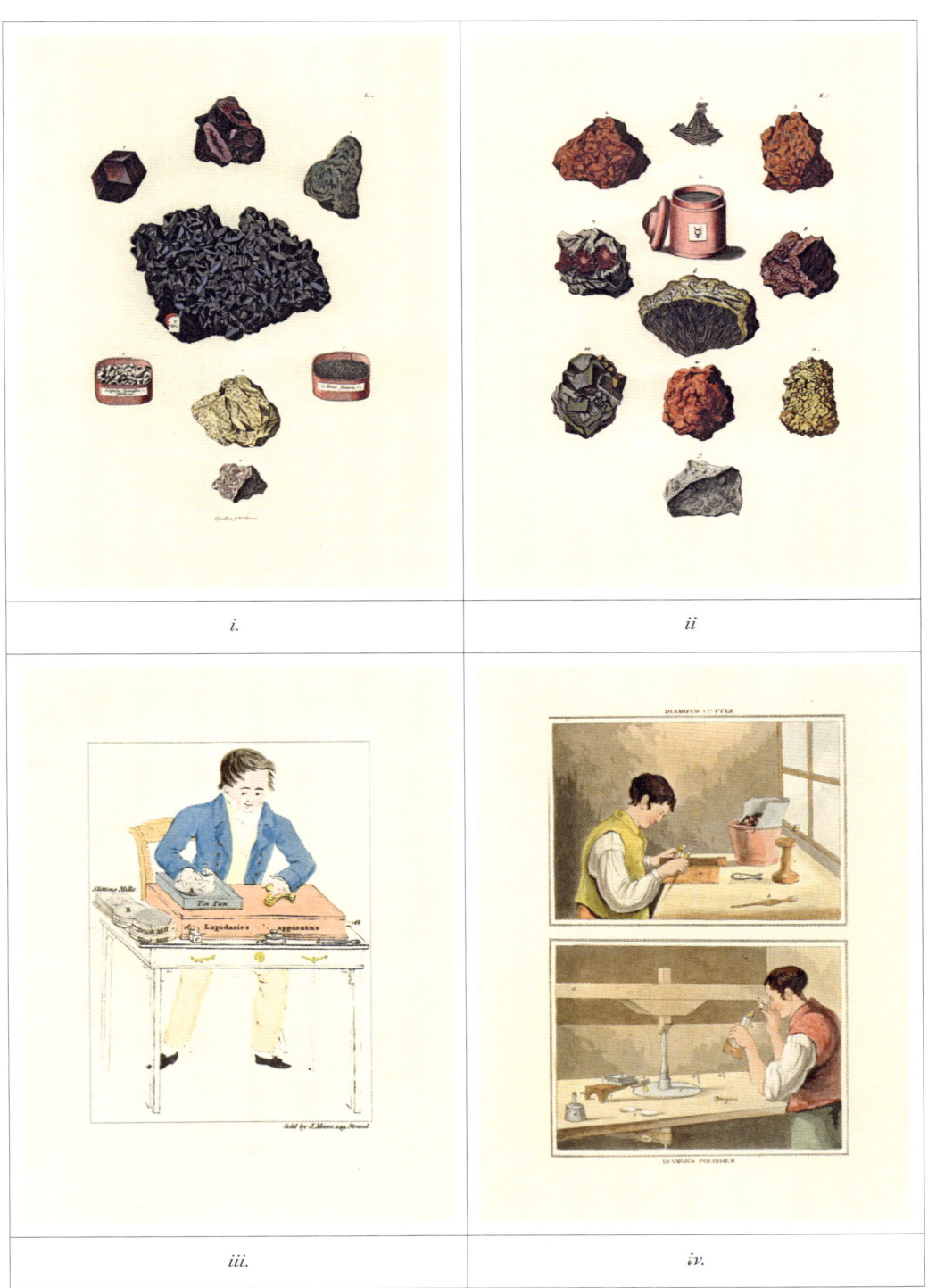

(i).   Varieties of tin ore, Georg Wolfgang Knorr, *Deliciae naturae selectae*, 1766.
(ii).   Varieties of minerals, Georg Wolfgang Knorr, *Deliciae naturae selectae*, 1766.
(iii).   Mineralogist at work, John Mawe, *Familiar Lessons on Mineralogy and Geology*, 1826.
(iv).   Diamond cutter (above) and polisher (below), John Mawe, *A Treatise on Diamonds*, 1823.

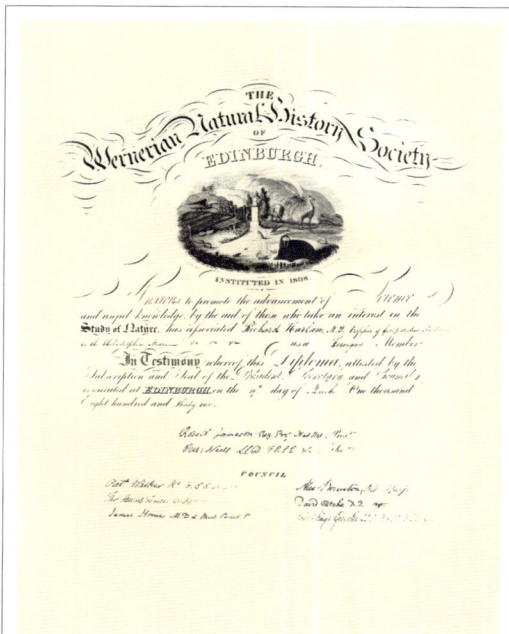

i.

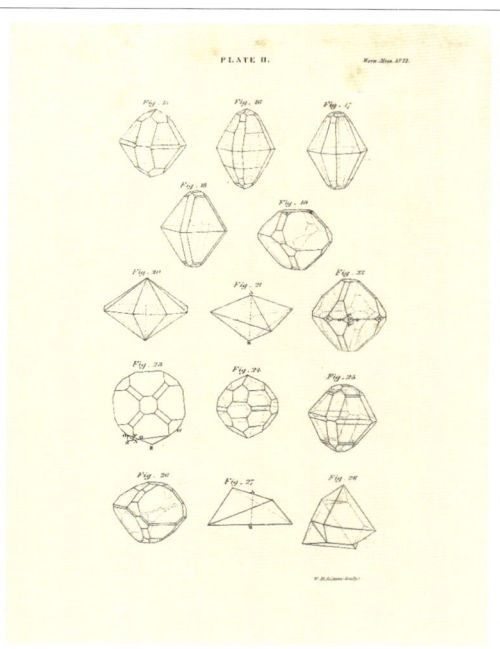

ii.

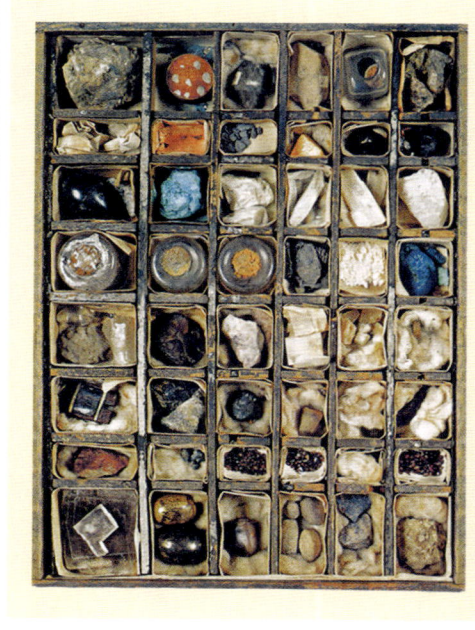

iii.

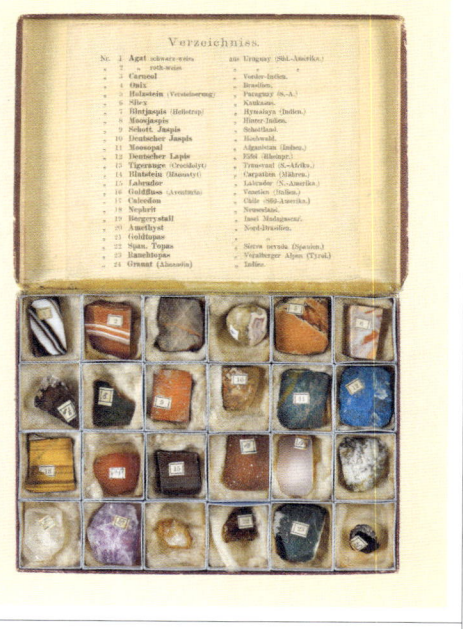

iv.

(i).   Membership certificate to the Wernerian Natural History Society of Edinburgh, 1831.
(ii).   Crystallizations of copper pyrites, *Memoirs of the Wernerian Natural History Society*, 1822.
(iii).   Cabinet drawer of minerals, Utrecht, the Netherlands, *c.* 1670.
(iv).   Mineral collection in a cardboard display box, Vienna, Austria, 1880.

high-quality colour printing was still a few decades away. By creating a large sheet of colour, to the satisfaction of the artist, which could then be cut up into smaller pieces, Syme could at least guarantee a degree of quality control.

THE INFLUENCE OF WERNER'S CLASSIFICATION SYSTEM ON MINERALOGY

Syme's book was generally favourably received, but his specific nomenclature was not used in the major textbooks on mineralogy published in the 19th century. One of the first, and most important, publications on systematic mineralogy after 1821 was *A System of Mineralogy: Including an Extended Treatise on Crystallography* by the American geologist and mineralogist James Dwight Dana (1813-1845), published in 1837. The strength of his mineral classification system is shown by the fact that a version of it – though substantially updated and modified – is still in use today. He includes a section on external characteristics using an unmodified version of the original Wernerian colour nomenclature of 1774, rather than either of Syme's or Jameson's systems, even though Jameson's *Treatise* is cited in the bibliography. As late as the 1850s, the fourth edition of *Dana's System of Mineralogy* was still using the original Werner nomenclature.

The Edinburgh mineralogist Robert Allan (1836-1863) published *A Manual of Mineralogy* in 1834. He was not a pupil of Jameson, but was strongly influenced by another Wernerian, Wilhelm Haidinger (1795-1871), who had visited Edinburgh in 1822. Allan, too, adopts the original Werner colour scheme rather than the Syme variation. In 1849, James Nicol (1810-1879), who had attended Jameson's lectures as a student, though his main interests were art and divinity, published his *Manual of Mineralogy* using the Wernerian system of colour nomenclature. When Thomas Thomson (1773-1852), professor of chemistry at Glasgow University, published his *Outlines of Mineralogy, Geology and Mineral Analysis* in 1836, he also adopted the Werner nomenclature.[21]

Syme's book was used in many sciences other than mineralogy, but as a guide in the field or laboratory rather than a systematic nomenclature for minerals. As the science of mineralogy progressed through the 19th and early 20th centuries, the need for a nomenclature such as Werner's or Syme's declined, and later textbooks incorporated external characteristics into the descriptions of individual minerals.

NOTES—(1). Dixon 2014. (2). The first translation was into Hungarian, by Ferentz Benkö; see p. 20 in this book and Kazmer 2002. (3). In German *Neues und wohleingerichtetes Mineral- und Bergwercks-Lexikon*, 1730. (4). *Curieuses und reales Natur-, Kunst-, Berg-, Gewerck- und Handlungs-Lexicon*, 1736. (5). The Werner family had been involved in the production of iron for over a hundred years, initially in Thuringia (Weida) then later in Silesia. (6). The collection was taken to Brazil, eventually becoming part of the collections of the National Museum of Brazil, and unfortunately was destroyed in the fire there in 2018. (7). Although diligent in his law studies, his interest in science and mineralogy was not forgotten. Together with some fellow students – Johann Samuel Traugott Gehler (1751-1795), Friedrich Callisch (1754-1783) and Nathanael Gottfried Leske (1751-1786) – Werner formed a small group to discuss psychology, astronomy and mineralogy. (8). *Försök til Mineralogie eller Mineral Rikets Upställning*; Cronstedt 1770. (9). Students were also now required to keep a journal or diary which they were to hand in regularly. (10). This theory was opposed by the Plutonist school led by the Scottish geologists James Hutton (1726-1797) and others. It was the Neptunist view that was later taught by Robert Jameson in Edinburgh. (11). Sweet 1976. (12). He had also had an interest in natural history and taxidermy, which continued into later life as he built up a large collection of stuffed birds in the University Museum. He showed this Syme and the great American ornithologist John James Audubon (1785-1851) when he visited Edinburgh. (13). Eddy 2002. (14). Bomare 1762. (15). Usually referred to as the Leskean Cabinet.16). His eponymous scale of mineral hardness is still used today. (17). Mohs 1825, originally published in German in 1822 and 1824. (18). In 1800, Scotland had five universities to serve a population of about 1.6 million, whereas England had only two with a population of 7.7 million. (19). Jameson had published the table separately in 1804, as *Tabular View of the External Characters of Minerals for the Use of Students of Oryctognosy* (20). Simonini, 2018. (21). For the development of geology from mineralogy, see Laudan 1987.

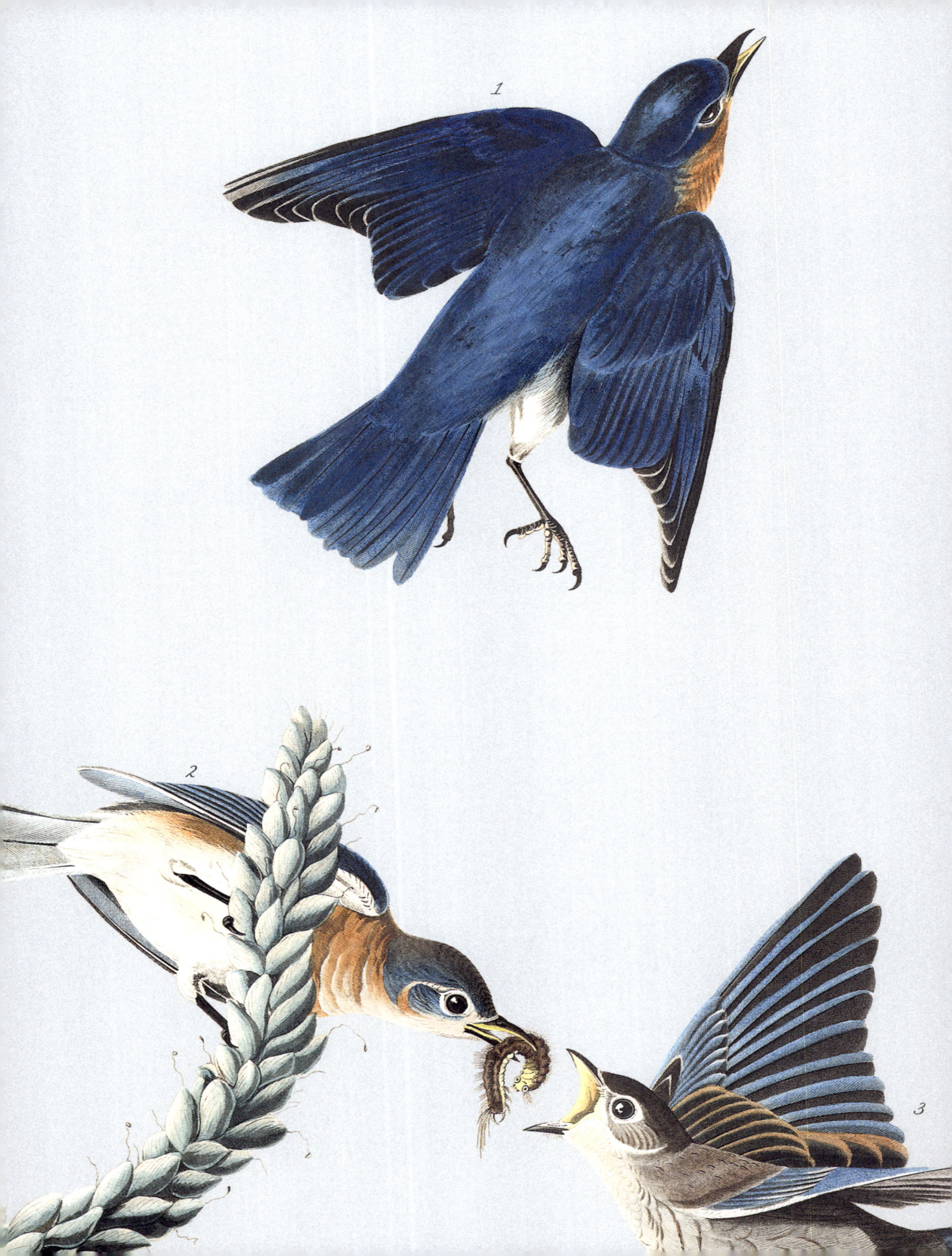

ii.

BLUES
AND
PURPLES.

BLUES.

BLUES

No.	Names	Colours	ANIMAL	VEGETABLE	MINERAL
24	Scotch Blue		Throat of Blue Titmouse.	Stamina of Single Purple Anemone.	Blue Copper Ore.
25	Prussian Blue		Beauty Spot on Wing of Mallard Drake.	Stamina of Bluish Purple Anemone.	Blue Copper Ore
26	Indigo Blue				Blue Copper Ore.
27	China Blue		Rhynchites Nitens	Back Parts of Gentian Flower.	Blue Copper Ore from Chessy.
28	Azure Blue.		Breast of Emerald-crested Manakin	Grape Hyacinth. Gentian.	Blue Copper Ore.
29	Ultra marine Blue.		Upper Side of the Wings of small blue Heath Butterfly.	Borrage.	Azure Stone or Lapis Lazuli.
30	Flax-flower Blue.		Light Parts of the Margin of the Wings of Devils Butterfly.	Flax flower.	Blue Copper Ore
31	Berlin Blue.		Wing Feathers of Jay.	Hepatica.	Blue Sapphire.
32	Verditter Blue				Lenticular Ore.
33	Greenish Blue			Great Fennel Flower.	Turquois. Flour Spar.
34	Greyish Blue.		Back of blue Titmouse	Small Fennel Flower.	Iron Earth.

PURPLES.

PURPLES.

Nº	Names	Colours	ANIMAL	VEGITABLE	MINERAL
35	Bluish Lilac Purple.		Male of the Lebellula Depressa.	Blue Lilac.	Lepidolite.
36	Bluish Purple.		Papilio Argeolus. Azure Blue Butterfly.	Parts of White and Purple Crocus.	
37	Violet Purple.			Purple Aster.	Amethyst.
38	Pansy Purple.		Chrysomela Goettingensis.	Sweet-scented Violet.	Derbyshire Spar.
39	Campanula Purple.			Canterbury Bell. Campanula Persicifolia.	Fluor Spar.
40	Imperial Purple.			Deep Parts of Flower of Saffron Crocus.	Fluor Spar.
41	Auricula Purple.		Egg of largest Blue-bottle, or Flesh Fly.	Largest Purple Auricula.	Fluor Spar.
42	Plum Purple.			Plum.	Fluor Spar.
43	Red Lilac Purple.		Light Spots of the upper Wings of Peacock Butterfly.	Red Lilac. Pale Purple Primrose.	Lepidolite.
44	Lavender Purple.		Light Parts of Spots on the under Wings of Peacock Butterfly.	Dried Lavender Flowers.	Porcelain Jasper.
45	Pale Blackish Purple.				Porcelain Jasper.

BLUES.

No.	Names.	Colours.	ANIMAL.		
24	*Scotch Blue.*		*Throat of Blue Titmouse.*		
25	*Prussian Blue.*		*Beauty Spot on Wing of Mallard Drake.*		
26	*Indigo Blue.*				
27	*China Blue.*		*Rhynchites Nitens.*		
28	*Azure Blue.*		*Breast of Emerald-crested Manakin.*		
29	*Ultra-marine Blue.*		*Upper Side of the Wings of small blue Heath Butterfly.*		
30	*Flax-flower Blue.*		*Light Parts of the Margin of the Wings of Devil's Butterfly.*		
31	*Berlin Blue.*		*Wing Feathers of Jay.*		
32	*Verditter Blue.*				
33	*Greenish Blue.*				
34	*Greyish Blue.*		*Back of blue Titmouse*		

Syme's 1821 edition included three of Werner's original blues (numbers 26, 28, and 31) and two renamed from Werner's original blues – Sky Blue renamed 'Greenish Blue' (number 33) and Smalt Blue renamed 'Greyish Blue' (number 34). In addition, there were five blues from his own 1814 system (numbers 25, 27, 29, 30 and 32) and one newly introduced blue (24).

BLUES.

	VEGETABLE.		MINERAL.	
	Stamina of Single Purple Anemone.		Blue Copper Ore.	
	Stamina of Bluish Purple Anemone.		Blue Copper Ore.	
			Blue Copper Ore.	
	Back Parts of Gentian Flower.		Blue Copper Ore from Chessy.	
	Grape Hyacinth. Gentian.		Blue Copper Ore.	
	Borrage.		Azure Stone or Lapis Lazuli.	
	Flax flower.		Blue Copper Ore.	
	Hepatica.		Blue Sapphire.	
			Lenticular Ore.	
	Great Fennel Flower.		Turquois. Flour Spar.	
	Small Fennel Flower.		Iron Earth.	

24. SCOTCH BLUE.

(i).   *Throat of Blue Titmouse.* [*Eurasian blue tit*; Cyanistes caeruleus]
(ii).   *Stamina of Single Purple Anemone.* [Anemone]
(iii).   *Blue Copper Ore.* [*Azurite*; Copper mineral]

ANIMAL.

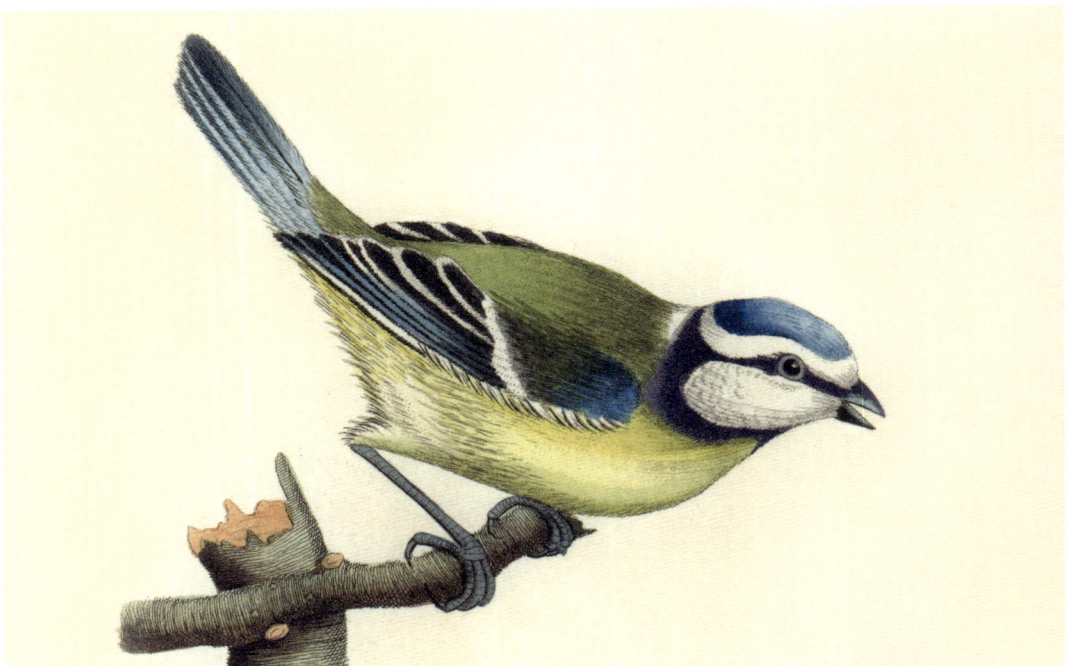

MINERAL.

Scotch Blue, is Berlin blue, mixed with a considerable portion of velvet black, a very little grey, and a slight tinge of carmine red. [W]

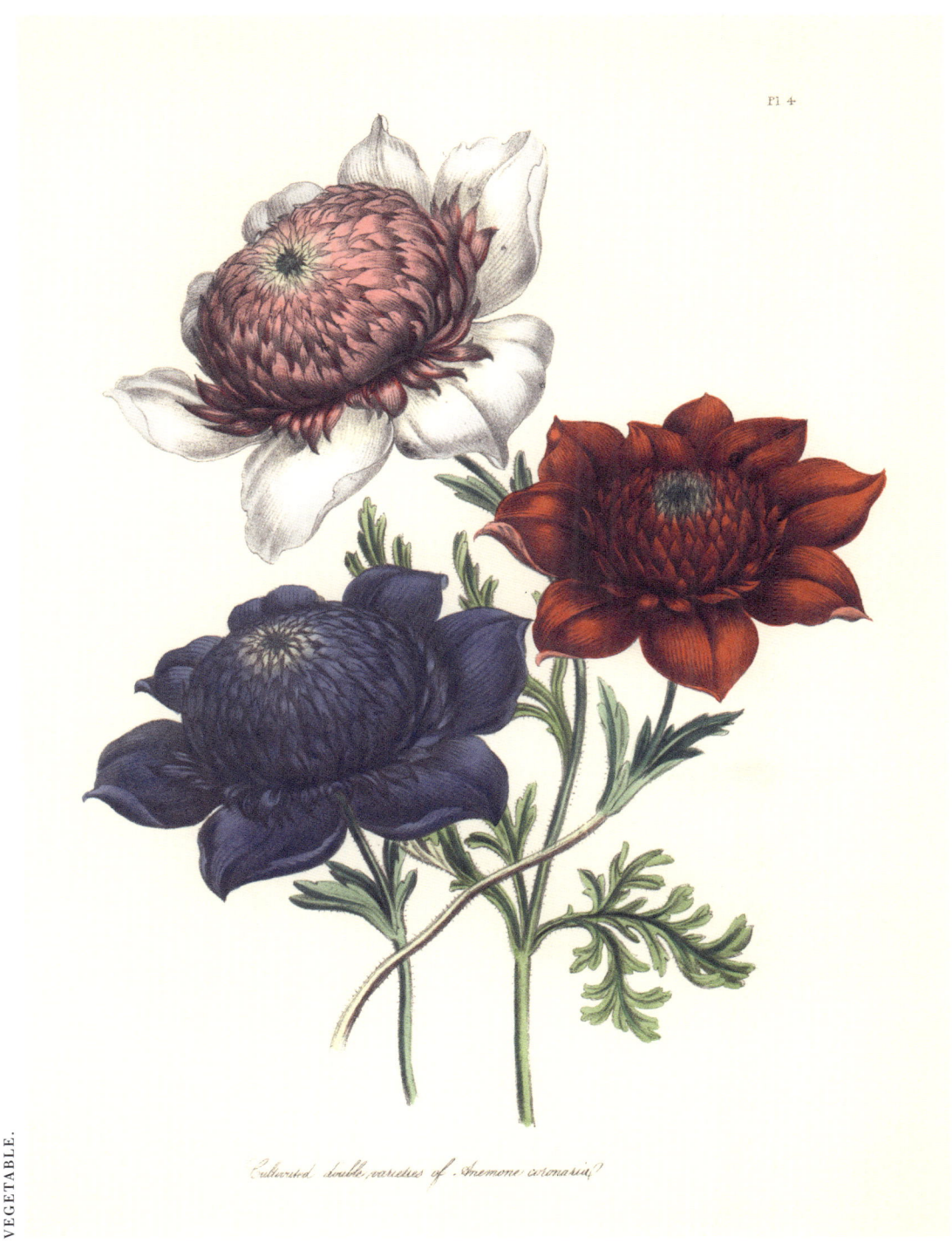

Pl 4

Cultivated double varieties of Anemone coronaria.

ANIMAL.
John Gould, *Birds of Europe*, Vol. 3, 1832–37. Scotch Blue is visible on the throat feathers of the Eurasian blue tit.

VEGETABLE.
Jane Loudon, *The Ladies' Flower Garden of Ornamental Perennials*, Vol. 1, 1849. Scotch Blue is visible on the stamina of the purple anemone (below left).

MINERAL.
Louis Simonin, *Underground Life*, 1869. Scotch Blue is visible on the azurite (centre).

25. PRUSSIAN BLUE.

(i). *Beauty Spot on Wing of Mallard Drake.*
[Anas platyrhynchos]
(ii). *Stamina of Bluish Purple Anemone.* [Anemone]
(iii). *Blue Copper Ore.* [*Azurite*; *Copper mineral*]

Prussian Blue, is Berlin blue, with a considerable portion of velvet black, and a small quantity of indigo blue.

ANIMAL.

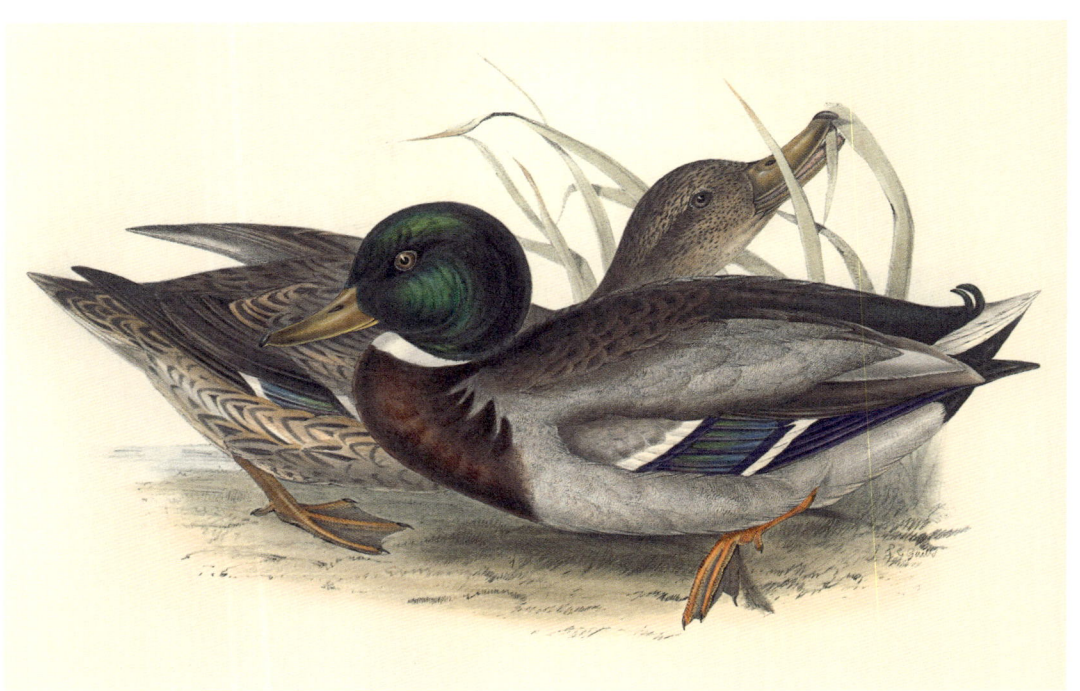

VEGETABLE.

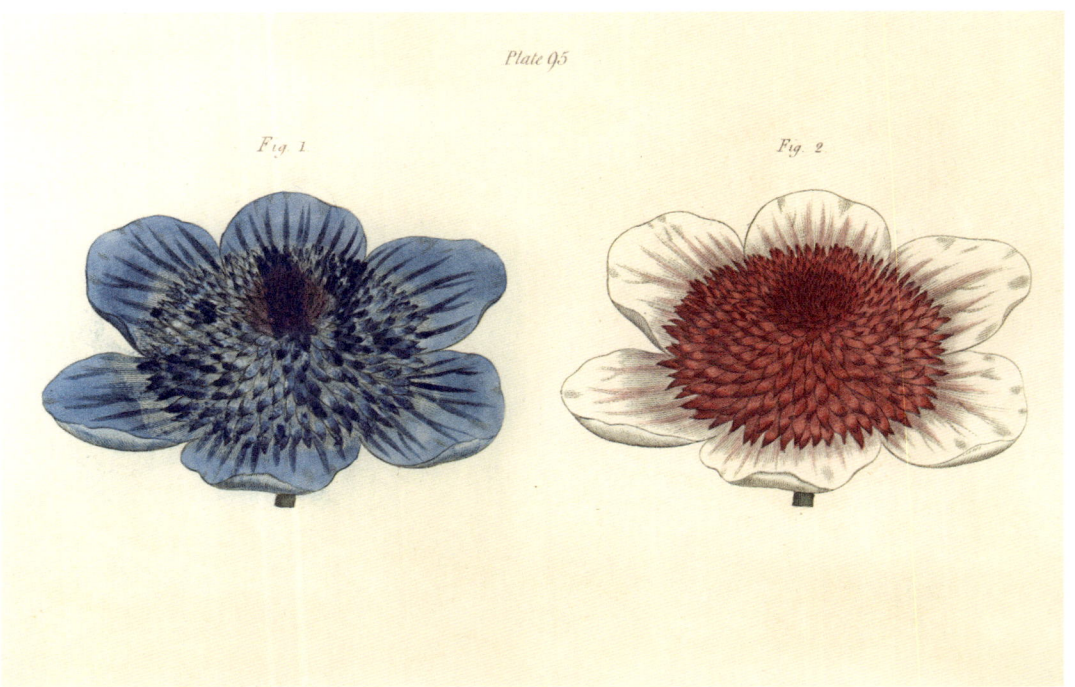

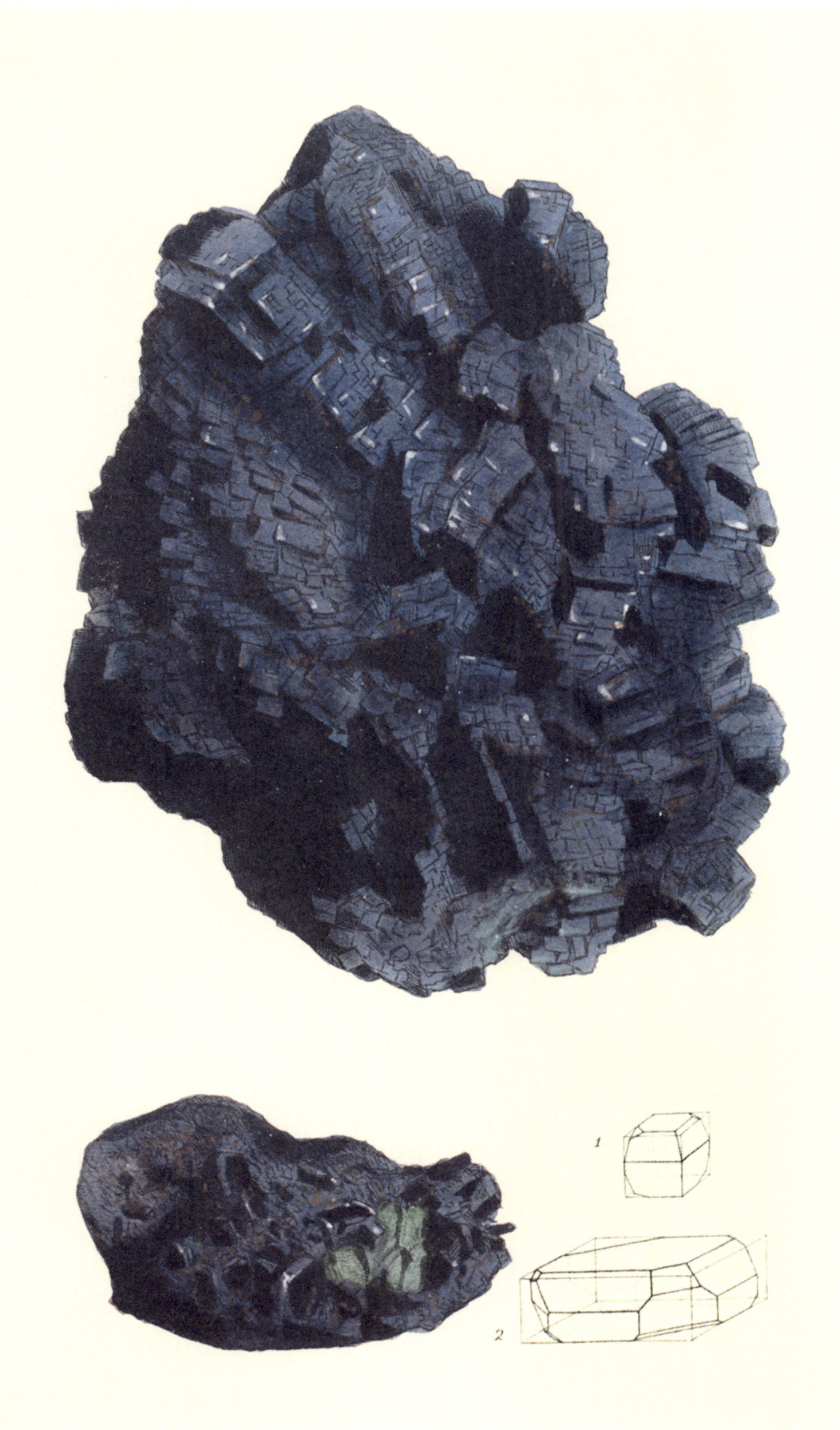

MINERAL.

ANIMAL.
John Gould, *Birds of Europe*, Vol. 5, 1832–37. Prussian Blue is visible on the beauty spot on the wing feathers of the mallard drake.

VEGETABLE.
F. Sansom, *Anemone coronaria*, hand-coloured copperplate engraving, 1805. Prussian Blue is visible on the stamina of the blue anemone (left).

MINERAL.
James Sowerby, *Exotic Mineralogy*, 1811. Prussian Blue is visible on the azurite (both specimens).

26. INDIGO BLUE.

(i). ———————
(ii). ———————
(iii). *Blue Copper Ore.* [*Azurite*; *Copper mineral*]

Indigo Blue, is composed of Berlin blue, a little black, and a small portion of apple green. †

† *Syme should have applied a [W] notation in this instance, as Indigo Blue appears in Werner's original list of colours.*

ANIMAL.

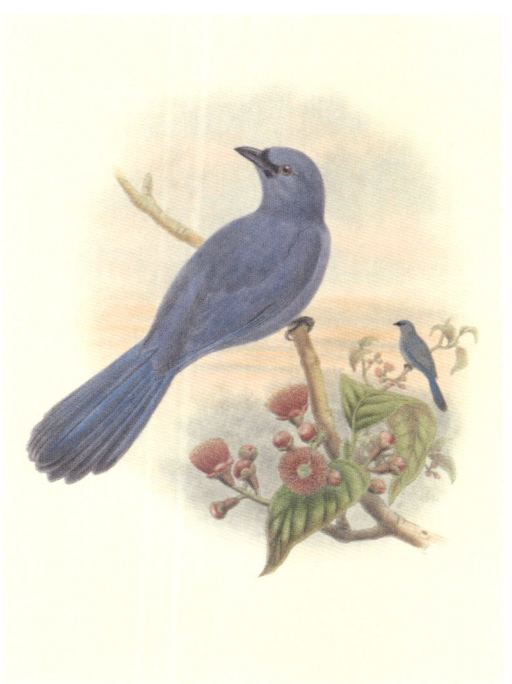

VEGETABLE.

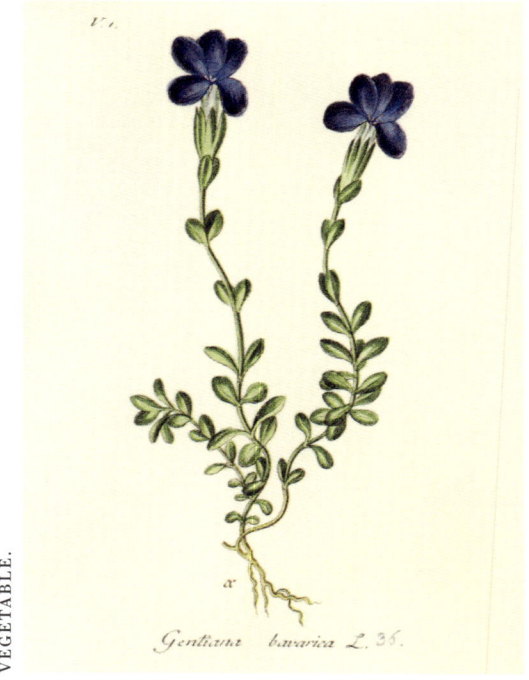

Gentiana bavarica L. 36.

ANIMAL.
John Gould, *Birds of New Guinea and the Adjacent Papuan Islands*, 1875–88. Indigo Blue is visible on the feathers of the blue cuckooshrike.*

VEGETABLE.
Jacob Sturm, *Deutschlands Flora in abbildungen nach der Natur*, 1798. Indigo Blue is visible on the petals of the Bavarian gentian.*

MINERAL.
James Sowerby, *Exotic Mineralogy*, 1811. Indigo Blue is visible on the azurite.

MINERAL.

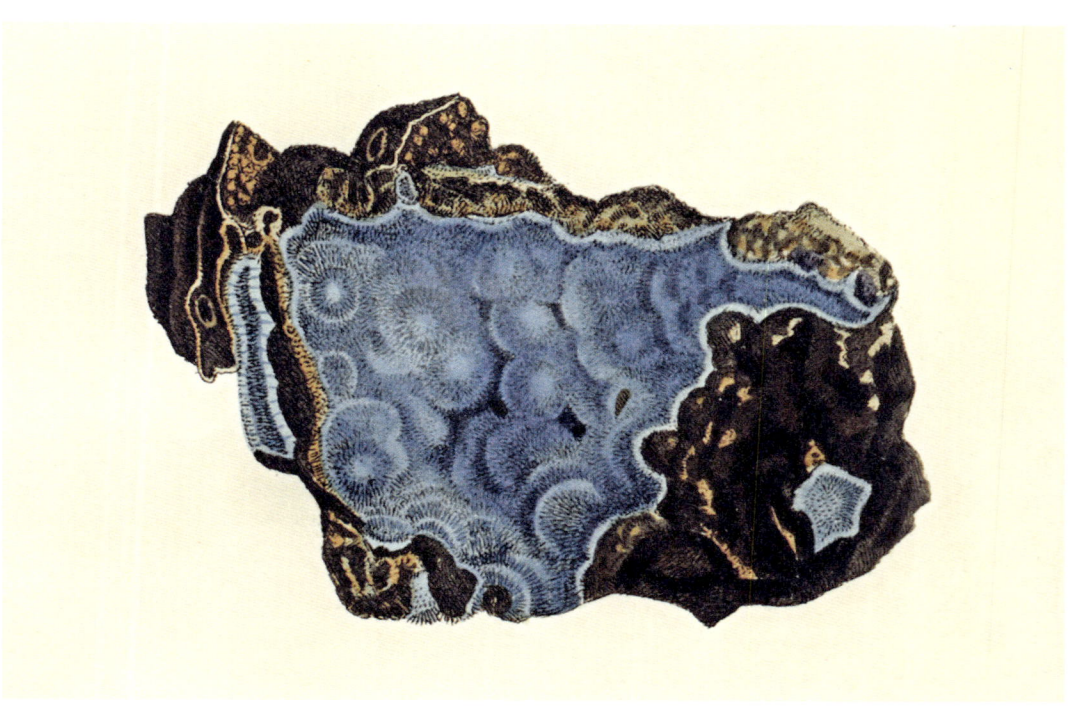

27. CHINA BLUE.

(i). *Rhynchites Nitens.* [*Weevil*; Rhynchites nitens]
(ii). *Back Parts of Gentian Flower.* [Gentiana]
(iii). *Blue Copper Ore from Chessy.* [*Chessylite*; *Azurite*;
Copper mineral]

China Blue, is azure blue, with a little Prussian blue in it.

ANIMAL.

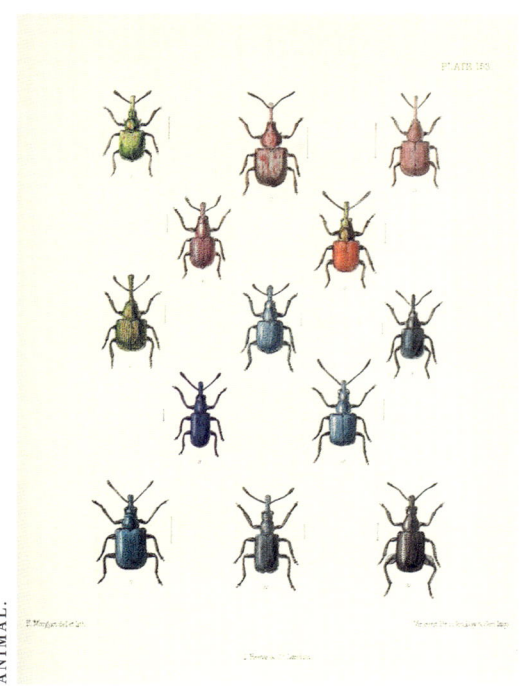

VEGETABLE.

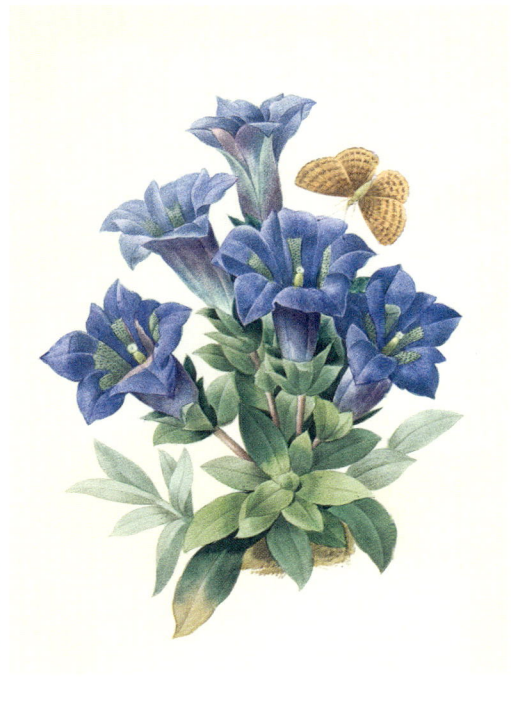

MINERAL.

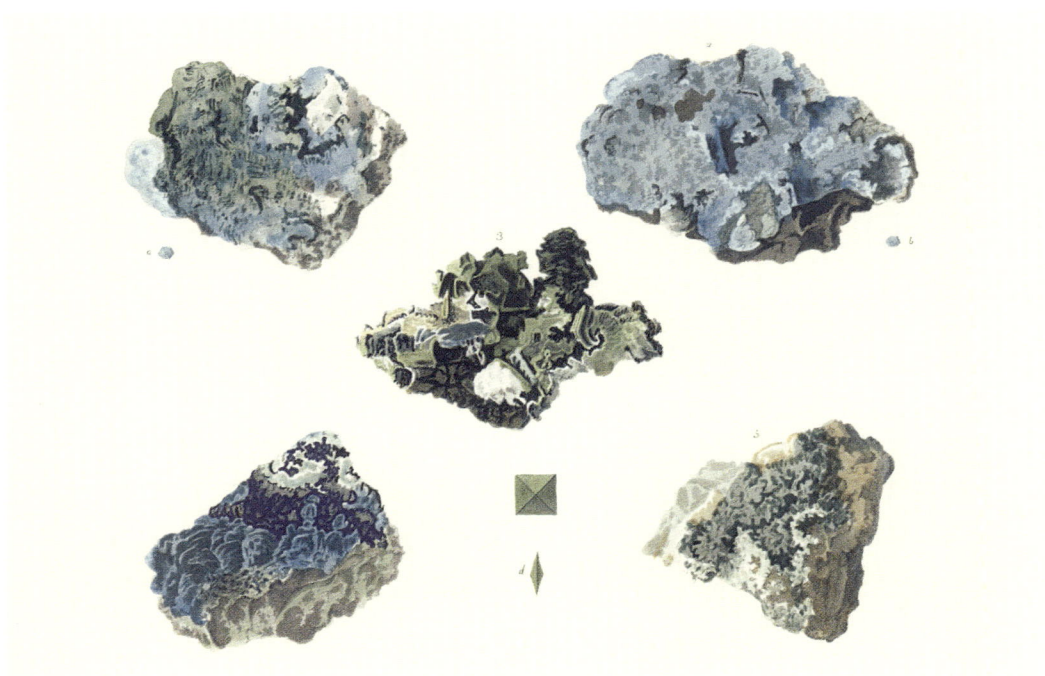

ANIMAL.
W. W. Fowler,
The Coleoptera of the British Islands,
Vol. 5, 1891.
China Blue is visible on the back of weevils (fourth row, left).

VEGETABLE.
Pierre-Joseph Redouté,
Choix des plus belles fleurs, 1833.
China Blue is visible on the petals of the gentian.

MINERAL.
Philip Rashleigh,
Specimens of British Minerals, 1797.
China Blue is visible on the azurite (bottom row, left).

(i).   *Breast of Emerald-crested Manakin.* [*Blue manakin*;
        Chiroxiphia caudata]
(ii).   *Grape Hyacinth.* [Muscari] *Gentian.* [Gentiana]
(iii). *Blue Copper Ore.* [*Azurite*; *Copper mineral*]

Azure Blue, is Berlin blue, mixed with a little carmine red: it is a burning colour. [W]

ANIMAL.

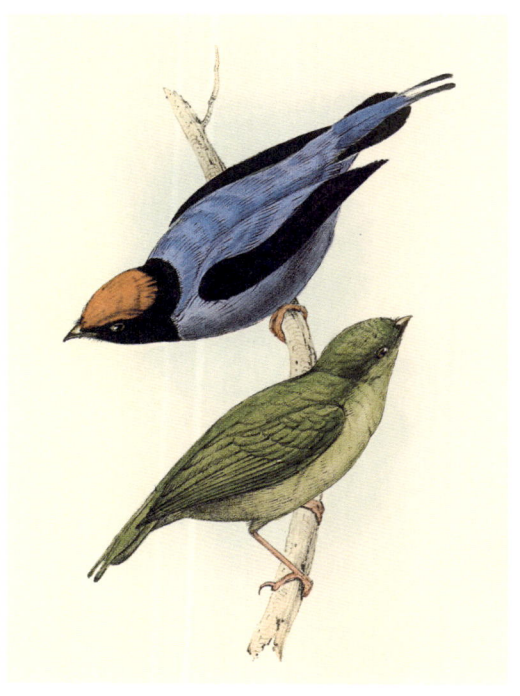

VEGETABLE.

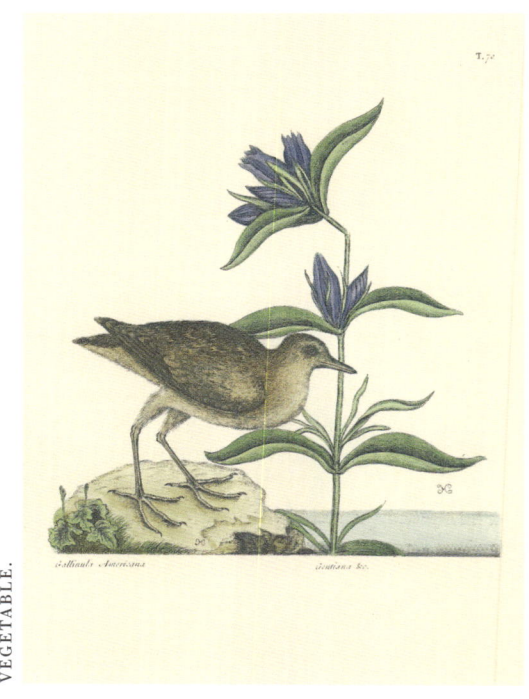

MINERAL.

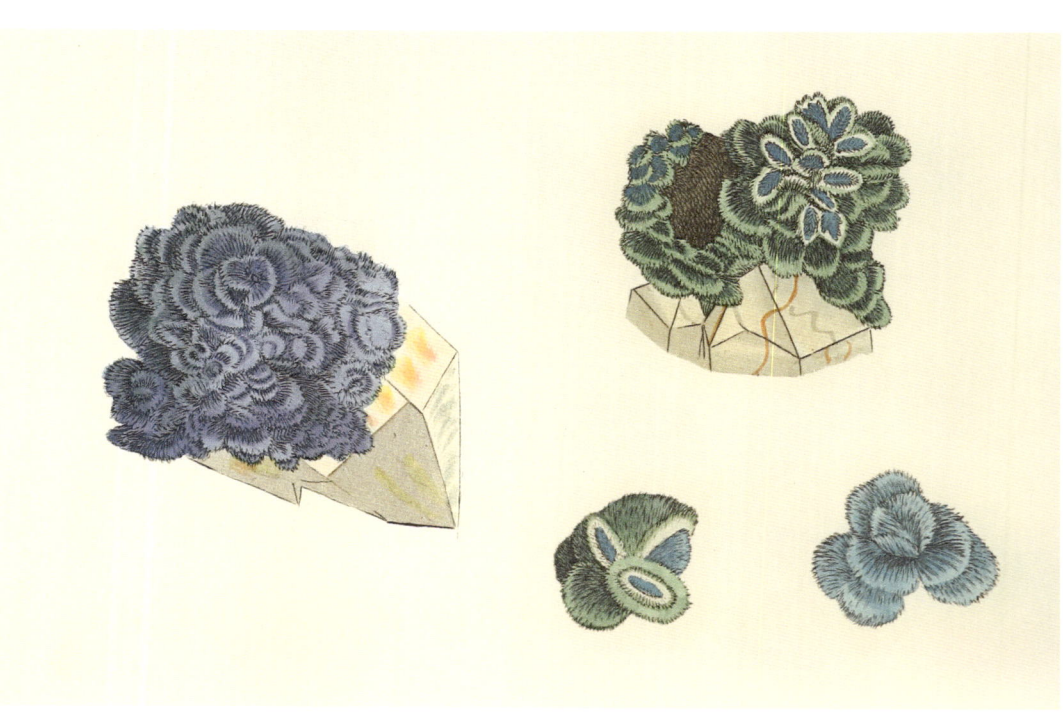

ANIMAL.
William Swainson,
A Selection of the Birds of Brazil and Mexico, 1841.
Azure Blue is visible on the breast feathers of the blue manakin (above).

VEGETABLE.
Mark Catesby,
The Natural History of Carolina, Florida, and the Bahama Islands, Vol. 1, 1754.
Azure Blue is visible on the petals of the gentian.

MINERAL.
James Sowerby,
British Mineralogy, Vol. 1, 1802–17.
Azure Blue is visible on the azurite (left).

29. ULTRAMARINE BLUE.

(i).   *Upper Side of the Wings of small blue Heath Butterfly.*
        [*Small heath*; Coenonympha pamphilus]

(ii).   *Borrage.* [*Borage*; Borago officinalis]

(iii).   *Azure Stone or Lapis Lazuli.* [*Metamorphic rock*]

Ultramarine Blue, is a mixture of equal parts Berlin and azure blue.

ANIMAL.

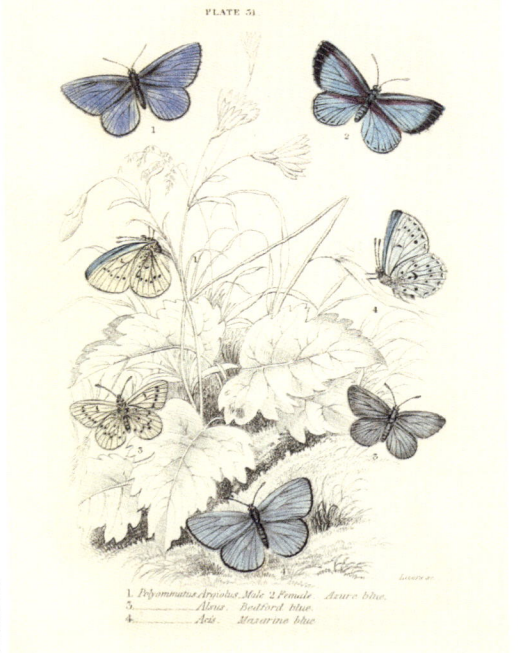

VEGETABLE.

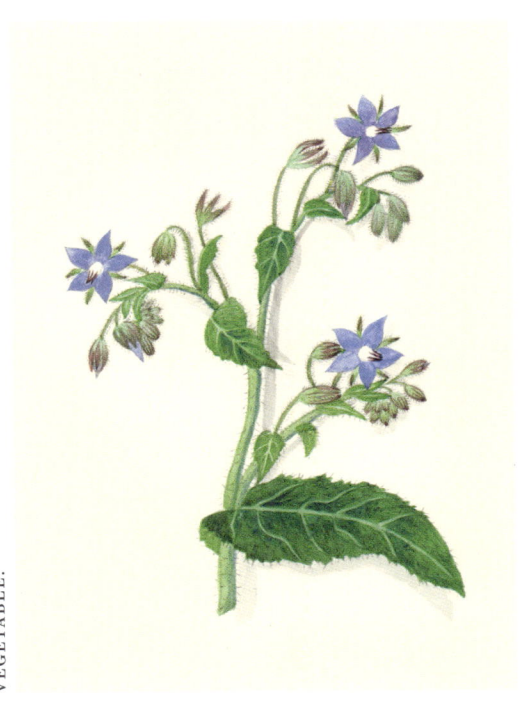

MINERAL.

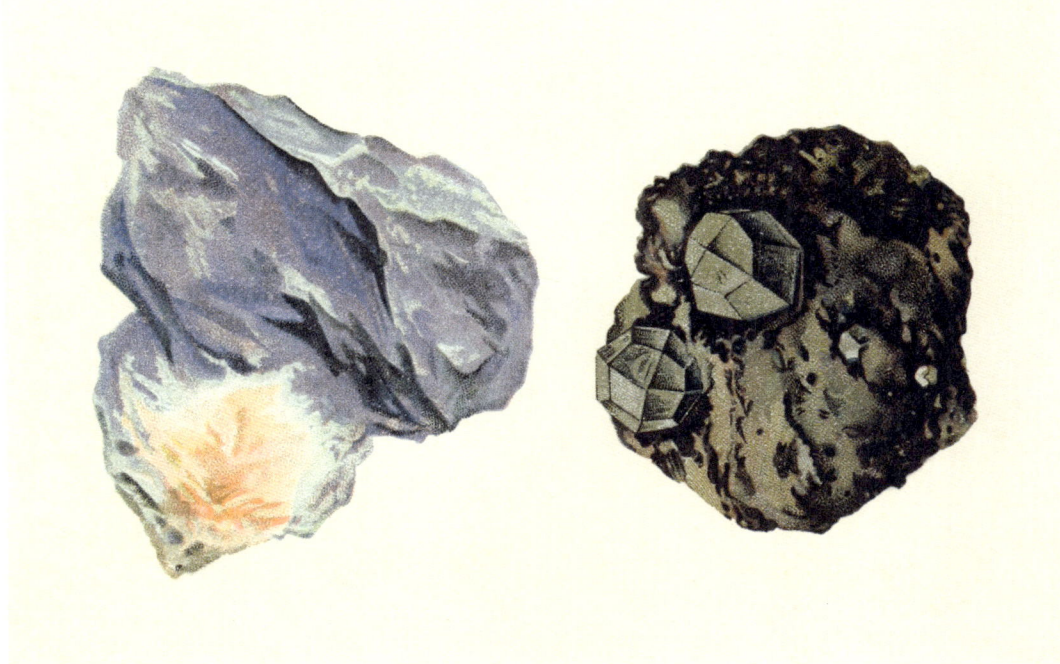

ANIMAL.
James Duncan,
British Butterflies, 1840.
Ultramarine Blue is visible on the wings of the small heath butterfly.

VEGETABLE.
Margaret Plues,
Borago officinalis, borage, watercolour, 1858.
Ultramarine Blue is visible on the petals of the borage.

MINERAL.
Leonard Spencer,
The World's Minerals, 1916.
Ultramarine Blue is visible on the lapis lazuli (left).

30. FLAX-FLOWER BLUE.

(i).   *Light Parts of the Margin of the Wings of Devil's Butterfly.*
         [*Small tortoiseshell*; Aglais urticae]
(ii).   *Flax flower.* [Linum perenne]
(iii).   *Blue Copper Ore.* [*Azurite*; Copper mineral]

Faux-flower Blue, is Berlin blue, with a slight tinge of ultramarine blue.

ANIMAL.

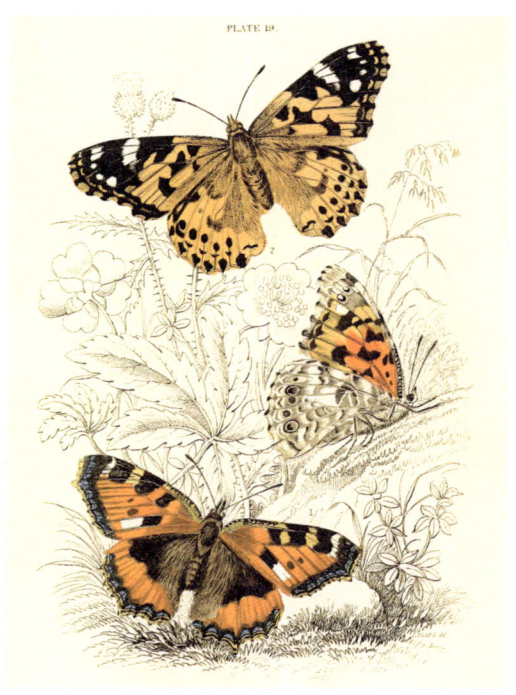

VEGETABLE.

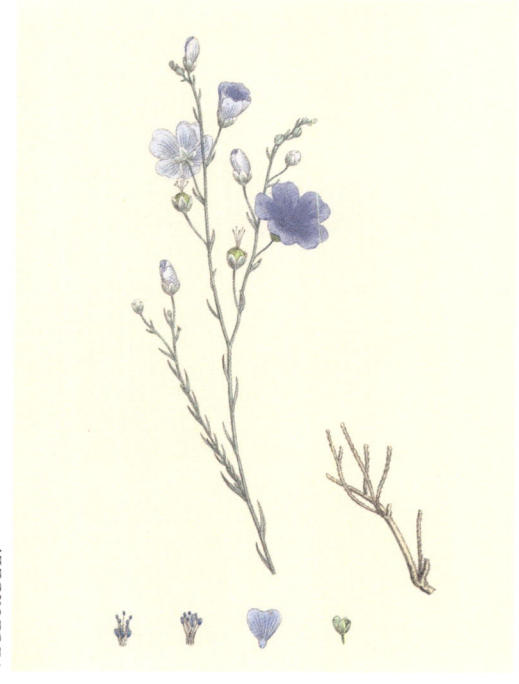

ANIMAL.
Georg Wolfgang
Knorr, *Deliciae
naturae selectae*, 1766.
Flax-flower Blue is
visible on the edges of
the wings of the small
tortoiseshell (bottom).

VEGETABLE.
*Linum perenne,
Perennial Flax*,
Watercolour, 1863.
Flax-flower Blue is
visible on the petals
of the flax.

MINERAL.
Gotthilf Heinrich
von Schubert,
*Naturgeschichte
des Tier-, Pflanzen-
und Mineralreichs*, 1886.
Flax-flower Blue is
visible on the azurite
(bottom row, left).

MINERAL.

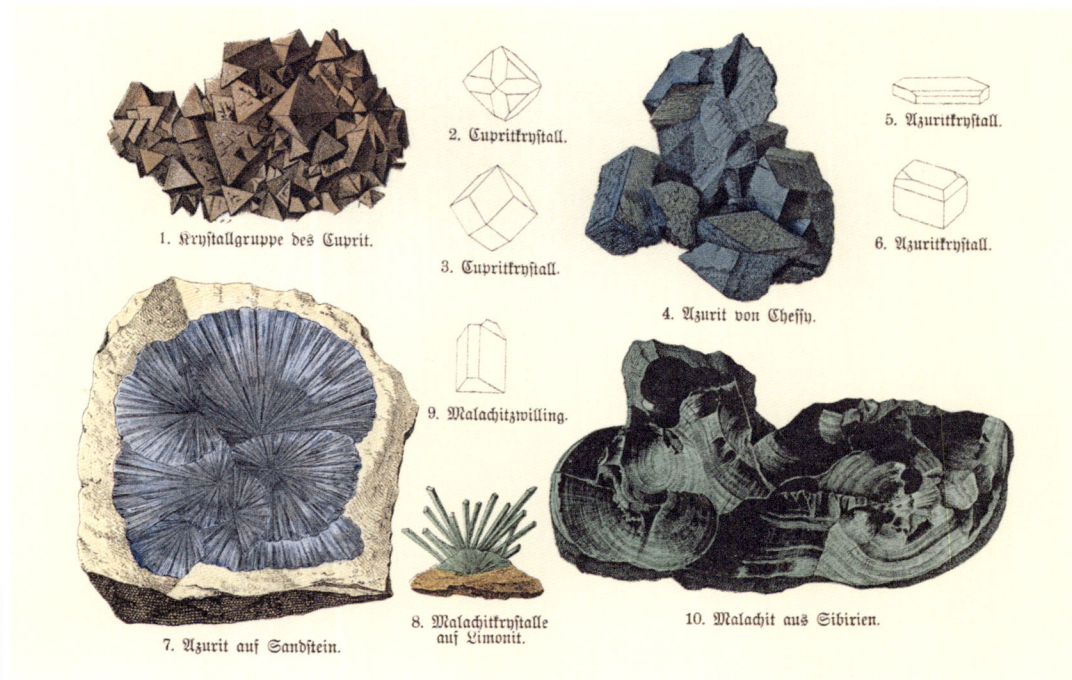

31. BERLIN BLUE.

(i).   *Wing Feathers of Jay.* [Garrulus glandarius]
(ii). *Hepatica.* [*Liverwort*; Anemone hepatica]
(iii). *Blue Sapphire.* [*Corundum mineral*]

Berlin Blue, is the pure, or the characteristic colour of Werner. [W]

ANIMAL.

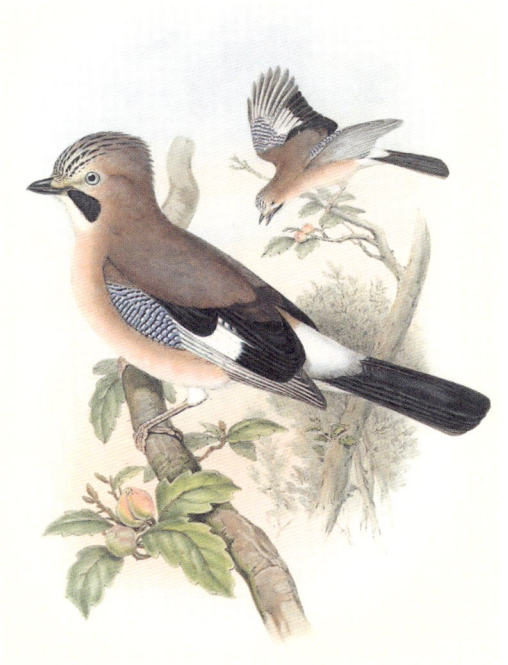

VEGETABLE.

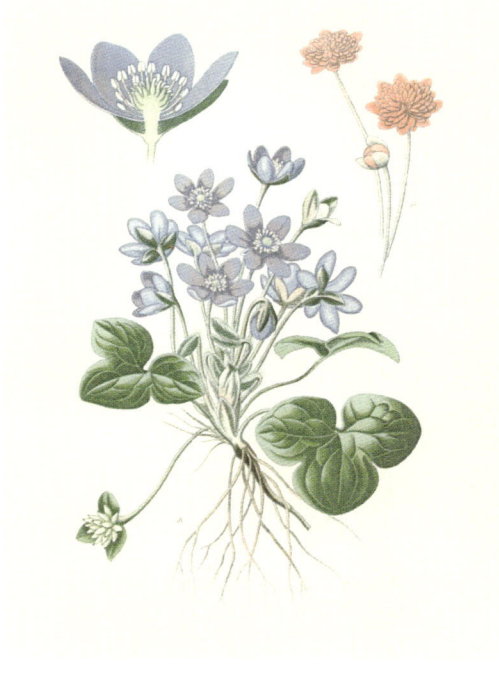

ANIMAL.
John Gould, *Birds of Great Britain*, Vol. 3, 1862–73. Berlin Blue is visible on the wing feathers of the jay.

VEGETABLE.
Edward Step, *Favourite Flowers of Garden and Greenhouse*, Vol. 1, 1896. Berlin Blue is visible on the petals of the liverwort.

MINERAL.
George Frederick Kunz, *Gems and Precious Stones of North America*, 1890. Berlin Blue is visible on the sapphire (bottom left). The other specimens, excepting the diamond (top row, second from left) and the ruby (centre right), are also sapphires, but exhibit different shades of blue.

MINERAL.

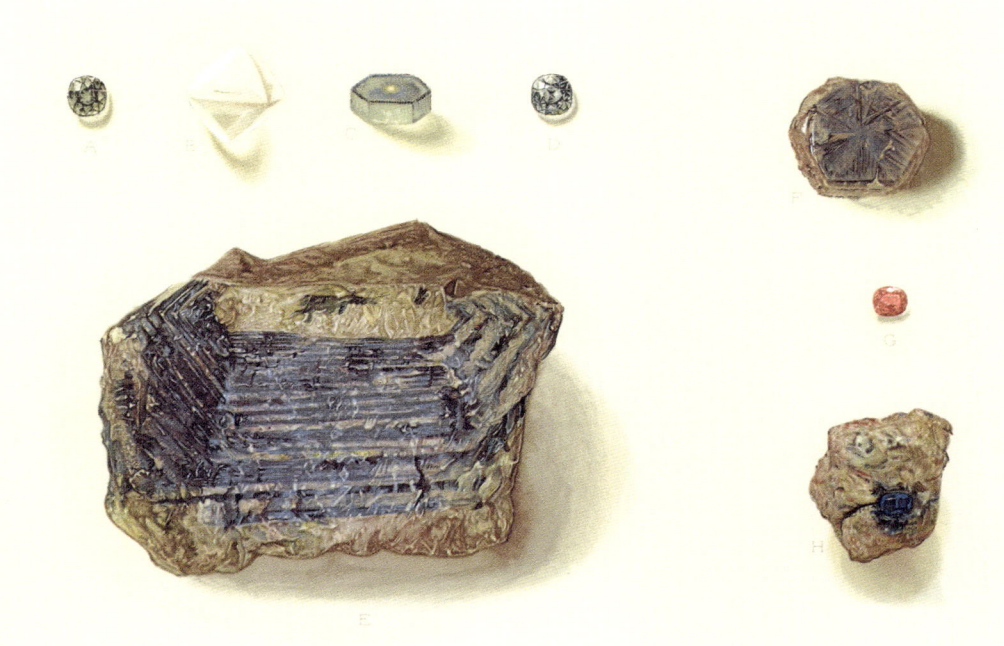

32. VERDITTER BLUE.

(i). ————————
(ii). ————————
(iii).   *Lenticular Ore.* [*Blue Copper Ore*, *Azurite*, *Copper mineral*]

Verditter Blue, is Berlin blue, with a small portion of verdigris green.

ANIMAL.

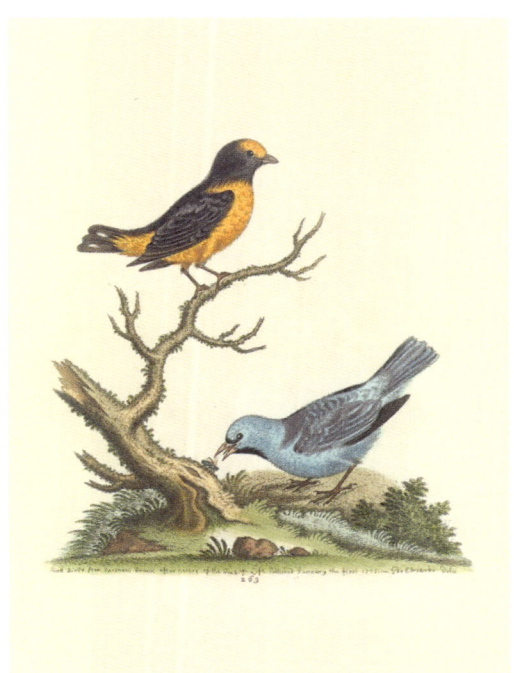

VEGETABLE.

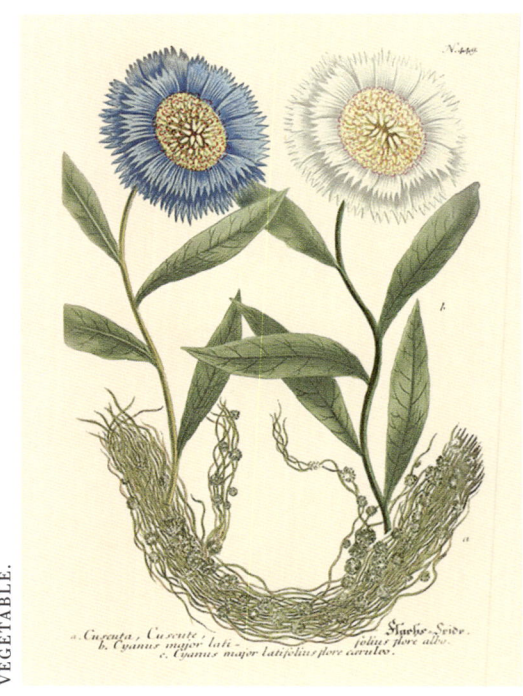

ANIMAL.
George Edwards,
*Gleanings of
Natural History*, 1858.
Verditter Blue is
visible on the breast
feathers of the blue
manakin (below).*

VEGETABLE.
Johann Wilhelm
Weinmann,
*Phytanthoza
iconographia*, 1737.
Verditter Blue is visible
on the petals of the
cornflower (left).*

MINERAL.
Philip Rashleigh,
*Specimens of British
Minerals*, 1797.
Verditter Blue is
visible on the azurite.

MINERAL.

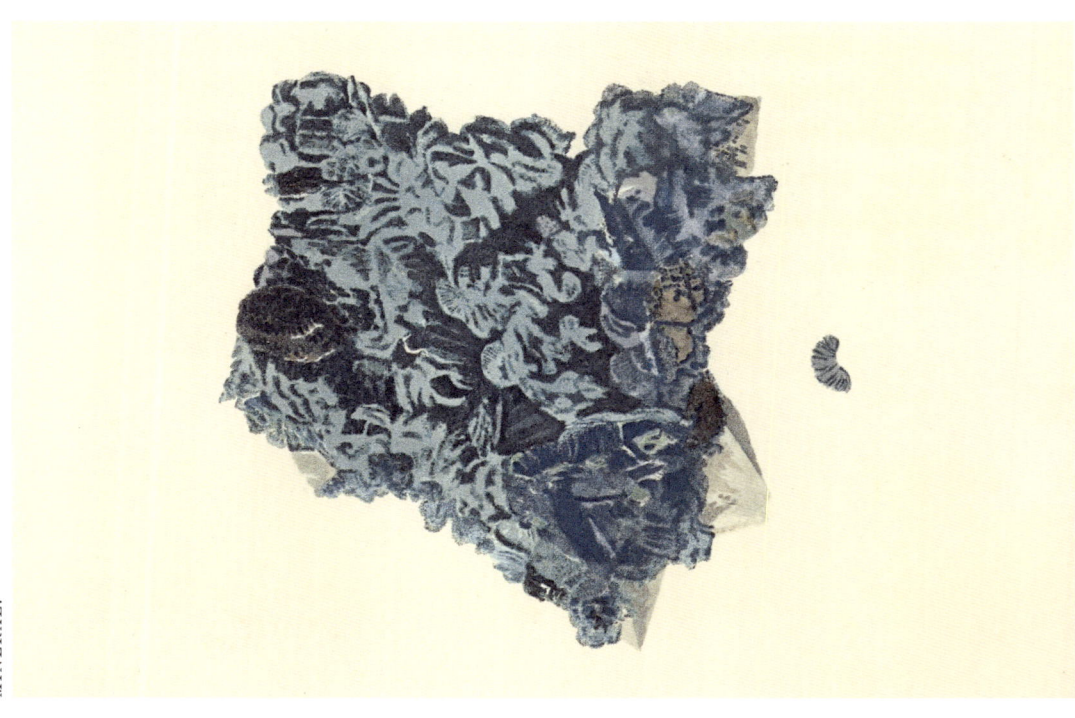

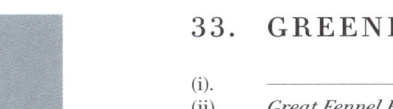

33. GREENISH BLUE.

(i). ————
(ii).   *Great Fennel Flower.* [*Love-in-a-mist*; Nigella]
(iii). *Turquois.* [*Turquoise*; Phosphate mineral]
       Flour Spar. [*Fluorite*; Fluorspar; Calcium Fluoride]

Greenish Blue, the sky blue of Werner, is composed of Berlin blue, white, and a little emerald green. [W]

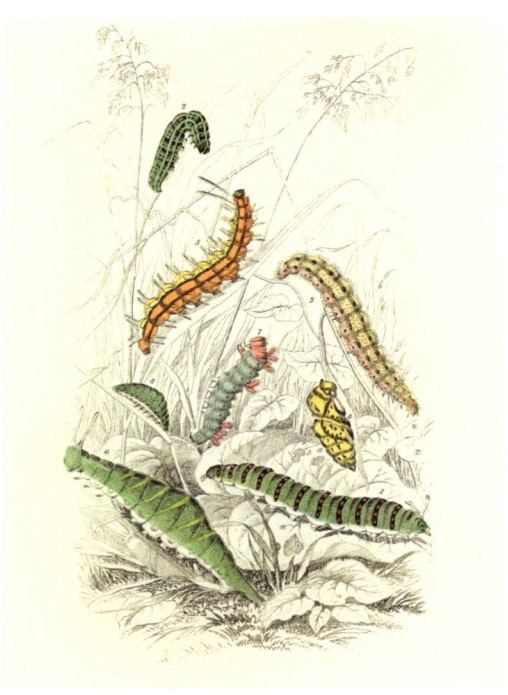

ANIMAL.

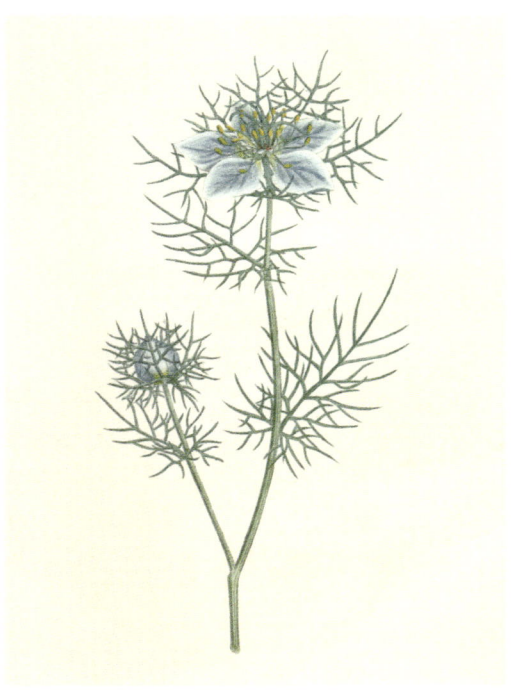

VEGETABLE.

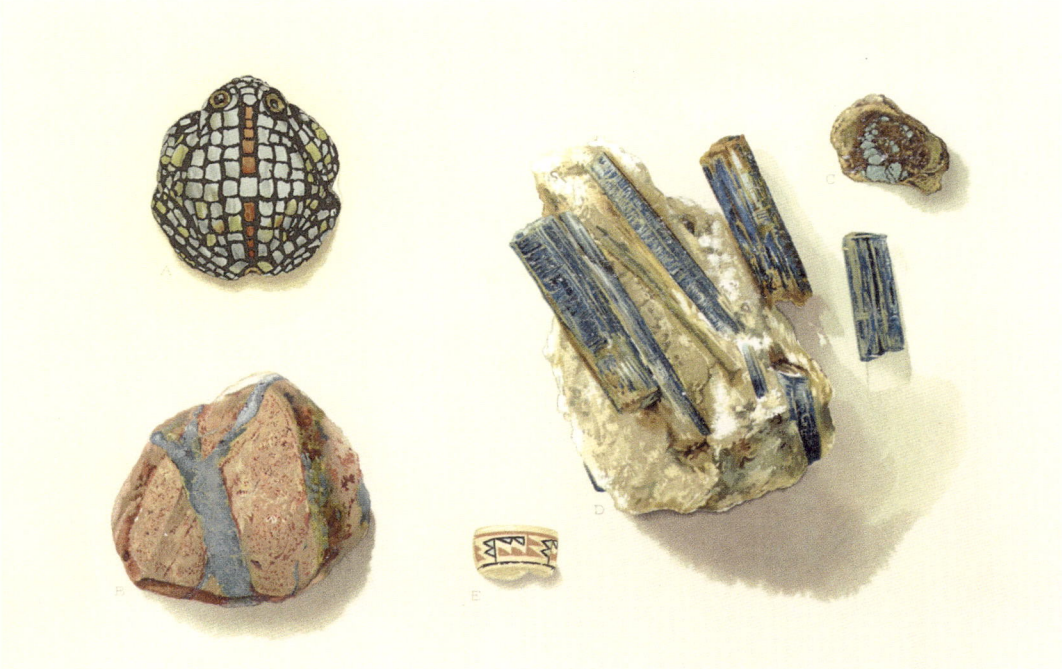

MINERAL.

ANIMAL.
James Duncan, *British Butterflies*, 1840. Greenish Blue is visible on the caterpillar of the pale yellow clouded butterfly (bottom row, right).*

VEGETABLE.
The Botanical Magazine, 1787–89. Greenish Blue is visible on the petals of the fennel flower.

MINERAL.
George Frederick Kunz, *Gems and Precious Stones of North America*, 1890. Greenish Blue is visible on the turquoise (all specimens except the kyanite embedded in rock, centre right).

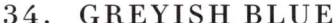

34. GREYISH BLUE.

(i).   *Back of blue Titmouse.* [*Eurasian blue tit*; Cyanistes caeruleus]
(ii).   *Small Fennel Flower.* [*Love-in-a-mist*; Nigella]
(iii). *Iron Earth.* [*Iron ore*; ore]

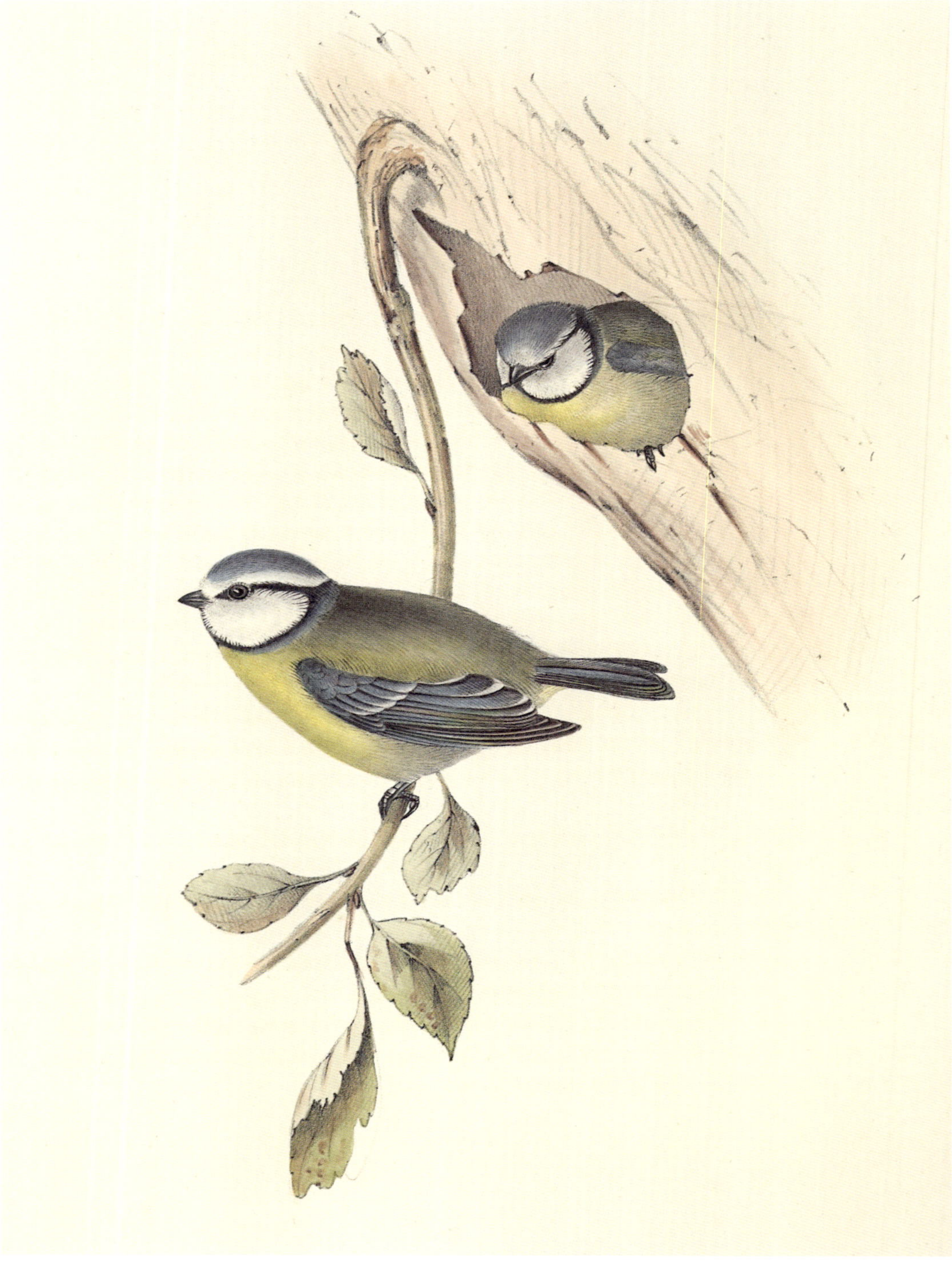

ANIMAL.

106.   II. BLUES AND PURPLES.

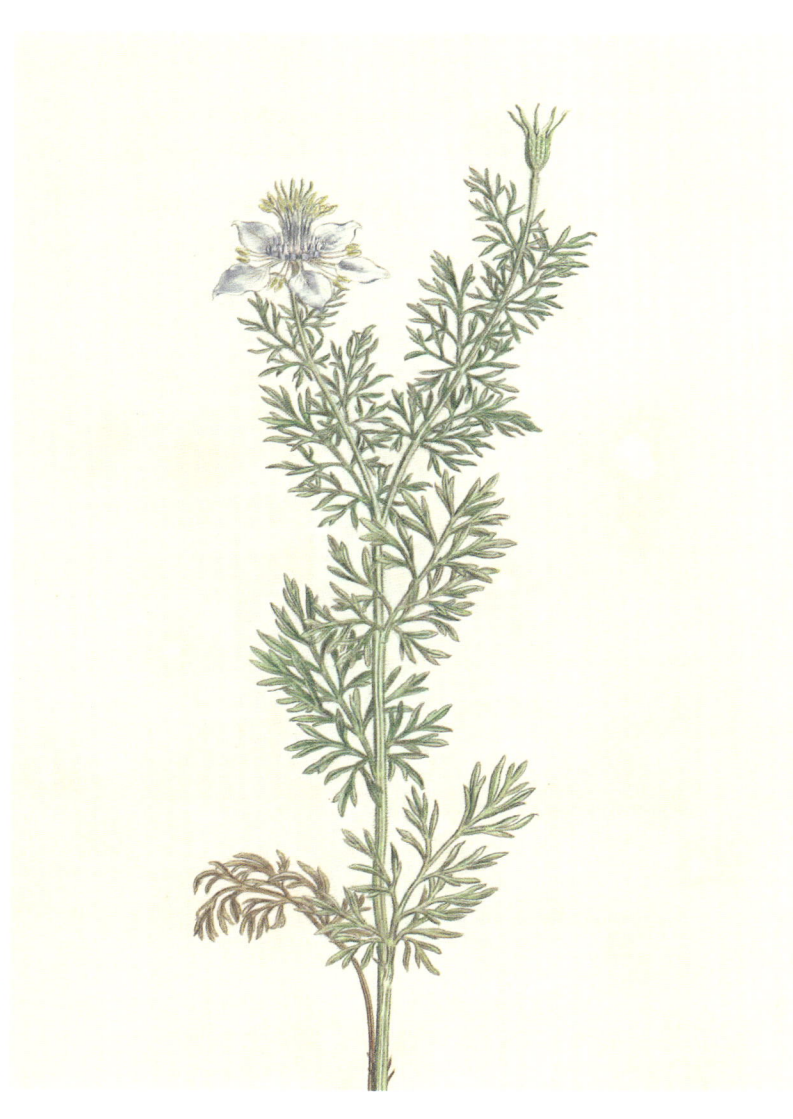

*Greyish Blue, the smalt
blue of Werner, is composed
of Berlin blue, with white,
a small quantity of grey,
and a hardly perceptible
portion of red. [W]*

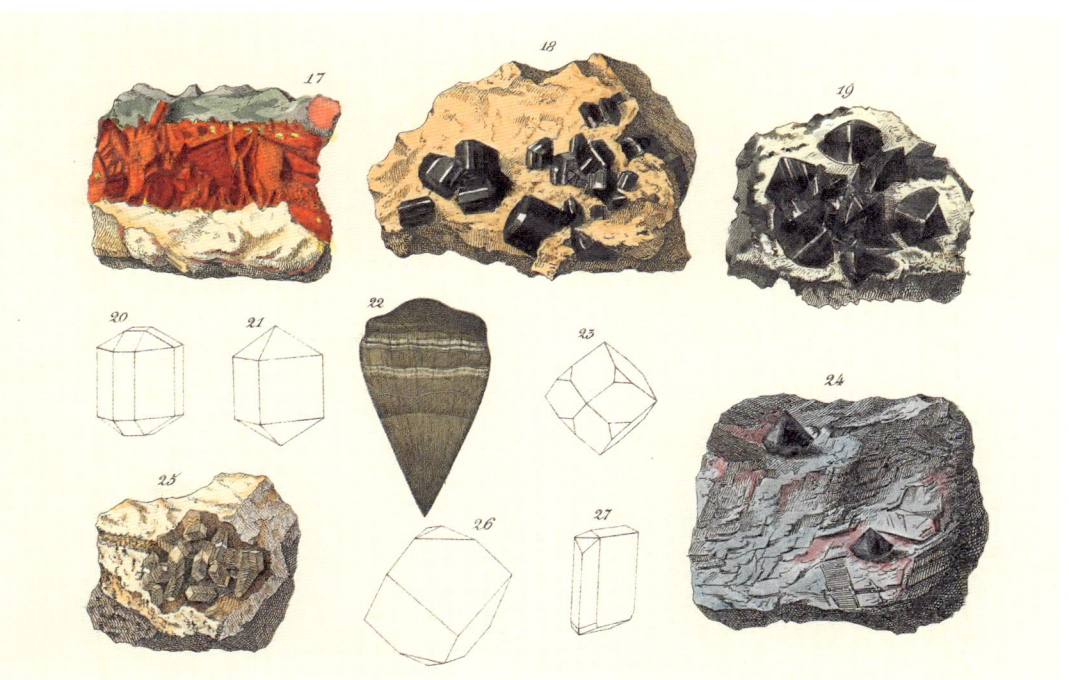

ANIMAL.
John Gould, *Birds of
Europe*, Vol. 3, 1832–37.
Greyish Blue is visible
on the back feathers
of the Eurasian blue tit.

VEGETABLE.
J. Sibthorp and
J. E. Smith, *Flora
graeca*, Vol. 6, 1828.
Greyish Blue
is visible on the petals
of the fennel flower.

MINERAL.
Johann Gottlob
Kurr, *The Mineral
Kingdom*, 1859.
Greyish Blue is visible
on the iron ore
(bottom row, right).

PURPLES.

No.	Names.	Colours.	ANIMAL.		
35	*Bluish Lilac Purple.*		*Male of the Lebellula Depressa.*		
36	*Bluish Purple.*		*Papilio Argeolus. Azure Blue Butterfly.*		
37	*Violet Purple.*				
38	*Pansy Purple.*		*Chrysomela Goettingensis.*		
39	*Campanula Purple.*				
40	*Imperial Purple.*				
41	*Auricula Purple.*		*Egg of largest Blue-Bottle, or Flesh Fly.*		
42	*Plum Purple.*				
43	*Red Lilac Purple.*		*Light Spots of the upper Wings of Peacock Butterfly.*		
44	*Lavender Purple.*		*Light Parts of Spots on the under Wings of Peacock Butterfly.*		
45	*Pale Blackish Purple.*				

*Syme's 1821 edition
included one purple
from the Kirwan system
(number 36) and seven
purples from his own
1814 edition (numbers
35, 38, 39, 40, 41, 43, 45).
Number 37 is likely
derived from Werner's
Violet Blue, number 42
from Jameson's Plum
Blue and number 44 from
Picardet's Lavender Blue.*

PURPLES.

	VEGETABLE.			MINERAL.	
	Blue Lilac.			Lepidolite.	
	Parts of White and Purple Crocus.				
	Purple Aster.			Amethyst.	
	Sweet-scented Violet.			Derbyshire Spar.	
	Canterbury Bell. Campanula Persicifolia.			Fluor Spar.	
	Deep Parts of Flower of Saffron Crocus.			Fluor Spar.	
	Largest Purple Auricula.			Fluor Spar.	
	Plum.			Fluor Spar.	
	Red Lilac. Pale Purple Primrose.			Lepidolite.	
	Dried Lavender Flowers.			Porcelain Jasper.	
				Porcelain Jasper.	

(i).   *Male of the Lebellula Depressa.* [*Broad-bodied chaser dragonfly*; Libellula depressa]
(ii).   *Blue Lilac.* [Syringa]
(iii). *Lepidolite.* [*Silicate mineral*]

Bluish Lilac Purple, is bluish purple and white.

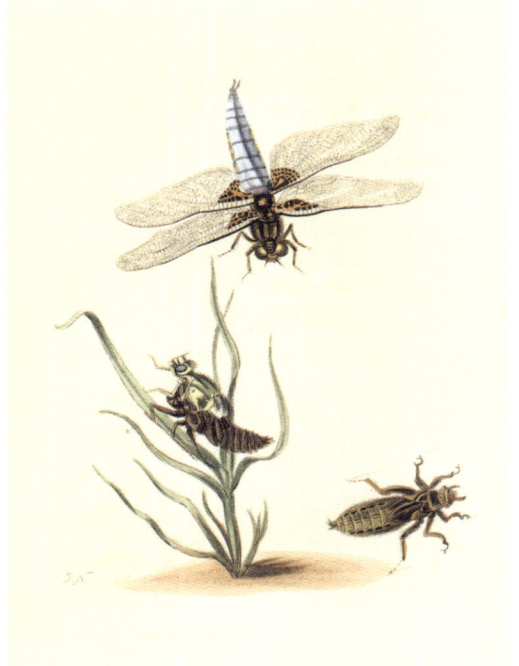

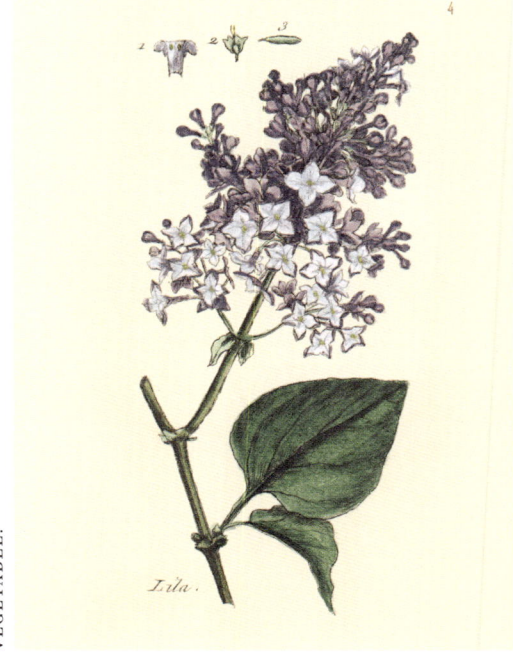

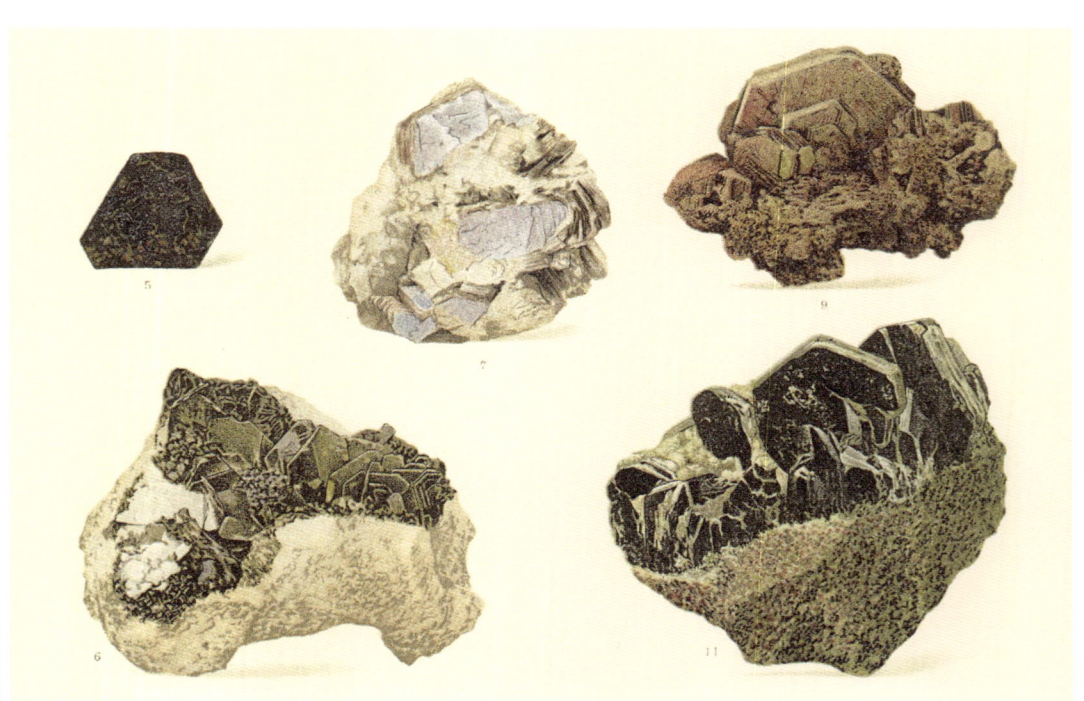

110.   II. BLUES AND PURPLES.

ANIMAL.

VEGETABLE.

MINERAL.

ANIMAL.
George Shaw and
Frederick P. Nodder,
*The Naturalist's
Miscellany*, 1789–1813.
Bluish Lilac Purple
is visible on the body
of the broad-bodied
chaser dragonfly.

VEGETABLE.
Pierre Bulliard,
Flora Parisiensis,
1776–83.
Bluish Lilac Purple
is visible on the
petals of the lilac.

MINERAL.
Reinhard Brauns,
*The Mineral
Kingdom*, Vol. 2, 1912.
Bluish Lilac Purple
is visible on the
lepidolite (top row,
centre).

36. BLUISH PURPLE.

(i). *Papilio Argeolus. Azure Blue Butterfly.* [*Holly blue*; Celastrina argeolus]
(ii). *Parts of White and Purple Crocus.* [Crocus]
(iii). ——————————

Bluish Purple, is composed of about equal parts of Berlin blue and carmine red.

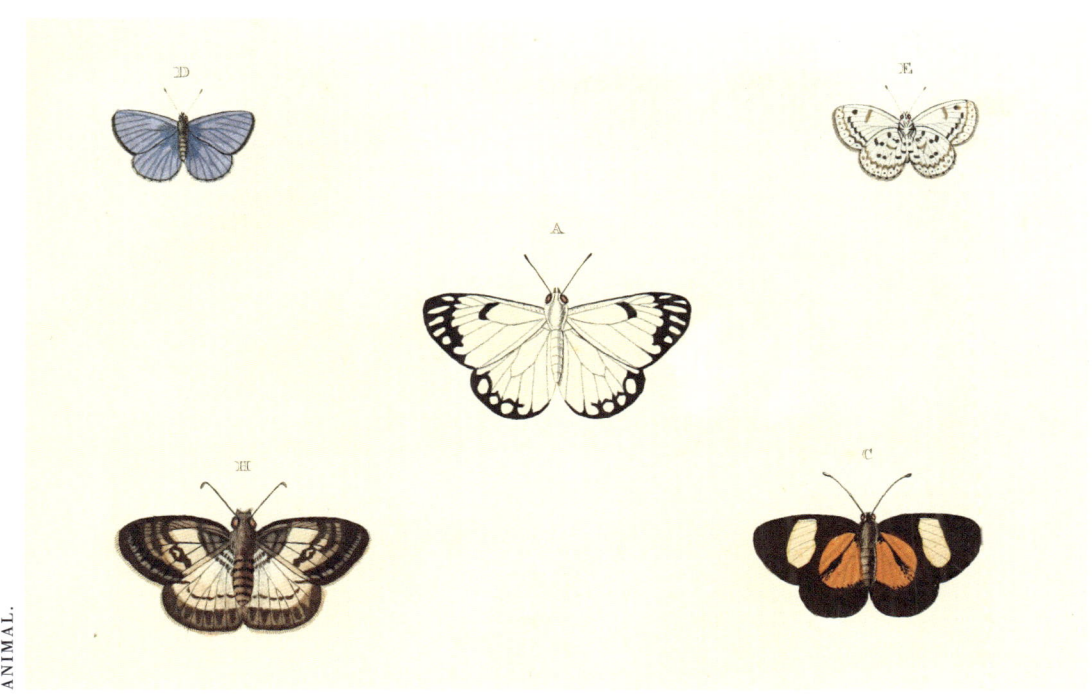

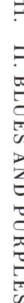

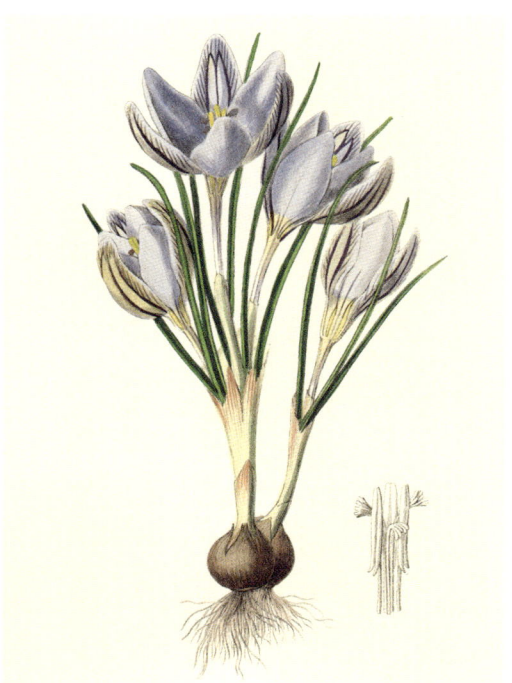

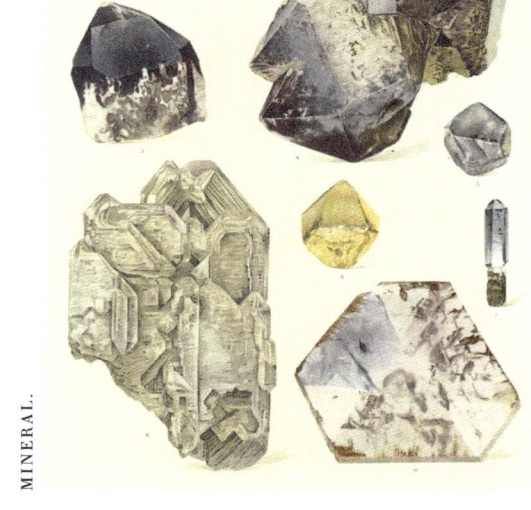

ANIMAL.
Pieter Cramer and Caspar Stoll, *De Uitlandsche Kapellen*, Vol. 3, 1782. Bluish Purple is visible on the wings of the holly blue (top row, left).

VEGETABLE.
John Lindley, *Edwards's Botanical Register*, 1829–47. Bluish Purple is visible on the petals of the crocus.

MINERAL.
Reinhard Brauns, *The Mineral Kingdom*, Vol. 2, 1912. Bluish Purple is visible on the amethyst (all specimens except centre, which is citrine).*

37. VIOLET PURPLE.

(i). ———————
(ii). *Purple Aster.* [Aster]
(iii). *Amethyst.* [Quartz]

Violet Purple, violet blue of Werner, is Berlin blue mixed with red, and a little brown. [W]

ANIMAL.

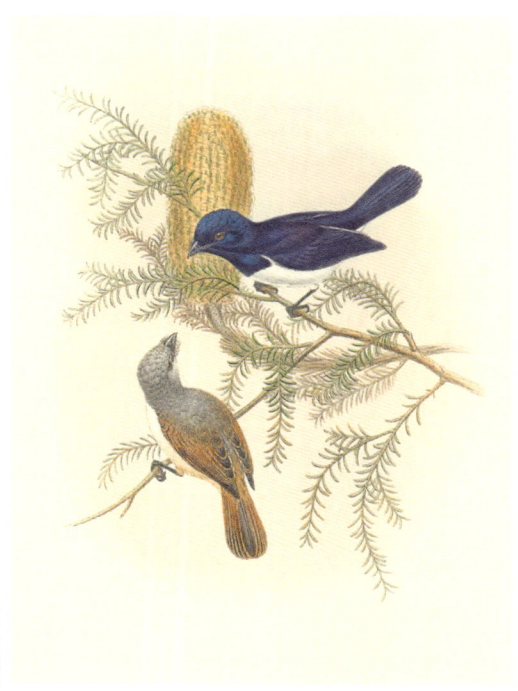

VEGETABLE.

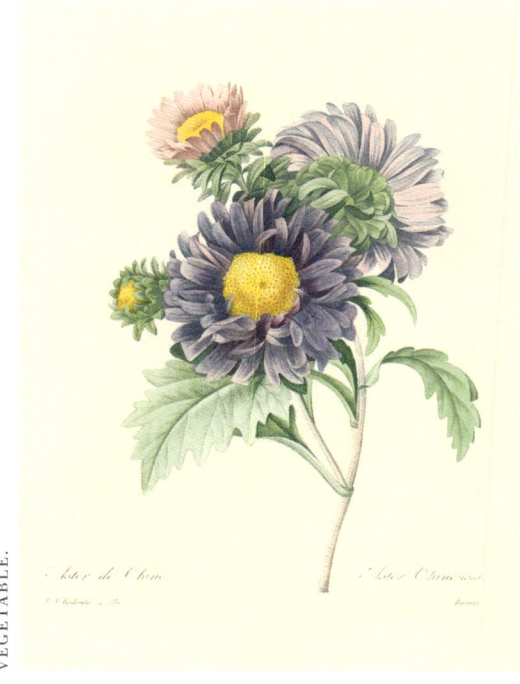

ANIMAL.
John Gould, *Birds of New Guinea and the Adjacent Papuan Islands*, 1875–88.
Violet Purple is visible on the wing feathers of the male steel-backed flycatcher (above).*

VEGETABLE.
Pierre-Joseph Redouté, *Choix des plus belles fleurs*, 1833.
Violet Purple is visible on the petals of the aster.

MINERAL.
George Frederick Kunz, *Gems and Precious Stones of North America*, 1890.
Violet Purple is visible on the amethyst (all specimens).

MINERAL.

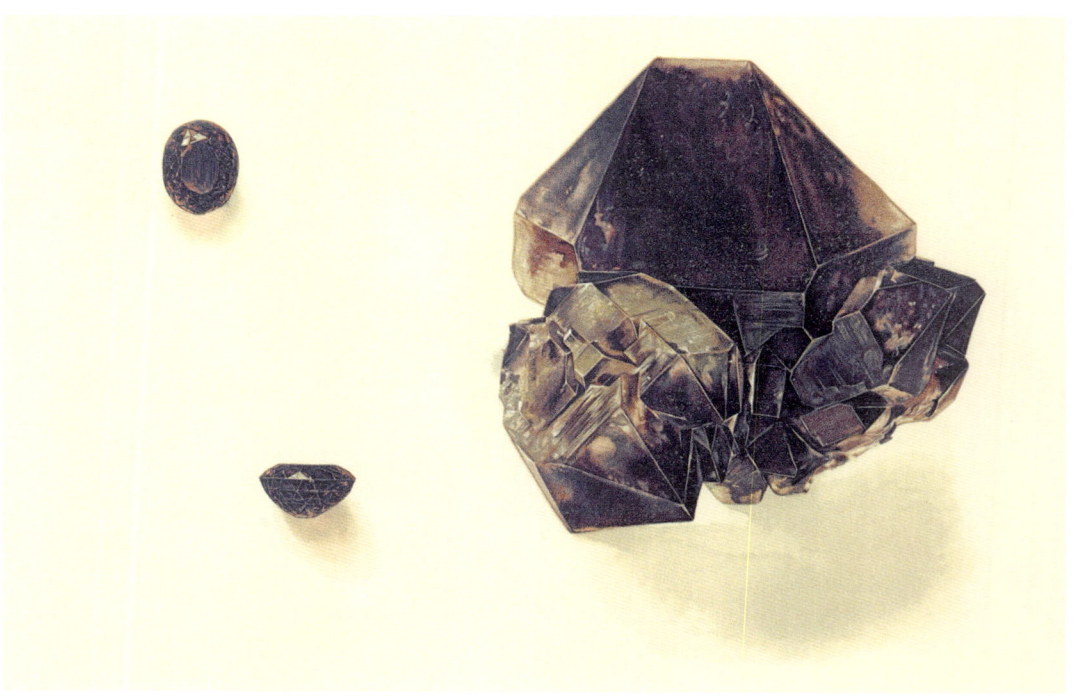

38. PANSY PURPLE.

(i).   *Chrysomela Goettingensis.*
         [*Small bloody-nosed beetle*; Timarcha goettingensis]
(ii).   *Sweet-scented Violet.*
         [*Sweet violet*; *wood violet*; Viola odorata]
(iii).   *Derbyshire Spar.* [*Blue John*; *Fluorite*; *Calcium Fluoride*]

Pansy Purple, is indigo blue, with carmine red, and a slight tinge of raven black.

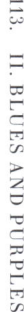

ANIMAL.

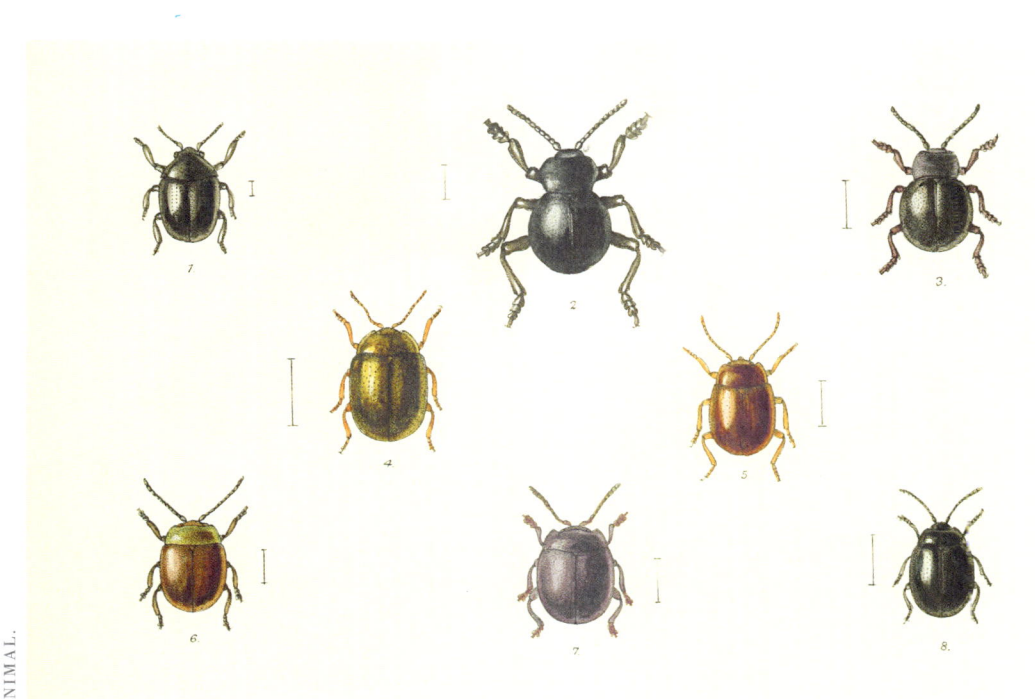

VEGETABLE.

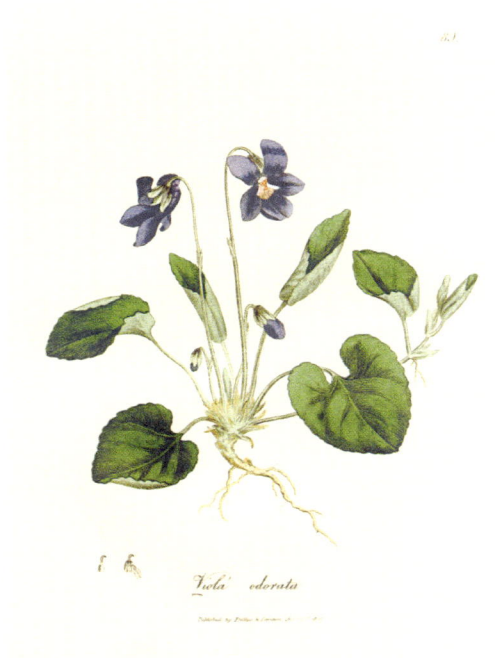

Viola odorata

MINERAL.

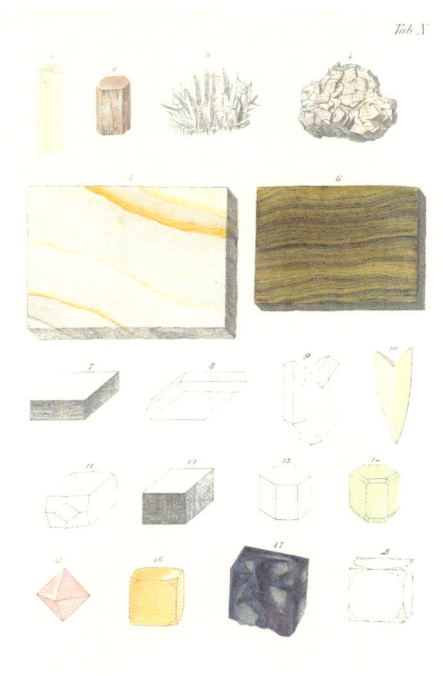

ANIMAL.
W. W. Fowler,
*The Coleoptera
of the British Islands*,
Vol. 4, 1891.
Pansy Purple is visible
on the back of the small
bloody-nosed beetle
(bottom row, centre).

VEGETABLE.
William Woodville,
Medical Botany, 1832.
Pansy Purple is visible
on the petals of the
sweet violet.

MINERAL.
Johann Gottlob
Kurr, *The Mineral
Kingdom*, 1859.
Pansy Purple is visible
on the fluorite (bottom
row, centre right).

39. CAMPANULA PURPLE.

(i).   ─────────

(ii).   *Canterbury Bell. Campanula Persicifolia.*
        [*Peach-leaved bellflower*; Campanula persicifolia]

(iii). *Fluor Spar.* [*Fluorite*; *Fluorspar*; *Calcium Fluoride*]

Campanula Purple, is ultramarine blue and carmine red, about equal parts of each: it is the characteristic colour.

ANIMAL.

VEGETABLE.

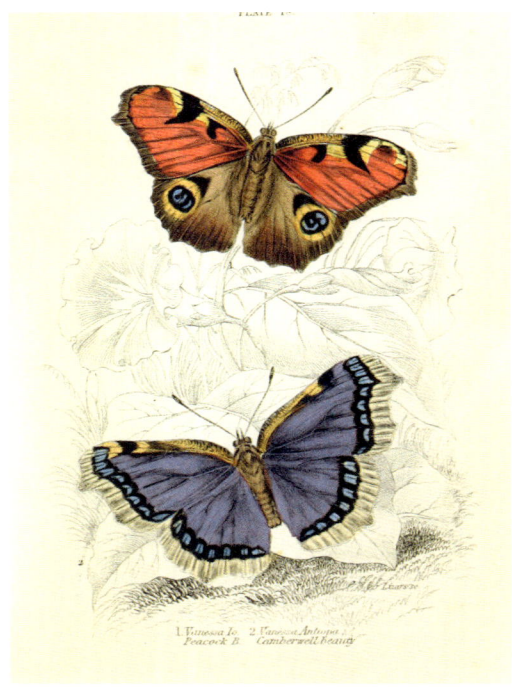

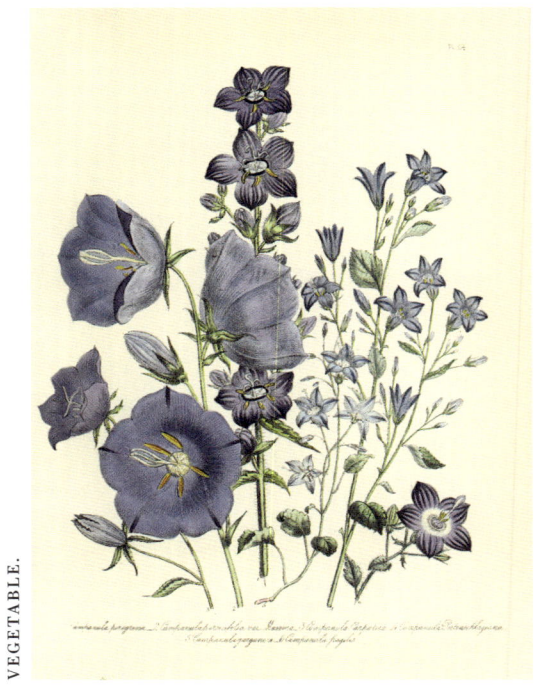

ANIMAL.
James Duncan, *British Butterflies*, 1840. Campanula Purple is visible on the wings of the Camberwell Beauty (below).*

VEGETABLE.
Jane Loudon, *The Ladies' Flower-Garden of Ornamental Perennials*, Vol. 1, 1849. Campanula Purple is visible on the petals of the peach-leaved bellflower (centre).

MINERAL.
Johann Gottlob Kurr, *The Mineral Kingdom*, 1859. Campanula Purple is visible on the fluorite (left).

MINERAL.

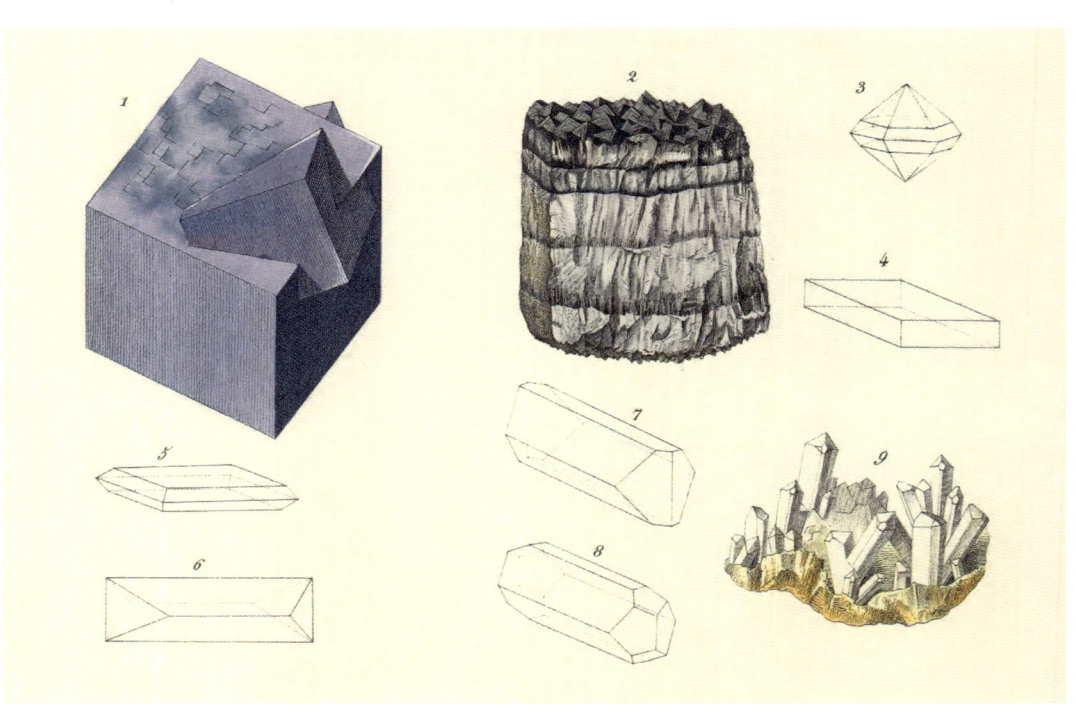

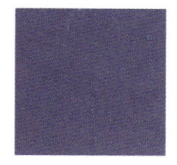

40. IMPERIAL PURPLE.

(i).
(ii). *Deep Parts of Flower of Saffron Crocus.* [*Autumn crocus;* Crocus sativus]
(iii). *Fluor Spar.* [*Fluorite; Fluorspar; Calcium Fluoride*]

Imperial Purple, is azure and indigo blue, with carmine red, about equal parts of each.

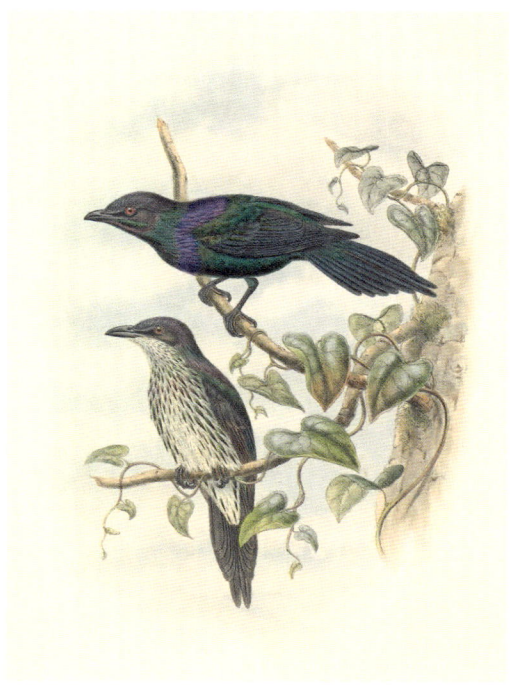

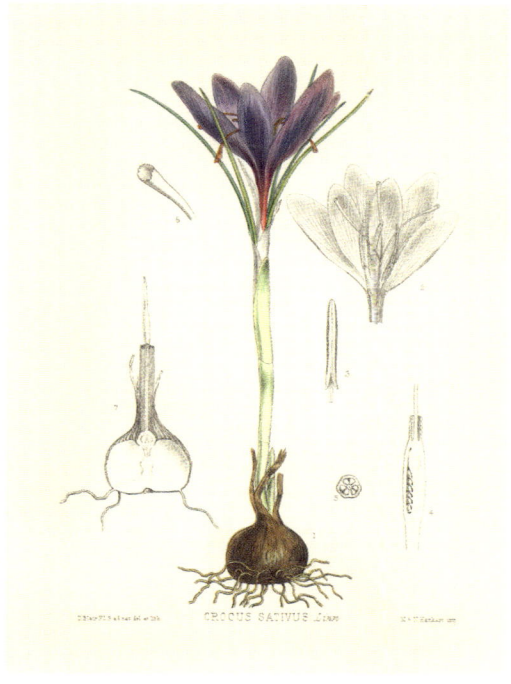

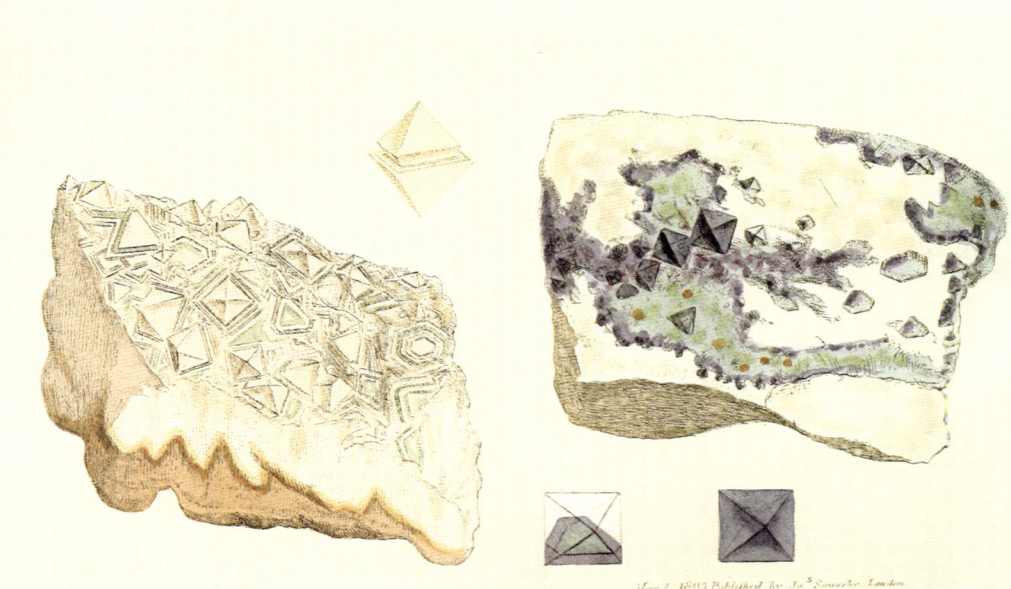

ANIMAL.
John Gould, *The Birds of New Guinea and the Adjacent Papuan Islands*, 1875–88. Imperial Purple is visible on the feathers of the metallic starling.*

VEGETABLE.
Robert Bentley and Henry Trimen, *Medicinal Plants*, 1880. Imperial Purple is visible on the petals of the saffron crocus.

MINERAL.
James Sowerby, *British Mineralogy*, Vol. I, 1802–17. Imperial Purple is visible on the fluorite (right). It is embedded within a lump of chalk.

(i).   *Egg of largest Blue-bottle, or Flesh Fly*
        [Calliphora vomitoria].
(ii).   *Largest Purple Auricula.* [*Bear's ear*; Primula auricula]
(iii).   *Fluor Spar.* [*Fluorite*; Fluorspar; *Calcium Fluoride*]

Auricula Purple, is plum purple, with indigo blue and much carmine red.

116.   II. BLUES AND PURPLES.

ANIMAL.

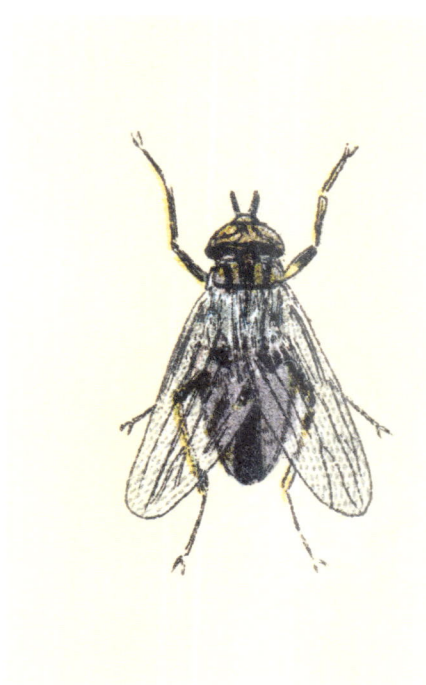

VEGETABLE.

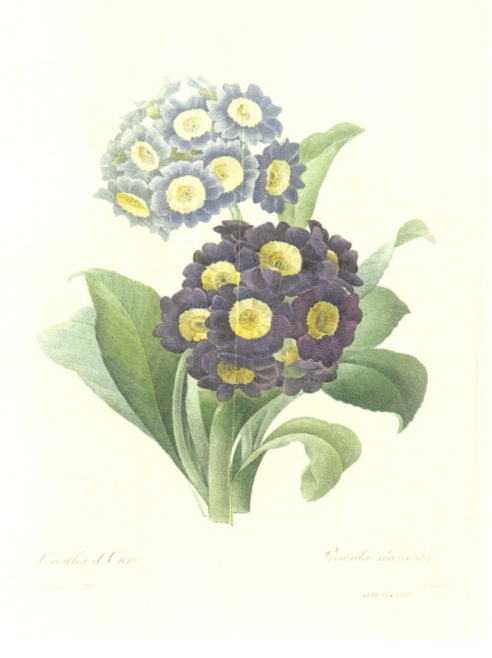

Cirollis d'Ours   *Primula discolor*

ANIMAL.
Common flesh fly,
ink, date unknown.
Auricula Purple is
visible on the back
of the flesh fly.

VEGETABLE.
Pierre-Joseph
Redouté, *Choix des
plus belles fleurs*, 1833.
Auricula Purple is
visible on the petals
of the bear's ear.

MINERAL.
Reinhard Brauns,
*The Mineral
Kingdom*, Vol. 1, 1912.
Auricula Purple is
visible on the fluorite
(centre row, second
from right).

MINERAL.

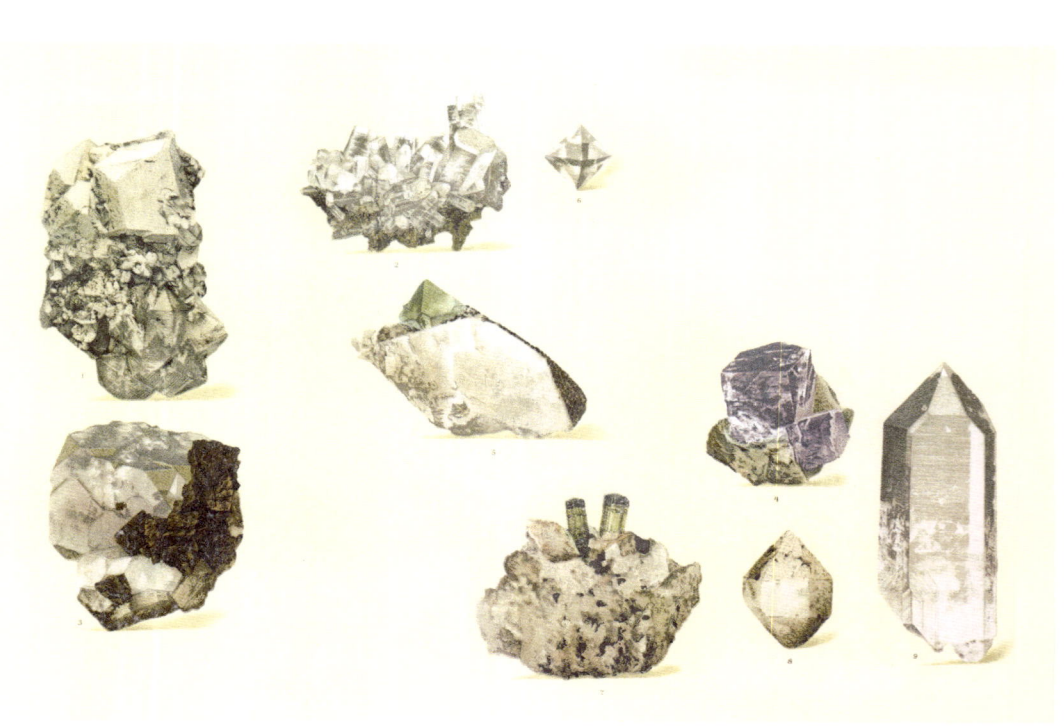

42. PLUM PURPLE.

(i). ──────────
(ii). *Plum.* [Prunus subg. Prunus]
(iii). *Fluor Spar.* [*Fluorite; Fluorspar; Calcium Fluoride*]

Plum Purple, the plum blue of Werner, is composed of Berlin blue, with much carmine red, a very little brown, and an almost imperceptible portion of black. [W]

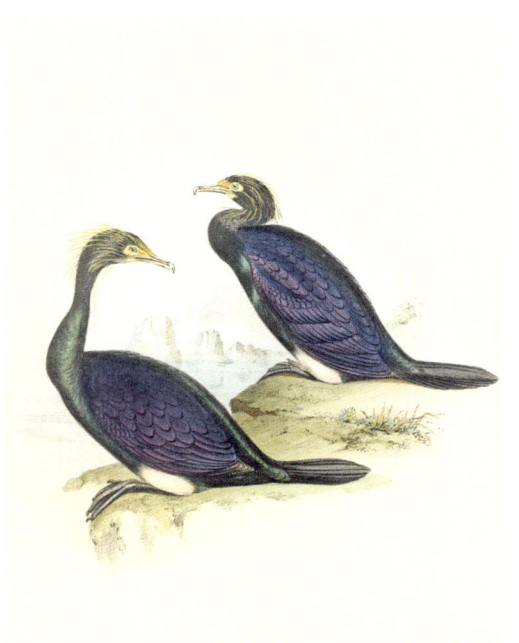

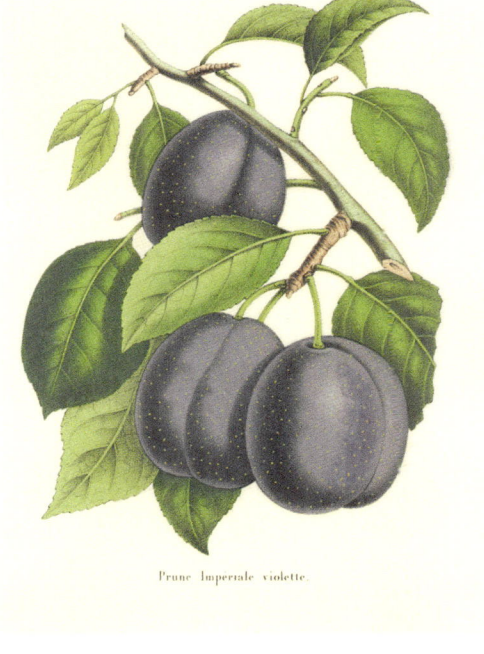

Prune Imperiale violette.

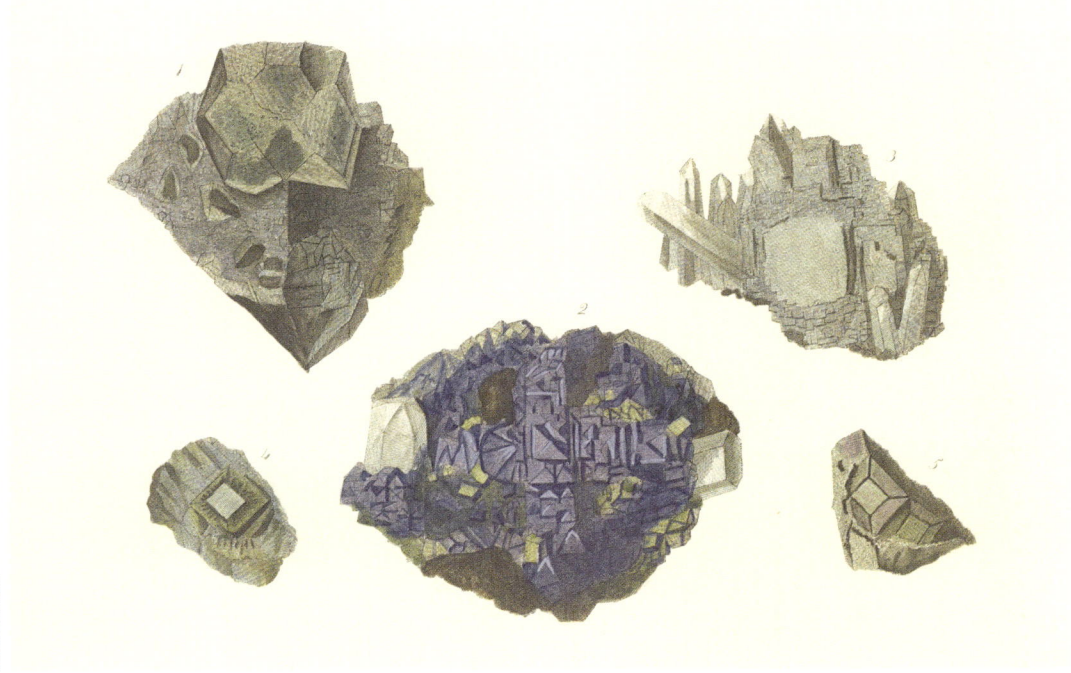

MINERAL.

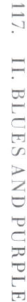

ANIMAL.
Richard Brinsley Hinds,
The Zoology of the Voyage of HMS Sulphur, 1843.
Plum Purple is visible on the wing feathers of the spectacled cormorant.*

VEGETABLE.
Charles Morren,
La Belgique horticole, journal des jardins,
Vol. 6, 1856.
Plum purple is visible on the skin of the plum.

MINERAL.
Philip Rashleigh,
Specimens of British Minerals, 1797.
Plum Purple is visible on the fluorite (bottom row, centre).

43. RED LILAC PURPLE.

(i).   *Light Spots of the upper Wings of Peacock Butterfly.*
        [Aglais io]
(ii).   *Red Lilac.* [Syringa]
        Pale Purple Primrose. [Primula vulgaris]
(iii).   *Lepidolite.* [*Silicate mineral*]

Red Lilac Purple, is campanula purple, with a considerable portion of snow white, and a very little carmine red.

ANIMAL.

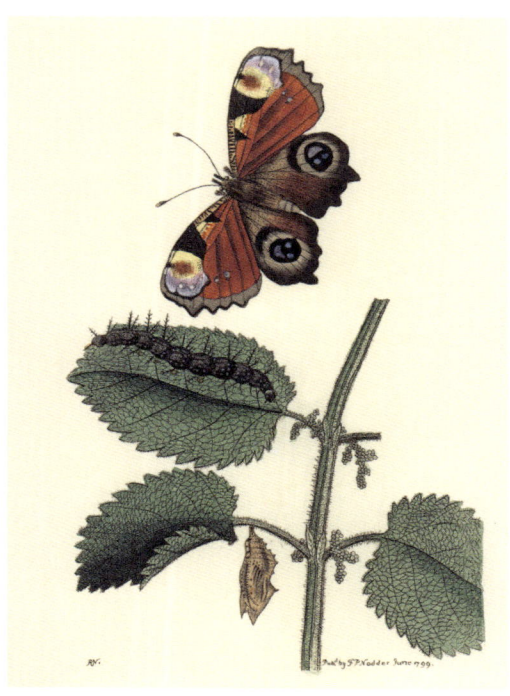

VEGETABLE.

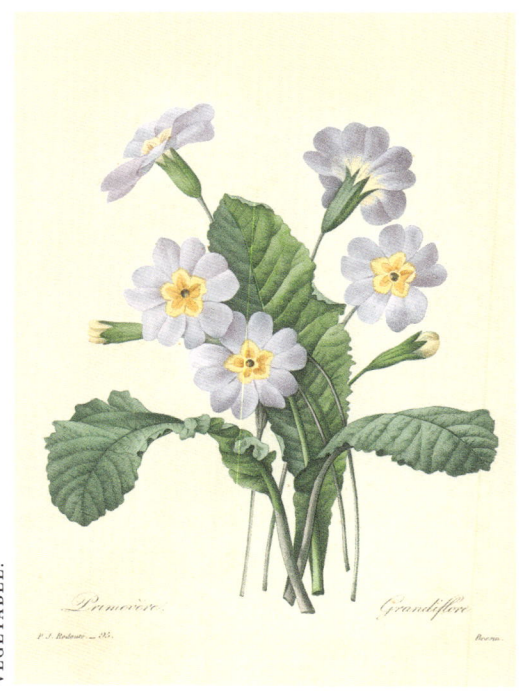

MINERAL.

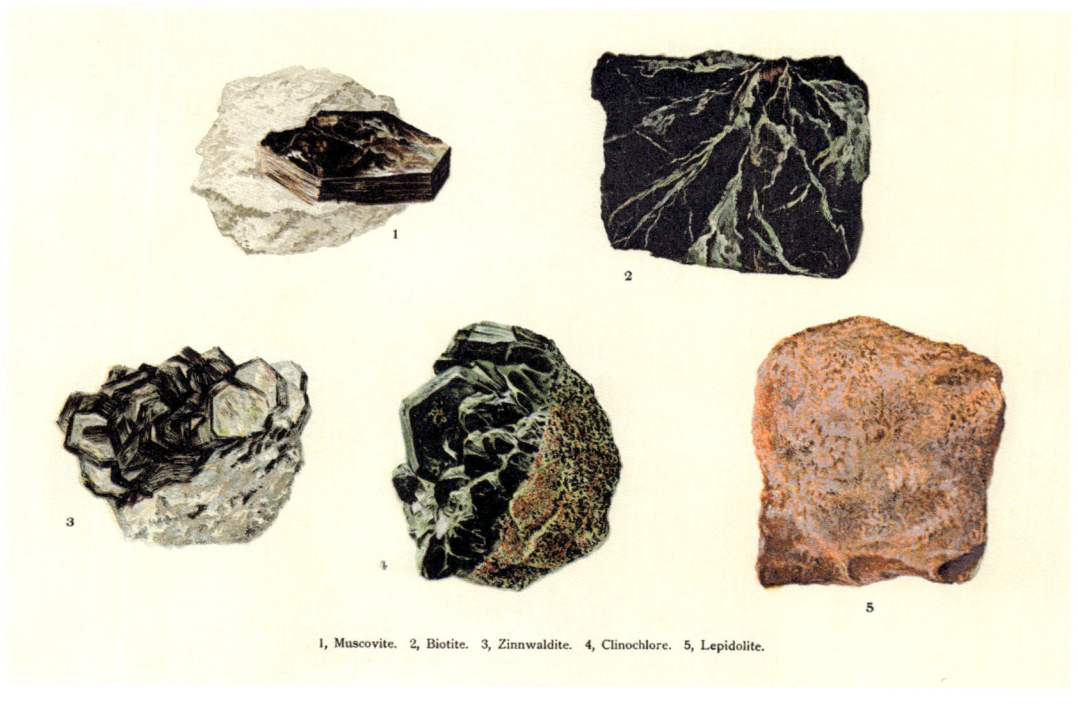

1, Muscovite. 2, Biotite. 3, Zinnwaldite. 4, Clinochlore. 5, Lepidolite.

ANIMAL.
George Shaw and Frederick P. Nodder, *The Naturalist's Miscellany*, 1789–1801. Red Lilac Purple is visible on the light spots on the wings of the peacock butterfly.

VEGETABLE.
Pierre-Joseph Redouté, *Choix des plus belles fleurs*, 1833. Red Lilac Purple is visible on the petals of the primrose.

MINERAL.
Leonard Spencer, *The World's Minerals*, 1916. Red Lilac Purple is visible on the lepidolite (bottom row, right).

44. LAVENDER PURPLE.

(i).   *Light Parts of Spots on the under Wings of Peacock Butterfly.* [Aglais io]
(ii).   *Dried Lavender Flowers.* [Lavandula]
(iii). *Porcelain Jasper.* [*Silica*]

Lavender Purple, the lavender blue of Werner, is composed of blue, red, and a little brown and grey. [W]

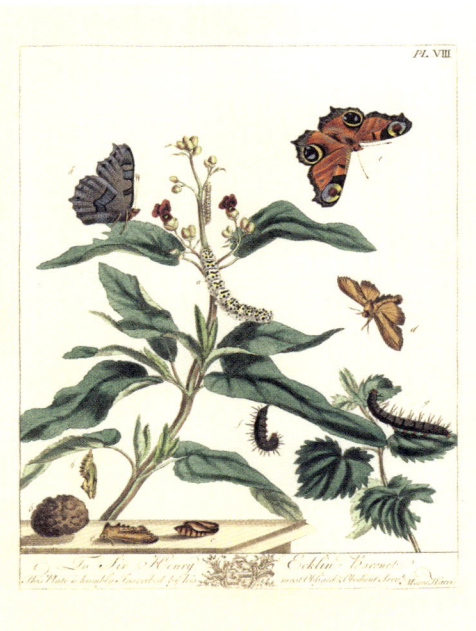

ANIMAL.

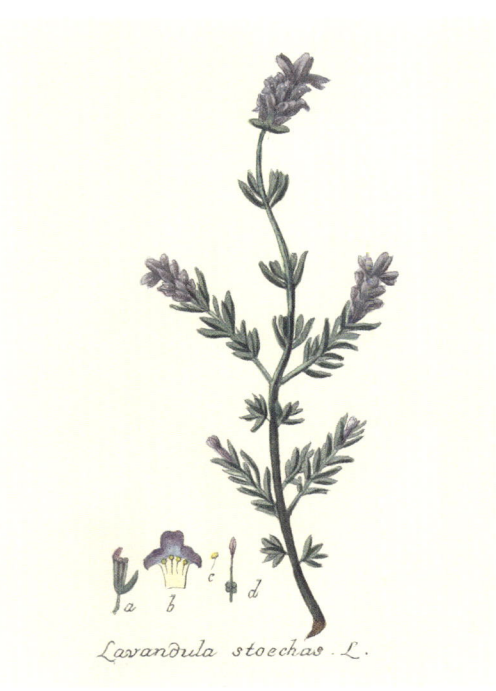

VEGETABLE.

Lavandula stoechas. L.

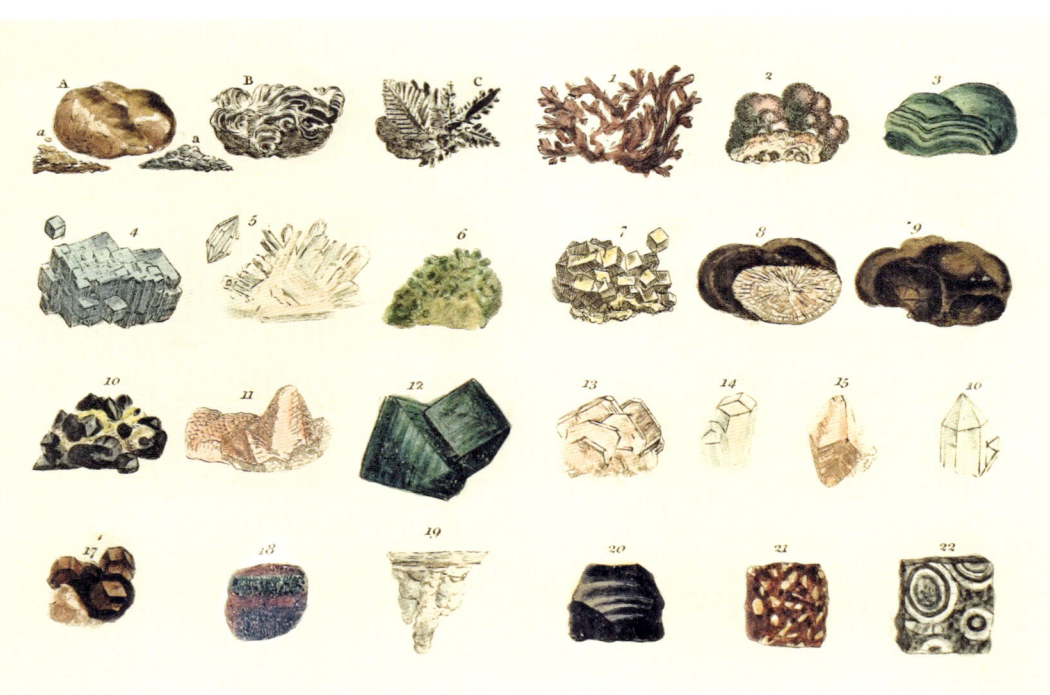

MINERAL.

ANIMAL.
John O. Westwood, *The Aurelian; a Natural History of English Moths and Butterflies*, 1840. Lavender Purple is visible on the light parts of the spots on the underwings of the peacock butterfly (above left).

VEGETABLE.
Johannes Zom, *Icones plantarum medicinalium*, 1779. Lavender Purple is visible on the petals of the lavender.

MINERAL.
John Mawe, *Familiar Lessons on Mineralogy and Geology*, 1826. Lavender Purple is visible on the jasper (bottom row, second from left).

45. PALE BLACKISH PURPLE.

(i).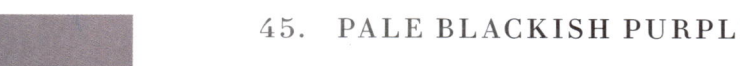

(ii).

(iii). *Porcelain Jasper.* [*Silica*]

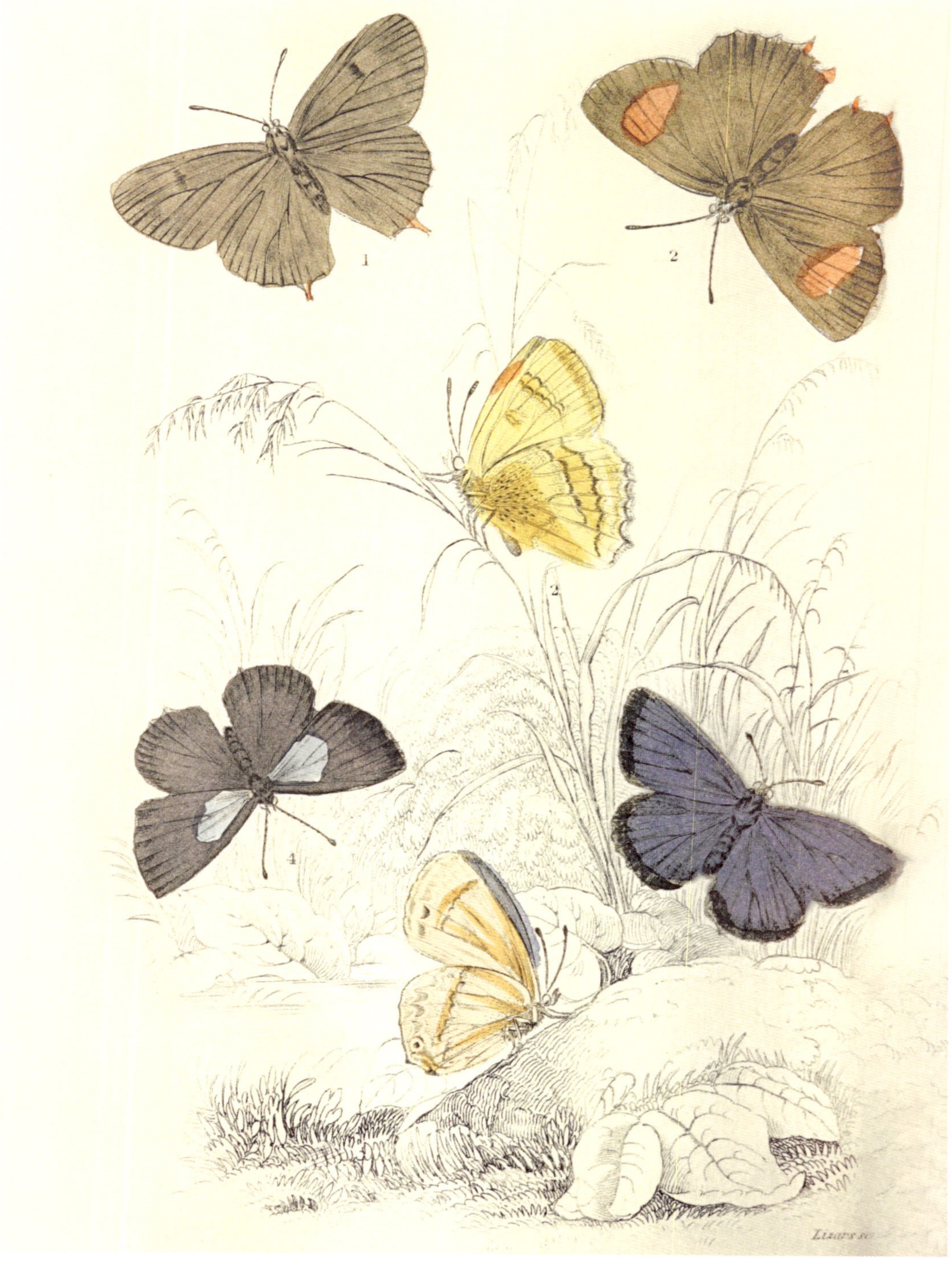

Pale Blackish Purple, is
lavender purple mixed
with a little red and black.

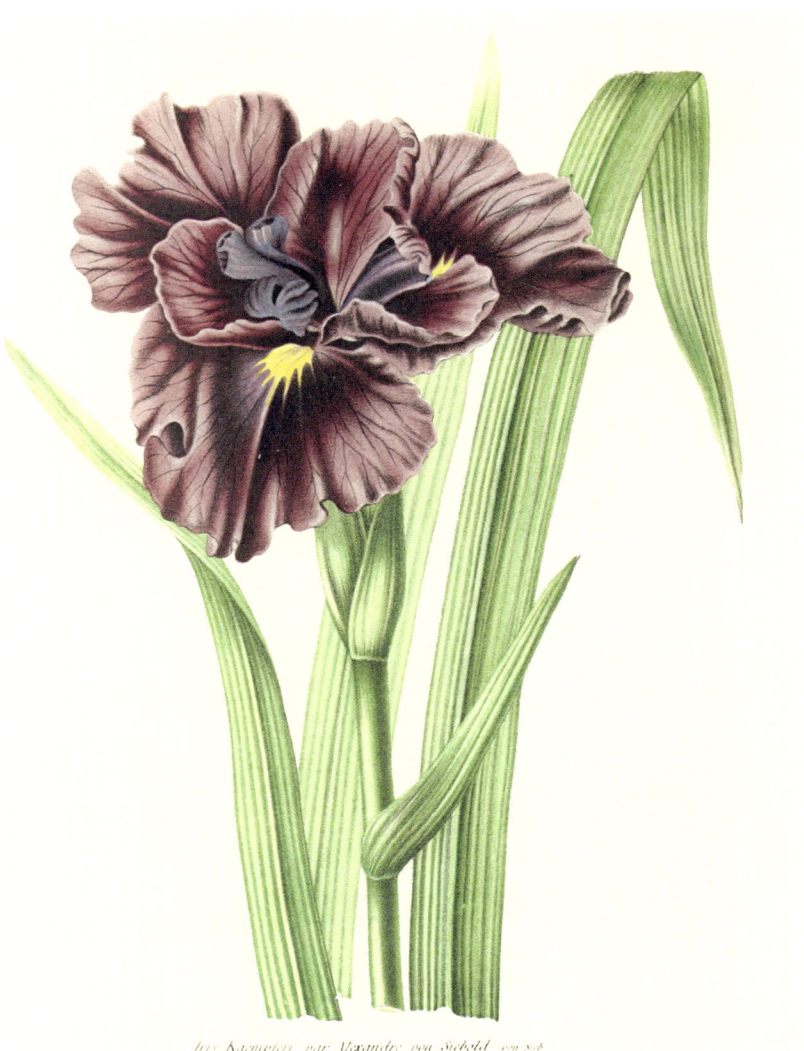

Iris Kaempferi var Alexandre von Siebold von Sieb.

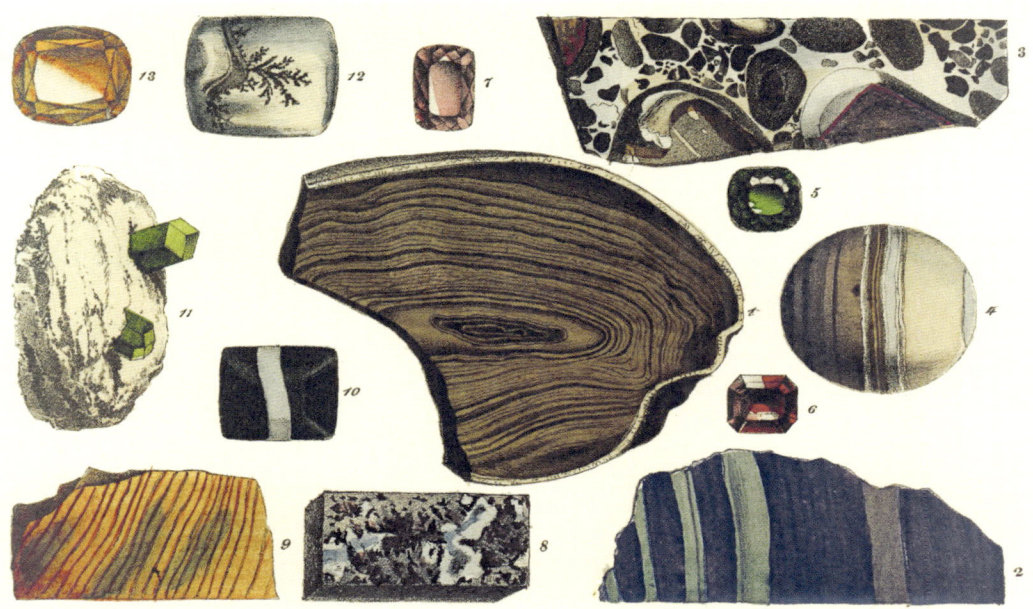

ANIMAL.
James Duncan,
British Butterflies, 1840.
Pale Blackish Purple
is visible on the wings
of the purple hairstreak
(bottom row, right).*

VEGETABLE.
Cornelis Antoon
Jan Abraham
Oudemans, *Neerland's
Plantentuin*, 1865.
Pale Blackish Purple
is visible on the inner
petals of the iris.*

MINERAL.
Lewis Feuchtwanger,
*A Popular Treatise
on Gems, in Reference
to their Scientific
Value*, 1859.
Pale Blackish Purple
is visible on the jasper
(bottom row, right).

2. COLOURS IN ZOOLOGY: SUBJECTIVE OR SYSTEMATIC?

Exploration and a field guide to colour for the great naturalists.

BY ELAINE CHARWAT.

For Carl Linnaeus (1707-1778), one of the pioneers of modern taxonomy, colour as a means of classifying animals was acceptable only if firmly linked to structure and form, as he sought to distance himself from naïve and confusing pre-Enlightenment schemes of classification. While he used colours for descriptions of particular species or individuals, especially birds, the fundamental criteria remained anatomical. Interestingly, one of Linnaeus's uses of colour as an important distinguishing attribute in the animal kingdom refers to humans. In the tenth edition of *Systema naturae* (1758-59), which marked the beginning of the scientific naming of animals in (Western) zoology, the first term Linnaeus uses to characterize American, European, Asian and African people is their 'colour': red, white, (pale) yellow and black. Using 'skin colour' to identify people as different varieties of *Homo sapiens* produced a legacy that would cast a shadow over anthropology and biology that stretches into the present day. It is also encountered in a later standard colour scheme, when Patrick Syme (1774-1845) in his *Werner's Nomenclature of Colours* used 'human skin' as the example from the animal kingdom of the colour 'flesh red' (i.e. pinkish).

Linnaeus's almost exact contemporary and critic, Georges-Louis Leclerc, Comte de Buffon (1707-1788), in his *Histoire naturelle des oiseaux* (1770-85), highlighted the dilemma of using colours as reliable criteria in serious scientific endeavour. He was opposed to Linnaeus's use of minute anatomical details or internal organs for identification and classification, and suggested that colour, as one of the 'main and essential' features, should be used instead.[1] In ornithology, especially, colours were the most important, and often the only, means of identifying and classifying birds. It is no coincidence that common (and scientific) bird names in many languages make extensive use of colour descriptors. For instance the wonderfully bicolour English name 'black redstart' (*Phoenicurus ochruros*), or 'Hausrotschwanz' in German and 'Rougequeue noir' in French. But even as Buffon advocated the use of colours in this way, he also acknowledged that there was no 'language' available to correctly express them in all their different manifestations.[2] They were fugitive, emotive, constantly changing with the movements of the birds.[3] He therefore advocated adding coloured plates for birds, partly to make up for this lack of a 'language'.

In order to 'tame' colours and to make them of practical use in a scientific context increasingly dominated by large-scale explorations and the collecting of animals, colours needed to be standardized. This was by no means a new endeavour; in the 17th and 18th centuries (but extending back to the ancient Greeks), natural philosophy looked closely at colours in nature, how they came into being and were perceived. However, it remained for 18th- and 19th-century naturalists, practitioners and artists to successfully turn colour into a standard trait that could be reliably identified and named when describing an animal. Colour shifted from volatile to stable, from subjective to standardized, from intuitive to scientific, but, crucially, became a characteristic that could be pinned down and widely communicated.

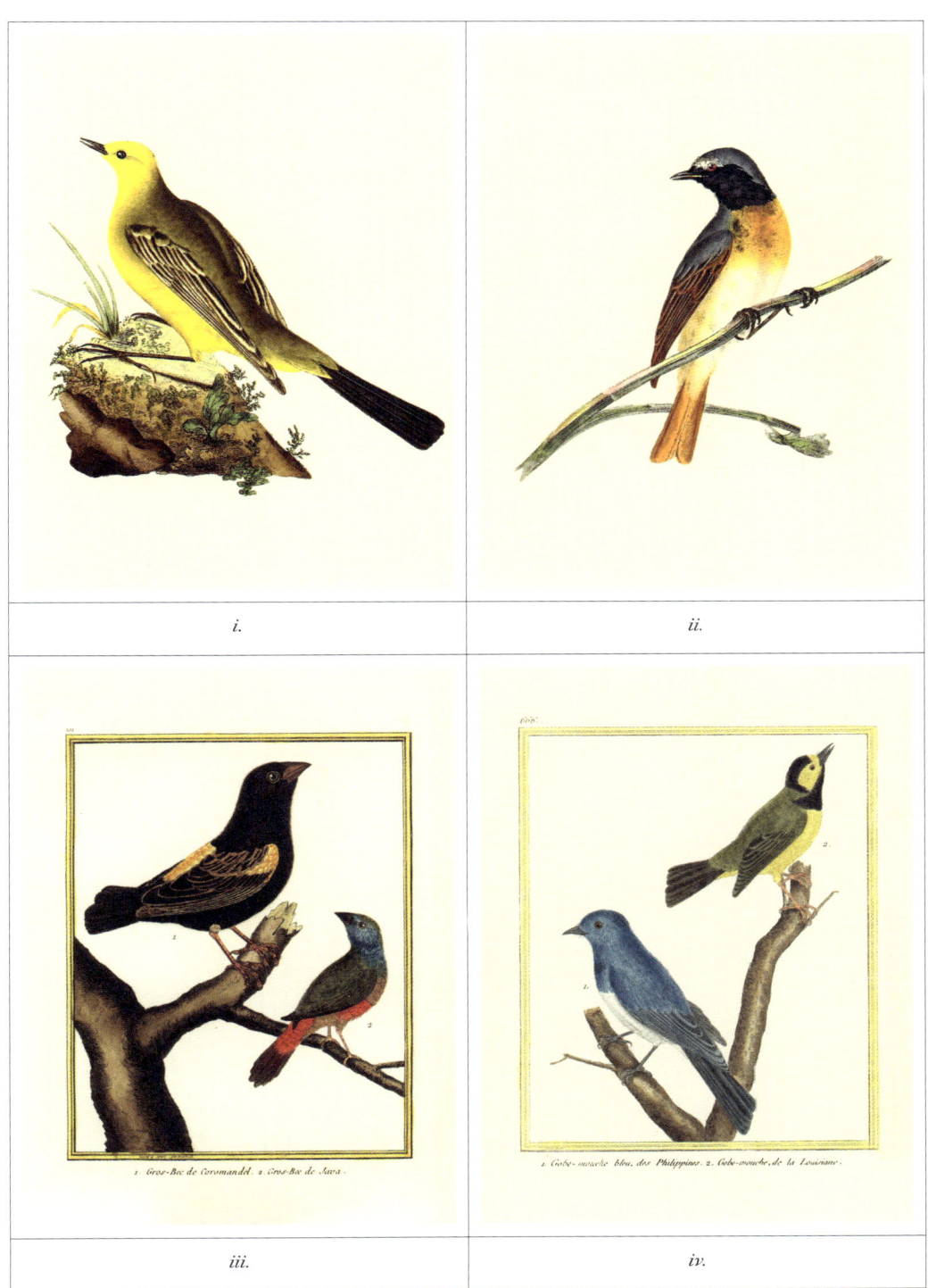

i.

ii.

iii.

iv.

(i).   Yellow wagtail, Edward Donovan, *The Natural History of British Birds*, 1794.
(ii).   Redstart, Edward Donovan, *The Natural History of British Birds*, 1794.
(iii). Two species of grosbeak, Comte de Buffon, *Histoire naturelle des oiseaux*, 1749–1804.
(iv).   Two species of flycatcher, Comte de Buffon, *Histoire naturelle des oiseaux*, 1749–1804.

Four Ruffs, *c.*1800. *In the West the practice of ornithology as a scientific discipline began in the 17th century. Taxidermy birds were made to aid study or for display, particularly in the 19th century.*

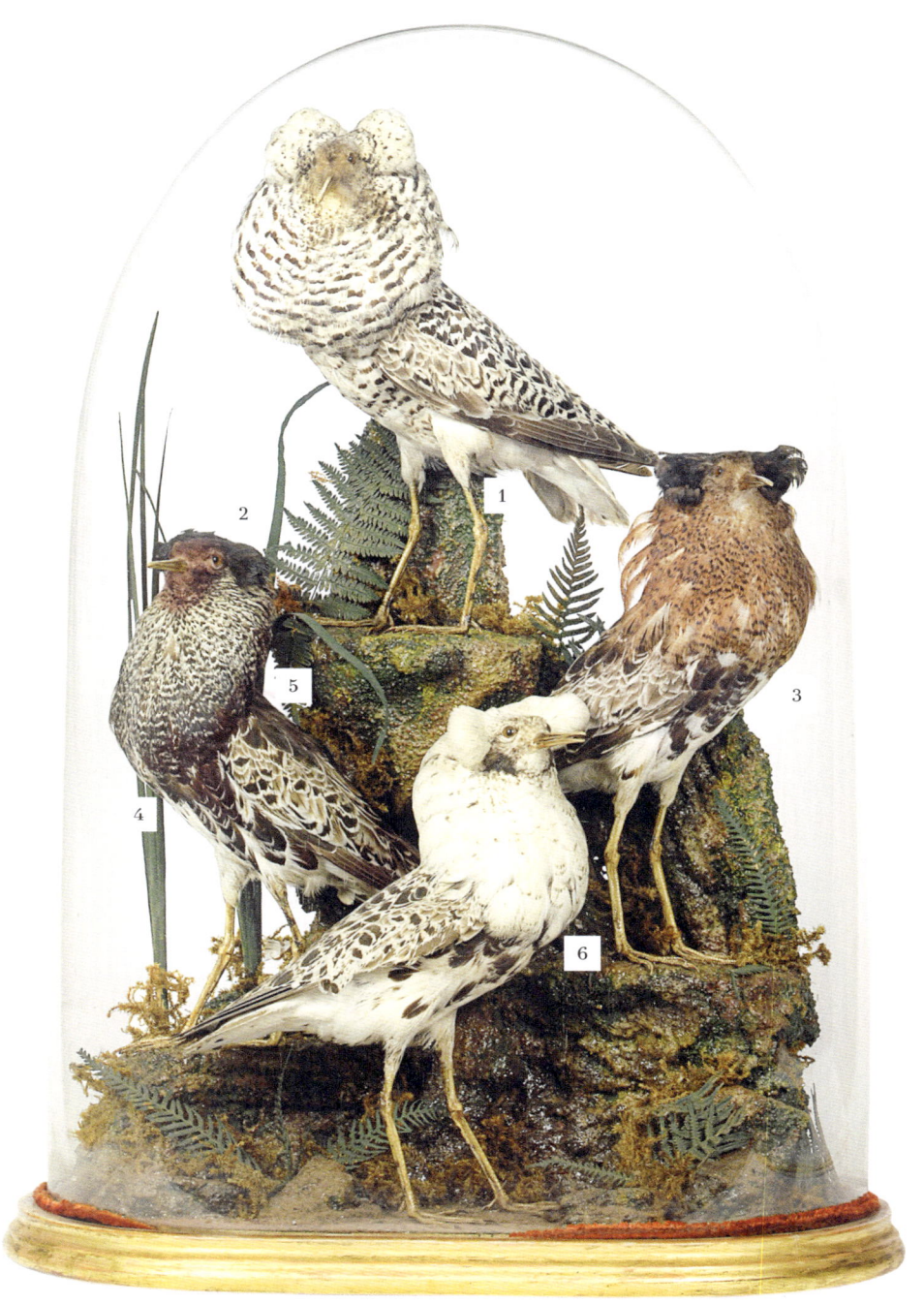

1		THIGH FEATHER.	2		HEAD FEATHER.	3		BREAST FEATHER.
		1. Snow White.			*79. Brownish Orange.*			*81. Deep Reddish Orange.*
4		BREAST FEATHER.	5		MANTLE FEATHER.	6		BREAST FEATHER.
		98. Chocolate Red.			*102. Umber Brown.*			*4. Yellowish White.*

ORNITHOLOGY.

Fourteen South
American birds,
c. 1870. *Taxidermy
birds mounted
under glass domes
were a popular
part of 19th-century
interior decor.*

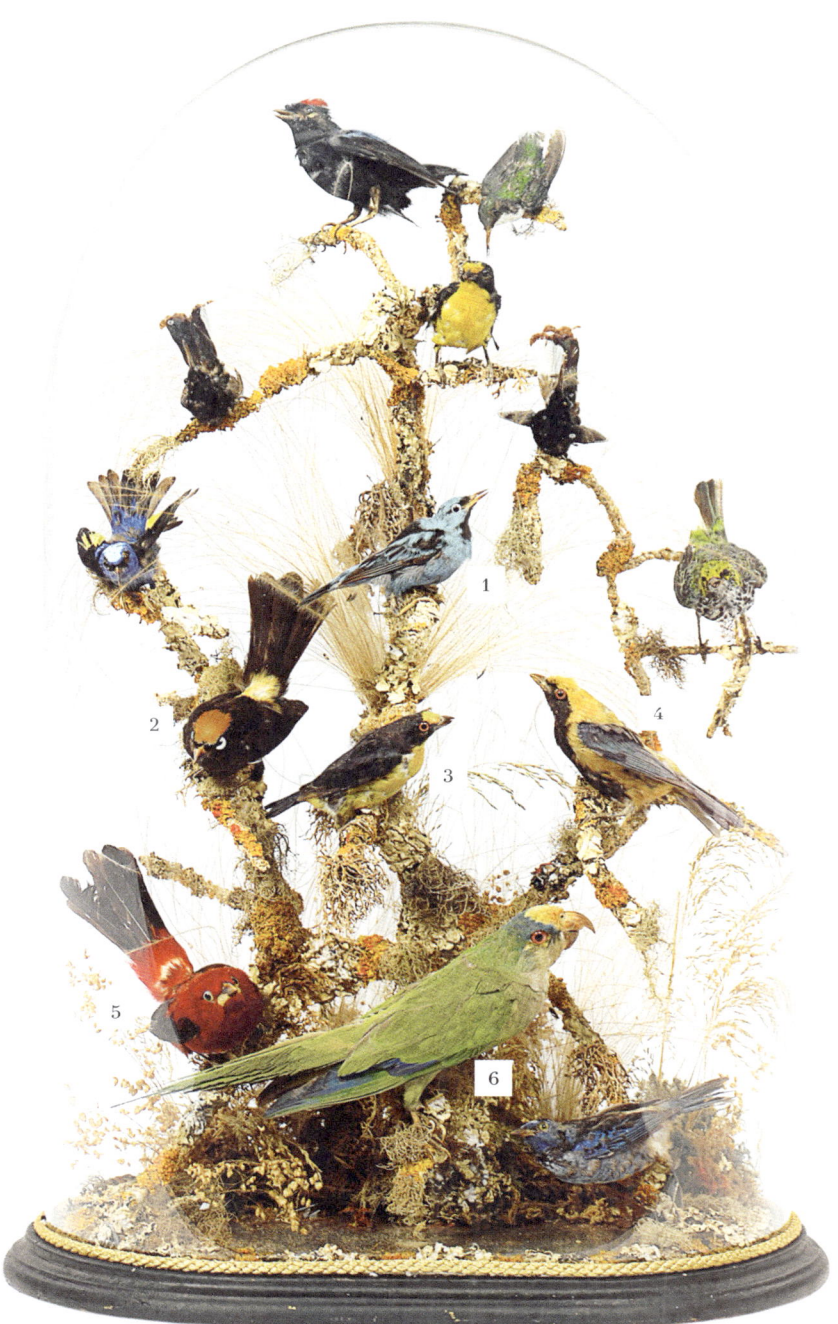

1		BLUE DACNIS.	2		EUPHONIA.	3		EUPHONIA.
		32. Verditter Blue.			*78. Orpiment Orange.*			*68. Saffron Yellow.*
4		YELLOW-BACKED ORIOLE.	5		SCARLET TANAGER.	6		AMAZON PARROT.
		33. Greenish Blue.			*84. Scarlet Red.*			*57. Pistachio Green.*

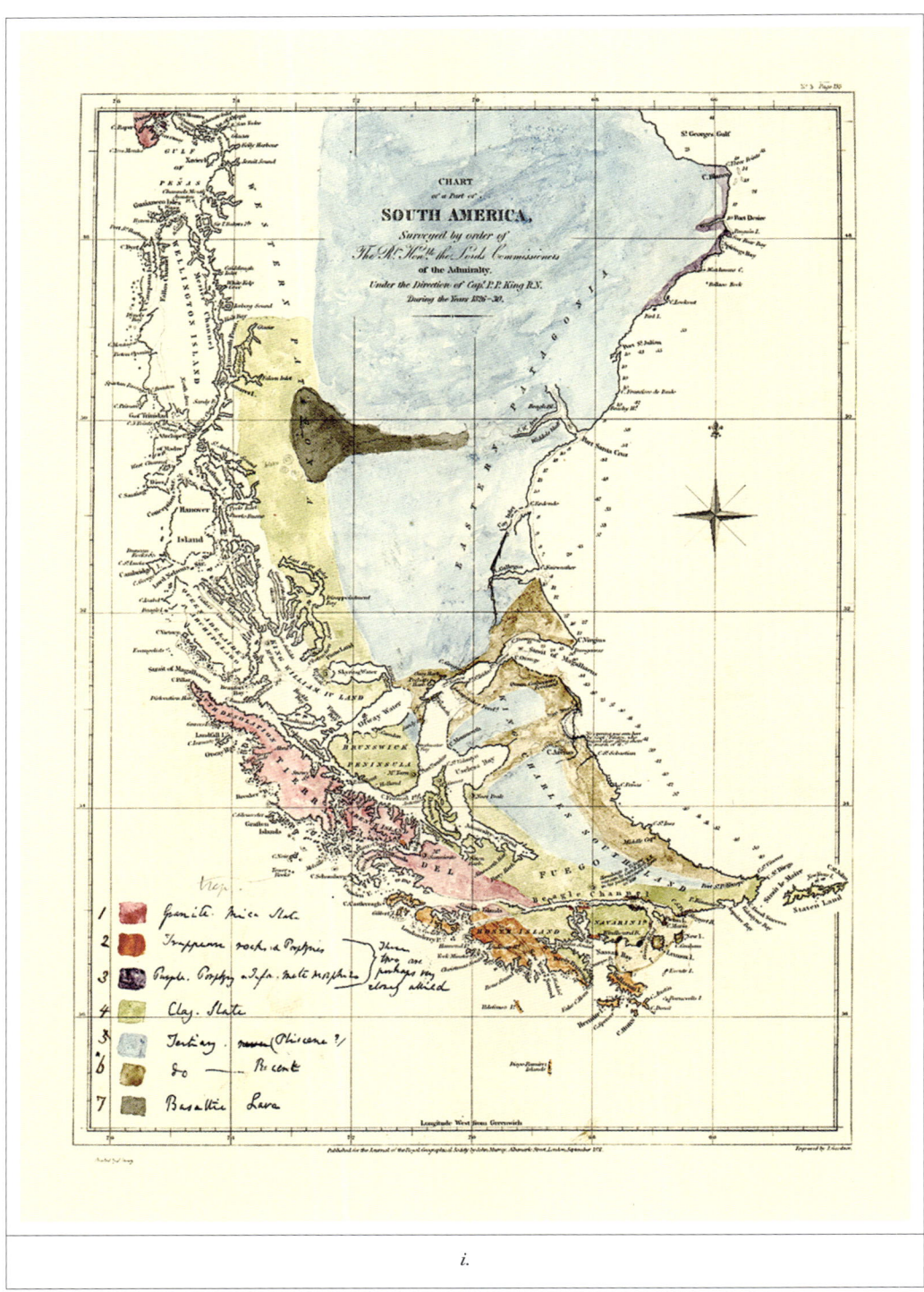

i.

(i).   Hand-coloured geological map of the southern tip of South America and
        the islands off its coast, created by Charles Darwin during his voyage on HMS
        Beagle, between 1831 and 1836. The key concern of Darwin's geological work here
        was to understand the changing relation between the levels of the land and sea.

In addition to describing and identifying birds, colours could be applied to insects and marine creatures. However, one great disadvantage was that organisms living in water often immediately lost their colours when brought to the surface or killed. On board a rolling ship, this often resulted in a hectic juggling of struggling creatures, reference books and notebooks in order to record the 'true' colours of these animals before they faded.

In the first half of the 19th century, the reference book that was being thus juggled and consulted would most likely have been Patrick Syme's. His was one of the earliest of such colour schemes encompassing all three kingdoms of nature: animal, vegetable and mineral. And one of the naturalists using it was Charles Darwin.

CHARLES DARWIN AND THE *NOMENCLATURE OF COLOURS*

In August 1832, Charles Darwin (1809–1882) was only a few heady months into his five-year voyage (1831–36) on HMS *Beagle* and still finding his feet as a naturalist, collector and explorer. Describing some of the 'marvellous' South American animals to be collected, listed and shipped to Britain, he expressed his thoughts in a letter to J. S. Henslow (1796–1861), his mentor and the person instrumental in securing his position as a gentleman naturalist on board. Darwin emphasized the importance of meticulously recording the animals' colours even if it slowed down the process of collecting:

> But I have come to the conclusion, that two animals with their original colour and shape noted down, will be more valuable to Naturalists than six with only dates and place.[4]

This was more than just a casual comment. The use of colours in the identification and classification of animals was an important element of Darwin's voyage. In his later work, he would use this data to look beyond mere descriptions, and discern how colours could be indicative of different processes of selection.

In his *Beagle Zoology Notes*, he recorded his first encounter with 'an octopus' on 28 January 1832 at the Cape Verde Islands. This seems to be the moment when Darwin, almost with a jolt, recollected the importance of recording colours scientifically on his expedition, having come face to face with the great colour- and shape-shifter of the sea, the cuttlefish. It had

> the Chamælion like power of changing the colour of its body.— The general colour of animal was French grey with numerous spots of bright yellow. — the former of these colours varied in intensity.— the other entirely disappeared & then again returned.— Over the whole body there were continually passing clouds, varying in colour from a 'hyacinth red' to a 'Chesnut brown'.[5]

Apart from the yellow, which remains unqualified except for being 'bright', all the colour terms in this extraordinarily vivid passage are taken straight from Syme's *Werner's Nomenclature of Colours*. A copy of the second edition of 1821 was included in the *Beagle's* library for Darwin's use, and from this point in time, he consulted it throughout his journey.

Syme's colour nomenclature had been on Darwin's mind even when preparing for the voyage. In the autumn of 1831, he exchanged a flurry of excited letters with Henslow in Cambridge, asking him for advice and help regarding his expedition. Before an impending visit, Darwin wrote to Henslow on 9 September 1831, discussing books and equipment for his journey, and asking him for references to scientific papers. Across the top of the first page of this letter, almost as an afterthought, Darwin had written: 'I will write again before I come to Cambridge. Keep Syme on colours in your mind.'[6]

A copy of the second edition of Syme's *Werner's Nomenclature of Colours* (1821) can still be found in Darwin's library at his home, Down House, just outside London. However, the condition of this copy is 'spotless', so is unlikely to have been the one Darwin used

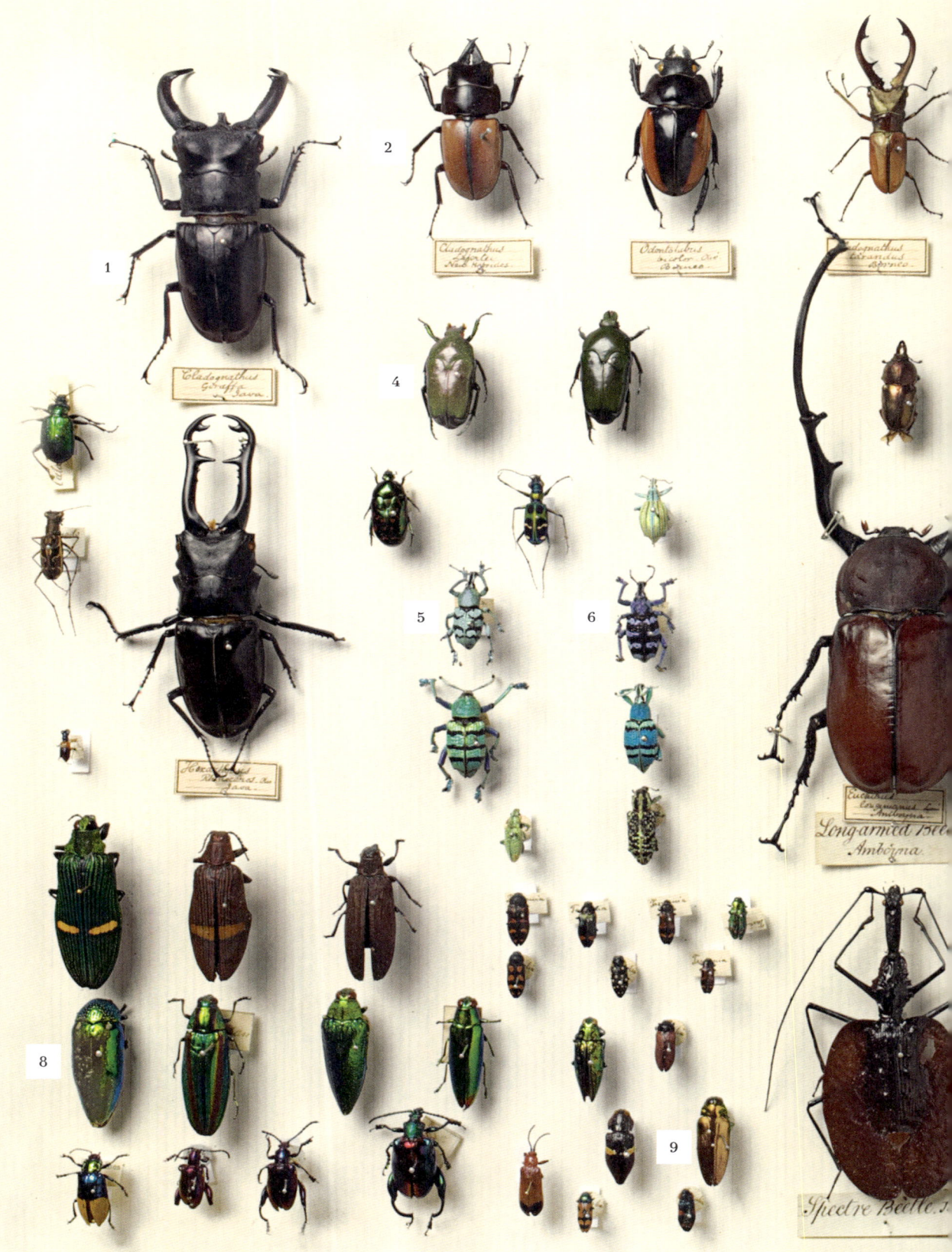

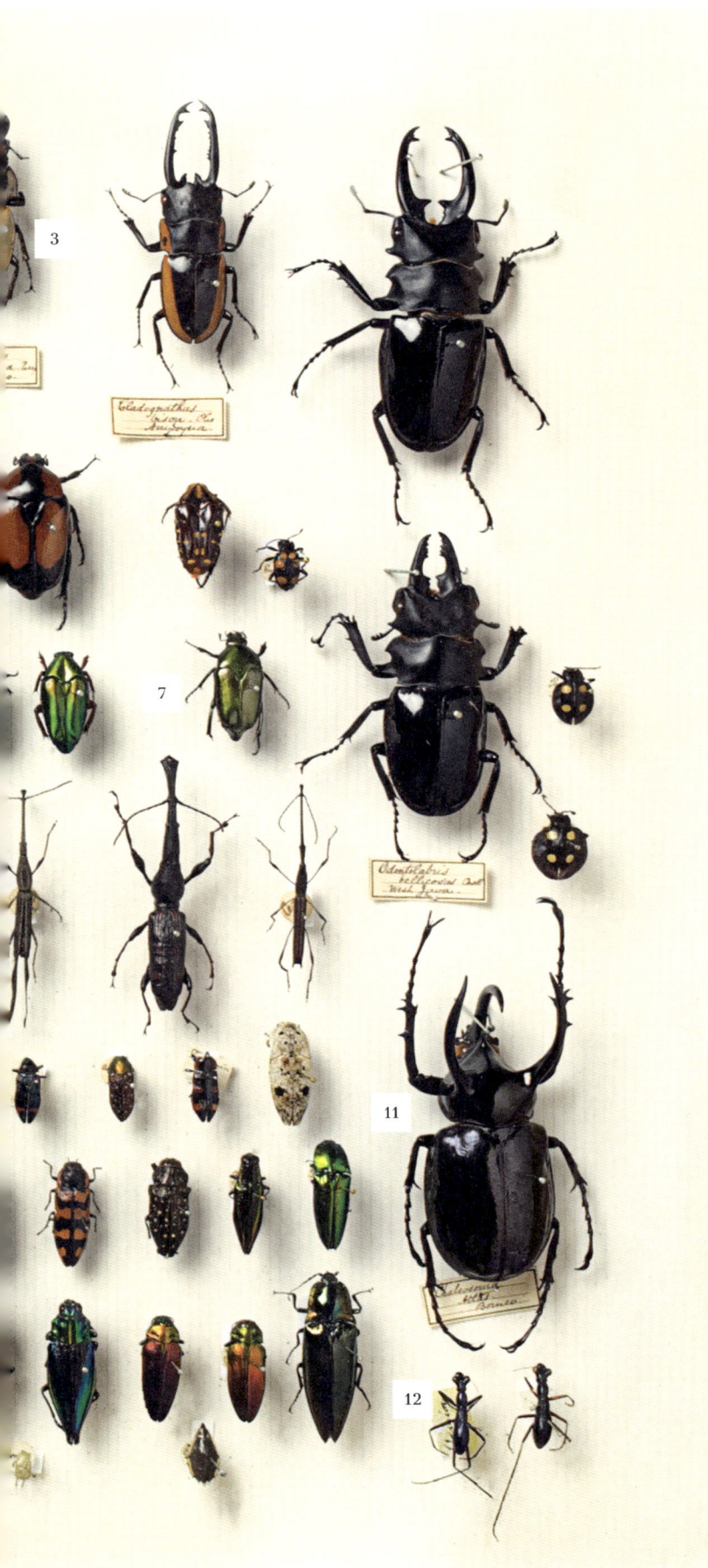

129. 2. COLOURS IN ZOOLOGY: SUBJECTIVE OR SYSTEMATIC?

ENTOMOLOGY.

Entomology is the branch of zoology concerned with the study of insects. *Introduction to Entomology* by William Kirby (1759-1850) and William Spence (1783-1860), published between 1815 and 1826, is considered the study's foundational text, and the science developed rapidly in the 18th and 19th centuries. This display case of Asian beetles comes from the collection of Alfred Russel Wallace (1823-1913), an eminent British naturalist and a prolific collector.

COLOUR REFERENCES.

1		HEXARTHRIUS RHINOCEROS.
		20. Pitch, or Brownish Black.
2		PROSOPOCOILUS LAFERTEI.
		81. Deep Reddish Orange.
3		ODONTOLABIS BROOKEANA.
		76. Dutch Orange.
4		ISCHIOPSOPHA SP.
		56. Sap Green.
5		EUPHOLUS CHEVROLATI.
		32. Verditter Blue.
6		EUPHOLUS LINNEI.
		29. Ultramarine Blue.
7		ISCHIOPSOPHA SP.
		60. Oil Green.
8		STERNOCERA AEQUISIGNATA.
		55. Duck Green.
9		BELIONOTA SP.
		78. Orpiment Orange.
10		TEMOGNATHA MITCHELLII.
		95. Cochineal Red.
11		CHALCOSOMA ATLAS.
		19. Greenish Black.
12		TRICONDYLA SP.
		24. Scotch Blue.

so extensively on the voyage.[7] According to Darwin's son Francis, a copy of Syme's 1821 edition was given to Cambridge's 'Botany School', and is identified in its 1911 catalogue as being 'a record of the [Beagle] voyage'. The entry adds that Darwin had 'recorded some observations in the volume itself: on a blank page at the beginning is written: "Beak of female ash grey, male nearly black, legs &c. exact dutch yellow".'[8] This annotation might be matched with Darwin's description in his *Beagle Zoology Notes* of the striated caracara (Darwin's 'Caracara novae-zelandae', now *Phalcoboenus australis*), a bird of prey of the Falkland Islands: 'legs & skin about beak bright "dutch orange", beak "ash-grey", in the male it is nearly black'.[9] It is interesting how Syme's 'dutch orange' becomes 'dutch yellow' in the note – a reminder that no system of colours can fully eliminate a subjective impression.

Later, in a letter written in 1860, Darwin would remark how a peacock's tail feather made him 'sick' – it seemed to contradict his theory of natural selection, its colours being so flamboyant and obvious to predators. The exuberant beauty of colours in nature triggered the idea of a different kind of selection at work – sexual selection. In the same letter, Darwin also mentioned 'Black Pigs in the Everglades' in the context of an ongoing speculation whether there might be a correlation between an animal's colour and its immunity to poison.[10] Darwin also looked closely at cultivated plants and animals, noting that there were much greater differences between individuals than in the same species in nature, the result of the Victorians deliberately breeding animals and plants for unusual colours and patterns.

One thing is certain – Syme's *Werner's Nomenclature of Colours* sharpened Darwin's eye for the beauty and the science of animal colours, just as Syme postulated in his introduction: 'the eye, by practice will become ... correct'.

NEW COLOURS IN THE FAR NORTH

In contrast to Darwin, John Richardson (1787-1865), a naval surgeon and naturalist,

could already be regarded as an 'old hand' at a particular type of voyage of discovery – Arctic exploration – when he wrote the *Appendix to Captain Parry's Journal of a Second Voyage for the Discovery of a North-west Passage* (1825). Although he had not been part of the expedition of 1821-23 under William Parry (1790-1855), Richardson had accompanied John Franklin (1786-1847) on his ill-fated 1819-22 Coppermine Expedition, also in search of the Northwest Passage. His energy apparently undiminished by the starvation and hardship he had experienced, Richardson not only worked on the official natural history account of Franklin's expedition, but also summarized and edited the zoological notes for Parry's voyage, as well as examining specimens collected – all in the short interval before he returned to Canada with Franklin in 1825. In his introduction (dated 1824) to the *Appendix to Captain Parry's Journal* Richardson notes that:

> The colours used in the descriptions are to be found in an excellent little work entitled, *Werner's Nomenclature of Colours* by Patrick Syme, Edinburgh, 1821, now frequently referred to by several eminent naturalists and comparative anatomists of this country.[11]

It might be expected that animal colours in the Arctic would be much less varied and vivid than those Darwin would later observe in the equatorial regions, but Richardson's descriptions are crammed with colour labels taken from Syme. Shades of white are a notable feature, as well as changes from winter to summer fur or plumage, which Richardson meticulously records, for example, for the ermine, Arctic fox and 'polar hare'. He also notes the importance of fur colour for the fur trade. As might be expected, Richardson seems to find Syme's shades of white almost lacking to describe the manifold, richly textured whites he encounters. Syme's 'snow-white' is a favourite in this environment of course (for instance for the ermine's 'winter habit'[12]), indicating the colour's role in animal camouflage. Sometimes,

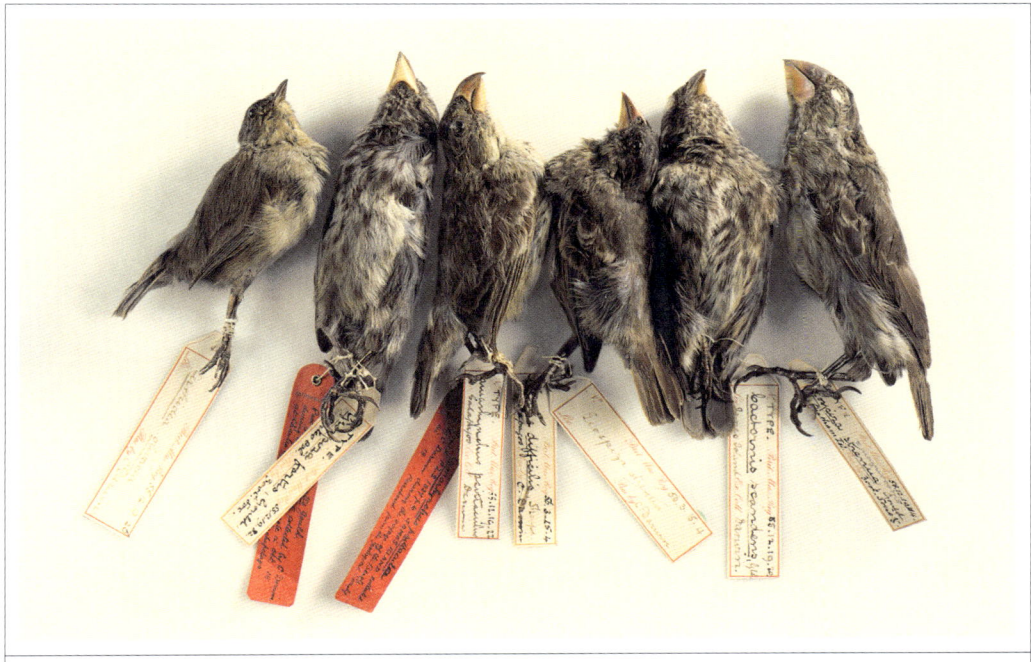

i.

ii.   iii.

(i).   Finches collected from the Galapagos Islands during the second voyage of HMS *Beagle,* 1831–36.
(ii–iii).   Pages from the catalogue of collected specimens made by Charles Darwin and his assistant
            Syms Covington during their voyage on the HMS *Beagle*, entitled *Catalogue for Specimens
            in Spirit of Wine.* Werner's colour standards are used to describe specimens, including
            Chesnut Brown (ii) and Dutch Orange (iii).

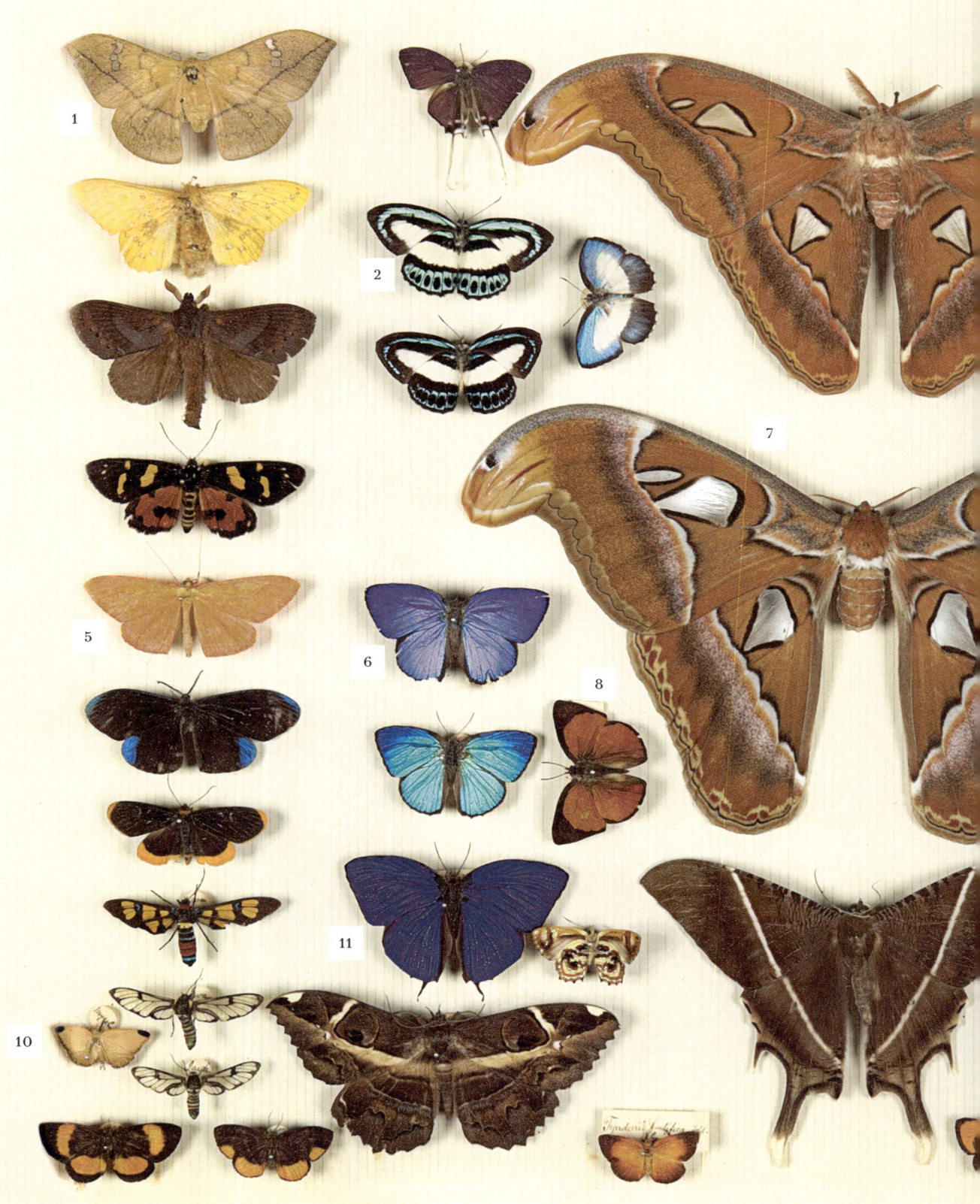

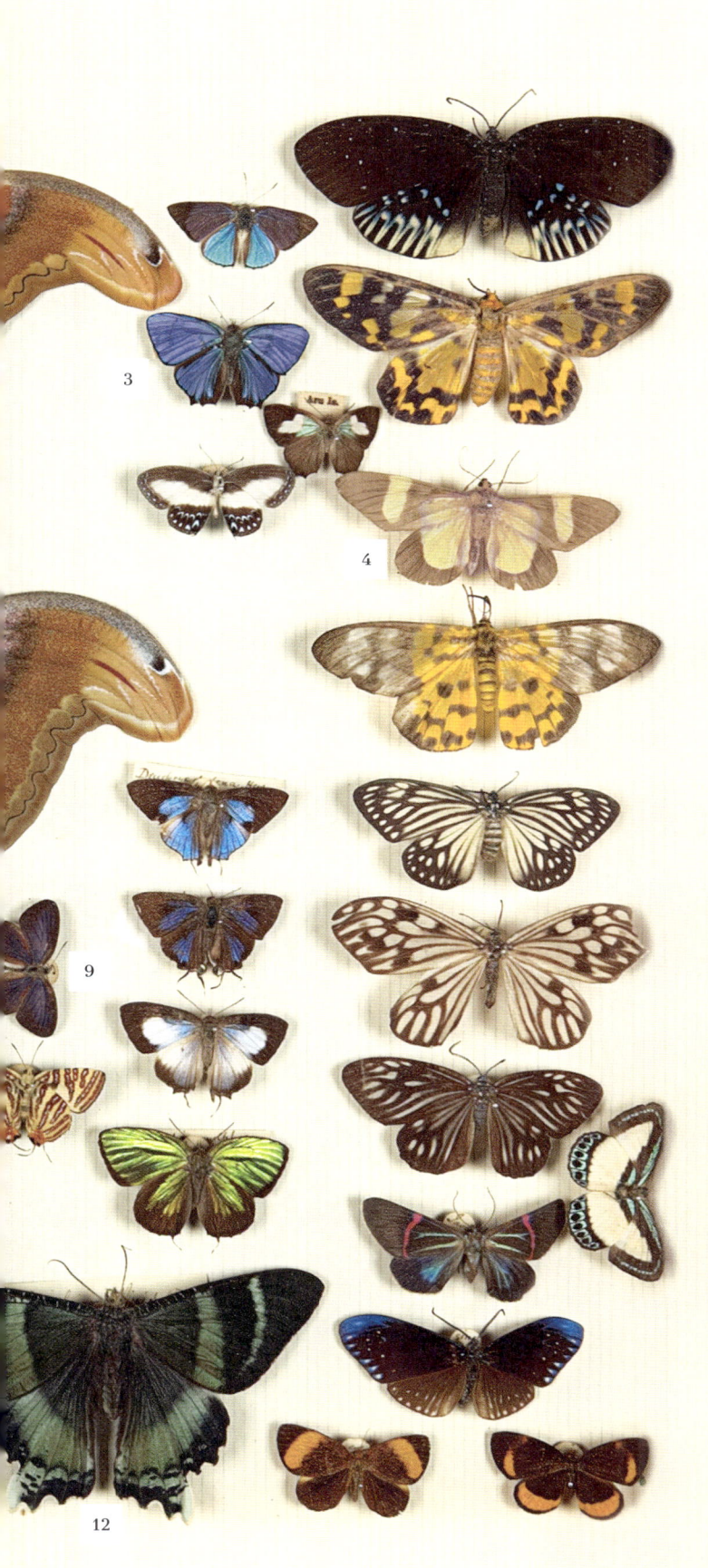

LEPIDOPTEROLOGY.

Lepidopterology, the study of moths and butterflies, grew in stature through an increased interest in science and nature following the Renaissance in Europe, and was developed further by explorers, scientists and naturalists in the 19th century. This board is from the collection of the 'father of biogeography' Alfred Russel Wallace (1823–1913). His butterfly collection aided him in the development of his theories of speciation and natural selection.

COLOUR REFERENCES.

1		CRICULA TRIFENESTRATA.
		76. Dutch Orange.
2		DANIS DANIS.
		50. Verdigris Green.
3		HYPOCHRYSOPS SP.
		29. Ultramarine Blue.
4		CELERENA SP.
		67. King's Yellow.
5		EUMELEA SP.
		78. Orpiment Orange.
6		ARHOPALA SP.
		31. Berlin Blue.
7		ATTACUS ATLAS.
		69. Gallstone Yellow.
8		HYPOCHRYSOPS SP.
		82. Tile Red.
9		HYPOCHRYSOPS SP.
		41. Auricula Purple.
10		COMELLA LAETIFICA.
		77. Buff Orange.
11		ARHOPALA SP.
		42. Plum Purple.
12		ALCIDES ORONTES.
		57. Pistachio Green.

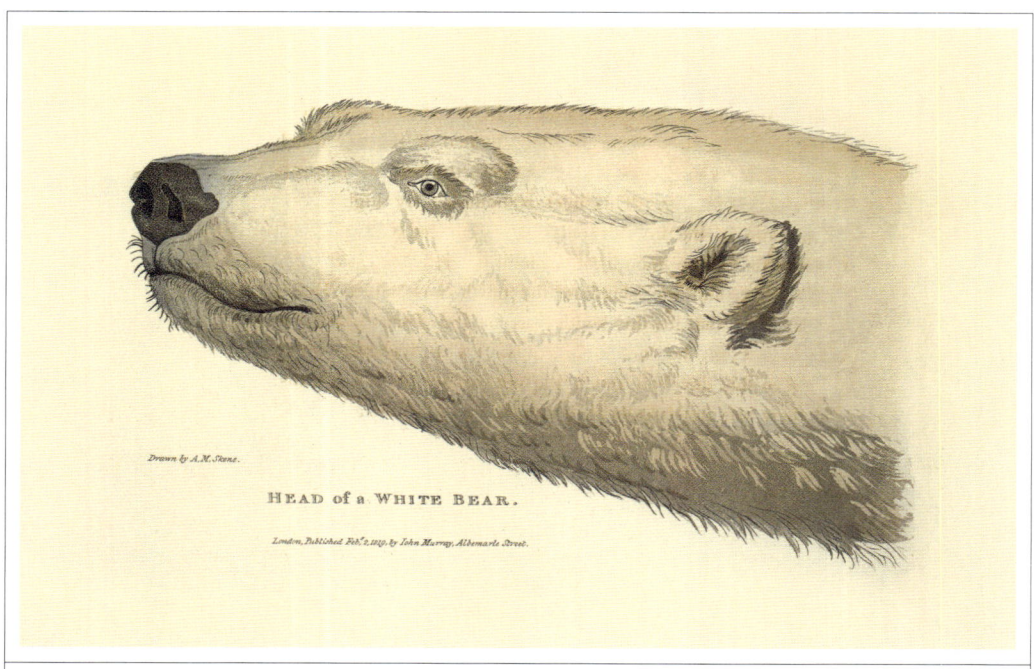

i.

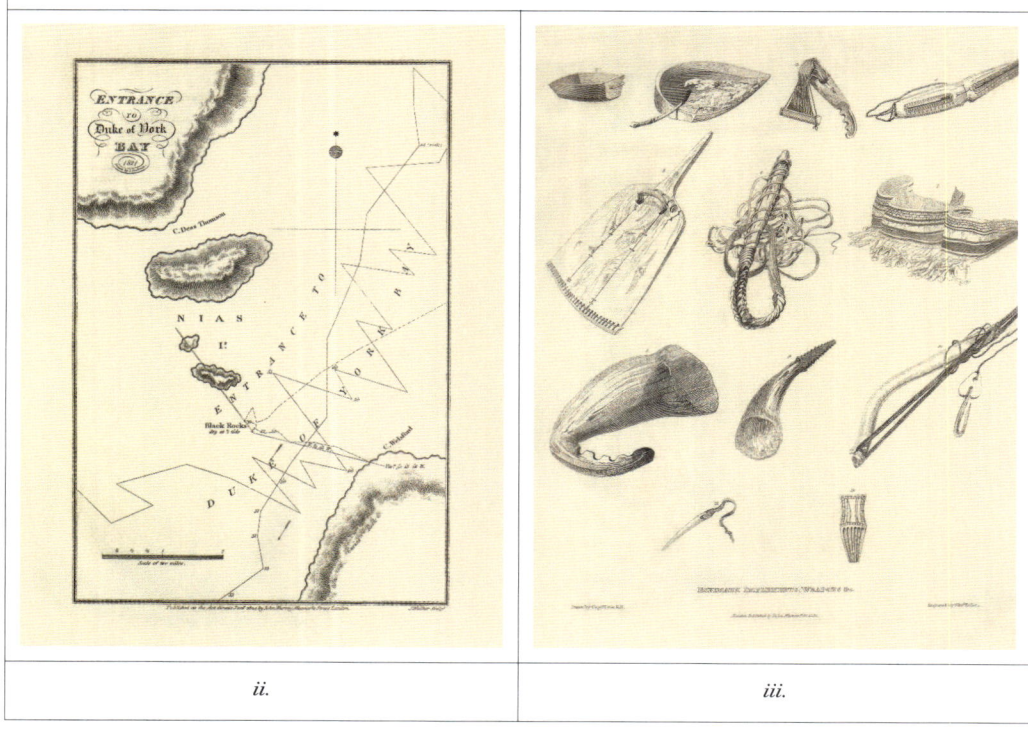

ii.   *iii.*

(i).   'Head of a White Bear', William Edward Parry, *Appendix to Captain Parry's Journal of a Second Voyage for the Discovery of a North-west Passage*, 1825.

(ii–iii).   Pages from William Edward Parry's *Journal of a Second Voyage for the Discovery of a North-west Passage*, entitled 'Entrance to Duke of York Bay' (ii) and 'Eskimaux Instruments, Weapons &c' (iii).

however, he adds personal colour examples or impressions, as in the case of the 'foetal' young of the rough seal: '... a yellowish white colour like raw silk'[13]. For the 'Lapland finch', he uses a feast of browns, including Syme's blackish-brown, yellowish-brown and clove-brown, all to describe the same female individual. He even employs an alternative shade of white for her, which leans towards the brown: rusty-white.[14]

In his account of his second expedition with Franklin (1825–27), published in 1829 and entitled *Fauna boreali-americana*, Richardson again explicitly mentions his use of Syme's colour system.[15] His new approach in incorporating Syme's *Nomenclature* was clearly considered useful by later naturalists: *Fauna boreali-americana* was available in the *Beagle* library, and Darwin noted it in one of his 1838 journals under 'Books to be read'.[16] To Richardson, Syme's book was a field guide of colours, allowing exact identification of little-known animals while on the voyage, as well as when writing accurate and vivid descriptions for a popular and scientific audience. It is no surprise that Charles Darwin, as a novice at voyages of discovery, would find it equally useful.

CHROMATOMETERS AND BUTTERFLIES: ANIMAL COLOURS IN ART AND SCIENCE

As Syme noted in the foreword to the first edition of his *Werner's Nomenclature of Colours* (1814), reliable colour standards were a necessity for taxonomy. Colours were of no use if there was confusion about their individual perception and names. Once this was resolved, 'description, figure, and colour combined form the most perfect representation, and are next to seeing the object itself'. Considering the emphasis on representation – art – as a taxonomic tool for science, it is not surprising that many of the leading attempts to produce a working colour scheme (either for personal or general use) came from natural history artists like Syme, a 'flower-painter' in Edinburgh. There was a long tradition of artists who had grappled with this issue, mainly in the field of botany, such as James Sowerby (1757–1822).

While Sowerby's work focused on botany (see pp. 172–75), he also created the plates for *Zoology of New Holland*, by George Shaw (1751–1813), published in 1794, drawing on the earliest expeditions to Australia, and presenting some of its animals to the public for the very first time. In the description accompanying Sowerby's plate of the aptly named 'Nonpareil parrot', Shaw notes: 'It may indeed be doubted whether any bird can exhibit a plumage more elegant, or colours of a nobler hue. These are so accurately expressed on the plate ... that it becomes unnecessary to particularize them here.'[17] Just as Syme postulated, the colours on the plate were as good as the 'object itself'.

Like other natural history illustrators, Sowerby experimented with developing and using colour schemes. In 1809, he published his *A New Elucidation of Colours*. Instead of providing colour swatches like Syme's, he developed a 'chromatometer', essentially a template to use together with a standard prism, which allowed the spectral colours to be exactly defined by their position on the template. This had the advantage of using 'true' colours for determination, instead of colours represented by pigments – which could vary according to the mix, type of paper, fading etc. However, using the chromatometer and prism was unwieldy and difficult to master – definitely not practical on expeditions or in the field. Therefore, Sowerby also provided a 'chromatic scale' which reproduced and defined 63 colours obtained from mixing three primary colours (yellow, red, blue) in a grid-like structure (and in his list also added five whites).

When considering the colour references for the animal kingdom in Syme's *Nomenclature*, it is interesting to note that around two thirds are to birds, with insects making up much of the remaining third. Mammals are largely ignored, as are fish. Mammals were still mainly classified according to their anatomical morphology (especially bone structure). As for fish, it was not possible for most people to observe live fish at this time, so references to them would not have been very helpful. Birds and insects, however, had always been particularly noted

OOLOGY.

Oology often involves the collecting of eggs, an activity that became popular in the 19th century as a scientific pursuit, but by the 20th century was increasingly regarded as a hobby rather than a scientific discipline. It is now illegal in the UK and restricted in the US. The pages shown below are taken from *British Oology*, 1833, by William Chapman Hewitson (1806–1878). In the book's introduction Hewitson describes his love for nature and the pleasure he derives from egg collecting, before going on to describe the eggs, breeding habits, nest construction and clutch size of over 200 species of birds that bred in Britain.

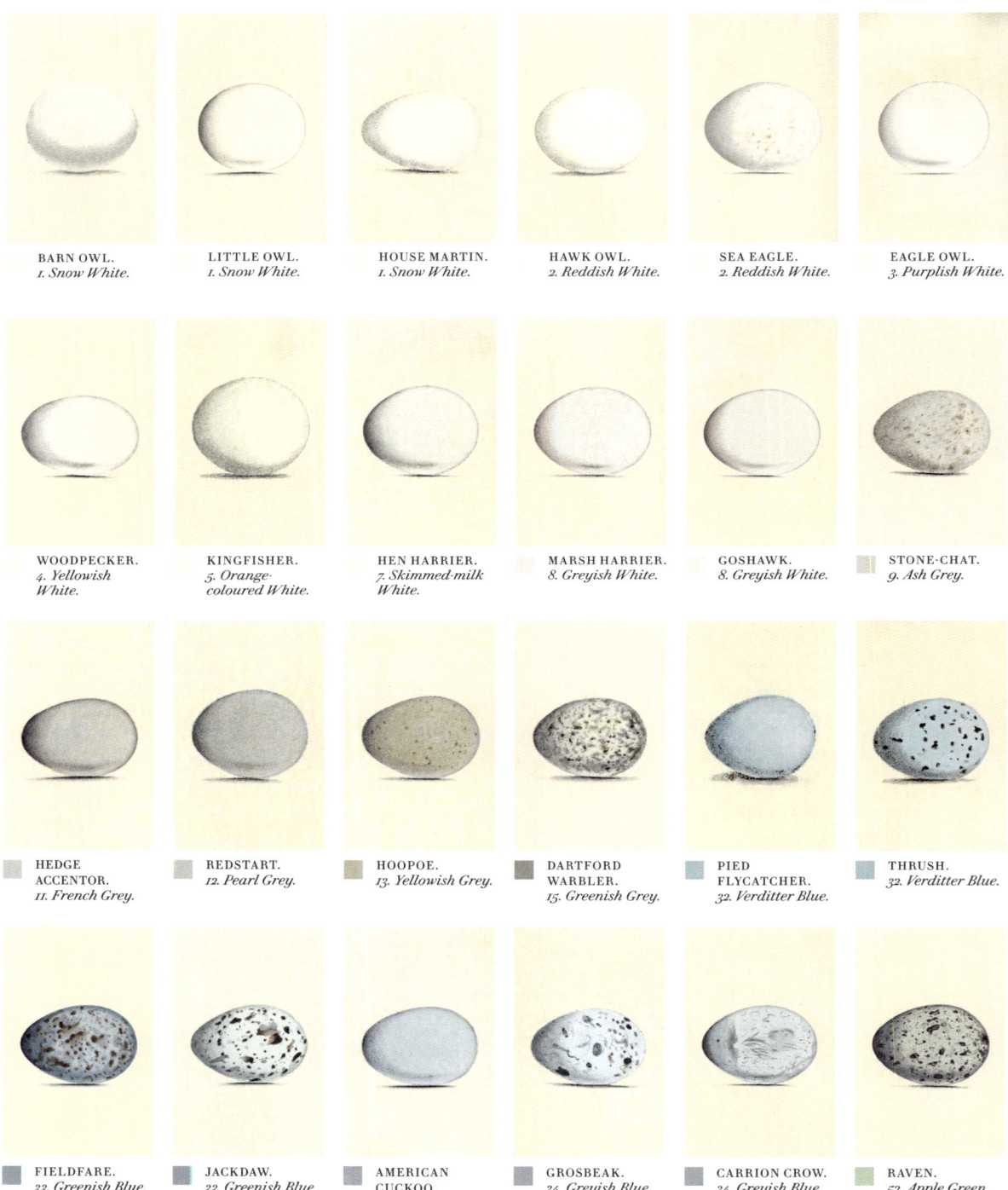

BARN OWL. *1. Snow White.*	**LITTLE OWL.** *1. Snow White.*	**HOUSE MARTIN.** *1. Snow White.*	**HAWK OWL.** *2. Reddish White.*	**SEA EAGLE.** *2. Reddish White.*	**EAGLE OWL.** *3. Purplish White.*
WOODPECKER. *4. Yellowish White.*	**KINGFISHER.** *5. Orange-coloured White.*	**HEN HARRIER.** *7. Skimmed-milk White.*	**MARSH HARRIER.** *8. Greyish White.*	**GOSHAWK.** *8. Greyish White.*	**STONE-CHAT.** *9. Ash Grey.*
HEDGE ACCENTOR. *11. French Grey.*	**REDSTART.** *12. Pearl Grey.*	**HOOPOE.** *13. Yellowish Grey.*	**DARTFORD WARBLER.** *15. Greenish Grey.*	**PIED FLYCATCHER.** *32. Verditter Blue.*	**THRUSH.** *32. Verditter Blue.*
FIELDFARE. *33. Greenish Blue.*	**JACKDAW.** *33. Greenish Blue.*	**AMERICAN CUCKOO.** *34. Greyish Blue.*	**GROSBEAK.** *34. Greyish Blue.*	**CARRION CROW.** *34. Greyish Blue.*	**RAVEN.** *52. Apple Green.*

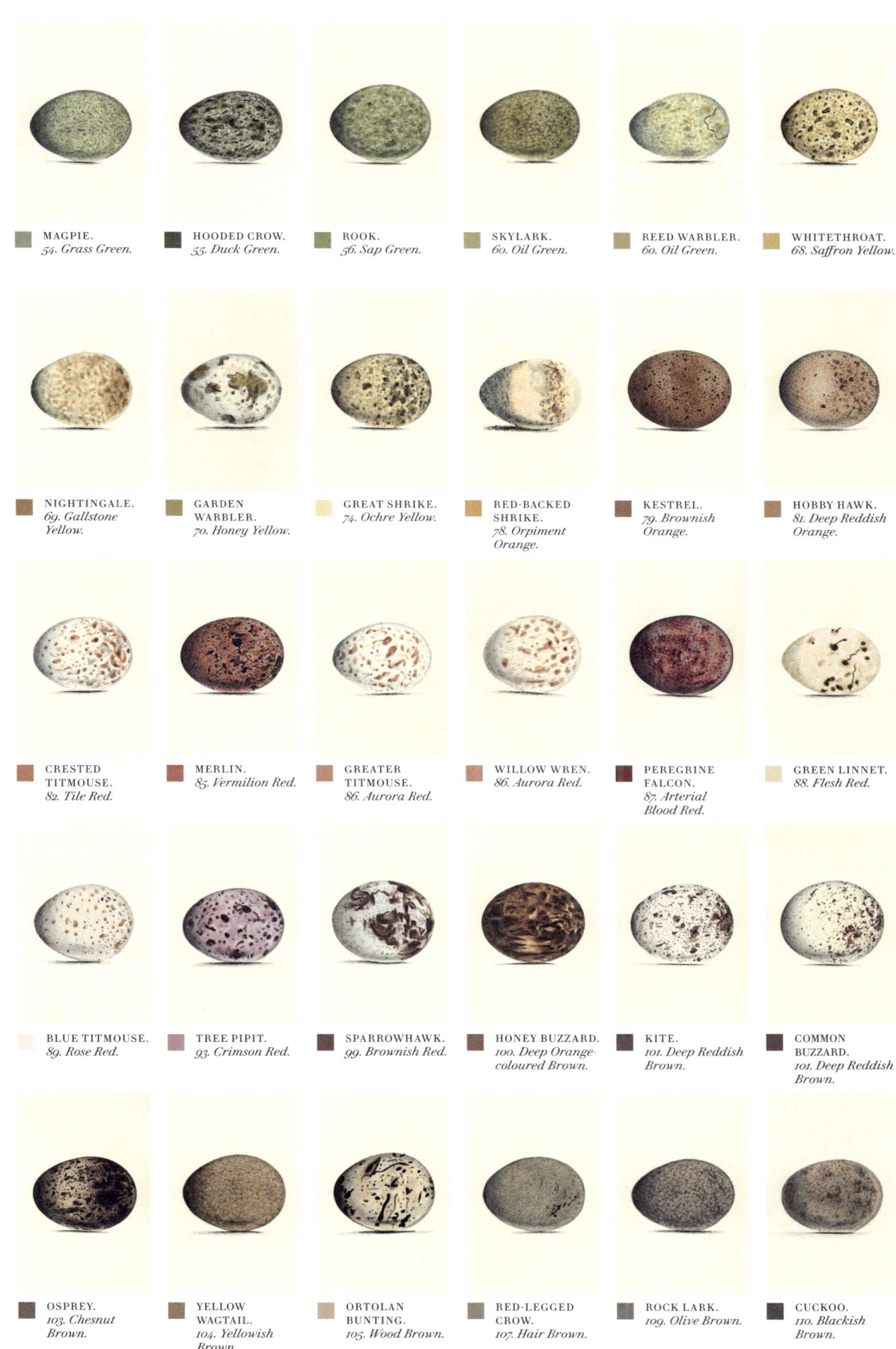

MAGPIE.
54. Grass Green.

HOODED CROW.
55. Duck Green.

ROOK.
56. Sap Green.

SKYLARK.
60. Oil Green.

REED WARBLER.
60. Oil Green.

WHITETHROAT.
68. Saffron Yellow.

NIGHTINGALE.
69. Gallstone Yellow.

GARDEN WARBLER.
70. Honey Yellow.

GREAT SHRIKE.
74. Ochre Yellow.

RED-BACKED SHRIKE.
78. Orpiment Orange.

KESTREL.
79. Brownish Orange.

HOBBY HAWK.
81. Deep Reddish Orange.

CRESTED TITMOUSE.
82. Tile Red.

MERLIN.
85. Vermilion Red.

GREATER TITMOUSE.
86. Aurora Red.

WILLOW WREN.
86. Aurora Red.

PEREGRINE FALCON.
87. Arterial Blood Red.

GREEN LINNET.
88. Flesh Red.

BLUE TITMOUSE.
89. Rose Red.

TREE PIPIT.
93. Crimson Red.

SPARROWHAWK.
99. Brownish Red.

HONEY BUZZARD.
100. Deep Orange-coloured Brown.

KITE.
101. Deep Reddish Brown.

COMMON BUZZARD.
101. Deep Reddish Brown.

OSPREY.
103. Chesnut Brown.

YELLOW WAGTAIL.
104. Yellowish Brown.

ORTOLAN BUNTING.
105. Wood Brown.

RED-LEGGED CROW.
107. Hair Brown.

ROCK LARK.
109. Olive Brown.

CUCKOO.
110. Blackish Brown.

for their colours, which were extensively used in their identification and description. This, in turn, obliged the artists to determine colours as accurately and systematically as the taxonomists who classified the animal. It is hardly surprising, therefore, that taxonomists of birds or insects in particular might also become colour taxonomists – and vice versa.

Moses Harris (1730–*c.* 1788) was a pioneer in that respect. Both an entomologist and artist specializing in engravings, he attempted to identify and classify colours as much as he focused on describing and classifying insects. In his *An Exposition of English Insects* (published in London in 1776), he proposed a 'Scheme of colours', treating colours almost like his living subjects. Acknowledging that the terms he used for colours and 'teints' were 'little known but to painters', he therefore provided a colour wheel. Its practical use was to clarify the terms he used to an audience unfamiliar with painting, and, just as Syme would later emphasize, to 'enable the reader to judge of the variety of teints that adorn the several parts of the insect'.[18] Here, already, ways of seeing had become ways of knowing, of being able to identify.

In another book, *The English Lepidoptera* (1775), Harris added an illustration showing a system for colour-coding the anatomical parts of a butterfly on a schematic drawing, particularly the many complicated wing 'membranes' and 'tendons', which he regarded as essential for the identification of different species. Colour-coding anatomical parts for identification and, especially, teaching, was a method used to great effect in the later part of the 19th century and first half of the 20th century in zoological publications, wall-charts and models, and is still widely used in scientific illustrations and digital 3D models today.

COLOUR SYSTEMATICS

As the natural sciences became increasingly 'professionalized' through the course of the 19th century, and with technical innovations and the flood of new species being discovered, taxonomy – of both animals and colours – became increasingly sophisticated. In the first half of the century schemes like Syme's had facilitated a multitude of new discoveries and their classification, but by the end of the century and in the early 20th century, an updated approach was needed.

These developments took shape in the work of the American ornithologist Robert Ridgway (1850–1929), whose career spanned this period. He published two major works on using colour systematics for the classification of birds. In his 1886 *A Nomenclature of Colors for Naturalists and Compendium of Useful Knowledge for Ornithologists* he proposed a new colour system (comprising 186 samples of named colours) and a colour dictionary (with colour terms in English, Latin, German, French, Spanish, Italian, Norwegian/Danish), which were integrated into a simple overall system for bird identification. Just like Syme, he saw the necessity of defining standards for colour terminology, and just like Syme's nomenclature, his system was prompted by a 'want' felt by ornithologists working in the field. As Ridgway realized:

Undoubtedly one of the chief *desiderata* of naturalists, both professional and amateur, is a means of identifying the various shades of colors named in descriptions, and of being able to determine exactly what name to apply to a particular tint which is desired to designate in an original description.[19]

He deplored the lack of modern publications of this kind, and mentioned Syme's 1821 edition as being the most recent he had been able to consult. While acknowledging its usefulness, he also summarized some of its major shortcomings: 'the colors have become so modified by time, that in very few cases do they correspond with the tints they were intended to represent'.[20] It had occurred to Ridgway, however, to use the commercially produced 'artists' colors' of his time (among them aniline dyes and pigments), with their much improved 'fixity'. He also tackled the 'arbitrariness' of tints and shades named after a familiar object, like

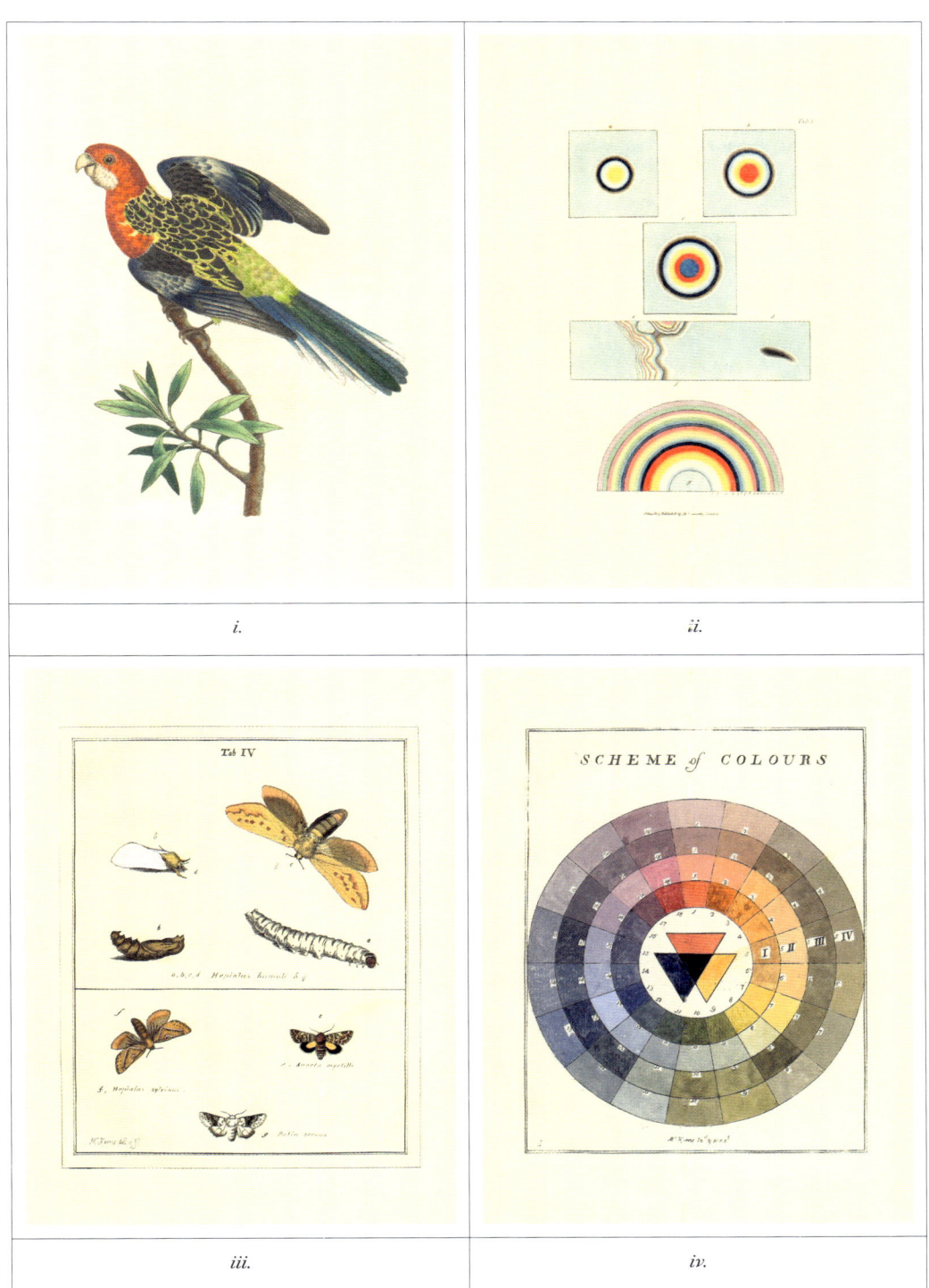

(i).   Eastern rosella parrot, George Shaw, *Zoology of New Holland*, Vol. 1, 1794.
(ii).   Plate 1, James Sowerby, *A New Elucidation of Colours, Original Prismatic, and Material*, 1809.
(iii).   Varieties of moth, Moses Harris, *An Exposition of English Insects*, 1776.
(iv).   Scheme of colours, Moses Harris, *An Exposition of English Insects*, 1776.

Shells collected on HMS *Endeavour*, 1768–71. *The shells featured in this tray were collected from the beaches of Brazil, Tahiti, New Zealand and Australia during Captain Cook's first expedition around the world. Sir Joseph Banks was the voyage's official botanist.*

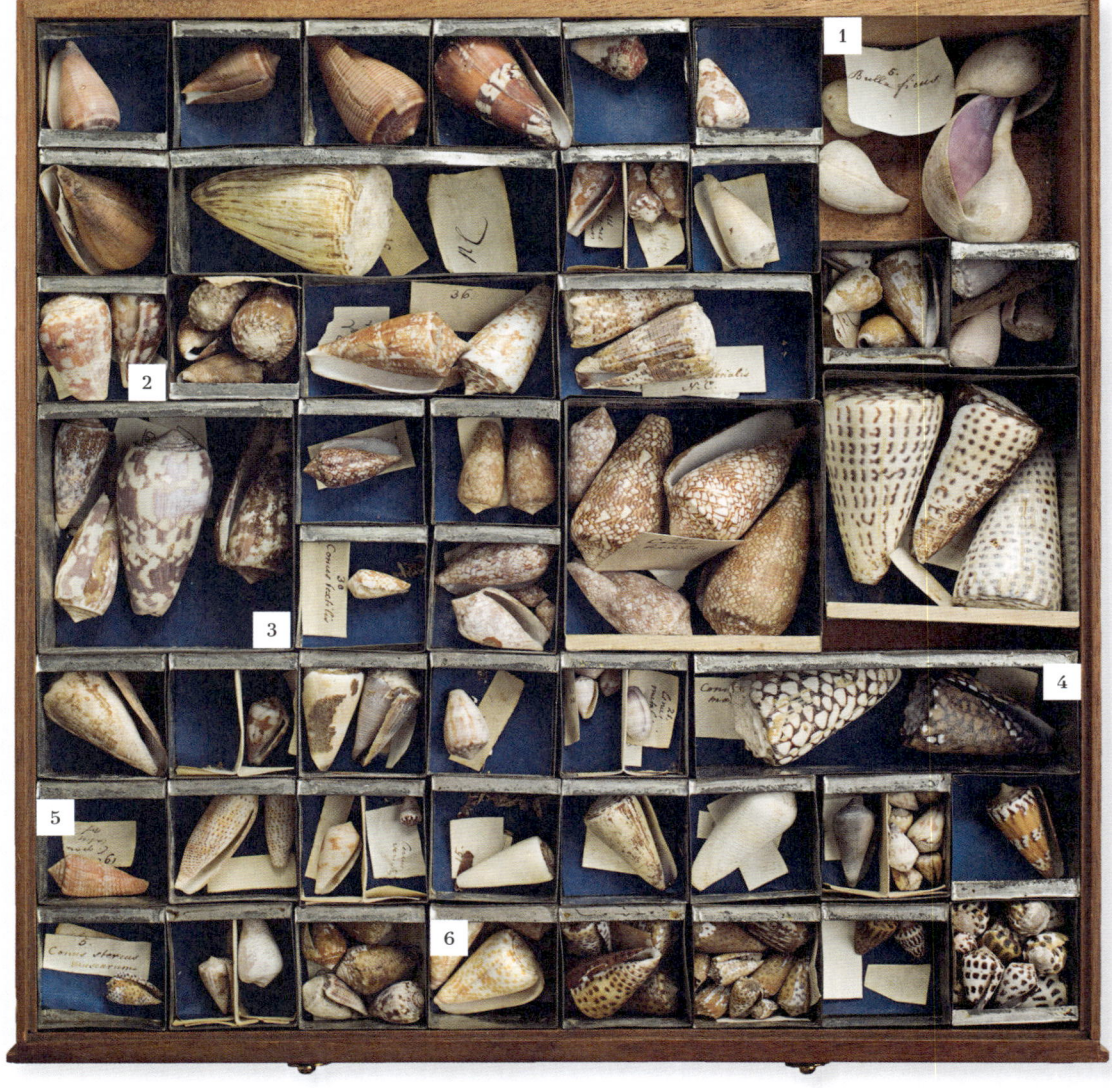

1		FICUS FICUS.	2		CONUS ERMINEUS.	3		CONUS STRIATUS.
		93. Crimson Red.			*82. Tile Red.*			*43. Red Lilac Purple.*
4		CONUS MARMOREUS.	5		CONUS GRANULATUS.	6		CONUS TESSULATUS.
		104. Yellowish Brown.			*86. Aurora Red.*			*5. Orange-coloured White.*

CHARLES DARWIN'S SHELLS.

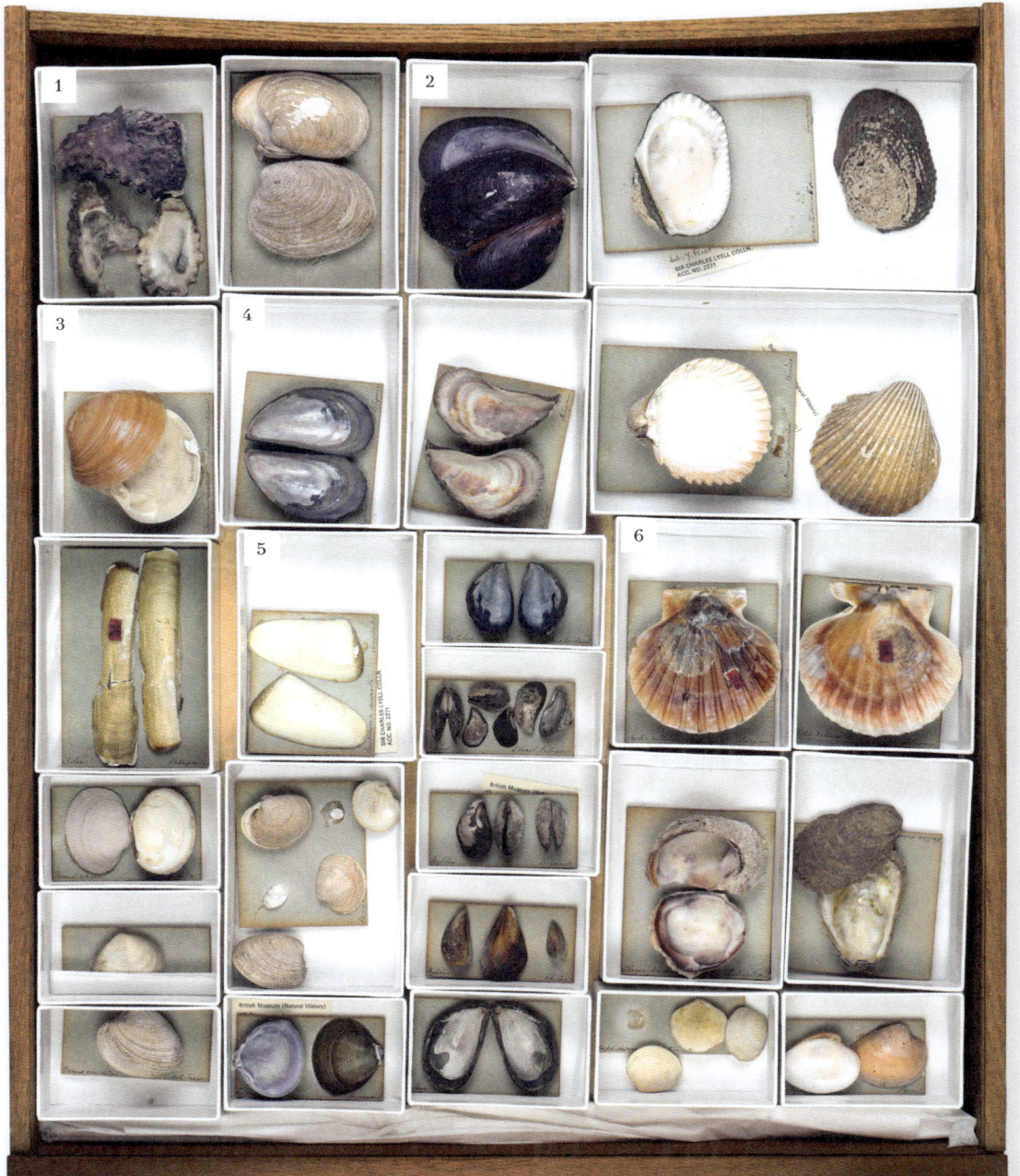

Shells collected on HMS *Beagle*, 1831–36. *The shells in this drawer were collected by Charles Darwin from various localities during the voyage of HMS* Beagle *around South America. The expedition provided Darwin with his first real training in natural history.*

1	SACCOSTREA CUCULLATA.	2	MYTILUS SP.	3	EUCALLISTA PURPURATA.
	40. *Imperial Purple.*		24. *Scotch Blue.*		80. *Reddish Orange.*
4	MYTILUS SP.	5	MESODESMA DONACIUM.	6	PECTEN SP.
	36. *Bluish Purple.*		7. *Skimmed-milk White.*		83. *Hyacinth Red.*

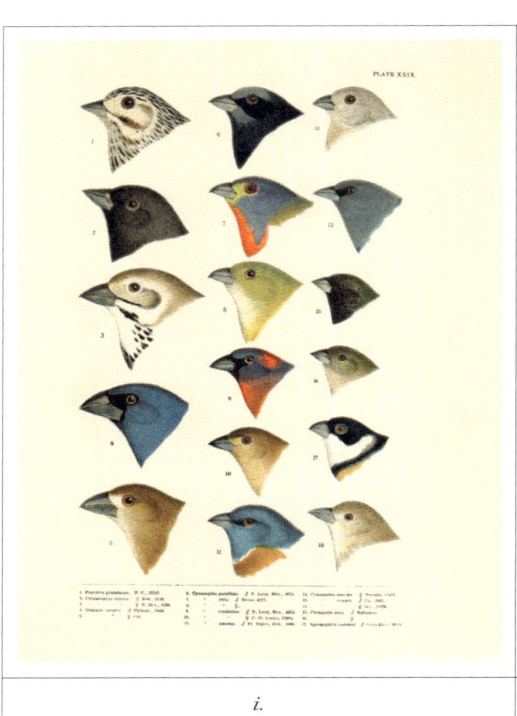

i.

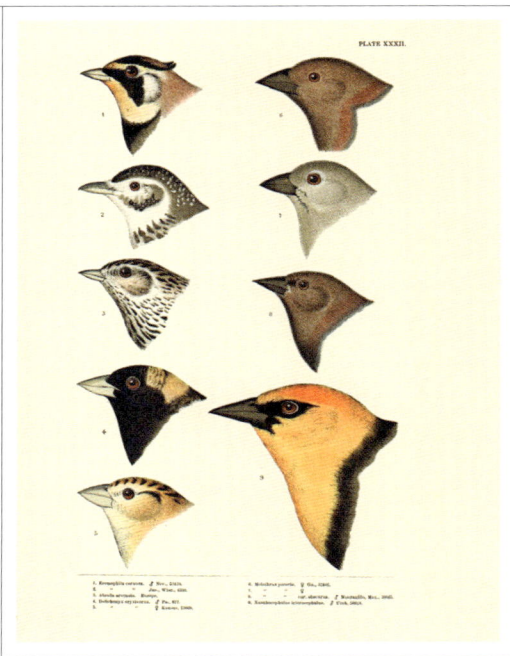

ii.

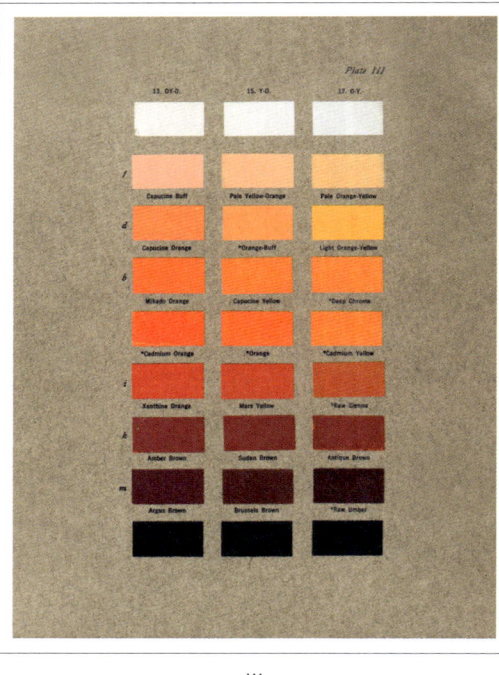

iii.

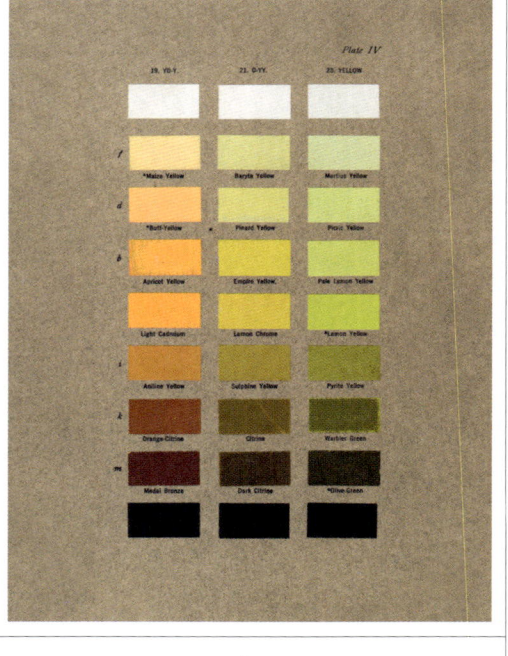

iv.

(i). Varieties of finch, Spencer Fullerton Baird, Thomas Mayo Brewer and Robert Ridgway,
      A History of North American Birds, Vol. 1, 1905.

(ii). Varieties of lark, Spencer Fullerton Baird, Thomas Mayo Brewer and Robert Ridgway,
      A History of North American Birds, Vol. 1, 1905.

(iii–iv). Colour charts, Robert Ridgway, *Color Standards and Color Nomenclature*, 1912.

the ones used by Syme (such as 'hair-brown, ash-color, lilac, etc.'), noting that this 'varies so much in color that the name without ... fixed standard would be practically valueless'.

Ridgway's work on colour systematics led him to pioneer the modern field-guide concept in his *A History of North American Birds* (1905). The visual effectiveness of a precise use of colours can be seen especially in the striking plates, in which the heads of easily confused species of birds are depicted almost like comparative colour swatches, making a first-glance comparison and identification quick and easy, especially for amateur bird-watchers in the field.

The importance Ridgway placed on colour systematics is demonstrated by his return to it towards the end of his career with his *Color Standards and Color Nomenclature* in 1912. Here, he developed his earlier system, criticizing his own shortcomings as much as he had once criticized Syme's – those in his case being an inadequate number of colours and their 'unscientific' arrangement. Through its scope and enhanced 'objectivity', his new work could not only be applied in ornithology, but, like Syme's *Nomenclature*, would also be 'for the use of the zoologist, the botanist, the pathologist, or the mineralogist'.[21] It is still regarded as a standard reference across the arts and sciences. Ridgway's colour analysis utilizes the actual solar spectrum, precisely determining colour, hue, tint, shade, tone, scale, and providing well over a thousand colour swatches on 53 plates, foreshadowing the Pantone charts of today.

Ridgway also turned his considerable taxonomic faculties to the results of a return to that most emblematic of locations of a voyage of discovery – the Galapagos Islands, the famed destination of the voyage of the *Beagle*, and in particular to 'Darwin's finches'. From specimens collected by an expedition of the US Fish Commission Steamer *Albatross* in 1888, Ridgway became the first to describe the Española cactus finch (*Geospiza conirostris*). With a precision similar to Richardson's description of the far north Lapland finch, Ridgway deftly characterizes the female finch, which a more casual observer might consider particularly hard to identify and distinguish:

> Above dull sooty; anterior lower parts similar, but indistinctly streaked with pale grayish buffy, this gradually increasing posteriorly until it becomes the prevailing colour and the sooty reduced to broad streaks.[22]

This was a 'serious' colour description for the first official zoological record of an individual from one of the most noted groups of animals in science – still considered 'living proofs' of Darwin's theories of natural selection and adaptation today.

From Darwin's use of colours and Syme's *Nomenclature*, throughout the 19th and early 20th centuries, zoologists and zoological artists continued to draw on earlier sources, constantly applying and perfecting them in line with their needs for identification and description in the field, and for classification and taxonomy. Such colour schemes evolved as zoology, systematics and the sciences in general changed, but also in tandem with artistic, technological and societal developments (such as an increasing number of amateur ornithologists), and therefore also reflect much wider changes in the natural sciences, as well as in art and in society.

NOTES – (1). Lyon 1976, p. 140. (2). Buffon 1770, pp. viii–ix. (3). Jones 2013, pp. 88–89. (4). Darwin Correspondence Project, Letter no. 178. (5). Keynes 2000, p. 9. (6). Barlow 1967, p. 41. (7). Keynes 2000, p. 10. (8). Rutherford 1908, p. X. (9). Keynes 2000, p. 211. (10). Darwin Correspondence Project, 'Letter no. 2743'. (11). Parry 1825, p. 287. (12). Parry 1825, p. 294. (13). Parry 1825, p. 333. (14). Parry 1825, p. 346. (15). Richardson 1829–37, Vol. I, p. xxxv. (16). Darwin, C. R. 'Books to be read' and 'Books Read' notebook (1838–51), CUL-DAR119. Transcribed by Kees Rookmaaker. Darwin Online. P. iv [2r]. (17). Shaw 1794, Vol. I, p. 3. (18). Harris 1776, p. iv. (19). Ridgway 1886, p. 9. (20). Ridgway 1886, p. 10. (21). Ridgway 1912, Preface, p. i. (22). Ridgway 1890, p. 106.

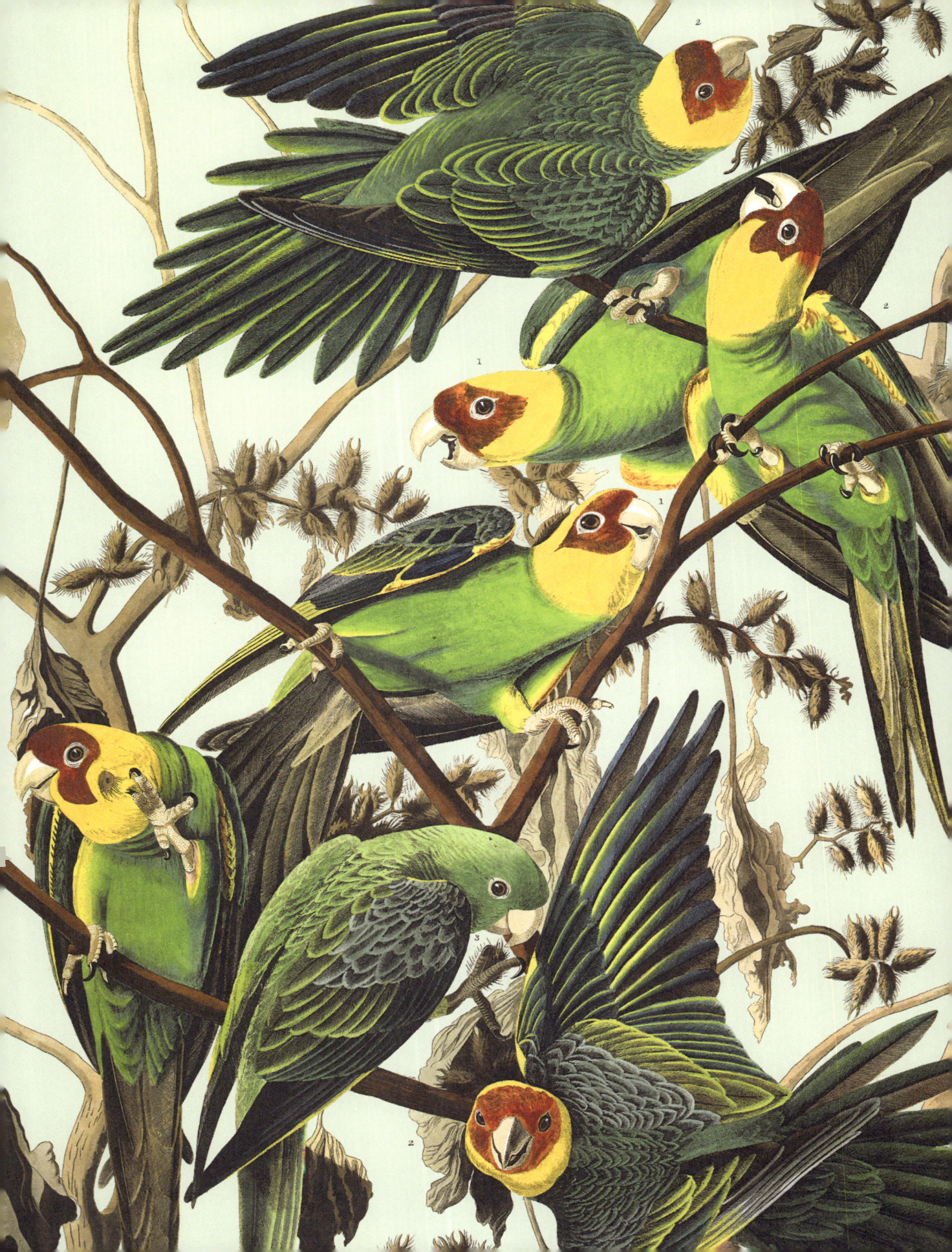

iii.

GREENS.

GREENS.

N°.	Names	Colours	ANIMAL	VEGITABLE	MINERAL
46	Celandine Green.		Phalæna Margaritaria.	Back of Tussilage Leaves.	Beryl.
47	Moun-tain Green.		Phalæna Viridaria.	Thick-leaved Cudweed, Silver-leaved Almond.	Actynolite Beryl.
48	Leek Green.			Sea Kale. Leaves of Leeks in Winter.	Actynolite Prase.
49	Blackish Green.		Elytra of Meloe Violaceus.	Dark Streaks on Leaves of Cayenne Pepper.	Serpentine.
50	Verdigris Green.		Tail of small Long-tailed Green Parrot.		Copper Green.
51	Bluish Green.		Egg of Thrush.	Under Disk of Wild Rose Leaves.	Beryl.
52	Apple Green.		Under Side of Wings of Green Broom Moth.		Crysoprase.
53	Emerald Green.		Beauty Spot on Wing of Teal Drake.		Emerald.

GREENS.

No.	Names	Colours	ANIMAL.	VEGETABLE.	MINERAL.
54	Grass Green		Scarabæus Nobilis.	General Appearance of Grass Fields. Sweet Sugar Pear	Uran Mica.
55	Duck Green		Neck of Mallard	Upper Disk of Yew Leaves.	Ceylanite
56	Sap Green.		Under Side of lower Wings of Orange tip Butterfly.	Upper Disk of Leaves of woolly Night Shade.	
57	Pistachio Green.		Neck of Eider Drake	Ripe Pound Pear. Hypnum like Saxifrage.	Crysolite.
58	Asparagus Green.		Brimstone Butterfly.	Variegated Horse-Shoe Geranium.	Beryl.
59	Olive Green.			Foliage of Lignum vitæ.	Epidote Olvene Ore.
60	Oil Green.		Animal and Shell of common Water Snail.	Nonpareil Apple from the Wall.	Beryl
61	Siskin Green.		Siskin.	Ripe Coalmar Pear. Irish Pitcher Apple.	Uran Mica.

No.	Names.	Colours.	ANIMAL.		
46	Celandine Green.		Phalaena Margaritaria.		
47	Mountain Green.		Phalaena Viridaria.		
48	Leek Green.				
49	Blackish Green.		Elytra of Meloe Violaceus.		
50	Verdigris Green.		Tail of small Long-tailed Green Parrot.		
51	Bluish Green.		Egg of Thrush.		
52	Apple Green.		Under Side of Wings of Green Broom Moth.		
53	Emerald Green.		Beauty Spot on Wing of Teal Drake.		

The first chart of greens in Syme's 1821 edition included four of Werner's original greens (numbers 47, 48, 50, 52), three greens from the Picardet system (numbers 46, 49 and 53) and one green from the Lenz system (number 51).

GREENS (i).

VEGETABLE.		MINERAL.	
Back of Tussilago Leaves.		Beryl.	
Thick leaved Cudweed, Silver-leaved Almond.		Actynolite Beryl.	
Sea Kale, Leaves of Leeks in Winter.		Actynolite Prase.	
Dark Streaks on Leaves of Cayenne Pepper.		Serpentine.	
		Copper Green.	
Under Disk of Wild Rose Leaves.		Beryl.	
		Crysoprase.	
		Emerald.	

(i).   *Phalaena Margaritaria*. [Glyphodes margaritaria]
(ii).   *Back of Tussilago Leaves*. [*Coltsfoot*; Tussilago farfara]
(iii).   *Beryl*. [*Silicate mineral*]

Celandine Green, is composed of verdigris green and ash grey. [W]

ANIMAL.

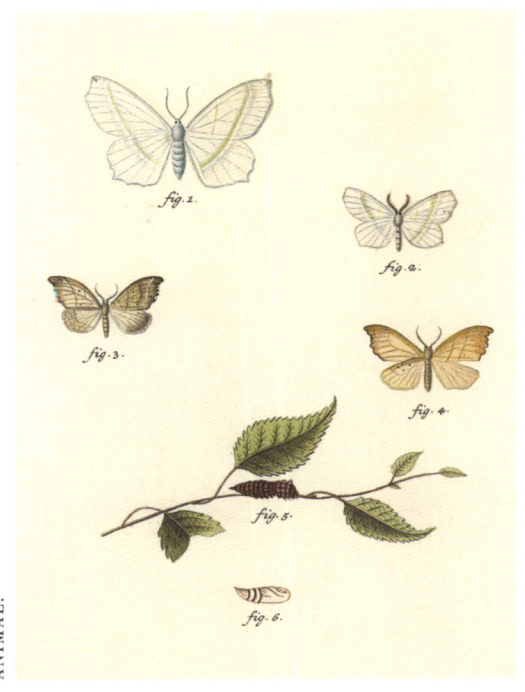

VEGETABLE.

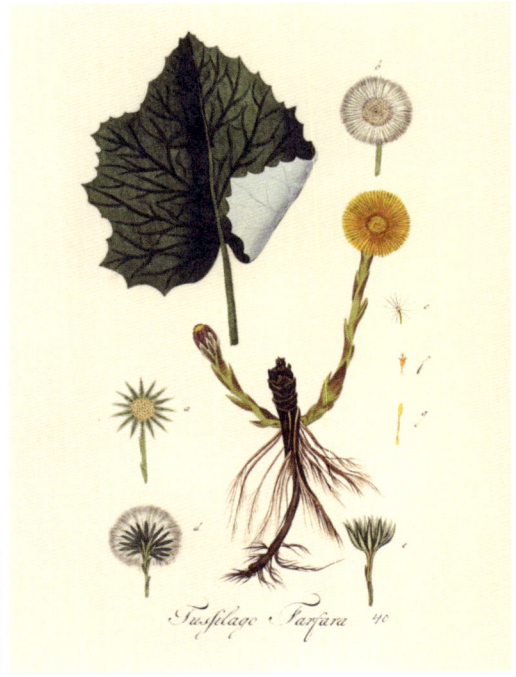

Tussilago Farfara 40.

ANIMAL.
Eugenius Johann
Christoph Esper,
*Die Schmetterlinge
in Abbildungen
nach der Natur*, 1786.
Celandine Green is
visible on the wings
of the *Glyphodes
margaritaria* (top row).

VEGETABLE.
Tussilago farfara,
watercolour, date
unknown.
Celandine Green
is visible on the
reverse of the leaves
of the coltsfoot.

MINERAL.
*Precious stones
selection*,
illustration, 1898.
Celandine Green is
visible on the beryl
(second row, second
from left). It is
embedded within
white topaz.

MINERAL.

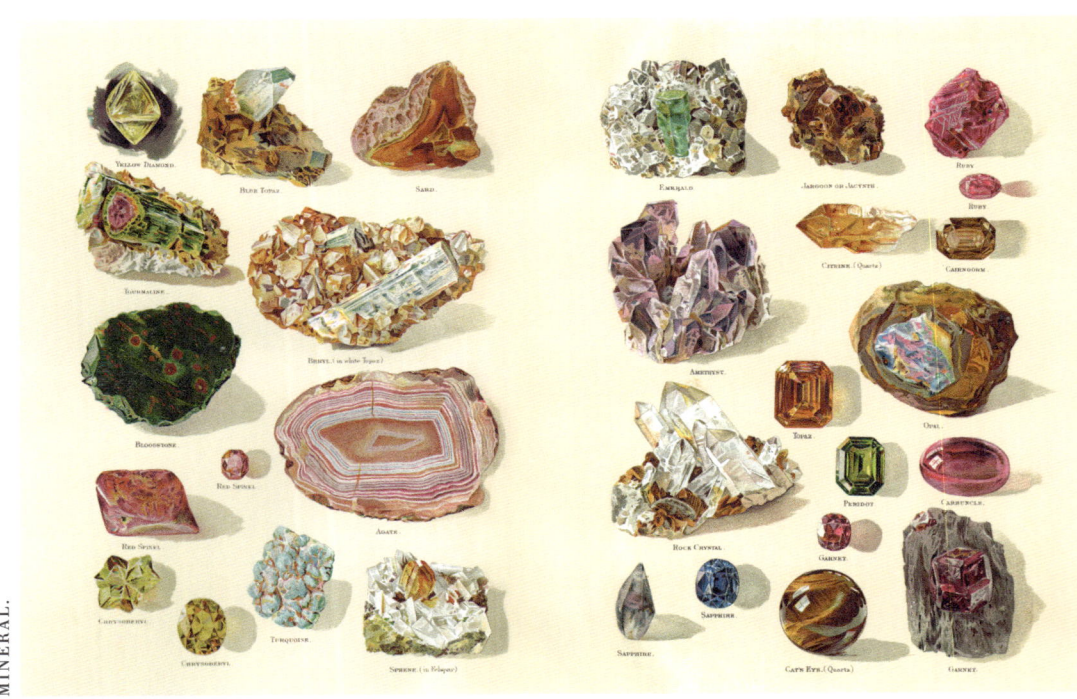

47. MOUNTAIN GREEN.

(i). *Phalaena Viridaria.* [Phalaena viridaria]
(ii). *Thick-leaved Cudweed.* [Gnaphalium]
       Silver-leaved Almond. [Prunus dulcis]
(iii). *Actynolite.* [*Actinolite; Silicate mineral*]
       Beryl. [*Silicate mineral*]

Mountain Green, is composed of emerald green, with much blue and a little yellowish grey. [W]

ANIMAL.

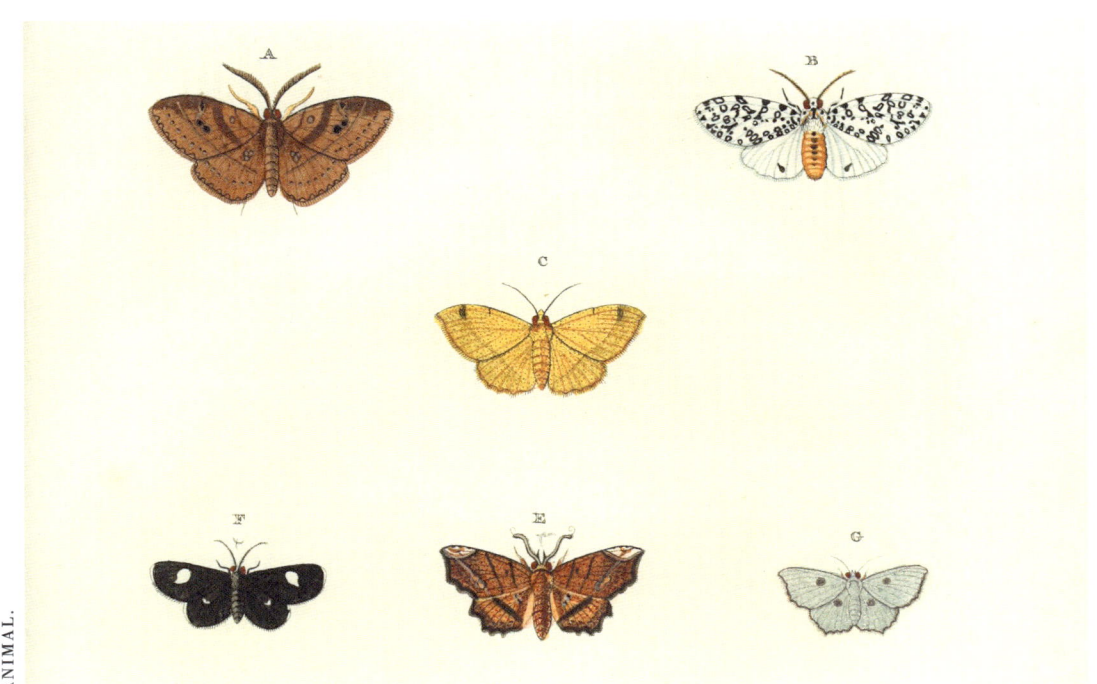

VEGETABLE.

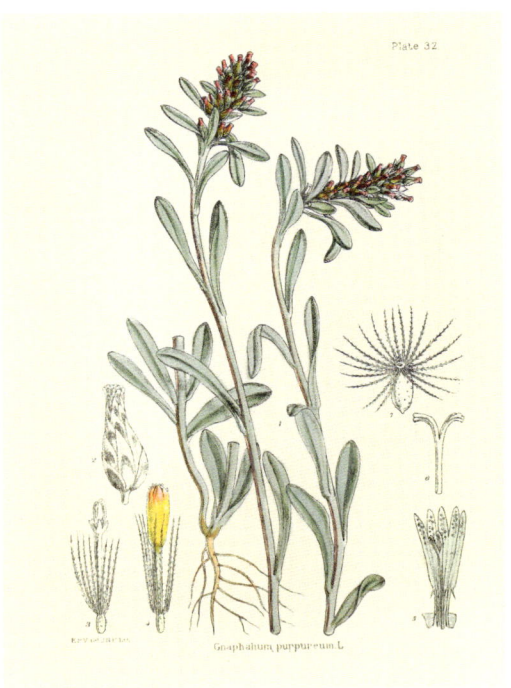

MINERAL.

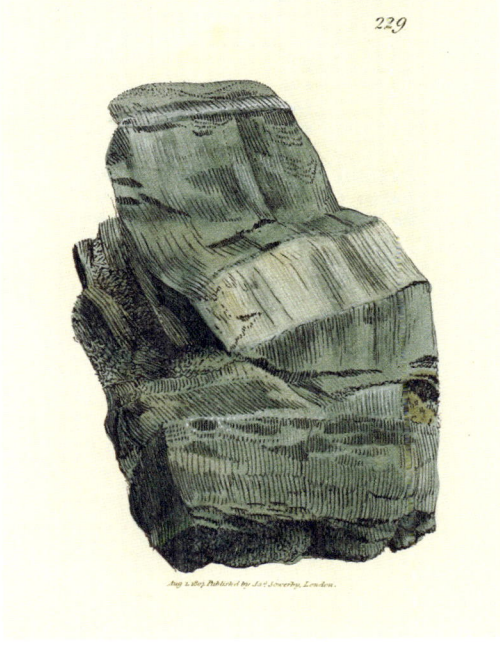

ANIMAL.
Pieter Cramer and Caspar Stoll, *De Uitlandsche Kapellen*, Vol. 4, 1782. Mountain Green is visible on the wings of the *Phalaena viridaria* (bottom row, right).

VEGETABLE.
E. F. Vallentin-Bertrand and E. M. Cotton, *Illustrations of the Flowering Plants and Ferns of the Falklands Islands*, 1921. Mountain Green is visible on the leaves of the cudweed.

MINERAL.
James Sowerby, *British Mineralogy*, Vol. 3, 1802–17. Mountain Green is visible on the actinolite.

48. LEEK GREEN.

(i). ————————
(ii). *Sea Kale.* [Crambe maritima]
Leaves of Leeks in Winter. [Allium porrum]
(iii). *Actynolite.* [*Actinolite; Silicate mineral*] *Prase.* [*Silica*]

Leek Green, is composed of emerald green, with a little brown and bluish grey. [W]

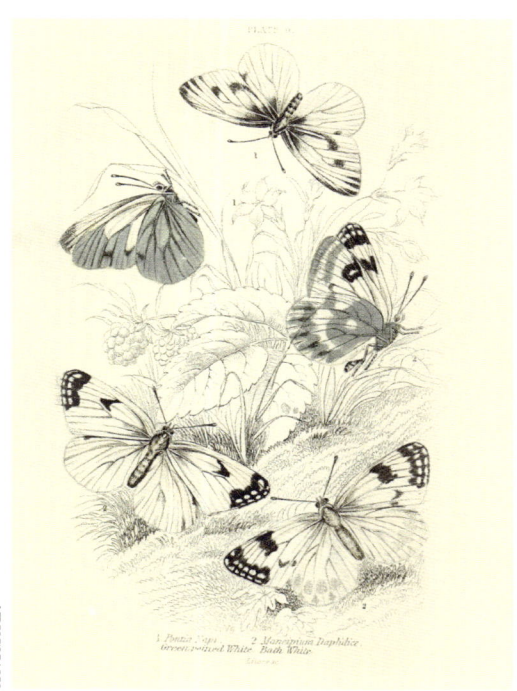

ANIMAL.

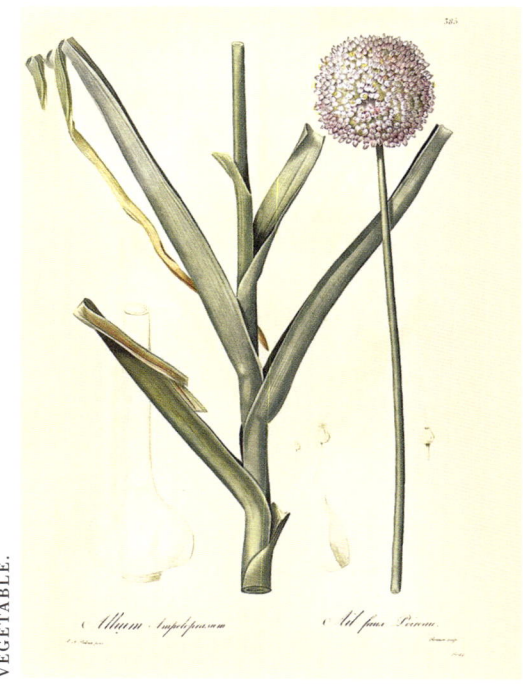

VEGETABLE.

Allium Ampelprasum *Ail faux Poireau*

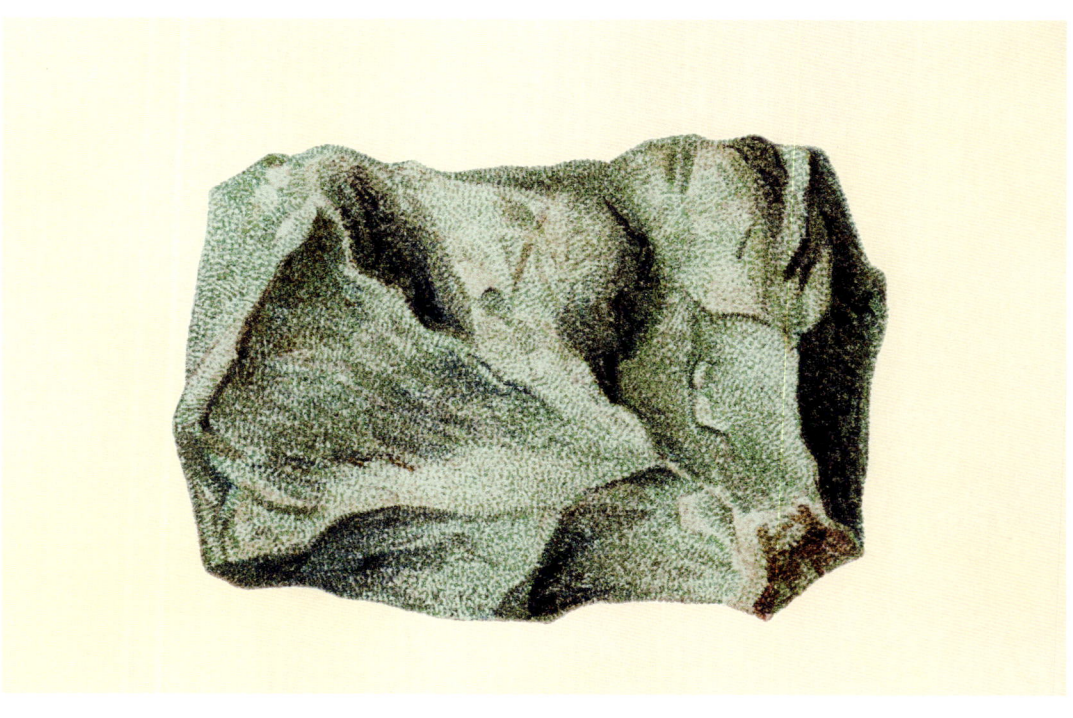

MINERAL.

ANIMAL.
James Duncan,
British Butterflies, 1840.
Leek Green is visible
on the underwings of
the green-veined white
butterfly (centre).*

VEGETABLE.
Pierre-Joseph Redouté,
Les Liliacées, 1805.
Leek Green is visible
on the leaves of the leek.

MINERAL.
Natural chyroprase,
illustration, date
unknown.
Leek Green is
visible on the prase.

49. BLACKISH GREEN.

(i).   *Elytra of Meloe Violaceus.* [*Violet oil beetle*; Meloe violaceus]
(ii).   *Dark Streaks on Leaves of Cayenne Pepper.* [Capsicum annuum]
(iii).   *Serpentine.* [*Silicate mineral*]

Blackish Green, is grass green mixed with a considerable portion of black. [W]

ANIMAL.

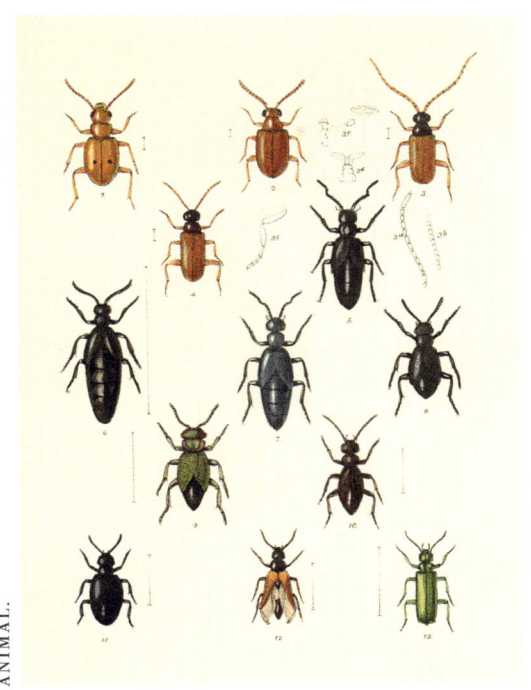

VEGETABLE.

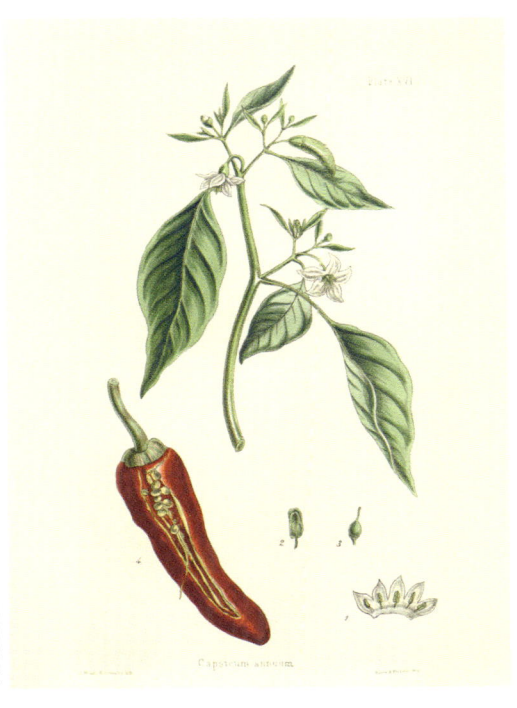

MINERAL.

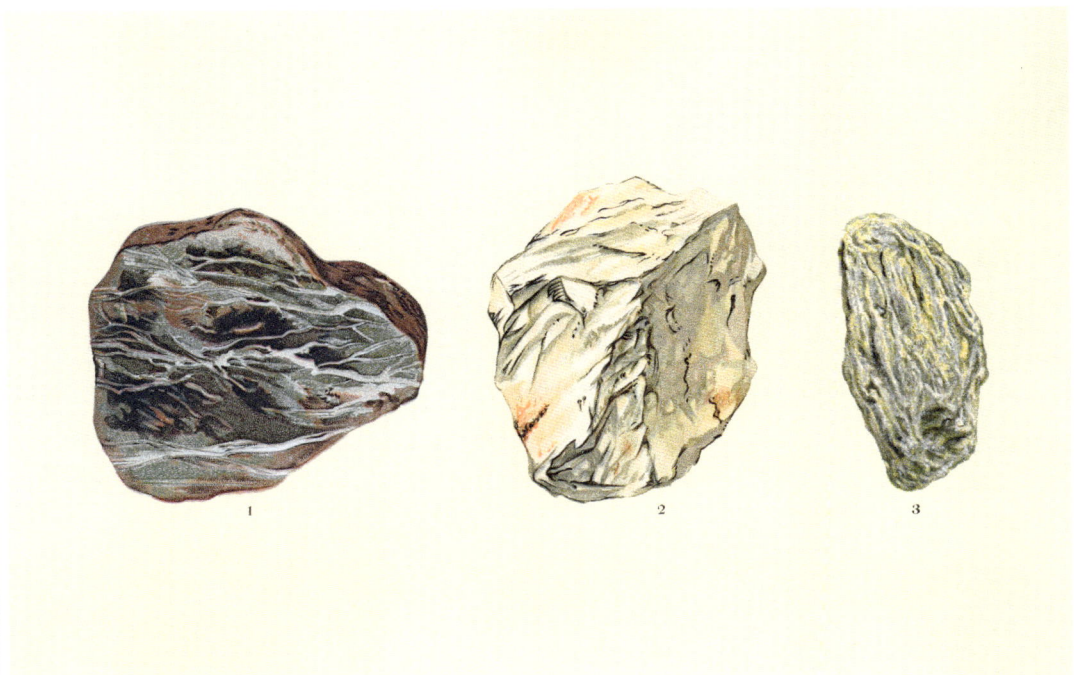

ANIMAL.
W. W. Fowler,
The Coleoptera of the British Islands, Vol. 5, 1891.
Blackish Green is visible on the back of the violet oil beetle (third row, centre).

VEGETABLE.
Edward Hamilton,
The Flora Homoeopathica, 1852.
Blackish Green is visible on the dark streaks on the leaves of the cayenne pepper.

MINERAL.
Leonard Spencer,
The World's Minerals, 1916.
Blackish Green is visible on the serpentine (left).

50. VERDIGRIS GREEN.

(i).   *Tail of small Long-tailed Green Parrot.*
         [*Long-tailed parakeeet*; Psittacula longicauda]
(ii).   ——————
(iii).   *Copper Green.* [*Metal*]

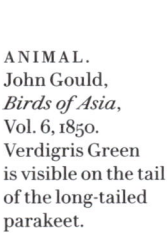

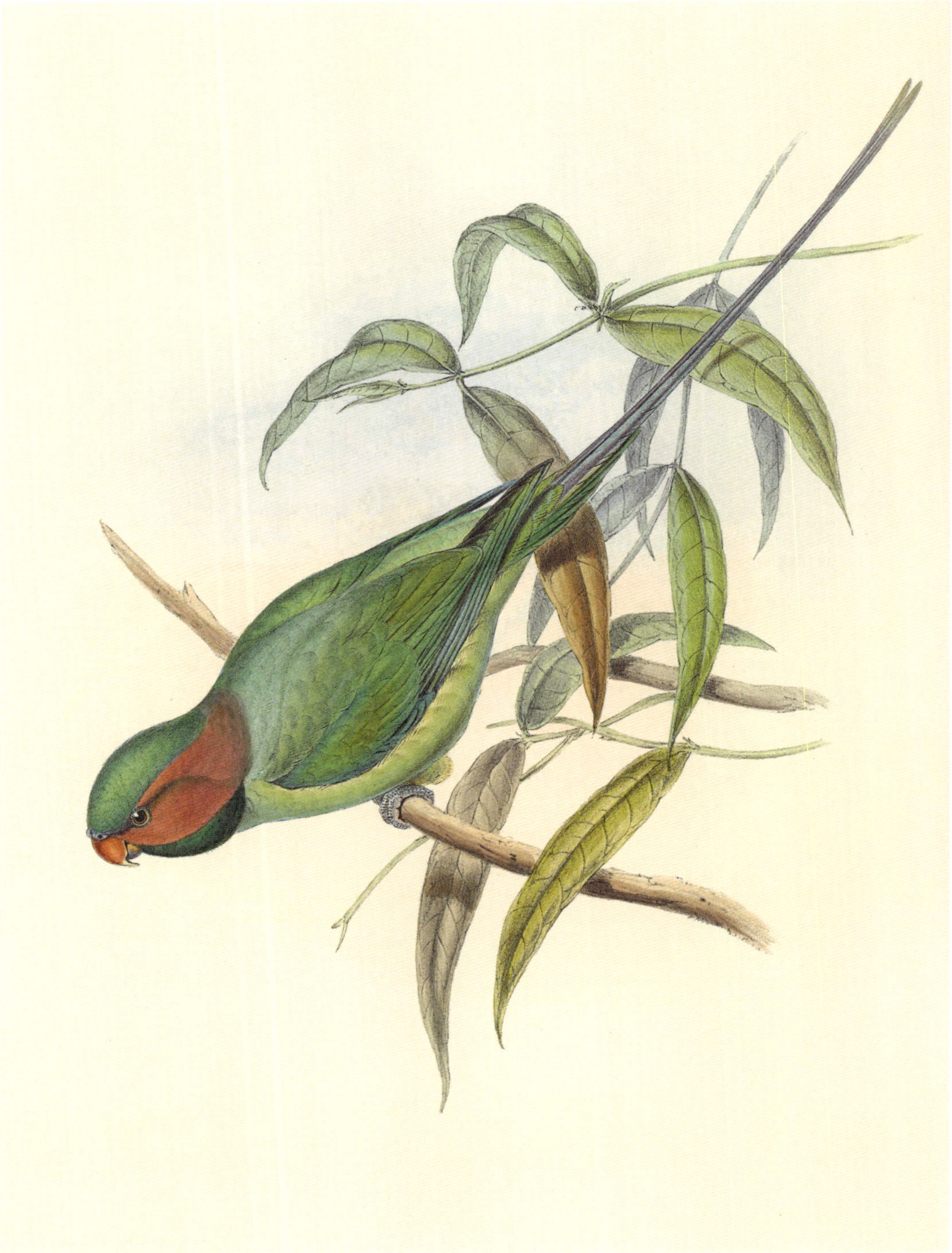

ANIMAL.
John Gould,
Birds of Asia,
Vol. 6, 1850.
Verdigris Green
is visible on the tail
of the long-tailed
parakeet.

VEGETABLE.
*Curtis's Botanical
Magazine*, 1832.
Verdigris Green is
visible on the stem
of the *Pilosocereus
lanuginosus* cactus.*

MINERAL.
Louis Simonin,
*Underground
Life*, 1869.
Verdigris Green
is visible on the
green copper
carbonate (centre).

ANIMAL.

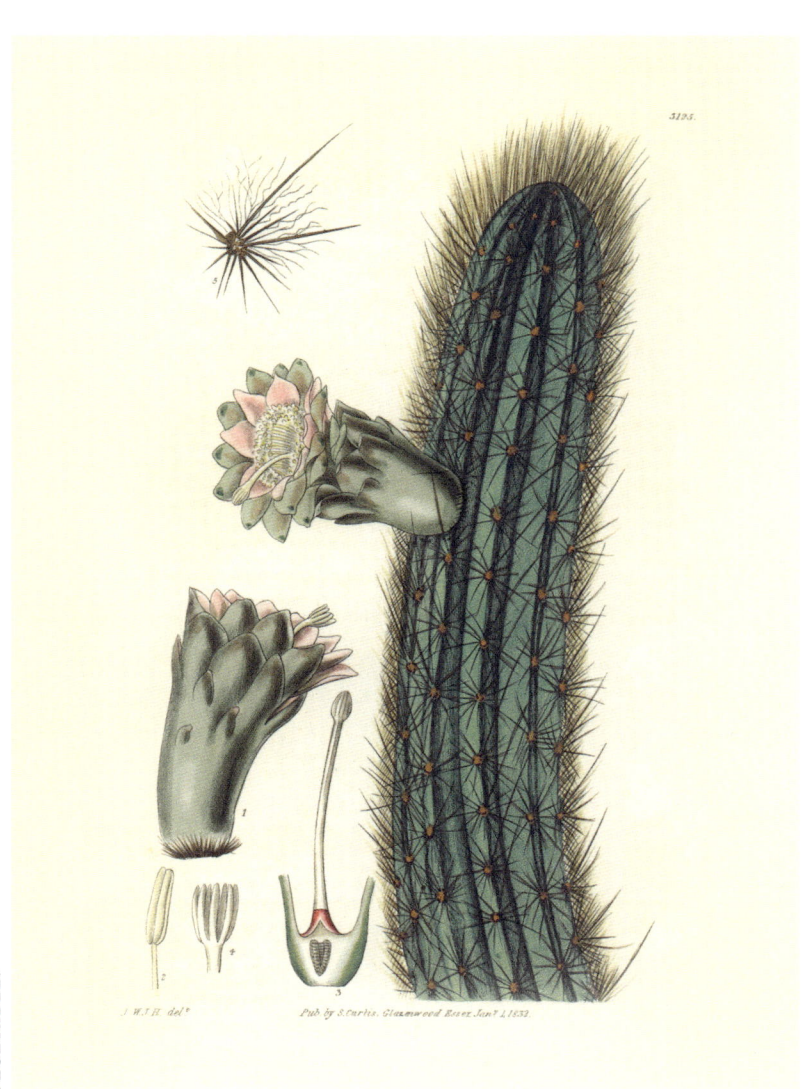

VEGETABLE.

Verdigris Green, is
composed of emerald
green, much Berlin blue,
and a little white. [W]

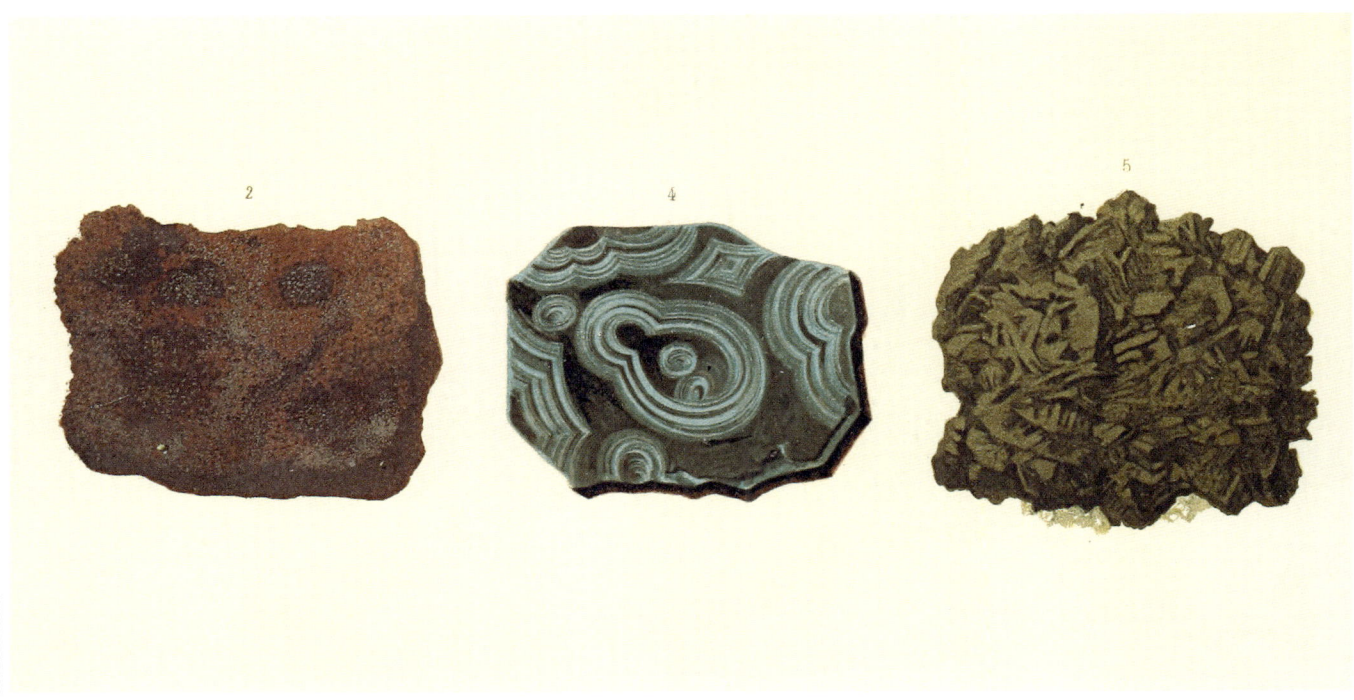

MINERAL.

51. BLUISH GREEN.

(i).   *Egg of Thrush.* [Turdidae]
(ii).   *Under Disk of Wild Rose Leaves.* [*Dog rose*; Rosa canina]
(iii). *Beryl.* [*Silicate mineral*]

Bluish Green, is composed of Berlin blue, and a little lemon yellow and greyish white.

ANIMAL.

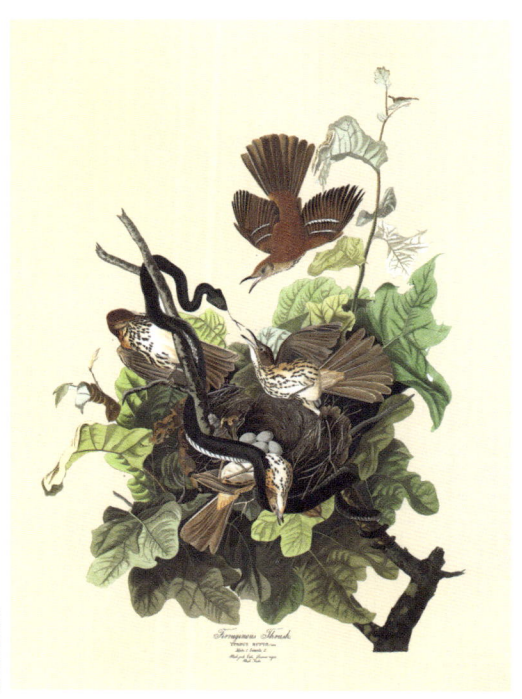

VEGETABLE.

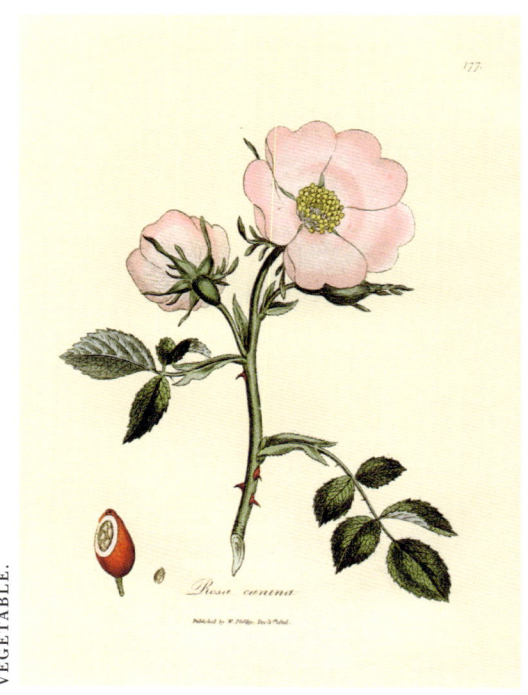

MINERAL.

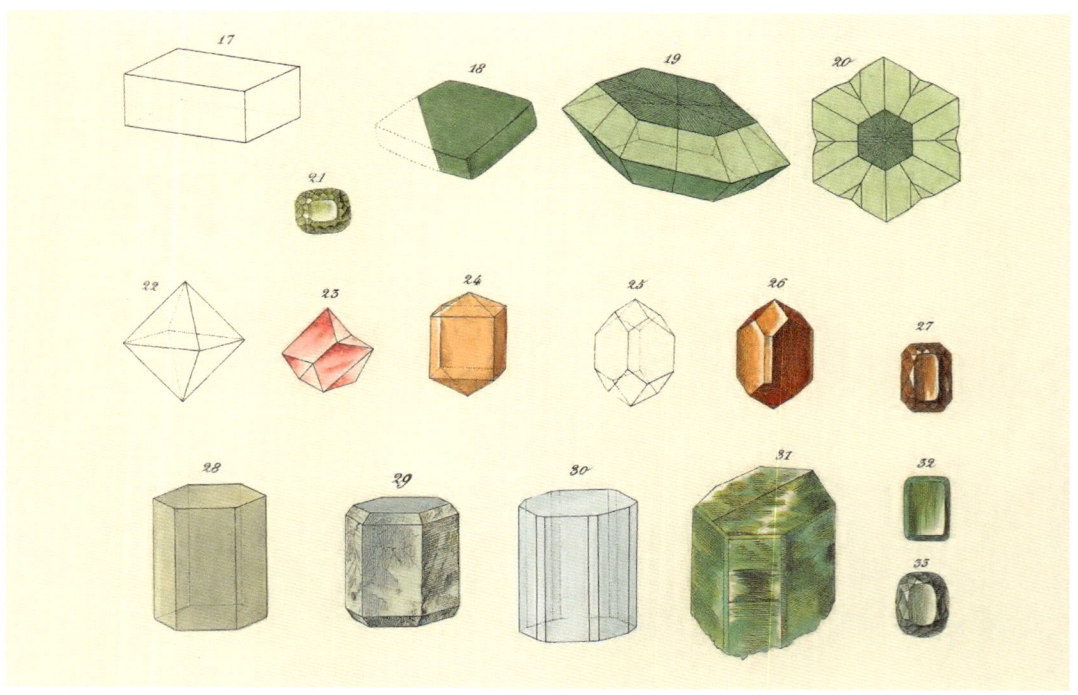

ANIMAL.
John James
Audubon, *Birds of
America*, 1827–38.
Bluish Green is
visible on the shell
of the thrush's egg.

VEGETABLE.
William Woodville,
Medical Botany, 1832.
Bluish Green is visible
on the underside of
the dog rose leaves.

MINERAL.
Johann Gottlob
Kurr, *The Mineral
Kingdom*, 1859.
Bluish Green is visible
on the beryl (bottom
row, far left and left
of centre).

52. APPLE GREEN.

(i).   *Under Side of Wings of Green Broom Moth.*
        [Ceramica pisi]
(ii).   ————————
(iii).   *Crysoprase.* [*Chrysoprase; Silica*]

Apple Green, is emerald green mixed with a little greyish white. [W]

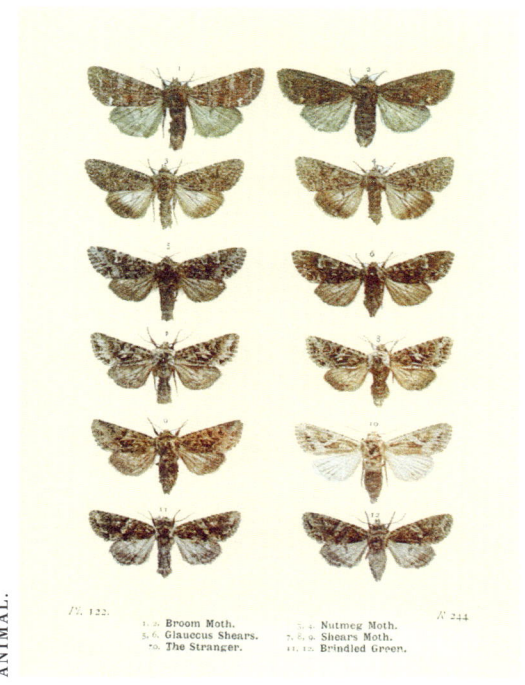

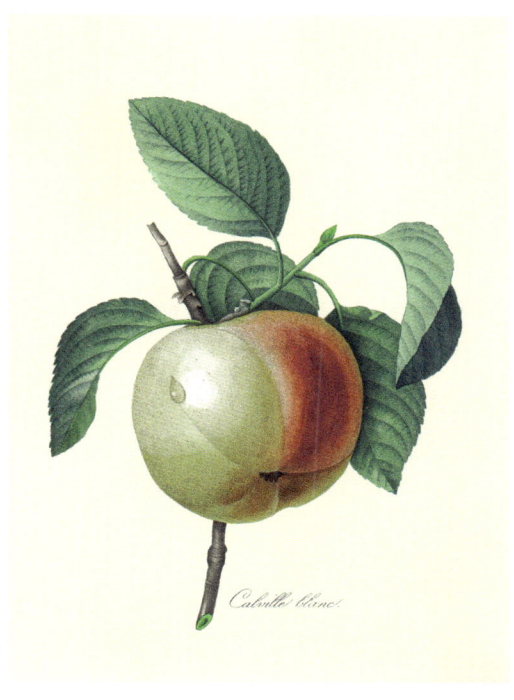

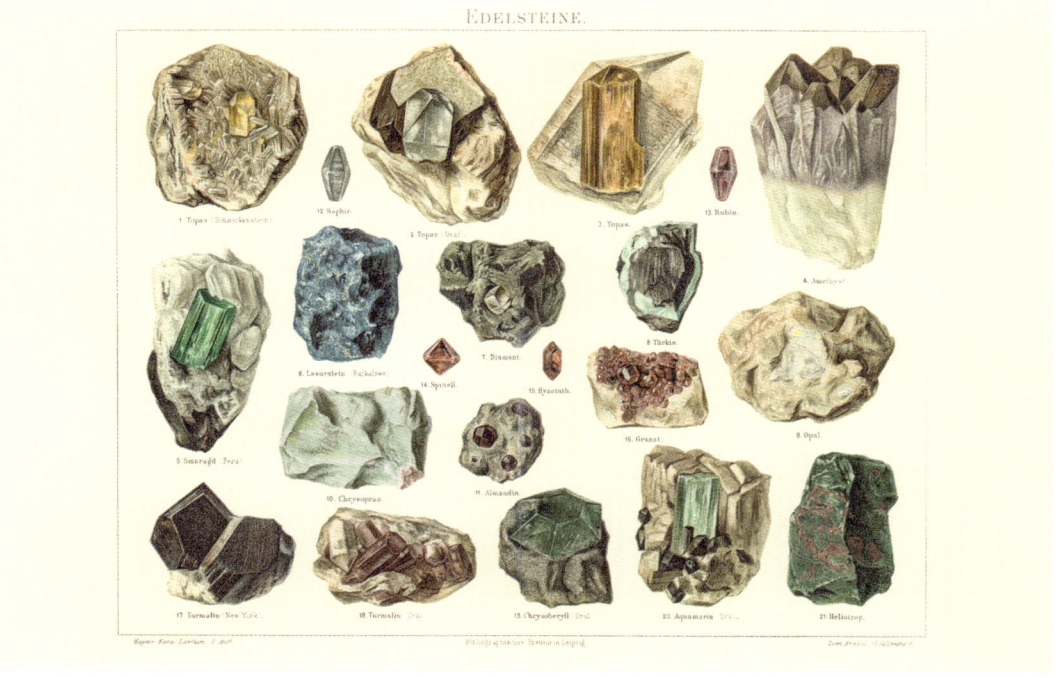

ANIMAL.
Richard South,
The Moths of the British Isles, 1920.
Apple Green is visible on the under side of the wing of the broom moth (top row).

VEGETABLE.
Pierre-Joseph Redouté,
Choix des plus belles fleurs, 1833.
Apple Green is visible on the skin of the apple.*

MINERAL.
Meyers Konversations-Lexikon, 1895–97.
Apple Green is visible on the chrysoprase (bottom row, centre).

(i).   *Beauty Spot on Wing of Teal Drake.*
       [*Eurasian teal*; Anas crecca]

(ii).   ————————

(iii).   *Emerald.* [*Beryl*; *Silicate mineral*]

Emerald Green, is the characteristic colour of Werner; he gives no description of the component parts of any of the characteristic colours; it is composed of about equal parts of Berlin blue and gamboge yellow.

ANIMAL.

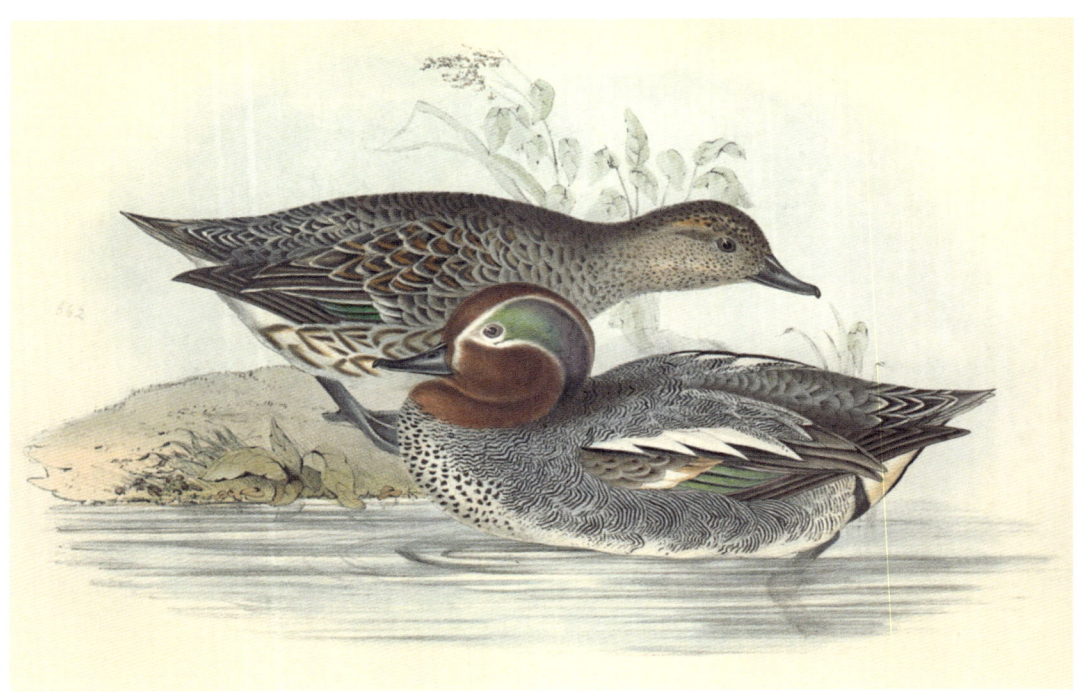

MINERAL.

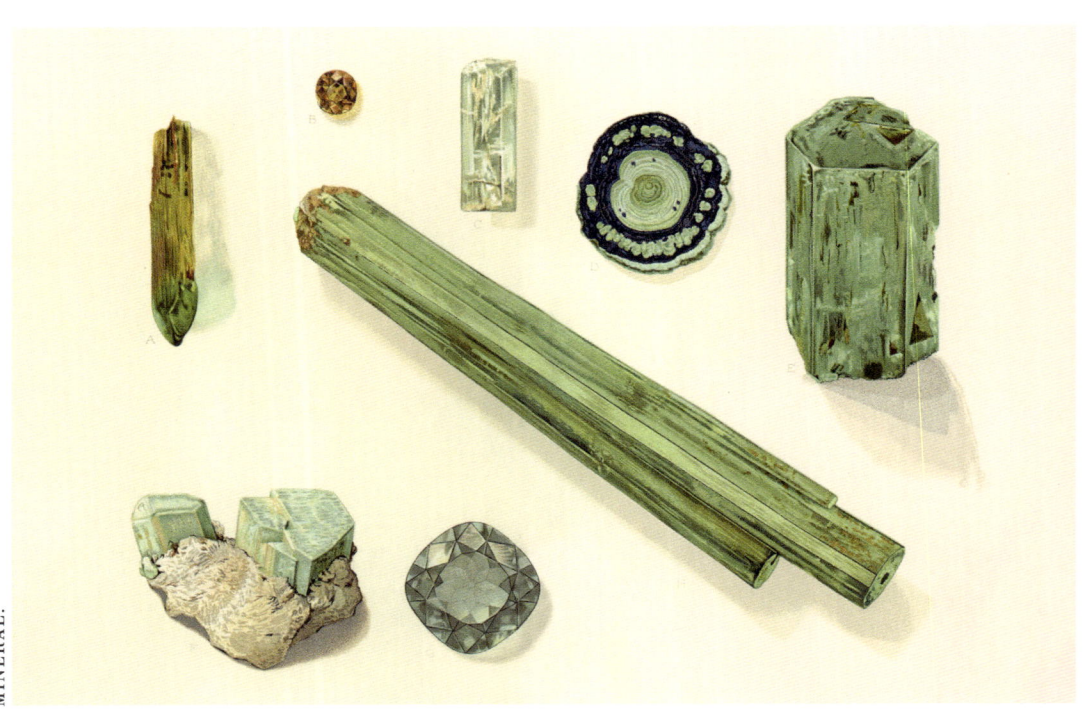

ANIMAL.
John Gould, *Birds of Europe*, Vol. 5, 1832–37. Emerald Green is visible on the beauty spot on the wing of the Eurasian teal.

VEGETABLE.
Cornelis Antoon Jan Abraham Oudemans, *Neerland's Plantentuin*, 1865. Emerald Green is visible on the leaves of the *Ficus*.*

MINERAL.
George Frederick Kunz, *Gems and Precious Stones of North America*, 1890. Emerald Green is visible on the emerald (top row, right).

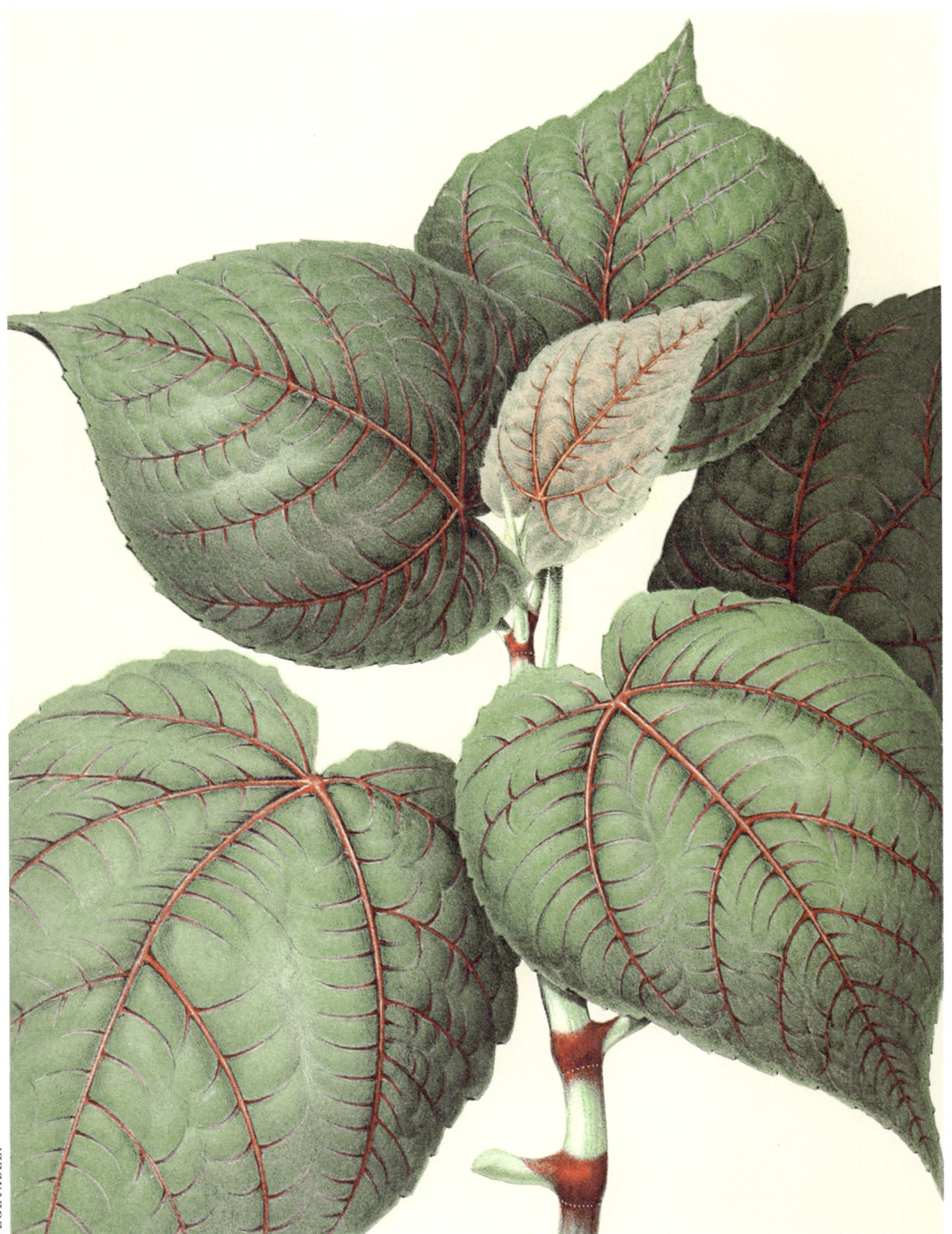

No.	Names.	Colours.	ANIMAL.		
54	Grass Green.		Scarabaeus Nobilis.		
55	Duck Green.		Neck of Mallard.		
56	Sap Green.		Under Side of lower Wings of Orange tip Butterfly.		
57	Pistachio Green.		Neck of Eider Drake.		
58	Asparagus Green.		Brimstone Butterfly.		
59	Olive Green.				
60	Oil Green.		Animal and Shell of common Water Snail.		
61	Siskin Green.		Siskin.		

The second chart of greens in Syme's 1821 edition included one of Werner's original greens (number 54), three greens from the Picardet system (numbers 57, 58 and 59), one green from the Lenz system (number 60), one green from the Jameson system (number 61) and two greens from his own 1814 edition (numbers 55 and 56).

GREENS (ii).

VEGETABLE.		MINERAL.	
General Appearance of Grass Fields. Sweet Sugar Pear.		Uran Mica.	
Upper disk of Yew Leaves.		Ceylonite.	
Upper Disk of Leaves of woody Night Shade.			
Ripe Pound Pear. Hypnum like Saxifrage.		Crysolite.	
Variegated Horse-Shoe Geranium.		Beryl.	
Foiliage of Lignum vitae.		Epidote Olvene Ore.	
Nonpareil Apple from the Wall.		Beryl.	
Ripe Coalmar Pear. Irish Pitcher Apple.		Uran Mica.	

54. GRASS GREEN.

(i).   *Scarabaeus Nobilis.* [*Noble chafer*; Gnorimus nobilis]
(ii).   *General Appearance of Grass Fields.* [Poaceae]
       Sweet Sugar Pear. [Pyrus communis]
(iii).   *Uran Mica.* [*Torbernite*; *Phosphate mineral*]

Grass Green, is emerald green mixed with a little lemon yellow. [W]

ANIMAL.

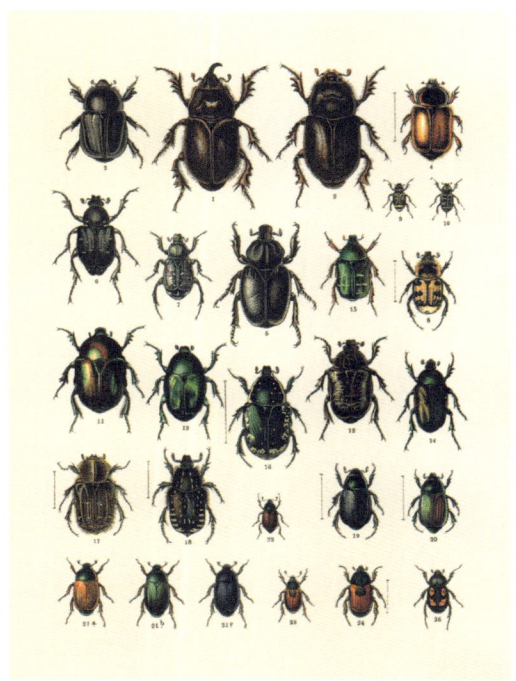

VEGETABLE.

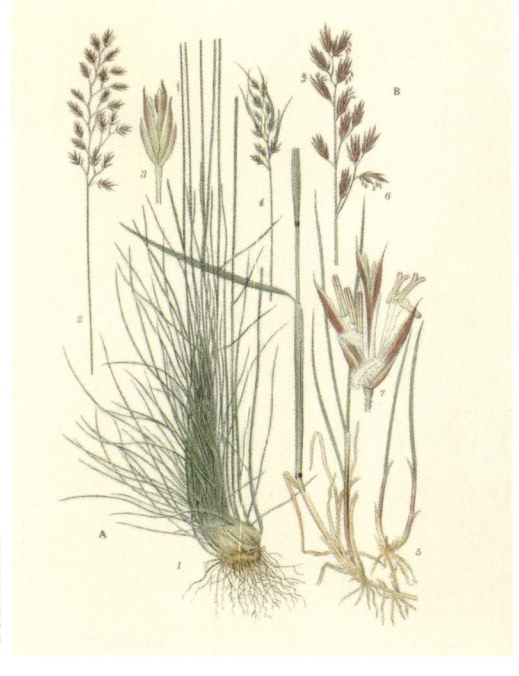

ANIMAL.
Georgiy Jacobson, *Beetles of Russia and Western Europe*, 1905. Grass Green is visible on the back of the noble chafter (second row, left of centre).

VEGETABLE.
A. Mentz and C. H. Ostenfeld, *Billeder af Nordens Flora*, Vol. 2, 1917. Grass Green is visible on the stems of the multiple varieties of grass.

MINERAL.
Torbernite mineral, lithograph, 1967. Grass Green is visible on the torbernite.

MINERAL.

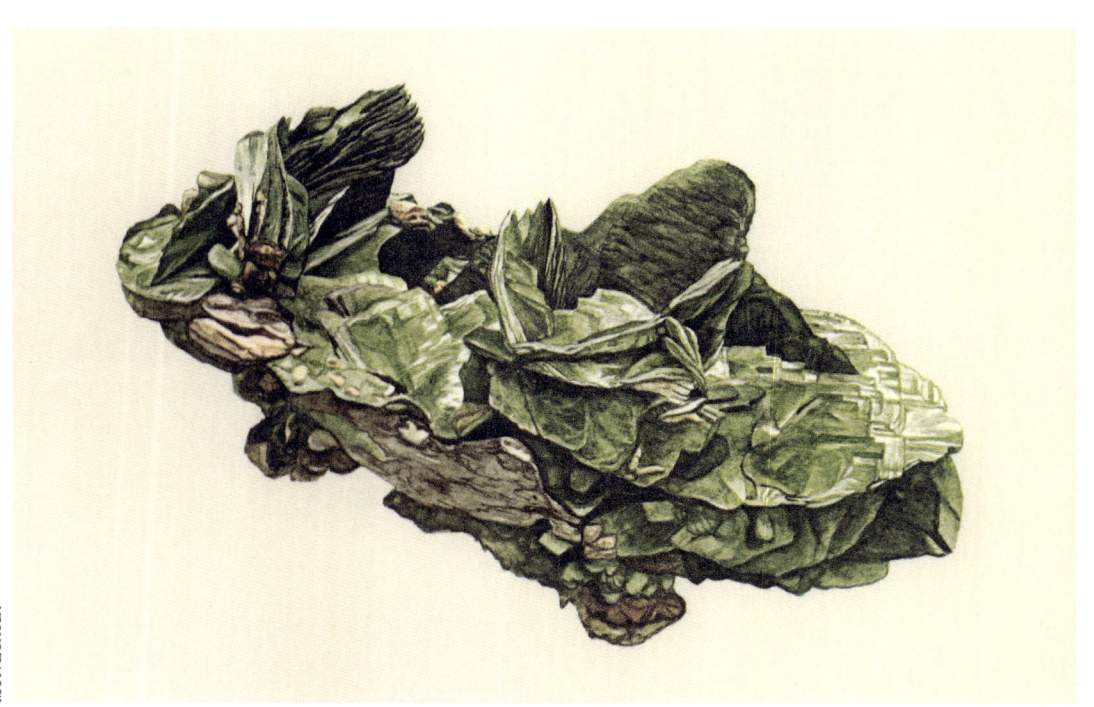

55. DUCK GREEN.

(i). *Neck of Mallard.* [Anas platyrhynchos]
(ii). *Upper Disk of Yew Leaves.* [Taxus baccata]
(iii). *Ceylonite.* [*Spinel mineral*]

Duck Green, a new colour of Werner's, added since the publication of his nomenclature; it is composed of emerald green, with a little indigo blue, much gamboge yellow, and a very little carmine red. [W]

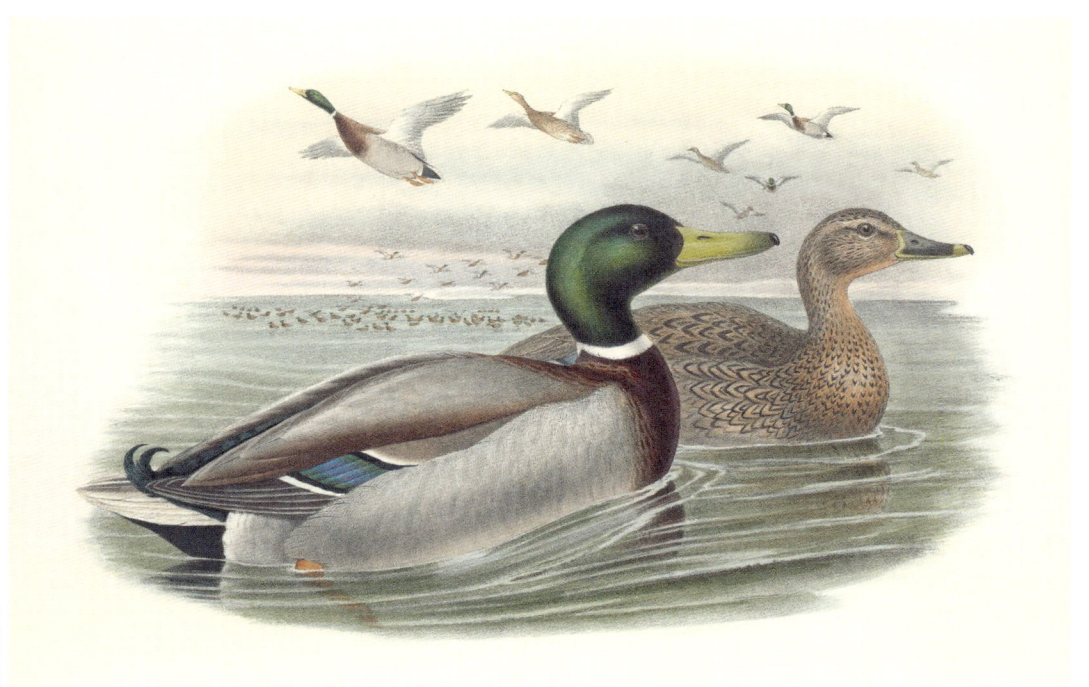

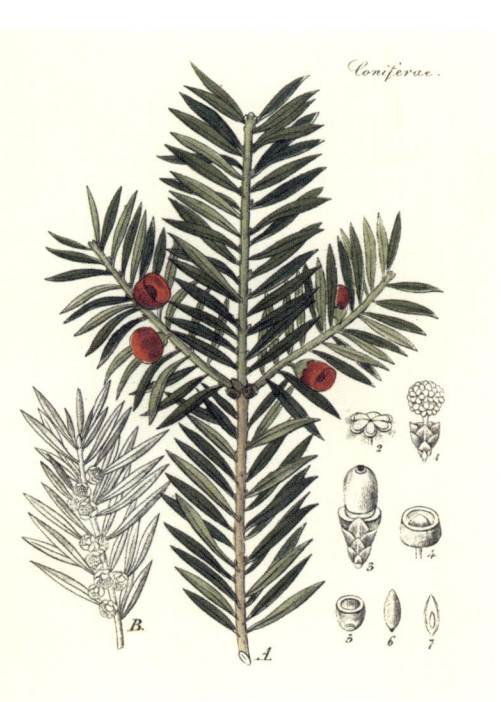

VEGETABLE.

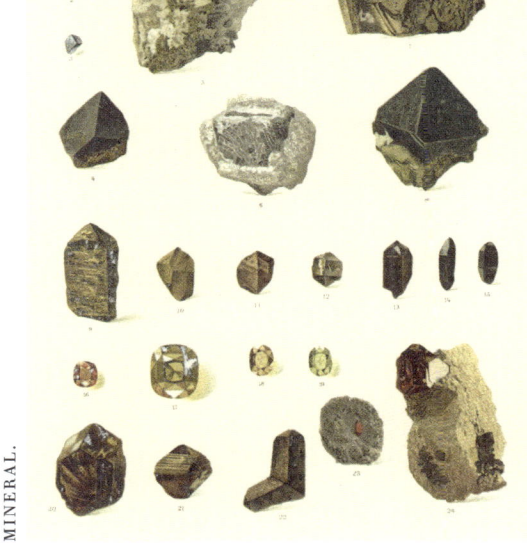

MINERAL.

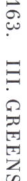

ANIMAL.
John Gould, *Birds of Europe*, Vol. 5, 1832–37. Duck Green is visible on the neck feathers of the drake mallard.

VEGETABLE.
Willibald Artus, *Sämmtlicher Medicinisch-pharmaceutischer Gewächse*, 1876. Duck Green is visible on the leaves of the yew.

MINERAL.
Reinhard Brauns, *The Mineral Kingdom*, Vol. 2, 1912. Duck Green is visible on the ceylonite (second row, right).

56. SAP GREEN.

(i).   *Under Side or lower Wings of Orange tip Butterfly.*
        [Anthocharis cardamines]
(ii).   *Upper Disk of Leaves of woody Night Shade.*
        [*Bittersweet nightshade*; Solanum dulcamara]
(iii). ——————————

Sap Green, is emerald green, with much saffron yellow, and a little chesnut brown.

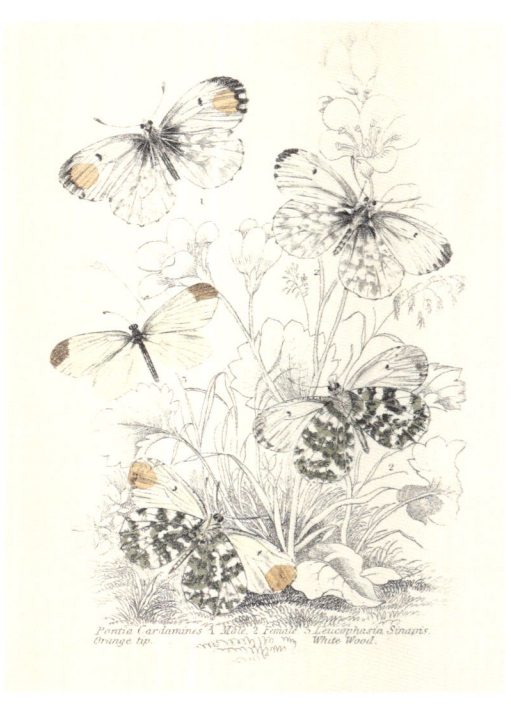

ANIMAL.

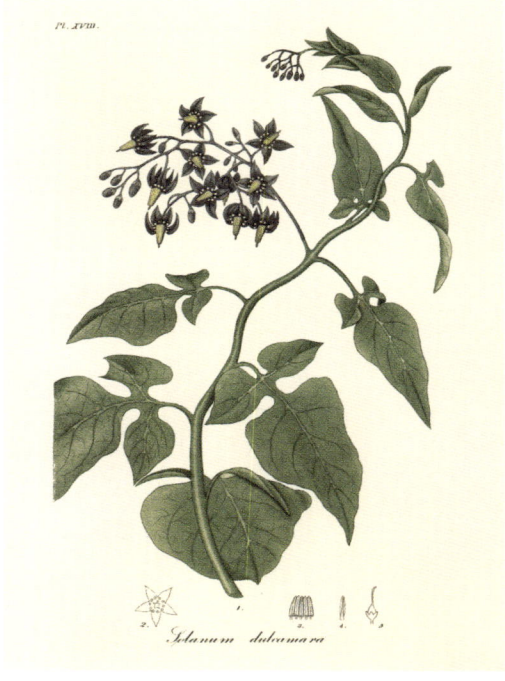

VEGETABLE.

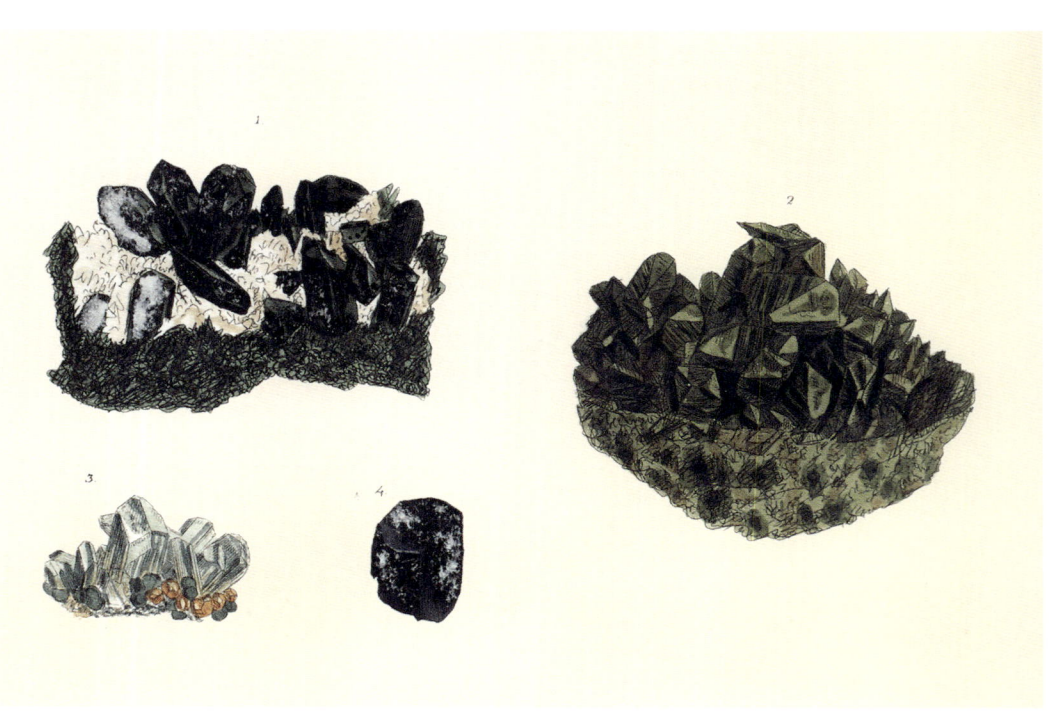

MINERAL.

164.   III. GREENS.

ANIMAL.
James Duncan,
British Butterflies, 1840.
Sap Green is visible
on the underside of
the wing of the orange
tip butterfly (bottom
row, left).

VEGETABLE.
Jacob Bigelow,
*American Medical
Botany*, Vol. 1, 1817.
Sap Green is visible
on the leaves of the
bittersweet nightshade.

MINERAL.
James Sowerby,
Exotic Mineralogy, 1811.
Sap Green is
visible on the augite
(all specimens).*

57. PISTACHIO GREEN.

(i).   *Neck of Eider Drake.* [*St Cuthbert's Duck*; Somateria mollissima]
(ii).   *Ripe Pound Pear.* [Pyrus]
        Hypnum like Saxifrage. [*Rockfoils*; Saxifraga]
(iii). *Crysolite.* [*Chrysolite*; Silicate mineral]

Pistachio Green, is emerald green mixed with a little lemon yellow, and a small quantity of brown. [W]

ANIMAL.

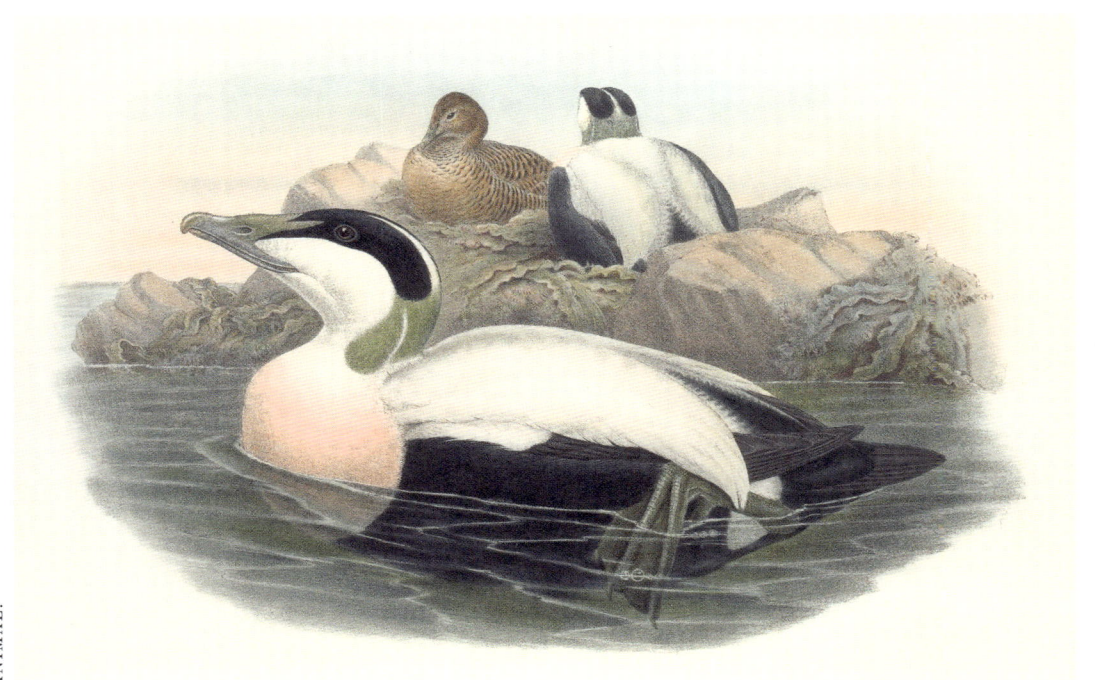

VEGETABLE.

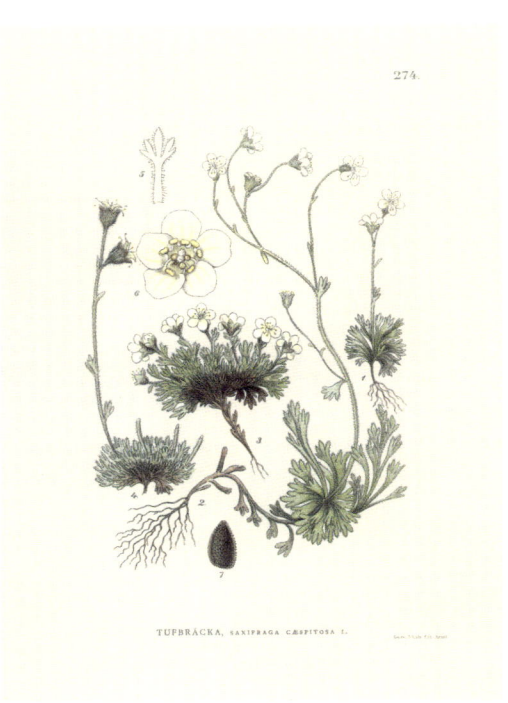

TUFBRÄCKA, SAXIFRAGA CÆSPITOSA L.

MINERAL.

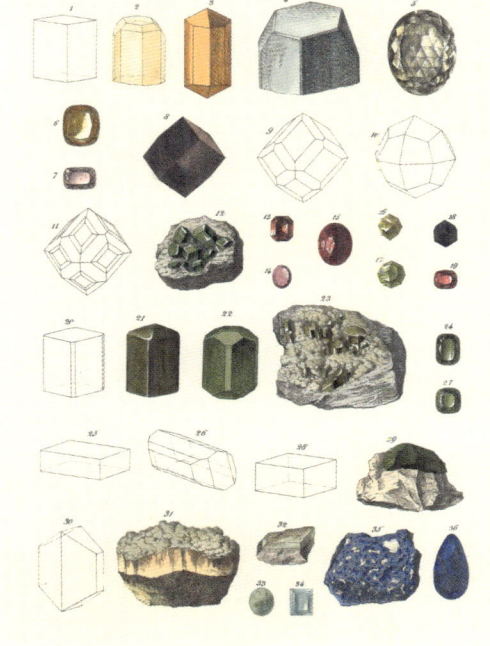

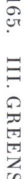

ANIMAL.
John Gould, *Birds of Great Britain*, Vol. 5, 1862–73. Pistachio Green is visible on the neck of the eider drake.

VEGETABLE.
Carl Lindman, *Bilder ur Nordens Flora*, 1905. Pistachio Green is visible on the leaves of the rockfoil.

MINERAL.
Johann Gottlob Kurr, *The Mineral Kingdom*, 1859. Pistachio Green is visible on the chrysolite (sixth from the top, right).

58. ASPARAGUS GREEN.

(i). *Brimstone Butterfly.* [Gonepteryx rhamni]
(ii). *Variegated Horse-Shoe Geranium.* [Pelargonium zonale]
(iii). *Beryl.* [*Silicate mineral*]

Asparagus Green, is pistachio green, mixed with much greyish white. [W]

ANIMAL.

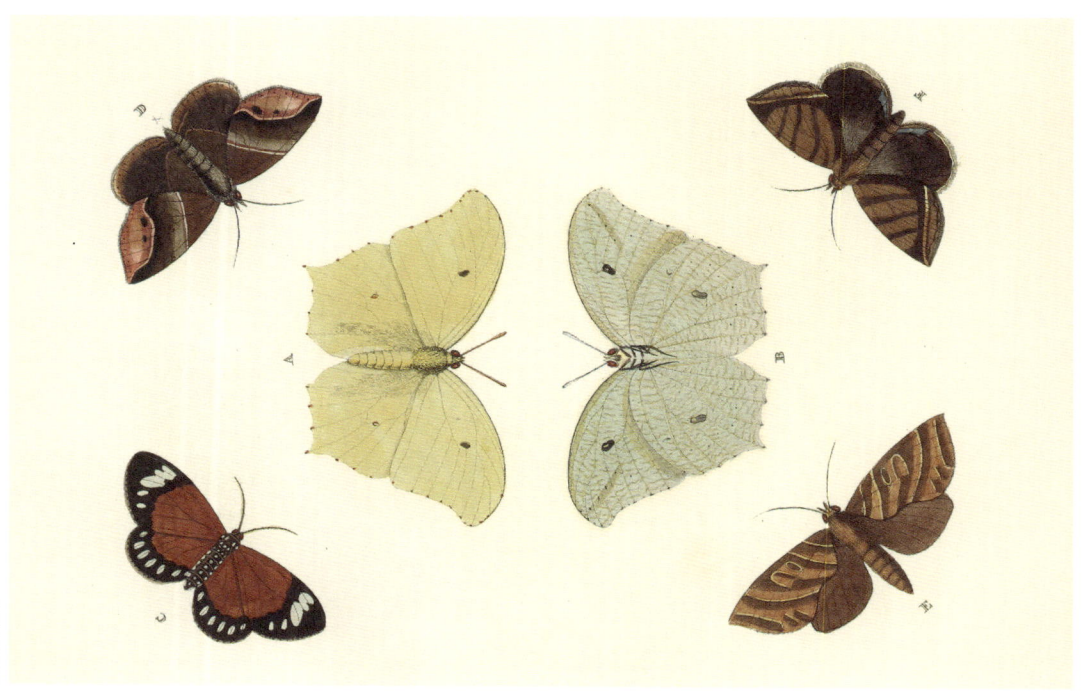

ANIMAL.
Pieter Cramer and Caspar Stoll, *De Uitlandsche Kapellen*, Vol. 2, 1782. Asparagus Green is visible on the wings of the brimstone butterfly (centre row, right).

VEGETABLE.
Louis van Houtte and Charles Lemaire, *Flowers of the Gardens and Hothouses of Europe*, 1857. Asparagus Green is visible on the leaves of the horseshoe geranium.

MINERAL.
Leonard Spencer, *The World's Minerals*, 1916. Asparagus Green is visible on the beryl (bottom row).

VEGETABLE.

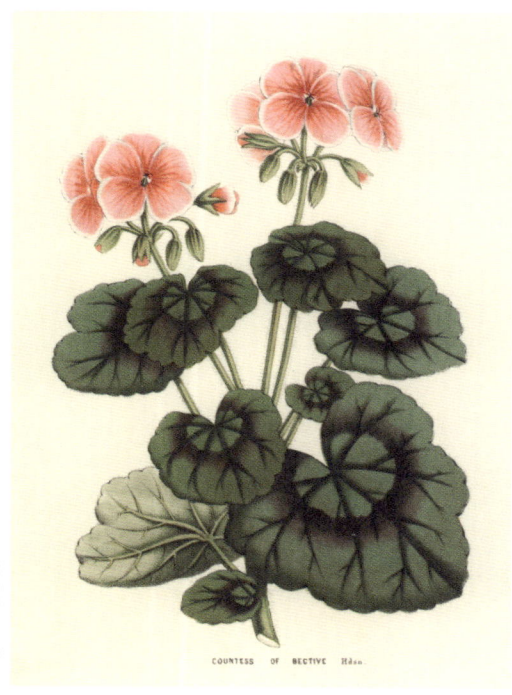

COUNTESS OF BECTIVE H&co.

MINERAL.

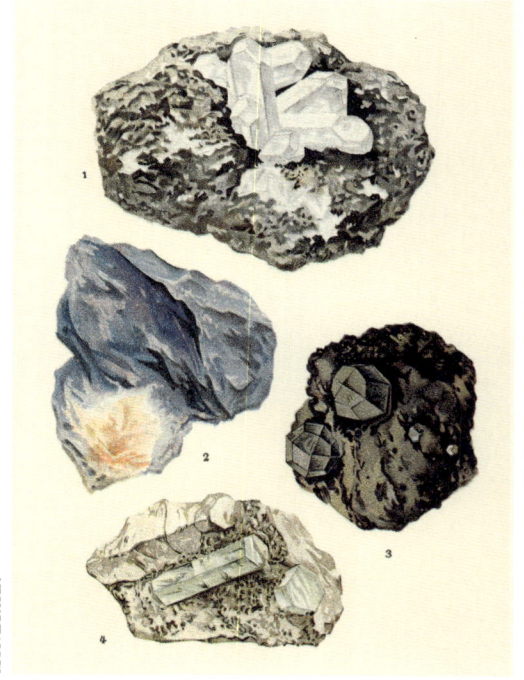

(i).   _____
(ii).   *Foilage on Lignum vitae.* [*Guayacan*; Lignum vitæ]
(iii). *Epidote.* [*Silicate mineral*]
        Olvene Ore. [*Olivine ore*; *Silicate mineral*]

Olive Green, is grass green mixed with much brown. [W]

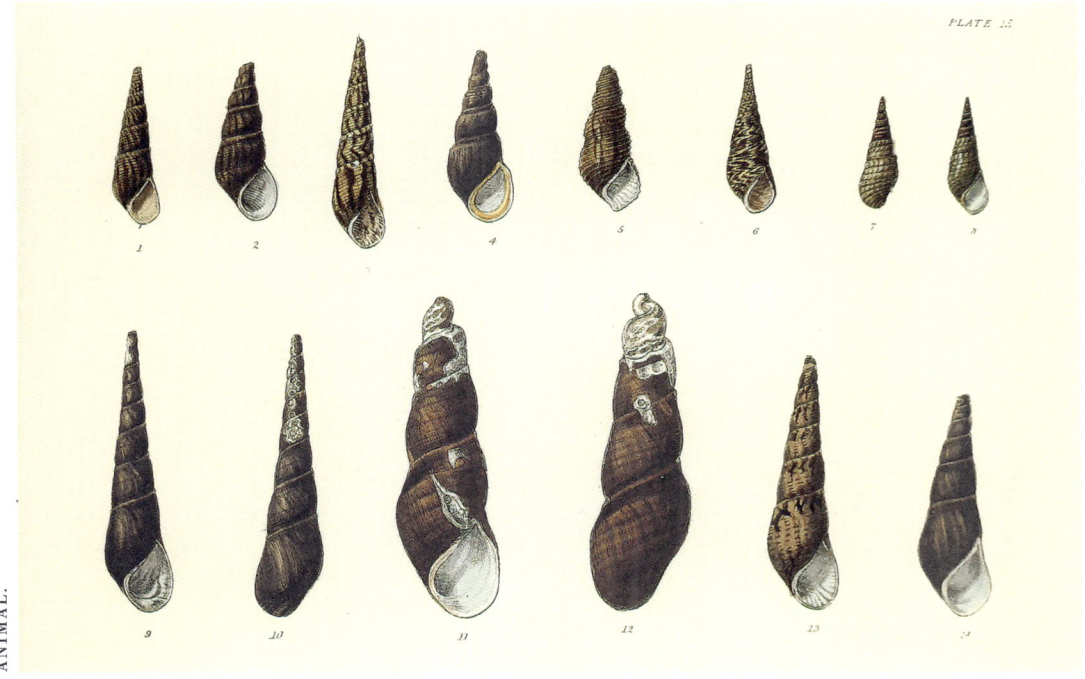

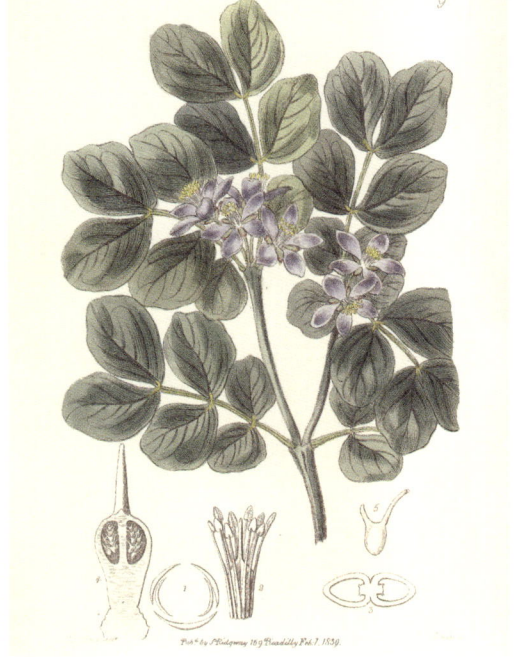

VEGETABLE.

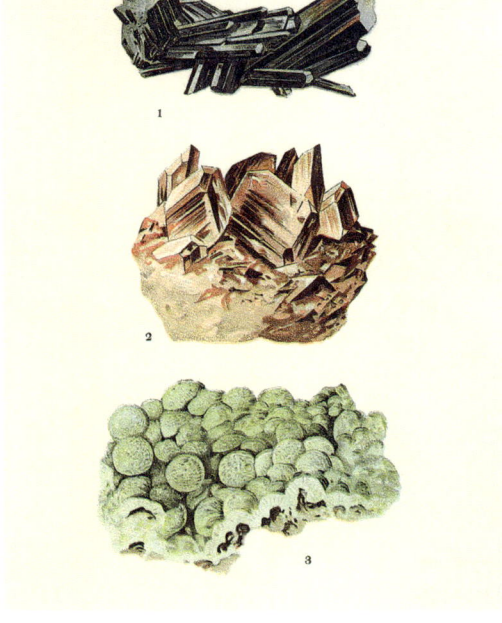

MINERAL.

ANIMAL.
Richard Brinsley Hinds, *The Zoology of the Voyage of HMS Sulphur*, 1843. Olive Green is visible on the quilted melania shell (top row, right).*

VEGETABLE.
John Lindley, *Edwards's Botanical Register*, 1829–47. Olive Green is visible on the leaves of the guayacan.

MINERAL.
Leonard Spencer, *The World's Minerals*, 1916. Olive Green is visible on the epidote (top row).

60. OIL GREEN.

(i). *Animal and Shell of common Water Snail.* [*Freshwater snail; Gastropod mollusc*]
(ii). *Nonpareil Apple from the Wall.* [Malus domestica]
(iii). *Beryl.* [*Silicate mineral*]

ANIMAL.

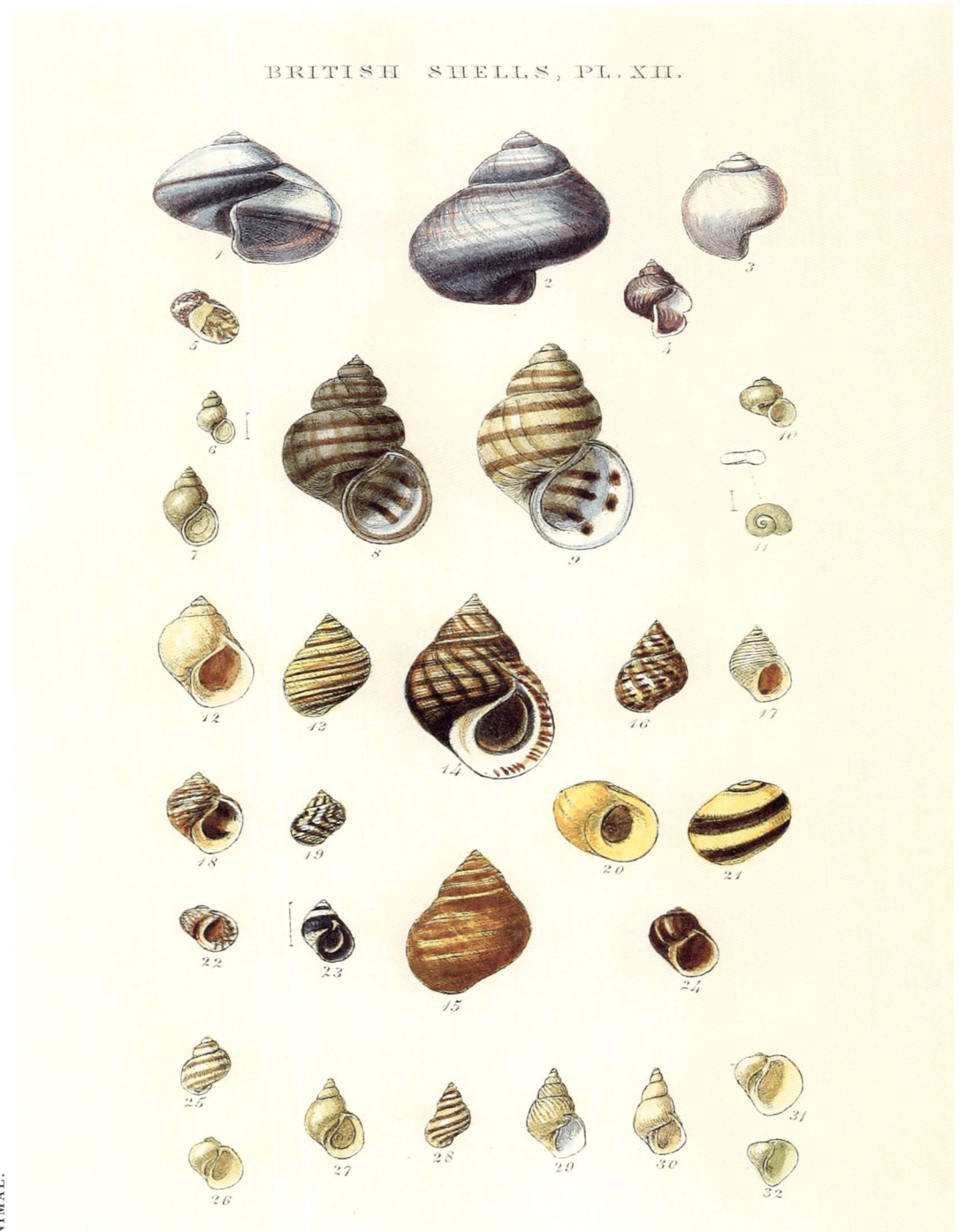

BRITISH SHELLS, PL. XII.

Oil Green, is emerald
green mixed with lemon
yellow, chesnut brown,
and yellowish grey. [W]

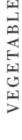

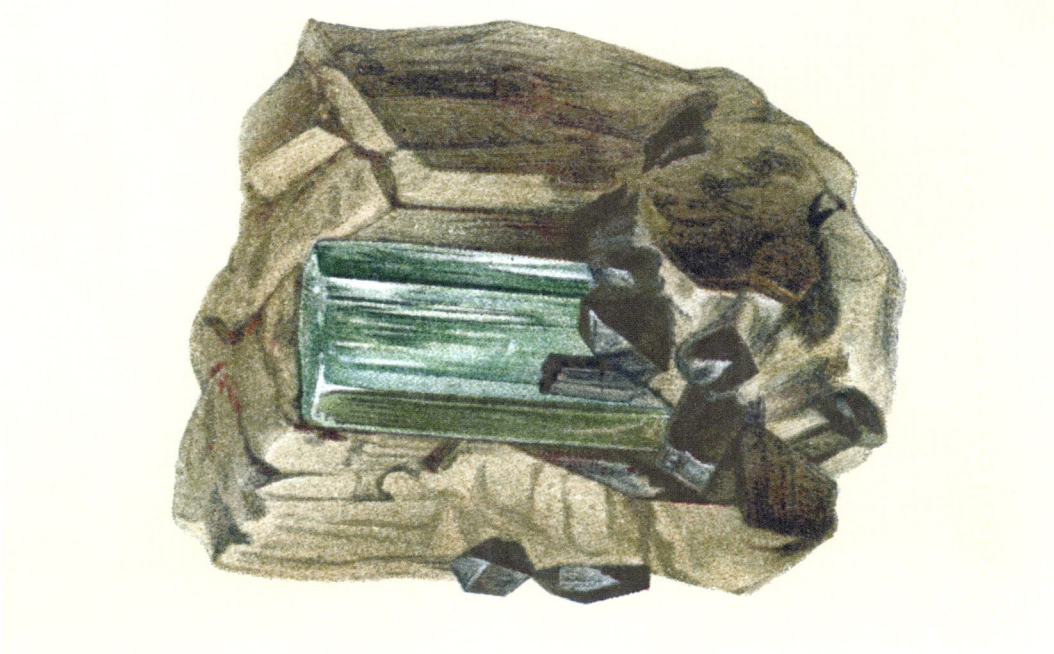

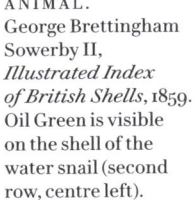

MINERAL.

ANIMAL.
George Brettingham
Sowerby II,
*Illustrated Index
of British Shells*, 1859.
Oil Green is visible
on the shell of the
water snail (second
row, centre left).

VEGETABLE.
Johann Wilhelm
Weinmann,
*Phytanthoza
iconographia*, 1737.
Oil Green is visible on
the skin of the apple.

MINERAL.
*Noble Beryl from
Ural*, illustration, 1800s.
Oil Green is visible
on the beryl.

61. SISKIN GREEN.

(i).　　*Siskin.* [*Eurasian siskin*; Spinus spinus]
(ii).　　*Ripe Coalmar Pear.* [Pyrus communis]
　　　　Irish Pitcher Apple. [Malus domestica]
(iii).　*Uran Mica.* [*Torbernite*; *Phosphate mineral*]

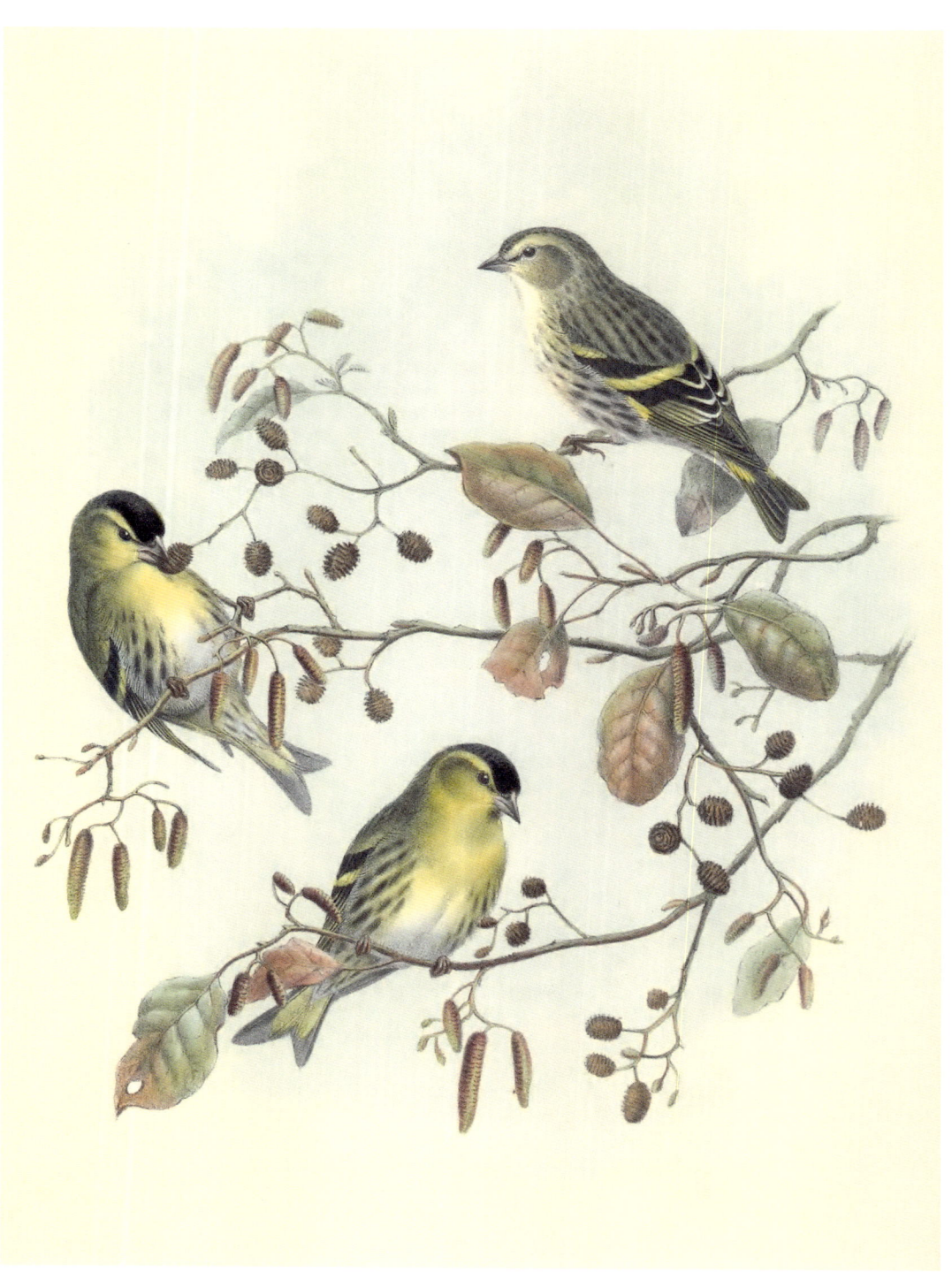

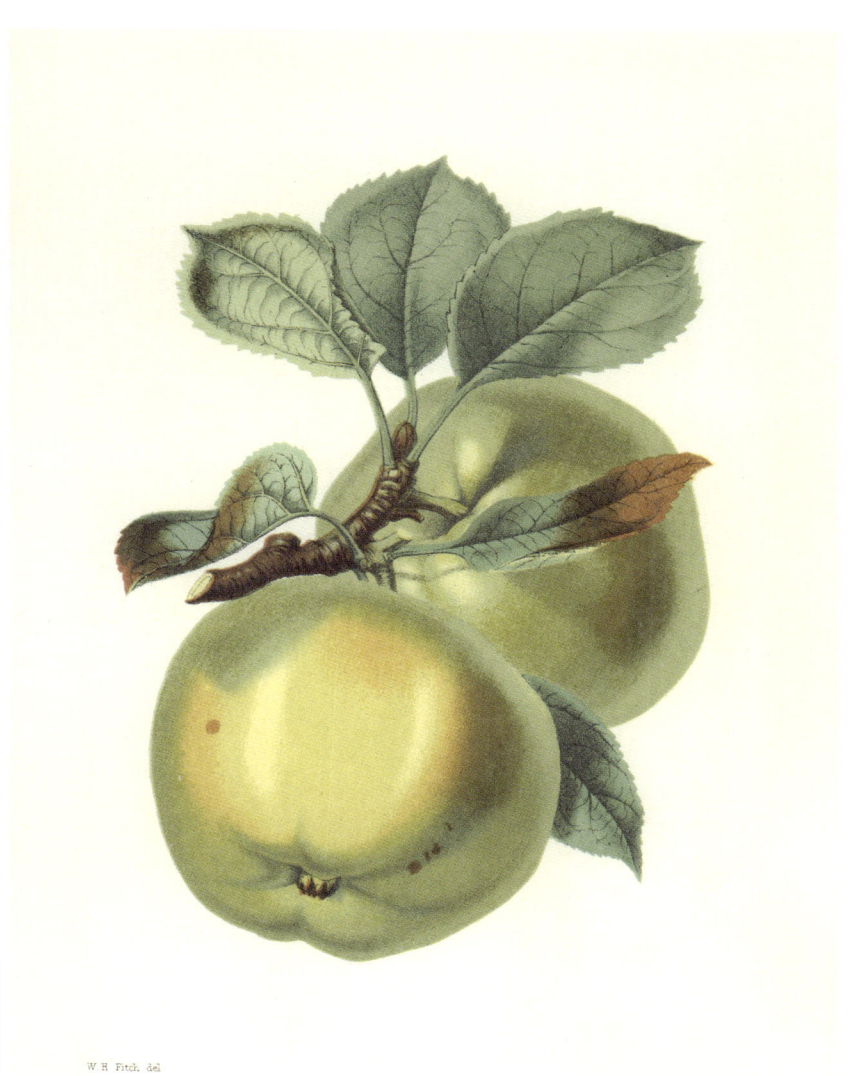

W H Fitch. del

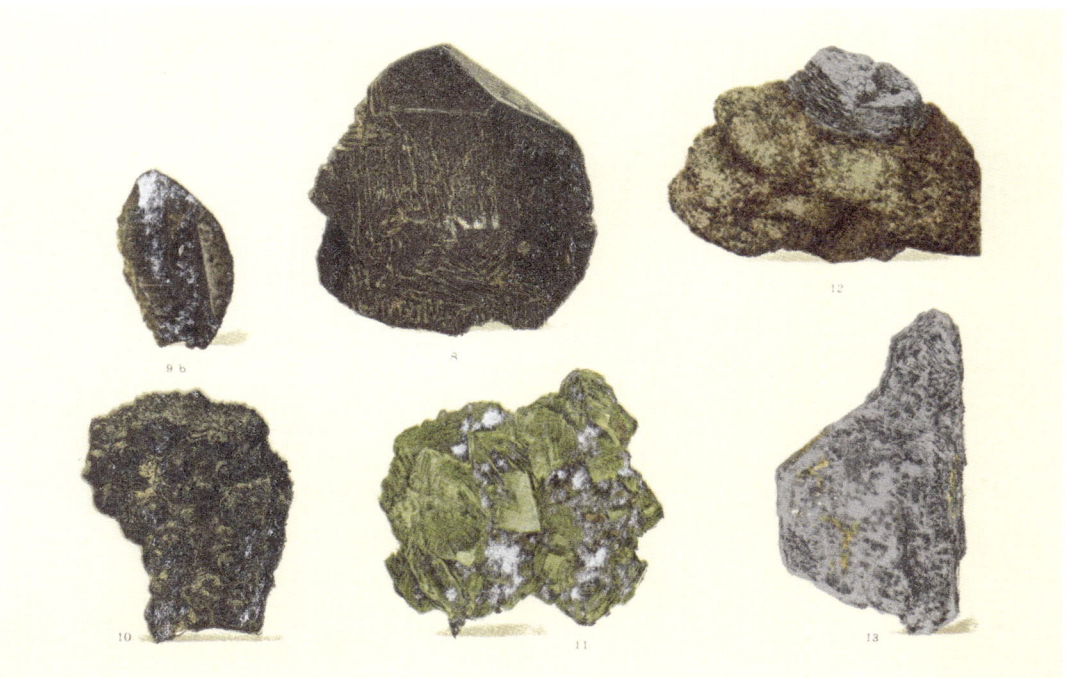

9 b

8

12

10

11

13

ANIMAL.
John Gould, *Birds of Great Britain*, Vol. 3, 1862–73. Siskin Green is visible on the breast feathers of the Eurasian siskin.

VEGETABLE.
Robert Hogg, *The Florist and Pomologist*, 1878–84. Siskin Green is visible on the skin of the apple.

MINERAL.
Reinhard Brauns, *The Mineral Kingdom*, Vol. I, 1912. Siskin Green is visible on the torbernite (bottom row, centre).

3. SYME'S COLOUR CHART IN BOTANY: ORIGIN AND IMPACT.

Flower-painting manuals and a colour standard for botanists.

BY GIULIA SIMONINI.

Patrick Syme (1774–1845) was the most renowned Scottish flower painter of his day, but he also painted other subjects.[1] An undated album in the National Galleries of Scotland, for instance, contains 67 watercolours by him, including several studies of flowers, fruits, insects, birds and bats.[2] One, in which Syme's painterly skills are particularly evident, is a magnificent watercolour depicting peas and broad beans.[3] At the age of 29, in 1803, he took over the art teaching practice of his brother,[4] and in 1810 he published his first book, *Practical Directions for Learning Flower-Drawing*. This was addressed to his clientele – 'ladies in the country', who could not afford to pay a 'master'. It was one of a host of manuals published at the beginning of the 19th century which provided colour-mixing instructions for painting progressively coloured flower studies.

From 1811, two Edinburgh-based learned societies, the Caledonian Horticultural Society and the Wernerian Natural History Society, employed Syme as draughtsman. For the latter, he was 'designated painter of objects in natural history'.[5] The society's founder, Professor of Natural History at the University of Edinburgh, Robert Jameson (1774–1854), encouraged and assisted Syme in compiling his renowned book, *Werner's Nomenclature of Colours* (1814; second edition 1821). Syme provided a colour nomenclature explicitly designed for naturalists and referenced with actual colour swatches. Between 1801 and 1814, only two other publications supplying a similar colour

chart had been printed in Great Britain: an English edition of Carl Ludwig Willdenow's *Grundriss der Kräuterkunde* (1805) and James Sowerby's *A New Elucidation of Colours, Original Prismatic, and Material* (1809), both discussed below. Nevertheless, Syme's colour chart was perhaps the only one used by English-speaking botanists until 1886, and numerous 19th-century English-speaking naturalists also referenced it in their works, making Syme's colour terminology highly influential.

COLOURS IN ENGLISH FLOWER-PAINTING MANUALS

Colour samples and colour names had appeared in how-to books on botanical illustration – a genre which became very popular towards the end of the 18th century – but in a less structured way. Many artists, Syme included, authored these manuals, perhaps to supplement their income.[6] One such was the naturalist and scientific illustrator James Sowerby (1757–1822). His book *An Easy Introduction to Drawing Flowers According to Nature* (1788) was addressed to 'Young Beginners, who are fond of delineating flowers ... to facilitate Botanical Studies and blend Amusement with Improvement.' Whereas Syme's manual contains recipes for mixing different colours, Sowerby's work included instructions on a few schematic mixtures of the three primaries, yellow, red and blue (Sowerby 1788, notes to plate X). In

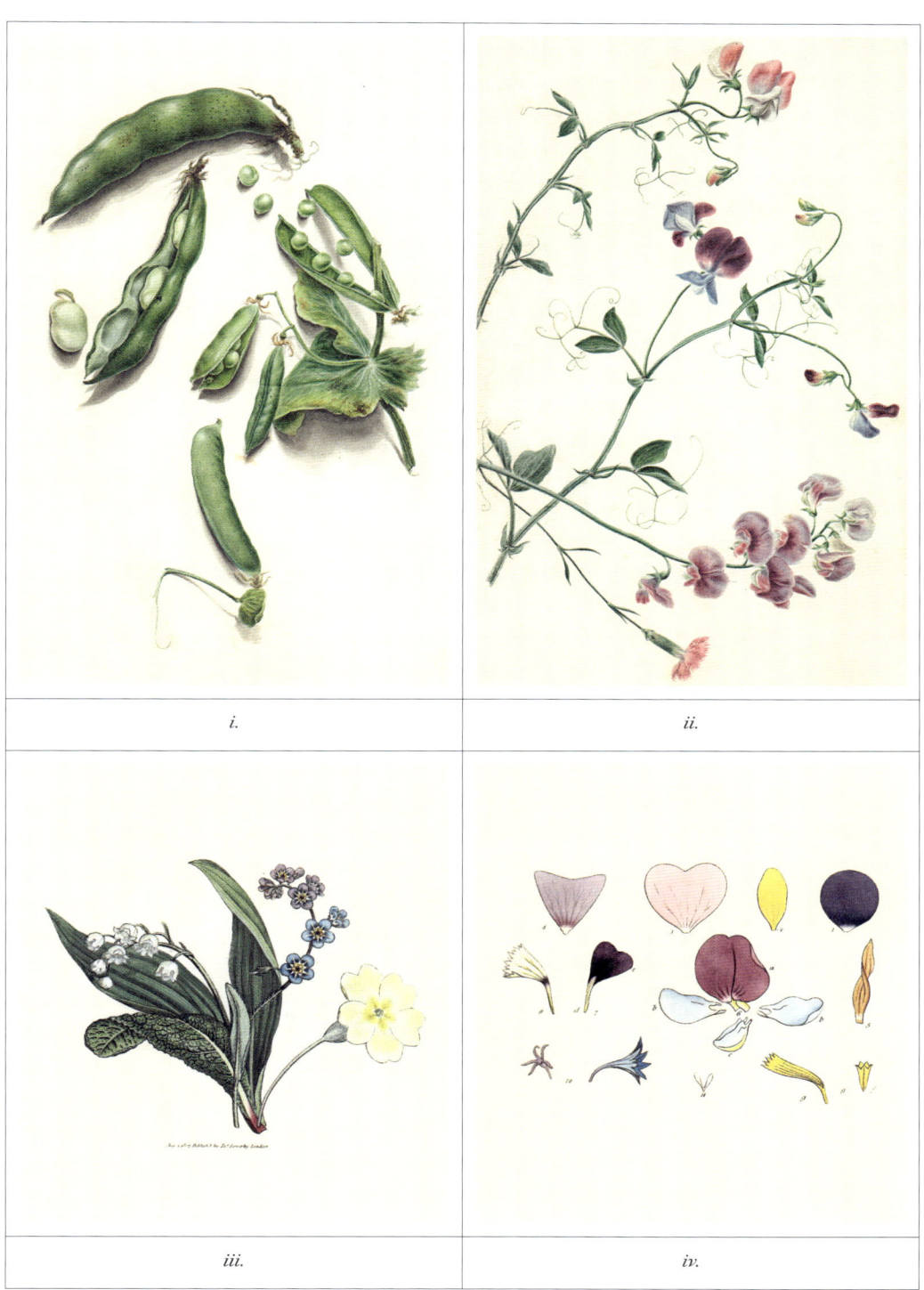

i.

ii.

iii.

iv.

(i).   Patrick Syme, *Peas and Beans*, watercolour, date unknown.
(ii).   Patrick Syme, *Sweet Peas*, watercolour, date unknown.
(iii).   Demonstration of opaque colours, James Sowerby, *A Botanical Drawing-book*, 1788.
(iv).   Petals, James Sowerby, *A Botanical Drawing-book*, 1788.

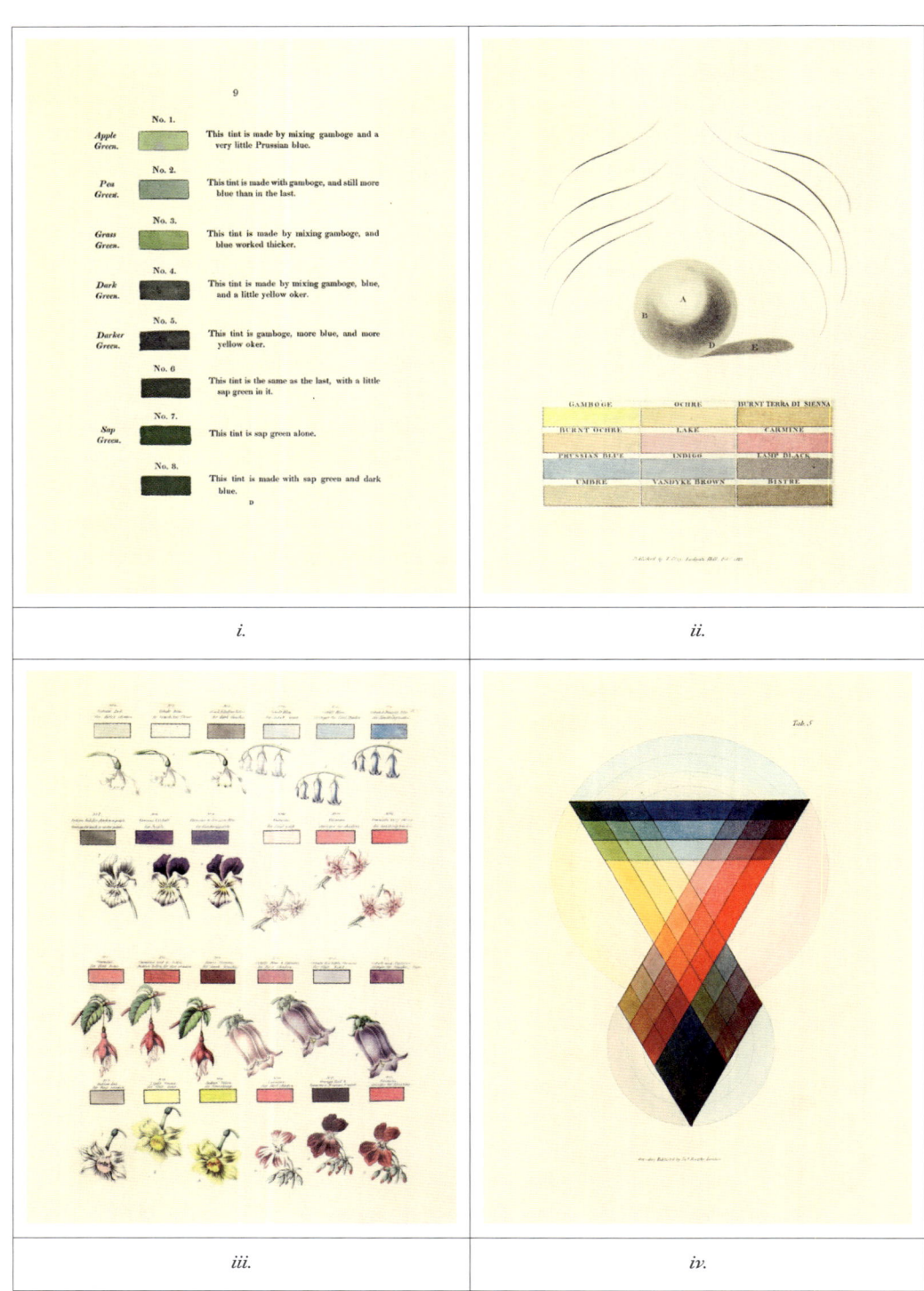

(i).   Chart of greens, George Brookshaw, *A New Treatise on Flower Painting*, 1818.
(ii). Pigments, François Louis Thomas Francia, *A Series of Progressive Lessons, Intended to Elucidate the Art of Flower Painting in Water Colours*, 1824.
(iii). Colours 1–12, James Andrews, *Lessons in Flower Painting*, 1836.
(iv). Chromatic scale, James Sowerby, *A New Elucidation of Colours, Original, Prismatic, and Material*, 1809.

A Practical Essay on Flower Painting in Water Colours (1810), the drawing master Edward Pretty (1792-1865) likewise recommended the use of just three 'primitive colours', but he did include a 'Tablet of Colours' displaying a grey tonal scale washed with Indian ink and a further 24 colour samples,[7] only 11 of which were supplied with colour terms.

The number of colour terms increased in the colour chart printed in *A New Treatise on Flower Painting* (1797), which was first published anonymously but whose author was most probably the cabinetmaker and flower painter George Brookshaw (1751-1823). Here 59 colour swatches were arranged over numerous pages to show many of the paints and mixtures necessary for painting flowers.[8] Among the pigment and colour names, 20 were later used by Syme, including sap green, apple green and grass green. Brookshaw's manual was, however, an exception, as usually such colour charts were labelled with pigment and dye names, not colour terms or mixes. This is evident in both *A Series of Progressive Lessons, Intended to Elucidate the Art of Flower Painting in Water Colours* (1815) by the artist François Louis Thomas Francia (1772-1839) and *Lessons in Flower Painting: A Series of Easy and Progressive Studies, Drawn and Coloured After Nature* (1835) by the flower painter James Andrews (1801-1876). Apart from the colour samples included for the purposes of teaching, it seems developers of these colour charts had virtually no interest in providing colour instead of pigment names. Indeed, they often favoured the use of numbers rather than colour terms, perhaps following the so-called painting by numbers technique used throughout his life by the great botanical artist Ferdinand Bauer (1760-1826).[9]

The scarcity of standard English colour terms in flower-painting manuals is evidence of the lack of interest of these artists in the subject, and this left it to botanists to select appropriate colour names to describe the specimens they studied. Colour terminology was therefore the naturalists' realm rather than that of painters. Sowerby, who was both a naturalist and a talented draughtsman, attempted a standardization of colour appearances and colour names. At the end of the second edition of his flower-painting manual, Sowerby referred to a list of colour terms that would appear in a forthcoming publication by him, promising 'an Essay for a new and universal Chromatic Scale, or List of Colours. It being a great desideratum in the present state of our knowledge in natural researches.'

The list and the chromatic scale duly appeared in *A New Elucidation of Colours, Original Prismatic, and Material* (1809). Sowerby identified 68 English and Latin colour terms (including five variants of white), which he named using compound terms such as yellowish green and bluish grey.[10] However, his system seems not to have appealed to naturalists, perhaps because they considered the colour terminology too abstract (see also p. 135). Moreover, it involved the use of a prism and his colour chart depicted small colour samples combined in a single diagram, making it difficult when comparing flower specimens and less practical in the field. In spite of Sowerby's attempt, in 1813 the naturalist Thomas Forster (1789-1860) was still calling for the compilation of 'a systematic arrangement of colours' with reference to 'the proportions of the various mixtures'.[11]

When in 1814 Syme released his colour nomenclature, the scientific community, botanists included, therefore greeted it with enthusiasm. Syme, indeed, explicitly encouraged botanists, along with others, to use his work. Yet in addition to Sowerby's version, Syme's colour chart had been preceded by one other using English colour terms, also specifically designed for botanists. This was the English edition of Carl Ludwig Willdenow's *Grundriss der Kräuterkunde*, translated with the title *The Principles of Botany, and of Vegetable Physiology* in 1805 (see p. 178). Its origin, like Syme's book, can be traced to the teachings of the father of modern mineralogy, Abraham Gottlob Werner (1749-1817).

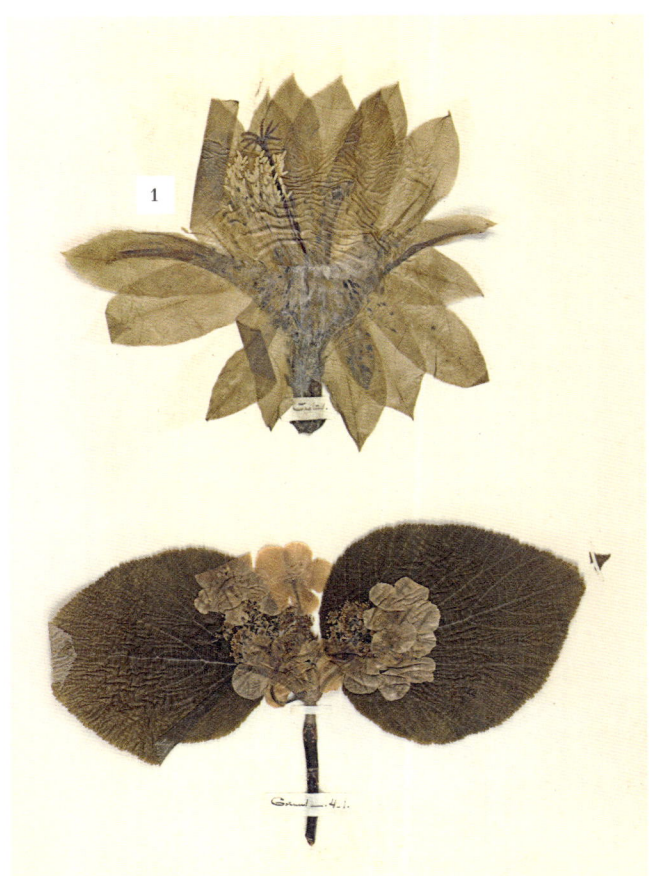

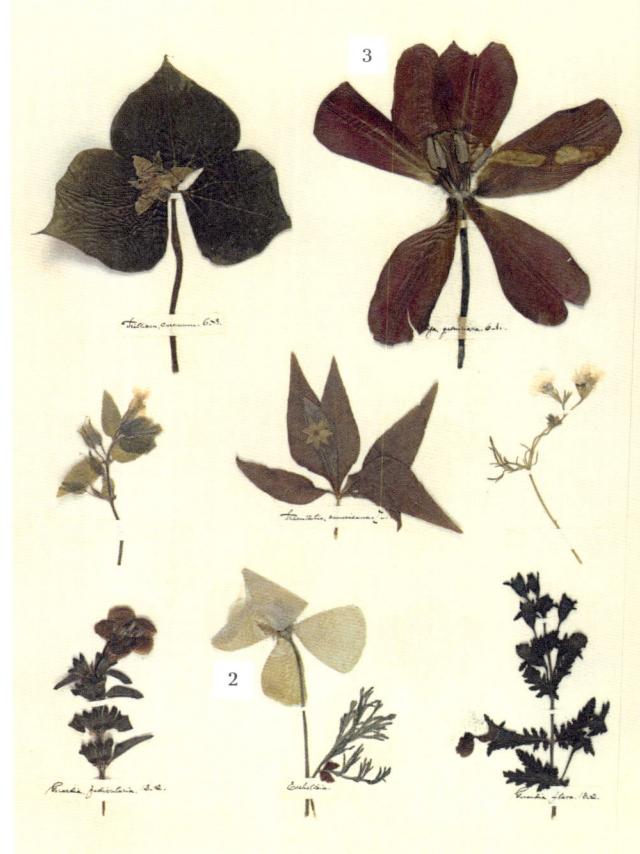

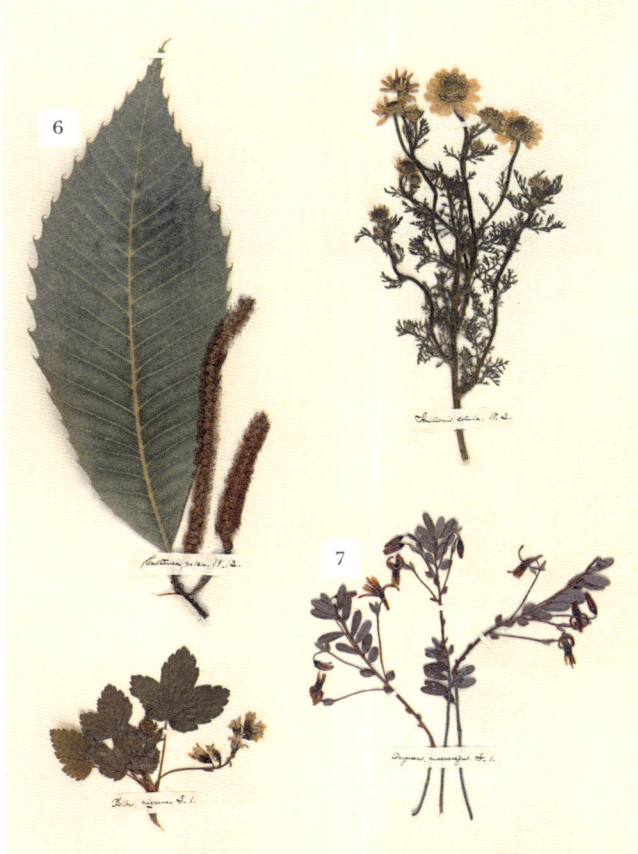

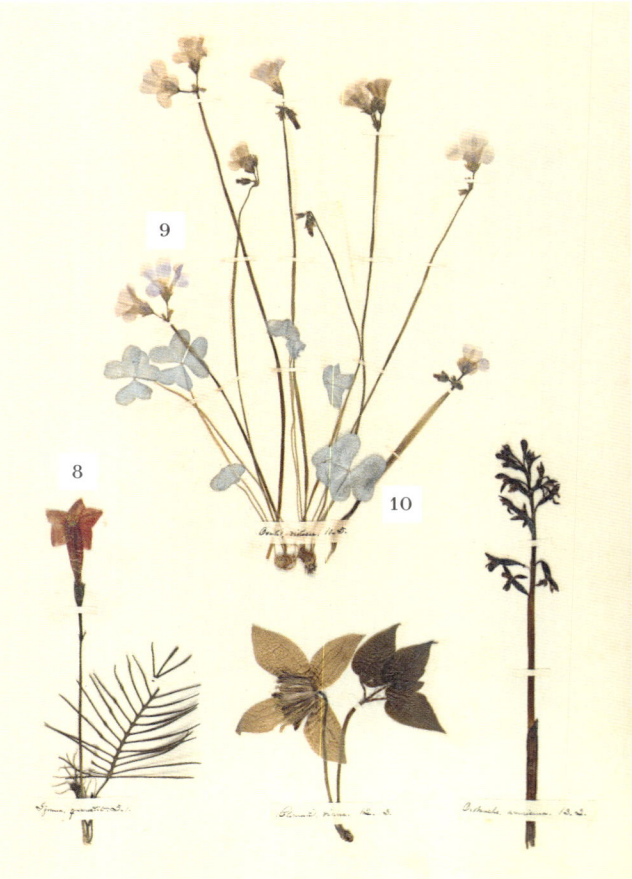

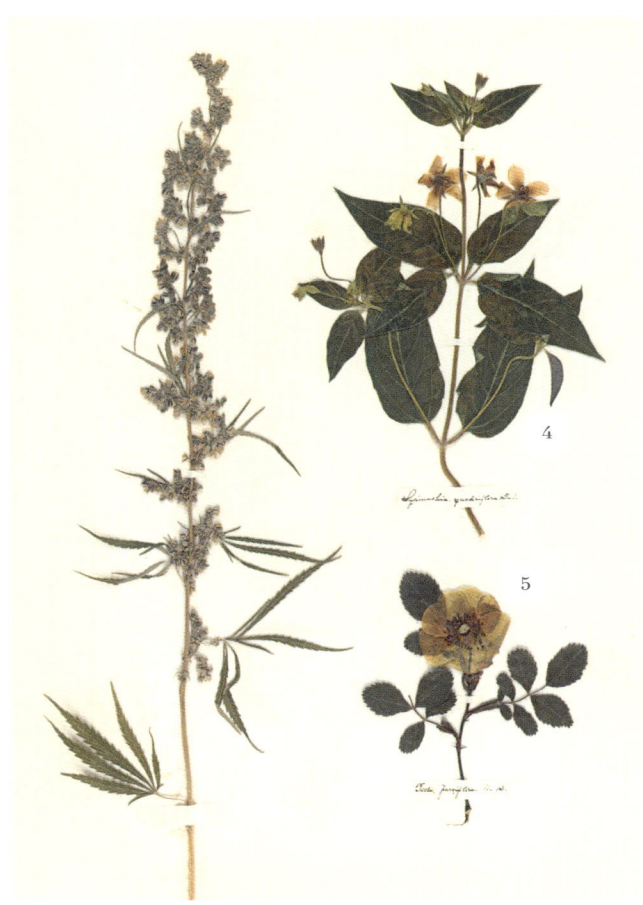

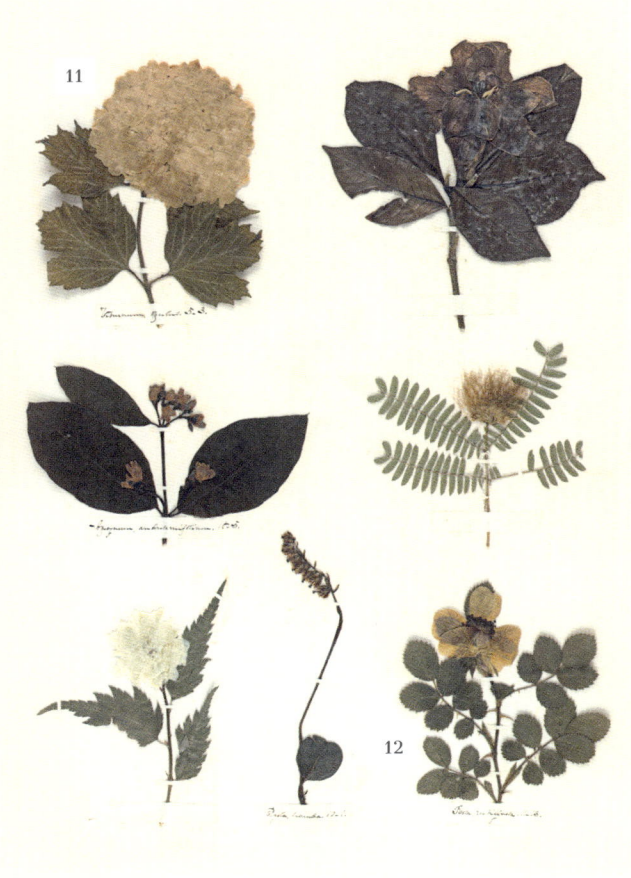

EMILY DICKINSON'S HERBARIUM.

As a young girl the poet Emily Dickinson (1830–1886) had an avid interest in botany, studying the subject from the age of nine, and completing her *Herbarium* by the time she was fourteen. The album contains 424 pressed plants and flowers, many with labels, collected from the Amherst, Massachusetts, region where she lived. Dickinson was well known as a gardener in Amherst, and her poems and letters are full of references to the natural world.

COLOUR REFERENCES.

1		CACTUS.
		70. Honey Yellow.
2		ESCHSCHOLZIA.
		72. Wine Yellow.
3		COMMON GARDEN TULIP.
		99. Brownish Red.
4		LYSIMACHIA QUADRIFLORA.
		55. Duck Green.
5		CAROLINA ROSE.
		68. Saffron Yellow.
6		SWEET CHESTNUT.
		59. Olive Green.
7		CRANBERRY.
		49. Blackish Green.
8		CYPRESS VINE.
		84. Scarlet Red.
9		VIOLET WOOD-SORREL, PETAL.
		43. Red Lilac Purple.
10		VIOLET WOOD-SORREL, LEAF.
		51. Bluish Green.
11		GUELDER ROSE.
		6. Greenish White.
12		SWEET BRIAR.
		48. Leek Green.

MINERALS AND BOTANY: SCIENTIFIC COLOUR TERMINOLOGY

Although colour terms were essential for scientists when describing the appearance of a specimen, no common universal terminology existed in the 18th century. Carl Linnaeus (1707–1778), in his *Philosophia botanica* (1751), even cautioned botanists to 'not put too much trust in colour', deeming it an unnecessary accident for the identification and classification of plants.[12] Nonetheless, he did produce a restricted colour nomenclature comprising 38 colour terms for plants and an even more limited one for minerals.[13] For the former his main colour categories were *hyalinus* (transparent), *albus* (white), *cinereus* (ash grey), *niger* (black), *luteus* (yellow), *ruber* (red), *purpureus* (purple), *caeruleus* (blue) and *viridis* (green). His colour terminology for minerals, set out in *Systema naturae*, consisted of *opacum* (dark), *diaphanum* (semi-transparent), *pellucidum* (pellucid), *hyalinum* (transparent), *tinctum* (coloured), *reflexio* (reflecting) and *refractio* (refracting).

Contrary to Linnaeus, Werner considered colour as the most obviously distinguishable and reliable property of minerals.[14] He therefore developed an extensive mineral colour terminology consisting of 54 terms subdivided into eight main colours,[15] which he published in his book *Von den äusserlichen Kennzeichen der Fossilien* in 1774. Werner's colour nomenclature was quickly adopted by his students and followers, though his book did not include a colour chart. In 1805, Robert Jameson, a former student, stated in his own book that Werner had hoped to publish colour charts, 'but never had leisure to get them executed'.[16] In preparation for this unrealized project, after 1774 Werner compiled hundreds of handwritten sheets with an expanded colour terminology featuring equivalent names in numerous languages, English and Latin included.[17] These were later used by his students and followers to develop colour charts for their own textbooks based on Werner's method, Syme included.

The Berlin botanist Carl Ludwig Willdenow (1765–1812) probably relied on one of Werner's new colour lists for his colour nomenclature and colour chart in his successful botanical textbook *Grundriss der Kräuterkunde* (1792), later translated into English.[18] However, mindful of Linnaeus's teaching, Willdenow maintained that his colours should be used only 'in describing the Lichens and Fungi: being not so variable in these plants as in others'.[19] His colour chart has 36 colour samples with Latin names, and is linked to a colour nomenclature of 40 terms in Latin and German. The four colours not illustrated in the colour chart are *hyalinus* (transparent), *lacteus* (milky white), *albus* (white) and *albidus* (whitish).[20] Of the Latin terms used by Willdenow, 23 can be found in Werner's handwritten colour nomenclatures. These are *cyaneus*, *coeruleus*, *caesius*, *prasinus*, *luteus*, *aureus*, *ochraceus*, *sulphureus*, *ferrugineus*, *badius/hepaticus*, *lateritius*, *coccineus*, *carneus*, *sanguineus*, *roseus*, *violaceus*, *ater*, *niger*, *cinereus*, *griseus*, *lividus*, *lacteus* and *albus*. Others, such as *azuleus* (azure), *aerogineus* (copper green), *aurantius* (orange) and *brunus* (brown), are reminiscent of Werner's Latin terms.[21] Given the enthusiastic reception of Werner's method, it was perhaps Willdenow's friend Alexander von Humboldt, (1769–1859) who recommended that he include a colour chart in his publication. Willdenow had met Humboldt in 1788 at one of his private botany lessons,[22] before Humboldt studied under Werner at Freiberg between 1791 and 1792.[23] It is possible that while there he sent Willdenow a copy of Werner's new colour list.

Evidence for the circulation of Werner's colour terminology can be found in other books, too. In the preface to his *Versuch einer Mineralogie* (1794), Franz Joseph Anton Estner (1739–1801) revealed that in 1790 Werner's student Johann Friedrich Wilhelm Widenmann (1764–1798) had given him an old chart ('eine alte Tabelle'), probably a copy of Werner's new colour nomenclature.[24] Likewise, in 1805, in his 'Advertisement' in *A Treatise on the External Characters of Minerals*, Jameson stated that he had received the 'Tabular View' with the expanded colour terminology directly from Werner, which he had already published separately in 1804.

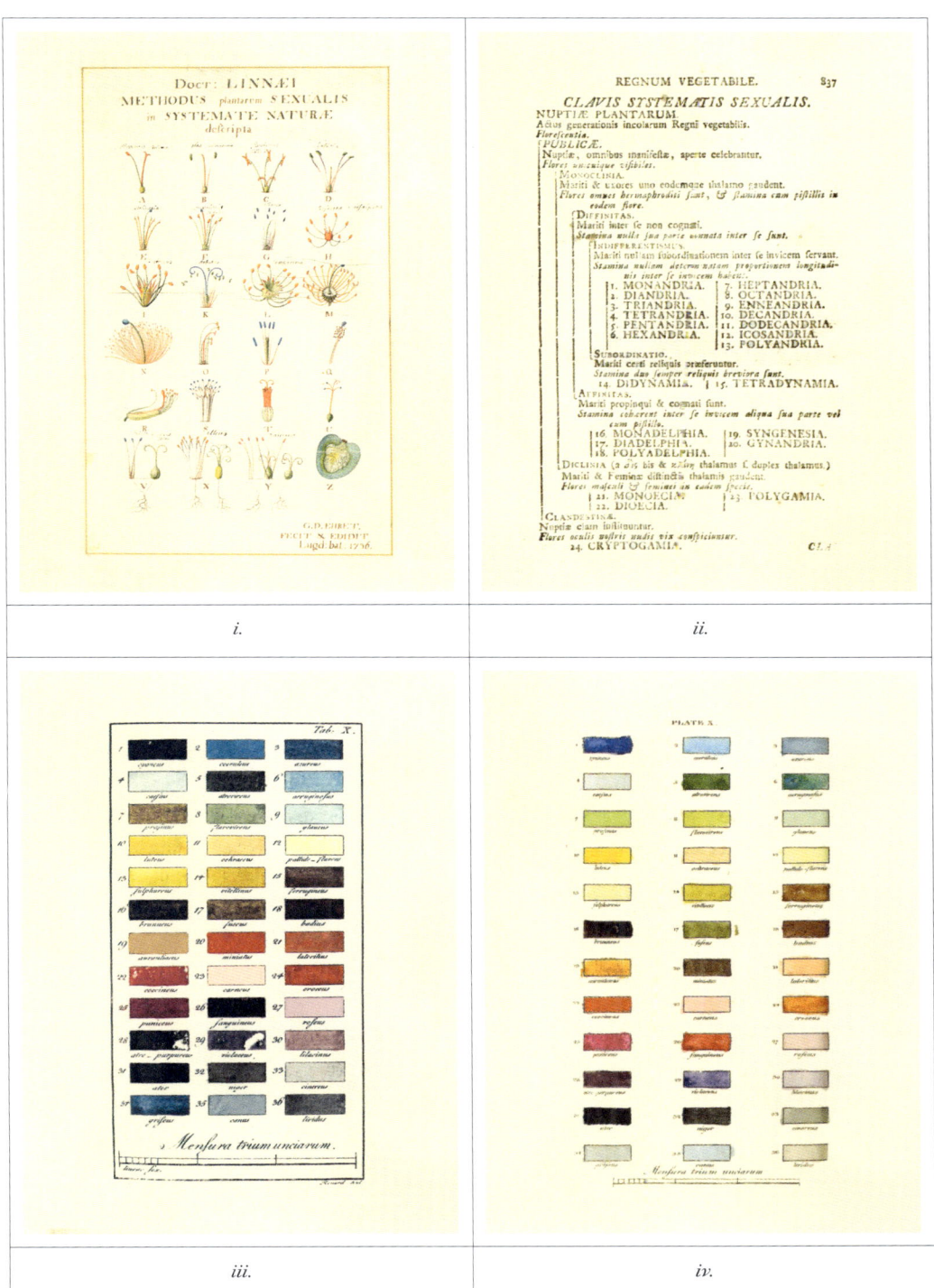

i.

ii.

iii.

iv.

(i).   Illustration of the sexual system of plants, Carl Linnaeus, *Systema naturae*, 1736.
(ii).   Description of the sexual system of plants, Carl Linnaeus, *Systema naturae*, 1758.
(iii).   Colour chart, Carl Ludwig Willdenow, *Grundriss der Kräuterkunde zu*
         Vorlesungen entworfen, 1792.
(iv).   Colour chart, Carl Ludwig Willdenow, *The Principles of Botany*, 1805.

The Botanical Register, subsequently known as *Edwards's Botanical Register*, was an illustrated horticultural magazine, published between 1815 and 1847. It was founded by Sydenham Edwards (1768–1819), who edited the first five volumes, as well as providing the paintings to be engraved by others. Following Edwards's death in 1819 it was edited by James Ridgway (dates unknown) and then by John Lindley (1799–1865) from 1829. The plates shown here are taken from Volume 5, 1819. The *Register* pairs illustrations of plant species with short descriptions of their characteristics.

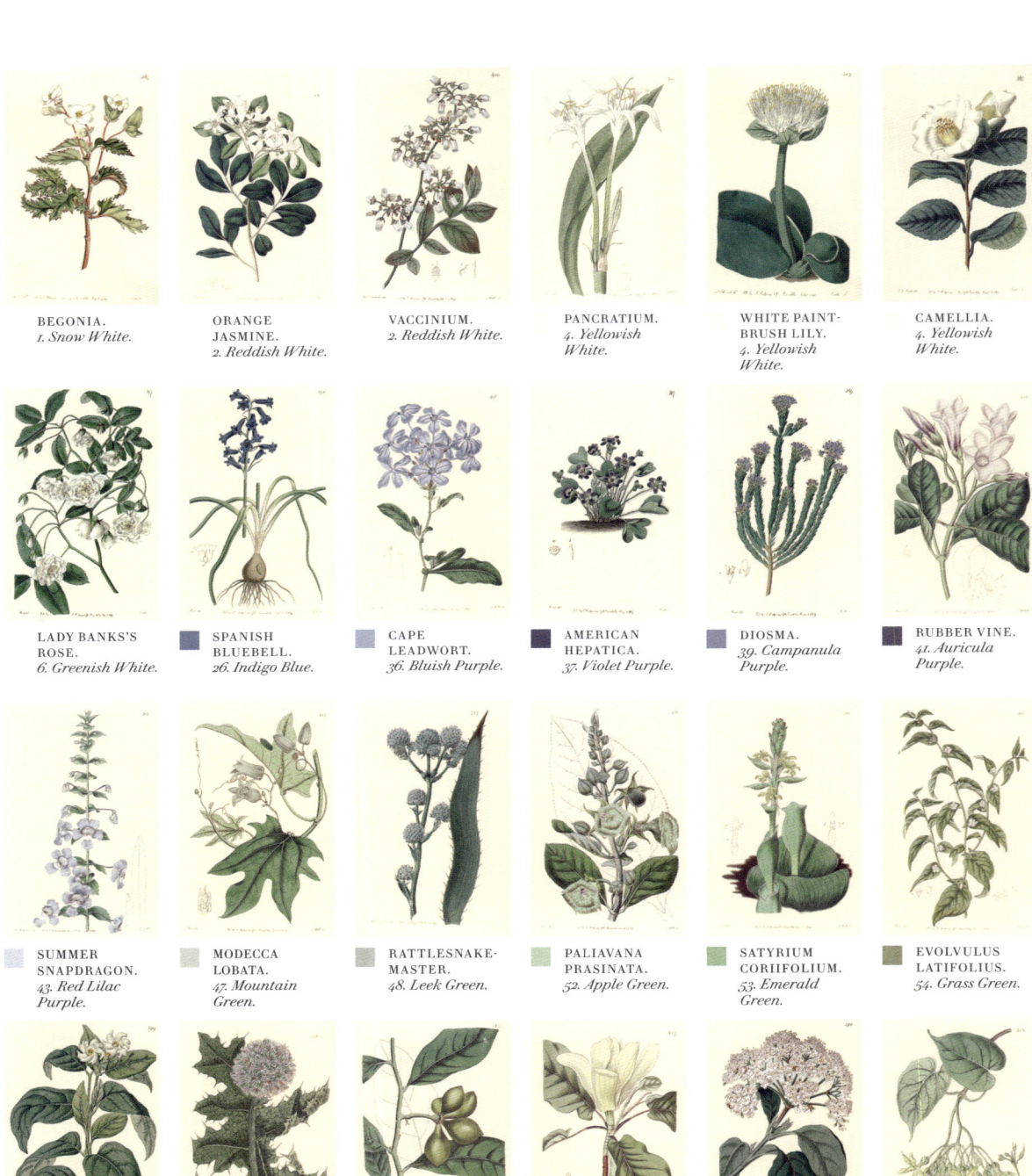

BEGONIA.
1. Snow White.

ORANGE JASMINE.
2. Reddish White.

VACCINIUM.
2. Reddish White.

PANCRATIUM.
4. Yellowish White.

WHITE PAINT-BRUSH LILY.
4. Yellowish White.

CAMELLIA.
4. Yellowish White.

LADY BANKS'S ROSE.
6. Greenish White.

SPANISH BLUEBELL.
26. Indigo Blue.

CAPE LEADWORT.
36. Bluish Purple.

AMERICAN HEPATICA.
37. Violet Purple.

DIOSMA.
39. Campanula Purple.

RUBBER VINE.
41. Auricula Purple.

SUMMER SNAPDRAGON.
43. Red Lilac Purple.

MODECCA LOBATA.
47. Mountain Green.

RATTLESNAKE-MASTER.
48. Leek Green.

PALIAVANA PRASINATA.
52. Apple Green.

SATYRIUM CORIIFOLIUM.
53. Emerald Green.

EVOLVULUS LATIFOLIUS.
54. Grass Green.

NIGHT-FLOWERING JASMINE.
54. Grass Green.

GLANDULAR GLOBE-THISTLE.
55. Duck Green.

ARTABOTRYS ODORATISSIMUS.
56. Sap Green.

PYRAMID MAGNOLIA.
58. Asparagus Green.

LAURUSTINE.
59. Olive Green.

WEST COAST CREEPER.
61. Siskin Green.

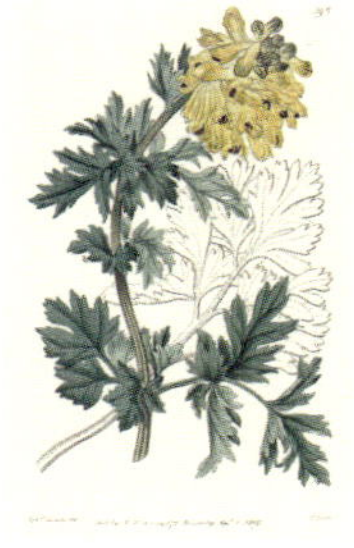

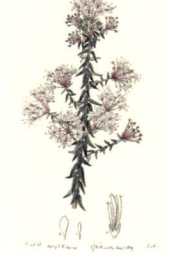

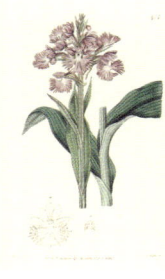

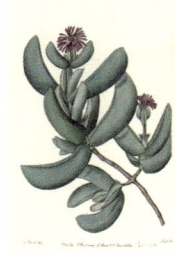

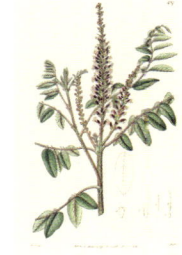

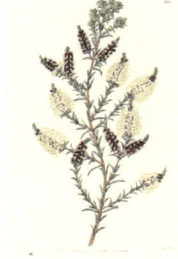

SIBERIAN CORYDALIS. *66. Gamboge Yellow.*

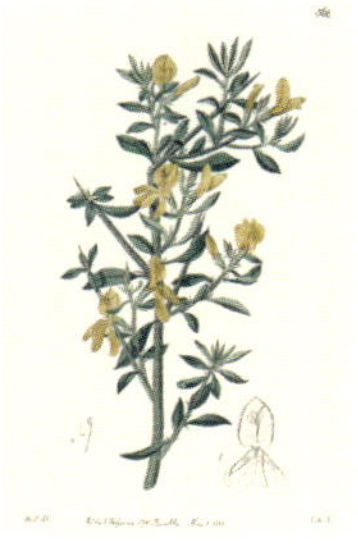

SPARTIUM. *68. Saffron Yellow.*

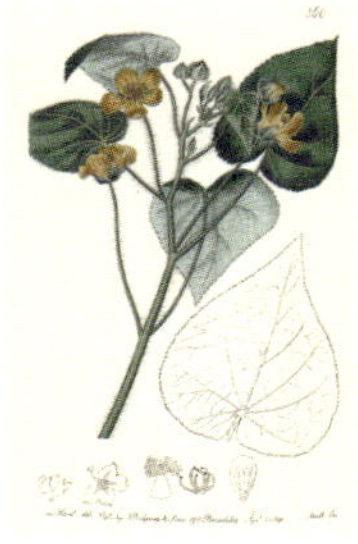

LARGE-LEAVED SIDA. *70. Honey Yellow.*

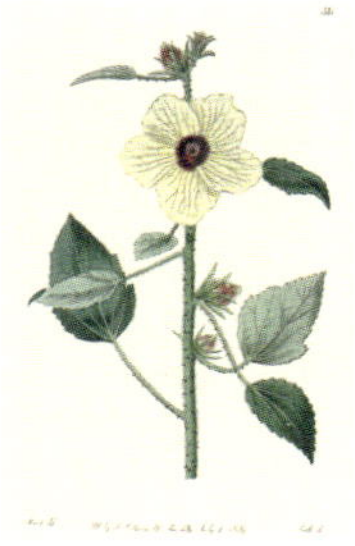

SWAMP HIBISCUS. *71. Straw Yellow.*

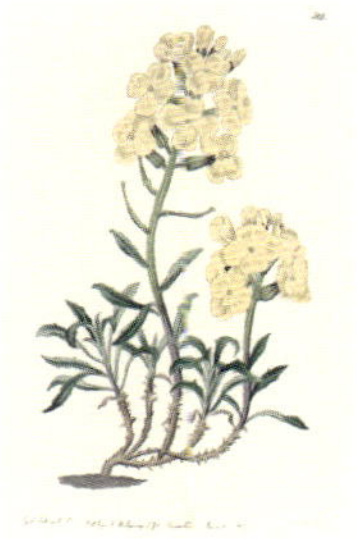

ERYSIMUM DIFFUSUM. *73. Sienna Yellow.*

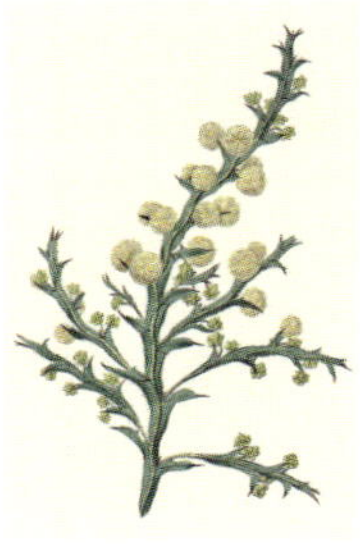

WINGED WATTLE. *74. Ochre Yellow.*

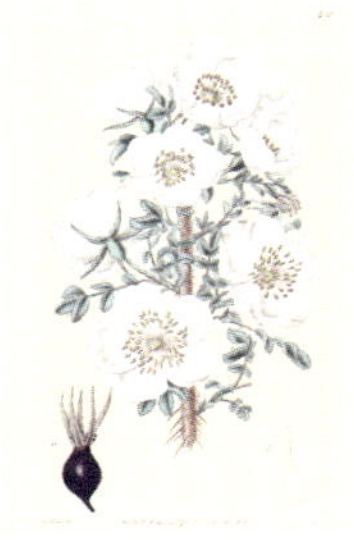

SCOTCH ROSE. *75. Cream Yellow.*

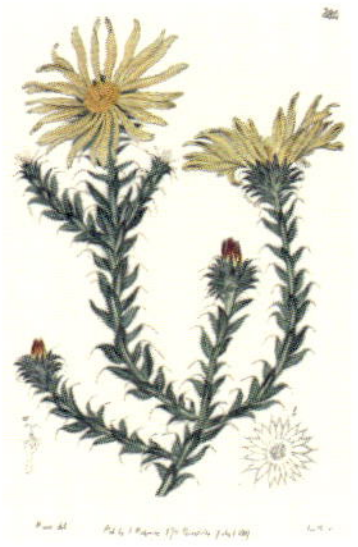

CULLUMIA. *76. Dutch Orange.*

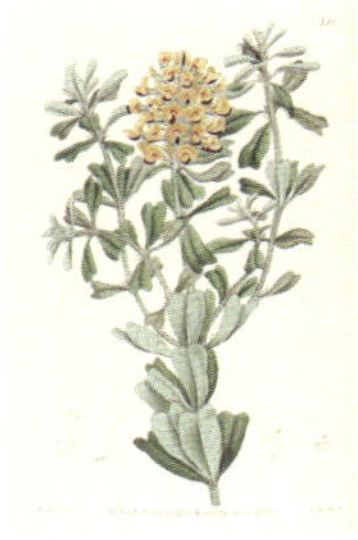

HEART-LEAVED POISON. *77. Buff Orange.*

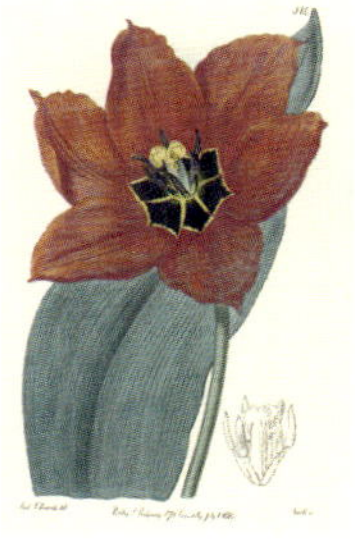

COMMON TULIP. *83. Hyacinth Red.*

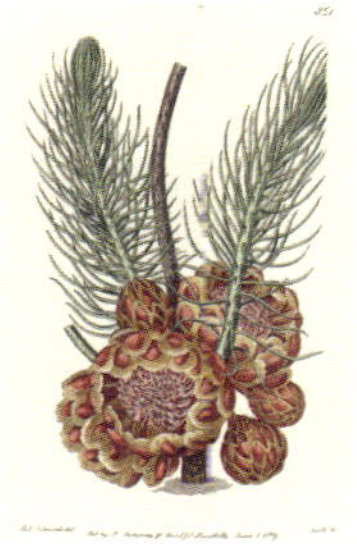

PROTEA. *84. Scarlet Red.*

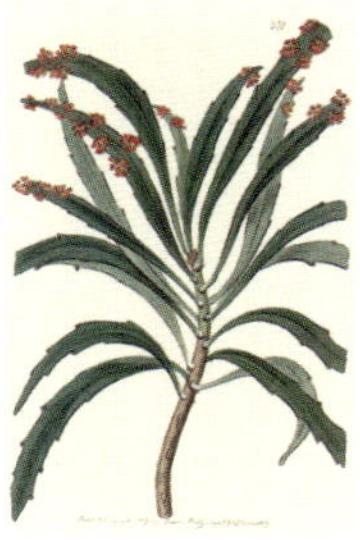

PHYLLANTHUS ANGUSTIFOLIUS. *84. Scarlet Red.*

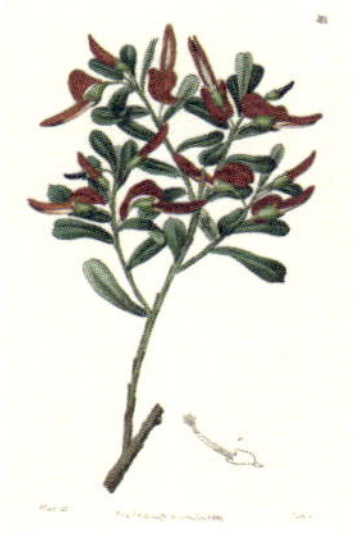

CORAL BUSH. *84. Scarlet Red.*

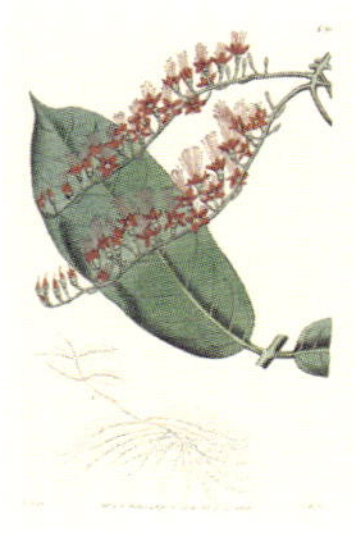

SCARLET COMB. *84. Scarlet Red.*

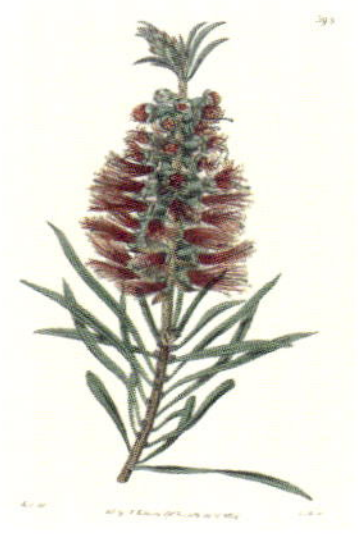

BOTTLEBRUSH. *85. Vermilion Red.*

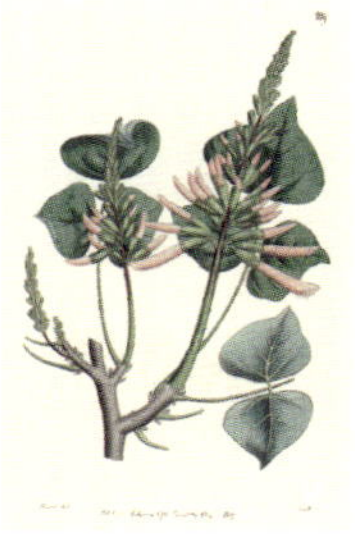

CORAL TREE. *86. Aurora Red.*

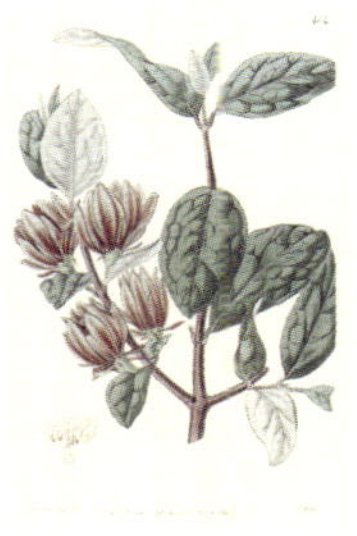

EASTERN SWEETSHRUB. *87. Arterial Blood Red.*

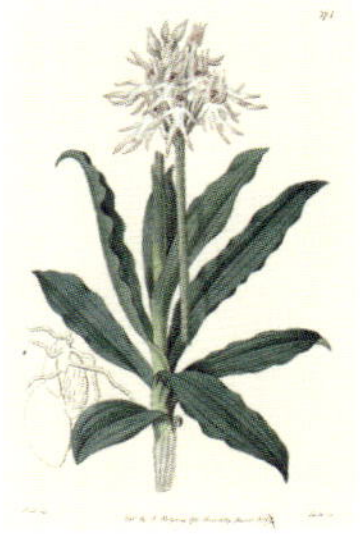

ITALIAN ORCHID. *89. Rose Red.*

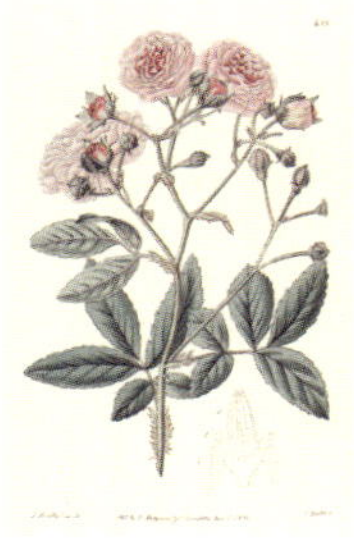

ROSA MULTI-FLORA CARNEA. *90. Peach Blossom Red.*

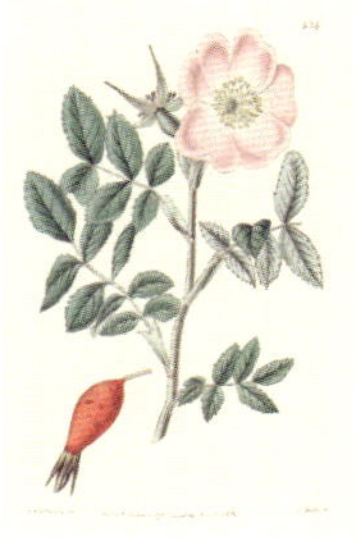

ALPINE ROSE. *90. Peach Blossom Red.*

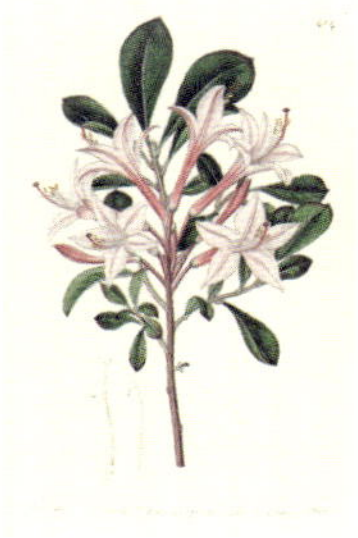

SWAMP HONEYSUCKLE. *90. Peach Blossom Red.*

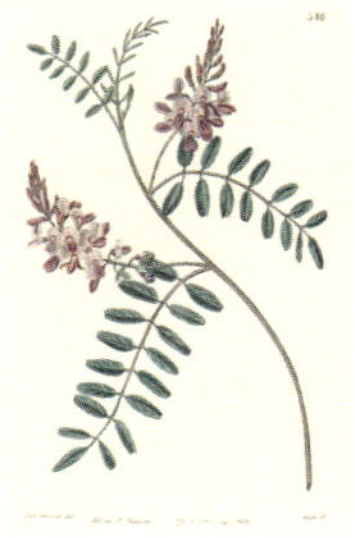

AUSTRALIAN INDIGO. *91. Carmine Red.*

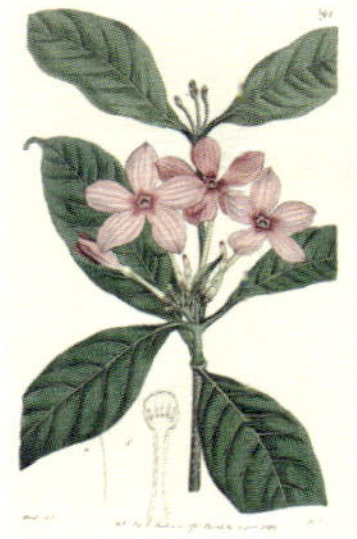

CERBERA. *91. Carmine Red.*

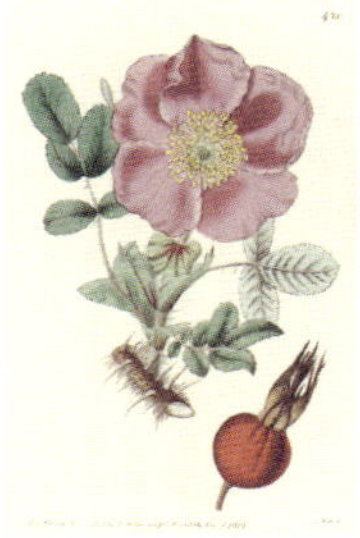

BEACH ROSE. *91. Carmine Red.*

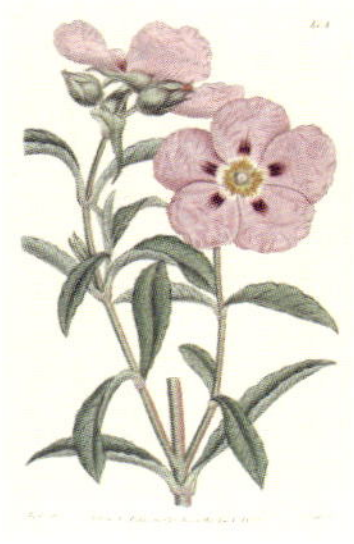

ORCHID ROCKROSE. *92. Lake Red.*

DIOSMA CILIATA. *93. Crimson Red.*

SMALL PURPLE FRINGED ORCHID. *93. Crimson Red.*

FIG MARIGOLD. *94. Purplish Red.*

FALSE INDIGO-BUSH. *94. Purplish Red.*

GREY HONEY-MYRTLE. *95. Cochineal Red.*

181.   3. SYME'S COLOUR CHART IN BOTANY: ORIGIN AND IMPACT.

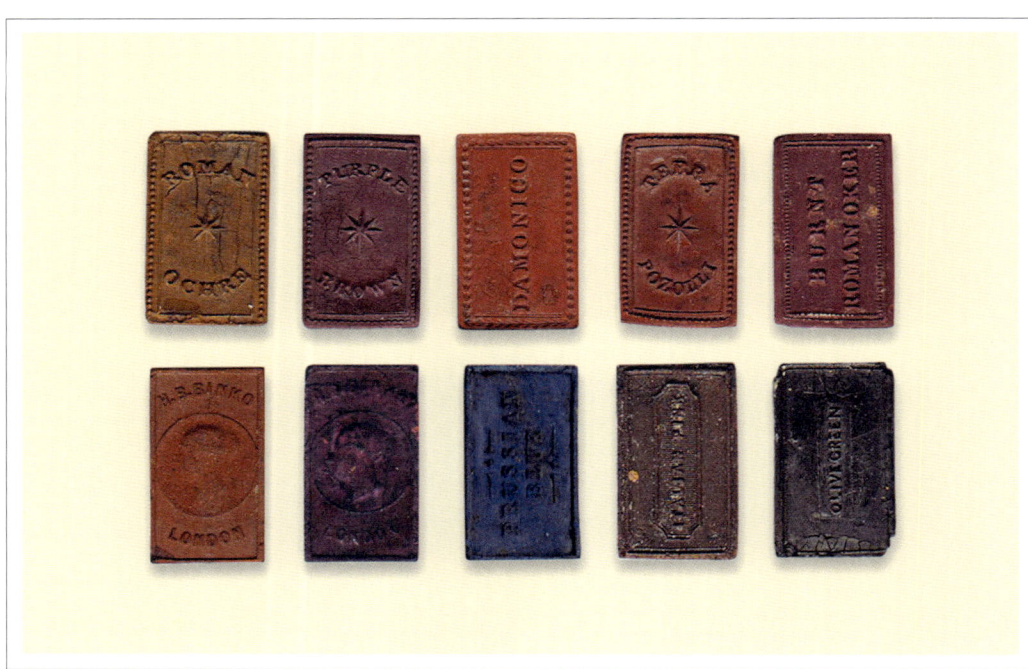

i.

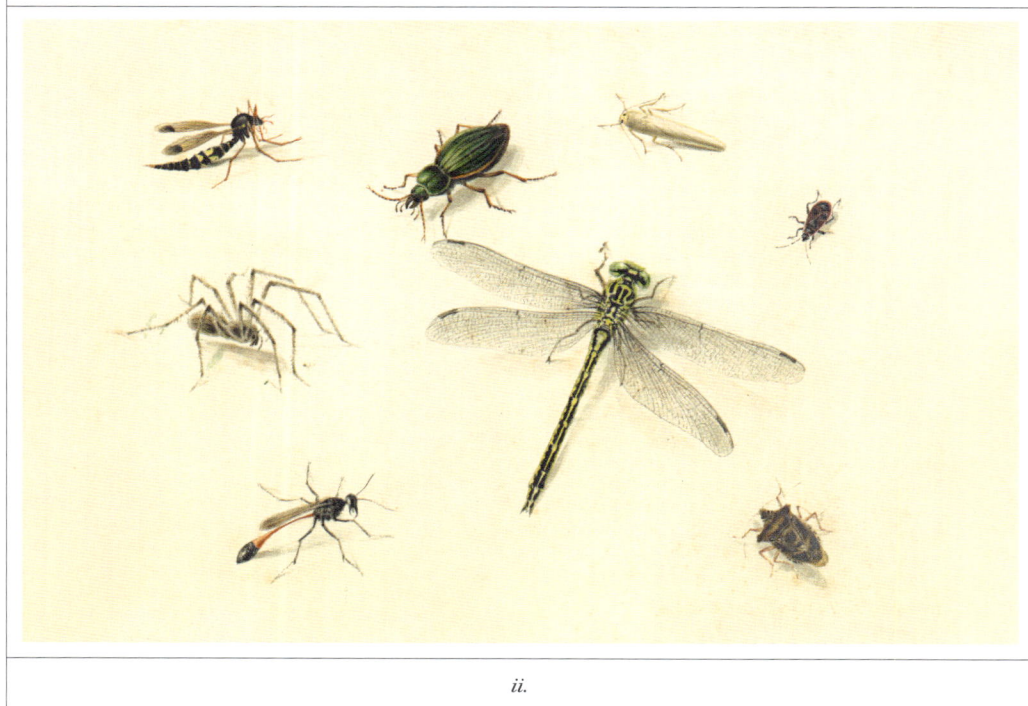

ii.

(i).   Watercolour blocks of the artist suppliers Henry Boch Binko, *c.* 1800s
           (bottom row, left three blocks), Giovanni Arzone, *c.* 1830 (top row),
           and Waring & Dimes, *c.* 1840–42 (bottom row, right two blocks).

(ii).   Patrick Syme, *Spider, Beetles and Insects*, watercolour, date unknown.

Willdenow's colour chart and nomenclature appeared in all the later reprints and translations of his textbook. In 1799 the Berlin pharmacist Friedrich Gottlob Hayne (1763–1832) included his own re-worked version of Willdenow's colour chart with colour samples at the sides and several roots at the centre of the plate. Plate X of the English edition is instead an almost identical colour chart to the original one; the colour terms are in Latin, with their English equivalents supplied in the main text. The Scottish engraver and map maker Daniel Lizars Sr (1760–1812), who signed all other nine plates 'D Lizars Sculpt', made this plate too. This edition was printed by the Edinburgh University Press for William Blackwood (1776–1834), also the publisher of Syme's *Werner's Nomenclature of Colours*. Syme knew of it and relied on it for some new colour terms.

SYME'S COLOUR TERMINOLOGY

The colour terminology used by Syme in *Werner's Nomenclature of Colours* was probably derived from Jameson's *Tabular View of the External Characters of Minerals* (1804), which rested in turn on Werner's new colour nomenclature. Jameson provided 80 colour terms (or 84 if we count the four lead-grey sub-varieties as independent colours, see p. 34), the majority of which are also found in Syme's book. However, Syme extended the colour nomenclature to 108 terms in the first edition of his book in 1814, and to 110 terms in the second edition in 1821, resulting from the creation of two new main colour groups, orange and purple, along with further hues identified by him.[25]

Some of Syme's new colour terms can be traced to other books mentioned above, and many are obviously loans from painters' pigments and dyes, which Syme likely used to manufacture his colour swatches. Among Syme's terms are gamboge yellow, Sienna yellow, sap green, lake red and umber brown, some of which also featured in Brookshaw's and Francia's flower-painting manuals. For five of his new colour terms Syme drew on Sowerby's *A New Elucidation of Colours* (1809) for

inspiration: reddish orange, brownish orange, deep orange-coloured brown, bluish purple and pale blackish purple. Other colour terms indicate the scientific advances being made at the time, for instance he divided blood red into two different hues, 'arterial' and 'veinous', no doubt as a result of the research on blood circulation by the Scottish surgeon John Hunter (1728–1793). Finally, Syme adopted four colour terms from the English edition of Willdenow's textbook, namely bluish green, saffron yellow, lilac and blackish grey. Syme used lilac for creating two colour varieties: bluish lilac purple and red lilac purple. Some of the remaining terms were coined by Syme, while others already commonly used in English, such as French grey, were popularized by Syme and adopted into the scientific colour terminology.[26]

What sets Syme's book apart was that it combined an extensive chart presenting simple colours and colour mixtures with a nomenclature and references to the natural world – animal, vegetable and mineral – for colour comparison. It was 'a NOMENCLATURE of colours with proper coloured examples of the different tints, as a general standard to refer to in the description of any object'. Thus it provided a colour terminology that scientists could use to pick the most suitable colour term to describe an object from the natural world in a standardized way. For the mineral examples Syme drew on Jameson's work but selected the animal and vegetable examples himself, perhaps feeling qualified to do so having trained as a botanist and entomologist.

His botanical references range from the straightforward – 'Chesnuts' [*sic*] for 'Chesnut Brown' or 'Hawthorn Blossom' for 'Yellowish White' – to the very specific – that for 'Cochineal Red' is 'Under Disk of decayed leaves of None-so-pretty' and for 'Velvet Black' it is 'Black of Red and Black West-Indian Peas'. And even with all his botanical knowledge he was not able always to come up with a suitable reference, as is also the case for minerals and animals.

Syme's most significant contribution to colour systems was not only to have selected 110 colour names from different sources, but also

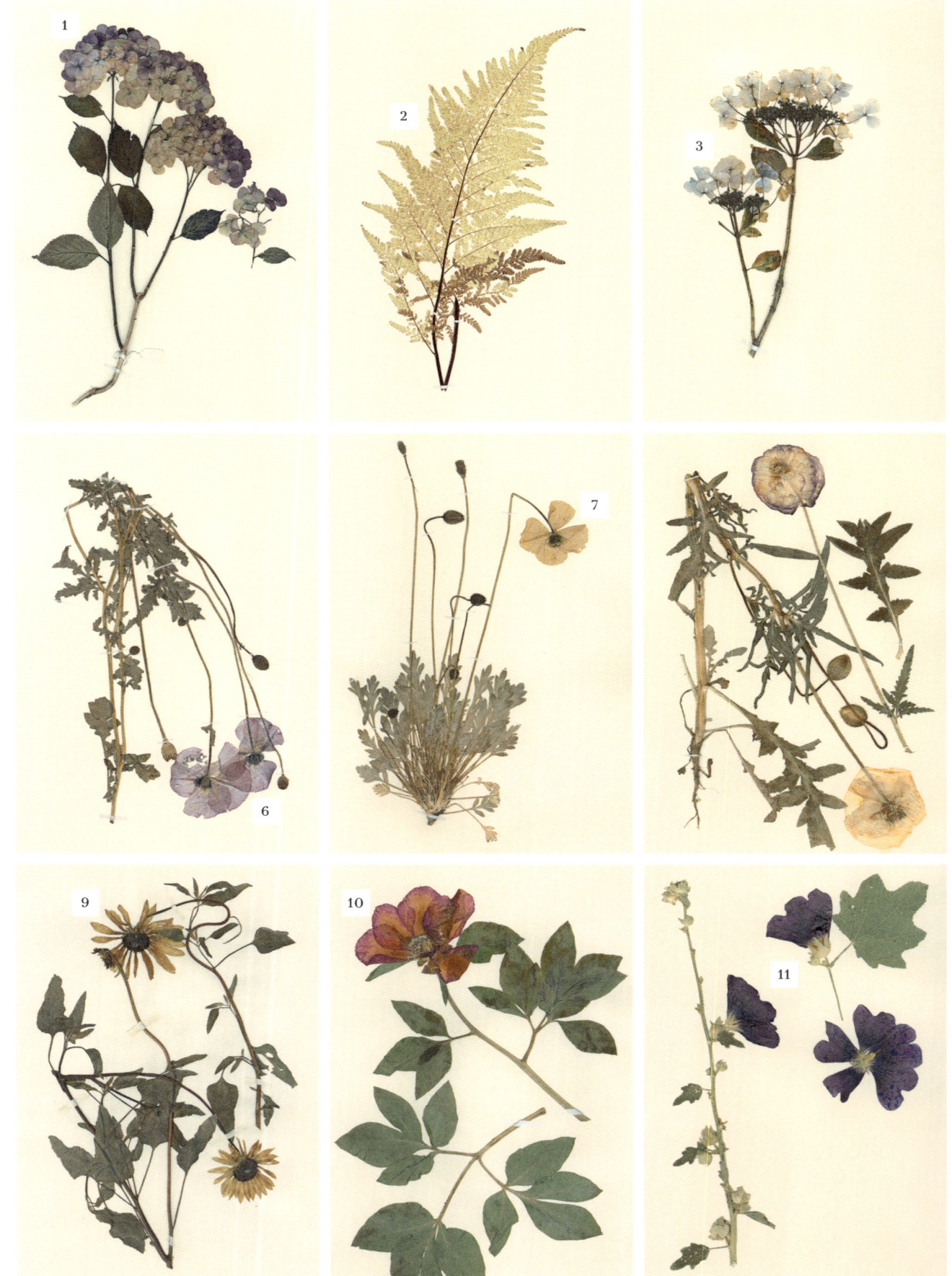

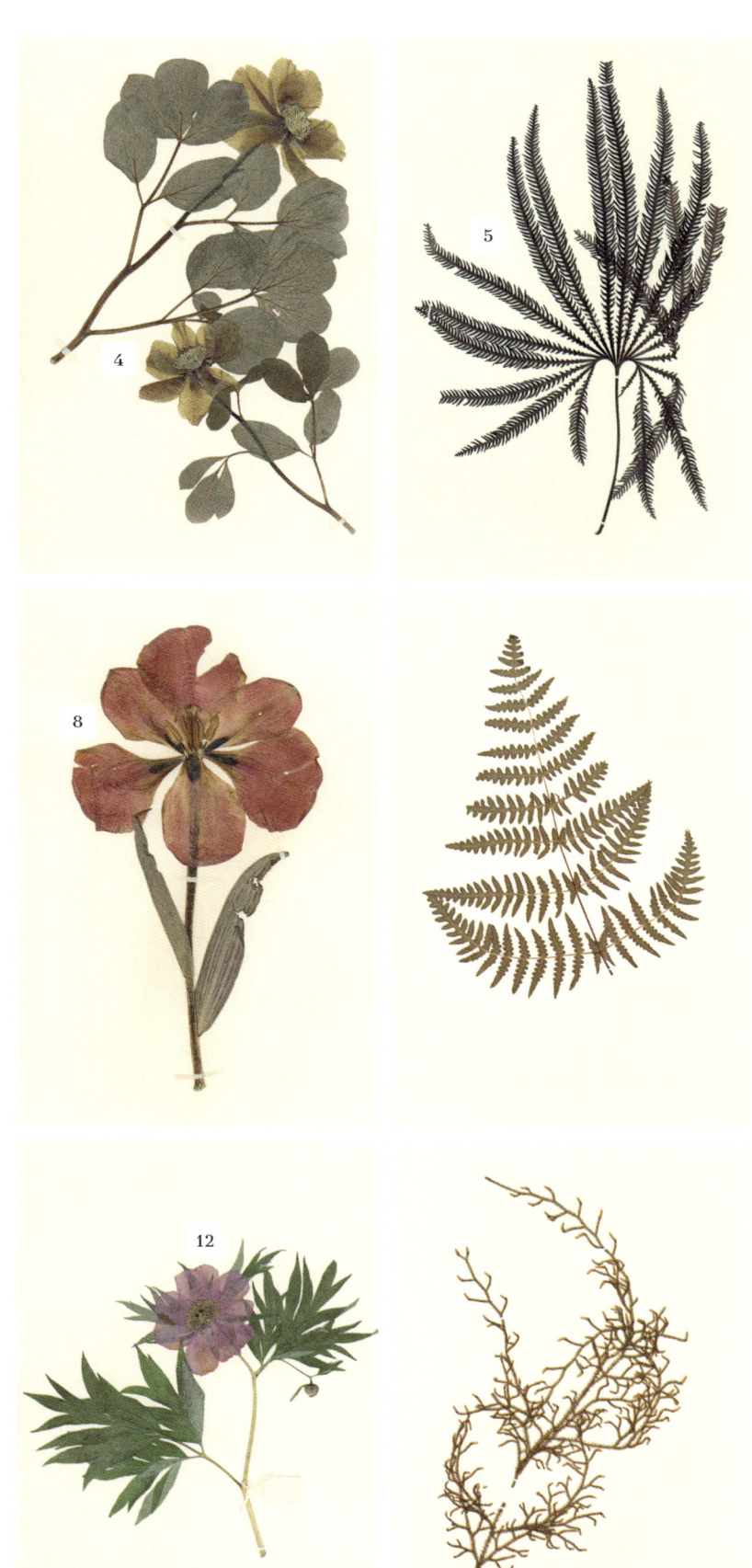

THE NATURAL HISTORY MUSEUM HERBARIUM.

A herbarium is a collection of preserved plant specimens, stored with their associated data for scientific study. The herbarium at the Natural History Museum, London, contains over 2 million specimens from all over the world, collected from the 17th century onwards. It includes species obtained on famed voyages, including that of HMS *Endeavour* and HMS *Beagle,* and by prominent naturalists, including Sir Joseph Banks (1743–1820) and James Sowerby (1757–1822).

COLOUR REFERENCES.

1		HYDRANGEA PREZIOSA.
		42.. Plum Purple.
2		YELLOW FERN.
		66. Gamboge Yellow.
3		HYDRANGEA MACROPHYLLA.
		32. Verditter Blue.
4		CORAL PEONY.
		68. Saffron Yellow.
5		MATONIA PECTINATA FERN.
		102. Umber Brown.
6		CORN POPPY.
		43. Red Lilac Purple.
7		ARCTIC POPPY.
		77. Buff Orange.
8		RED RIDING HOOD TULIP.
		84. Scarlet Red.
9		SUNFLOWER.
		76. Dutch Orange.
10		DWARF PEONY.
		91. Carmine Red.
11		TURKISH HOLLYHOCK.
		40. Imperial Purple.
12		VEITCH'S PEONY.
		93. Crimson Red.

to have radically transformed the colour chart from an educational tool for painters and some naturalists into a practical working instrument for all naturalists. Moreover, with Syme's publication and his explicit encouragement of botanists to use it, the Linnaean reservations about colour were finally overcome.

COLOUR TERMS AND CHARTS FOR BOTANISTS IN EUROPE AFTER SYME

An example of the reception of Syme's colour terms by English-speaking botanists can be seen in the use of French grey in the prestigious series *The Botanical Register* edited by Sydenham Edwards (1768–1819) and John Lindley (1799–1865).[27] Even though the great botanist Sir William Jackson Hooker (1785–1865) made use of *Werner's Nomenclature of Colours* for describing plants in *Appendix to Captain Parry's Journal...* (1825), as John Richardson (1787–1865) did for animals, he relied on Syme's standard colours for his *Supplement to the English Botany* (1834), at least to render the colours of a lichenized fungus.[28] That Syme's type of colour chart was a radical novelty for botanical science is demonstrated by the botanist William P. C. Barton (1786–1856), who in the advertisement for the third volume of *A Flora of North America* (1823) lamented that he had been unable to reproduce Syme's colour samples as he had anticipated in the first volume, where he had provided a black-and-white copy of Syme's *Werner's Nomenclature of Colours*:

> It was the intention of the Author ... to add the tints of *Werner's Nomenclature of Colours* to Vol. II. Upon repeated experiments with the tints, it was found that the best watercolours produced in their combinations, fading and evanescent tints – and the Author was acquainted with no other mode of colouring them. He believes the tints of Werner's Book to be dyed by mineral solutions, and afterwards they are evidently pasted in squares, opposite to the columns of names. Hence it was impossible for him

to add the tints, which he intended to do under the idea that they were reproduced by the common colour in use.

It seems that Barton had not grasped the intended function of Syme's book to provide standard colour terms, believing that it was also a guide for mixing pigments and dyes.[29]

Colour charts specifically for botanists were published occasionally after the appearance of Syme's in 1814, though general attempts at classifying colours for naturalists were more frequent. In 1815, for instance, the French painter and chemist Léonor Mérimée (1757–1836) wrote an essay on colours for naturalists and included three circular colour charts with 83 nuances, or shades, and 96 corresponding terms in French and Latin.[30] Later, in 1825, the Scottish horticulturist George Sinclair (1787–1834) included a 'Diagram of Colours' in his *Hortus ericæus woburnensis*, consisting of a colour circle subdivided into 270 hues and two colour scales (for grey and brown) created by George Hayter (1792–1871), later Principal Painter in Ordinary to Queen Victoria.[31] The general tendency after this in English-language botanical textbooks was for colour nomenclatures without samples of colour. This is not to say that English naturalists and scientists were not interested in colour standardization. On the contrary, James David Forbes (1809–1868) and Francis Galton (1822–1911) proposed two different ways of producing colour standards using mosaic tesserae instead of colour charts painted on paper,[32] a solution aimed at overcoming the problem of fading and colour light-fastness.

Further attempts appeared in Germany, France, the United States and Italy. In 1834, the playwright Wilhelm Gerhard (1780–1858) included a colour chart in his history of the cultivation and classification of dahlias, illustrating 48 predominantly red, yellow and purple hues for the identification of these plants, as well as a colour nomenclature with terms in German, Latin, French, Italian and English.[33] Among his textual sources he includes Mérimée's essay, but strangely not

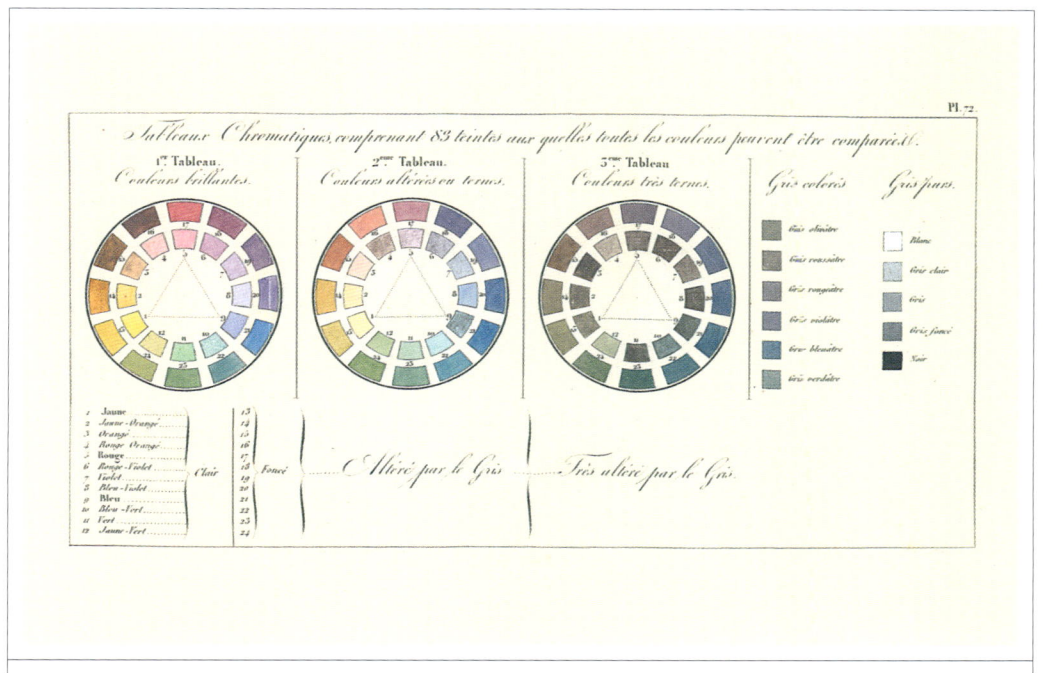

i.

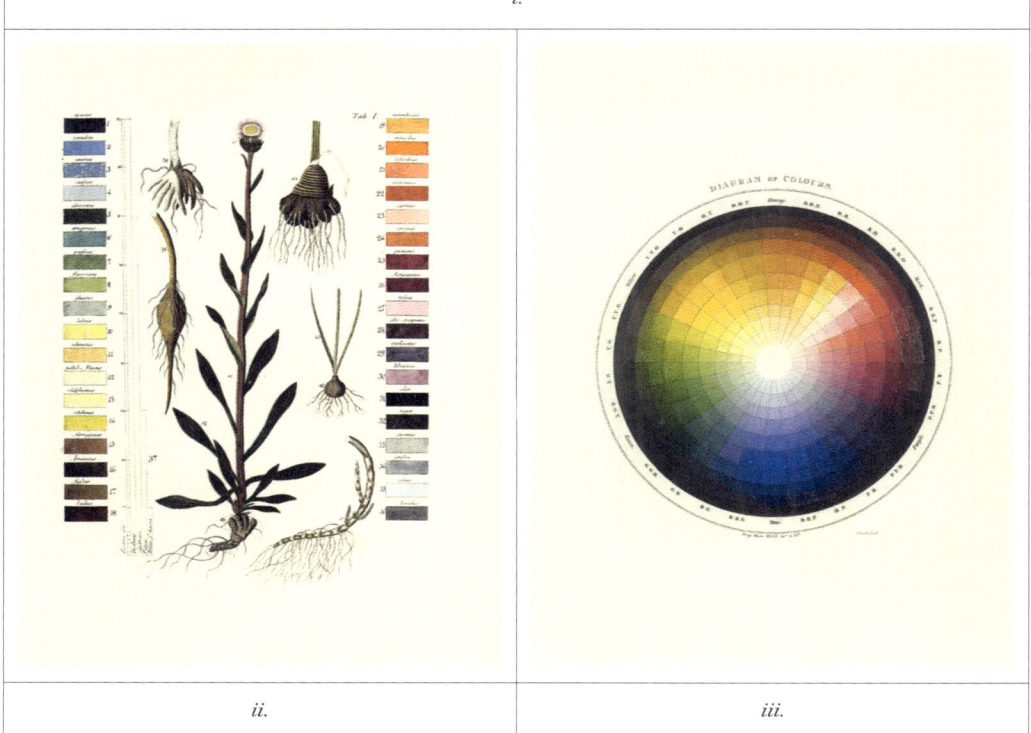

ii.   iii.

(i).   Tableaux chromatique, Léonor Mérimée, *Mémoire sur les lois générales de la coloration appliquées à la formation d'une échelle chromatique, à l'usage des naturalistes*, 1815.
(ii). Plate 1, Friedrich Gottlob Hayne, *Termini botanici iconibus illustrati*, 1799.
(iii). Diagram of Colours, George Hayter, *Hortus ericæus woburnensis*, 1825.

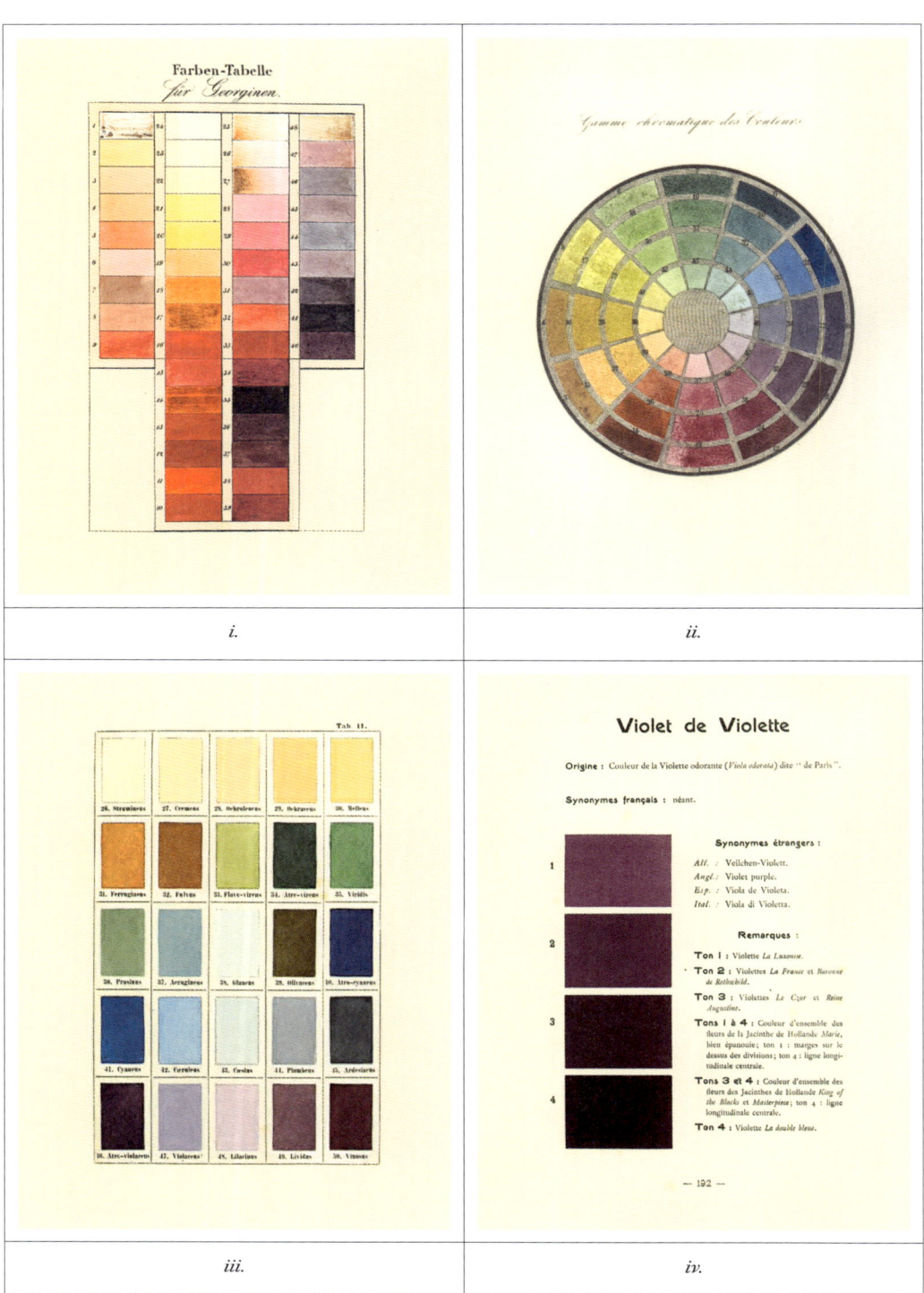

(i).   Colour chart for dahlias, Wilhelm Gerhard, *Zur Geschichte, Cultur und Classification der Georginen oder Dahlien*, 1836.
(ii).   Gamme chromatique des couleurs, Ragonot-Godefroy, *Traité sur la culture des œillets*, 1842.
(iii).   Chromotaxy scale, Plate II, Pier Andrea Saccardo, *Chromotaxia seu nomenclator colorum*, 1894.
(iv).   Chart of purples, René Oberthür and Henri Dauthenay, *Répertoire de couleurs*, 1905.

Syme's publication. Another type of flower inspired a certain Monsieur Ragonot-Godefroy, perhaps a pseudonym for the botanist Pierre Boitard (1789-1859), to publish his treatise on the cultivation of carnations in 1842, entitled *Traité sur la culture des œillets*. In this, he provided a colour circle subdivided into 48 hues – which he called a 'Gamme chromatique des Couleurs'. It was clearly inspired by Mérimée's attempt,[34] though Ragonot-Godefroy used numbers instead of words to indicate the colours.

Then, in 1886, the American ornithologist Robert Ridgway (1850-1929) published *A Nomenclature of Colors for Naturalists*, which included 186 colour samples using names drawn from Syme's work (see also pp. 30-31) and translated, where possible, into six other languages. The design of Ridgway's colour chart is similar to Syme's, rather than the previous circular diagrams. A similar colour chart was published in 1891 by the botanist and mycologist Pier Andrea Saccardo (1845-1920), entitled *Chromotaxia*. Saccardo provided 50 colour samples accompanied by a polyglot colour nomenclature, including English colour names taken from Ridgway and thus indirectly from Syme. Like Syme's colour nomenclature, Ridgway's and Saccardo's systems were not addressed exclusively to botanists but to all naturalists. A colour chart that was explicitly made 'for the use of Florists' was developed by Ferdinand Schuyler Mathews (1854-1938) in 1895. Mathews's chart contains 36 numbered and named samples, although the majority are shades of red,[35] and is reminiscent

of Gerhard's colour chart for dahlias as it is primarily for botanists and horticulturists and lacks many relevant nuances.

This gap was finally filled in 1905, when the first standard colour catalogue for botanists appeared. *Répertoire de couleurs pour aider à la determination des couleurs des fleurs, des feuillages et des fruits* was the result of an international co-operation supported by the Société Française des Chrysanthémistes. It comprises 365 hues arranged in a total of 1,403 colour samples. For this feat, the authors, the secretary to the Roseraie de L'Haÿ, Henri Dauthenay (1857-1910), and the entomologist and printer René Oberthür (1852-1944), compiled an extensive colour nomenclature in six languages, including Latin, with the help of experts from England, Germany, Italy and Spain. The production of the catalogue relied on the famous colour system (1861) of Michel Eugène Chevreul (1786-1889) and on the use of high-quality inks provided by Charles Lorilleux's (1827-1893) company.[36] Even though Syme's work does not appear among the sources consulted by Dauthenay and Oberthür, some of their colour terms do seem to derive from it. 'Violet purple', 'primrose yellow', 'China blue' and 'gallstone yellow' had all been introduced to naturalists by Syme in 1814.[37] Syme's colour nomenclature had evidently permeated botanical terminology so deeply that, less than a century after its publication, the authors of the first standard colour nomenclature for botanists drew on its colour terms without realizing.

NOTES – (1). McEwan 1994, p. 566; Halsby and Harris 2001, p. 217. (2). Dixon 2014. (3). Edinburgh, The National Galleries of Scotland, *Peas and Beans*, date of creation unknown, watercolour over pen, ink and pencil, laid down onto album leaf with a pen and wash border, 32 × 20.9 cm, accession number D 3870.32. (4). Bénézit 2011; Dixon 2014. (5). *Dictionary of National Biography*. (6). Blunt and Stearn 1995, pp. 254-56. (7). Pretty 1810, plate 3. (8). Wood 1991, p. 303. (9). Lack and Ibáñez 1997; Lack 2015, pp. 35-41; Mabberley 2017, pp. 3-18. (10). Sowerby 1809, pp. 34-35. (11). Forster 1813, pp. 119, 121. (12). Linnaeus and Freer 2005, p. 229. (13). Linnaeus 1751, pp. 243-44. (14). Werner 1774, pp. 58-62. (15). Werner 1774, pp. 99-127. (16). Jameson 1805, p. 22. (17). Freiberg, TU Bergakademie, Universitätsbibliothek, Werner Nachlass, Handschriftlicher Nachlass, Bd. 13, pp. 84r-263v. (18). Between 1798 and 1829-1833, the Berlin publishing house Haude und Spener reprinted *Grundriss der Kräuterkunde* with amendments and additions a further six times. The book was also re-issued by other publishing houses, in particular in 1799 and 1805 by Ghelen, in 1808 by Bauer and in 1818 by Doll, all three based in Vienna. Already in 1794, the textbook had been translated into Danish by Henrik Steffens (1773-1845), into English in 1805, possibly by Maria Elizabetha Jacson (1755-1829), and, finally, into Dutch by Gerard Wttewaal (1776-1839) in 1819. (19). Willdenow 1805, pp. 197-99. (20). Willdenow 1792, pp. 236-39. (21). Compare Willdenow 1792, pp. 236-39, and Werner's manuscripts at Freiberg. (22). Wagenitz and Lack 2012, p. 3; Tkach et al. 2016, p. 13. (23). Wagenbreth 1967, p. 165. (24). Estner 1794:1, pp. 11-12. (25). Simonini 2018, §47. (26). Simonini 2018, §46. (27). *The Botanical Register*, Vol. V, 1819, pl. 417. (28). On Richardson and the colours of animals see p. 130; Hooker 1834, p. 2768. (29). Barton 1823, [p. ix] Advertisement. (30). Mérimée 1815. (31). Sinclair 1825, pp. 39-42; Wachsmuth 2014, p. 73. (32). Forbes 1849; Galton 1887. (33). Gerhard 1834, pp. 41-43; Wachsmuth 2014, p. 73. (34). Wachsmuth 2014, pp. 73-74. (35). Mathews 1895. The problem of light-fast pigment is stressed by Syme and by Mathews as well. (36). Dauthenay and Oberthür 1905, pp. 36-37. (37). The works consulted are listed in the section 'Principaux ouvrages consultés' at the beginning of the book. These colour terms correspond to the colours numbered 191, 19, 210, and 51 in *Répertoire de couleurs*.

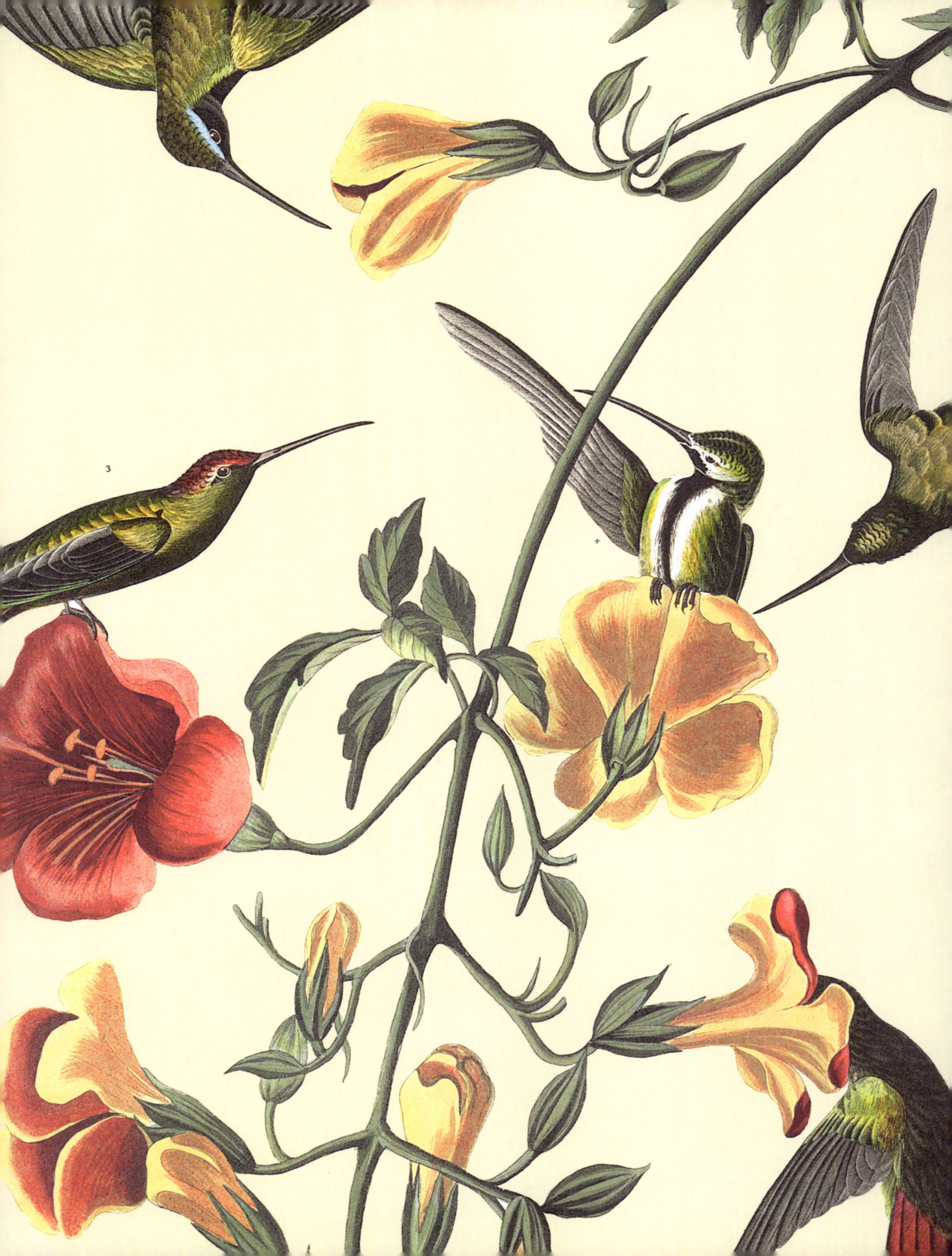

iv.

YELLOWS AND ORANGES.

YELLOWS (i).

YELLOWS.

No.	Names	Colours	ANIMAL	VEGETABLE	MINERAL
62	Sulphur Yellow.		Yellow Parts of large Dragon Fly.	Various Coloured Snap dragon.	Sulphur
63	Primrose Yellow.		Pale Canary Bird.	Wild Primrose	Pale coloured Sulphur.
64	Wax Yellow.		Larva of large Water Beetle.	Greenish Parts of Nonpareil Apple.	Semi Opal.
65	Lemon Yellow.		Large Wasp or Hornet.	Shrubby Goldylocks.	Yellow Orpiment.
66	Gamboge Yellow.		Wings of Goldfinch. Canary Bird.	Yellow Jasmine.	High coloured Sulphur.
67	Kings Yellow.		Head of Golden Pheasant.	Yellow Tulip. Cinque foil.	
68	Saffron Yellow.		Tail Coverts of Golden Pheasant.	Anthers of Saffron Crocus.	

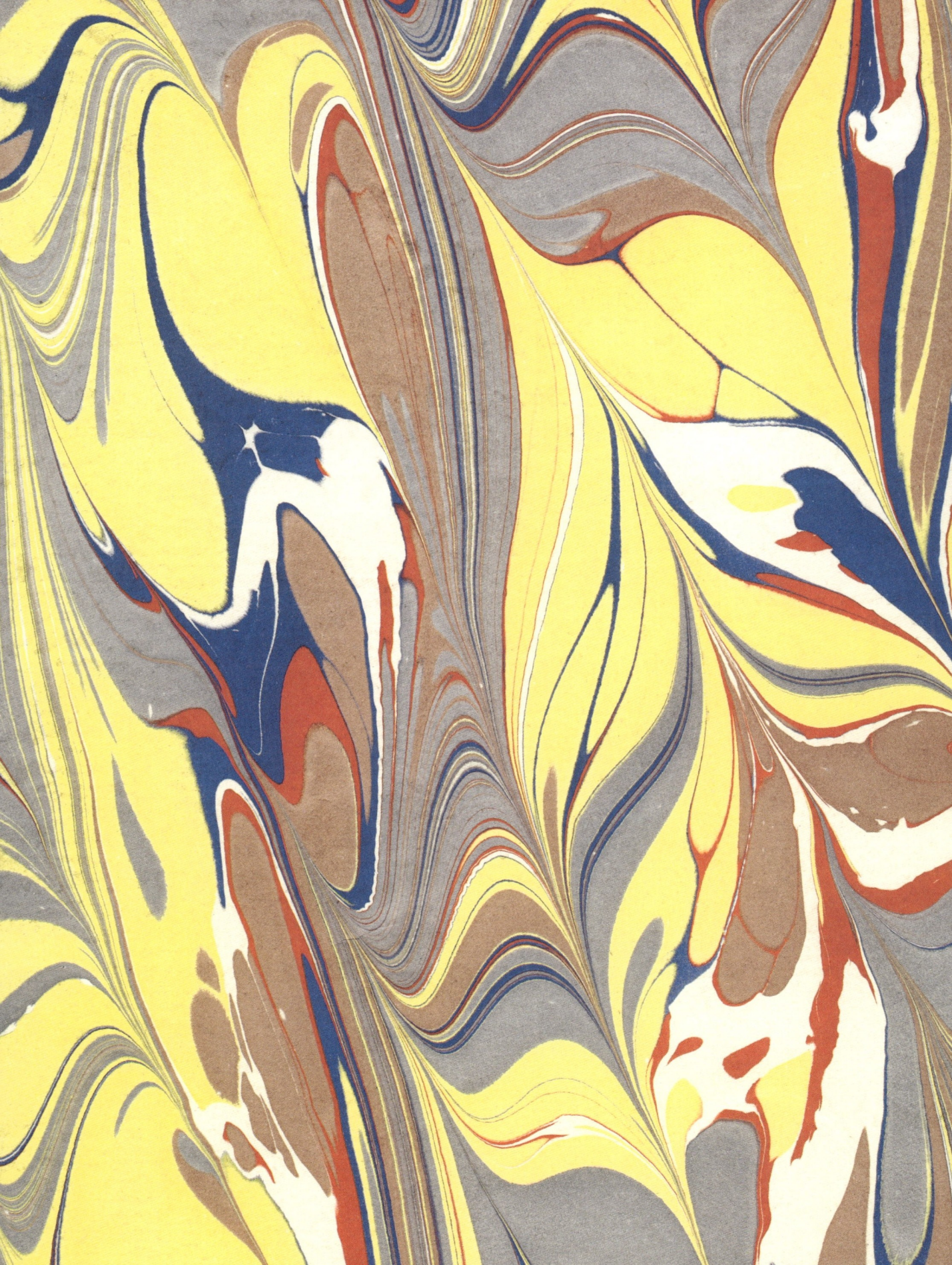

ORANGES.

ORANGE.

N?.	Names	Colours.	ANIMAL.	VEGITABLE.	MINERAL.
76	Dutch Orange.		Crest of Golden crested Wren.	Common Marigold, Seedpod of Spindle-tree.	Streak of Red Orpiment.
77	Buff Orange.		Streak from the Eye of the King Fisher.	Stamina of the large White Cistus.	Natrolite.
78	Orpiment Orange.		The Neck Ruff of the Golden Pheasant. Body of the Warty Newt.	Indian Cress.	
79	Brownish Orange.		Eyes of the largest Flesh-Fly.	Style of the Orange Lily.	Dark Brazilian Topaz.
80	Reddish Orange.		Lower Wings of Tyger Moth.	Hemimeris, Buff Hibiscus.	
81	Deep Reddish Orange.		Gold Fish lustre abstracted.	Scarlet Leadington Apple.	

YELLOWS.

N°.	Names	Colours	ANIMAL.	VEGITABLE.	MINERAL.
69	Gallstone Yellow.		Gallstones.	Marigold Apple.	
70	Honey Yellow.		Lower Parts of Neck of Bird of Paradise.		Fluor Spar.
71	Straw Yellow.		Polar Bear.	Oat Straw.	Scherlite. Calamine.
72	Wine Yellow.		Body of Silk Moth.	White Currants.	Saxon Topaz.
73	Sienna Yellow.		Vent Parts of Tail of Bird of Paradise.	Stamina of Honey-suckle.	Pale Brazilian Topax.
74	Ochre Yellow.		Vent Coverts of Red Start.		Porcelain Jasper.
75	Cream Yellow.		Breast of Teal Drake.		Porcelain Jasper.

No.	Names.	Colours.	ANIMAL.		
62	*Sulphur Yellow.*		*Yellow Parts of Large Dragon Fly.*		
63	*Primrose Yellow.*		*Pale Canary Bird.*		
64	*Wax Yellow.*		*Larva of large Water Beetle.*		
65	*Lemon Yellow.*		*Large Wasp or Hornet.*		
66	*Gamboge Yellow.*		*Wings of Goldfinch, Canary Bird.*		
67	*King's Yellow.*		*Head of Golden Pheasant.*		
68	*Saffron Yellow.*		*Tail Coverts of Golden Pheasant.*		

The first chart of yellows in Syme's 1821 edition included two of Werner's original yellows (numbers 62 and 65), one yellow from the Picardet system (number 64) and four yellows from his own 1814 edition (numbers 63, 66, 67 and 68).

YELLOWS (i).

VEGETABLE.		MINERAL.	
Various Coloured Snap dragon.		Sulphur.	
Wild Primrose.		Pale coloured Sulphur.	
Greenish Parts of Nonpareil Apple.		Semi Opal.	
Shrubby Goldylocks.		Yellow Orpiment.	
Yellow Jasmine.		High coloured Sulphur.	
Yellow Tulip. Cinque foil.			
Anthers of Saffron Crocus.			

62. SULPHUR YELLOW.

(i).   *Yellow Parts of large Dragon Fly.* [*Dragonfly*; Anisoptera]
(ii).   *Various Coloured Snap dragon.* [*Wild Snapdragon*;
         Yellow toadflax; Linaria vulgaris]
(iii).   *Sulphur.* [*Chemical element*]

Sulphur Yellow, is lemon yellow mixed with emerald green and white. [W]

ANIMAL.

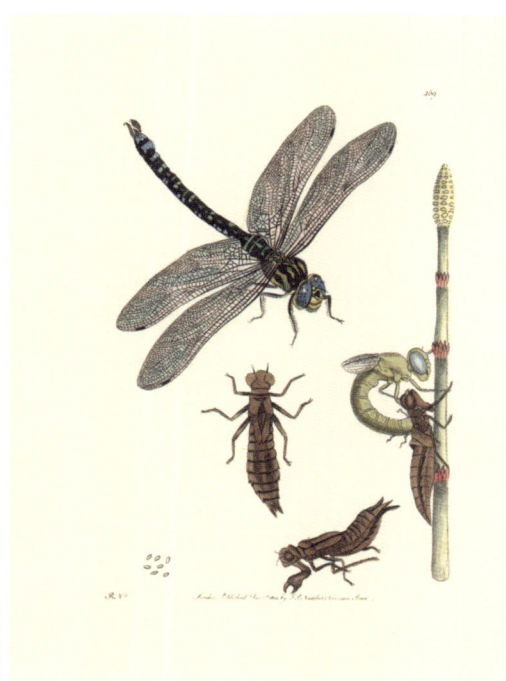

VEGETABLE.

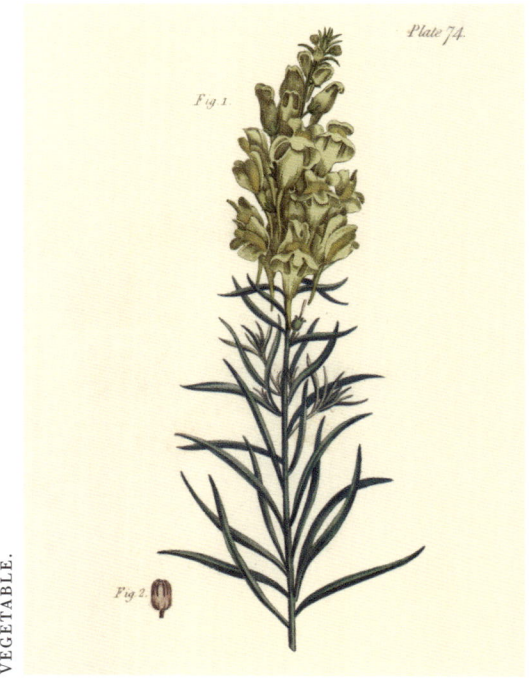

ANIMAL.
George Shaw and
Frederick P. Nodder,
*The Naturalist's
Miscellany*, 1789–1801.
Sulphur Yellow is
visible on the body
of the brown hawker
dragonfly (right).

VEGETABLE.
William Curtis,
*Lectures on Botany,
as delivered in the
Botanic Garden
at Lambeth*, 1805.
Sulphur Yellow is
visible on the petals
of the wild snapdragon.

MINERAL.
Leonard Spencer,
*The World's
Minerals*, 1916.
Sulphur Yellow is
visible on the sulphur.

MINERAL.

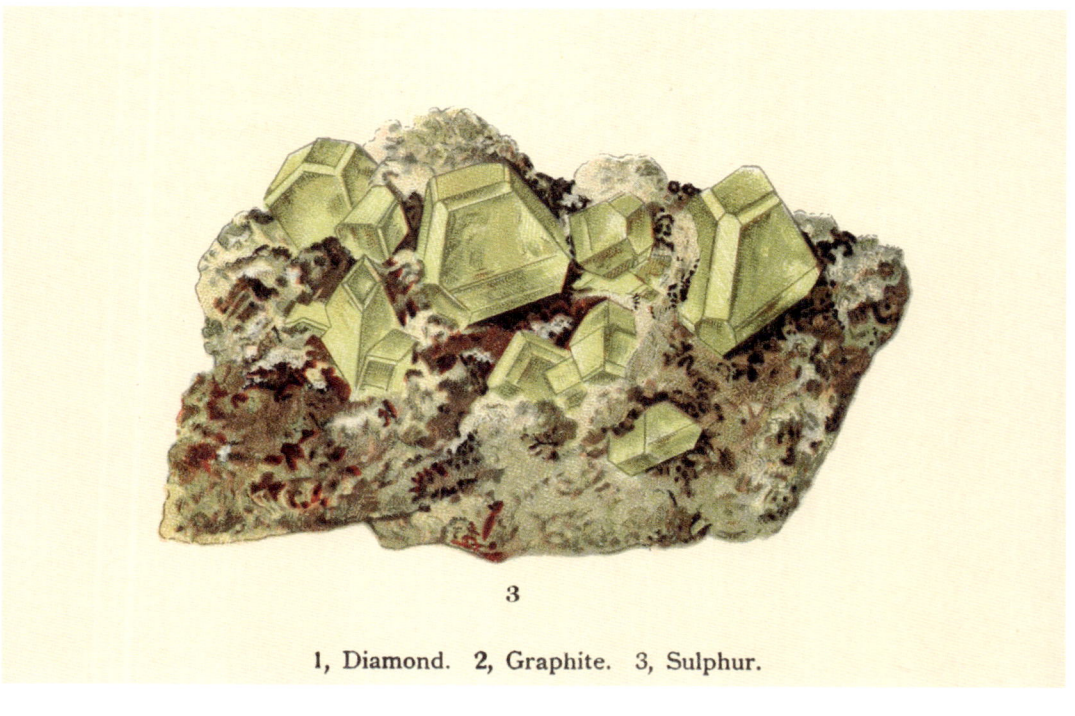

1, Diamond.   2, Graphite.   3, Sulphur.

63. PRIMROSE YELLOW.

(i).   *Pale Canary Bird.* [Serinus canaria domestica]
(ii).   *Wild Primrose.* [Primula vulgaris]
(iii).   *Pale coloured Sulphur.* [Chemical element]

Primrose Yellow, is gamboge yellow mixed with a little sulphur yellow, and much snow white.

ANIMAL.

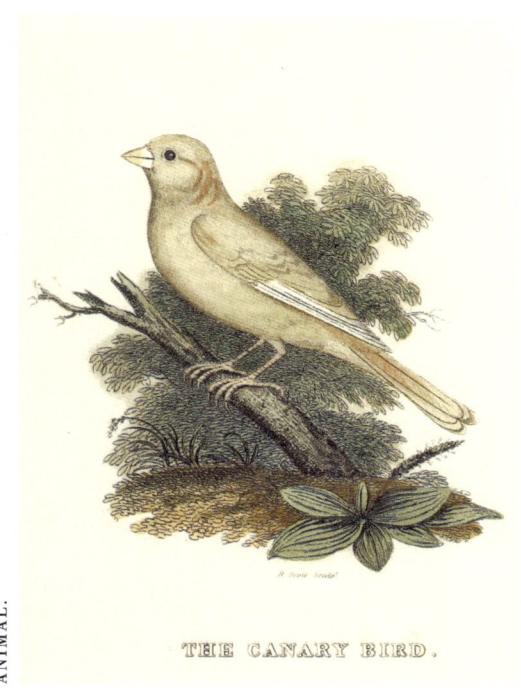

THE CANARY BIRD.

VEGETABLE.

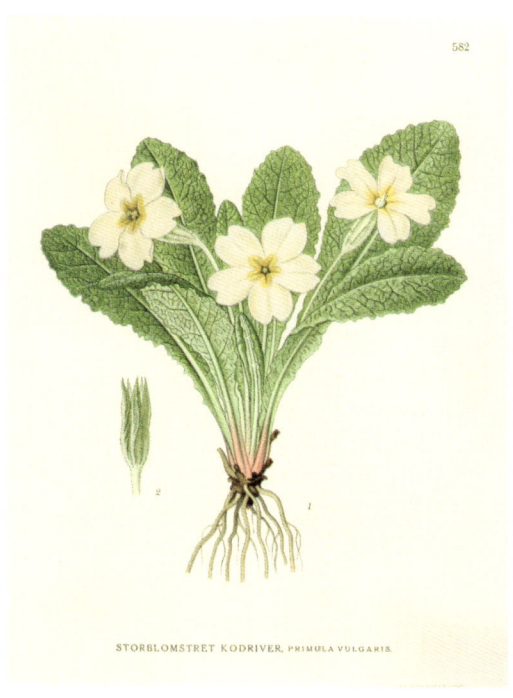

STORBLOMSTRET KODRIVER, PRIMULA VULGARIS.

MINERAL.

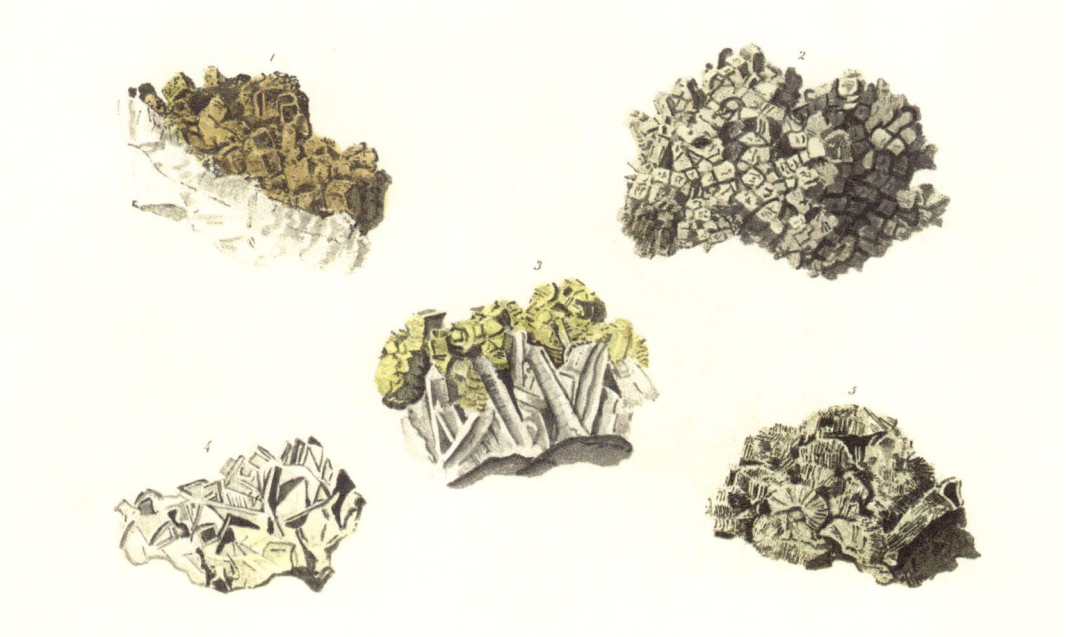

ANIMAL.
Patrick Syme,
A Treatise on British Song-birds, 1823.
Primrose Yellow is visible on the feathers of the canary.

VEGETABLE.
A. Mentz and C. H. Ostenfeld,
Billeder af Nordens Flora, Vol. 1, 1917.
Primrose Yellow is visible on the petals of the primrose.

MINERAL.
Philip Rashleigh,
Specimens of British Minerals, 1797.
Primrose Yellow is visible on the sulphurated pyrite (all specimens).

64. WAX YELLOW.

(i).   *Larva of large Water Beetle.* [Dytiscidae]
(ii).   *Greenish Parts of Nonpareil Apple.* [Malus domestica]
(iii). *Semi Opal.* [Silica]

Wax Yellow, is composed of lemon yellow, reddish brown, and a little ash grey. [W]

ANIMAL.

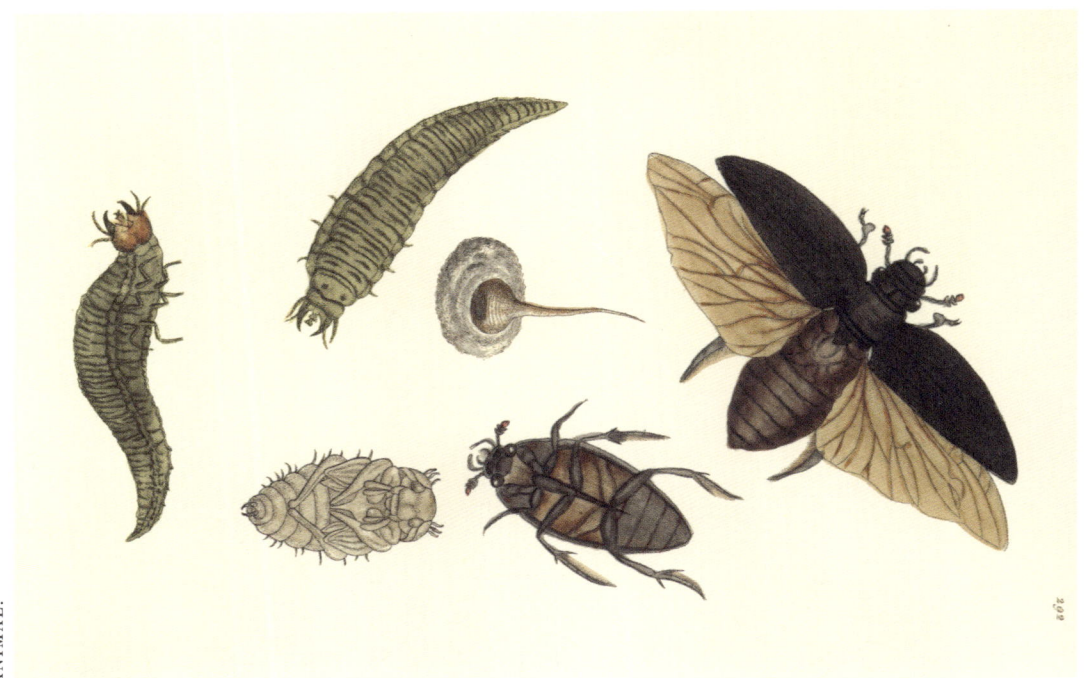

VEGETABLE.

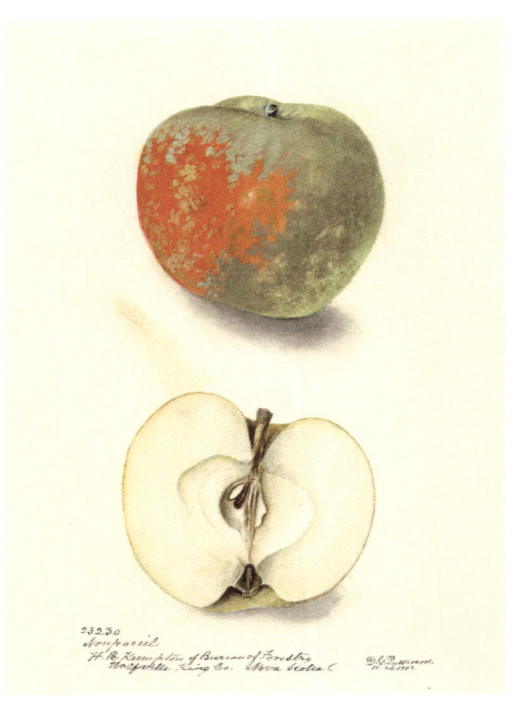

MINERAL.

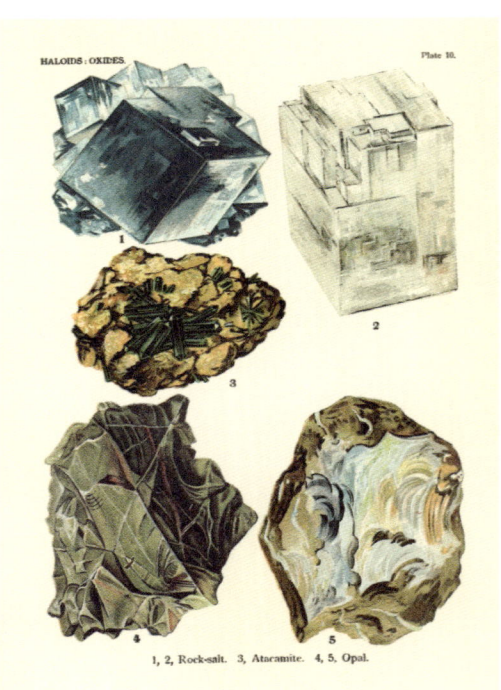

HALOIDS : OXIDES   Plate 16.

1, 2, Rock-salt.   3, Atacamite.   4, 5, Opal.

ANIMAL.
George Shaw and
Frederick P. Nodder,
*The Naturalist's
Miscellany,* 1789–1801.
Wax Yellow is visible
on the larvae of the
water beetle (left).

VEGETABLE.
Deborah Griscom
Passmore, *Nonpareil,*
watercolour, 1902.
Wax Yellow is
visible on the skin
of the apple.

MINERAL.
Leonard Spencer,
*The World's
Minerals,* 1916.
Wax Yellow is visible
on the opal (bottom
row, left and right).

65. LEMON YELLOW.

(i).   *Large Wasp.* [Vespula vulgaris] *Hornet.* [Vespa]
(ii).   *Shrubby Goldylocks.* [*Goldilocks aster,* Galatella linosyris]
(iii).   *Yellow Orpiment.* [*Sulphide mineral*]

Lemon Yellow, the characteristic colour of the yellow series of Werner, the colour of ripe lemons; it is found to be a mixture of gamboge yellow and a little ash grey: being a mixed colour, it cannot be adopted as the characteristic colour.... [W]

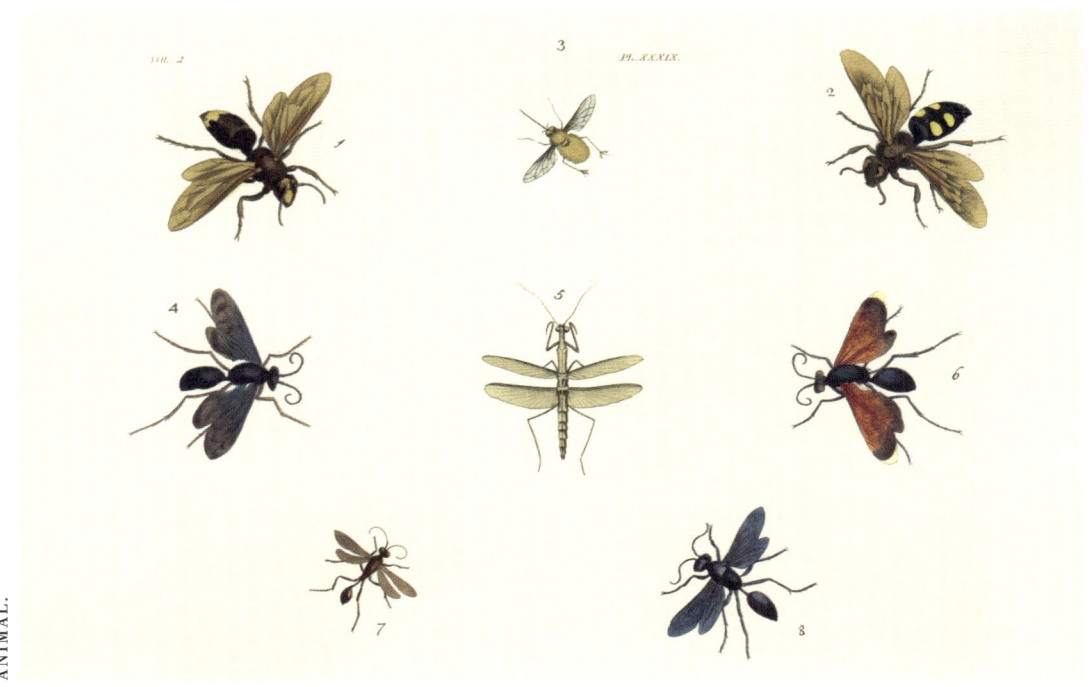

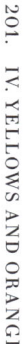

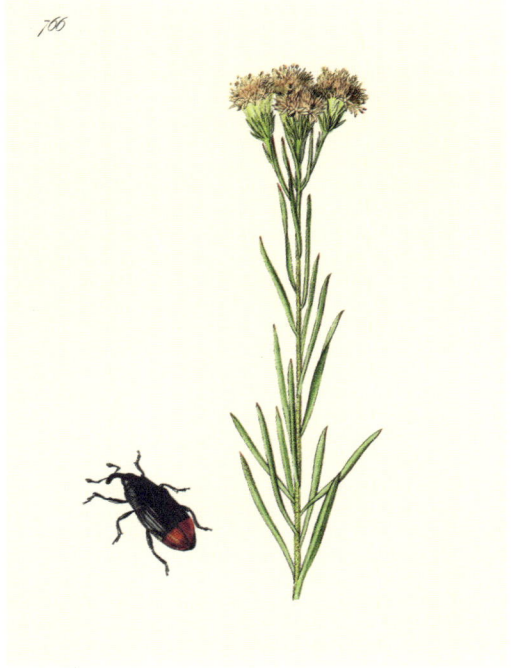

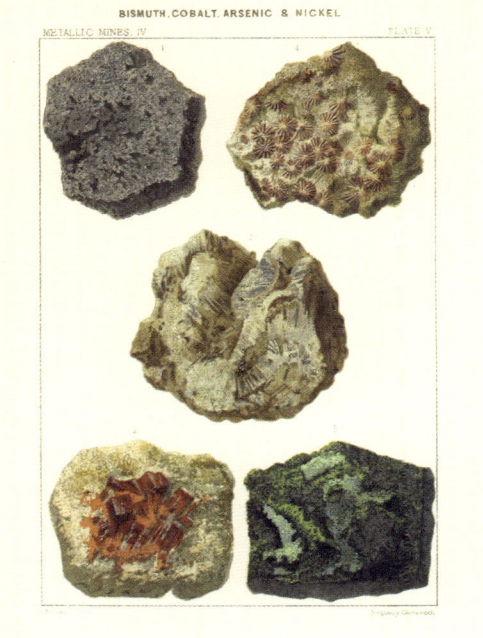

ANIMAL.
Dru Drury, *Illustrations of Exotic Entomology*, 1837. Lemon Yellow is visible on the wasp (top row, left).

VEGETABLE.
John Curtis, *British Entomology*, 1840. Lemon Yellow is visible on the petals of the Goldilocks aster.

MINERAL.
Louis Simonin, *Underground Life*, 1869. Lemon Yellow is visible on the orpiment (top row, right).

66. GAMBOGE YELLOW.

(i). *Wings of Goldfinch.* [Carduelis carduelis]
Canary Bird. [Serinus canaria domestica]
(ii). *Yellow Jasmine.* [Gelsemium sempervirens]
(iii). *High coloured Sulphur.* [*Chemical element*]

Gamboge Yellow, is the characteristic colour.

ANIMAL.

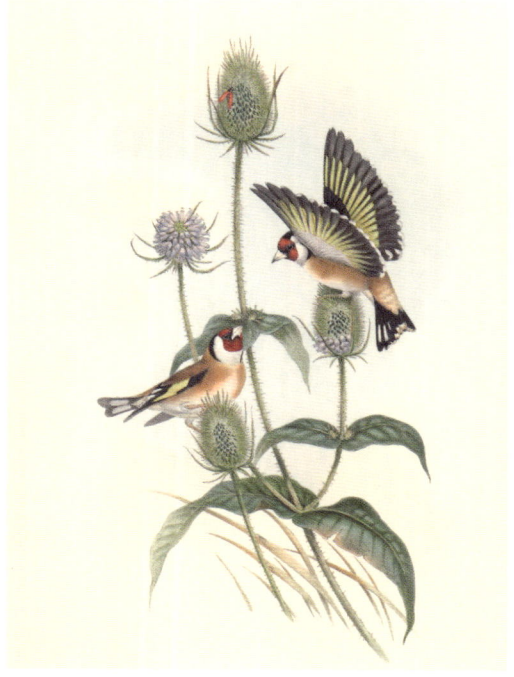

VEGETABLE.

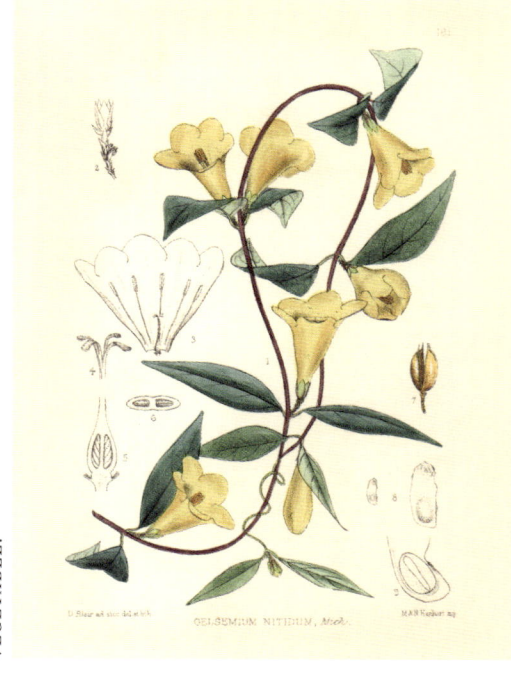

ANIMAL.
John Gould, *Birds of Great Britain*, Vol. 3, 1862–73. Gamboge Yellow is visible on the wing feathers of the goldfinch.

VEGETABLE.
Robert Bentley and Henry Trimen, *Medicinal Plants*, 1880 Gamboge Yellow is visible on the petals of the yellow jasmine.

MINERAL.
Reinhard Brauns, *The Mineral Kingdom*, Vol. 1, 1912. Gamboge Yellow is visible on the sulphur (all specimens).

MINERAL.

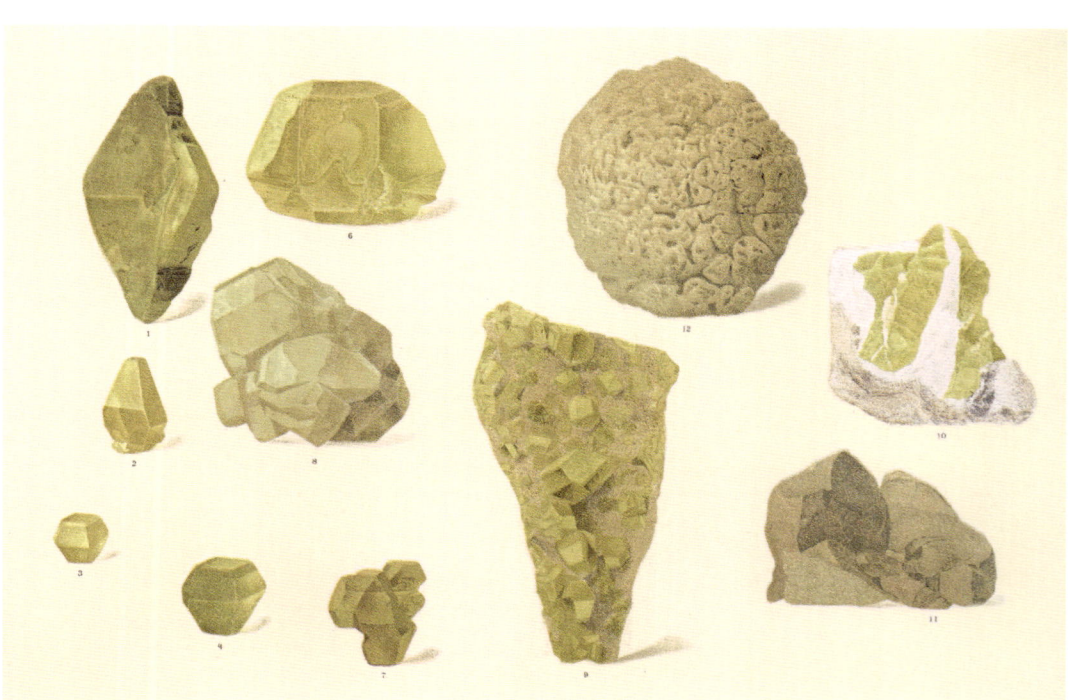

67. KING'S YELLOW.

(i).   *Head of Golden Pheasant.* [Chrysolophus pictus]
(ii). *Yellow Tulip.* [Tulipa] *Cinque foil.* [*Cinquefoil*; Potentilla]
(iii). ————————

*King's Yellow, is gamboge
yellow, with a small
portion of saffron yellow.*

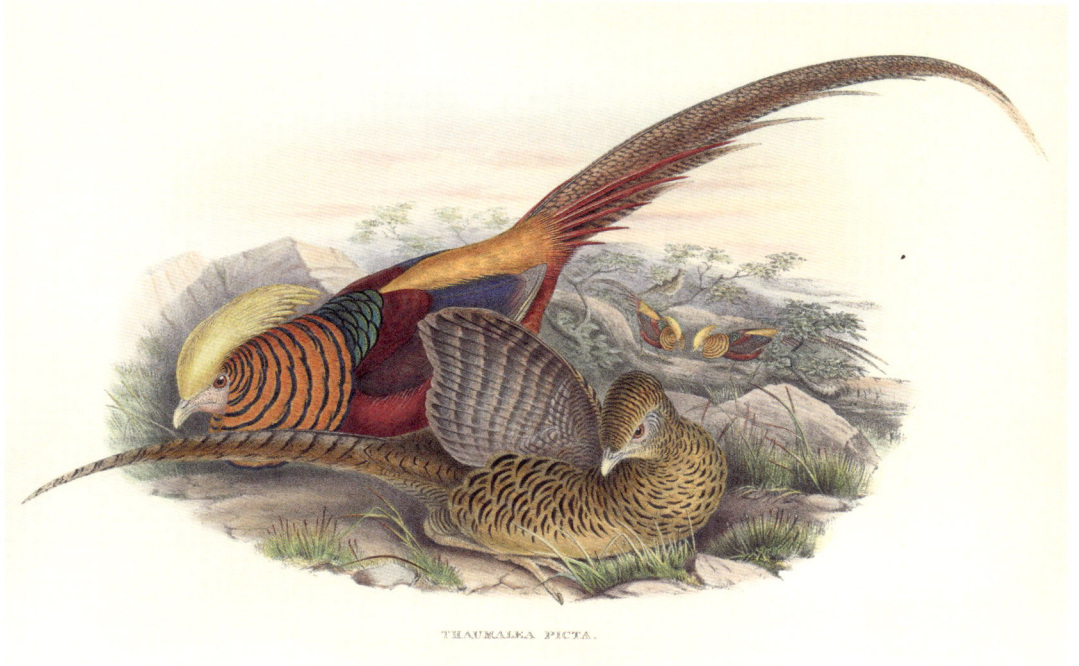

THAUMALEA PICTA.

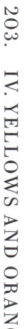

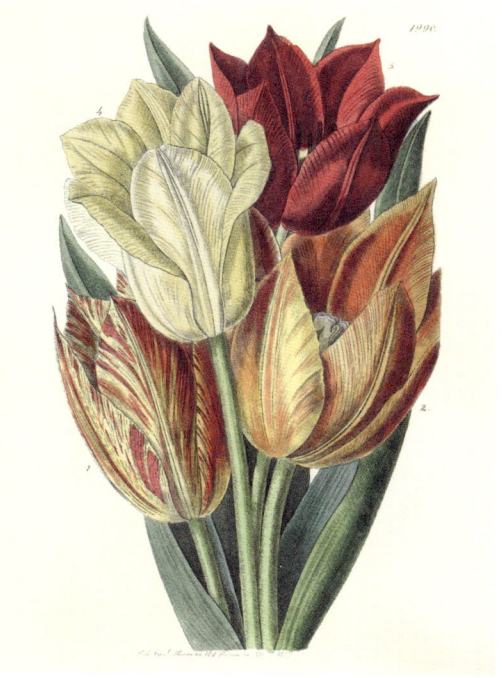

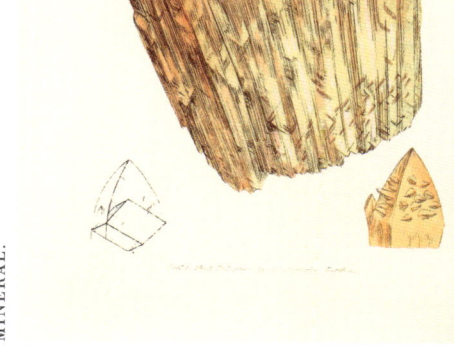

ANIMAL.
John Gould,
Birds of Australia,
Vol. 7, 1840–48.
King's Yellow is visible
on the head feathers
of the golden pheasant.

VEGETABLE.
John Lindley,
*Edwards's Botanical
Register*, 1829–47.
King's Yellow is visible
on the petals of the
yellow tulip.

MINERAL.
James Sowerby,
British Mineralogy,
Vol. 2, 1802–17.
King's Yellow
is visible on the
carbonate of lime.*

68. SAFFRON YELLOW.

(i).   *Tail Coverts of Golden Pheasant.* [Chrysolophus pictus]
(ii).   *Anthers of Saffron Crocus.* [*Autumn crocus*; Crocus sativus]
(iii).   ──────────────

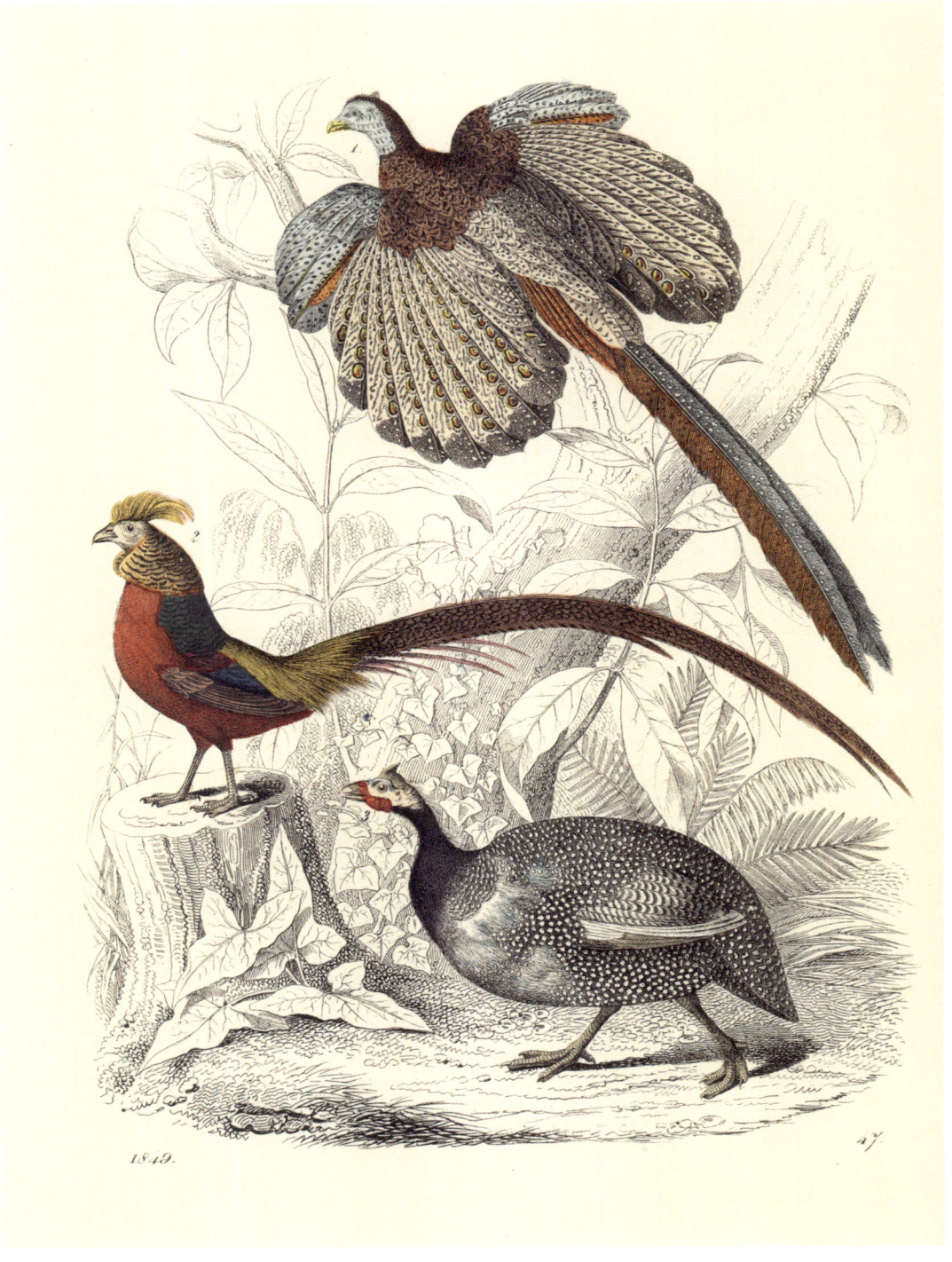

1849.   47.

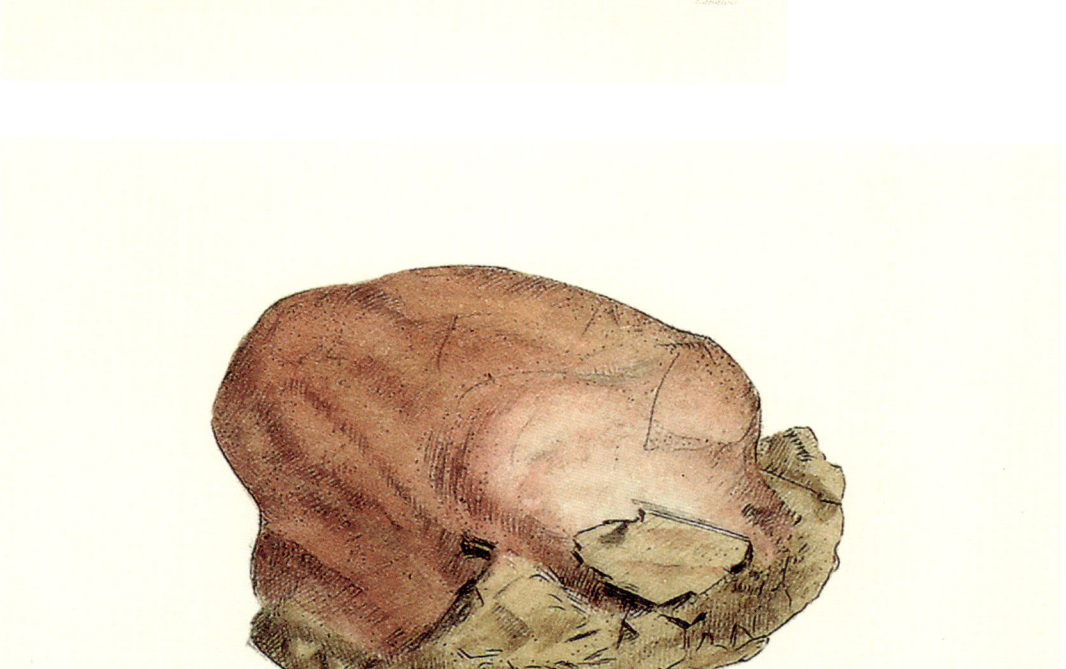

Saffron Yellow, is
gamboge yellow, with
gallstone yellow, about
equal parts of each.

VEGETABLE.

Crocus sativus.   Safran cultivé.

MINERAL.

ANIMAL.
Carl Hoffmann,
Book of the World, 1849.
Saffron Yellow is visible
on the tail feathers of
the golden pheasant
(centre).

VEGETABLE.
Pierre-Joseph
Redouté, *Choix des
plus belles fleurs*, 1833.
Saffron Yellow is
visible on the anthers
of the saffron crocus.

MINERAL.
James Sowerby,
Exotic Mineralogy, 1811.
Saffron Yellow is
visible on the sulphate
of magnesia.*

No.	Names.	Colours.	ANIMAL.		
69	*Gallstone Yellow.*		*Gallstones.*		
70	*Honey Yellow.*		*Lower Parts of Neck of Bird of Paradise.*		
71	*Straw Yellow.*		*Polar Bear.*		
72	*Wine Yellow.*		*Body of Silk Moth.*		
73	*Sienna Yellow.*		*Vent Parts of Tail of Bird of Paradise.*		
74	*Ochre Yellow.*		*Vent Coverts of Red Start.*		
75	*Cream Yellow.*		*Breast of Teal Drake.*		

The second chart of yellows in Syme's 1821 edition included four of Werner's original yellows (numbers 71, 72, 74 and 75), although he renamed Werner's Isabella Yellow 'Cream Yellow'. There is also one yellow from the Picardet system (number 70) and two yellows from his own 1814 edition (numbers 69 and 73).

YELLOWS (ii).

	VEGETABLE.		MINERAL.	
	Marigold Apple.			
			Fluor Spar.	
	Oat Straw.		Schorlite. Calamine.	
	White Currants.		Saxon Topaz.	
	Stamina of Honey-suckle.		Pale Brazilian Topaz.	
			Porcelain Jasper.	
			Porcelain Jasper.	

69. GALLSTONE YELLOW.

(i).   *Gallstones.* [Calculi]
(ii).   *Marigold Apple.* [Malus domestica]
(iii).   ——————

Gallstone Yellow, is gamboge yellow, with a small quantity of Dutch orange, and a minute proportion of honey yellow.

ANIMAL.

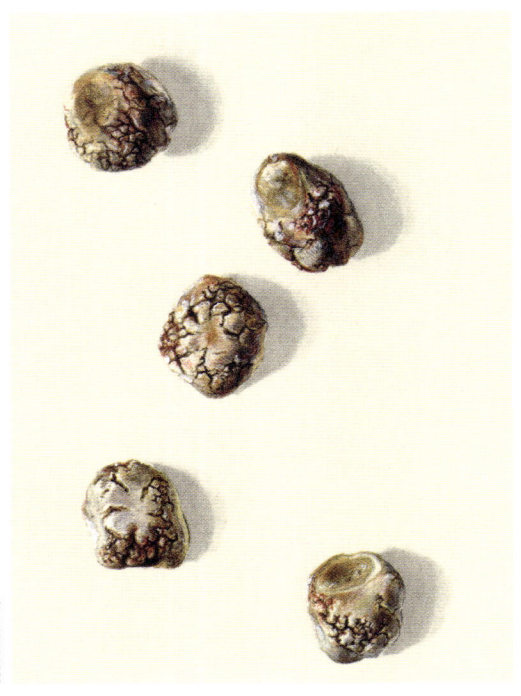

VEGETABLE.

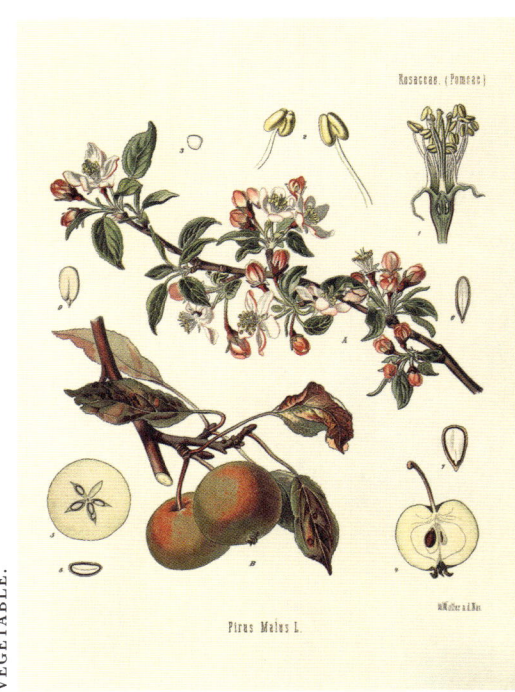

ANIMAL.
Hamlet Frederick Aitken, *Gallbladder and gallstones*, medical illustration, date unknown. Gallstone Yellow is visible on the gallstones (all specimens).

VEGETABLE.
Hermann Adolph Koehler, *Medicinal Plants*, 1887. Gallstone Yellow is visible on the skin of the apple.

MINERAL.
James Sowerby, *British Mineralogy*, Vol. I, 1802–17. Gallstone Yellow is visible on the native gold (all specimens).*

MINERAL.

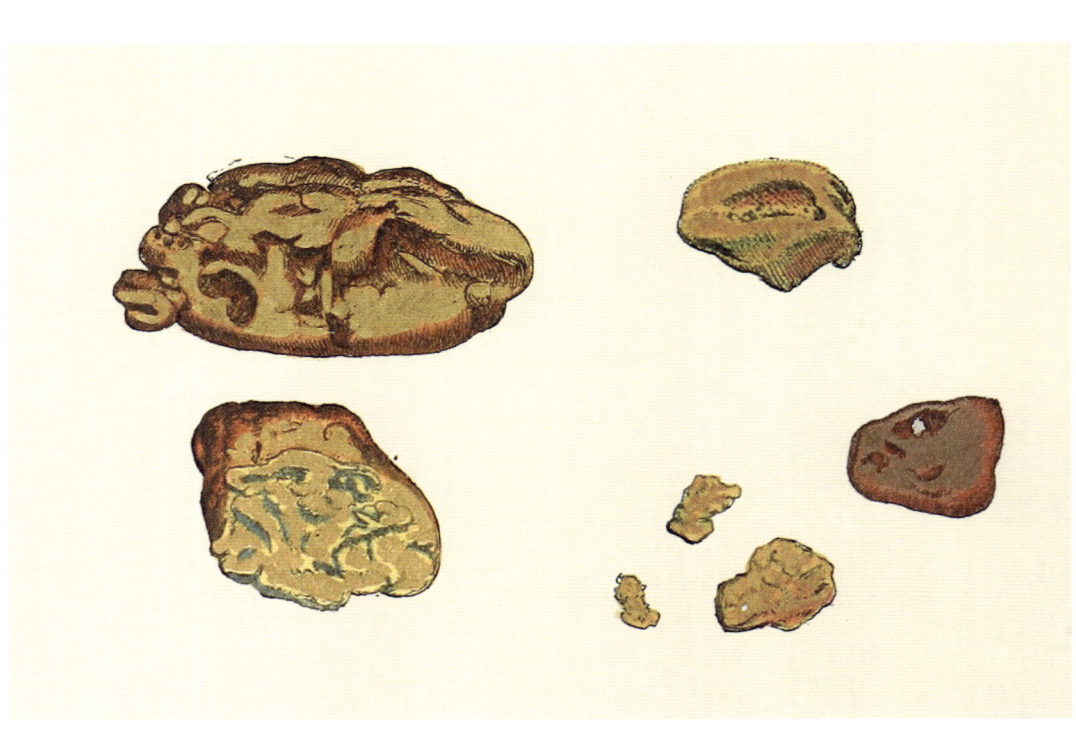

70. HONEY YELLOW.

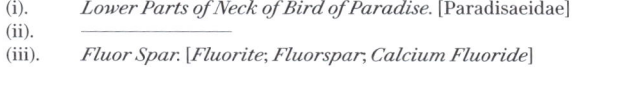

(i).   *Lower Parts of Neck of Bird of Paradise.* [*Paradisaeidae*]
(ii).   ———————
(iii).   *Fluor Spar.* [*Fluorite; Fluorspar, Calcium Fluoride*]

Honey Yellow, is sulphur yellow mixed with chesnut brown. [W]

ANIMAL.

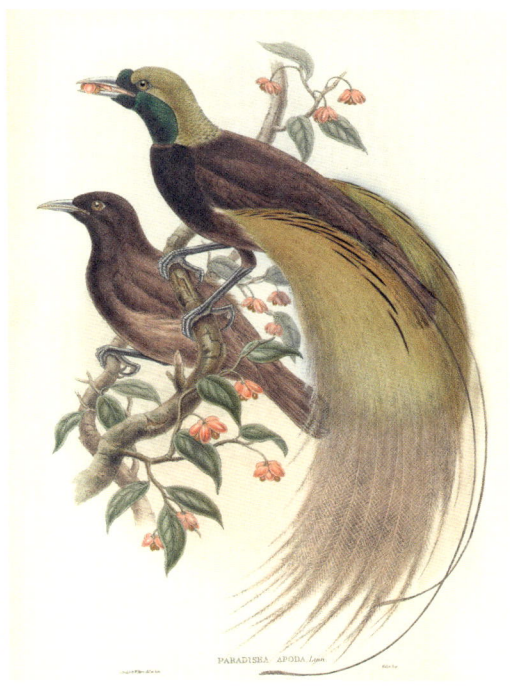

PARADISEA APODA. *Lyon.*

VEGETABLE.

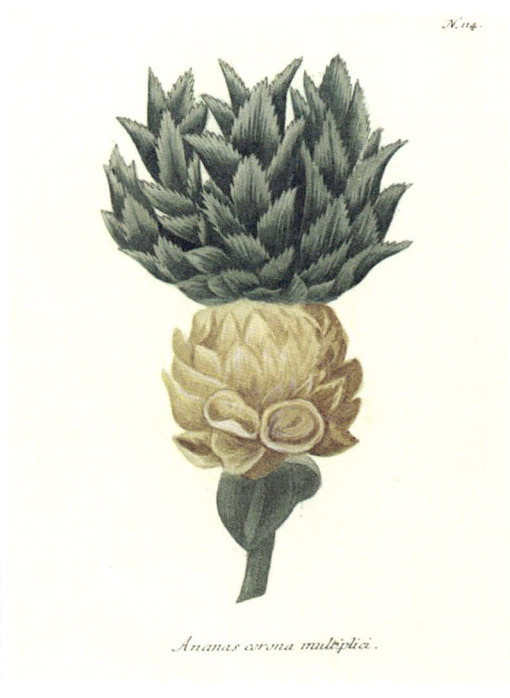

Ananas corona multiplici.

MINERAL.

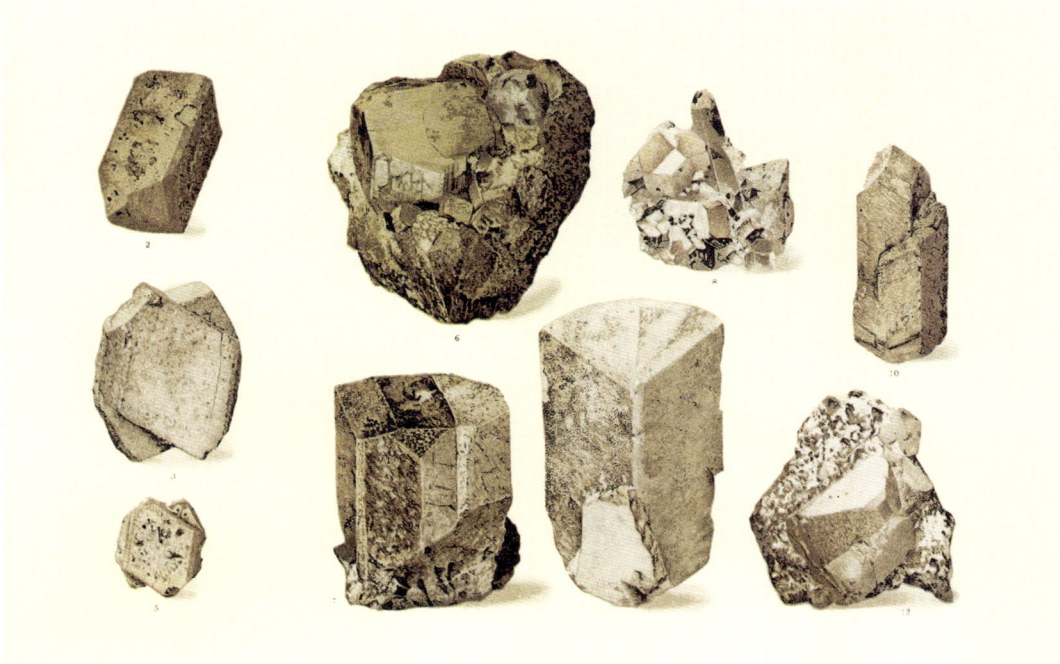

ANIMAL.
John Gould, *Birds of New Guinea and the Adjacent Papuan Islands*, 1875–88. Honey Yellow is visible on the lower neck feathers of the bird of paradise.

VEGETABLE.
Johann Wilhelm Weinmann, *Phytanthoza iconographia*, 1737. Honey Yellow is visible on the fruit of the ornamental 'corona' pineapple.*

MINERAL.
Reinhard Brauns, *The Mineral Kingdom*, Vol. 2, 1912. Honey Yellow is visible on the fluorite (top row, second from left). It is embedded within a piece of orthoclase.

71. STRAW YELLOW.

(i).   *Polar Bear.* [Ursus maritimus]
(ii).   *Oat Straw.* [Avena sativa]
(iii).   *Schorlite.* [*Scheelite*; *Tungstate mineral*]
       Calamine. [*Smithsonite*; *Zinc cabonate*]

Straw Yellow, is sulphur yellow mixed with much greyish white and a little ochre yellow. [W]

ANIMAL.

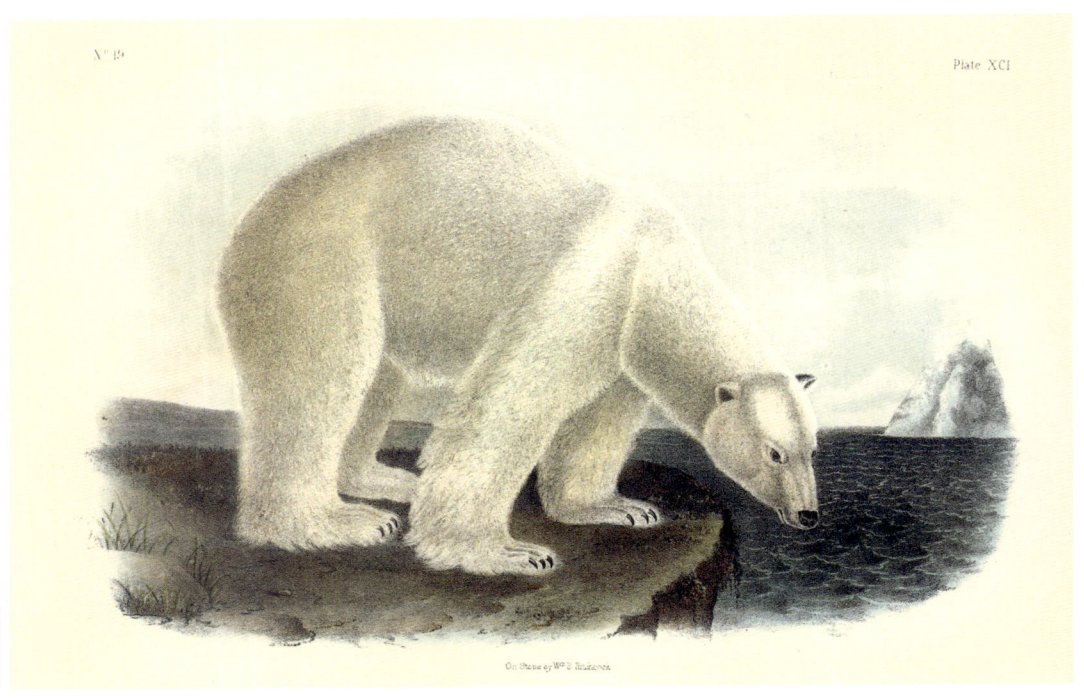

ANIMAL.
John James Audubon,
*The Quadrupeds
of North America*,
Vol. 3, 1849.
Straw Yellow is
visible on the fur
of the polar bear.

VEGETABLE.
E. Blackwell,
*Herbarium
Blackwellianum*,
Vol. 2, 1754.
Straw Yellow is
visible on the ear
of the oat straw.

MINERAL.
Philip Rashleigh,
*Specimens of British
Minerals*, 1797.
Straw Yellow is visible
on the calamine
(all specimens).

VEGETABLE.

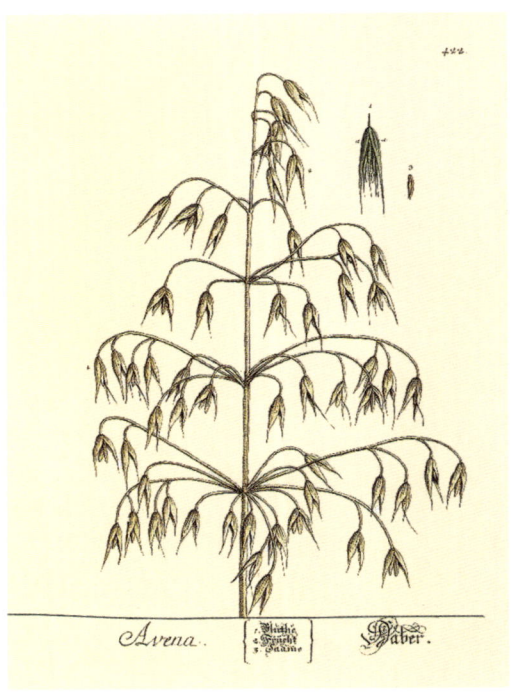

MINERAL.

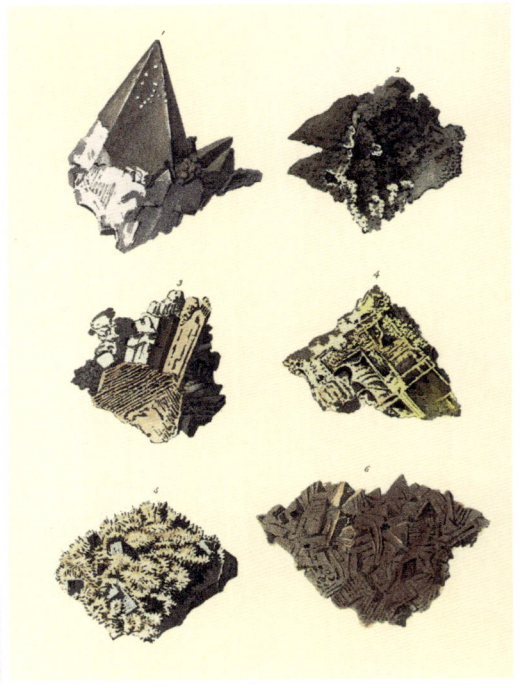

72. WINE YELLOW.

(i).   *Body of Silk Moth.* [Bombyx mori]
(ii).   *White Currants.* [Ribes rubrum]
(iii).   *Saxon Topaz.* [*Silicate mineral*]

Wine Yellow, is sulphur yellow mixed with reddish brown and grey, with much snow white. [W]

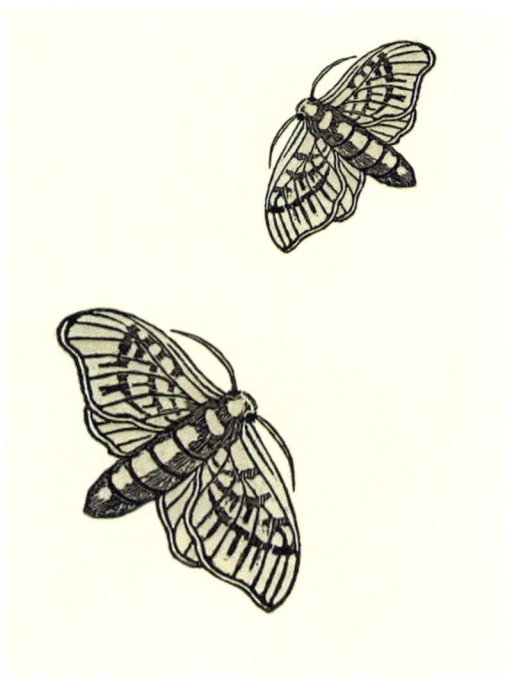

ANIMAL.

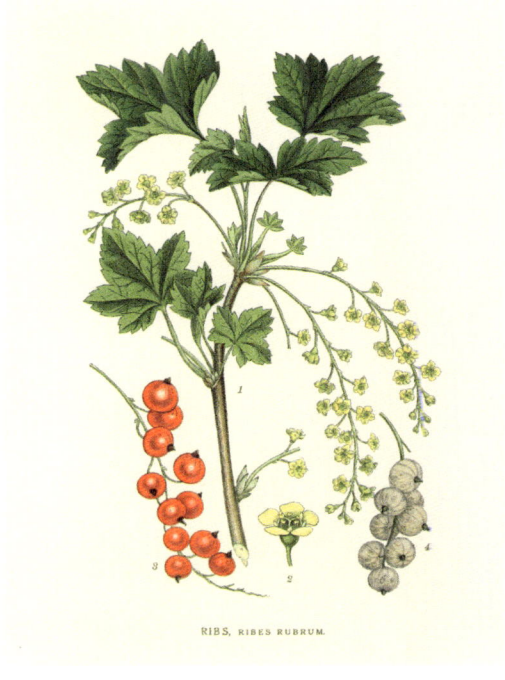

VEGETABLE.

RIBS, RIBES RUBRUM.

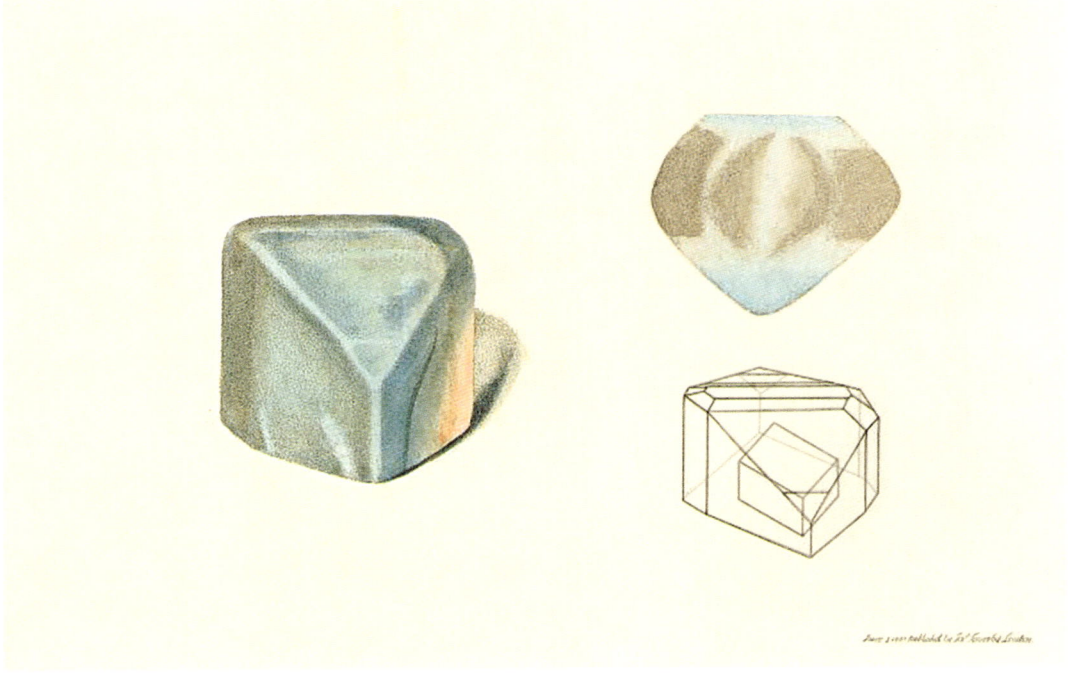

MINERAL.

ANIMAL.
Thomas Brown, *The Book of Butterflies, Sphinxes and Moths*, 1832. Wine Yellow is visible on the body of the silk moth (both specimens).

VEGETABLE.
A. Mentz and C. H. Ostenfeld, *Billeder af Nordens Flora*, Vol. 2, 1917. Wine Yellow is visible on the berries of the white currant (right).

MINERAL.
James Sowerby, *British Mineralogy*, Vol. 4, 1802-17. Wine Yellow is visible on the topaz (both specimens).

(i).   *Vent Parts of Tail of Bird of Paradise.* [Paradisaeidae]
(ii).   *Stamina of Honey-suckle.* [Lonicera periclymenum]
(iii). *Pale Brazilian Topaz.* [Silicate mineral]

Sienna Yellow, is primrose yellow, with a little ochre yellow.

IV. YELLOWS AND ORANGES.

212.

ANIMAL.

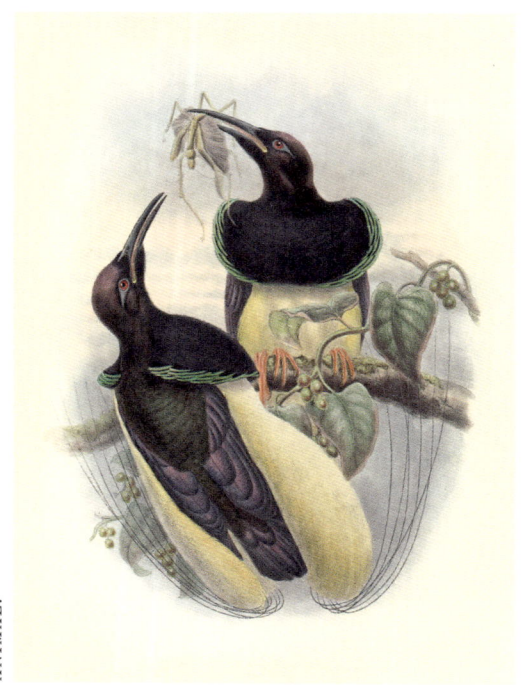

VEGETABLE.

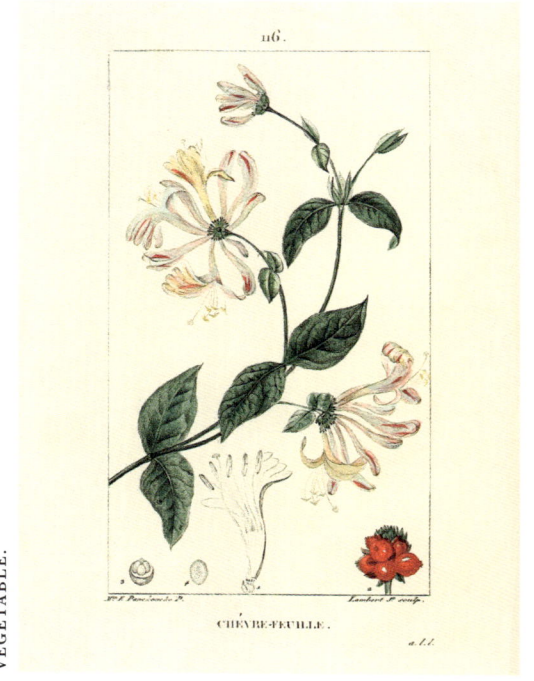

ANIMAL.
John Gould, *Birds of New Guinea and the Adjacent Papuan Islands*, 1875–88. Sienna Yellow is visible on the tail feathers of the bird of paradise.

VEGETABLE.
François-Pierre Chaumeton, *Flore médicale*, Vol. 2, 1833. Sienna Yellow is visible on stamina of the honeysuckle.

MINERAL.
Reinhard Brauns, *The Mineral Kingdom*, Vol. 2, 1912. Sienna Yellow is visible on the topaz (top row, left).

MINERAL.

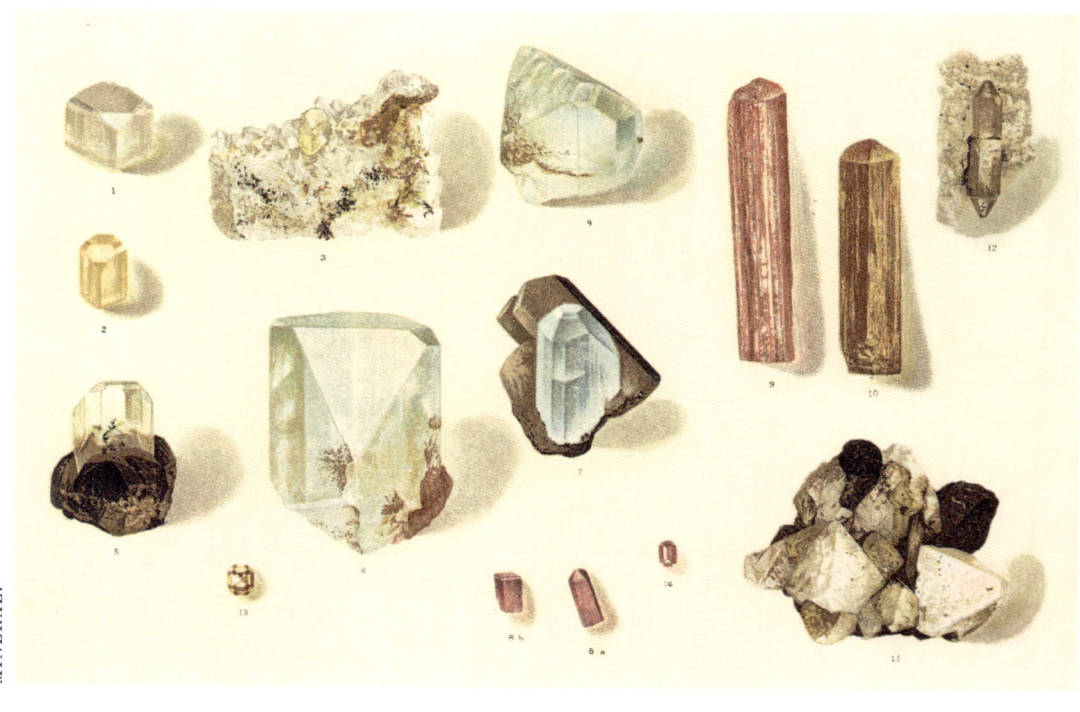

74. OCHRE YELLOW.

(i).   *Vent Coverts of Red Start.* [*Redstart*; Phoenicurus phoenicurus]

(ii).   ——————————

(iii).   *Porcelain Jasper.* [*Silica*]

Ochre Yellow, is Sienna yellow, with a little light chesnut brown. [W]

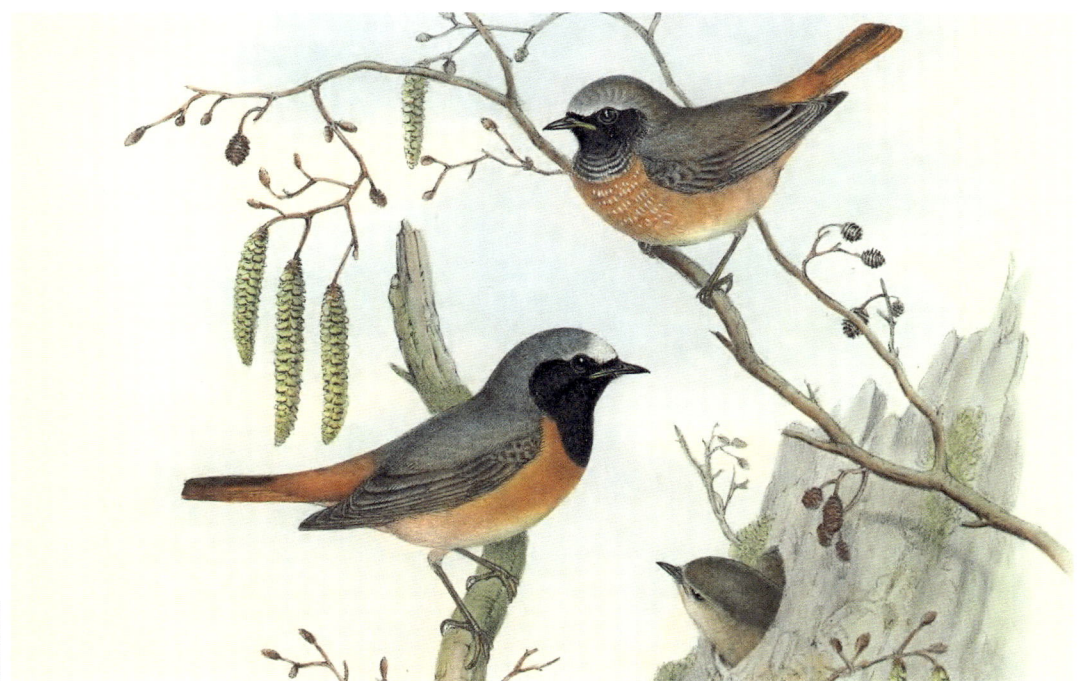

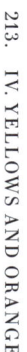

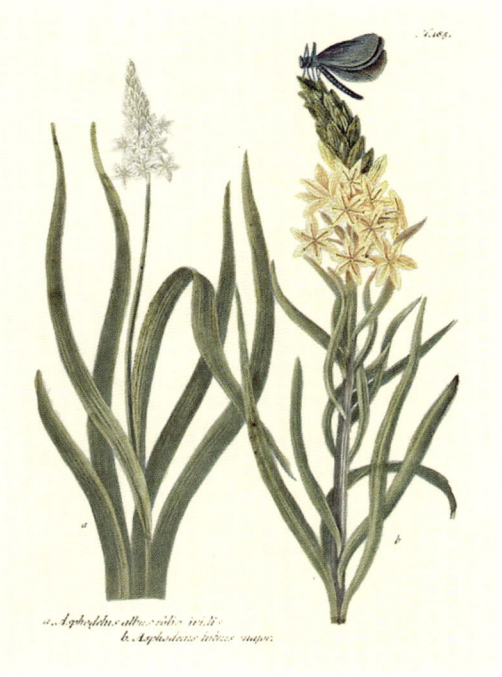

*a. Asphodelus albus ramosus mas.
b. Asphodelus luteus major.*

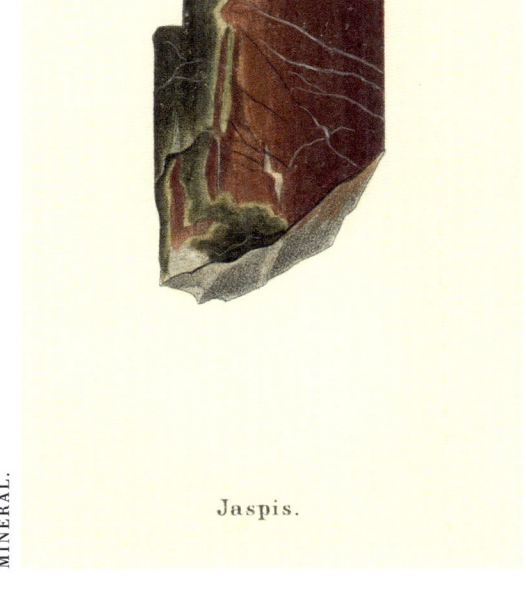

Jaspis.

ANIMAL.
John Gould, *Birds of Great Britain*, Vol. 2, 1862–73. Ochre Yellow is visible on the vent coverts, i.e. the feathers around the cloaca, of the red start.

VEGETABLE.
Johann Wilhelm Weinmann, *Phytanthoza iconographia*, 1737. Ochre Yellow is visible on the petals of the king's spear, or yellow asphodel (right).*

MINERAL.
Johann Carl Weber, *Die Mineralien*, 1871. Ochre Yellow is visible on the jasper.

75. CREAM YELLOW.

(i).   *Breast of Teal Drake.* [*Eurasian teal*; Anas crecca]
(ii).   ————————————
(iii). *Porcelain Jasper.* [*Silica*]

ANIMAL.

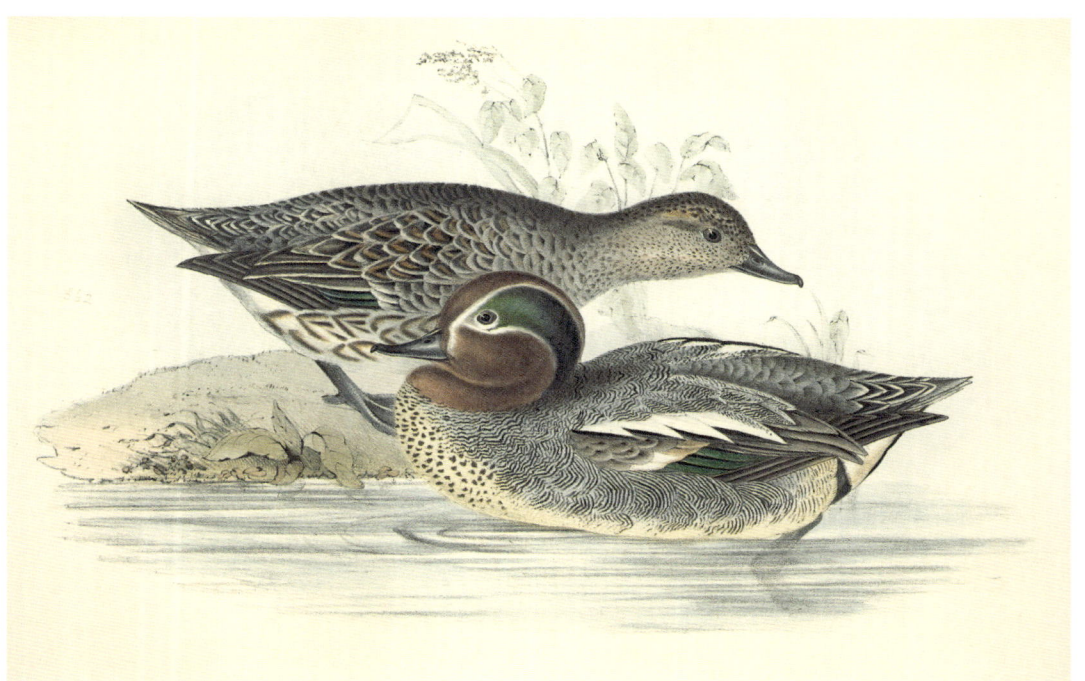

MINERAL.

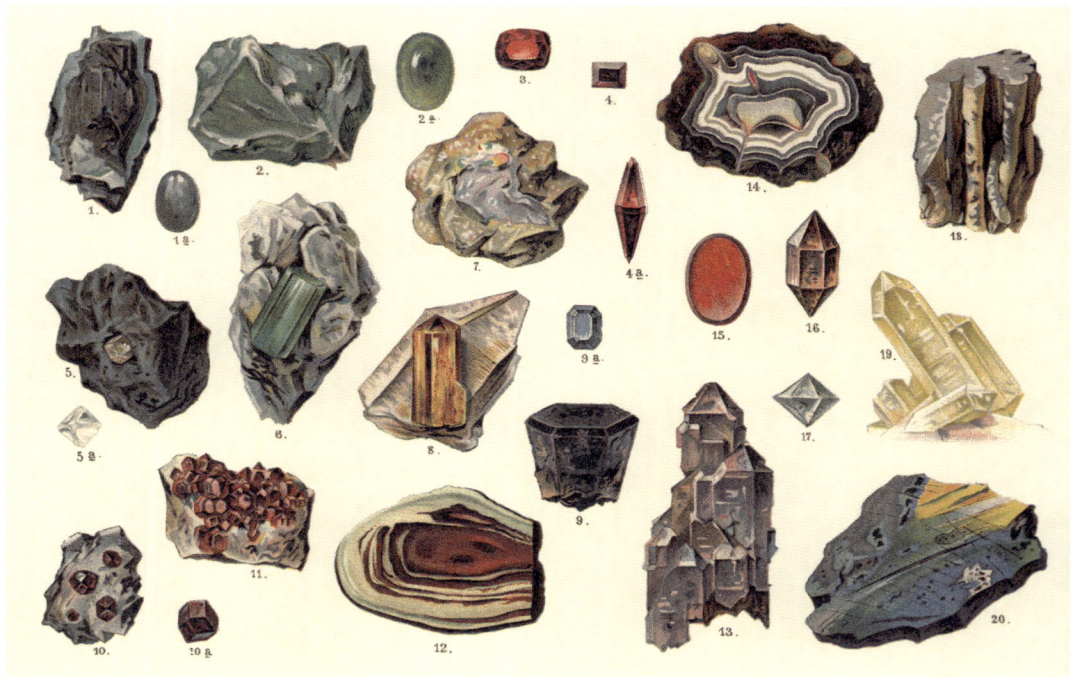

*Cream Yellow, is ochre yellow
mixed with a little white,
and a very small quantity
of Dutch orange. [W]* †*

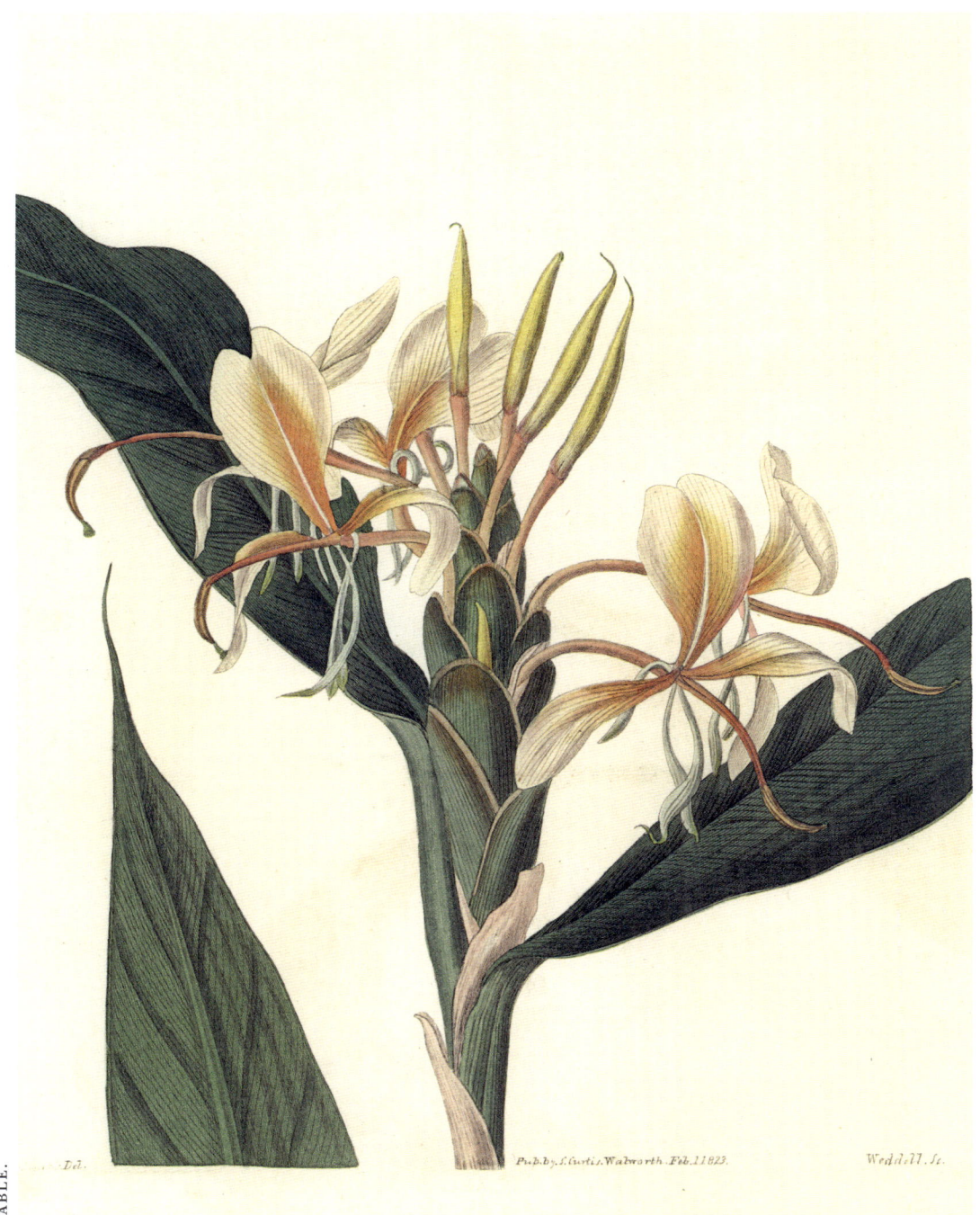

Pub. by S. Curtis. Walworth. Feb. 1. 1823.   Weddell. Sc.

VEGETABLE.

ANIMAL.
John Gould, *Birds of
Europe*, Vol. 5, 1832–37.
Cream Yellow is visible
on the breast feathers
of the Eurasian teal.

VEGETABLE.
*Curtis's Botanical
Magazine*, 1823.
Cream Yellow is visible
on the petals of the
yellow butterfly ginger.*

MINERAL.
Philip Rashleigh,
*Specimens of British
Minerals*, 1797.
Cream Yellow is visible
on the jasper (bottom
row, centre).

ORANGES.

No.	Names.	Colours.	ANIMAL.		
76	*Dutch Orange.*		*Crest of Golden crested Wren.*		
77	*Buff Orange.*		*Streak from the Eye of the King Fisher.*		
78	*Orpiment Orange.*		*The Neck Ruff of the Golden Pheasant, Belly of the Warty Newt.*		
79	*Brownish Orange.*		*Eyes of the largest Flesh Fly.*		
80	*Reddish Orange.*		*Lower Wings of Tyger Moth.*		
81	*Deep Reddish Orange.*		*Gold Fish lustre abstracted.*		

In his chart of oranges, Syme included one of Werner's original colours, Orange Yellow, which he renamed 'Dutch Orange' (number 76). All the remaining oranges in Syme's 1821 edition were taken from his 1814 edition.

ORANGES.

	VEGETABLE.		MINERAL.	
	Common Marigold, Seedpod of Spindle-tree.		Streak of Red Orpiment.	
	Stamina of the large White Cistus.		Natrolite.	
	Indian Cress.			
	Style of the Orange Lily.		Dark Brazilian Topaz.	
	Hemimeris, Buff Hibiscus.			
	Scarlet Leadington Apple.			

76. DUTCH ORANGE.

(i). *Crest of Golden crested Wren.*
      [*Goldcrest*; Regulus regulus]
(ii). *Common Marigold.* [Calendula] *Seedpod of Spindle tree.*
      [*European spindle*; Euonymus europaeus]
(iii). *Streak of Red Orpiment.* [*Sulphide mineral*]

Dutch Orange, the orange yellow of Werner, is gamboge yellow, with carmine red. [W]

ANIMAL.

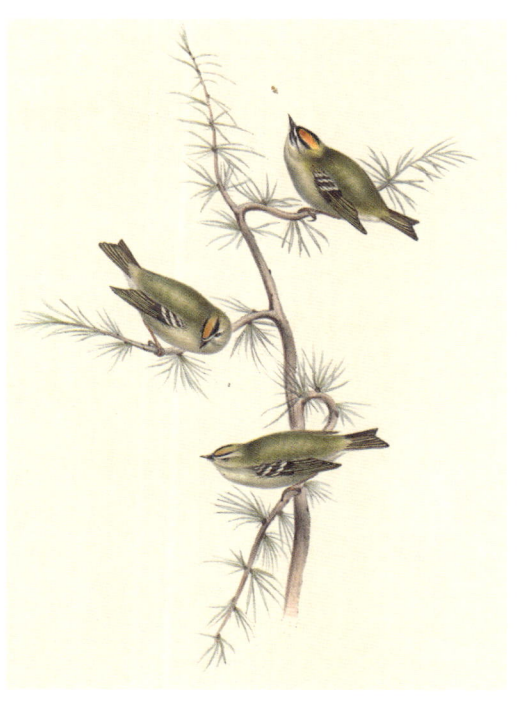

VEGETABLE.

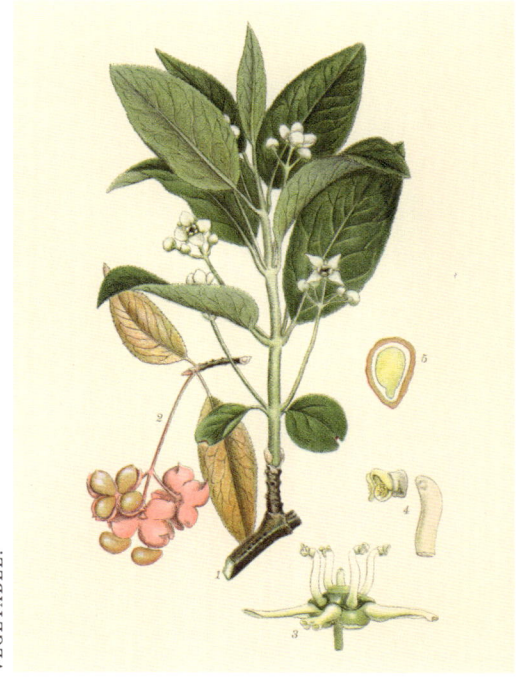

ANIMAL.
John Gould, *Birds of Europe*, Vol. 2, 1832–37. Dutch Orange is visible on the crest feathers of the goldcrest.

VEGETABLE.
A. Mentz and C. H. Ostenfeld, *Billeder af Nordens Flora*, Vol. 1, 1917. Dutch Orange is visible on the seedpod of the European spindle.

MINERAL.
Leonard Spencer, *The World's Minerals*, 1916. Dutch Orange is visible on the orpiment (top row, right).

MINERAL.

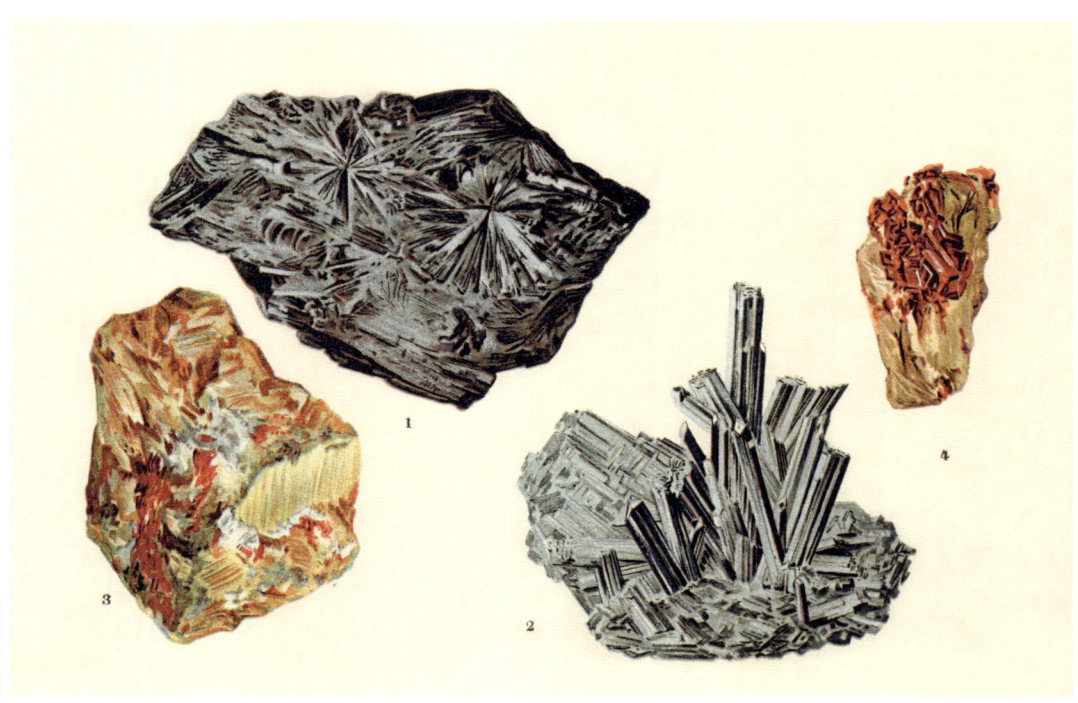

77. BUFF ORANGE.

(i). *Streak from the Eye of the King Fisher.*
[*Kingfisher*; Alcedo atthis]
(ii). *Stamina of the large White Cistus.* [Cistus]
(iii). *Natrolite.* [*Silicate mineral*]

Buff Orange, is Sienna yellow, with a little Dutch orange.

ANIMAL.

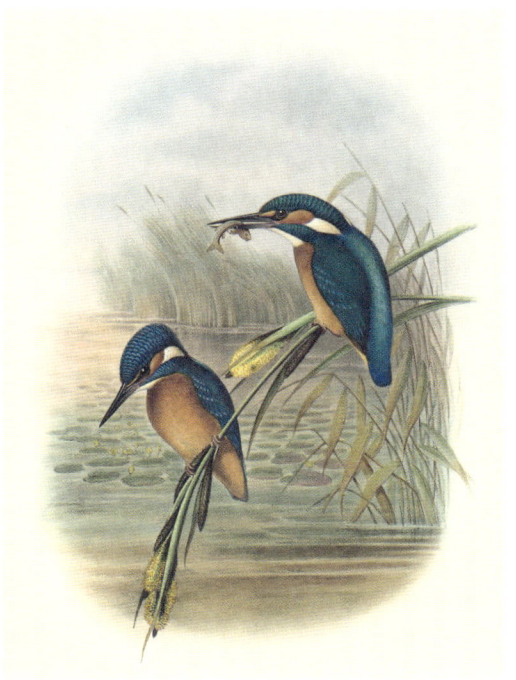

VEGETABLE.

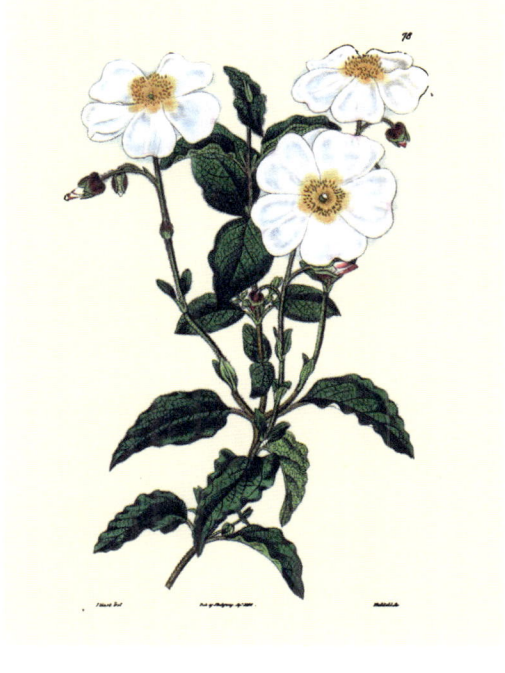

MINERAL.

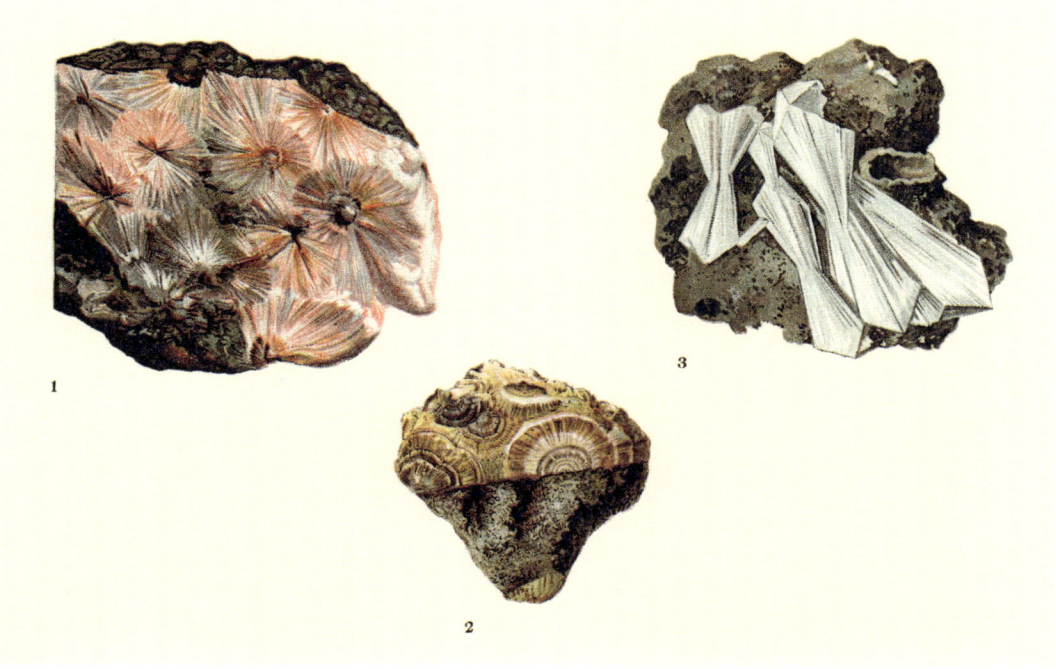

ANIMAL.
John Gould, *Birds of Great Britain*, Vol. 2, 1862–73. Buff Orange is visible on the feathers around the eye of the kingfisher.

VEGETABLE.
Robert Sweet, *Cistineae*, 1830. Buff Orange is visible on the stamina of the cistus.

MINERAL.
Leonard Spencer, *The World's Minerals*, 1916. Buff Orange is visible on the natrolite (bottom row).

78. ORPIMENT ORANGE.

(i). *The Neck Ruff of the Golden Pheasant.*
[Chrysolophus pictus] *Belly of the Warty Newt.*
[*Great crested newt*; Triturus cristatus]
(ii). *Indian Cress.* [*Garden nasturtium*; Tropaeolum majus]
(iii). ————————

Orpiment Orange, the characteristic colour, is about equal parts of gamboge yellow and arterial blood red.

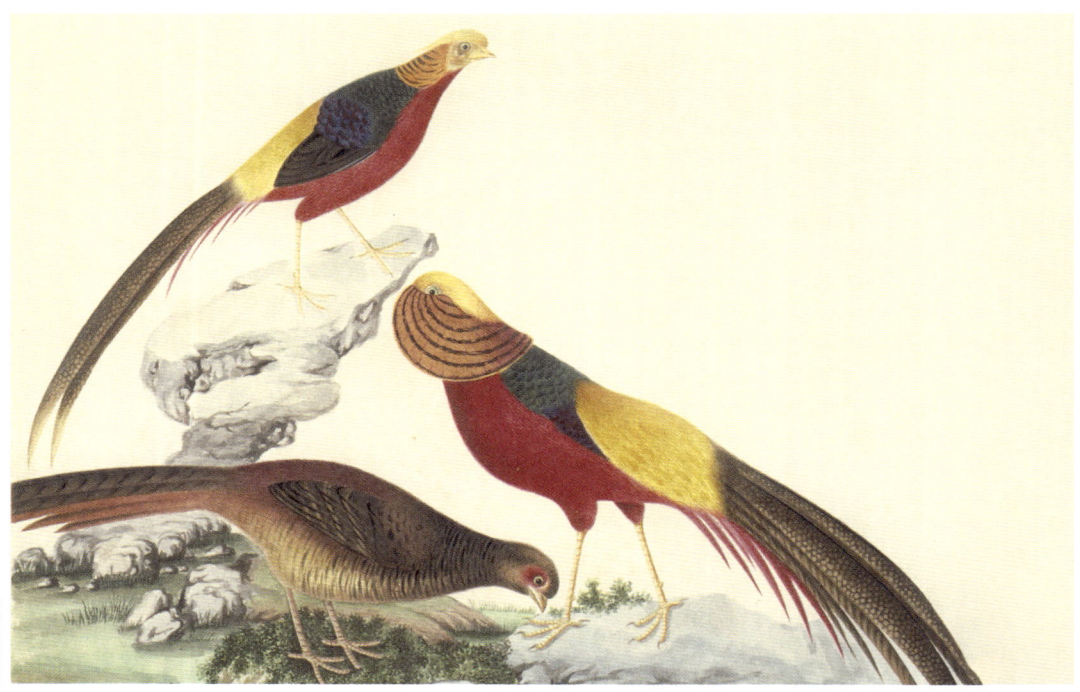

ANIMAL.

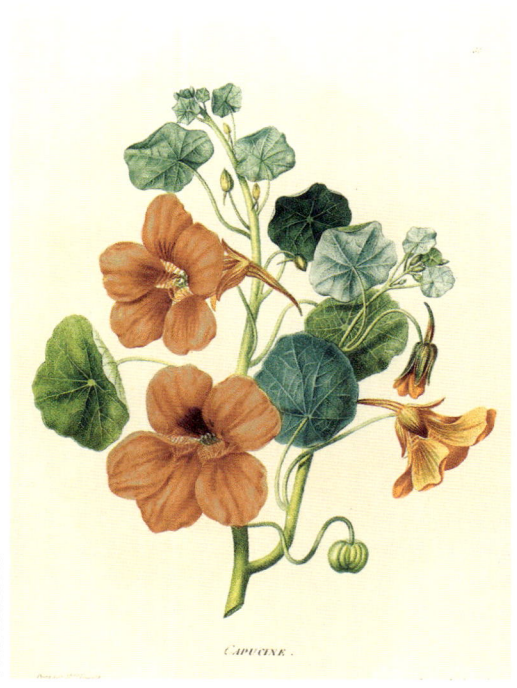

VEGETABLE.

CAPUCINE.

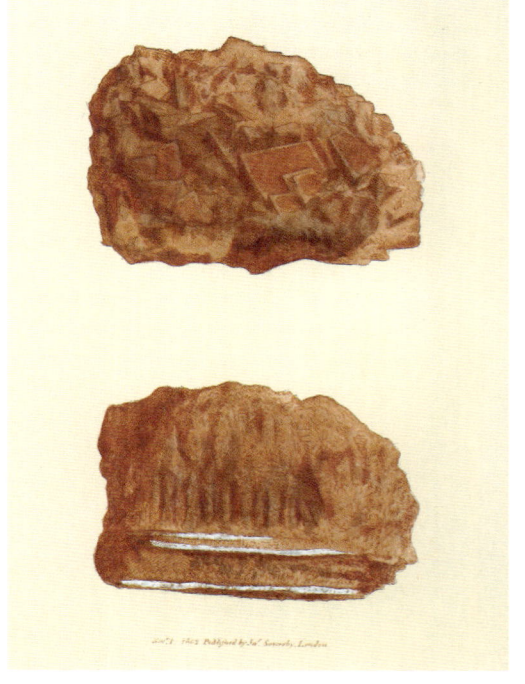

MINERAL.

ANIMAL.
John Reeves,
Chrysolophus pictus,
watercolour, c. 1812–31.
Orpiment Orange is
visible on the neck
ruff feathers of the
golden pheasant.

VEGETABLE.
Henriette Antoinette
Vincent, *Études de
fleurs et de fruits*, 1820.
Orpiment Orange is
visible on the petals
of the garden
nasturtium.

MINERAL.
James Sowerby,
British Mineralogy,
Vol. 1, 1802–17.
Orpiment Orange
is visible on the
carbonate of lime.*

79. BROWNISH ORANGE.

(i). *Eyes of the largest Flesh Fly.* [Sarcophagidae]
(ii). *Style of the Orange Lily.* [Lilium bulbiferum]
(iii). *Dark Brazilian Topaz.* [*Silicate mineral*]

Brownish Orange, is orpiment orange, with a little hyacinth red, and a small quantity of light chesnut brown.

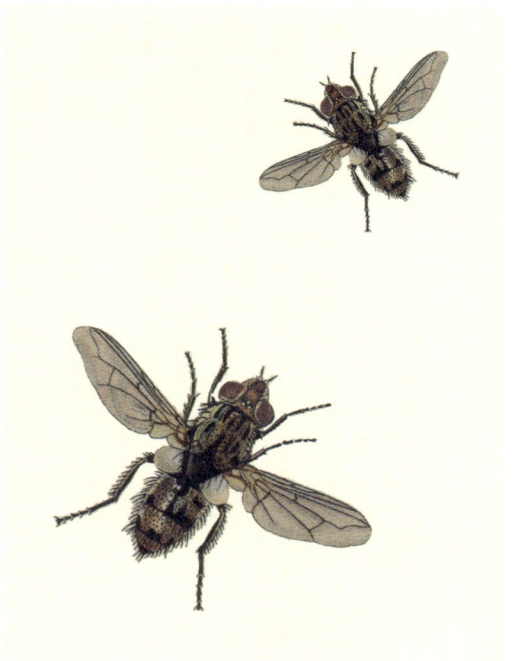

ANIMAL.

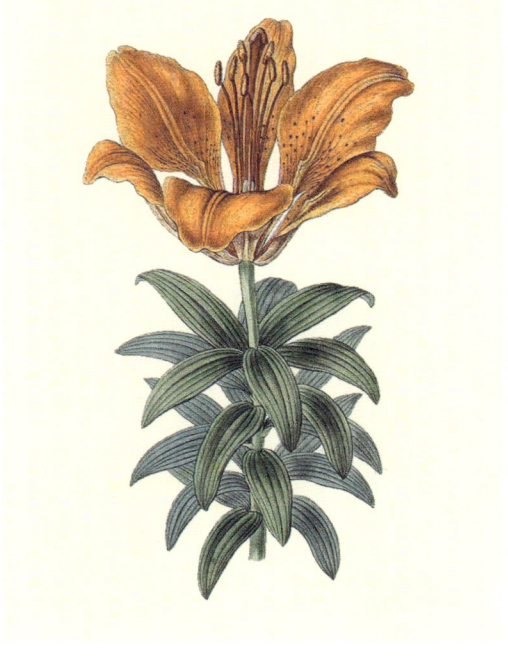

VEGETABLE.

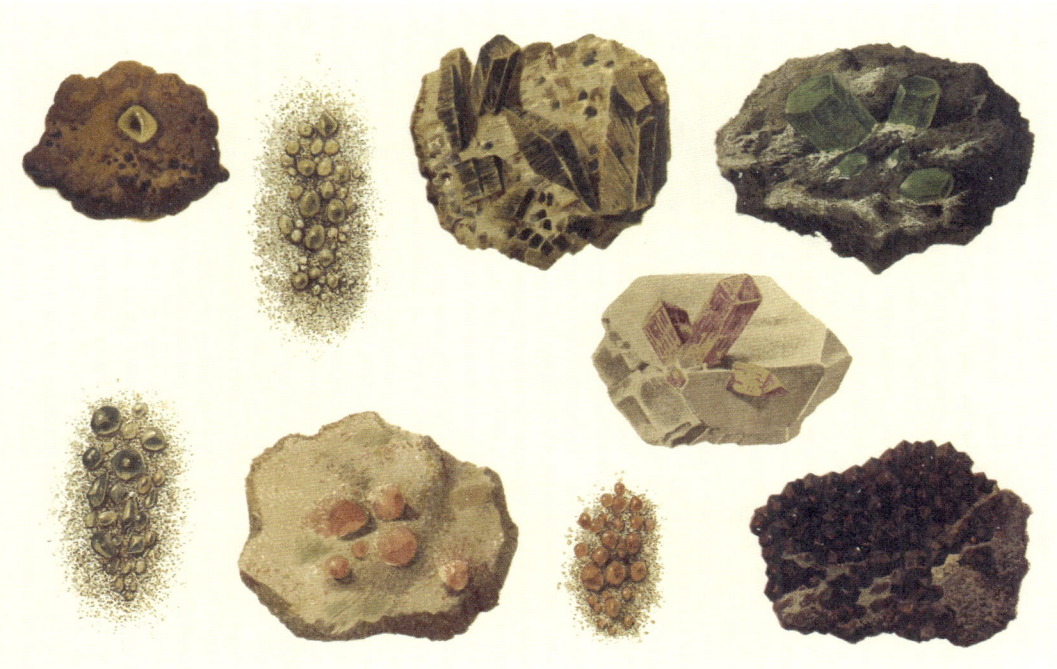

MINERAL.

ANIMAL.
John Curtis, *British Entomology*, 1840. Brownish Orange is visible on the eyes of the flesh fly.

VEGETABLE.
John Lindley, *Edwards's Botanical Register*, 1829–47. Brownish Orange is visible on the style of the lily.

MINERAL.
Louis Simonin, *Underground Life*, 1869. Brownish Orange is found on the topaz (centre row). The topaz is embedded within rock crystal.

80. REDDISH ORANGE.

(i).   *Lower Wings of Tyger Moth.* [*Tiger moth*; Arctia caja]
(ii).   *Hemimeris.* [Hemimeris] *Buff Hibiscus.* [Hibiscus]
(iii).   ———————

Reddish Orange, is buff orange mixed with a considerable portion of tile red.

ANIMAL.

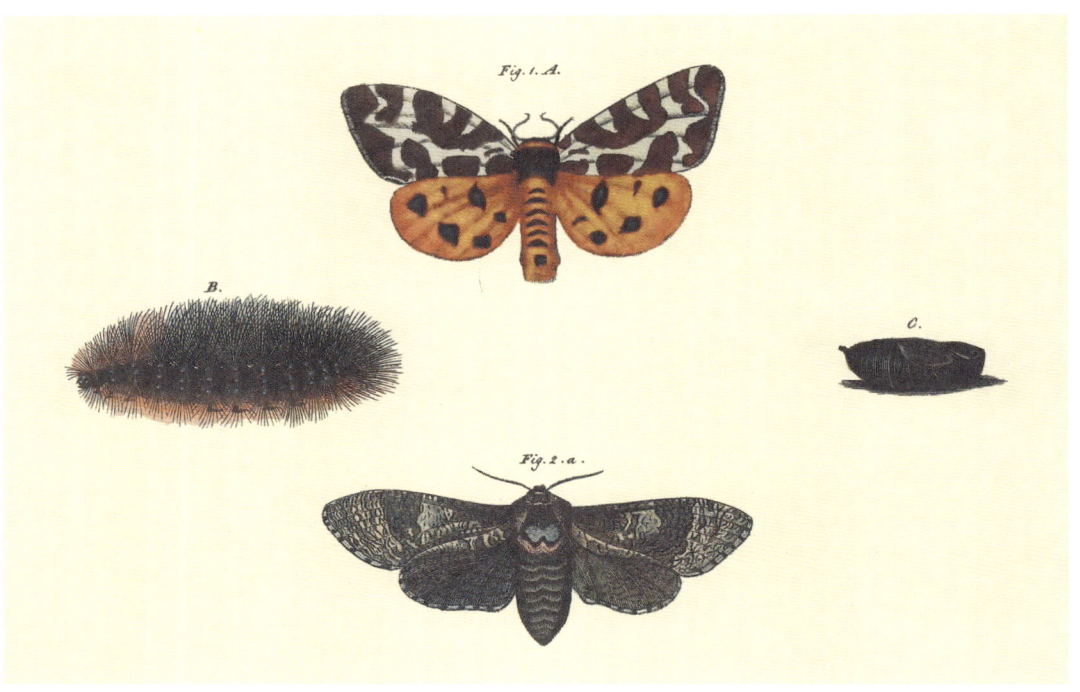

ANIMAL.
Friedrich Johann Bertuch, *Bilderbuch für Kinder*, 1802. Reddish Orange is visible on the lower wings of the tiger moth (top row).

VEGETABLE.
Lena Lowis, *Familiar Indian Flowers*, 1878. Reddish Orange is visible on the petals of the hibiscus.

MINERAL.
James Sowerby, *Exotic Mineralogy*, 1811. Reddish Orange is visible on the polyhalite.*

VEGETABLE.

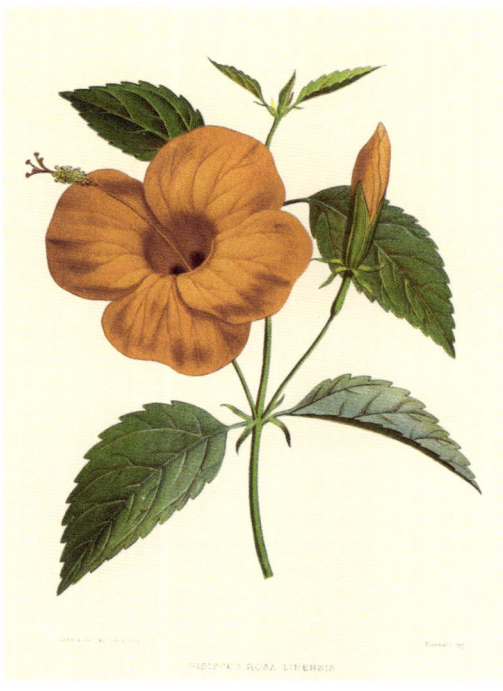

MINERAL.

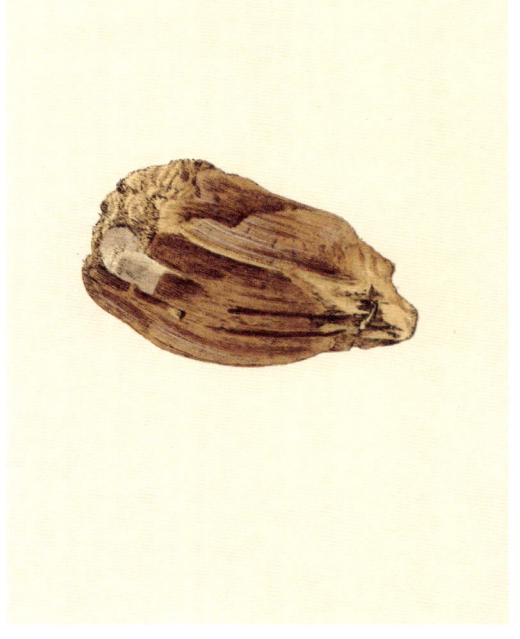

81. DEEP REDDISH ORANGE.

(i). *Gold Fish lustre abstracted.* [*Goldfish*; Carassius auratus]
(ii). *Scarlet Leadington Apple.* [Malus domestica]
(iii). ————————————

*Deep Reddish Orange,
is Dutch orange mixed
with much scarlet red.*

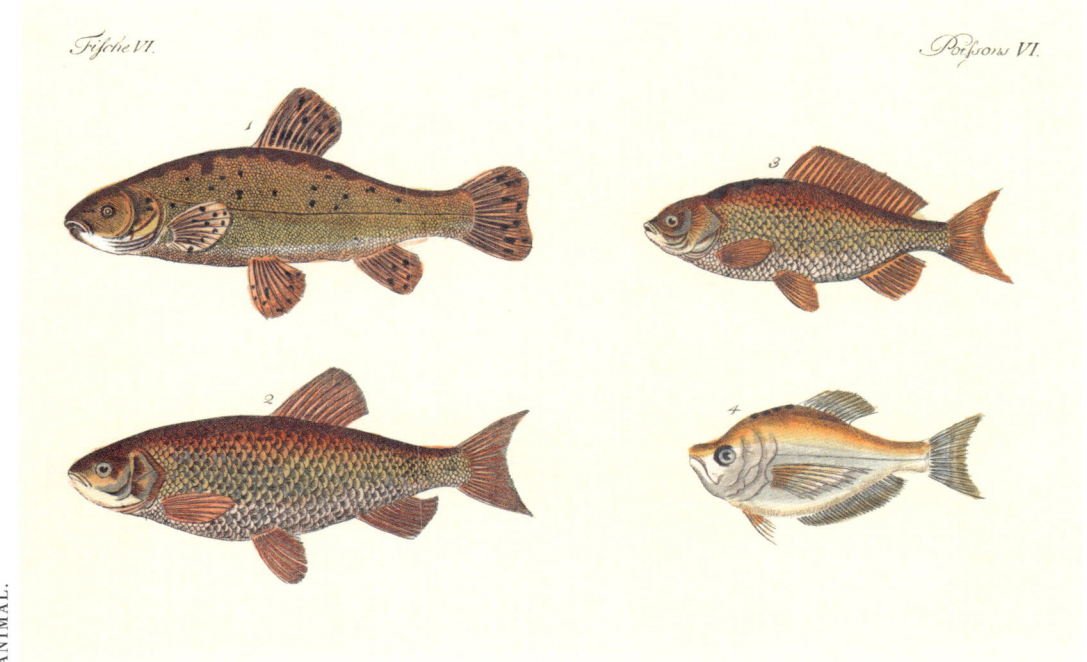

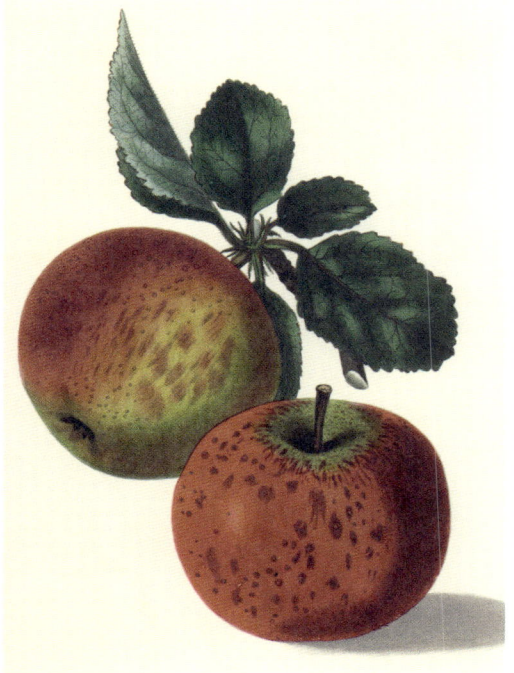

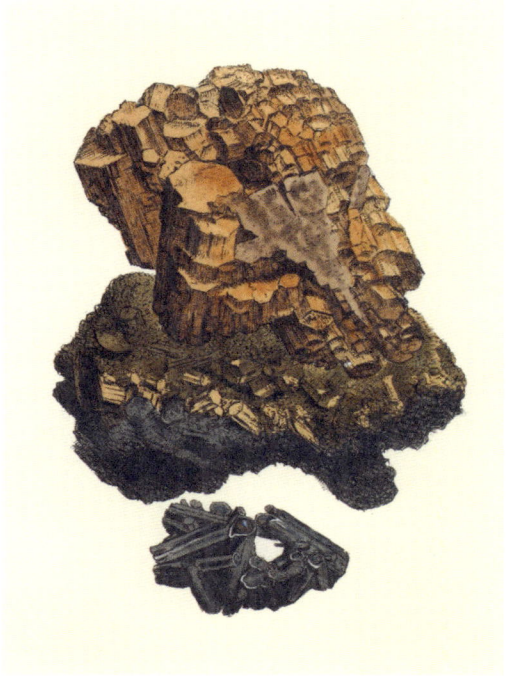

VEGETABLE.

MINERAL.

ANIMAL.
Friedrich Johann
Bertuch, *Bilderbuch
für Kinder*, 1802.
Deep Reddish Orange
is visible on the lustre
on the scales of the
goldfish (bottom left).

VEGETABLE.
Charles McIntosh,
Flora and Pomona,
1829.
Deep Reddish Orange
is visible on the skin
of the apple.

MINERAL.
James Sowerby,
Exotic Mineralogy, 1811.
Deep Reddish Orange
is visible on the lead
sulphide.*

4.

ONE FOR ALL?
WERNER'S NOMENCLATURE OF
COLOURS AS A GENERAL STANDARD
OF COLOUR AND ITS PARTICULAR
USE IN MEDICINE.

Morbid anatomy and colour tables for inflammation and skin diseases.

BY ANDRÉ KARLICZEK.

Werner's Nomenclature of Colours by Patrick Syme (1774-1845) was one of the most popular and widely used systems of colour reference in the 19th century and is still highly appreciated today.[1] Published in 1814, this small book, with its 108 colour swatches (110 in the second edition of 1821), is neither the first nor the most exhaustive of its kind, but in the development of the standardization of natural colours it marks a high point. Despite its meticulous workmanship, however, the success of *Werner's Nomenclature of Colours* was not assured. It could be argued that if it had been published around 100 years earlier, in all probability it would have shared the same fate as *A Catalogue of Simple and Mixt Colours*[2] of 1686, by the English naturalist Richard Waller (*c.* 1660-1715) – the earliest known attempt to establish a general standard of colour reference for the scientific description of plants and animals. Waller had learnt of the basic concept of colour nomenclature and samples from the Swedish miniature painter Elias Brenner (1647-1717), and his own table, with text in both English and Latin, provided instructions on how to reproduce the colours by mixing blue, red and yellow. Waller's treatise seems to have been

overlooked by scientists, and Syme's book too might have been barely noticed as a standard work on colour and languished in obscurity if it had appeared a century before, for the simple reason that at that time there was no call for it.

Patrick Syme referred to this himself in his preface, writing that specifying a colour is always useful if the colour of an object is to be described exactly, but only becomes necessary 'where colour forms a character'. Instead of the colour of a plant or animal being relevant *per se*, it was necessary for it to be recognized as an essential characteristic by scientists, which in turn gave rise to a need for standards of colour reference. The requirement for a scientific determination of colour first evolved in the second half of the 18th century. Colour gradually became a determining, rather than a secondary character, as well as being susceptible to analytical measurement. This in turn relied on two connected developments.

The first was the classification of nature following the work of Carl Linnaeus (1707-1778). In his *Systema naturae* of 1735 he divided all natural things into three kingdoms – animal, vegetable and mineral – and then, according to their common features and differences,

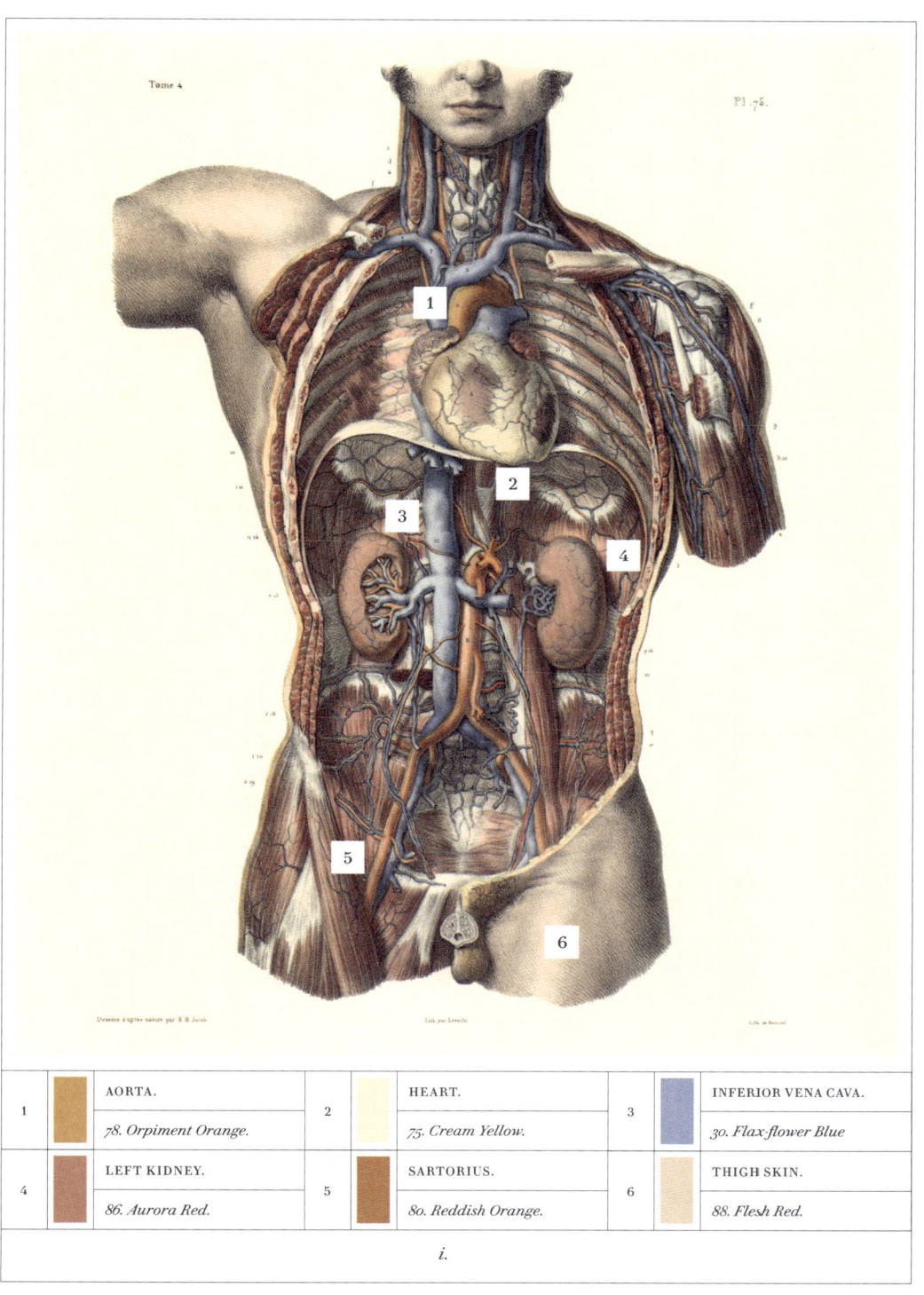

Tôme 4

Pl.75.

1		AORTA.	2		HEART.	3		INFERIOR VENA CAVA.
		78. Orpiment Orange.			*75. Cream Yellow.*			*30. Flax-flower Blue*
4		LEFT KIDNEY.	5		SARTORIUS.	6		THIGH SKIN.
		86. Aurora Red.			*80. Reddish Orange.*			*88. Flesh Red.*

i.

(i).   Marc Jean Bourgery, *Traité complet de l'anatomie
de l'homme,* 1831–54. Anantomical drawing showing
the blood vessels and organs of the thorax and abdomen.

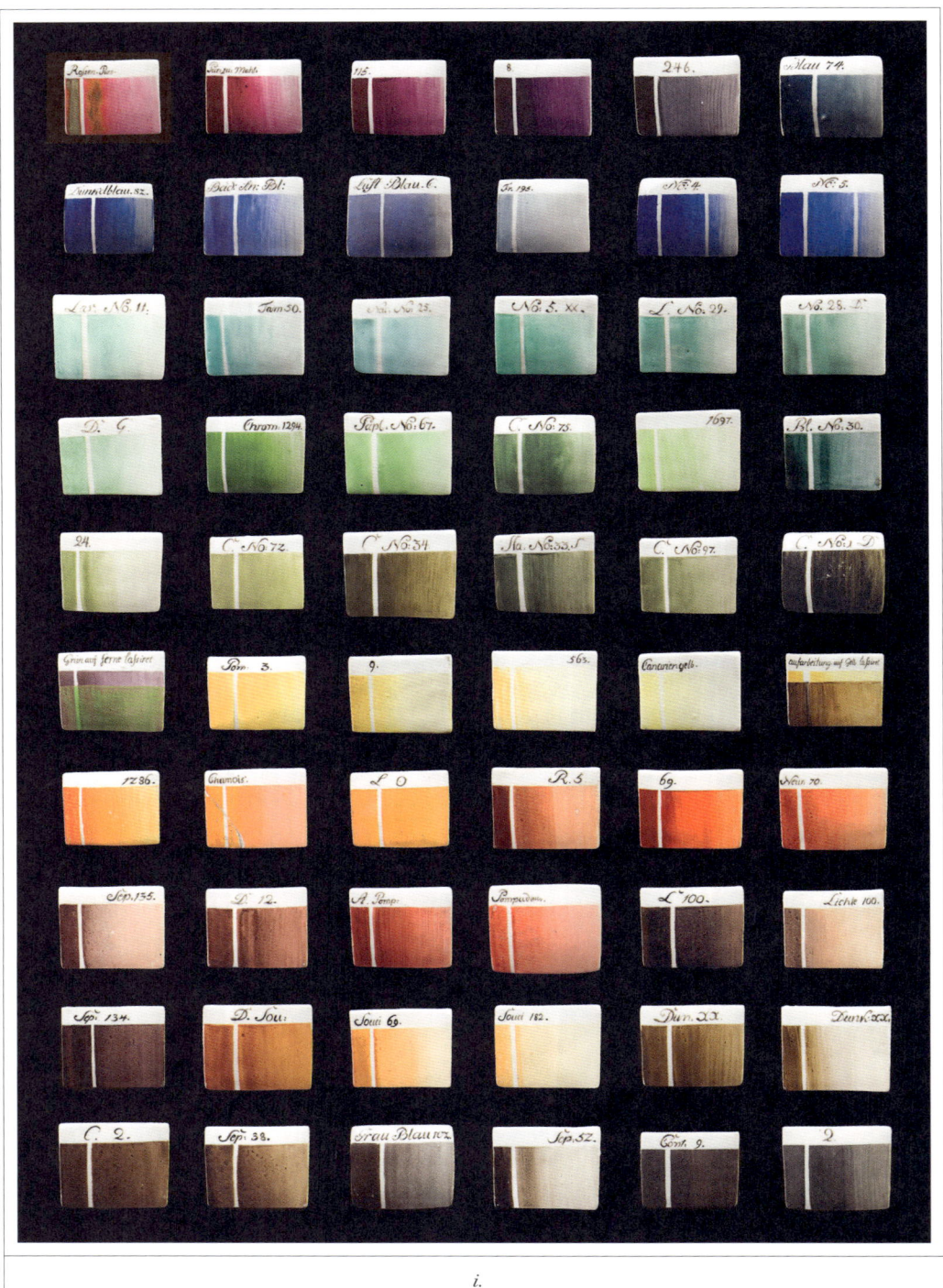

i.

(i).   Colour swatches applied to Meissen porcelain plates, from the
           collection of Abraham Gottlob Werner, *c.* 1814–17. The plates are
           described in the appendix to the 1823 catalogue of Werner's 'external
           characteristics' mineral collection, and it is likely he used them as
           a tool for teaching his pupils about colour gradation. There are 249
           tiles in total and they are approximately 5 × 3.9 cm (2 × 1 ½ in.) in size.

organized them into a system of classes, orders, genera and species. In the tenth edition of his work (1758–59), he introduced the system of binomial nomenclature, still in use today, by which living organisms are classified by genus and species names.[3] Second was the analytical quantification of nature through the use of instruments.

In the developing scientific thought of the 18th century, different colour usage contexts can be identified: general colour systems, colour reference systems, and colour scales that elucidate particular colour reference systems. Colour reference systems consist of a combination of colour names and swatches to provide a standard with reference to a visual example of each colour. This ensures a reliable, verifiable and comparative description of the colours of natural things. Such systems can be directed towards the requirements of individual areas of science – the tones of colour called for when describing butterflies are different from those needed for plants and mushrooms, or minerals. Colour scales go beyond a pure description towards precise measurement. The different tones of colour that make up a colour scale can determine the mass of a material or the course of certain processes and their observable transformations. Examples include the tables used in urinoscopy, the visual analysis of the colour of urine for medical purposes,[4] or the cyanometer,[5] an instrument for measuring the tones of blue in the skies as well as determining the mass of opaque particles.

COLOUR REFERENCE SYSTEMS
IN THE NATURAL SCIENCES

Colour reference systems, of which *Werner's Nomenclature of Colours* is one example, first appear after 1769 predominantly in German-speaking areas and in different variants.[6] In addition to colour tables that include the most frequently occurring colour tones found in nature, there are also extensive colour atlases, sometimes with more than 5,400 colour samples, which provide colour standards for general use and not just for natural history. A

system that addresses the needs of the natural scientist in describing the different colours found in the three kingdoms of nature must be much more complex if the demands of both specific scientific fields and the arts have to be accommodated. The more all-encompassing and subdivided a colour reference system is, the longer it takes to find and identify a distinct colour tone. The potential for uncertainty is increased when many hundreds of tones are distributed over numerous pages of a book, making it impossible to gain an overview.

A disadvantage of a standardization of colour such as *Werner's Nomenclature of Colours* that is directed not only towards natural scientists but also to a wider audience is that it runs the risk of prioritizing a greater variety of colour tones over a subject-specific usefulness.[7] In this Syme is not alone. In 1782, the artist and teacher Christian Friedrich Prange (1756–1836) published a colour lexicon aimed at artists, manufacturers and craftsmen, as well as natural scientists, with 4,608 colour samples. This was followed in 1794 by the anonymous Viennese *Farbenkabinet*, which contained no fewer than 5,000 colour swatches on coloured strips of paper pasted into the book, like Syme.

The question also arises of whether a swatch on paper can really give a true impression of colour as compared to objects in nature, where metallic colours, translucence, sheen and iridescence can affect colour perception. For colour comparisons mineralogists could use either a reference collection – a 'Colour-suite of Minerals' (see p. 74) – or tiny porcelain plates. Comparable natural history collections, for example of butterflies, beetles or dried plants (herbaria), are also well known.

COLOUR AND THE
DEVELOPMENT OF ANATOMY

One factor relevant to the use of colour swatches on paper in medicine is how the subject, and anatomy in particular, has been taught historically. Anatomy, the knowledge of the human body and its illnesses through cutting open bodies (from the Greek: ἀνά/aná 'open' and τομή/tomé 'cut'), was forbidden, or at least strongly disapproved of, from the 3rd century BC until the Renaissance in the West, especially under the influence of Christian moral beliefs. Following renewed interest in the physical structure of the body during the Renaissance, anatomy again became a focus of research from the 16th century on.[8] Public anatomical demonstrations gave the dissecting doctors and their audiences direct experience and knowledge of the actual appearance of human organs, building on the information from the ancient physicians and medical authorities.

A new tradition of illustrated anatomical books also appeared at this time, including *De humani corporis fabrica* (1543) by Andreas Vesalius (1514-1564). They were very elaborate productions and therefore expensive. In addition, they did not simply depict what was seen on the dissection table, but constructed ideal bodies in accordance with the developing concept of the human body as machine.[9] Such anatomical books were also always uncoloured. The physical structure of the organs was thought to be the most essential aspect, and colour as an independent characteristic was considered unreliable because of its great variability. Colour was treated as a secondary feature, for example as part of general presentations before the advent of clinical pictures. Lectures in anatomy were given on the basis of the great works of Vesalius or Justus Christian Loder (1753-1832),[10] but were supplemented by sections, practical anatomical exercises and demonstrations of anatomical preparations, as well as the use of moulages – models and casts taken from human body parts – in order to give students first-hand experience.

THE ROLE OF *WERNER'S NOMENCLATURE* IN MEDICINE

What role, then, did *Werner's Nomenclature of Colours* have in medicine? Syme had been appointed painter to the Wernerian Natural History Society, whose members included many respected artists and scientists – surgeons and anatomists among them. He specifically

recommends his book as an important aid in 'Morbid Anatomy', that is pathological anatomy, pointing out that conditions from inflammation to gangrene are 'strikingly marked' by colours.[11] Morbid, or pathological, anatomy – concerned with disease – like the systematic classification of natural history, was a relatively new scientific field at the time.[12] Methods were essentially based on a comparison of natural objects, in the case of pathological anatomy the diseased and healthy body. For such comparisons, a colour standard was essential because visual aspects, in addition to changes in the physical form of the organs, as well as consistency and smell (and to some extent taste), are significant and can be observed and recorded. Nevertheless, such changes should not be looked at in isolation – colour is not by itself a representative aspect and has to be considered in relation to the overall appearance of the body.

Around 1800, the ability to distinguish normal from abnormal, that is between health and sickness, was by no means established. As medicine was moving away from the ancient theory of the four humours in the relatively new direction of pathology based on physical anatomy, there were relatively few corpses available for examination whose individual, and family, medical histories were known. The normal condition of the organs themselves as a standard against which changes could be compared had not yet been definitively fixed, and neither the range of variation of healthy organ growth, nor the natural changes that occurred with age or as a result of the influence of the environment and life conditions, as well as degenerative processes after death, had been determined.[13] Given this, in the first half of the 19th century colour played no great part in theoretical concepts of medicine. Moreover, any attempt at a precise analysis of colour diagnostics using a paper-based colour standard during an autopsy, with corpses usually stored in cool vaults, would have been extremely difficult.

It is therefore not surprising to find that in the area of pathological anatomy, at least, *Werner's Nomenclature of Colours* did not find

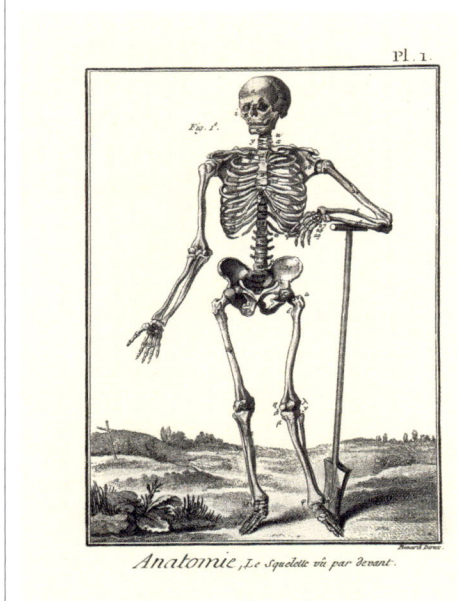

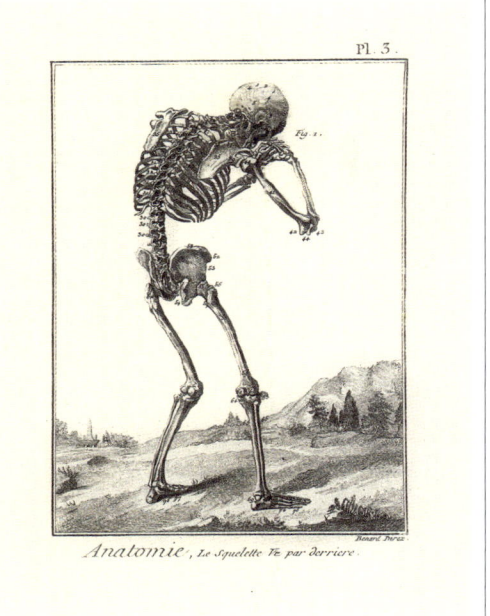

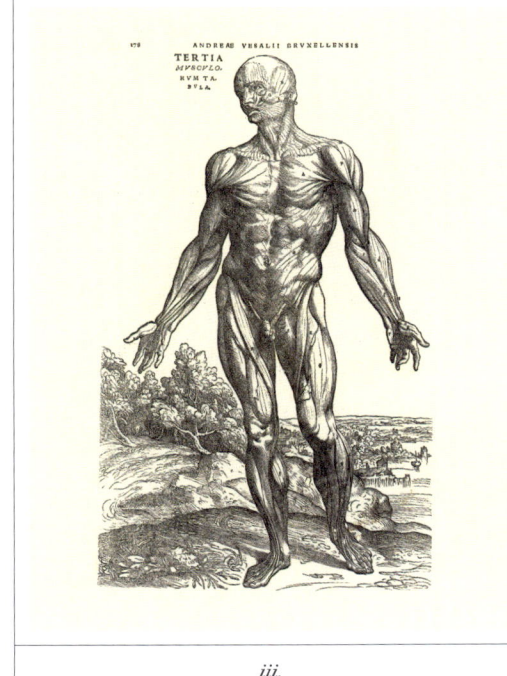

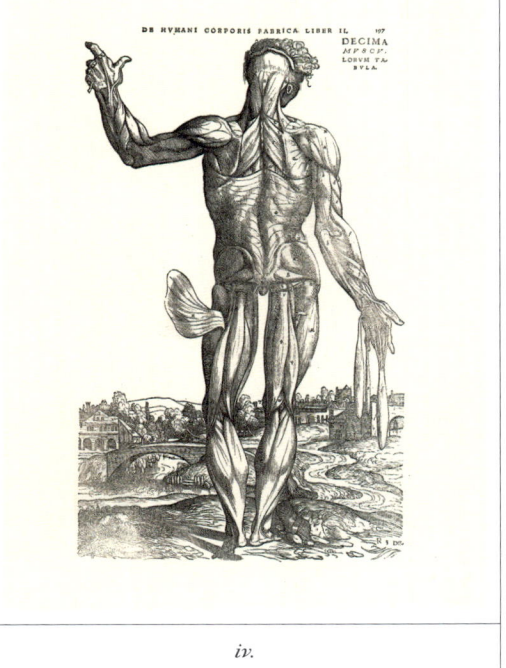

i.

ii.

iii.

iv.

(i).   Robert Bénard, *A human skeleton, seen from the front*, engraving, 1779.
(ii).   Robert Bénard, *A human skeleton, seen from the back*, engraving, 1779.
(iii). Muscles 3, Andreas Vesalius Bruxellensis, *De humani corporis fabrica libri septem*, 1543.
(iv).   Muscles 4, Andreas Vesalius Bruxellensis, *De humani corporis fabrica libri septem*, 1543.

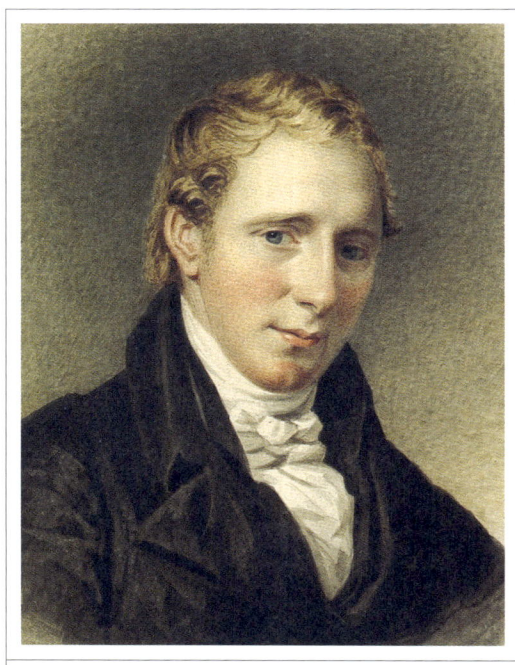

i.

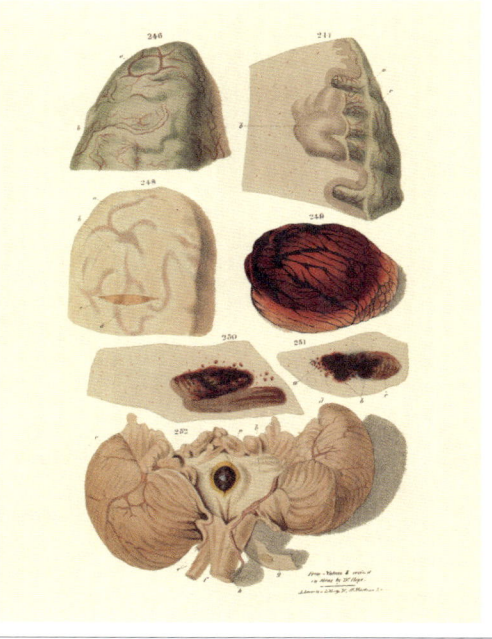

ii.

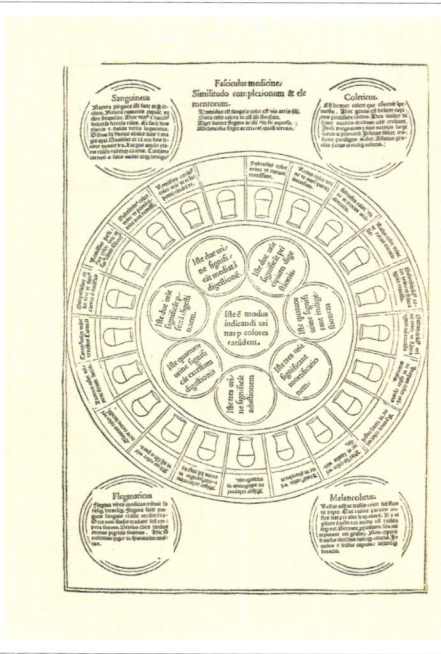

iii.

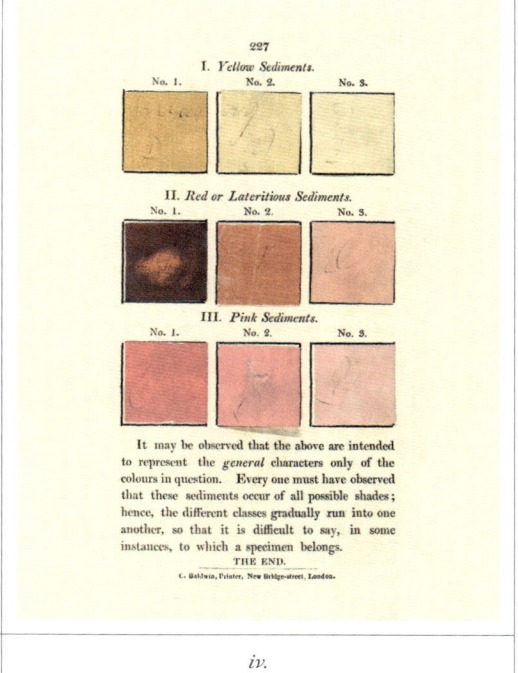

iv.

(i).   W. J. Thomson's watercolour portrait of anatomist John Gordon.
(ii).   Parts of the brain, James Hope, *Principles and Illustrations of Morbid Anatomy*, 1834.
(iii). Uroscopy wheel, Johannes de Ketham, *Fasciculus medicinae*, 1491.
(iv).   Colour chart for urine sediments, William Prout, *An Inquiry into the Nature and Treatment of Gravel, Calculus, and Other Diseases*, 1821.

any great resonance or application, despite the fact that it would have been useful for the comparison of colours and colour descriptions, and there was certainly demand for it. Occasional references to its use by physicians should be seen in the context of the fact that at that time natural scientists studied medicine or philosophy, and there was as yet no specific specialist training for botanists and zoologists. Such is the case of the Scottish physician John Richardson (1777–1865), who as a naval surgeon went on numerous expeditions (including with John Franklin to the Arctic Ocean) and used *Werner's Nomenclature of Colours* not in his work as a physician but for his descriptions of minerals, plants and animals (see also p. 130).

SPECIFIC USES OF *WERNER'S NOMENCLATURE* IN MEDICINE

The first clear, concrete use of *Werner's Nomenclature of Colours* in medicine is by the Scottish anatomist John Gordon (1786–1818) in 1817. Although he died at the age of only 32, Gordon served as President of the Royal Medical Society and is well known for his criticism of phrenology, popular in Europe at the time. Around 1800, Franz Joseph Gall (1758–1828), in association with Johann Spurzheim (1776–1832), had developed a theory, based on his observations and experiments, that the mental abilities and character of a person could be deduced from the impressions made on the surface of the skull by the brain. Among other objections, Gordon used his neuro-anatomical knowledge to contradict assumptions about different substances in the brain and refers to Syme in connection with one in particular:

The Grey Substance.-The term *grey*, or *cineritious*, which is generally applied to this substance, is calculated to convey an inaccurate idea of its colour to those who have not seen it. *Brown* is every where its predominating hue; and in most parts it is of that species of *Brown*, which is called by Werner in his Nomenclature of Colours, *Wood-Brown*.[14]

The reference to the specific colour sample in Syme is thus used to give the reader a more accurate impression of the brown colour of this substance in the brain, rather than grey as implied by its name. Since Gordon had studied medicine in Edinburgh, and his book was published by William Blackwood, who also published Syme, his familiarity with Werner's *Nomenclature of Colours* is not surprising.

Another context in which Syme's book was certainly used in medicine is provided by William Prout (1785–1850) in the field of urogenital pathology. Prout, who also studied medicine in Edinburgh, used the colour references in 1819 to characterize urinary stones by a specific colour or hue. His use of colours in this way was markedly different from the colour references found in urinoscopy at the end of the Middle Ages (see p. 227), as it was based on chemical analysis of the constituents, with the colours providing an accurate reference. Prout refers to *Werner's Nomenclature of Colours* in describing the colour and consisency of urinary stones, differentiating the exterior ('wax-yellow') and inner ('wood-brown') colouring.[15]

In 1821, Prout developed his own colour table to characterize urinary sediments without direct reference to Syme. It seems Prout felt the need to clarify his descriptions with his own colour swatches, perhaps because he was aware that *Werner's Nomenclature of Colours* was not well established or sufficiently familiar in a specialized medical context for him to be confident that his own readers would follow direct references to it.

In addition, Prout limited his table to nine colour tones which could be displayed on a single page, allowing for better ease of use. Using *Werner's Nomenclature of Colours* in such situations, with its far more extensive colour references, would entail having to consult several different pages and scrolling backwards and forwards, making it less practical. Even so, it might be wondered why Prout does not make recourse to Syme's nomenclature when developing his own colour swatches, or name him.

A third example of a usage in a medical context is illustrated by the Edinburgh-born optician James Hunter. In 1841 he published a chart of colour transformations to assist in the diagnosis of inflammations of the iris. Starting with the natural colours of the iris, the chart provides colour tones for various changes resulting from disease, which also can provide clues to other illnesses such as syphilis. Hunter's remarks concerning *Werner's Nomenclature* are particularly interesting:

> In originally framing the table, I compared the colours of the inflamed iris with the standard ones of Werner, and adopted his nomenclature. I have been induced, however, to change it partially, in preparing this paper for the press; because, without illustrations, many of Werner's names are not easily recognized or comprehended; such as 'pistachio green, siskin green, broccili brown,' &c; whilst others, such as 'apple green,' which resembles the bark, not the fruit; 'cochineal red,' which is a reddish brown, and not an arterial or crimson red, &c. are by no means happy, and very apt to mislead. The practical utility of a correct observation of the changes produced in the iris by inflammation is considerable, both in the diagnosis, and in the treatment of iritis.[16]

Hunter here highlights two difficulties that stand in the way of establishing a colour reference system that is useful for both general and specific purposes. The first relates to the names given to the colours that are taken from a natural object that the colour supposedly matches (grass green, copper red, lead grey etc). If a concept of colour is evoked without a colour swatch, an impression of the colour is conveyed only when the particular object is familiar from personal experience. The second problem, especially in medicine, is that an exactly determined tone of colour diagnosis is closely bound up with the correct therapy to be applied. Hunter writes that it is unsatisfactory to have only an approximate impression of the colour, and that personal observations and experience are still indispensable.

THE PLACE OF *WERNER'S NOMENCLATURE* IN THE HISTORY OF COLOUR REFERENCE SYSTEMS

That there was an urgent need for standardized references of colour within medicine was widely accepted in the first half of the 19th century. Internationally, many authors regretted the lack of specific standards that would allow them to differentiate transformations of colour resulting from illness. The Nuremberg dermatologist Heinrich Eichhorn wrote in 1827:

> A colour table is of inestimable worth for determining skin illnesses, similar to what is found in some branches of natural history, e.g. botany. It is self-evident that such colour tables, if they should serve their purpose properly, need to be constructed with considerable diligence and exactitude. It is well known that every exanthema [inflammatory rash] appears unique in its colours upon the skin; nevertheless, modifications of this colour by one and the same exanthema, e.g. scarlet fever, occur according to its character: syncopal [fainting], typhoidal, etc.; but it is precisely these modifications that are best compared with a colour table; only in this manner, if it is possible, is the greatest perfection achieved. How far the novice is able to remark on the differences in the colour of things, because they spring immediately to his eyes, is well known, and even if he is sufficiently practised in the differences of the usual characteristics of the external forms of skin ailments, the colour chart can be of the greatest use.[17]

Standards of colour designed for universal use in every area of science might not meet the specific needs of each discipline precisely, but as the above examples demonstrate, *Werner's Nomenclature of Colours* was clearly used in a medical context in the first half of the 19th century. That Syme's book circulated widely among scientific and medical circles is

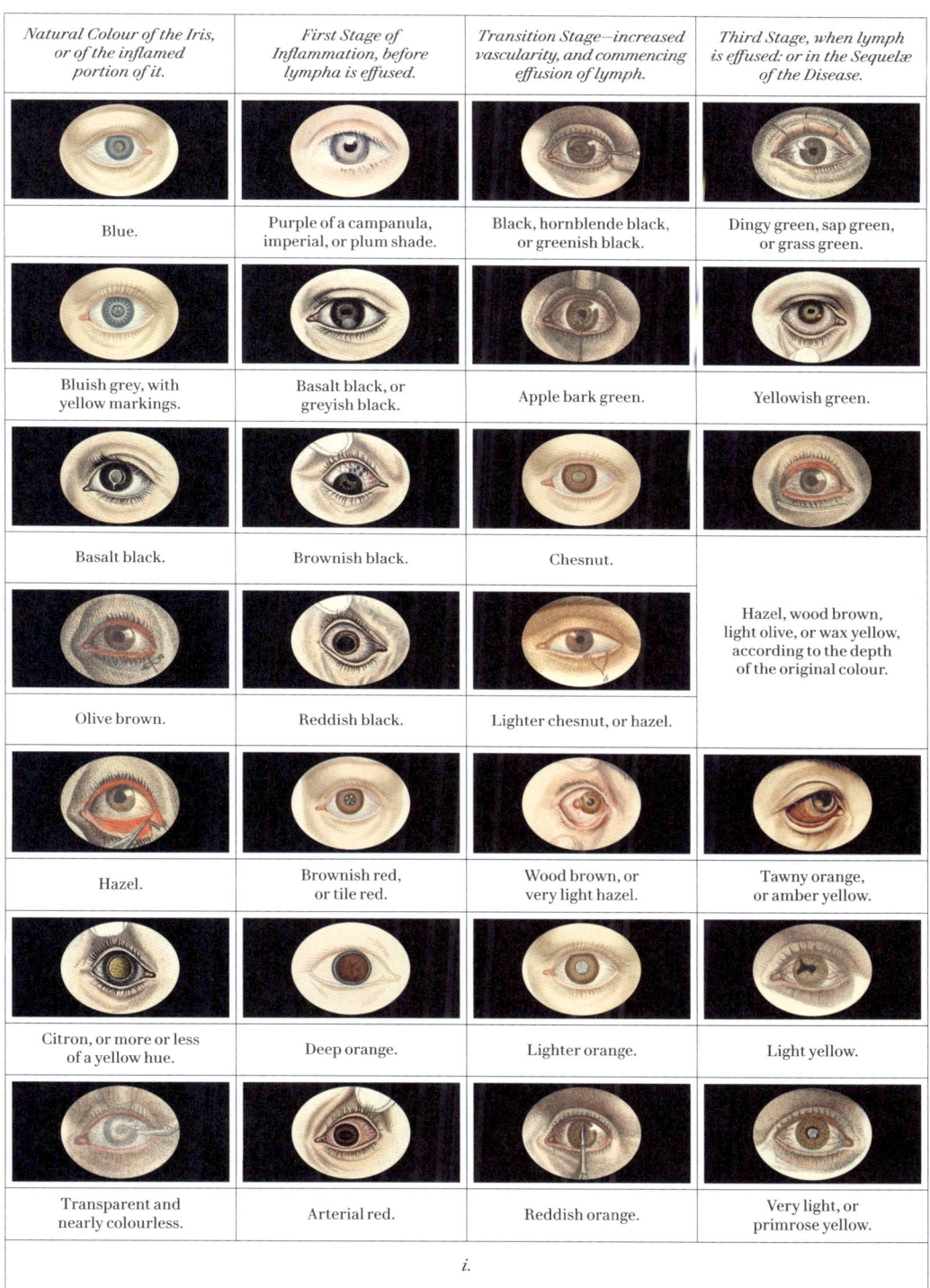

Natural Colour of the Iris, or of the inflamed portion of it.	First Stage of Inflammation, before lympha is effused.	Transition Stage—increased vascularity, and commencing effusion of lymph.	Third Stage, when lymph is effused: or in the Sequelæ of the Disease.
Blue.	Purple of a campanula, imperial, or plum shade.	Black, hornblende black, or greenish black.	Dingy green, sap green, or grass green.
Bluish grey, with yellow markings.	Basalt black, or greyish black.	Apple bark green.	Yellowish green.
Basalt black.	Brownish black.	Chesnut.	Hazel, wood brown, light olive, or wax yellow, according to the depth of the original colour.
Olive brown.	Reddish black.	Lighter chesnut, or hazel.	
Hazel.	Brownish red, or tile red.	Wood brown, or very light hazel.	Tawny orange, or amber yellow.
Citron, or more or less of a yellow hue.	Deep orange.	Lighter orange.	Light yellow.
Transparent and nearly colourless.	Arterial red.	Reddish orange.	Very light, or primrose yellow.

i.

(i).   James Hunter's 'Table of the more common Changes in the Colour of the Iris', 1841, with added illustrations. Hunter's table describes how different iris colours may appear at each stage of inflammation. Here medical illustrations of eyes have been matched to Hunter's descriptions.

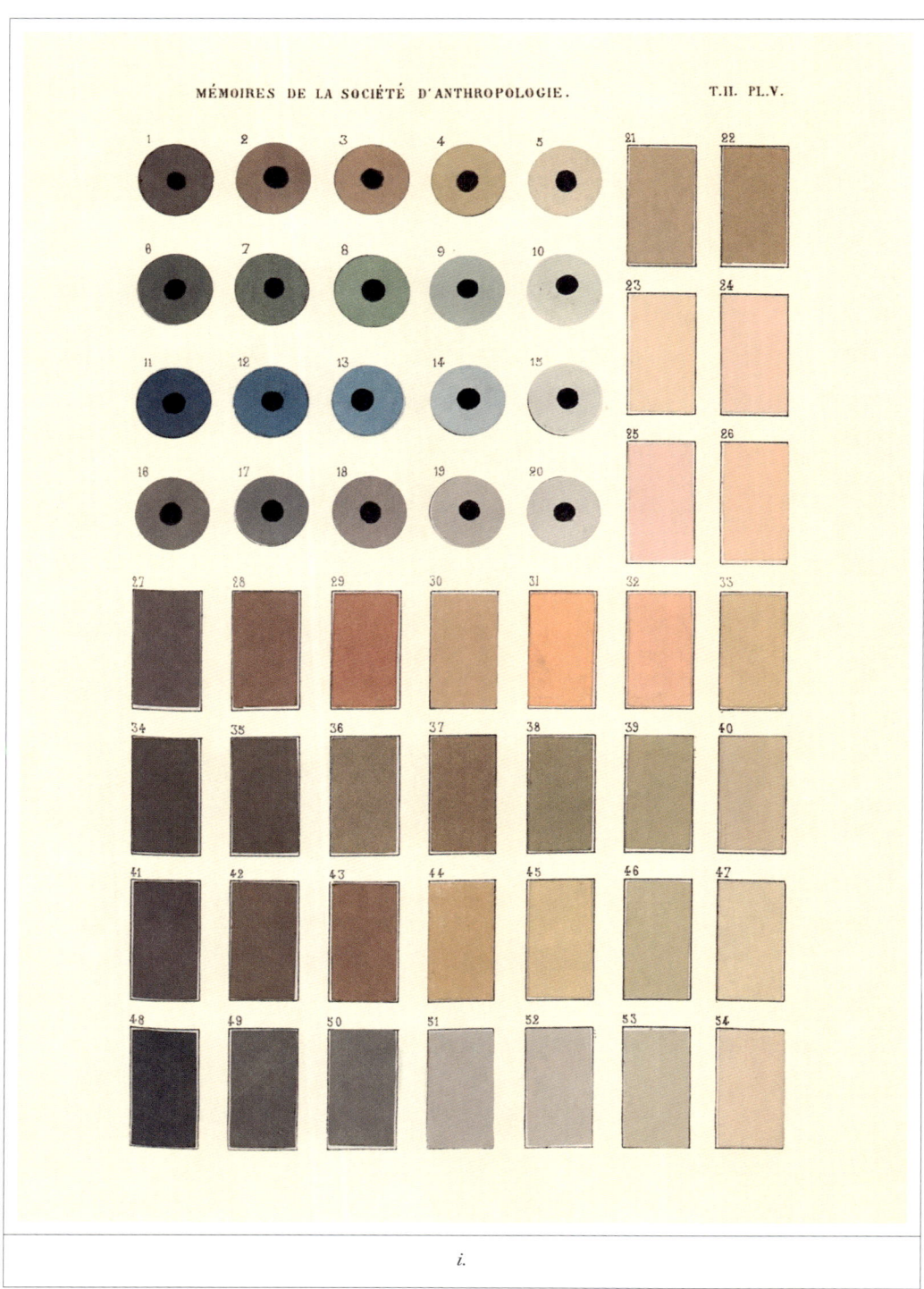

MÉMOIRES DE LA SOCIÉTÉ D'ANTHROPOLOGIE.   T.II. PL.V.

i.

(i).   Colour chart for the description of human colours in anthropology, Paul Broca,
         Instructions générales pour les recherches et observations anthropologiques,
         1865. Broca was a French physician known for his research on the brain,
         as well as for contributing to the development of anthropometry.

also certain. The particular role of scientific societies such as the Wernerian Natural History Society, with which Syme was associated, was one reason for its successful reception, along with the pre-eminent position of Edinburgh in the field of medicine around 1800 and the skills of the publisher William Blackwood, who facilitated the distribution of the book through donations to libraries. An entry in the library catalogue of the Medical Society of Edinburgh shows that Blackwood had already presented a copy there in 1814, the year of its publication.[18]

Certain technical limitations stood in the way of the creation and widespread use of general standards of colour at the time. It was only in the second half of the 19th century with the development of synthetic dyes and colours and improved printing methods that any increased distribution of identical colour swatches could be assured. The development of industrial colour printing (chromo-lithography) in 1837 by Godefroy Engelmann (1788–1839) was one necessary advance, together with the lithographic printing press (1871).[19] And with the discovery of organic coal tar colours a completely new range of affordable inks became available.[20] As a result, not only could colour swatch books be produced economically in very large quantities, but the chemical standardization of the new printing inks also meant that the colour swatches were identical and infinitely reproducible. It thus became much easier for a colour reference system to become recognized and more widely distributed, which in turn brought greater international and interdisciplinary use.

Changes to terminology also occurred. Later colour standards used mostly numerical references, as in the 1865 anthropological colour chart for the description of skin and eye colours[21] by Paul Broca (1824–1880), or straightforward colour names, as in the 1877 international colour scale of Otto Radde (1835–1908).[22]

In its nature and scale, Patrick Syme's *Werner's Nomenclature of Colours* perfectly corresponded with the needs of natural science and the technical and productive possibilities of the times. Its success, despite the lack of modern colour inks and industrial printing, makes it even more remarkable, and ensures its place in the history of scientific colour standards.

NOTES—(1). For detailed information see: Karliczek 2013b; Karliczek 2016; Karliczek 2018. An extensive list of colour reference systems can be found in the catalogue section of Karliczek and Schwarz (eds) 2016. A good overview of colour reference systems can be found in Kuehni and Schwarz 2008; Spillmann 2009. (2). Waller 1686. On Waller see also: Kusukawa 2015. (3). See Linnaeus 1735. (4). Urinoscopy is a tradition that reaches back into antiquity. Prior to the 19th century it was closely connected with the Hippocratic notion of the four humours (black bile, yellow bile, phlegm and blood). The tones of colour used since the Middle Ages and the urinoscopic colour tables are not actual measurements of values, but rather indices for certain illnesses on the basis of an accepted but not quantitatively and analytically determined excess of fluids. (5). See also: Breidbach and Karliczek 2011; Karliczek 2013b. (6). Jacob Christian Schäffer in 1769 with his *Entwurf einer allgemeinen Farbenverein* set out the formal rules for a useful scientific reference system. In essence this consists of a colour pattern that represents a consecutively numbered table with different tones of colour, together with an index of names that refers to the coloured pattern with an ordinal number and thereby provides a concrete visual impression of colour with its colour name. With recourse to Schäffer, the rules and major colours of Werner in his *Kennzeichen* of 1774 were taken up and circulated by his pupils. Schäffer 1769. Also relevant in this context is Giovanni Antonio Scopoli (1723–1788), who already in 1763 in his *Entomologia carniolica* had undertaken an attempt at the standardization of colour with the use of rotating and different coloured discs; his attempt, however, has not been acknowledged. See Karliczek 2016, pp. 300–1. (7). Prange 1782; Anonymous 1794. (8). For an overview of the history of anatomy see: Gerabek et al. 2007. (9). See Karliczek 2014. (10). *Tabvlae anatomicae quas ad illvstrandam hvmani corporis fabricam*, Weimar (1794–1803). (11). Syme 1814, p. 23. Giulia Simonini has noted that Syme's intended target audience was connected to the composition of the Wernerian Natural History Society in Edinburgh: 'This decision was certainly suggested by the desire to reach a greater audience, and it might have been encouraged by the presence of many experts in different fields within the Wernerian Society itself. The Society numbered among its members renowned geologists, physicists, engineers, botanists zoologists, explorers, surgeons, anatomists and also artists.' Simonini 2018. (12). For anatomical pathology, particularly the transition from the theory of humours to a knowledge of anatomy deduced from actual bodily parts, Giovanni Battista Morgagni's work is considered fundamental: *De sedibus et causis morborum per anatomen indagatis* (1767). (13). See in particular Karliczek 2014. (14). Gordon 1817, pp. 28–29. (15). Prout 1819. (16). Hunter 1841. (17). Eichhorn 1827. (18). See: Medical Society of Edinburgh, 1823, *Catalogue of the library of the Medical Society of Edinburgh, distributed in two parts ... : [with Appendices, 1823–26 and 1823–27.]: Edinburgh Medical Society.* Hay & Gall, p. 213. (19). For a short history of colour printing before 1800, see Grimm, Kleine-Tebbe and Stijnman 2011. (20). Engel 2009. (21). Broca 1865. For a general overview of the use of colour standards for describing human colours, see Karliczek and Schwarz, 'Mit Haut und Haar. Vom Merkmal zum Stigma – Farbbestimmungsmethoden am Menschen' in Karliczek and Schwarz 2016, pp. 13–62. (22). Radde 1877.

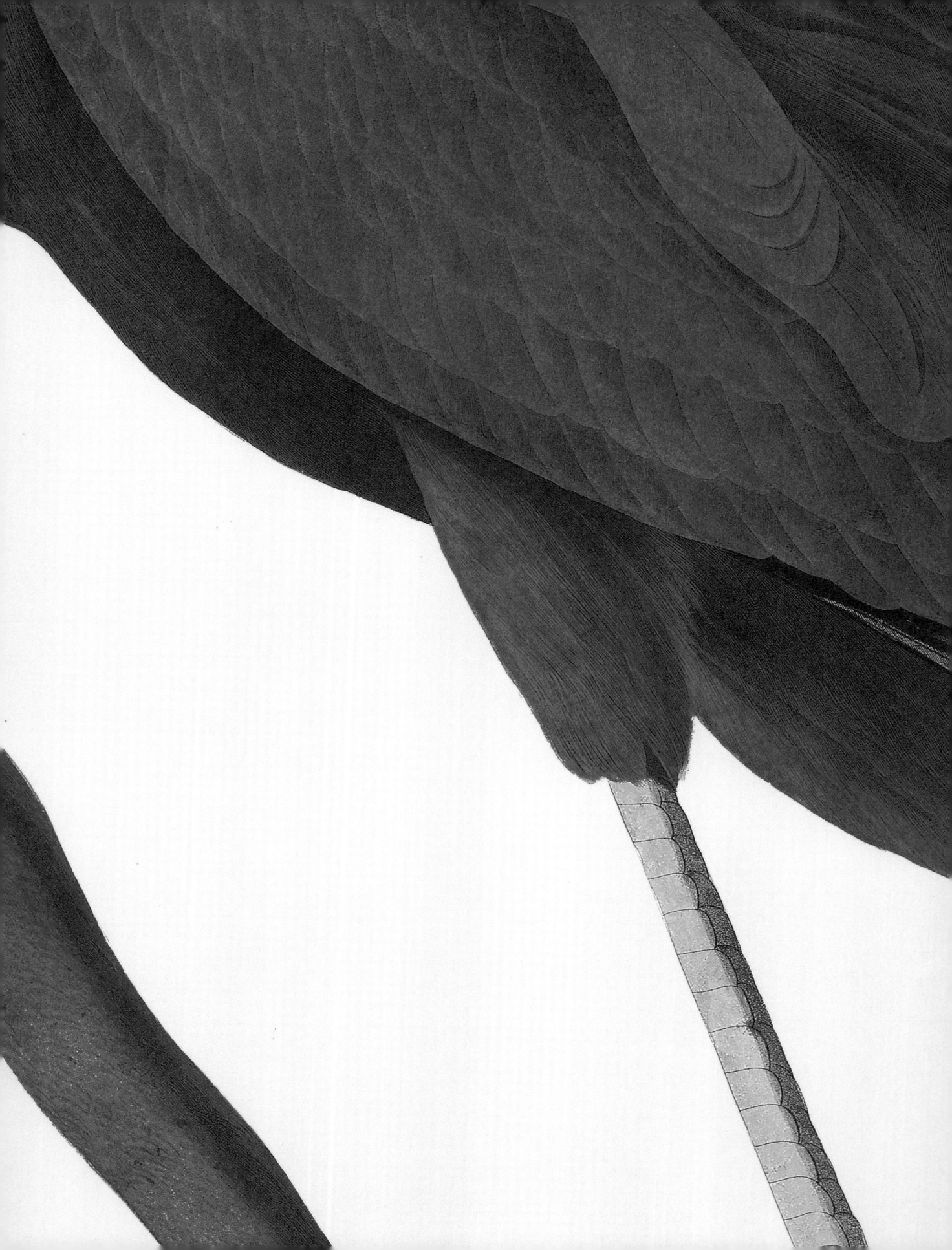

V.

REDS AND BROWNS.

RED.

Nº	Names.	Colours.	ANIMAL.	VEGETABLE.	MINERAL.
82	Tile Red.		Breast of the Cock Bullfinch.	Shrubby Pimpernel.	Porcelain Jasper.
83	Hyacinth Red.		Red Spots of the Lygœus Apterus Fly.	Red on the golden Rennette Apple.	Hyacinth.
84	Scarlet Red.		Scarlet Ibis or Curlew, Mark on Head of Red Grouse.	Large red Oriental Poppy, Red Parts of red and black Indian Peas.	Light red Cinnaber.
85	Vermillion Red.		Red Coral.	Love Apple.	Cinnaber.
86	Aurora Red.		Vent coverts of Pied Wood-Pecker.	Red on the Naked Apple.	Red Orpiment.
87	Arterial Blood Red.		Head of the Cock Gold-finch.	Corn Poppy, Cherry.	
88	Flesh Red.		Human Skin.	Larkspur.	Heavy Spar. Limestone.
89	Rose Red.			Common Garden Rose.	Figure Stone.
90	Peach Blossom Red.			Peach Blossom.	Red Cobalt Ore.

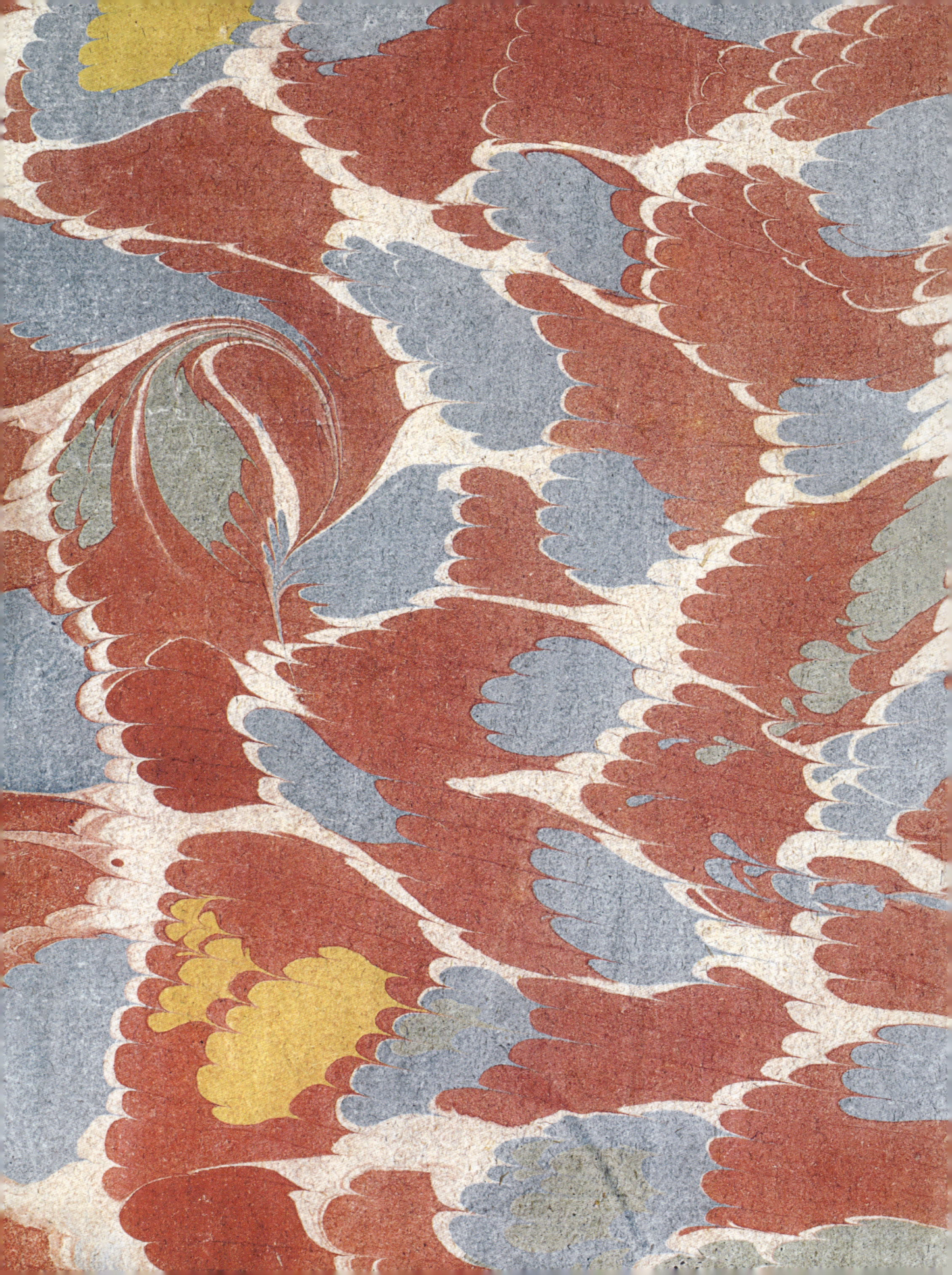

BROWNS.

BROWNS.

Nº	Names.	Colours.	ANIMAL.	VEGETABLE.	MINERAL.
100	Deep Orange-coloured Brown.		Head of Pochard. Wing coverts of Sheldrake.	Female Spike of Catstail Reed.	
101	Deep Reddish Brown.		Breast of Pochard, and Neck of Teal Drake.	Dead Leaves of green Panic Grass.	Brown Blende.
102	Umber Brown.		Moor Buzzard.	Disk of Rubeckia.	
103	Chesnut Brown.		Neck and Breast of Red Grouse.	Chesnuts.	Egyptian Jasper.
104	Yellowish Brown.		Light Brown Spots on Guinea-Pig. Breast of Hoopoe.		Iron Flint, and common Jasper.
105	Wood Brown.		Common Weasel. Light parts of Feathers on the Back of the Snipe.	Hazel Nuts.	Mountain Wood.
106	Liver Brown.		Middle Parts of Feathers of Hen Pheasant, and Wing coverts of Grosbeak.		Semi Opal.
107	Hair Brown.		Head of Pintail Duck		Wood Tin.
108	Broccoli Brown.		Head of Black headed Gull.		Zircon.
109	Clove Brown.		Head and Neck of Male Kestril.	Stems of Black Currant Bush.	Axinite, Rock Cristal.
110	Blackish Brown.		Stormy Petril. Wing Coverts of black Cock. Forehead of Foumart.		Mineral Pitch.

R E D .

Nº	Names.	Colours.	ANIMAL.	VEGETABLE.	MINERAL.
91	Carmine Red.			Raspberry. Cocks Comb. Carnation Pink.	Oriental Ruby.
92	Lake Red.			Red Tulip. Rose Officinalis.	Spinel.
93	Crimson Red.				Precious Garnet.
94	Purplish Red.		Outside of Quills of Terico.	Dark Crimson Officinal Garden Rose.	Precious Garnet.
95	Cochineal Red.			Under Disk of decayed Leaves of None-so-pretty.	Dark Cinnaber
96	Veinous Blood Red.		Veinous Blood.	Musk Flower, or dark Purple Scabious.	Pyrope.
97	Brownish Purple Red.			Flower of deadly Nightshade.	Red Antimony Ore.
98	Chocolate Red.		Breast of Bird of Paradise.	Brown Disk of common Marigold.	
99	Brownish Red.		Mark on Throat of Red-throated Diver.		Iron Flint.

No.	Names.	Colours.	ANIMAL.		
82	*Tile Red.*		*Breast of the Cock Bullfinch.*		
83	*Hyacinth Red.*		*Red Spots of the Lygœus Apterus Fly.*		
84	*Scarlet Red.*		*Scarlet Ibis or Curlew, Mark on Head of Red Grouse.*		
85	*Vermilion Red.*		*Red Coral.*		
86	*Aurora Red.*		*Vent coverts of Pied Wood-Pecker.*		
87	*Arterial Blood Red.*		*Head of the Cock Gold-finch.*		
88	*Flesh Red.*		*Human Skin.*		
89	*Rose Red.*				
90	*Peach Blossom Red.*				

The first chart of reds in Syme's 1821 edition included four of Werner's original reds (numbers 84, 86, 88 and 90), two reds from the Picardet system (numbers 83 and 89), one red from the Jameson system (number 82) and two reds from his own 1814 edition (numbers 85 and 87).

REDS (i).

VEGETABLE.		MINERAL.	
Shrubby Pimpernel.		Porcelain Jasper.	
Red on the golden Rennette Apple.		Hyacinth.	
Large red Oriental Poppy, Red Parts of red and black Indian Peas.		Light red Cinnaber.	
Love Apple.		Cinnaber.	
Red on the Naked Apple.		Red Orpiment.	
Corn Poppy. Cherry.			
Larkspur.		Heavy Spar, Limestone.	
Common Garden Rose.		Figure Stone.	
Peach Blossom.		Red Cobalt Ore.	

82. TILE RED.

(i).   *Breast of the Cock Bullfinch.* [Pyrrhula pyrrhula]
(ii).   *Shrubby Pimpernel.* [Anagallis]
(iii).   *Porcelain Jasper.* [*Silica*]

Tile Red, is hyacinth red mixed with much greyish white, and a small portion of scarlet red. [W]

ANIMAL.

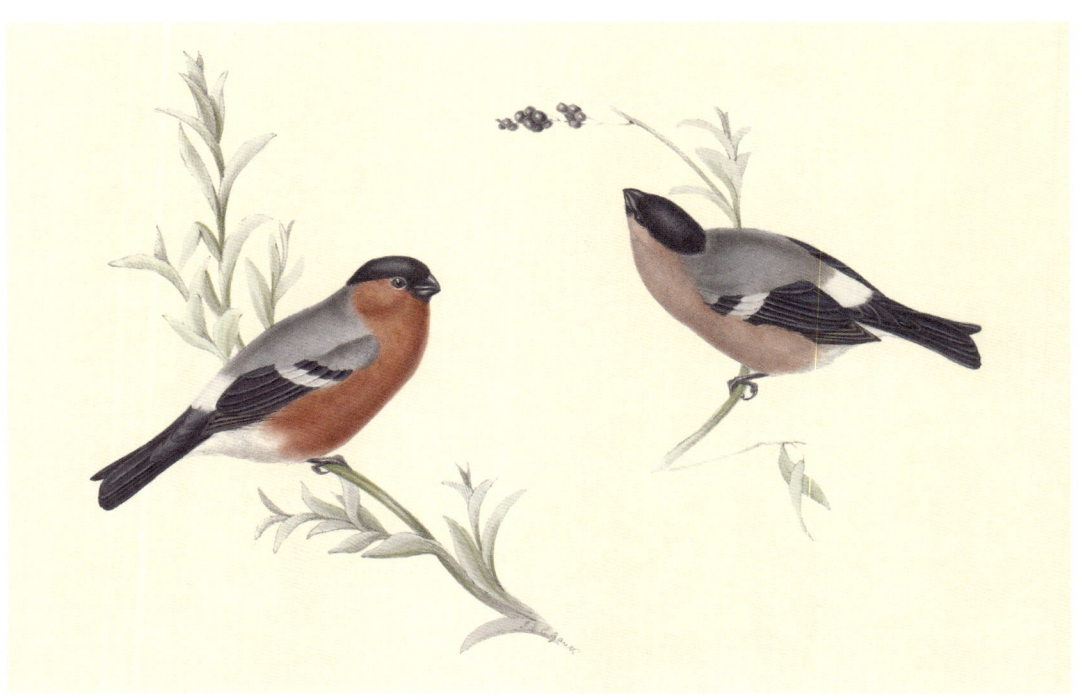

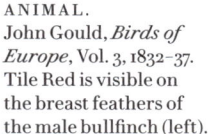

VEGETABLE.

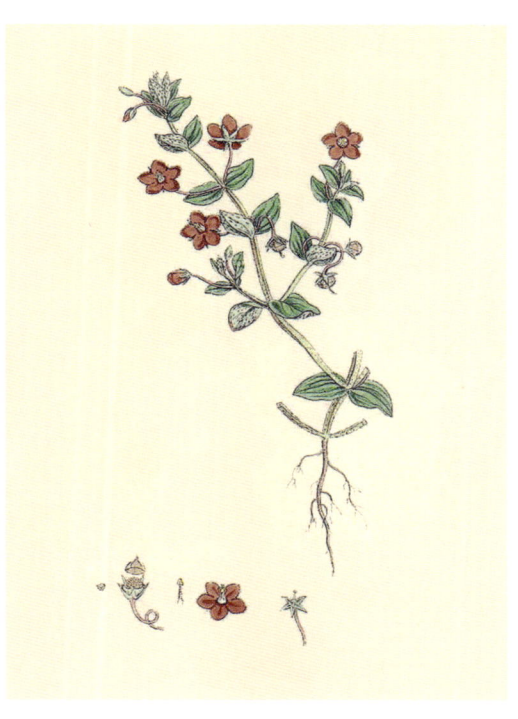

MINERAL.

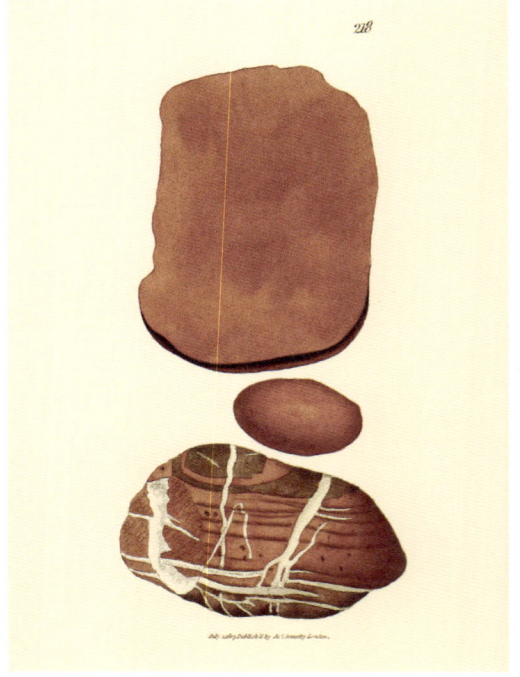

ANIMAL.
John Gould, *Birds of Europe*, Vol. 3, 1832–37. Tile Red is visible on the breast feathers of the male bullfinch (left).

VEGETABLE.
J. E. Smith, *English Botany*, 1863–99. Tile Red is visible on the petals of the pimpernel.

MINERAL.
James Sowerby, *British Mineralogy*, Vol. 3, 1802–17. Tile Red is visible on the jasper (all specimens).

83. HYACINTH RED.

(i).   *Red Spots of the Lygoeus Apterus Fly.*
       [*Black-and-Red-bug*; Lygaeus equestris]

(ii).   *Red on the golden Rennette Apple.*
       [*Reinette*; Malus domestica]

(iii).   *Hyacinth.* [*Jacinth*; *Silicate mineral*]

Hyacinth Red, is scarlet red, with lemon yellow and a minute proportion of brown.

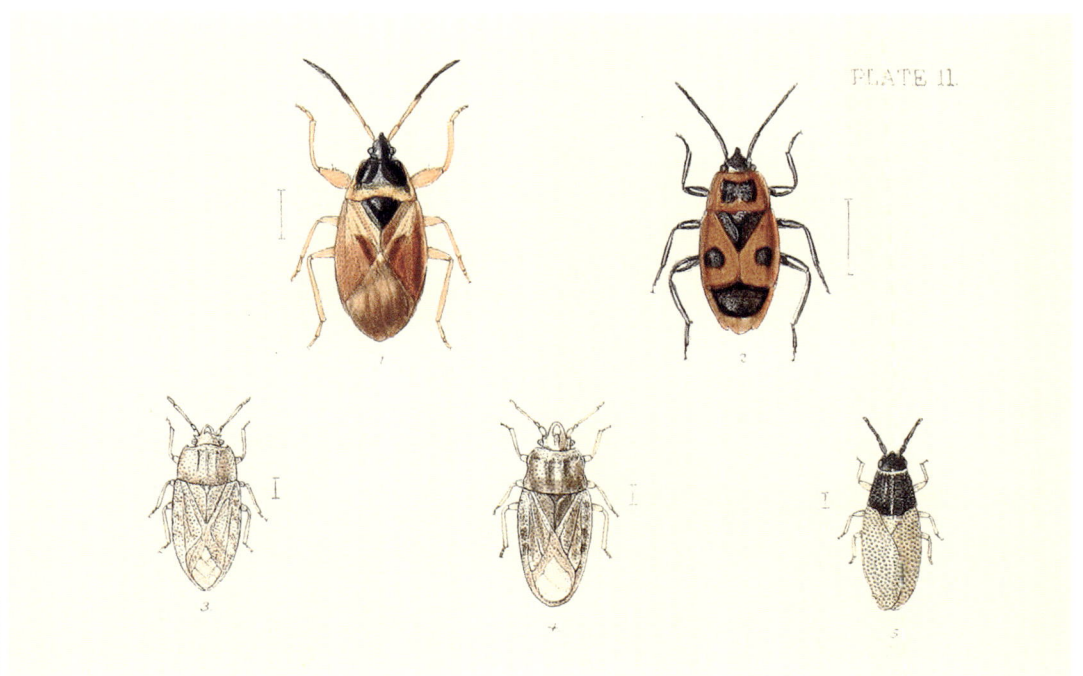

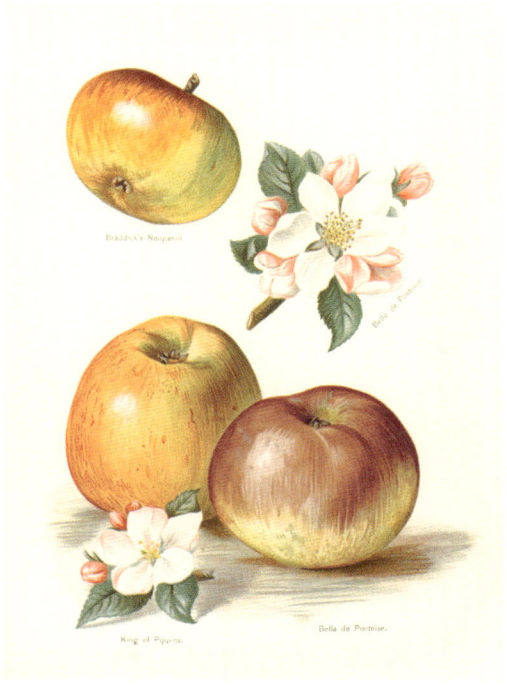

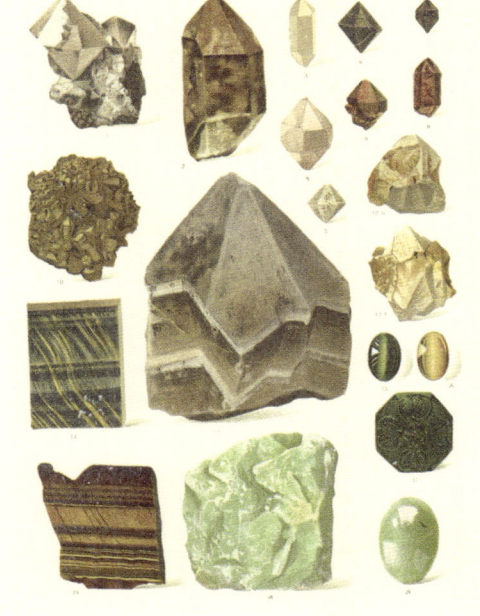

VEGETABLE.

MINERAL.

ANIMAL.
Edward Saunders,
The Hemiptera Heteroptera of the British Islands, 1892.
Hyacinth Red is visible on the black-and-red-bug (above right).

VEGETABLE.
John Wright,
The Fruit Growers Guide, Vol. 1, 1891–94.
Hyacinth Red is visible on the skin of the apple.

MINERAL.
Reinhard Brauns,
The Mineral Kingdom, Vol. 2, 1912.
Hyacinth Red is visible on the jacinth (two specimens, second row, top right).

84. SCARLET RED.

(i).   *Scarlet Ibis.* [Eudocimus ruber] *Curlew.* [Numenius]
        Mark on Head of Red Grouse. [Lagopus lagopus scotica]

(ii).   *Large red Oriental Poppy.* [Papaver orientale]
        Red Parts of red and black Indian Peas. [*Cowpea*; Vigna unguiculata]

(iii).   *Light red Cinnaber.* [*Cinnabar, Mercury Sulphide*]

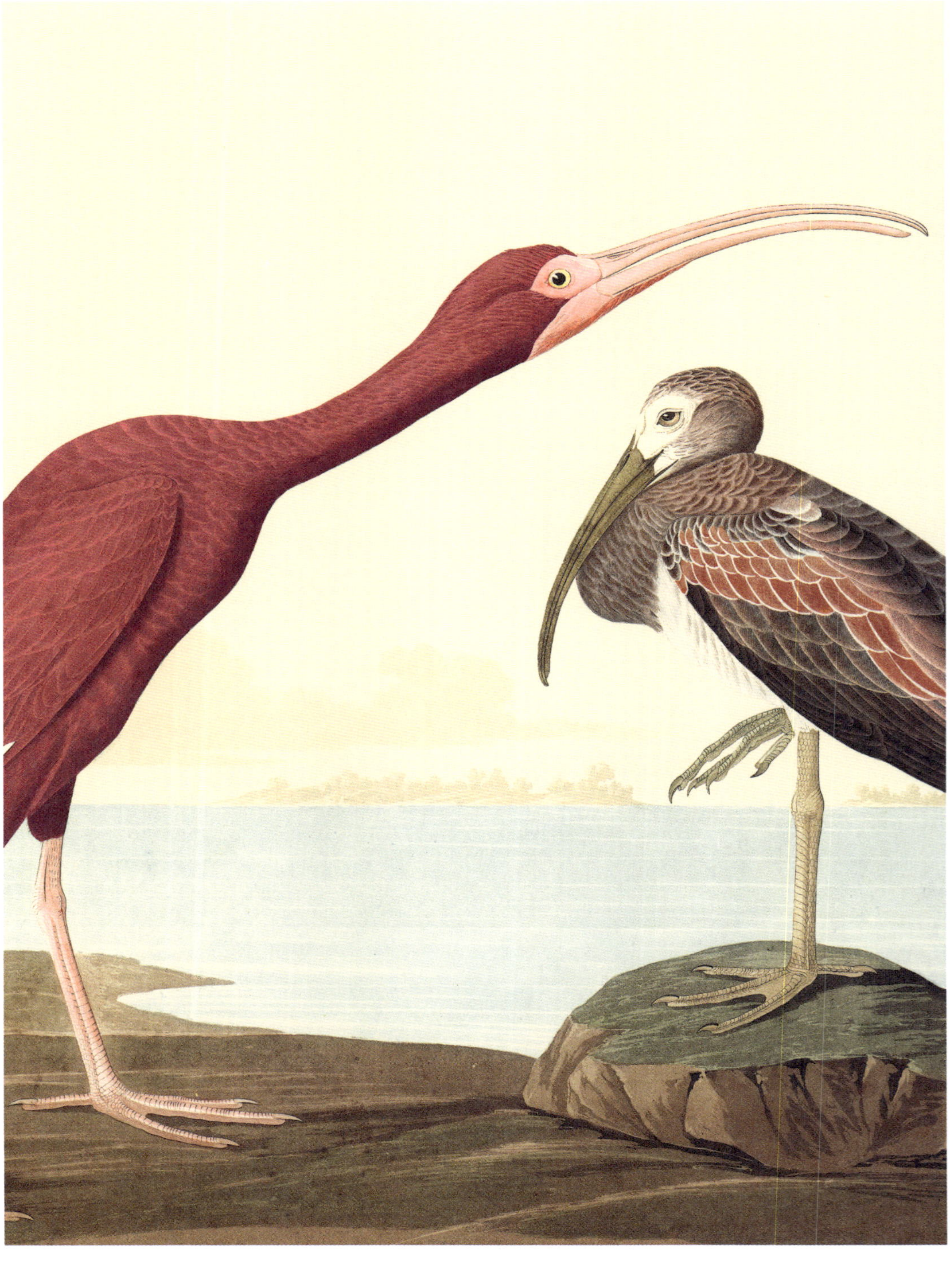

ANIMAL.

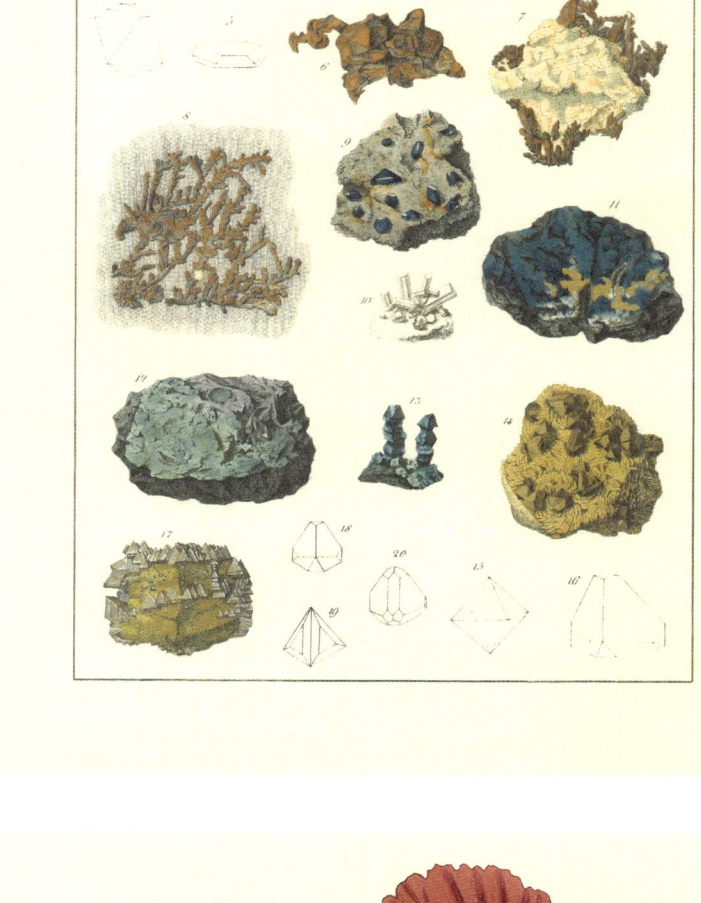

Scarlet Red, is arterial blood red, with a little gamboge yellow. †

† *Syme should have applied a [W] notation in this instance, as Scarlet Red appears in Werner's original list of colours.*

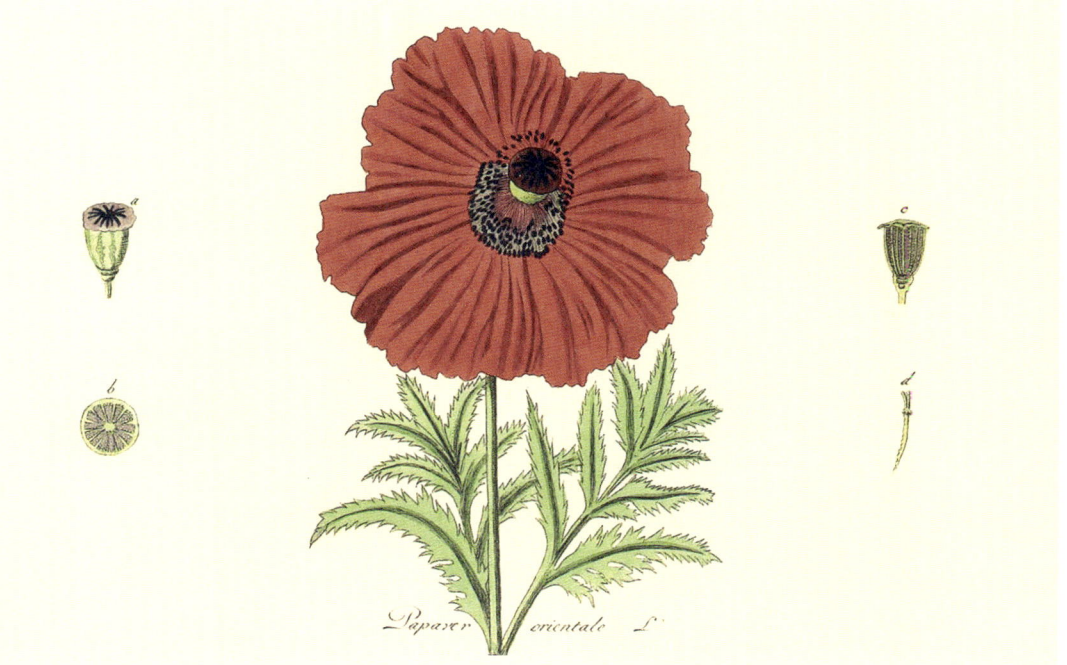

ANIMAL.
John James Audubon, *Birds of America*, 1827–38. Scarlet Red is visible on the feathers of the young scarlet ibis (right).

VEGETABLE.
J. Zorn and D. L. Oskamp, *Afbeeldingen der Artseny-gewassen*, 1796–1800. Scarlet Red is visible on the petals of the oriental poppy.

MINERAL.
Johann Gottlob Kurr, *The Mineral Kingdom*, 1859. Scarlet Red is visible on the cinnabar (top row, centre).

85. VERMILION RED.

(i).   *Red Coral.* [Corallium]
(ii).   *Love Apple.* [*Tomato*; Solanum lycopersicum]
(iii).   *Cinnaber.* [*Cinnabar; Mercury Sulphide*]

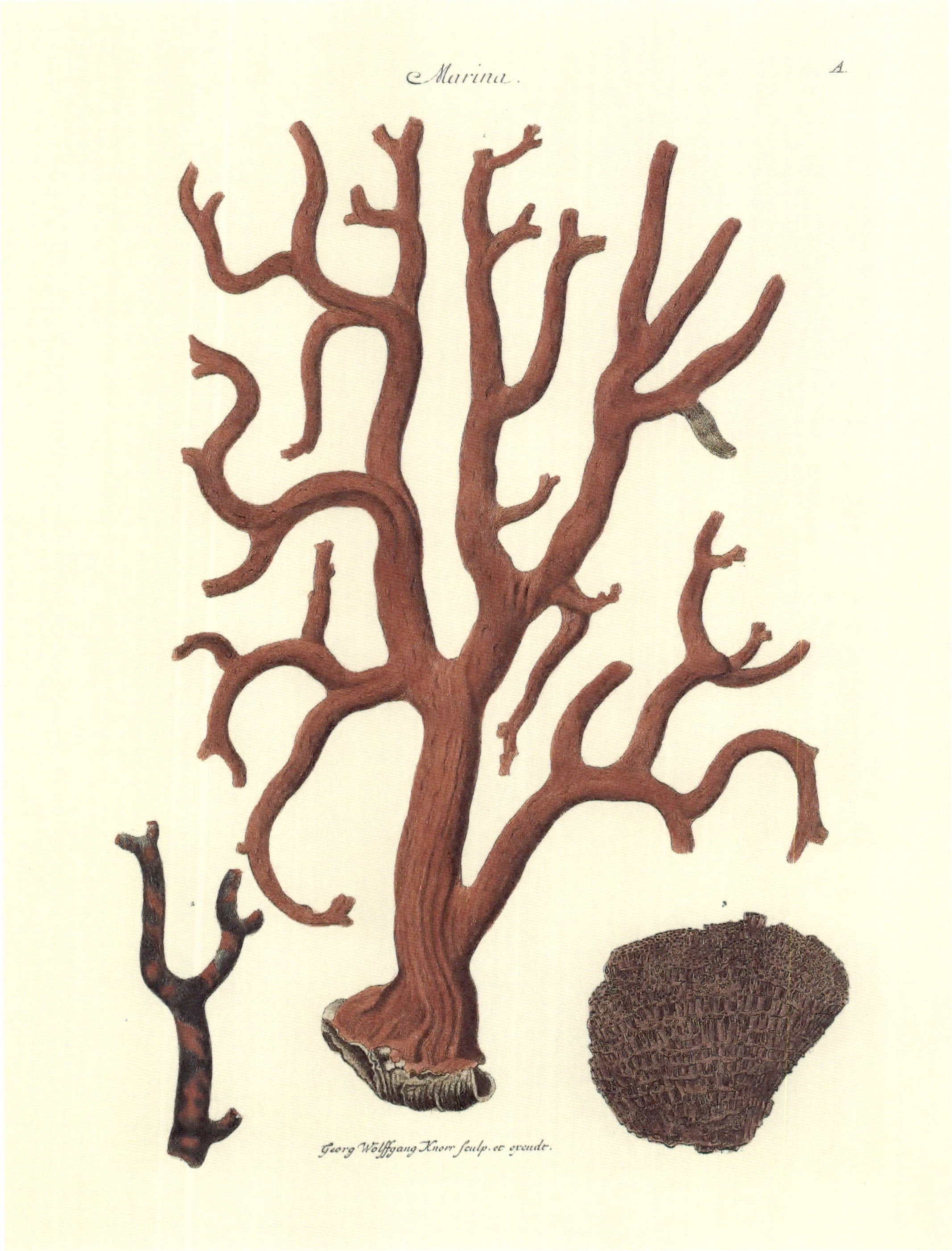

Marina.

A.

Georg Wolffgang Knorr sculp. et excudt.

*Vermilion Red,
is scarlet red, with
a minute portion
of brownish red.*

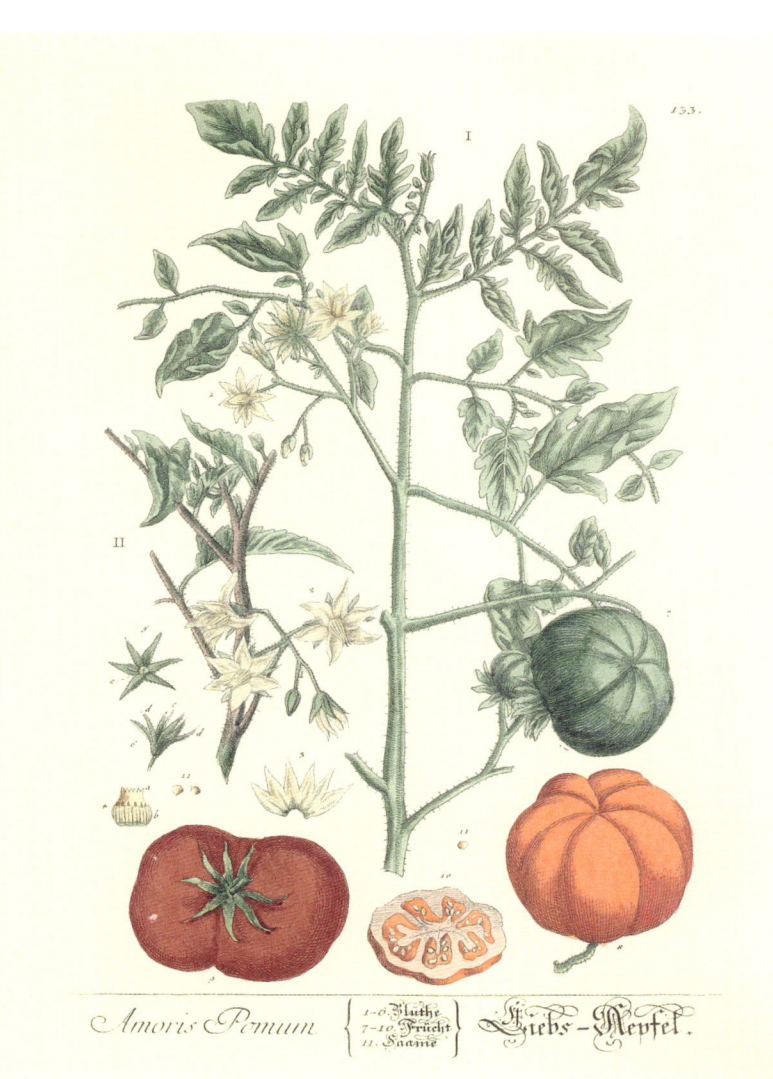

Amoris Pomum ⎨ *1–6. Bluthe*
7–10. Frucht
11. Saame ⎬ *Liebs-Aepfel.*

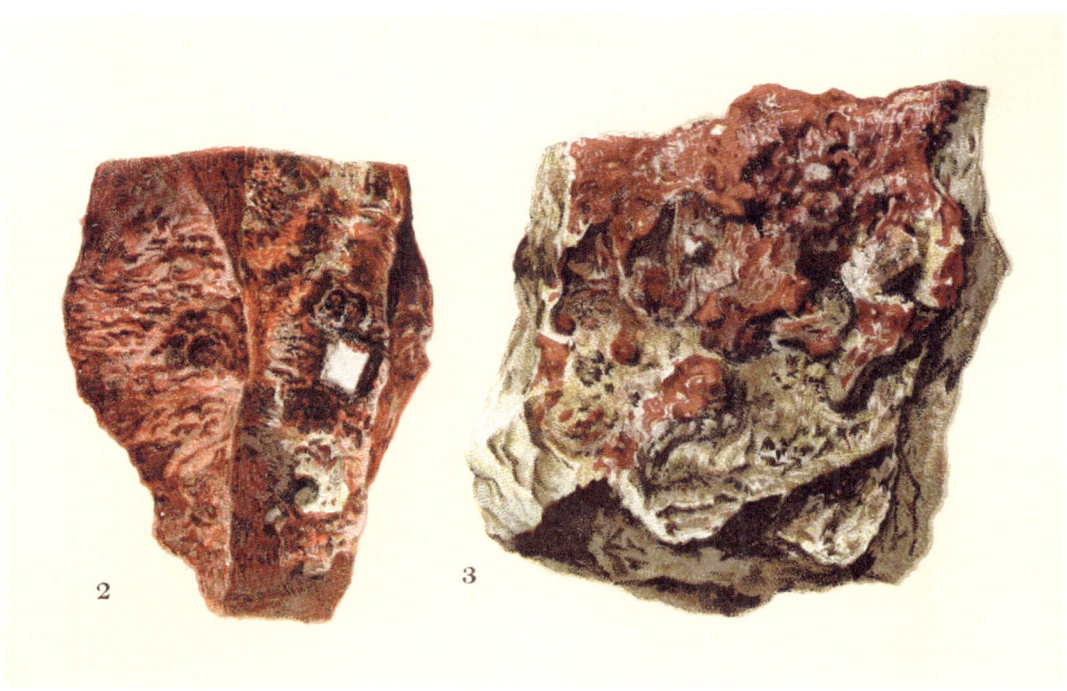

ANIMAL.
Georg Wolfgang Knorr,
*Deliciae naturae
selectae*, 1766.
Vermilion Red
is visible on the
coral (centre).

VEGETABLE.
E. Blackwell,
*Herbarium
Blackwellianum*,
Vol. 2, 1747–73.
Vermilion Red is
visible on the skin
of the tomato.

MINERAL.
Leonard Spencer,
*The World's
Minerals*, 1916.
Vermilion Red is
visible on the cinnabar
(both specimens).

86. AURORA RED.

(i).   *Vent coverts of Pied Wood-Pecker.*
        [*Great spotted woodpecker*; Dendrocopos major]
(ii).   *Red on the Naked Apple.* [Malus domestica]
(iii).   *Red Orpiment.* [*Sulphide mineral*]

Aurora Red, is tile red, with a little arterial blood red, and a slight tinge of carmine red. [W]

ANIMAL.

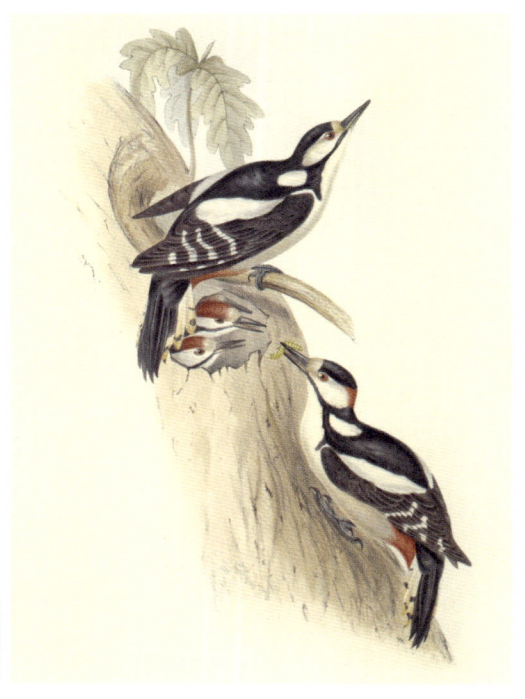

MINERAL.

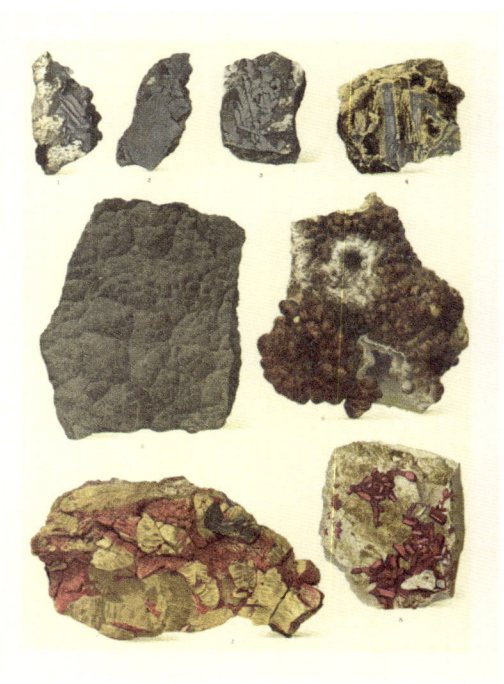

ANIMAL.
John Gould, *Birds of Europe*, Vol. 3, 1832–37. Aurora Red is visible on the vent coverts, i.e. the feathers around the cloaca, of the great spotted woodpecker.

VEGETABLE.
A. Poiteau, *Pomologie Française*, 1846. Aurora Red is visible on the skin of the apple.

MINERAL.
Reinhard Brauns, *The Mineral Kingdom*, Vol. 1, 1912. Aurora Red is visible on the orpiment (bottom row, left).

VEGETABLE.

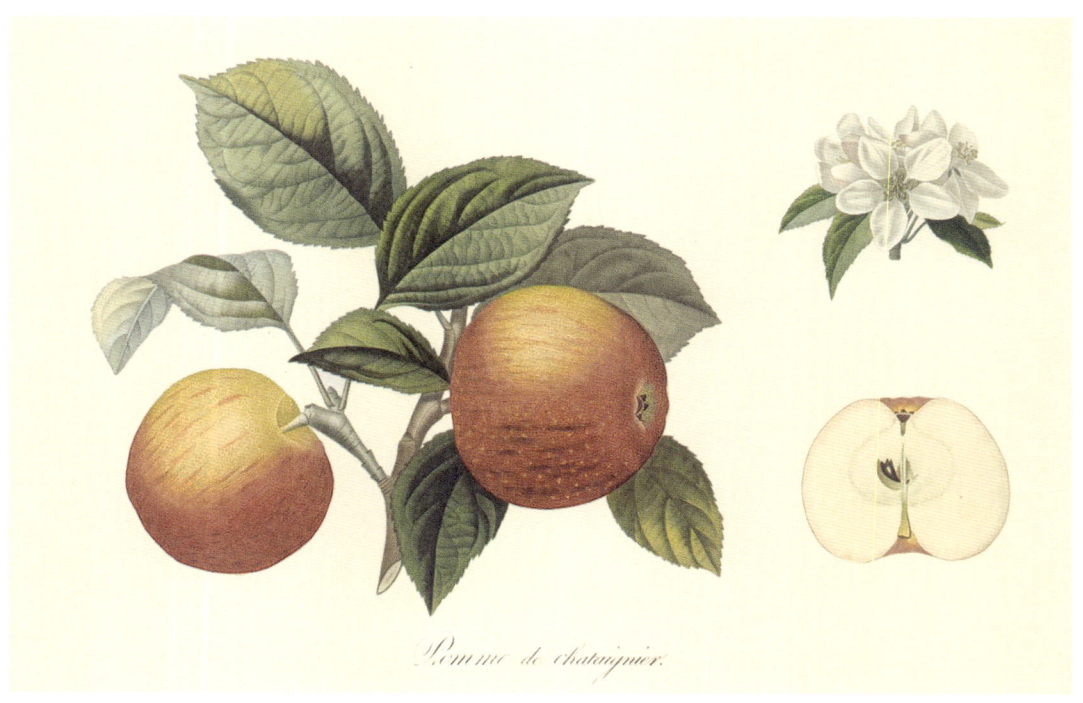

Pomme de chataignier.

*Arterial Blood Red,
is the characteristic
colour of the red series.*

(i).   *Head of the Cock Gold-finch.* [Carduelis carduelis]
(ii).   *Corn Poppy.* [*Common poppy;* Papaver rhoeas]
        Cherry. [Prunus]
(iii). ————————

ANIMAL.

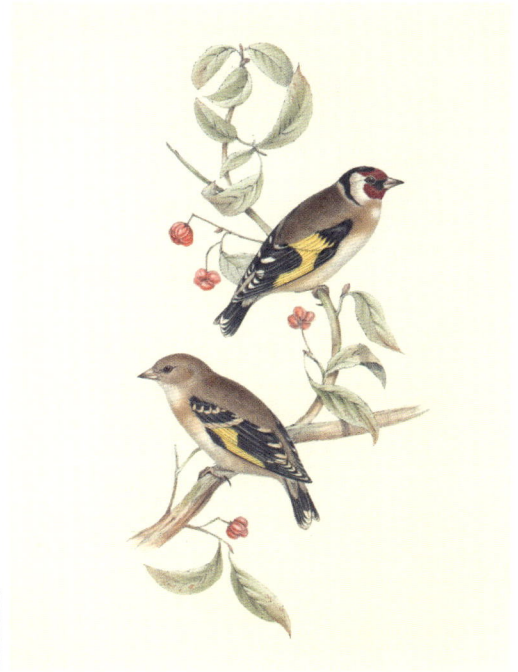

VEGETABLE.

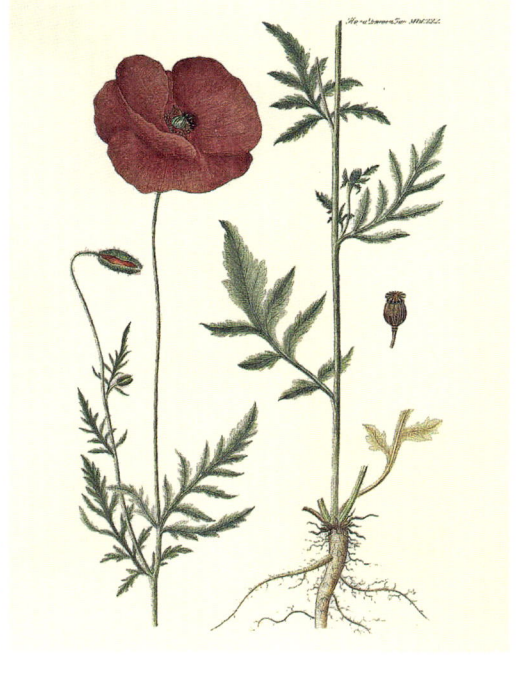

251.   V. REDS AND BROWNS.

MINERAL.

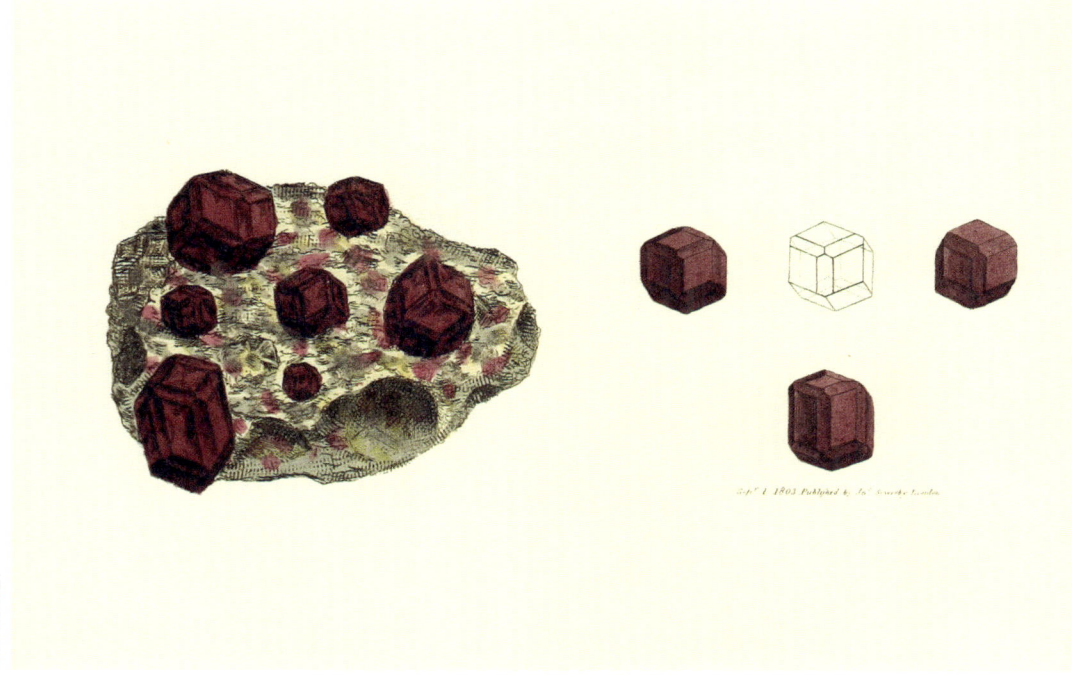

ANIMAL.
John Gould, *Birds of
Europe*, Vol. 3, 1832–37.
Arterial Blood Red is
visible on the head
feathers of the male
goldfinch (above).

VEGETABLE.
G. C. Oeder, *Flora
Danica*, 1761–1861.
Arterial Blood Red
is visible on the petals
of the common poppy.

MINERAL.
James Sowerby,
British Mineralogy,
Vol. 1, 1802–17.
Arterial Blood Red is
visible on the garnet.
The garnet is shown
embedded within
granite and detached.*

88. FLESH RED.

(i).   *Human Skin.* [Homo sapiens]
(ii).   *Larkspur.* [Consolida]
(iii).   *Heavy Spar.* [*Baryte*; *Barite*; *Barium Sulphate mineral*]
       Limestone. [*Carbonate sedimentary rock*]

Flesh Red, is rose red mixed with tile red and a little white. [W]

ANIMAL.

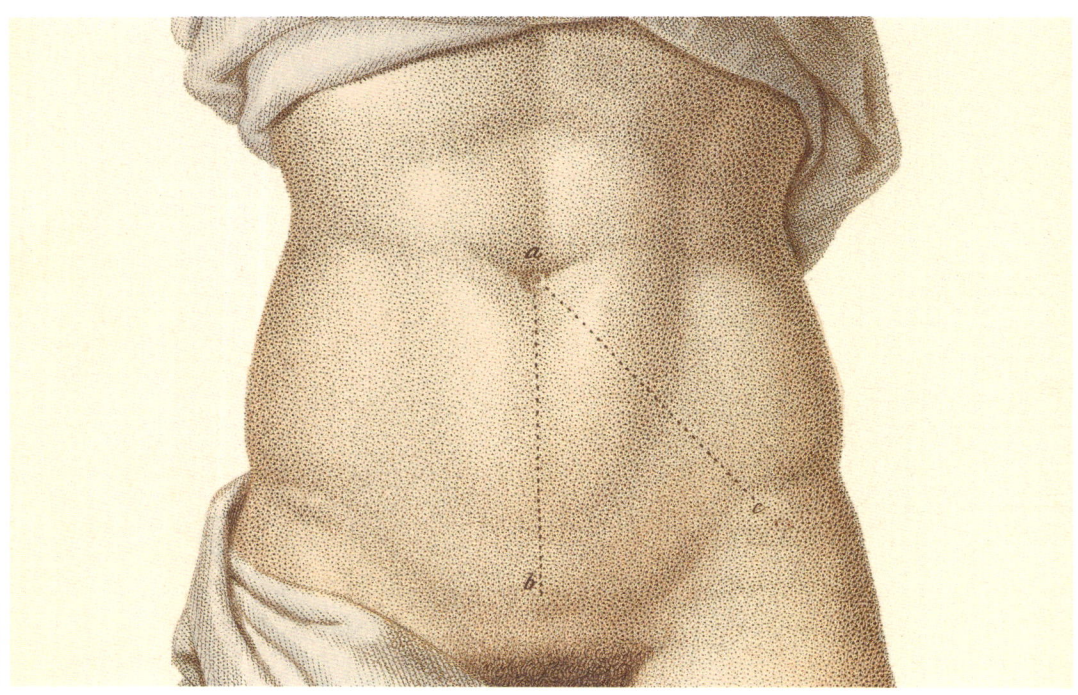

ANIMAL.
Claude Bernard and Charles Huette, *Précis iconographique de médecine opératoire et d'anatomie chirurgicale*, 1856. Flesh Red is visible on human skin.

VEGETABLE.
Johann Wilhelm Weinmann, *Phytanthoza iconographia*, 1737. Flesh Red is visible on the petals of the larkspur.

MINERAL.
James Sowerby, *British Mineralogy*, Vol. I, 1802–17. Flesh Red is visible on the baryte. It is embedded within iron ore.

VEGETABLE.

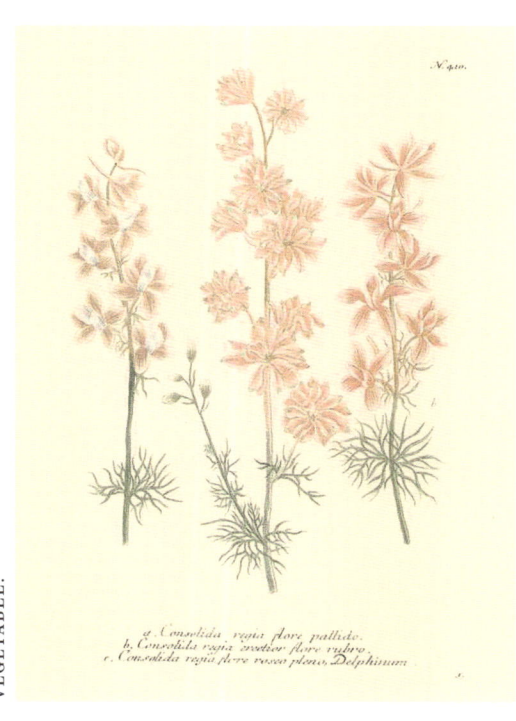

MINERAL.

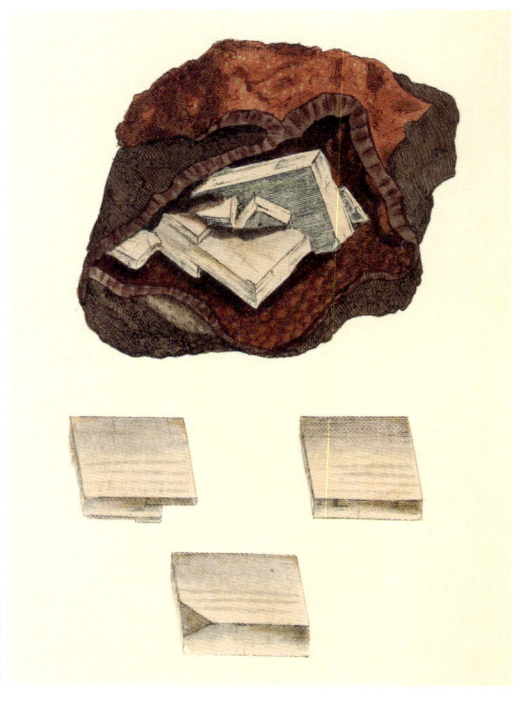

89. ROSE RED.

(i).
(ii). *Common Garden Rose.* [Rosa]
(iii). *Figure Stone.* [*Pagodite; agalmatolite; Silicate mineral*]

Rose Red, is carmine red, with a great quantity of snow white, and a very small portion of cochineal red. [W]

ANIMAL.

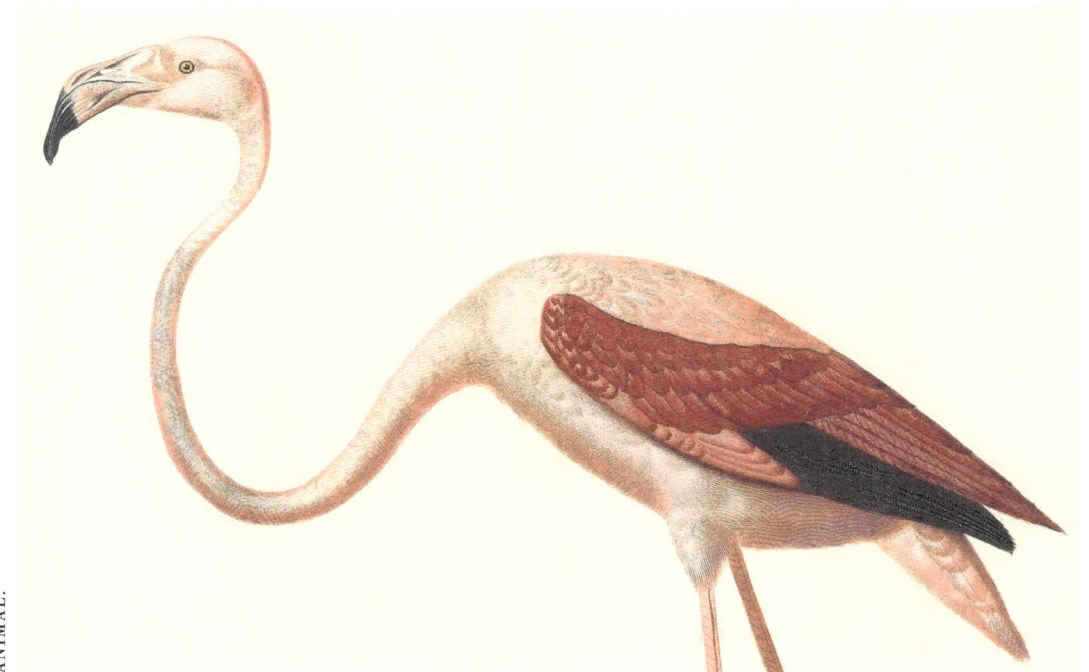

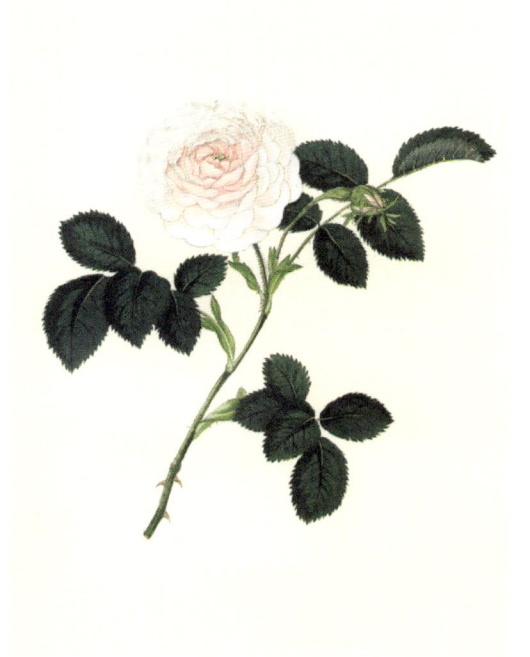

VEGETABLE.

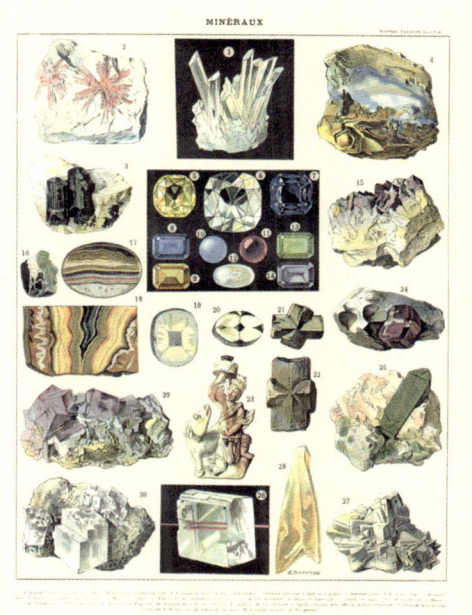

MINERAL.

ANIMAL.
Ramón de la Sagra,
*Histoire physique,
politique et naturelle
de l'île de Cuba,*
1798–1871.
Rose Red is visible
on the feathers
of the flamingo.*

VEGETABLE.
Carl Gottlob Rössig,
*Rosen nach der
Natur gezeichnet,*
Vol. I, 1802–20.
Rose Red is visible on
the petals of the rose.

MINERAL.
*Nouveau Larousse
illustré,* 1897–1904.
Rose Red is visible
on the statuette made
of pagodite (fourth
row, centre left).

(i).   ——————
(ii).   *Peach Blossom.* [Prunus persica]
(iii). *Red Cobalt Ore.* [Ore]

Peach Blossom Red, is lake red mixed with much white. [W]

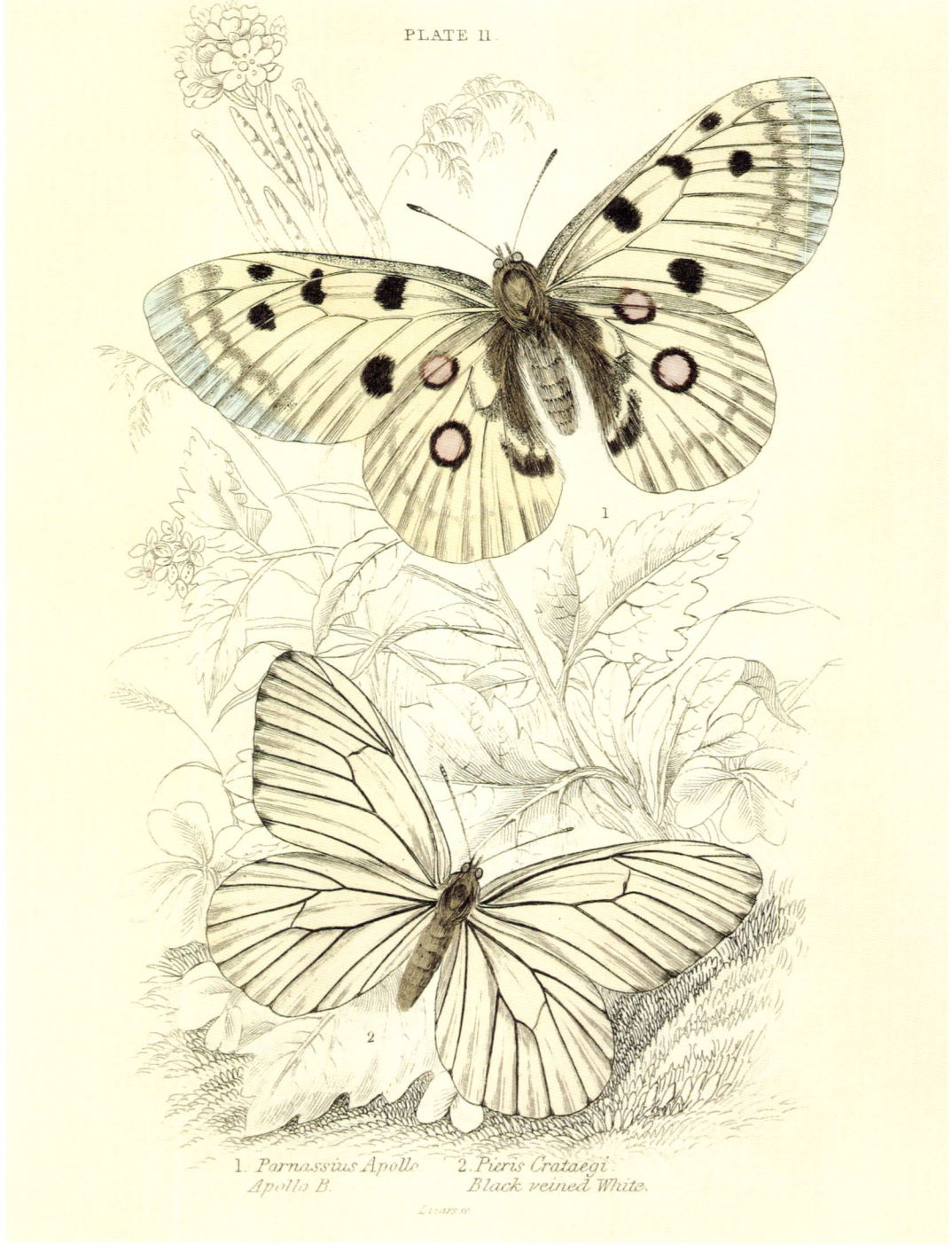

PLATE 11.

1. *Parnassius Apollo.*
   Apollo B.

2. *Pieris Crataegi.*
   Black veined White.

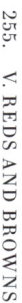
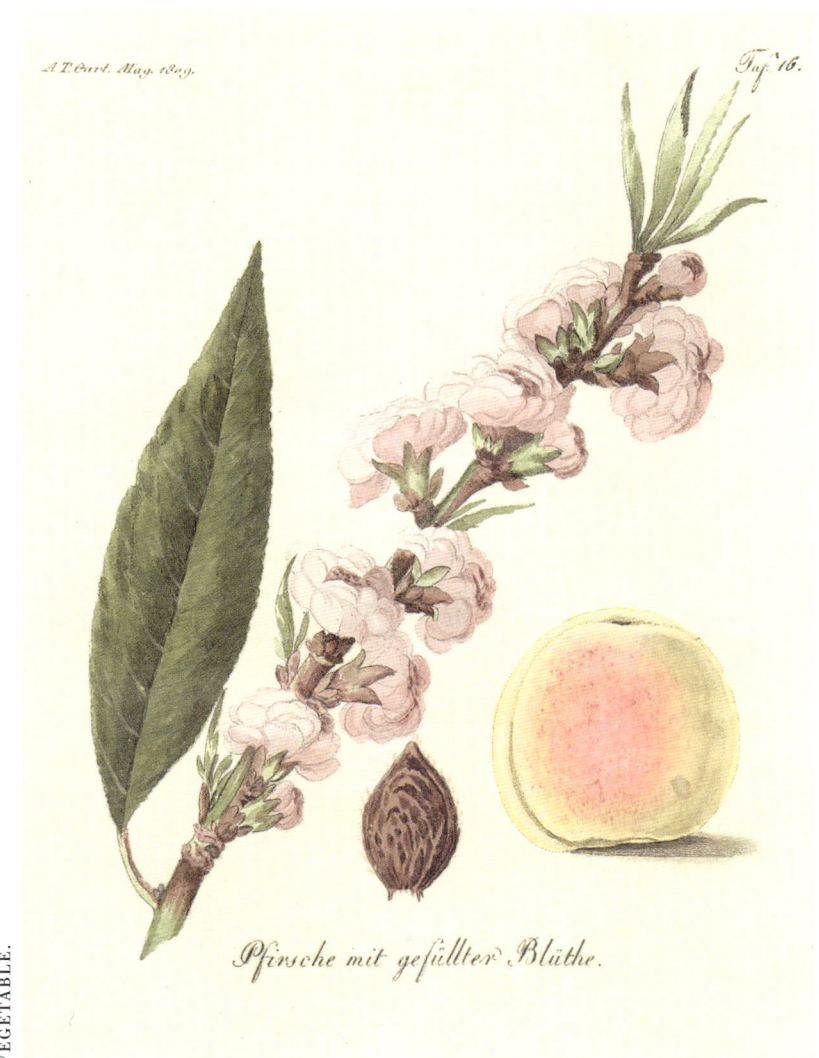

A.T. Curt. Mag. 1809. *Taf. 16.*

Pfirsche mit gefüllter Blüthe.

MINERAL.

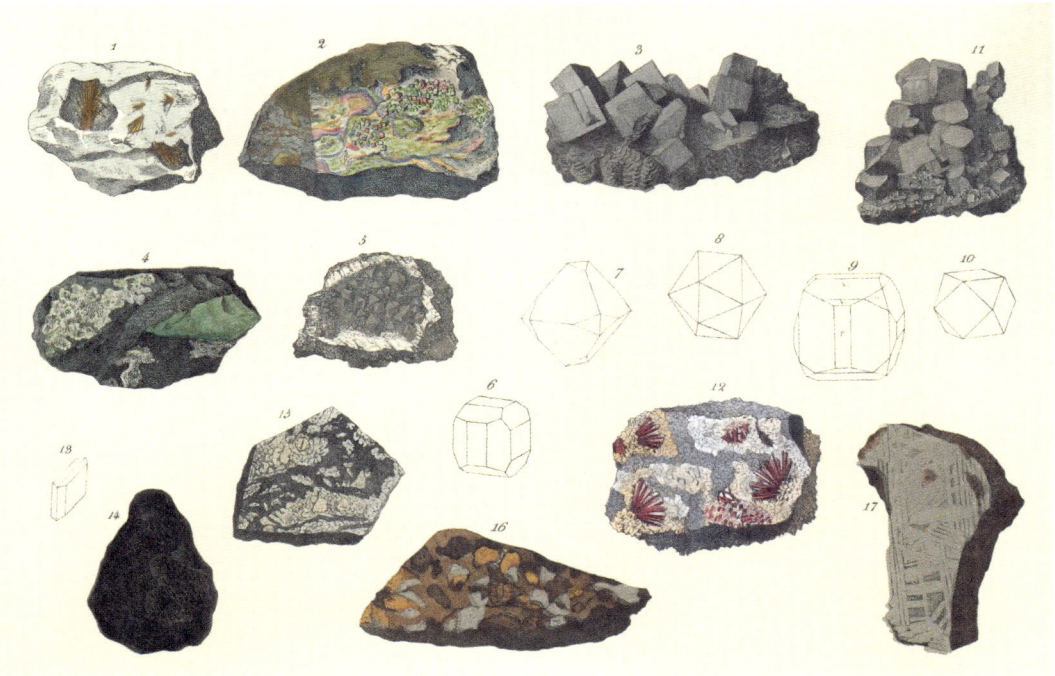

ANIMAL.
James Duncan,
British Butterflies, 1840.
Peach Blossom Red is
visible on the spots on
the wings of the Apollo
butterfly (above).*

VEGETABLE.
*Allgemeines teutsches
Garten-Magazin*,
Vol. 6, 1804–11.
Peach Blossom Red
is visible on the petals
of the peach blossom.

MINERAL.
Johann Gottlob
Kurr, *The Mineral
Kingdom*, 1859.
Peach Blossom Red
is visible on the cobalt
ore (bottom row,
second from right).

No.	Names.	Colours.	ANIMAL.		
91	*Carmine Red.*				
92	*Lake Red.*				
93	*Crimson Red.*				
94	*Purplish Red.*		*Outside of Quills of Terico.*		
95	*Cochineal Red.*				
96	*Veinous Blood Red.*		*Veinous Blood.*		
97	*Brownish Purple Red.*				
98	*Chocolate Red.*		*Breast of Bird of Paradise.*		
99	*Brownish Red.*		*Mark on Throat of Red-throated Diver.*		

The second chart of reds in Syme's 1821 edition included four of Werner's original reds (numbers 91, 93, 96 and 99), one red from the Picardet system (number 95), two reds from the Lenz system (numbers 94 and 97), although Syme renamed Columbine Red Purplish Red, and two reds from his own 1814 edition (numbers 92 and 98).

R E D S (ii).

VEGETABLE.		MINERAL.	
Raspberry, Cocks Comb, Carnation Pink.		Oriental Ruby.	
Red Tulip, Rose Officinalus.		Spinel.	
		Precious Garnet.	
Dark Crimson Official Garden Rose.		Precious Garnet.	
Under Disk of decayed Leaves of None-so-pretty.		Dark Cinnaber.	
Musk Flower, or dark Purple Scabious.		Pyrope.	
Flower of deadly Nightshade.		Red Antimony Ore.	
Brown Disk of common Marigold.			
		Iron Flint.	

91. CARMINE RED.

(i). ————

(ii). *Raspberry.* [Rubus idaeus] *Cocks Comb.* [*Cockscomb*; Celosia] *Carnation Pink.* [Dianthus caryophyllus]

(iii). *Oriental Ruby.* [*Corundum mineral*]

Carmine Red, the characteristic colour of Werner, is lake red, with a little arterial blood red. [W]

ANIMAL.

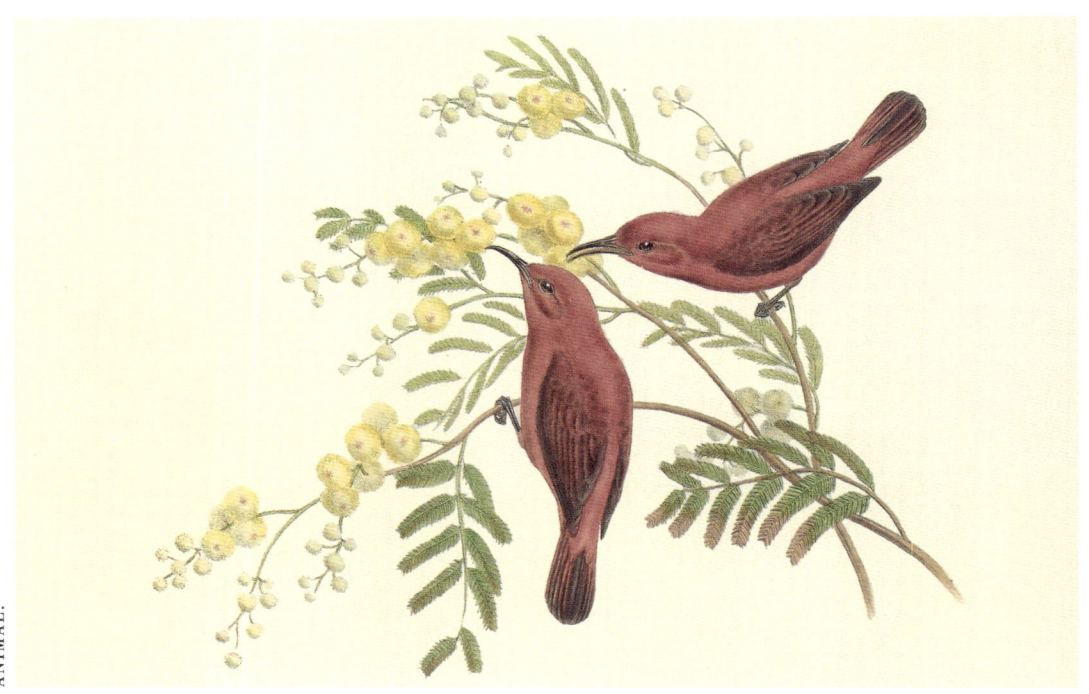

ANIMAL.
John Gould, *Birds of New Guinea and the Adjacent Papuan Islands*, 1875–88. Carmine Red is visible on the feathers of the red myzomela.*

VEGETABLE.
Johann Wilhelm Weinmann, *Phytanthoza iconographia*, 1737. Carmine Red is visible on the petals of the cockscomb.

MINERAL.
Reinhard Brauns, *The Mineral Kingdom*, Vol. 2, 1912. Carmine Red is visible on the ruby (five specimens, centre left).

VEGETABLE.

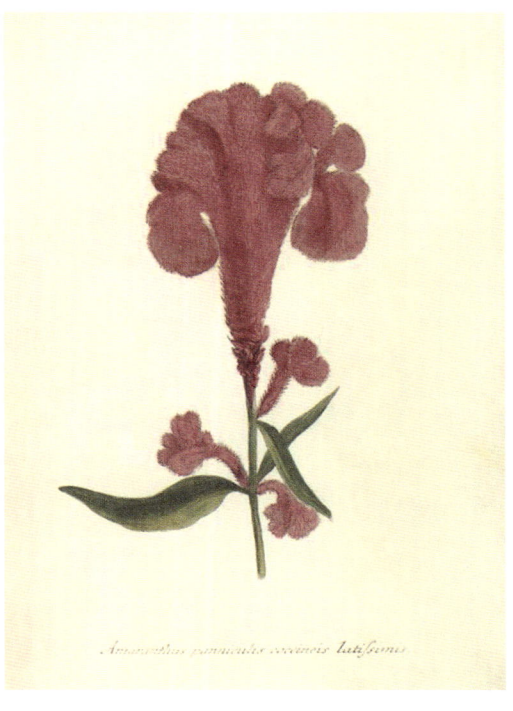

MINERAL.

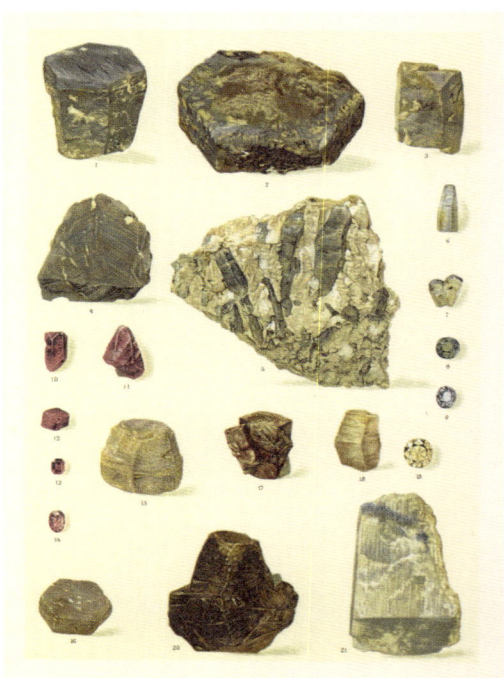

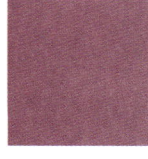

92. LAKE RED.

(i). ———————
(ii). *Red Tulip.* [Tulipa] *Rose Officinalus.*
[*French Rose*; Rosa gallica]
(iii). *Spinel.* [*Spinel mineral*]

259. V. REDS AND BROWNS.

Lake Red, the crimson red of Werner, is arterial blood red, with a portion of Berlin blue. [W] †

† *Syme erroneously applied a [W] notation in this instance, as he also included Werner's crimson red in his nomenclature.*

ANIMAL.

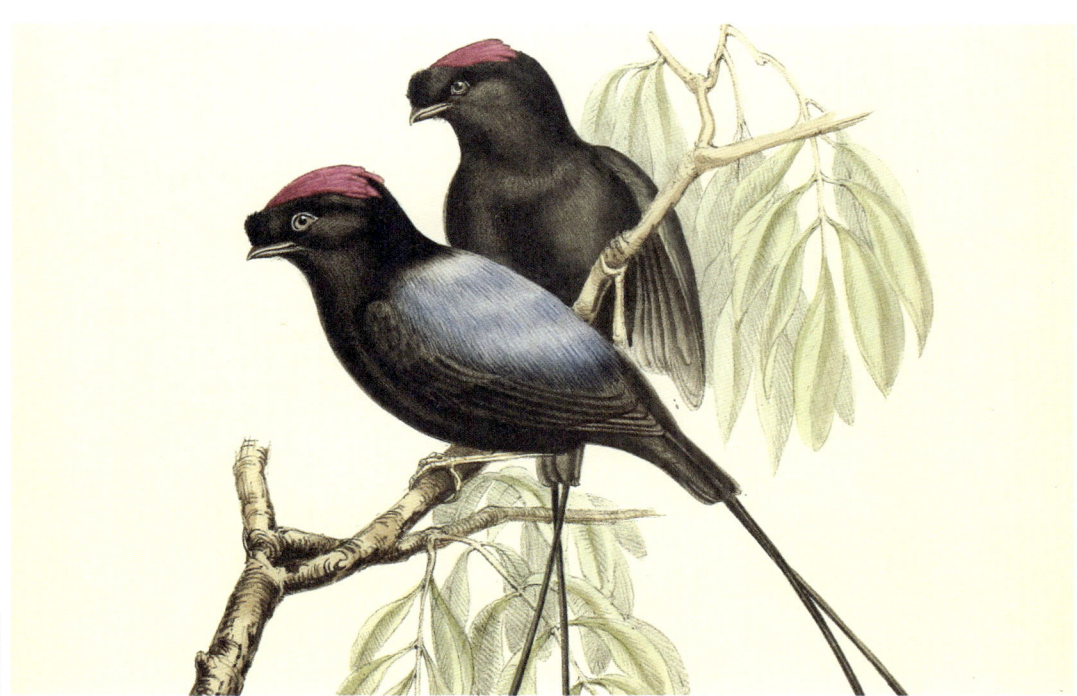

VEGETABLE.

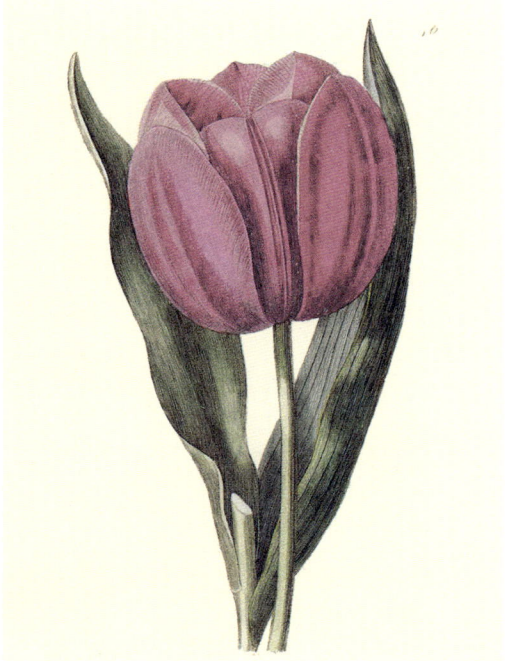

MINERAL.

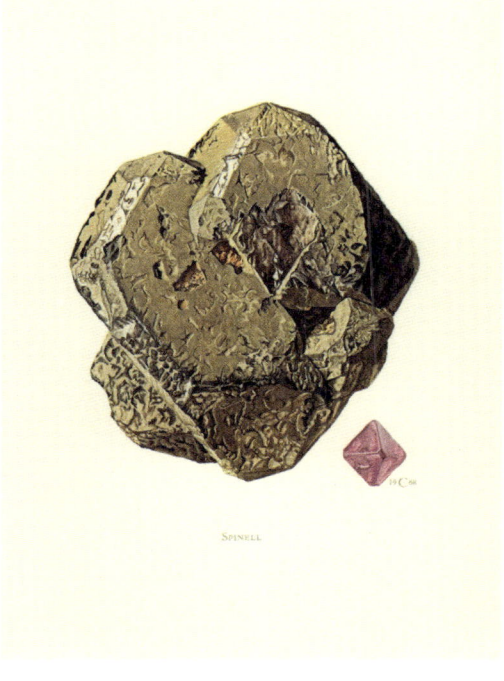

SPINELL.

ANIMAL.
Richard Brinsley Hinds, *The Zoology of the Voyage of HMS Sulphur*, 1843. Lake Red is visible on the head feathers of the long-tailed manakin.*

VEGETABLE.
John Lindley, *Edwards's Botanical Register*, 1829–47. Lake Red is visible on the petals of the tulip.

MINERAL.
Spinel, lithograph, 1968. Lake Red is visible on the spinel (right).

93. CRIMSON RED.

(i). ———————
(ii). ———————
(iii). *Precious Garnet.* [*Silicate mineral*]

Crimson Red, is carmine red, with a little indigo blue. [*W*]

260. V. REDS AND BROWNS.

ANIMAL.

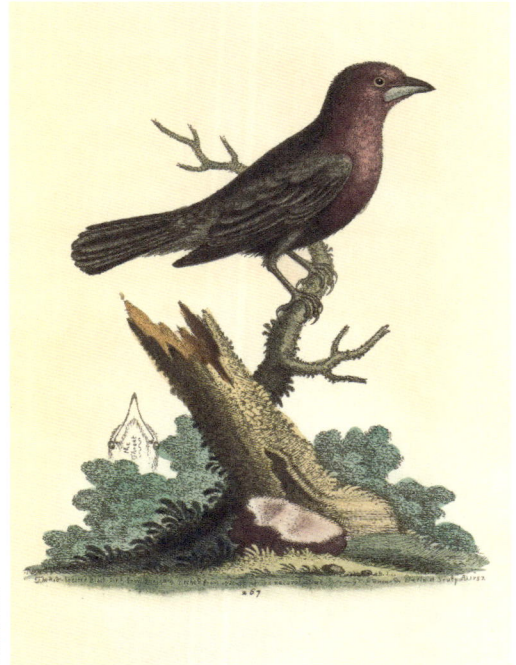

VEGETABLE.

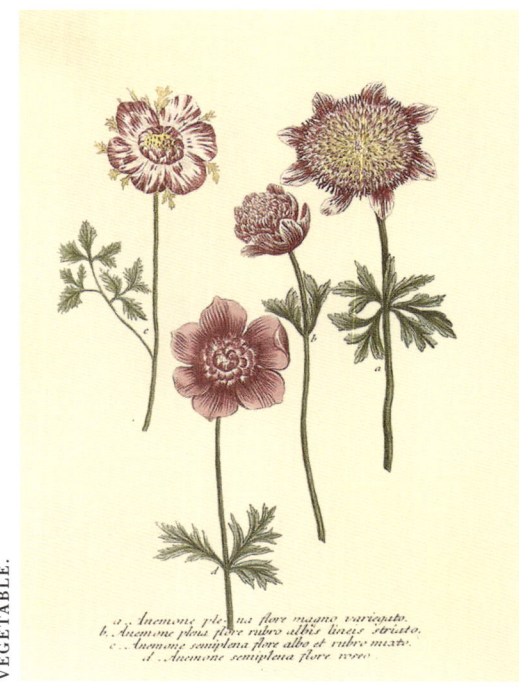

a. Anemone plena flore magno variegata.
b. Anemone plena flore rubro albis lineis striato.
c. Anemone semiplena flore albo et rubro mixto.
d. Anemone semiplena flore roseo.

MINERAL.

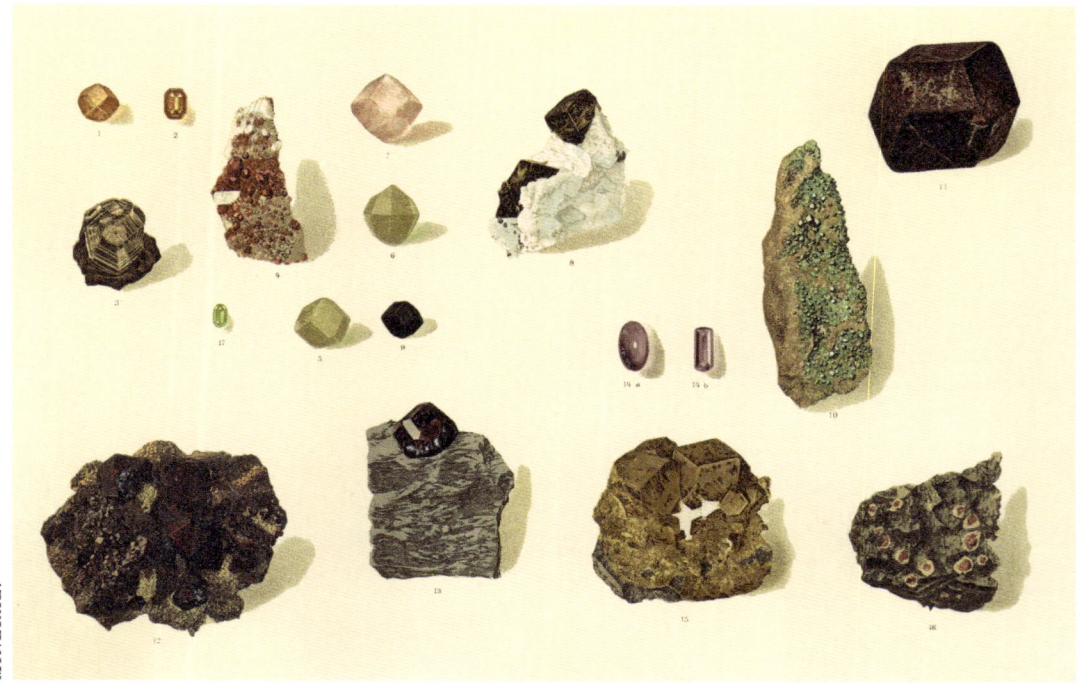

ANIMAL.
George Edwards,
Gleanings of Natural History, 1758.
Crimson Red is visible on the breast feathers of the red-breasted meadowlark.*

VEGETABLE.
Johann Wilhelm Weinmann,
Phytanthoza iconographia, 1737.
Crimson Red is visible on the petals of the anemones.*

MINERAL.
Reinhard Brauns,
The Mineral Kingdom, Vol. 2, 1912.
Crimson Red is visible on the garnet (two specimens, third row, second from right).

94. PURPLISH RED.

(i).   *Outside of Quills of Terico.*
       [*Turaco*; Musophagidae]
(ii).   *Dark Crimson Officinal Garden Rose.*
       [*French Rose*; Rosa gallica]
(iii). *Precious Garnet.* [*Silicate mineral*]

Purplish Red, the columbine red of Werner, is carmine red, with a little Berlin blue, and a small portion of indigo blue. [W]

ANIMAL.

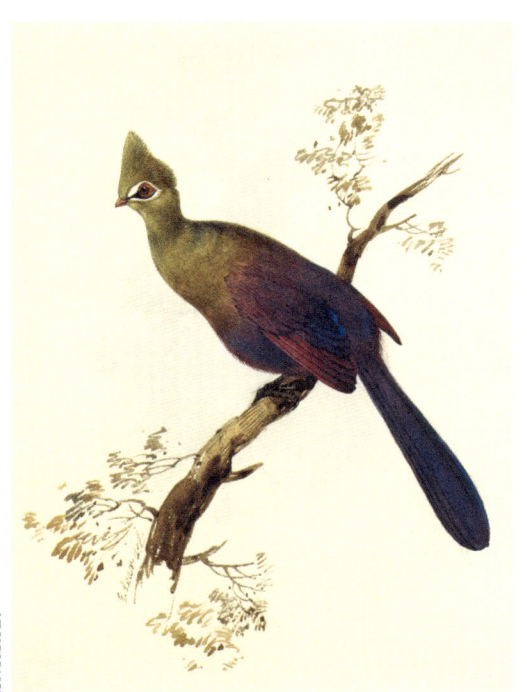

VEGETABLE.

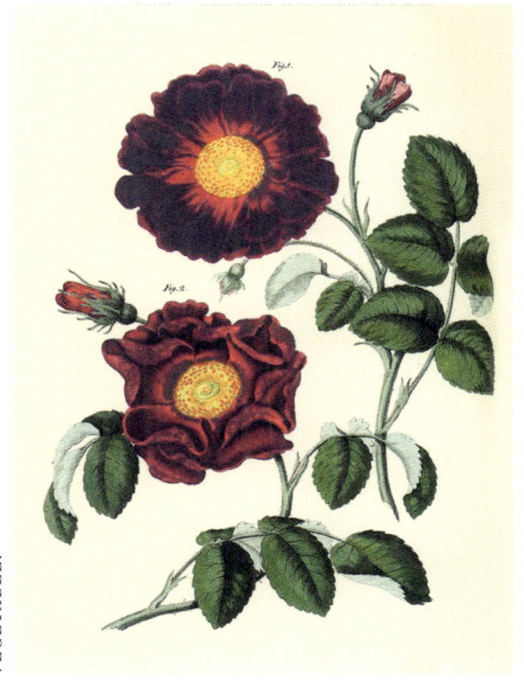

MINERAL.

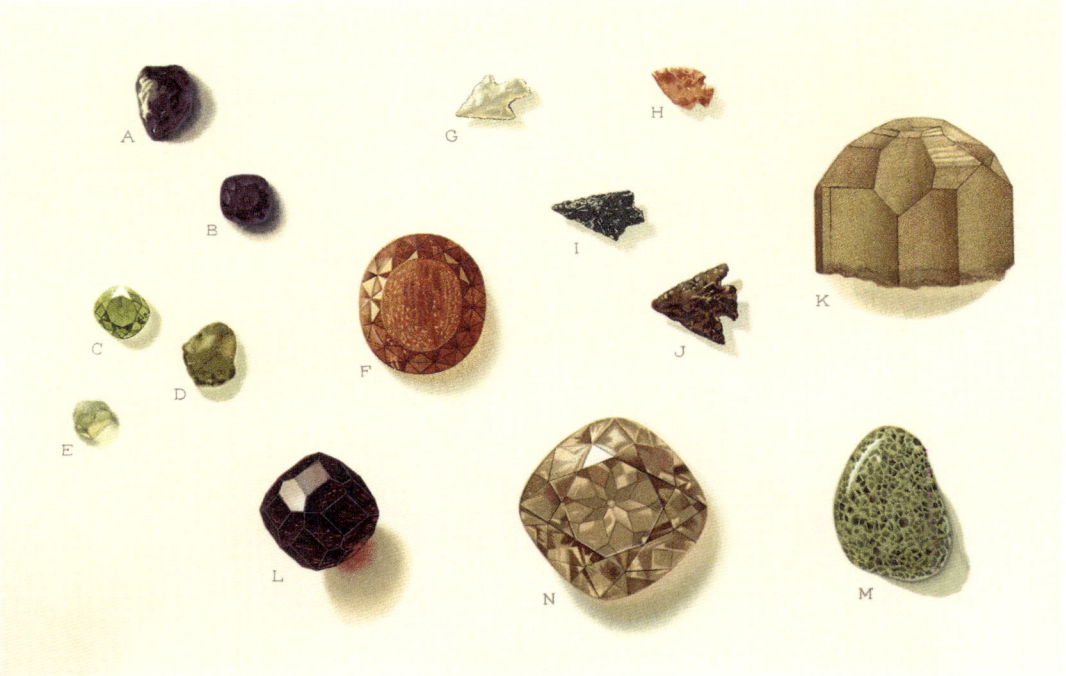

ANIMAL.
Edward Lear, *Tauraco persa*, watercolour, c. 1835. Purplish Red is visible on the feathers of the turaco.

VEGETABLE.
Friedrich Johann Bertuch, *Bilderbuch für Kinder*, 1802. Purplish Red is visible on the petals of the French rose.

MINERAL.
George Frederick Kunz, *Gems and Precious Stones of North America*, 1890. Purplish Red is visible on the garnet (two specimens, top left).

95. COCHINEAL RED.

(i). ——————————
(ii). *Under Disk of decayed Leaves of None-so-pretty.* [*Sweet William catchfly*; Silene armeria]
(iii). *Dark Cinnaber.* [*Cinnabar; Mercury sulphide*]

Cochineal Red, is lake red mixed with bluish grey. [W]

ANIMAL.

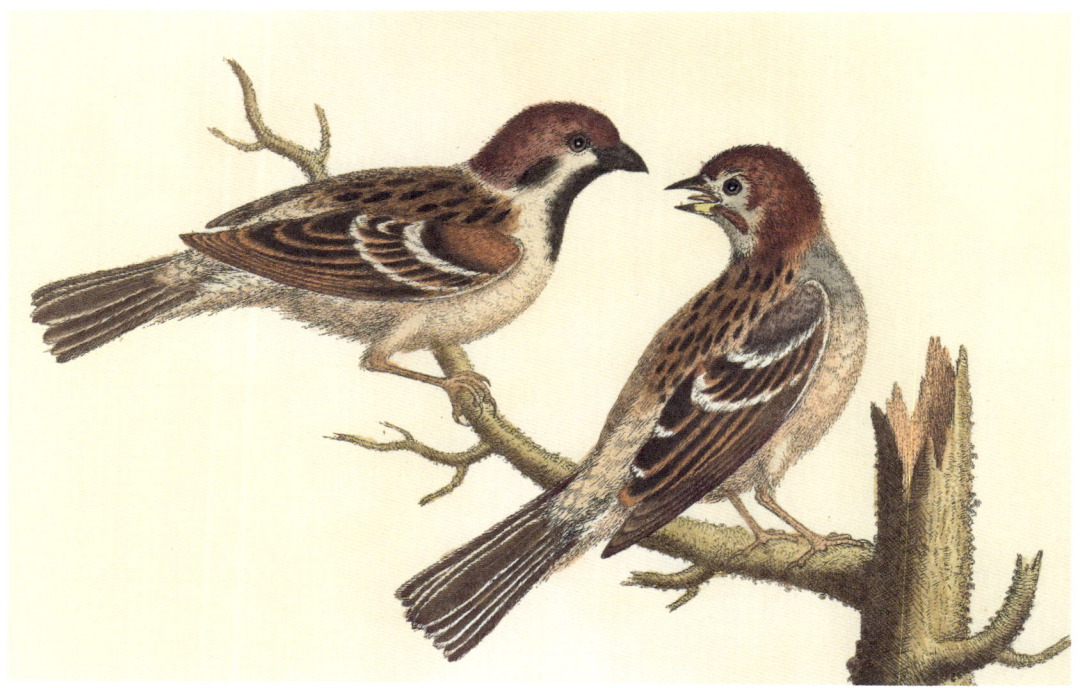

ANIMAL.
George Edwards, *Gleanings of Natural History*, 1858. Cochineal Red is visible on the head feathers of the Eurasian tree sparrow.*

VEGETABLE.
William Baxter, *British Phaenogamous Botany*, 1834–43. Cochineal Red is visible on the leaves of the Sweet William catchfly.

MINERAL.
Louis Simonin, *Underground Life*, 1869. Cochineal Red is visible on the cinnabar (bottom row).

VEGETABLE.

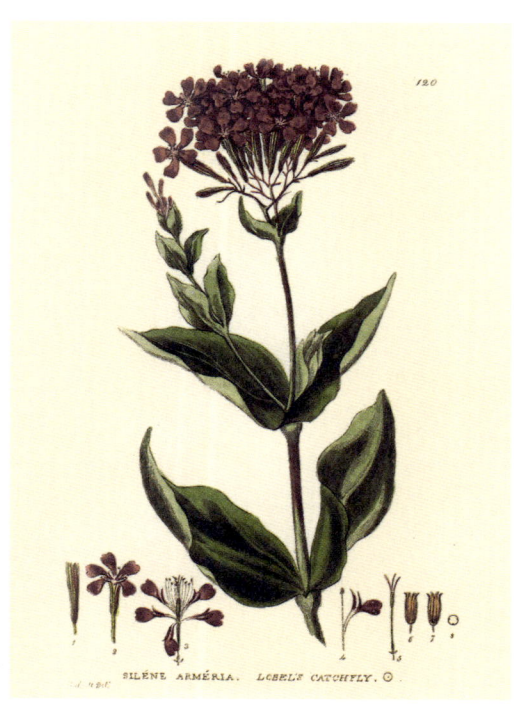

MINERAL.

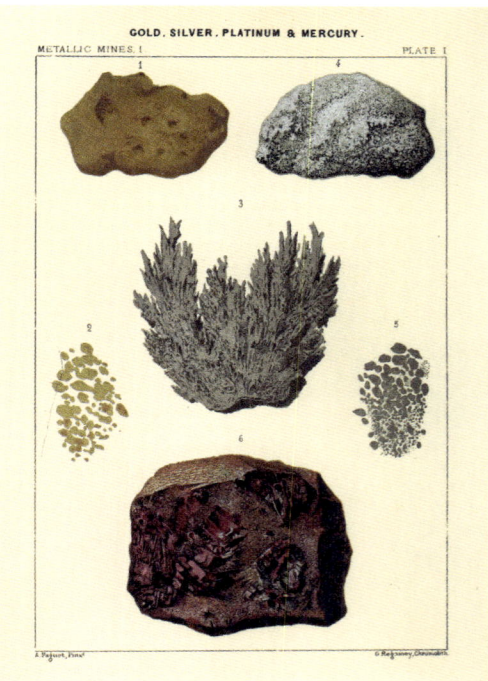

96. VEINOUS BLOOD RED.

(i).   *Veinous Blood.* [Sanguis]
(ii).   *Musk Flower.* [*Erythranthe moschata*; Mimulus moschatus]
        Dark Purple Scabious. [*Pincushion flower*; Scabiosa]
(iii).   *Pyrope.* [*Silicate mineral*]

Veinous Blood Red, is carmine red mixed with brownish black. [W]†

† *Veinous Blood Red is Syme's name for Werner's Blood Red.*

ANIMAL.

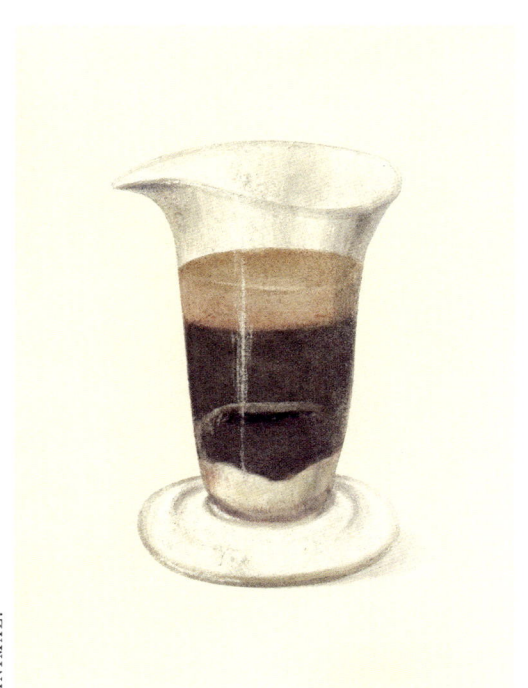

VEGETABLE.

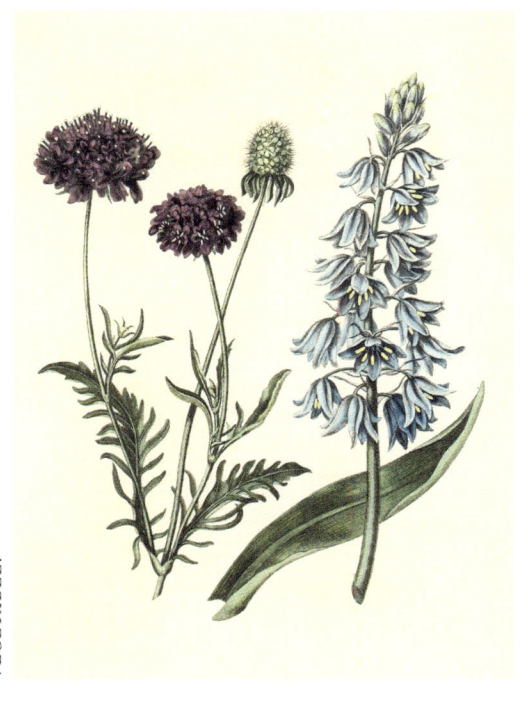

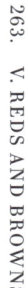

263. V. REDS AND BROWNS.

MINERAL.

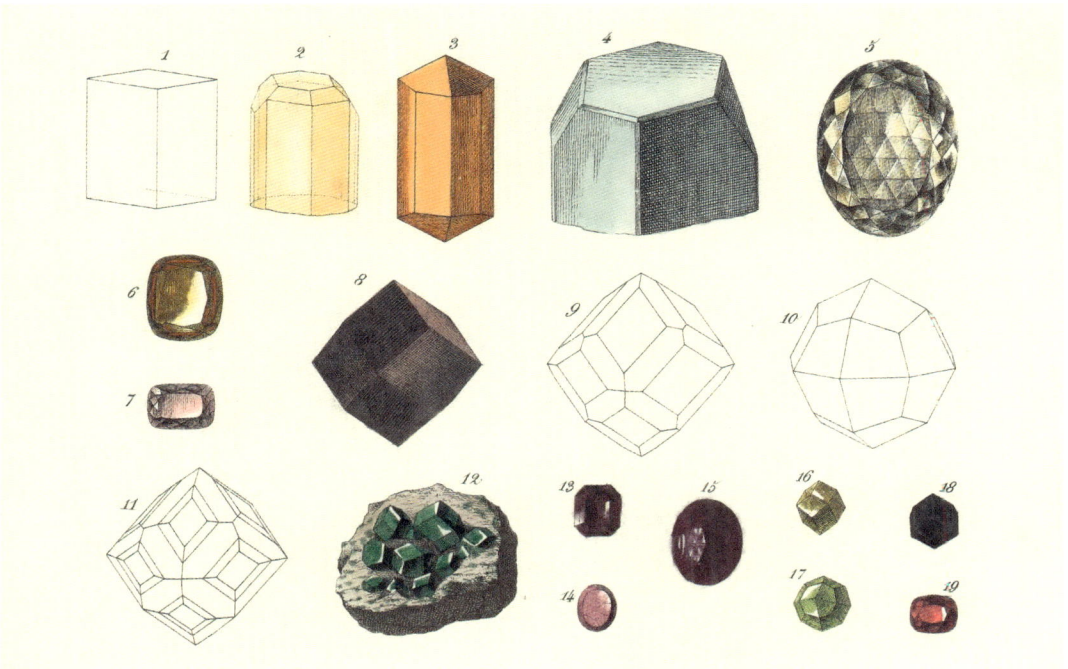

ANIMAL.
Thomas Godart, *Blood from a case of leukaemia*, watercolour, *c.* 1852–61. Veinous Blood Red is visible on the veinous blood.

VEGETABLE.
Sydenham Edwards, *The New Botanic Garden*, 1812. Veinous Blood Red is visible on the petals of the scabious (left).

MINERAL.
Johann Gottlob Kurr, *The Mineral Kingdom*, 1859. Veinous Blood Red is visible on the pyrope (third row, fourth specimen from right).

97. BROWNISH PURPLE RED.

(i).   ——————————
(ii).   *Flower of deadly Nightshade.* [*Deadly nightshade*;
          Belladonna; Atropa belladonna]
(iii).   *Red Antimony Ore.* [*Ore*]

*Brownish Purple Red,
the cherry red of Werner,
is lake red mixed with
brownish black, and a
small portion of grey. [W]*

ANIMAL.

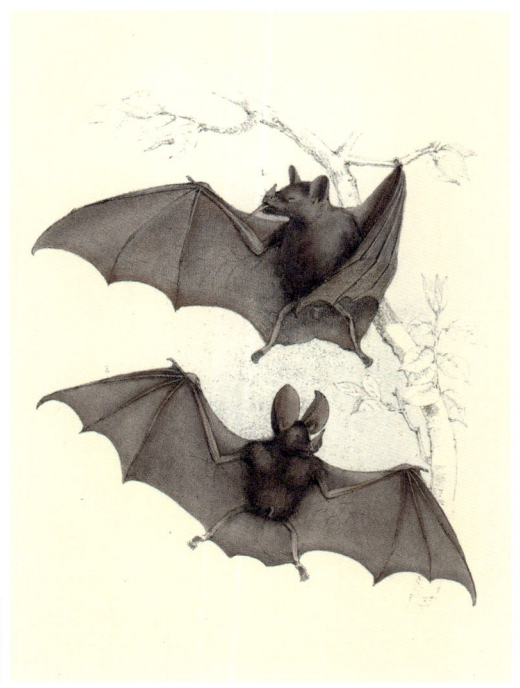

VEGETABLE.

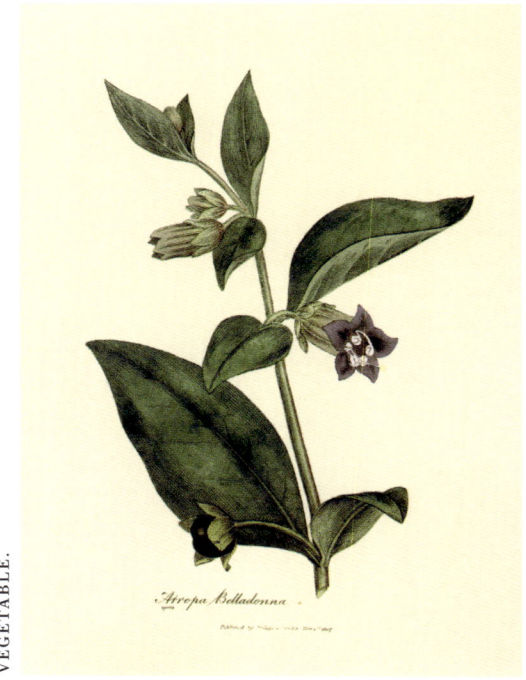

Atropa Belladonna

ANIMAL.
Richard Brinsley
Hinds, *The Zoology
of the Voyage of
HMS Sulphur*, 1843.
Brownish Purple
Red is visible on the
wings of the bat.*

VEGETABLE.
William Woodville,
Medical Botany,
Vol. 2, 1832.
Brownish Purple is
visible on the petals of
the deadly nightshade.

MINERAL.
Philip Rashleigh,
*Specimens of
British Minerals*, 1797.
Brownish Purple
is visible on the
antimony ore (above).

MINERAL.

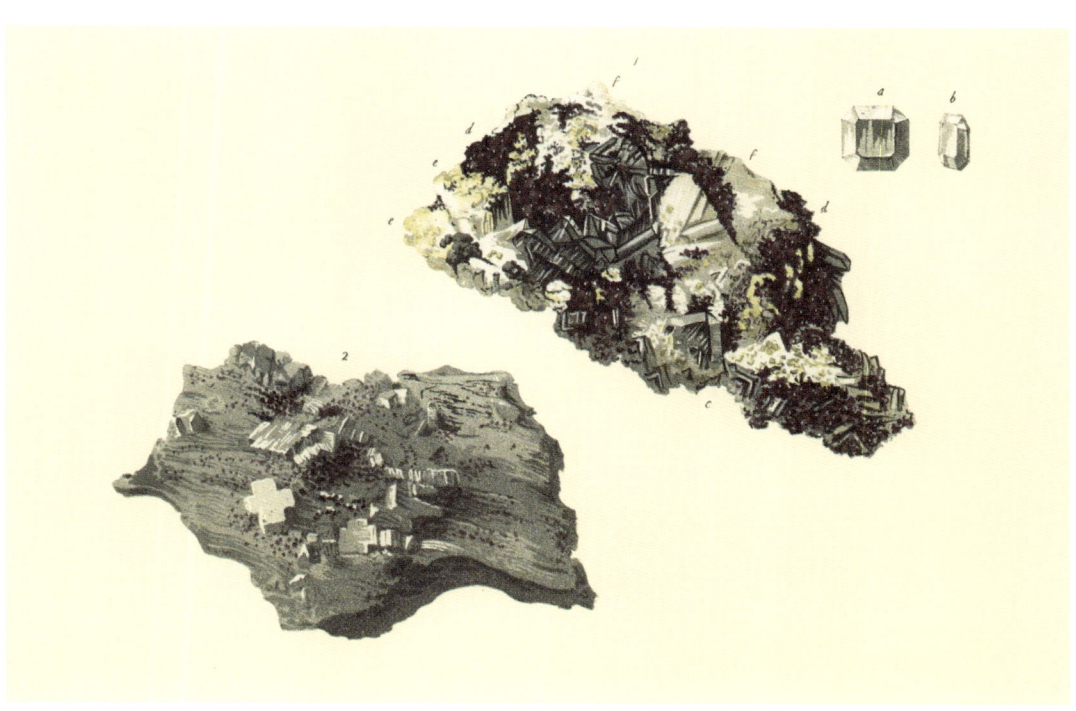

98. CHOCOLATE RED.

(i).   *Breast of Bird of Paradise.* [Paradisaeidae]
(ii).   *Brown Disk of common Marigold.* [Calendula]
(iii).   ————

Chocolate Red, is veinous blood red mixed with a little brownish red.

ANIMAL.

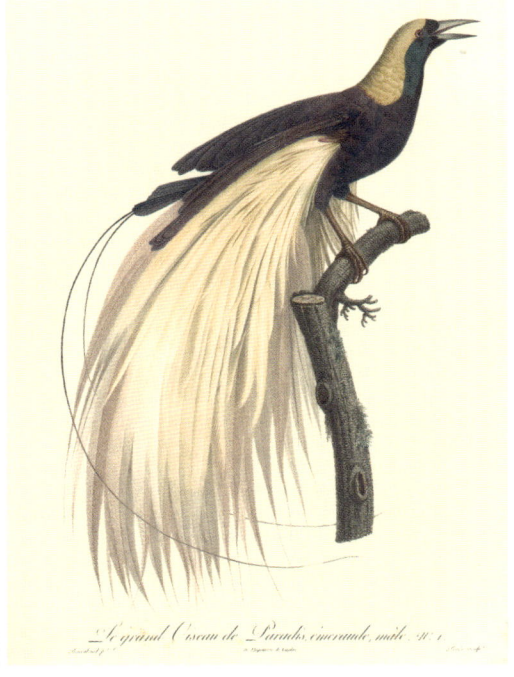

Le grand Oiseau de Paradis, émeraude, mâle.

VEGETABLE.

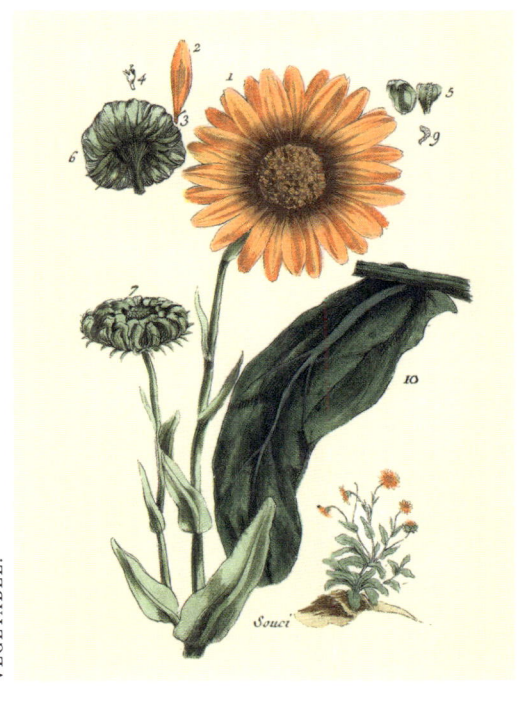

Souci

MINERAL.

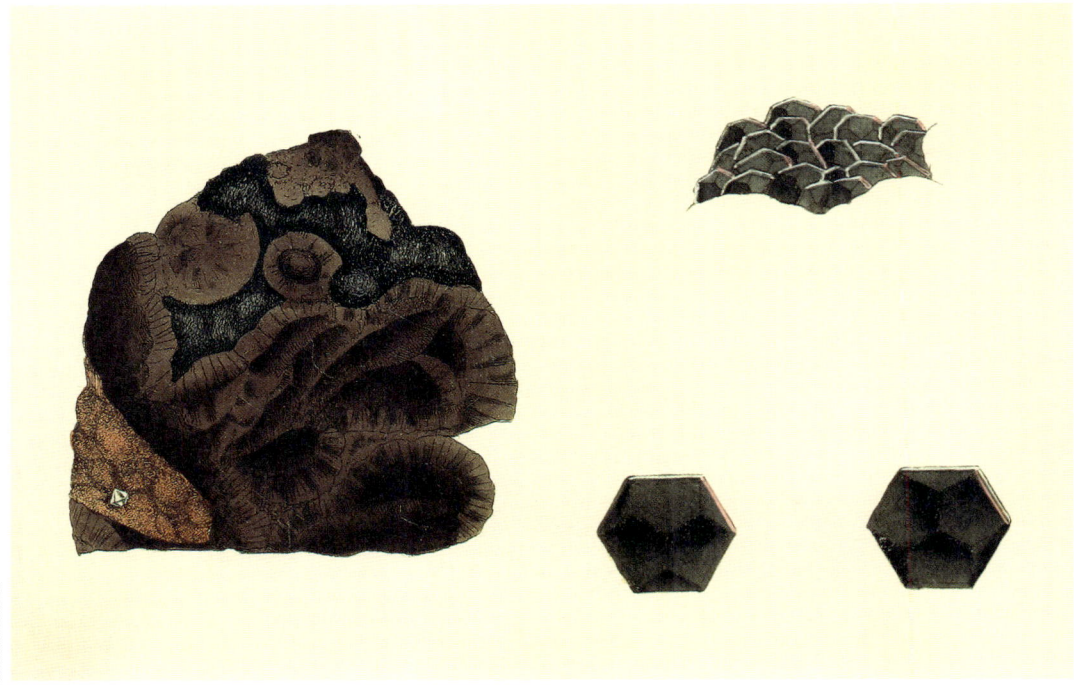

ANIMAL.
François Levaillant,
Le grand Oiseau de paradis, émeraude, mâle, engraving, 1801–06.
Chocolate Red is visible on the breast feathers of the bird of paradise.

VEGETABLE.
Pierre Bulliard,
Flora Parisiensis,
Vol. 5, 1776–81.
Chocolate Red is visible on the central disk of the marigold.

MINERAL.
James Sowerby,
British Mineralogy,
Vol. 1, 1802–17.
Chocolate Red is visible on the iron oxide (left).*

(i).   *Mark on Throat of Red-throated Diver.*
         [*Red-throated loon*; Gavia stellata]
(ii).   ————————
(iii).   *Iron Flint.* [*Quartz*]

ANIMAL.

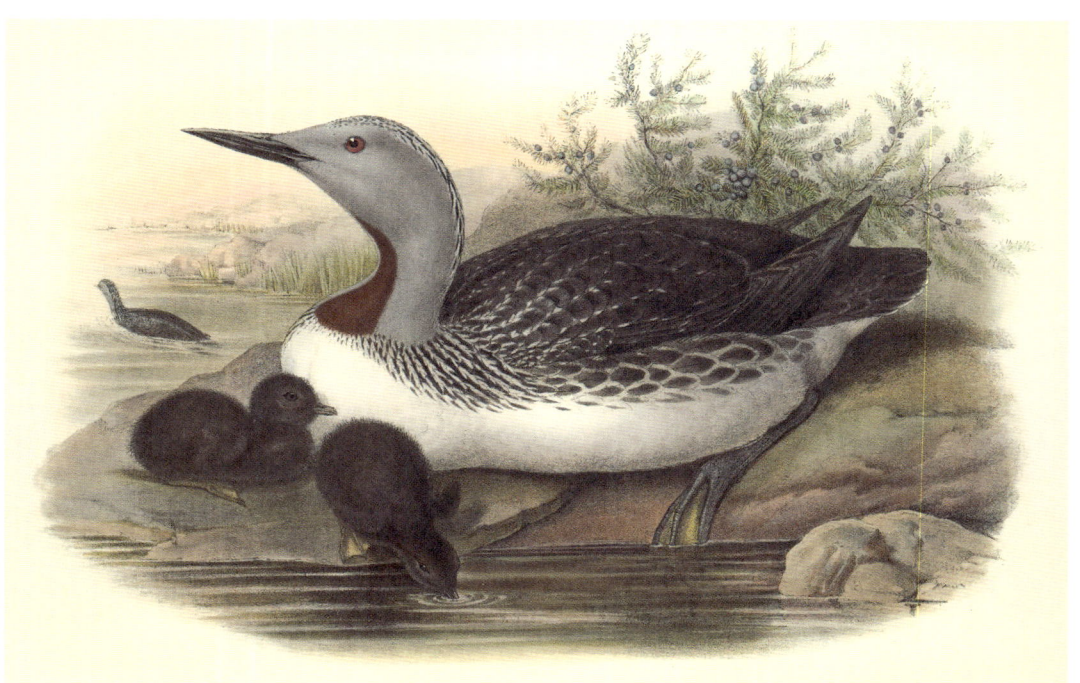

MINERAL.

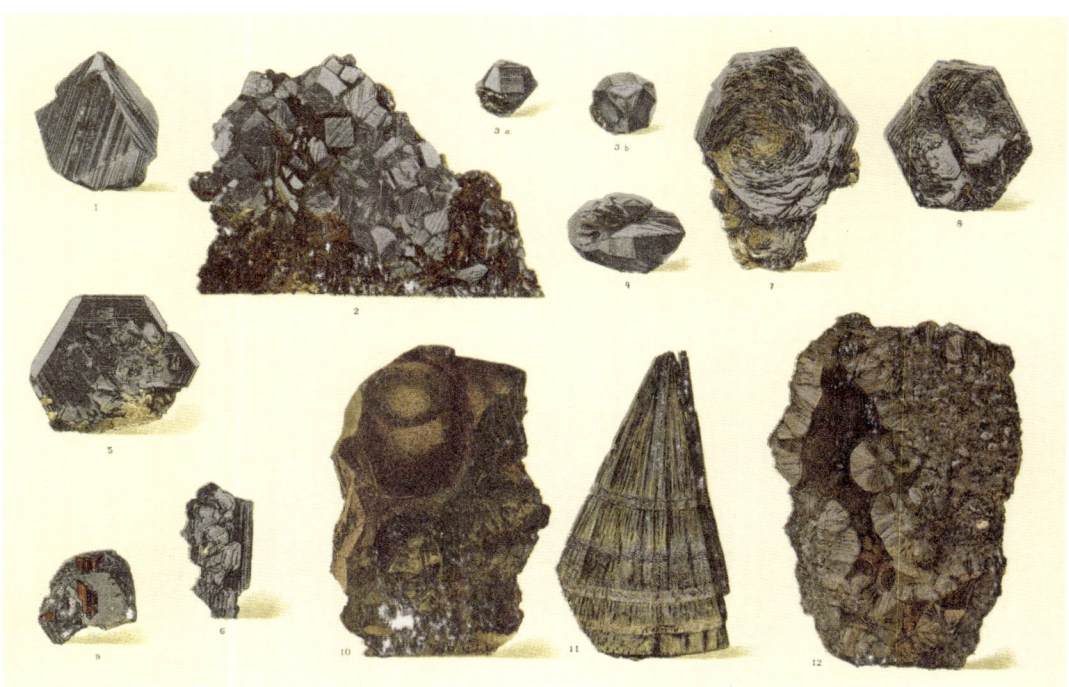

*Brownish Red, is chocolate
red mixed with hyacinth red,
and a little chesnut brown. [W]*

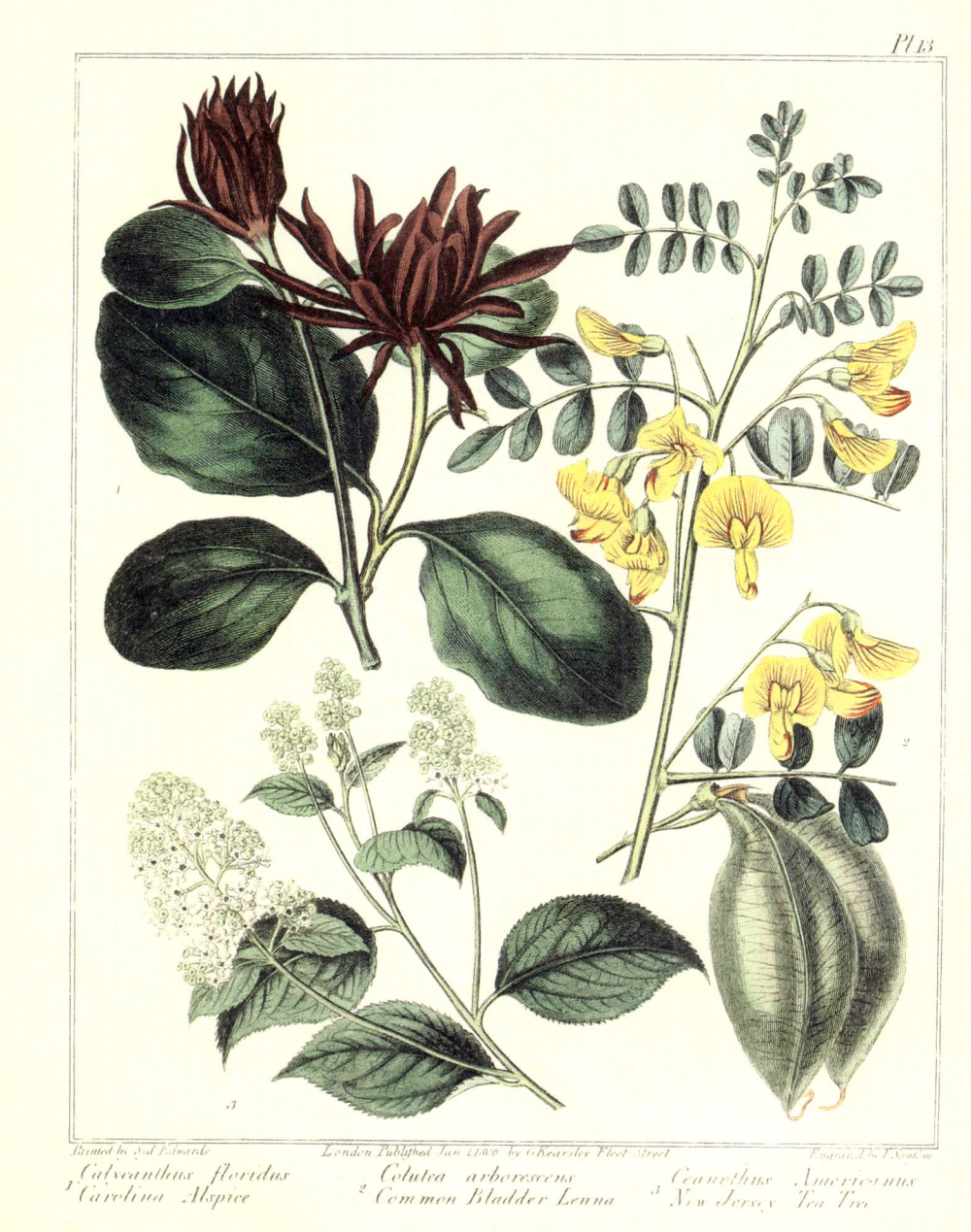

ANIMAL.
John Gould, *Birds
of Great Britain*,
Vol. 5, 1862–73.
Brownish Red is visible
on the throat feathers
of the red-throated loon.

VEGETABLE.
Johann Wilhelm
Weinmann,
*Phytanthoza
iconographia*, 1737.
Brownish Red is visible
on the petals of the
Carolina allspice.*

MINERAL.
Sydenham Edwards,
*The New Botanic
Garden*, 1812.
Brownish Red is
visible on the iron ore
(bottom row, centre).

BROWNS.

No.	Names.	Colours.	ANIMAL.		
100	Deep Orange-coloured Brown.		Head of Pochard, Wing coverts of Sheldrake.		
101	Deep Reddish Brown.		Breast of Pochard, and Neck of Teal Drake.		
102	Umber Brown.		Moor Buzzard.		
103	Chesnut Brown.		Neck and Breast of Red Grouse.		
104	Yellowish Brown.		Light Brown Spots on Guinea-Pig, Breast of Hoopoe.		
105	Wood Brown.		Common Weasel, Light parts of Feathers on the Back of the Snipe.		
106	Liver Brown.		Middle Parts of Feathers of Hen Pheasant, and Wing coverts of Grosbeak.		
107	Hair Brown.		Head of Pintail Duck.		
108	Broccoli Brown.		Head of Black headed Gull.		
109	Olive Brown.		Head and Neck of Male Kestril.		
110	Blackish Brown.		Stormy Petril Wing Coverts of black Cock. Forehead of Foumart.		

Syme's 1821 edition included four of Werner's original browns (numbers 104, 106, 109 and 110), two browns from the Lenz system (numbers 105 and 107), two browns from the Jameson system (numbers 103 and 108) and three browns from his own 1814 edition (numbers 100, 101 and 102).

BROWNS.

	VEGETABLE.		MINERAL.	
	Female Spike of Catstail Reed.			
	Dead Leaves of green Panic Grass.		Brown Blende.	
	Disk of Rubeckia.			
	Chesnuts.		Egyptian Jasper.	
			Iron Flint and common Jasper.	
	Hazel Nuts.		Mountain Wood.	
			Semi Opal.	
			Wood Tin.	
			Zircon.	
	Stems of Black Currant Bush.		Axinite, Rock Cristal.	
			Mineral Pitch.	

(i).   *Head of Pochard.* [*Common pochard*; Aythya ferina]
         Wing coverts of Sheldrake. [*Shelduck*; Tadorna]
(ii).   *Female Spike of Catstail Reed.* [*Cattail*; Typha]
(iii).   —————————

Deep Orange-coloured Brown, is chesnut brown, with a little reddish brown, and a small quantity of orange brown.

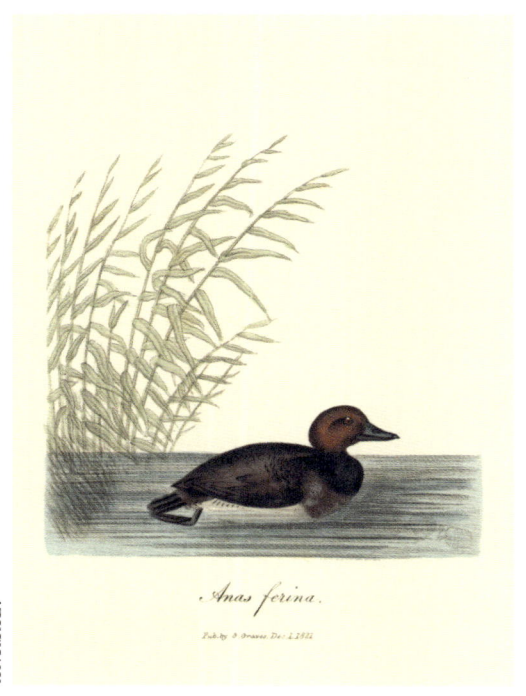

Anas ferina.

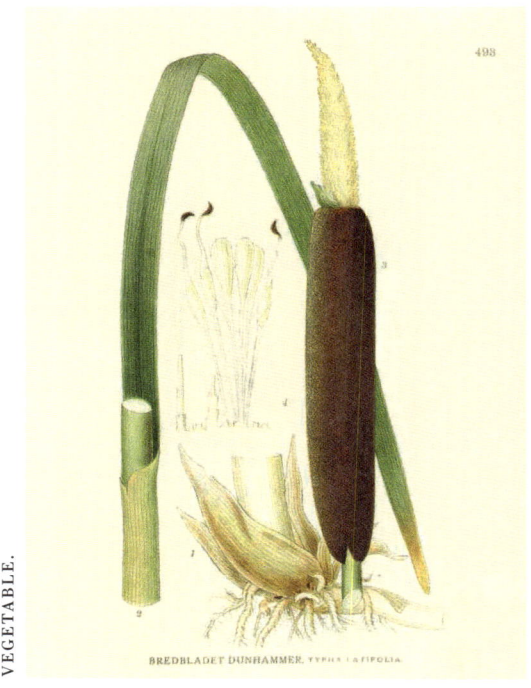

BREDBLADET DUNHAMMER, TYPHA LATIFOLIA.

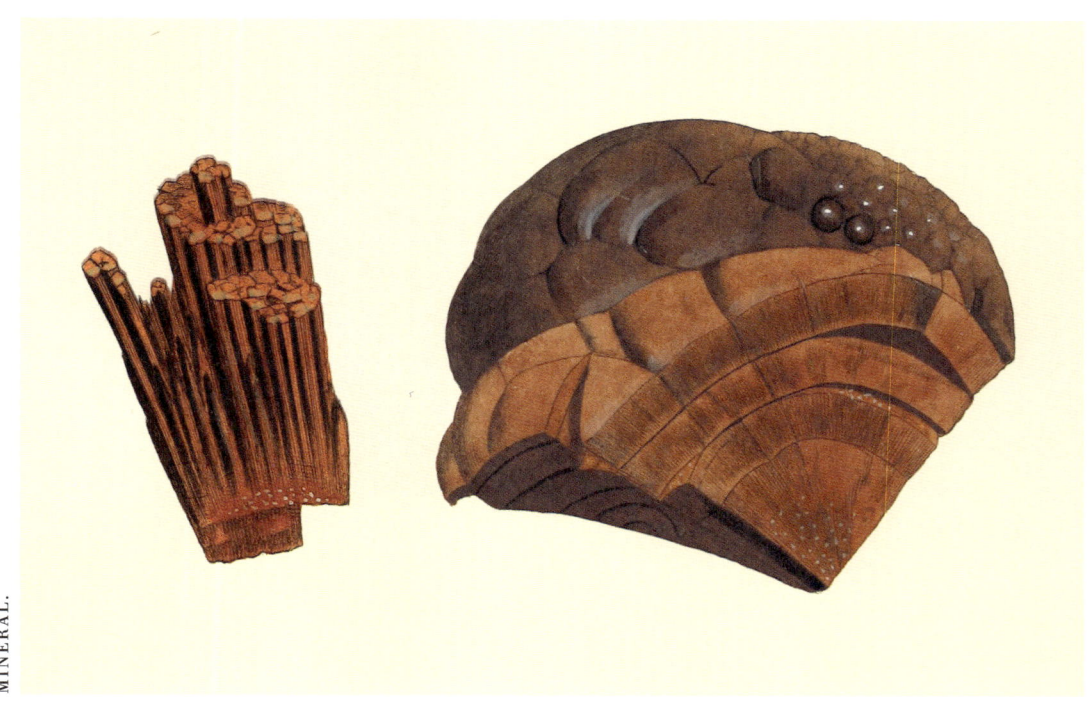

ANIMAL.

VEGETABLE.

MINERAL.

270.   V. REDS AND BROWNS.

ANIMAL.
George Graves,
*British
Ornithology*, 1821.
Deep Orange-
coloured Brown is
visible on the feathers
on the head of the
common pochard.

VEGETABLE.
J. W. Palmstruch,
Svensk Botanik,
Vol. 8, 1807.
Deep Orange-
coloured Brown is
visible on the spike
of the cattail reed.

MINERAL.
James Sowerby,
British Mineralogy,
Vol. 1, 1802–17.
Deep Orange-coloured
Brown is visible on
the the hematite
(both specimens).*

101. DEEP REDDISH BROWN.

(i).   *Breast of Pochard.* [*Common pochard*; Aythya ferina]
       Neck of Teal Drake. [*Eurasian teal*; Anas crecca]
(ii).   *Dead Leaves of green Panic Grass.* [Panicum]
(iii). *Brown Blende.* [*Sphalerite*; *Zincblende*; *Sulphide mineral*]

Deep Reddish Brown,
is chesnut brown, with
a little chocolate red.

ANIMAL.

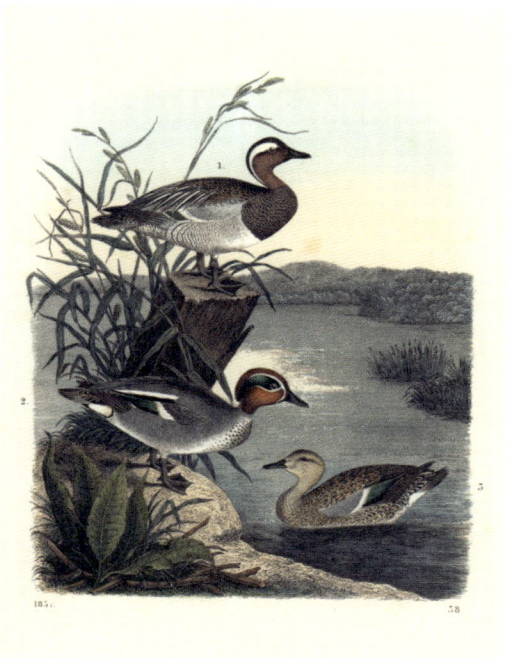

VEGETABLE.

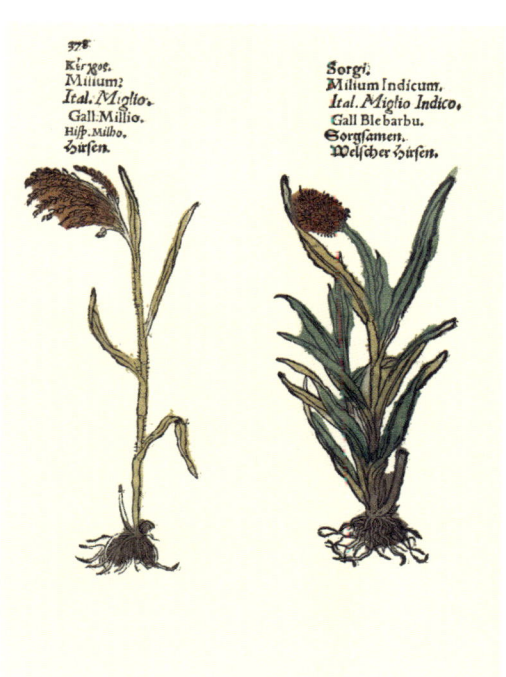

MINERAL.

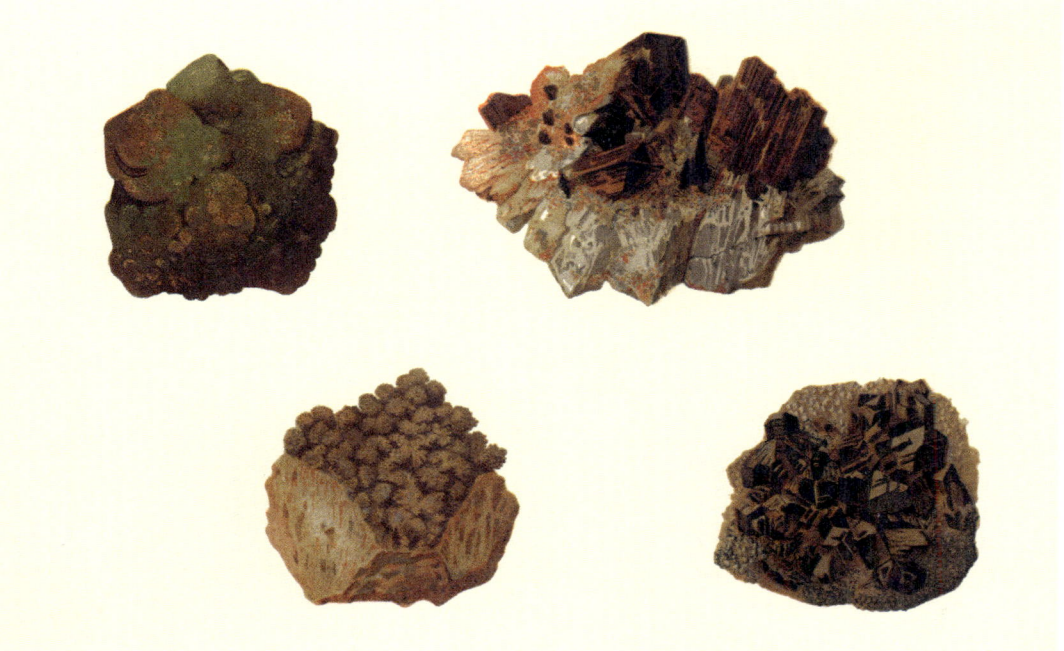

ANIMAL.
Carl Hoffmann,
Book of the World, 1857.
Deep Reddish Brown
is visible on the neck
feathers of the male
Eurasian teal (below left).

VEGETABLE.
Adam Lonicer,
Krauterbuch, 1557.
Deep Reddish Brown
is visible on the dead
leaves of the panic
grass (left).

MINERAL.
Frederic Brewster
Loomis, *Field Book
of Common Rocks
and Minerals,* 1923.
Deep Reddish Brown is
visible on the sphalerite
(bottom row, right).

(i).   *Moor Buzzard.* [*Marsh Harrier*; Circus aeruginosus]
(ii).   *Disk of Rubeckia.* [*Coneflower*; *Black-eyed Susan*; Rudbeckia]
(iii).   —————————

Umber Brown, is chesnut brown, with a little blackish brown.

ANIMAL.

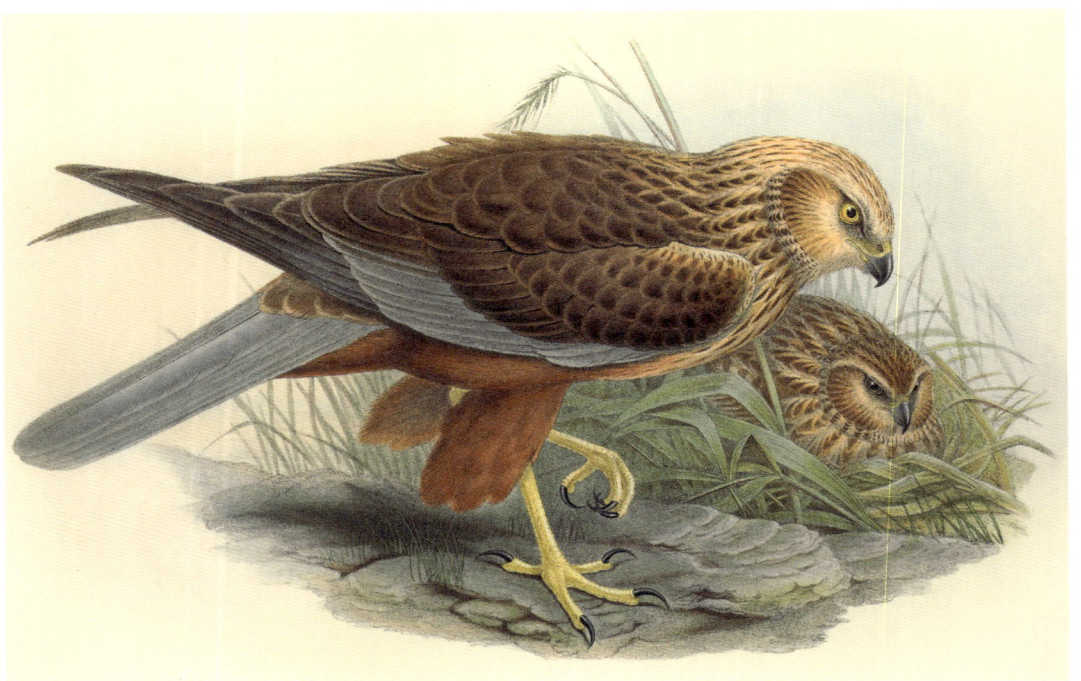

ANIMAL.
John Gould, *Birds of Great Britain*, Vol. 1, 1862–73. Umber Brown is visible on the feathers of the marsh harrier.

VEGETABLE.
J. H. Jaume Saint-Hilaire, *Flore et la pomone Françaises*, Vol. 4, 1828. Umber Brown is visible on the central disk of the coneflower.

MINERAL.
James Sowerby, *British Mineralogy*, Vol. 4, 1802–17. Umber Brown is visible on the oxide of tin (top row).*

VEGETABLE.

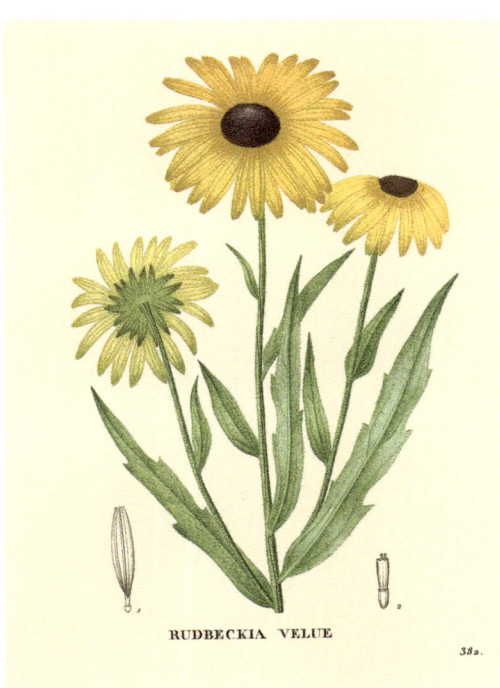

RUDBECKIA VELUE

MINERAL.

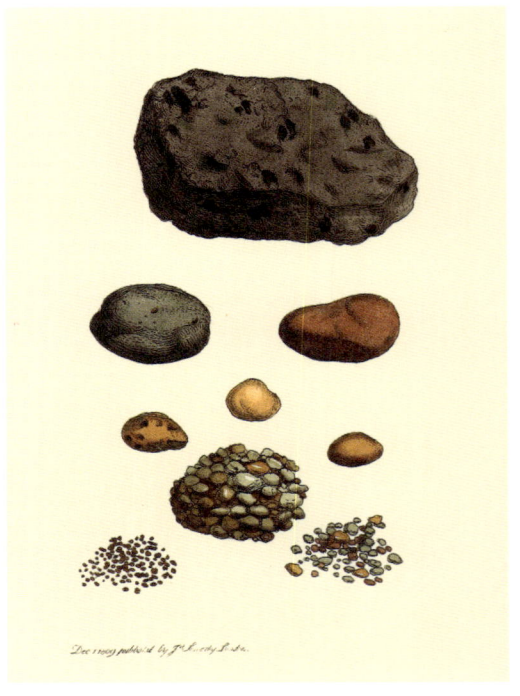

103. CHESNUT BROWN.

(i).   *Neck and Breast of Red Grouse.* [Lagopus lagopus scotica]
(ii).   *Chesnuts.* [Castanea *or* Aesculus]
(iii). *Egyptian Jasper.* [*Silica*]

Chesnut Brown, the characteristic colour of the browns of Werner's series, is deep reddish brown and yellowish brown. [W]

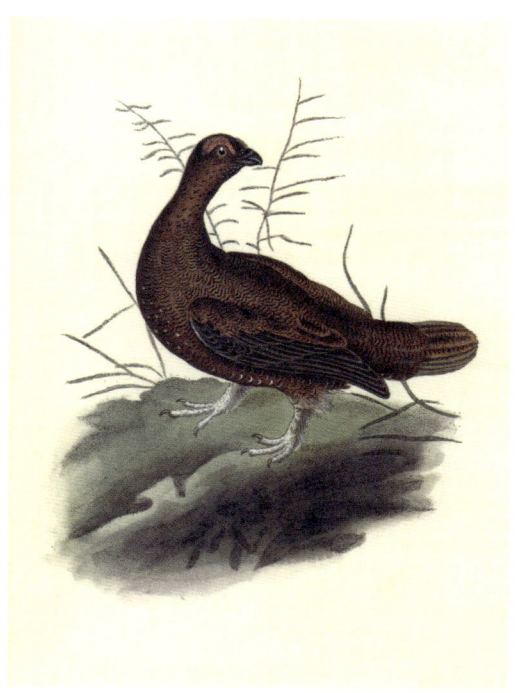

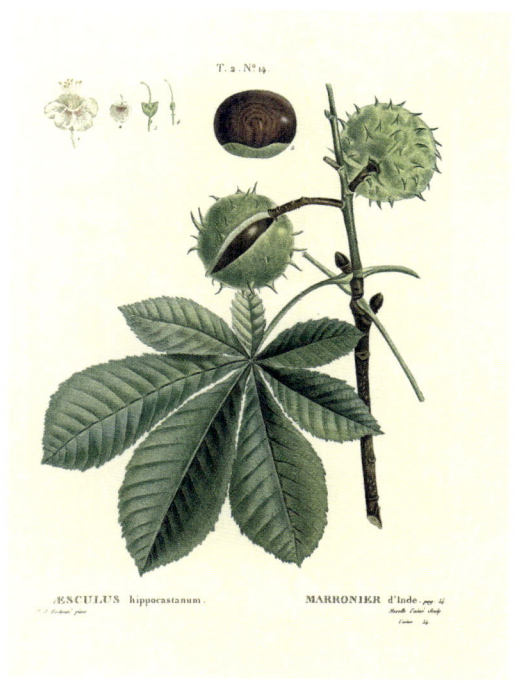

ÆSCULUS hippocastanum.   MARRONIER d'Inde.

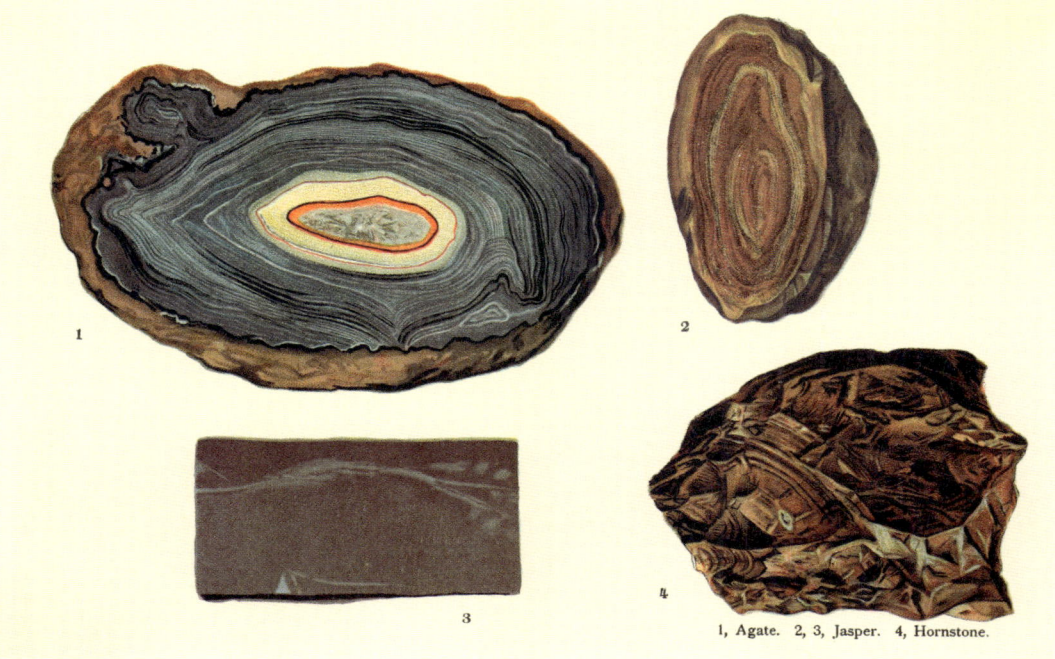

1, Agate. 2, 3, Jasper. 4, Hornstone.

ANIMAL.
Edward Donovan, *Natural History of British Birds,* 1794–1819. Chesnut Brown is visible on the neck and breast feathers of the red grouse.

VEGETABLE.
H. L. Duhamel du Monceau, *Traité des arbres et arbustes,* Vol. 2, 1800–19. Chesnut Brown is visible on the seed of the horse chestnut.

MINERAL.
Leonard Spencer, *The World's Minerals,* 1916. Chesnut Brown is visible on the jasper (top row, right and bottom row, left).

104. YELLOWISH BROWN.

(i).   *Light Brown Spots on Guinea-Pig.* [Cavia porcellus]
         Breast of Hoopoe. [Upupa epops]
(ii).   ———
(iii).   *Iron Flint.* [*Quartz*] *Common Jasper.* [*Silica*]

Yellowish Brown, is chesnut brown mixed with a considerable portion of lemon yellow. [W]

ANIMAL.

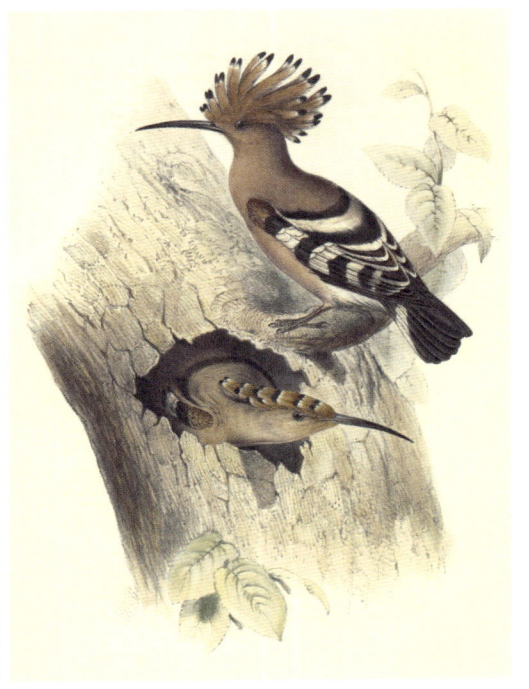

VEGETABLE.

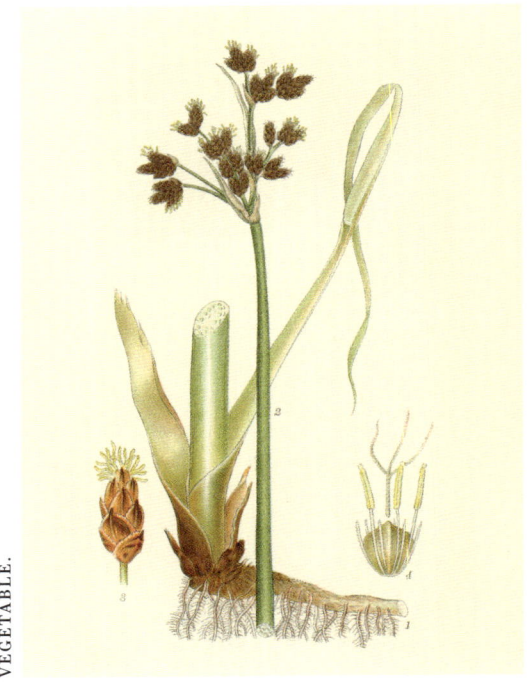

ANIMAL.
John Gould, *Birds of Europe*, Vol. 3, 1832–37. Yellowish Brown is visible on the breast feathers of the hoopoe.

VEGETABLE.
A. Mentz and C. H. Ostenfeld, *Billeder af Nordens Flora*, Vol. 2, 1917. Yellowish Brown is visible on the flower of the lakeshore bulrush.*

MINERAL.
Johann Gottlob Kurr, *The Mineral Kingdom*, 1859. Yellowish Brown is visible on the jasper (centre row, centre).

MINERAL.

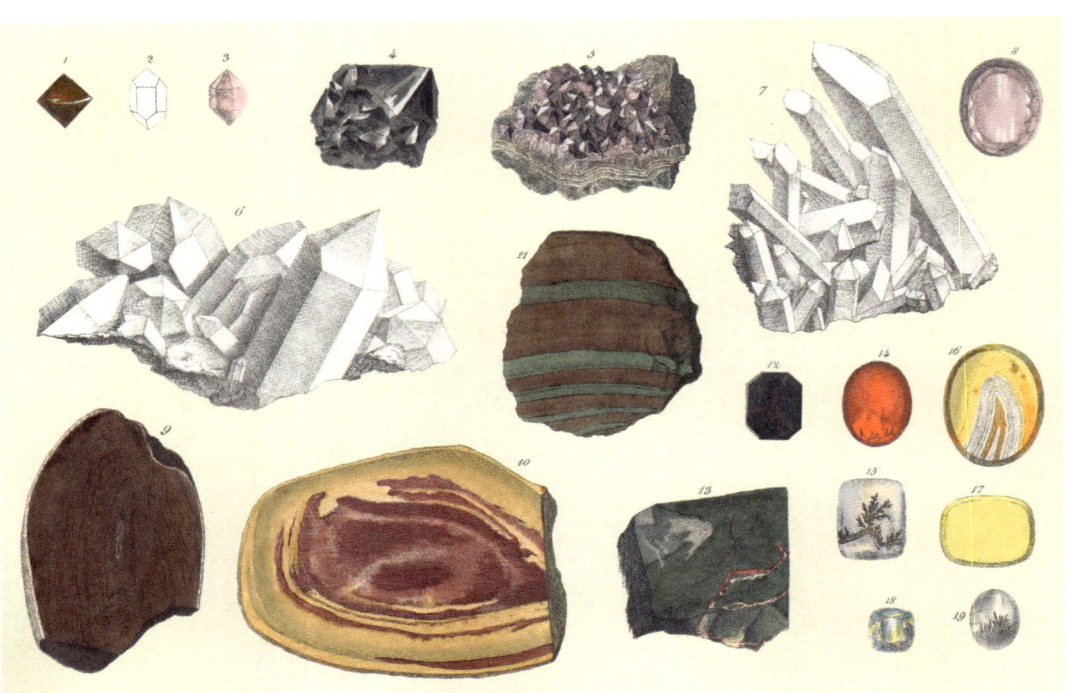

105. WOOD BROWN.

(i).   *Common Weasel.* [*Little weasel*; Mustela nivalis]
       Light parts of Feathers on the Back of the Snipe.
       [*Common snipe*; Gallinago gallinago]
(ii). *Hazel Nuts.* [*Hazelnut*; Corylus]
(iii). *Mountain Wood.* [*Silicate mineral*]

*Wood Brown, is
yellowish brown
mixed with ash grey.*

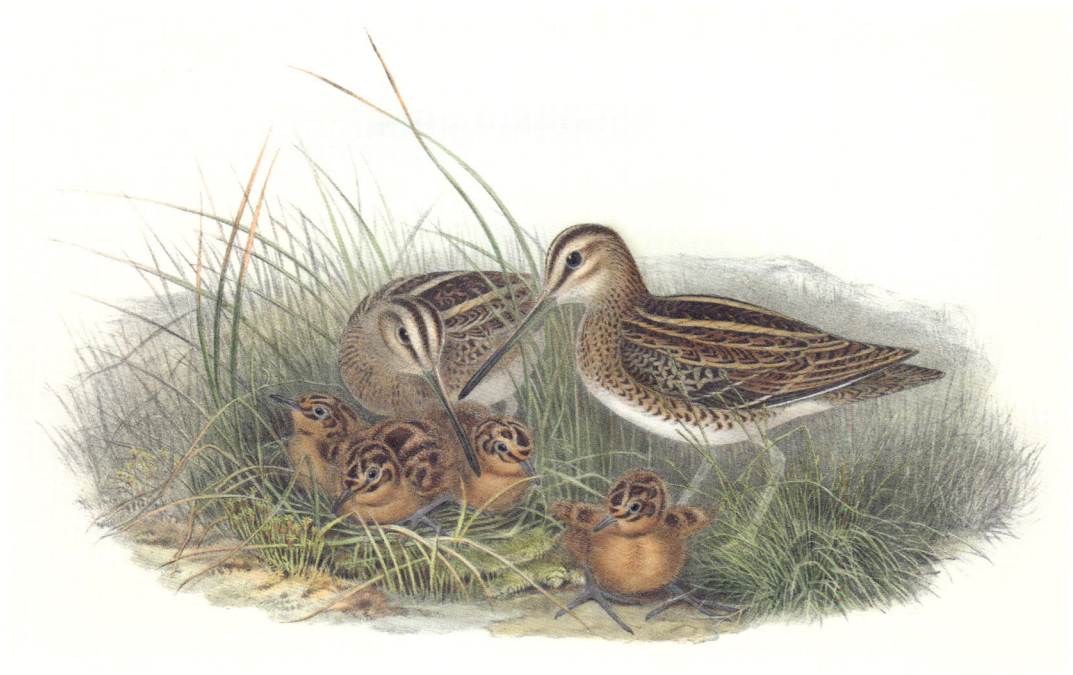

ANIMAL.

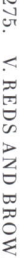

275.   V. REDS AND BROWNS.

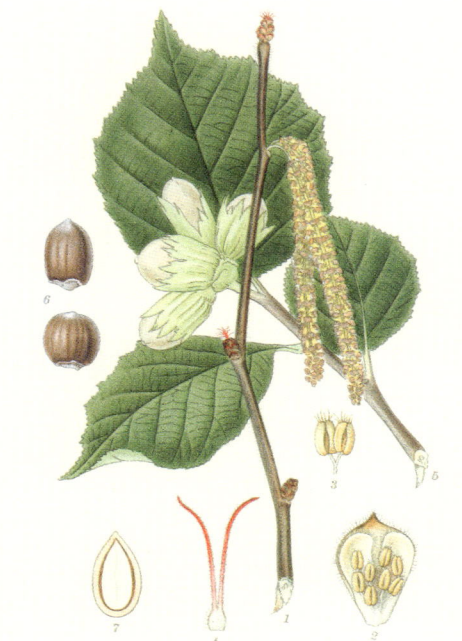

VEGETABLE.

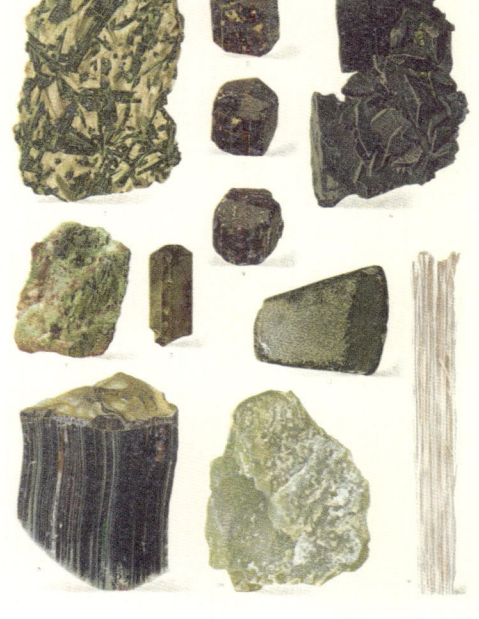

MINERAL.

ANIMAL.
John Gould, *Birds
of Great Britain*,
Vol. 4, 1862–73.
Wood Brown is visible
on the light feathers
on the back of the
common snipe.

VEGETABLE.
A. Mentz and C. H.
Ostenfeld, *Billeder
af Nordens Flora*,
Vol. 1, 1917.
Wood Brown is
visible on the shell
of the hazelnut.

MINERAL.
Reinhard Brauns,
*The Mineral
Kingdom*, Vol. 2, 1912.
Wood Brown is visible
on the mountain wood
(bottom row, right).

106. LIVER BROWN.

(i).   *Middle Parts of Feathers of Hen Pheasant.*
      [Phasianus colchicus]
      Wing coverts of Grosbeak. [Grosbeak]

(ii).   ————————

(iii).   *Semi Opal.* [*Silica*]

*Liver Brown, is chesnut
brown mixed with a little
black and olive green.* †

† *Syme should have applied a [W] notation in this
instance, as Liver Brown appears in Werner's
original list of colours.*

V. REDS AND BROWNS.

276.

ANIMAL.

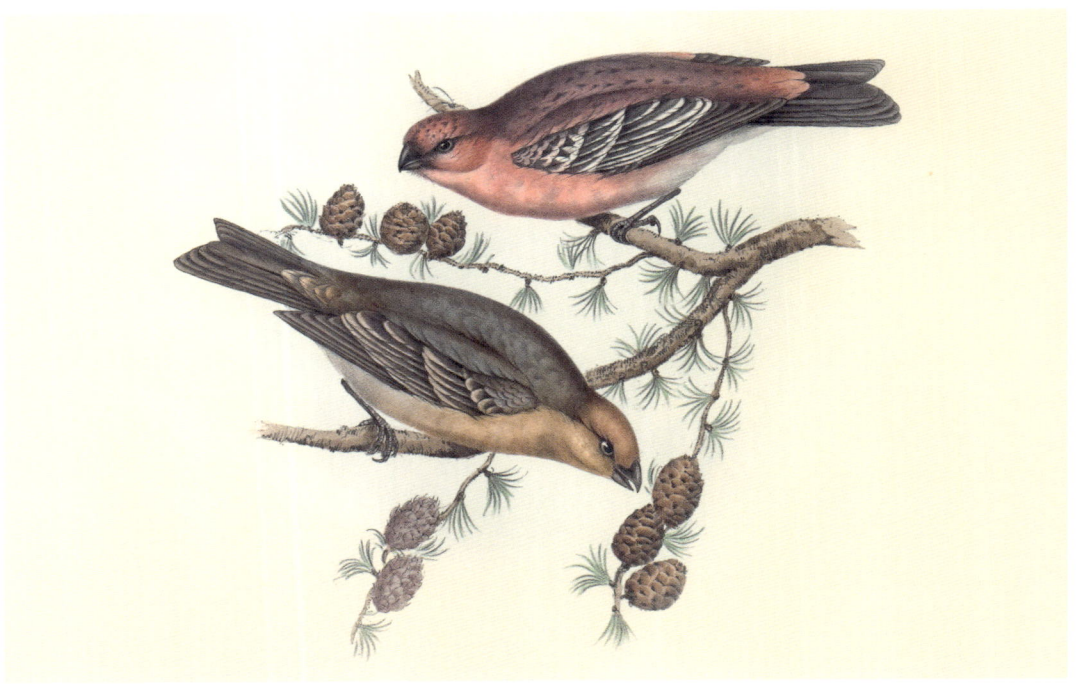

ANIMAL.
John Gould, *Birds of
Europe*, Vol. 3, 1832–37.
Liver Brown is visible
on the wing feathers
of the grosbeak.

VEGETABLE.
Johann Wilhelm
Weinmann,
*Phytanthoza
iconographia*, 1737.
Liver Brown is
visible on the seedpod
of the cashew.*

MINERAL.
Reinhard Brauns,
*The Mineral
Kingdom*, Vol. 2, 1912.
Liver Brown is visible
on the opal (second
row, centre).

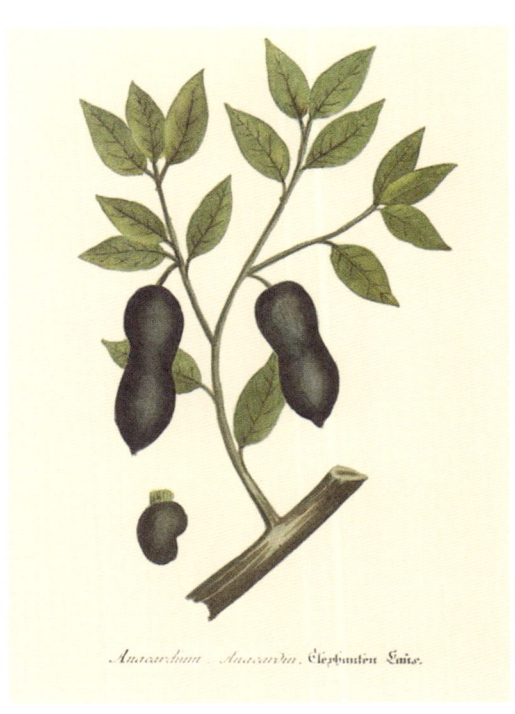

Anacardium Anacardia Elephanten Laus.

VEGETABLE.

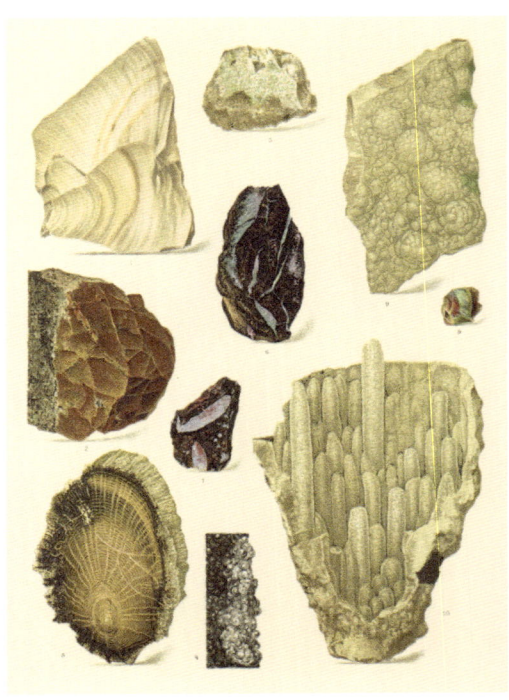

MINERAL.

107. HAIR BROWN.

(i).   *Head of Pintail Duck.* [*Northern pintail*; Anas acuta].
(ii). ———————————
(iii). *Wood Tin.* [*Tin oxide mineral*].

Hair Brown, is olive brown mixed with ash grey. [W]

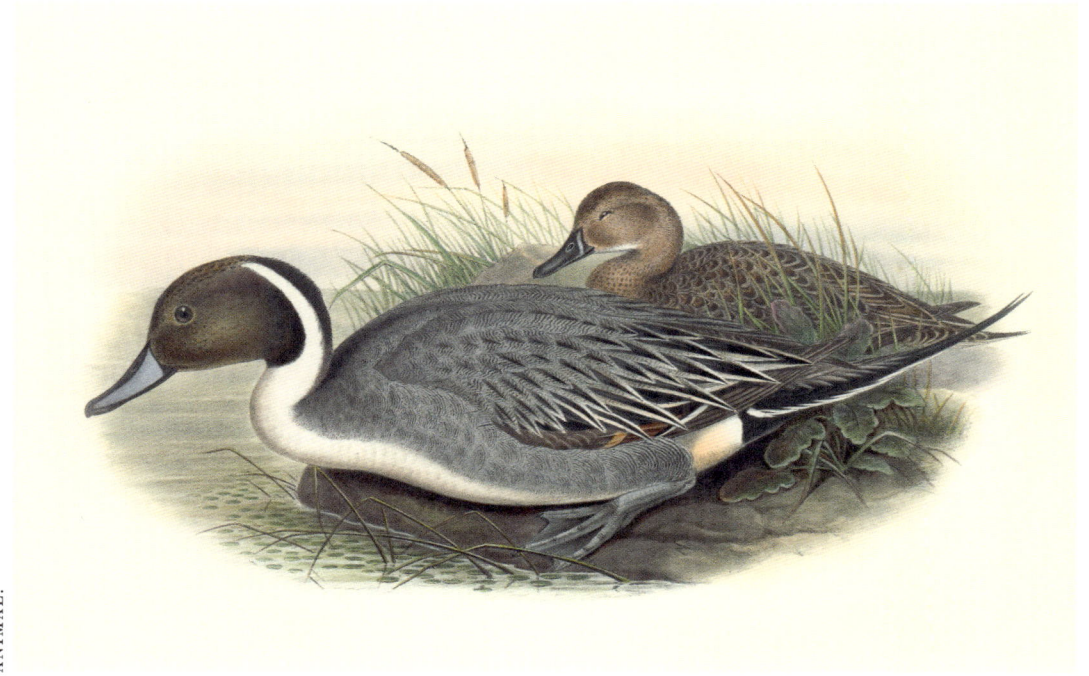

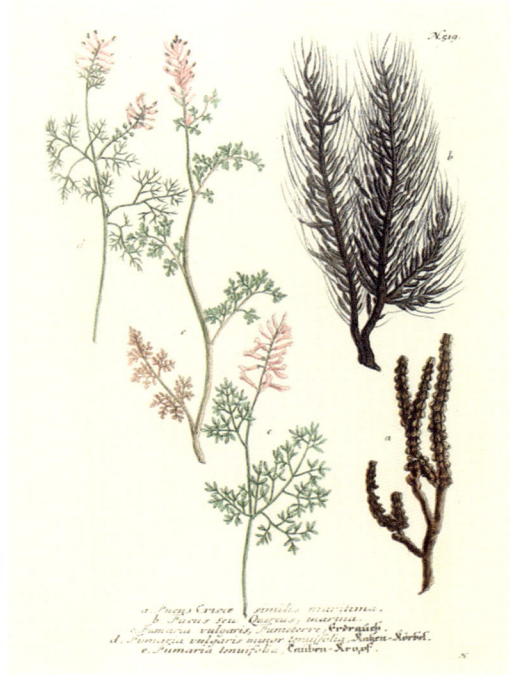

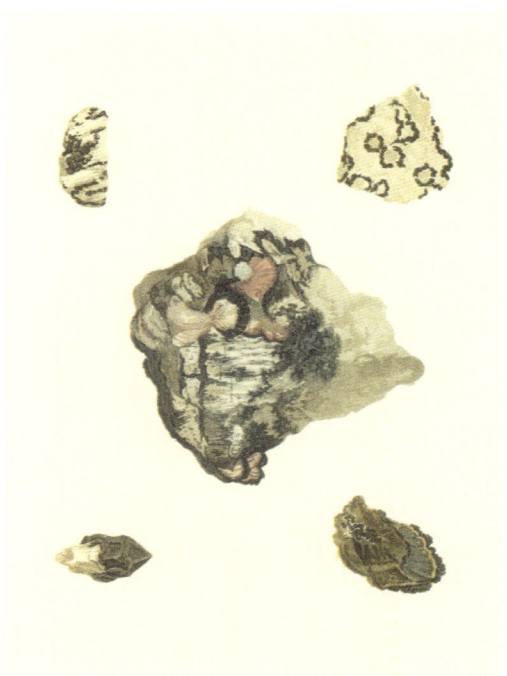

ANIMAL.
John Gould, *Birds of Great Britain*, Vol. 5, 1862–73. Hair Brown is visible on the head feathers of the northern pintail.

VEGETABLE.
Johann Wilhelm Weinmann, *Phytanthoza iconographia*, 1737. Hair Brown is visible on the fucus seaweed (top row, right).*

MINERAL.
Philip Rashleigh, *Specimens of British Minerals*, 1797. Hair Brown is visible on the wood tin (all specimens).

108. BROCCOLI BROWN.

(i).   *Head of Black headed Gull.* [Chroicocephalus ridibundus]
(ii).   ——————————
(iii).   *Zircon.* [*Silicate mineral*]

Broccoli Brown, is olive brown mixed with ash grey, and a small tinge of red. [W]

ANIMAL.

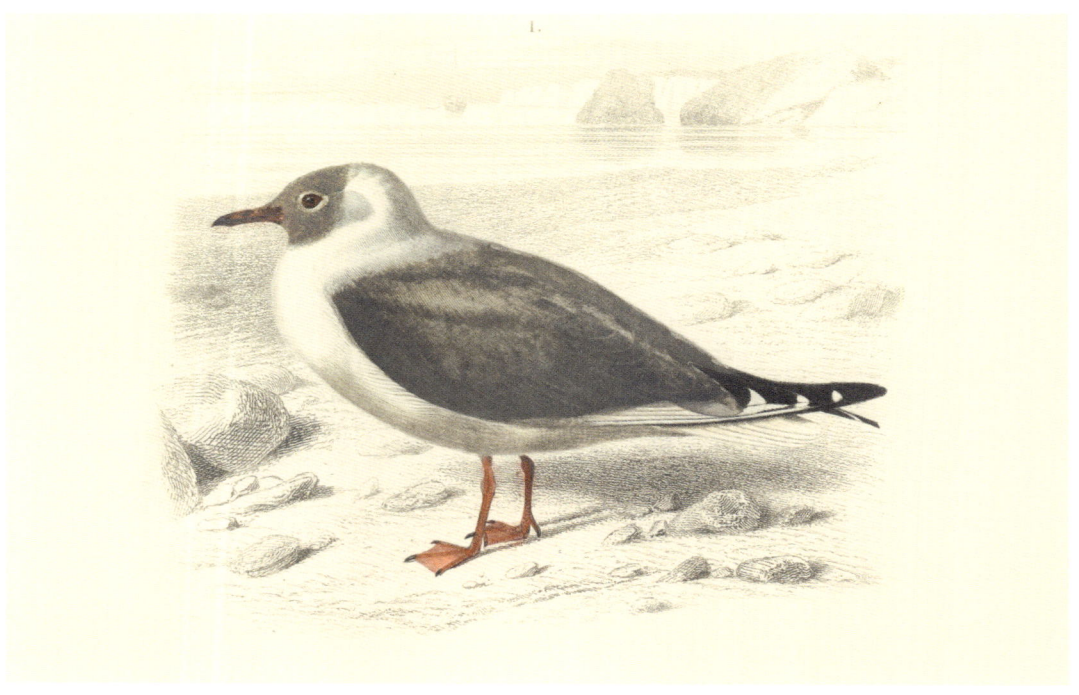

ANIMAL.
Charles d'Orbigny, *Dictionnaire universel d'histoire naturelle*, 1849. Broccoli Brown is visible on the head feathers of the black-headed gull.

VEGETABLE.
Johann Wilhelm Weinmann, *Phytanthoza iconographia*, 1737. Broccoli Brown is visible on the fruit of the *Commiphora*.*

MINERAL.
Leonard Spencer, *The World's Minerals*, 1916. Broccoli Brown is visible on the zircon (centre row, right). The zircon is embedded within a rock.

VEGETABLE.

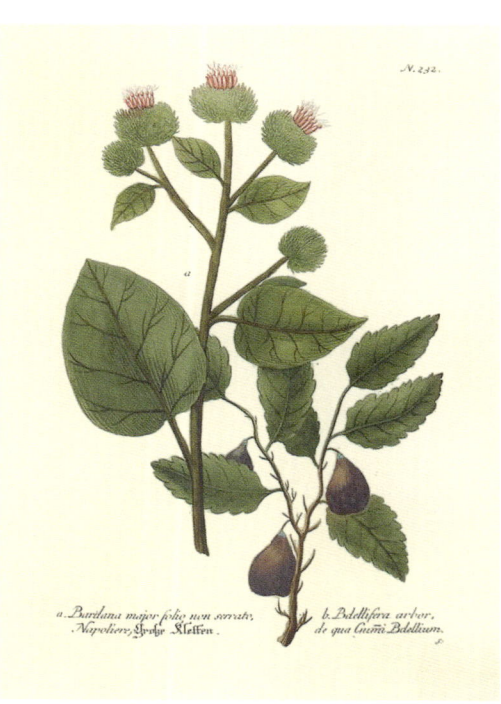

a. *Bardana major folio non serrato.* Napoliere, grobe Kletten.   b. *Bdellifera arbor, de qua Gumi Bdellium.*

MINERAL.

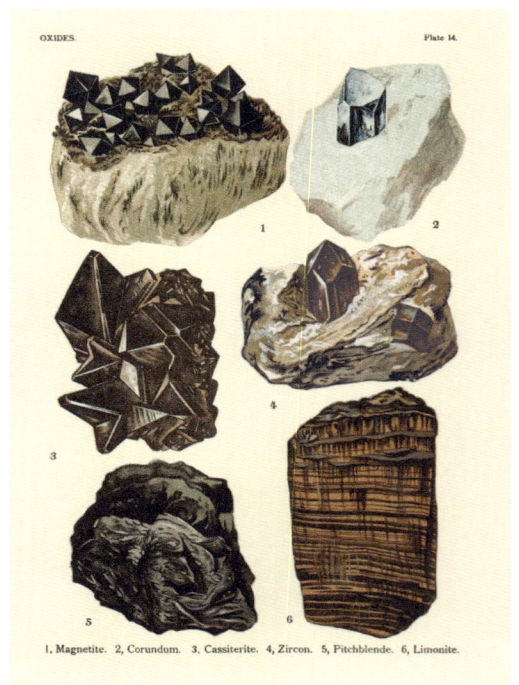

1. Magnetite.   2, Corundum.   3, Cassiterite.   4, Zircon.   5, Pitchblende.   6, Limonite.

109. OLIVE BROWN.

(i).   *Head and Neck of Male Kestril.*
         [*Common kestrel*; Falco tinnunculus]
(ii).   *Stems of Black Currant Bush.* [*Blackcurrant*; Ribes nigrum]
(iii).   *Axinite.* [*Silicate mineral*] *Rock Crystal.* [*Quartz*]

Olive Brown, is ash grey mixed with a little blue, red, and chesnut brown. [W]

ANIMAL.

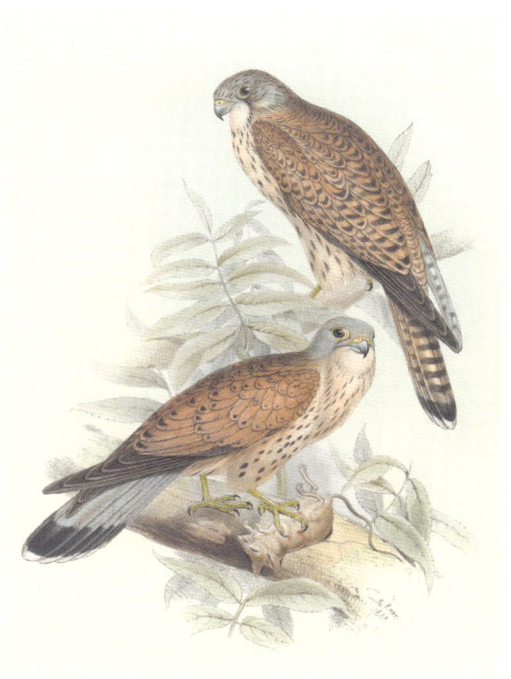

VEGETABLE.

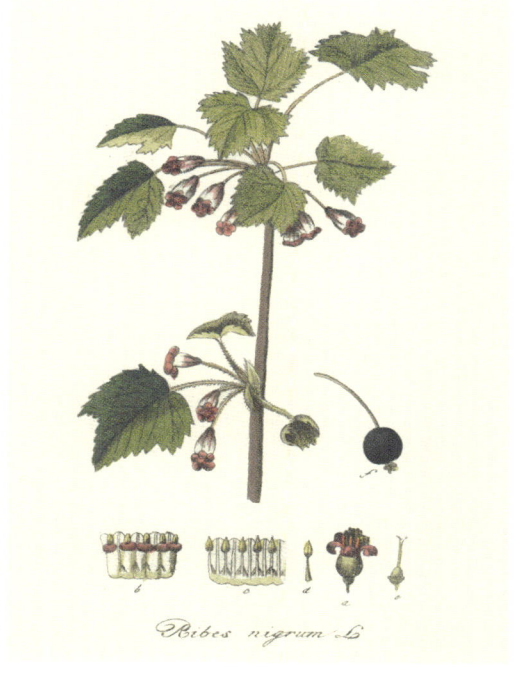

Ribes nigrum L.

MINERAL.

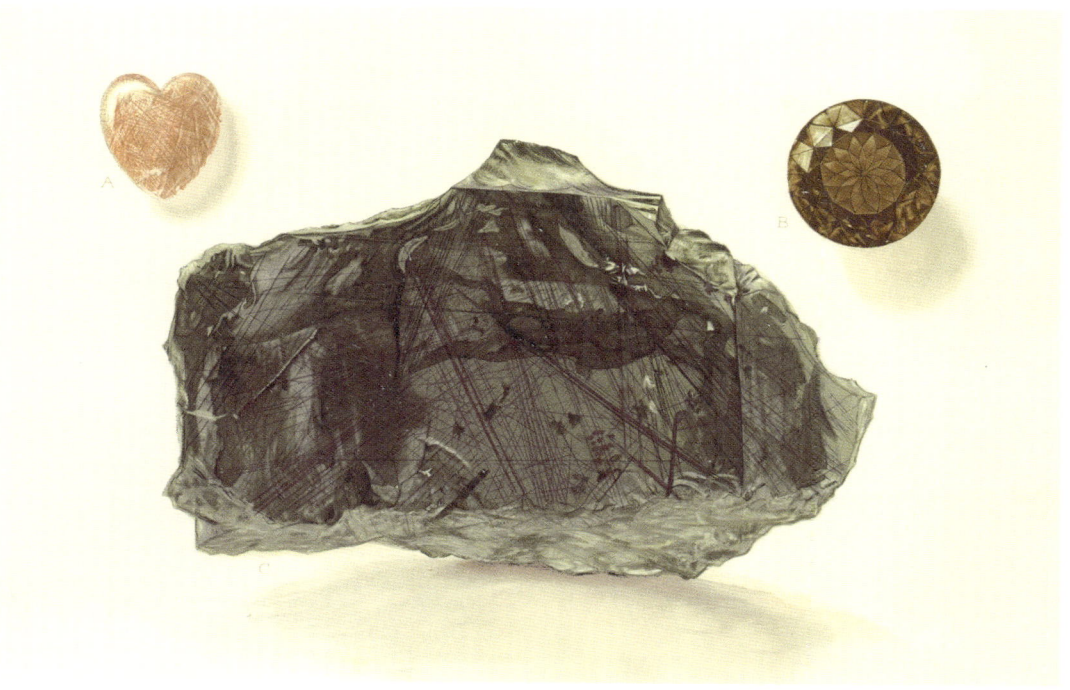

ANIMAL.
John Gould, *Birds of Europe*, Vol. 1, 1832–37.
Olive Brown is visible on the head and neck feathers of the common kestrel.

VEGETABLE.
J. Zorn and D. L. Oskamp, *Afbeeldingen der Artseny-gewassen*, 1796–1800.
Olive Brown is visible on the stem of the blackcurrant.

MINERAL.
George Frederick Kunz, *Gems and Precious Stones of North America*, 1890.
Olive Brown is visible on the axinite (bottom row).

110. BLACKISH BROWN.

(i).   *Stormy Petril.* [*Storm petrel*; Procellariiformes]
        Wing Coverts of black Cock. [*Black grouse*; Lyrurus tetrix]
        Forehead of Foumart. [*European polecat*; *Common ferret*; Mustela putorius]
(ii).   ——————
(iii).   *Mineral Pitch.* [*Asphalt*; *Bitumen*; Petroleum]

ANIMAL.

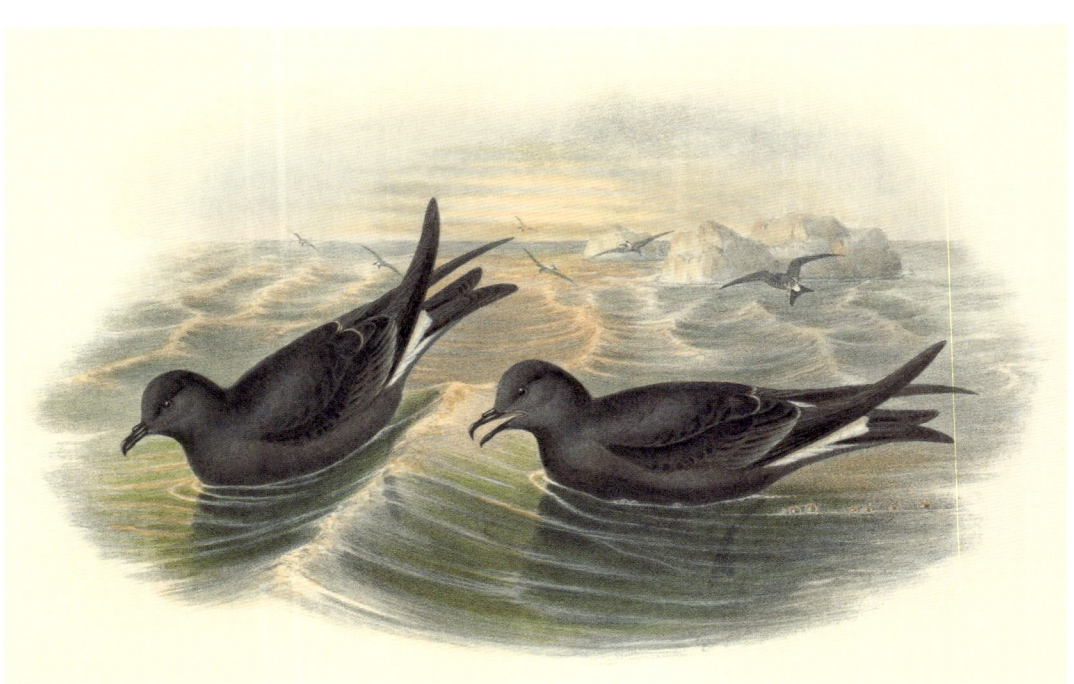

MINERAL.

Blackish Brown, is composed of chesnut brown and black. [W]

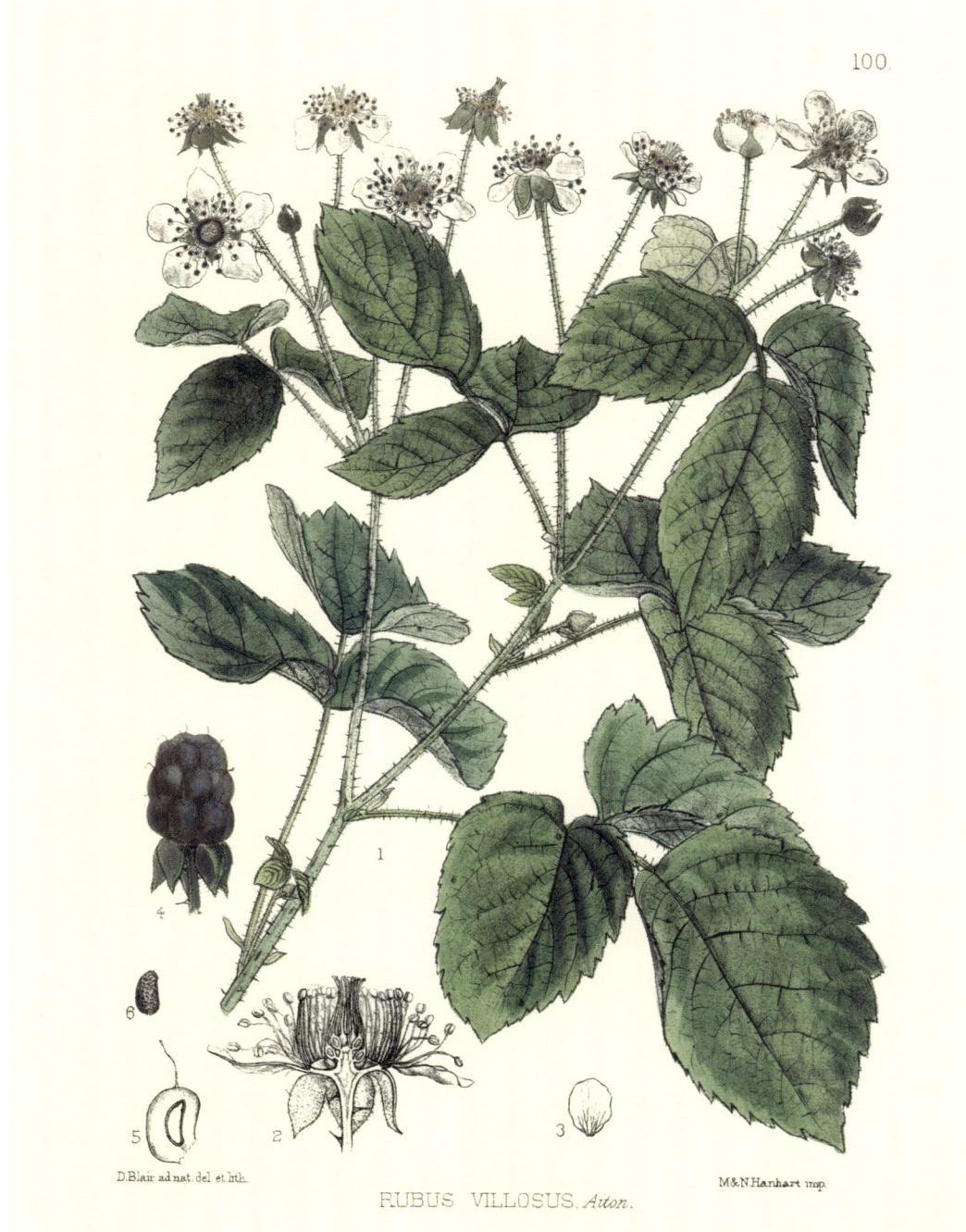

100.

1

4

6

5

2

3

D.Blair ad nat.del et lith.

RUBUS VILLOSUS, *Aiton.*

M&N.Hanhart imp.

ANIMAL.
John Gould, *Birds of Great Britain*, Vol. 5, 1862–73. Blackish Brown is visible on the feathers of the storm petrel.

VEGETABLE.
Robert Bentley and Henry Trimen, *Medicinal Plants*, 1880. Blackish Brown is visible on the skin of the blackberry.*

MINERAL.
Johann Gottlob Kurr, *The Mineral Kingdom*, 1859. Blackish Brown is visible on the pitch (bottom row, centre left).

No.	SYME'S COLOURS	CMYK	PANTONE	WINSOR & NEWTON	CARAN D'ACHE	LITTLE GREENE	FARROW & BALL
1		4-4-12-0	7527 U	Iridescent White	White	Loft White	Snow White
2		3-4-10-0	N/A	Flake White Hue	White	Flint	Pointing
3		5-4-10-0	COOL GRAY 1 U	Titanium White	Buff Titanium	Whitening	James White
4		4-4-13-0	7527 U	Iridescent White	Primerose	Slaked Lime	White Tie
5		3-4-12-0	N/A	Naples Yellow Light	Primerose	Stock	Orange Coloured White
6		5-4-12-0	7527 U	Iridescent White	Naples Ochre	Wood Ash	New White
7		6-5-12-0	7527 U	Zinc White	Primerose	Rolling Fog Pale	Skimmed Milk White
8		8-6-12-0	COOL GRAY 1 U	Iridescent White	Raw Umber 10%	French Grey Pale	School House White
9		15-11-16-2	2330 U	Silver	French Grey 10%	Bone China Blue Mid	Ash Grey
10		18-13-17-3	400 U	Pewter	French Grey 30%	Mono	Hardwick White
11		19-13-16-3	COOL GRAY 3 U	Davy's Gray	French Grey 10%	French Grey	Mizzle
12		20-15-17-4	420 U	Silver	Silver Grey	Gauze Dark	Purbeck Stone
13		19-16-31-7	4239 U	Davy's Gray	Olive Brown 10%	Portland Stone	French Gray
14		27-20-22-9	2331 U	Pewter	French Grey	Mid Lead Colour	Manor House Gray
15		33-24-30-16	415 U	Charcoal Grey	Raw Umber 50%	French Grey Dark	Treron
16		50-41-31-38	2334 U	Payne's Gray	Paynes Grey	Juniper Ash	Plummett
17		45-36-26-49	2336 U	Charcoal Grey	Graphite	Dolphin	Tanner's Brown
18		53-44-25-54	4287 U	Blue Black	Paynes Grey	Lamp Black	Railings
19		51-35-33-54	5463 U	Mars Black	Cassel Earth	Invisible Green	Off-black
20		51-44-29-57	4147 U	Perylene Black	Cassel Earth	Basalt	Paean Black
21		50-46-31-58	BLACK 5 U	Payne's Gray	Burnt Sienna	Chimney Black	Mahogany
22		64-50-29-69	BLACK 6 U	Ivory Black	Black	Basalt	Pitch Black
23		63-49-31-69	532 U	Lamp Black	Black	Chocolate Colour	Off-black
24		81-74-14-66	282 U	Blue Black	N/A	Thai Sapphire	Scotch Blue
25		91-82-9-58	280 U	Prussian Blue	Violet	Ultra Blue	N/A
26		57-42-8-22	4128 U	Indanthrene Blue	Prussian Blue	Mambo	Pitch Blue
27		74-68-9-37	2746 U	Ultramarine	Violet Brown	Purpleheart	N/A
28		52-39-9-20	7683 U	Prussian Blue	Phthalocyanine Blue	Mambo	Pitch Blue
29		50-31-2-5	285 U	Cerulean Blue	Prussian Blue	Sky Blue	Ultramarine Blue
30		43-27-6-7	2128 U	Ultramarine	Genuine Cobalt Blue	Tivoli	Cook's Blue
31		38-23-7-6	535 U	French Ultramarine	Light Cobalt Blue	Blue Verditer	Lulworth Blue
32		35-8-14-5	4170 U	Cobalt Turquoise Light	Light Malachite Green	Turquoise Blue	Arsenic
33		37-16-15-16	5493 U	Cobalt Green	Grey Blue	Celestial Blue	Green Blue
34		31-16-14-12	428 U	Viridian	Steel Grey	Grey Stone	Oval Room Blue
35		12-6-4-0	N/A	Manganese Blue	French Grey 10%	Bone China Blue Pale	Pale Powder
36		38-25-9-5	2115 U	French Ultramarine	Manganese Violet	Gauze Dark	N/A
37		73-67-15-40	7679 U	Mauve Blue Shade	Light Aubergine	Purpleheart	N/A
38		69-60-19-47	2765 U	Winsor Violet	Violet Brown	Purple Brown	Scotch Blue
39		49-40-9-9	272 U	Winsor Violet	Ultramarine Violet	Hortense	Pitch Blue
40		60-65-11-19	2370 U	Cobalt Violet	Violet	Purpleheart	N/A
41		59-65-17-38	2627 U	Permanent Mauve	Light Aubergine	Córdoba	Brinjal
42		67-64-15-36	2371 U	Winsor Violet	Violet Brown	N/A	Pelt
43		18-13-7-1	664 U	Mauve Blue Shade	Paynes Grey 30%	Gauze Mid	Calluna
44		41-32-20-17	5285 U	Mauve Blue Shade	Violet Grey	Arquerite	Brassica
45		62-51-20-36	2111 U	Winsor Violet	Sepia 50%	Juniper Ash	Imperial Purple
46		17-8-17-1	5595 U	Terre Verte	Light Malachite Green	Pearl Colour Mid	Green Ground
47		20-13-21-2	4288 U	Prussian Green	Olive Yellow	Portland Stone	Cooking Apple Green
48		27-18-25-6	COOL GRAY 5 U	Olive Green	Green Ochre	Pearl Colour Dark	Lichen
49		51-30-33-30	4198 U	Chrome Green Deep	Malachite Green	Livid	Studio Green
50		36-7-27-2	558 U	Permanent Green	Beryl Green	Green Verditer	Arsenic
51		23-11-16-2	441 U	Viridian	Steel Grey	Salix	Teresa's Green
52		27-7-34-2	4204 U	Prussian Green	Spring Green	Aquamarine	Breakfast Room Green
53		43-8-53-3	2255 U	Winsor Green	Cobalt Green	Spearmint	Emerald Green
54		36-22-55-19	5835 U	Olive Green	Moss Green	Citrine	Bancha
55		57-36-66-59	350 U	Prussian Green	Dark Sap Green	Olive Colour	Duck Green

No.	SYME'S COLOURS	CMYK	PANTONE	WINSOR & NEWTON	CARAN D'ACHE	LITTLE GREENE	FARROW & BALL
56		34-22-71-26	7748 U	Oxide of Chromium	Moss Green	Garden	Sap Green
57		31-19-63-17	5767 U	Sap Green	Olive Yellow	Boxington	Yeabridge Green
58		20-14-35-4	453 U	Olive Green	Raw Umber 10%	Kitchen Green	Green Ground
59		44-30-46-25	7735 U	Chrome Green Deep	Dark Sap Green	N/A	Green Smoke
60		23-26-61-19	5835 U	Olive Green	Green Ochre	Light Bronze Green	N/A
61		18-11-52-2	5865 U	Green Gold	Olive Yellow	Pale Lime	Breakfast Room Green
62		16-12-56-7	616 U	Green Gold	N/A	Oak Apple	N/A
63		8-8-30-1	468 U	Naples Yellow Light	Naples Ochre	Apple	Farrow's Cream
64		20-22-56-17	4505 U	Olive Green	Green Ochre	Light Bronze Green	Calke Green
65		11-14-48-6	4003 U	Cadmium Lemon	Yellow Ochre	Yellow-pink	Churlish Green
66		10-11-53-4	615 U	Winsor Yellow	Bismuth Yellow	Carys	Pale Hound
67		9-10-47-2	460 U	Transparent Yellow	Bismuth Yellow	Lemon Tree	Dayroom Yellow
68		13-25-67-13	4018 U	Green Gold	Raw Sienna	N/A	Sudbury Yellow
69		21-45-72-28	7574 U	Gold Ochre	Brown Ochre	Callaghan	India Yellow
70		22-33-69-24	7558 U	Yellow Ochre Pale	Green Ochre	Bath Stone	N/A
71		9-12-34-1	7500 U	Raw Umber Light	Naples Ochre	Ivory	House White
72		15-15-40-4	4545 U	Yellow Ochre Pale	Olive Brown 10%	Normandy Grey	Ball Green
73		9-13-37-2	7501 U	Raw Sienna	Naples Ochre	White Lead Dark	Dorset Cream
74		10-15-41-2	7402 U	Yellow Ochre	Naples Ochre	Woodbine	Yellow Ground
75		7-9-27-0	7500 U	Naples Yellow Light	Primerose	Custard	Pale Hound
76		14-30-70-3	7555 U	Yellow Ochre Light	Golden Bismuth	Mister David	Dutch Orange
77		13-25-58-0	156 U	Naples Yellow Deep	Yellow Ochre	Mortlake Yellow	Citron
78		16-42-75-5	7571 U	Raw Sienna	Raw Sienna	Yellow-pink	India Yellow
79		24-61-59-33	7587 U	Burnt Sienna	Burnt Sienna 50%	Tuscan Red	Preference Red
80		18-59-86-13	4013 U	Brown Ochre	Orange	Heat	Red Earth
81		17-53-60-20	7592 U	Transparent Maroon	Burnt Ochre	N/A	N/A
82		14-57-63-17	7585 U	Transparent Red Ochre	Burnt Ochre	Tuscan Red	Picture Gallery Red
83		18-62-67-27	7600 U	Indian Red	Perylene Brown	Bronze Red	Eating Room Red
84		14-78-65-25	2350 U	Scarlet Lake	Scarlet	Theatre Red	Incarnadine
85		15-71-62-23	7524 U	Transparent Red Ochre	Russet	N/A	Blazer
86		14-55-54-14	7619 U	Winsor Red	Burnt Ochre 50%	Orange Aurora	Red Earth
87		20-97-50-55	4102 U	Permanent Magenta	Crimson Aubergine	Baked Cherry	Radicchio
88		10-20-32-2	4675 U	Transparent Red Ochre	Brown Ochre 10%	Creamerie	Setting Plaster
89		9-12-19-0	7604 U	Rose Dore	Primerose	Julie's Dream	Tallow
90		9-16-18-0	7611 U	Rose Madder Genuine	Burnt ochre 10%	Pink Slip	Pink Ground
91		15-68-27-15	233 U	Permanent Carmine	Crimson Alizarine	Carmine	Rangwali
92		23-73-17-19	2062 U	Magenta	Purplish Red	Mischief	Lake Red
93		24-48-27-4	4036 U	Purple Lake	Sepia 10%	Dorchester Pink	Crimson Red
94		50-82-25-47	2355 U	Permanent Mauve	Crimson Aubergine	Adventurer	N/A
95		36-62-40-40	696 U	Purple Lake	Sepia 50%	Blush	Brinjal
96		60-61-39-61	2478 U	Purple Madder	Cassel Earth	Purple Brown	Paean Black
97		35-40-33-22	437 U	Permanent Mauve	Sepia 10%	Dolphin	Sulking Room Pink
98		53-61-42-58	2478 U	Raw Umber	Cassel Earth	Toad	Pelt
99		35-65-50-51	4056 U	Brown Madder	Burnt Sienna	Spanish Brown	Mahogany
100		28-62-57-40	499 U	Vandyke Brown	Burnt Ochre	Callaghan	Picture Gallery Red
101		42-64-44-53	4104 U	Mars Violet Deep	Burnt Sienna	Spanish Brown	Deep Reddish Brown
102		47-56-45-55	BLACK 5 U	Burnt Umber	Brown Ochre	Felt	Tanner's Brown
103		33-57-53-42	7603 U	Brown Madder	Brown Ochre	N/A	N/A
104		27-44-60-29	2317 U	Raw Umber	Green Ochre	Stone-dark-warm	London Stone
105		19-28-47-11	4249 U	Raw Umber Light	Olive Brown 10%	Stock Dark	Dead Salmon
106		49-54-47-56	412 U	Davy's Grey	Raw Umber	Chimney Brick	Salon Drab
107		33-35-49-25	4242 U	Raw Umber (Green)	Raw Umber	Grey Moss	Pigeon
108		30-33-42-18	7529 U	Raw Umber (Green)	Olive Brown 50%	Silt	Broccoli Brown
109		38-44-44-35	411 U	Davy's Grey	Sepia	Felt	Charleston Gray
110		55-52-46-58	412 U	Charcoal Grey	Cassel Earth	Attic II	Off-Black

INTRODUCTION.

—Aikin, A., 1815. *A Manual of Mineralogy. First American Edition* (Philadelphia: Solomon W. Conrad)
—Curry, W. (Jun.), 1834. *The Dublin University Magazine: A Literary and Political Journal* (Dublin: William Curry, Jun. and Company)
—Darwin, C. R., 1845. *Journal of Researches into the Natural History and Geology of the Countries Visited During the Voyage of H.M.S. Beagle Round the World under the Command of Captain Fitz Roy, R.N.* 2nd ed. (London: John Murray)
—Darwin, C. R., 1985. *The Correspondence of Charles Darwin, Volume 5: 1851–1855.* Edited by F. Burkhardt (Cambridge: Cambridge University Press)
—Darwin, C. R., 2016. *The Works of Charles Darwin,* P. H. Barrett and R. B. Freeman (eds), Vol. 3, *Journal of Researches,* Part 2 (London: Routledge)
—Emmerling, L. A., 1793–97. *Lehrbuch der Mineralogie,* 3 vols (Giessen: Georg Friedrich Hayer)
—Estner, F. J. A., 1794. *Versuch einer Mineralogie: für Anfänger und Liebhaber: Nach des herrn Bergcommissionsraths Werner's Methode* (Vienna: J. Georg Oehler)
—Eyssvogel, F. G., 1756. *Neu-Eröffnetes Magazin, Bestehend in einer Versammlung allerhand raren Künsten und besonderen Wissenschafften, Durch welche sich Alle Arten der Künstler sehr grossen Nutzen schaffen können* (Bamberg: Martin Göbhardt)
—Hamm, E. P., 2001. 'Unpacking Goethe's collections: the public and the private in natural-historical collecting', *The British Journal for the History of Science* 34, 275–300.
—Hartley, S. D., 2001. *Robert Jameson, Geology and Polite Culture, 1796–1826: Natural Knowledge Enquiry and Civic Sensibility in Late Enlightenment Scotland* (PhD: The University of Edinburgh)
—Jameson, L., 1854. 'Biographical memoir of the late Professor Jameson', *Edinburgh New Philosophical Journal* 57, 1–49
—Jameson, R., 1804. *Tabular View of the External Characters of Minerals for the Use of Students of Oryctognosy*
—Jameson, R., 1805. *A Treatise on the External Characters of Minerals* (Edinburgh: Bell & Bradfute)
—Jameson, R., 1811. 'On Colouring Geognostical Maps', *Memoirs of the Wernerian Natural History Society. Vol. I. For the years 1808,-9,-10* (Edinburgh: Bell & Bradfute), 149–61
—Jameson, R., 1816. *A Treatise on the External, Chemical, and Physical Characters of Minerals,* 2nd ed. (Edinburgh: Archibald Constable & Co.)
—Jameson, R., 1821. *Manual of Mineralogy: Containing an Account of Simple Minerals and also a Description and Arrangement of Mountain Rocks* (Edinburgh: Archibald Constable & Co.)
—Kirwan, R., 1794 [1784]. *Elements of Mineralogy,* 2nd ed. (London: P. Elmsly)
—Latreille, P. A., 1803–4. *Histoire naturelle, générale et particulière des crustacés et des insectes,* Vol. 1 (Paris: F. Dufart)
—Lenz, J. G., 1799 [1791]. *Mineralogisches Handbuch durch weitere Ausführung des Wernerschen Systems,* 3rd ed. (Hildsburghausen: Johann Gottfried Hanisch)

—Lenz, J. G., 1793. *Grundriss der Mineralogie, nach dem neuesten Wernerschen System* (Hildsburghausen: Johann Gottfried Hanisch)
—Lenz, J. G., 1794. *Mustertafeln der bis Jetzt Bekannten Einfachen Mineralien.* (Jena: Losten des Verfassers)
—Lenz, J. G., 1798. *Mineralogisches Taschenbuch für Anfänger und Liebhaber,* Vol. 1 (Erfurt: Henningschen Buchhandlung)
—Lenz, J. G., 1800. *System der äusseren Kennzeichen der Mineralien in deutscher, lateinischer, italienischer, französischer, dänischer und ungarischer Sprache, mit erläuternden Anmerkungen* (Bamburg and Würzburg: Tobias Göbhard)
—Lenz, J. G., 1806. *Tabellen über das gesammte Mineralreich* (Jena: Göpferdt)
—Lenz, J. G., 1819. *Die Metalle: ein Handbuch für Freunde der Mineralogie. Platin, Gold, Quecksilber, Silber und Kupferordnung,* Vol. 1 (Giessen: C. G. Müller)
—Lenz, J. G., 1822. *Handbuch der vergleichenden Mineralogie: ein tabellarisches Hülfsbuch zur alsbaldigen Auffindung und Bestimmung der Mineralien.* Vol. 1 (Giessen: C. G. Müller)
—Lewis, D., 2012. *The Feathery Tribe. Robert Ridgway and the Modern Study of Birds* (New Haven: Yale University Press)
—Linnaeus, C., 1735. *Systema naturae, sive Regna tria naturae systematice proposita per classes, ordines, genera, & species,* 1st ed. (Leiden: Theodorum Haak)
—Ludwig, C. F., 1803–4. *Handbuch der Mineralogie nach A. G. Werner,* 2 vols (Leipzig: Siegfried Lebrecht Crusius)
—Mawe, J., 1813. *A Treatise on Diamonds and Precious Stones* (London: Longman, Hurst, Rees, Orme and Brown)
—Morrell, J. B., 1972. 'Science and Scottish University reform: Edinburgh in 1826', *The British Journal for the History of Science* 6, 39–56
—Picardet [Guyton de Morveau], C., 1790. *Traité des caractères extérieurs des fossiles* (Dijon: L.-N. Frantin)
—Rees, A., 1819. *The Cyclopædia; Or, Universal Dictionary of Arts, Sciences, and Literature,* Vol. 38 (London: Longman, Hurst, Rees, Orme and Brown)
—Ridgway, R., 1886. *A Nomenclature of Colors for Naturalists, and Compendium of Useful Knowledge for Ornithologists* (Boston: Little, Brown, and Company)
—Ridgway, R., 1912. *Color Standards and Color Nomenclature* (Washington, DC: The author)
—Saccardo, P. A., 1891. *Chromotaxia seu Nomenclator colorum polyglottus additis speciminibus coloratis ad usum botanicorum et zoologorum* (Padua: Typis seminarii)
—Schäffer, J. C., 1769. *Entwurf einer allgemeinen Farbenverein, oder Versuch und Muster einer gemein-nützlichen Bestimmung und Benennung der Farben* (Regensburg: Emanuel Adam Weiss)
—Secord, J. A., 1991(a). 'Edinburgh Lamarckians: Robert Jameson and Robert E. Grant', *Journal of the History of Biology* 24, 1–18
—Secord, J. A., 1991(b). 'The discovery of a vocation: Darwin's early geology', *The British Journal for the History of Science* 24, 133–57
—Simonini, G., 2018. 'Organising colours:

Patrick Syme's colour chart and nomenclature for scientific purposes', *XVII-XVIII. Revue de la Société d'études anglo-américaines des XVIIe et XVIIIe siècles,* 75, 1–25
—Sowerby, J., 1804–17. *British Mineralogy: or, Coloured Figures Intended to Elucidate the Mineralogy of Great Britain,* 5 vols (London: R. Taylor and Co.)
—Sowerby, J., 1811. *Exotic Mineralogy: or, Coloured Figures of Foreign Minerals, as a Supplement to British Mineralogy* (London: Benjamin Meredith)
—Struve, H., 1797. *Méthode analytique des fossiles, fondée sur leurs caractères extérieur* (Paris: C. Pougens)
—Syme, P., 1814. *Werner's Nomenclature of Colours: with additions, arranged so as to render it highly useful to the arts and sciences, particularly zoology, botany, chemistry, mineralogy, and morbid anatomy. Annexed to which are examples selected from well-known objects in the animal, vegetable, and mineral kingdoms* (Edinburgh: William Blackwood and T. Cadell); 2nd ed., 1821
—Weaver, T., 1805. *A Treatise on the External Characters of Fossils, translated from the German of Abraham Gottlob Werner* (Dublin: M. N. Mahon)
—Werner, A. G., 1774. *Von den äusserlichen Kennzeichen der Fossilien.* (Leipzig: Siegfried Lebrecht Crusius)
—Widenmann, J. F. W., 1794. *Handbuch des oryktognostischen Theils der Mineralogie* (Leipzig: Siegfried Lebrecht Crusius)
—Wilkinson, J. G., 1858. *On Colour and on the Necessity for a General Diffusion of Taste Among All Classes* (London: John Murray)
—Zappe, J. M. R., 1804. *Mineralogisches Handlexicon* (Vienna: Anton Doll)

WERNER'S MINERALOGICAL SYSTEM.

—Agricola, G., 1556 (1950). *De re Metallica* (translated from the first Latin Edition of 1556 by H. C. Hoover in 1950) (New York: Dover Publications)
—Allan, R., 1834. *A Manual of Mineralogy Comprehending the More Recent Discoveries in the Mineral Kingdom* (Edinburgh: Adam and Charles Black)
—Bomare, J.- C. V. de, 1762. *Minéralogie, ou nouvelle exposition du règne mineral* (Paris: Vincent)
—Cronstedt, A. F., 1770. *An Essay Towards a System of Mineralogy* (translated by Gustav von Engestrom, revised by Emanuel Mendes da Costa) (London: Edward and Charles Dilly)
—Dana, J. D., 1837. *A System of Mineralogy: Including an Extended Treatise on Crystallography* (New Haven: Durrie & Peck and Herrick & Noyes)
—Dixon, L., 2014. 'Syme, Patrick (1774–1845), flower painter', *Oxford Dictionary of National Biography* (online edition)
—Eddy, M. D., 2002. 'Scottish chemistry, classification and the early mineralogical career of the "ingenious" Rev. Dr John Walker (1746 to 1779)', *British Journal for the History of Science* 35, 411–38
—Gehler, J. K., 1757. *De characteribus fossilium externis* (Leipzig: Officina Langenhemiana)
—Hübner, J., 1736. *Curieuses und Reales Natur- Kunst- Berg- Gewerck- und Handlungs-Lexicon,* 7th ed. (Leipzig: Gleditsch)

—Jameson, R., 1804. *System of Mineralogy,* Vol. 1 (Edinburgh: Archibald Constable and Co.)
—Jameson, R., 1805. *System of Mineralogy,* Vol. 2 (Edinburgh: Bell & Bradfute)
—Jameson, R., 1805. *See Introduction*
—Jameson, R., 1808. *System of Mineralogy,* Vol. 3 (Edinburgh: William Blackwood)
—Jameson, R., 1820. *A System of Mineralogy, in which Minerals are Arranged According to the Natural History Method,* Vol. 1 (Edinburgh: Archibald Constable & Co.)
—Kazmer, M., 2002. 'Werner's first translator: Ferenc Benkő, Hungarian priest, mineralogist, professor', in Albrecht, H. and Ladwig, R. (eds), *Abraham Gottlob Werner and the Foundation of the Geological Sciences* (Freiburger Forschungshefte D 207, Verlag der Technischen Universität Bergakademie Freiberg), 161–71
—Laudan, R., 1987. *From Mineralogy to Geology: The Foundations of a Science 1650–1830* (Chicago: University of Chicago Press)
—Linnaeus, C., 1735. *See Introduction*
—Memoirs of the Wernerian Natural History Society, Vol. I, for the years 1808,-9,-10, 1811 (Edinburgh: Bell & Bradfute)
—Mohs, F., 1825. *Treatise on Mineralogy, or the Natural History of the Mineral Kingdom,* Vol. 1 (translated by Wilhelm Haidinger) (Edinburgh: Archibald Constable)
—Nicol, J., 1849. *Manual of Mineralogy, or the Natural History of the Mineral Kingdom* (Edinburgh: Adam and Charles Black)
—Simonini, G., 2018. *See Introduction*
—Sweet, J. M., 1976. *The Wernerian Theory of the Neptunian Origin of Rocks* (New York: Hafner Press)
—Syme, P., 1814. *See Introduction*
—Weaver, T., 1805. *See Introduction*
—Werner, A. G., 1774. *See Introduction*
—Werner, A. G., 1791. *Ausführliches und systematisches Verzeichnis des Mineralien-kabinets des weiland kurfürstlich, sächsischen Berghauptmans Hernn Karl Eugen Pabst von Ohain* (Leipzig and Annaberg: Grazischen Buchhandlung)
—Zeisig, J. C. (Minerophilus or Minerophilo Freibergensi), 1730. *Neues und wohleingerichtetes Mineral- und Bergwercks-Lexikon* (New Mining Lexicon) (Chemnitz: Johann Christoph and Johann David Stösseln)

COLOURS IN ZOOLOGY.

—Baird, S. F., Brewer, T. M. and Ridgway, R., 1905. *A History of North American Birds* (Boston: Little, Brown, and Company)
—Barlow, N. (ed.), 1967. *Darwin and Henslow. The Growth of an Idea* (London: Bentham-Moxon Trust, John Murray)
—Buffon, Comte de, 1770. *Histoire naturelle des oiseaux. Tome 1* (Paris: L'Imprimerie Royale)
—Darwin, C. R., 'Books to be read' and 'Books Read' notebook. (1838–51) CUL-DAR119. Transcribed by Kees Rookmaaker. Darwin Online, http://darwin-online.org.uk/
—Darwin Correspondence Project, 'Letter no. 178', Darwin, C., to J. S. Henslow [23 July –] 15 August [1832],

https://www.darwinproject.ac.uk/letter/DCP-LETT-178.xml
— Darwin Correspondence Project, 'Letter no. 192', Darwin, C., to J. S. Henslow [*c.* 26 October–] 24 November [1832], https://www.darwinproject.ac.uk/letter/DCP-LETT-192.xml
— Darwin Correspondence Project, 'Letter no. 2743', Darwin, C. to Asa Gray, 3 April [1860], https://www.darwinproject.ac.uk/letter/DCP-LETT-2743.xml
— Harris, M., 1775. *The English Lepidoptera, or the Aurelian's Pocket Companion…* (London: Printed for J. Robson)
— Harris, M., 1776. *An Exposition of English Insects* (London: Printed for the author by Messrs. Robson and Dilly)
— Jones, W. J., 2013. *German Colour Terms: A Study in Their Evolution from Earliest Times to the Present* (Amsterdam/Philadelphia: John Benjamins)
— Keynes, R. (ed.), 2000. *Charles Darwin's Zoology Notes & Specimen Lists from H.M.S. Beagle* (Cambridge: Cambridge University Press)
— Linnaeus, C., 1758. *Systema naturae…*, 10th ed. (Stockholm: Laurentii Salvii)
— Lyon, J., 1976. 'The "Initial Discourse" to Buffon's *Histoire naturelle*: the first complete English translation', *Journal of the History of Biology* 9, 133–81
— Parry, W. E. (ed.), 1825. *Appendix to Captain Parry's Journal of a Second Voyage for the Discovery of a North-west Passage…* (London: John Murray)
— Richardson, J., 1829–37. *Fauna Boreali-Americana; or the Zoology of the Northern Parts of British America* (London: John Murray)
— Ridgway, R., 1886. *See Introduction*
— Ridgway, R., 1890. 'Scientific results of explorations by the U.S. Fish Commission Steamer *Albatross*. No. I. Birds collected on the Galapagos Islands in 1888', in *Proceedings of the United States National Museum*, Vol. XII, 101–28 (Washington, DC: Government Printing Office)
— Ridgway, R., 1912. *Color Standards and Color Nomenclature* (Washington, DC: The author)
— Rutherford, H. W., 1908. *Catalogue of the library of Charles Darwin now in the Botany School, Cambridge … with an Introduction by Francis Darwin* (Cambridge: Cambridge University Press)
— Shaw, G., 1794. *Zoology of New Holland* (London: John Sowerby; printed by J. Davis)
— Sowerby, J., 1809. *A New Elucidation of Colours, Original Prismatic, and Material* (London: Richard Taylor)
— van Wyhe, J. (ed.), 2002–. *The Complete Work of Charles Darwin Online* (http://darwin-online.org.uk)

SYME'S COLOUR CHART IN BOTANY.

— Barton, W. P. C., 1823. *A Flora of North America Illustrated by Coloured Figures Drawn from Nature*, Vol. III (Philadelphia: H. C. Carey and I. Lea)
— Bénezit, E.-C., 2011. 'Patrick Syme', in *Benezit Dictionary of Artists*, online ed.
— Blunt, W. and Stearn, W. T., 1995. *The Art of Botanical Illustration*, new ed. (Woodbridge: Antique Collector's Club)
— Brown, G. [Brookshaw, G.], 1797. *A New Treatise on Flower Painting: Containing the Most Familiar and Easy Instructions; with Directions How to Mix the Various Tints, and Obtain a Complete Knowledge by Practice Alone* (London: Printed for the author)
— Dauthenay, H. and Oberthür, R., 1905. *Répertoire de couleurs pour aider à la détermination des couleurs des fleurs, des feuillages et des fruits. Publié par la Société française des chrysanthémistes…* (Paris: for La Société française des chrysanthémistes)
— Dixon, L., 2014. *See Werner's Mineralogical System*
— Edwards, S. T. and Lindley, J., 1819. *The Botanical Register: Consisting of Coloured Figures of Exotic Plants Cultivated in British Gardens with Their History and Mode of Treatment*, Vol. V (London: Printed for James Ridgway)
— Estner, F. J. A., 1794. *See Introduction*
— Forbes, J. D., 1849. 'Hints towards a classification of colours', *Philosophical Magazine*, Third Series, 34, 161–78
— Forster, T., 1813. 'On a systematic arrangement of colours', *The Philosophical Magazine* 42, 119–21
— Galton, F., 1887. 'Notes on permanent colour types in mosaic', *Journal of the Anthropological Institute* 16, 145–47
— Gerhard, W., 1834. *Zur Geschichte, Cultur und Classification der Georginen oder Dahlie* (Leipzig: Baumgärtner)
— Halsby, J. and Harris, P., 2001. *The Dictionary of Scottish Painters: 1600 to the Present*, 3rd ed. (Edinburgh: Canongate)
— Hooker, W. J., 1834. *Supplement to the English Botany of the Late Sir J. E. Smith and Mr. Sowerby: The Descriptions, Synonyms, and Places of Growth*, Vol. II (London: C. E. Sowerby)
— Jameson, R., 1804. *See Werner's Mineralogical System*
— Jameson, R., 1805. *See Introduction*
— Lack, H.-W., 2015. *The Bauers: Joseph, Franz & Ferdinand. Masters of Botanical Illustration. An Illustrated Biography* (Munich: Prestel)
— Lack, H.-W. and Ibáñez, M. V., 1997. 'Recording colour in late eighteenth century botanical drawings: Sydney Parkinson, Ferdinand Bauer and Thaddäus Haenke', *Curtis's Botanical Magazine* 14, 87–100
— Linnaeus, C., 1751. *Philosophia Botanica in qua explicantur fundamenta botanica cum definitionibus partium, exemplis terminorum, observationibus rariorum, adjectis figuris aeneis* (Stockholm: Gottfried Kiesewetter)
— Linnaeus, C. and Freer, S., 2005. *Linnaeus' Philosophia Botanica*. 2nd ed. (Oxford: Oxford University Press)
— Mabberley, D. J., 2017. *Painting by Numbers: The Life and Art of Ferdinand Bauer* (Sydney: New South Publishing)
— McEwan, P. J. M., 1994. *Dictionary of Scottish Art & Architecture* (Woodbridge: Antique Collectors' Club)
— Mathews, F. S., 1895. 'A chart of correct colors of flowers Arranged by F. Schuyler Mathews for the use of Florists', *American Florist* 11, 34
— Mérimée, J.-F. L., 1815. 'Mémoire sur les lois générales de la coloration appliquées à la formation d'une échelle chromatique, à l'usage des naturalistes', in C. F. Brisseau de Mirbel, *Élémens de Physiologie végétale et de Botanique*, Vol. 2 (Paris: Magimel), 909–24
— Parry, W. E. (ed.), 1825. *See Colours in Zoology*
— Pretty, E., 1810. *A Practical Essay on Flower Painting in Water Colours* (London: S. and J. Fuller)
— Ragonot-Godefroy [P. B.?], 1842. *Traité sur la culture des œillets; suivie d'une nouvelle classification pouvant aussi s'appliquer aux genres rosier, dahlia, chrysanthème, et a tous ceux qui sont nombreux en variétés* (Paris: Audot)
— Ridgway, R., 1886. *See Introduction*
— Saccardo, P. A., 1891. *See Introduction*
— Simonini, G., 2018. *See Introduction*
— Sinclair, G., 1825. *Hortus ericæus woburnensis: Or, A Catalogue of Heaths in the Collection of the Duke of Bedford, at Woburn Abbey. Alphabetically and Systematically Arranged.* (London: J. Moyes)
— Sowerby, J., 1788. *An Easy Introduction to Drawing Flowers According to Nature* (London: The Author)
— Sowerby, J., 1809. *See Colours in Zoology*
— Syme, P., 1810. *Practical Directions for Learning Flower-Drawing. Illustrated by Coloured Drawings* (Edinburgh: Printed for the Author by George Ramsay & Company)
— Syme, P., 1814. *See Introduction*
— Tkach, N., Heuchert, B., Krüger, C., Heklau, H., Marx, D., Braun, U., and Röser, M., 2016. 'Type material in the herbarium of the Martin Luther University Halle-Wittenberg of species based on collections from Alexander von Humboldt's American expedition between 1799 and 1804 in its historical context', *Schlechtendalia* 29, 1–107
— Wachsmuth, B., 2014. 'Farbentafeln für Gärtner und Pflanzenfreunde', *Zandera* 29, 70–89
— Wagenbreth, O., 1967. 'Werner-Schüler als Geologen und Bergleute und ihre Bedeutung für die Geologie und den Bergbau des 19. Jahrhunderts' in Rösler, H. J. (ed.), Über die Entwicklung der Mineralsystematik in der ersten Hälfte des 19. Jahrhunderts durch die Schüller A. G. Werners, Freiberger Forschungshefte. C 223: Mineralogie-Lagerstättenlehre (Leipzig: VEB Deutscher Verlag für Grundstoffindustrie), 163–78
— Wagenitz, G. and Lack, H.-W., 2012. 'Carl Ludwig Willdenow (1765–1812), ein Botanikerleben in Briefen', *Annals of the History and Philosophy of Biology* (formerly *Jahrbuch für Geschichte und Theorie der Biologie*) 17, 1–289
— Werner, A. G., 1774. *See Introduction*
— Willdenow, C. L., 1792. *Grundriss der Kräuterkunde zu Vorlesungen entworfen* (Berlin: Haude und Spener)
— Willdenow, C. L., 1805. *The Principles of Botany, and of Vegetable Physiology* (Edinburgh: William Blackwood)
— Wood, L., 1991. 'George Brookshaw: the case of the vanishing cabinet-maker I', *Apollo* 133, 301–6

ONE FOR ALL?

— Anonymous, 1794. *Wiener Farben-kabinet; oder vollständiges Musterbuch aller Natur-, Grund- und Zusammen-setzungsfarben mit 5000 nach der Natur gemalten Abbildungen und der Bestimmung des Namens einer jeden Farbe, dann einer ausführlichen Beschreibung aller Farbengeheimnisse* (Vienna and Prague: Schönfeld)
— Breidbach, O. and Karliczek, A., 2011. 'Himmelblau – das Cyanometer des Horace-Bénédict de Saussure (1740–1799)', *Sudhoffs Archiv. Zeitschrift für Wissenschaftsgeschichte* 95, 3–29
— Broca, P., 1865. *Instructions générales pour les recherches et observations anthropologiques (anatomie et physiologie)* (Paris: Victor Masson et Fils)
— Eichhorn, H., 1827. 'Allgemeine Bemerkungen über die Terminologie der Hautkrankheiten', *Archiv für medizinische Erfahrungen im Gebiete der praktischen Medizin, Chirurgie, Geburtshülfe und Staatsarzneikunde* 50, 432–77
— Engel, A., 2009. *Farben der Globalisierung. Die Entstehung moderner Märkte für Farbstoffe 1500–1900* (Frankfurt am Main: Campus-Verlag)
— Gerabek, W. E., Haage, B. D., Keil, G. and Wegner, W. (eds), 2007. *Enzyklopädie Medizingeschichte* (Berlin: Walter De Gruyter)
— Gordon, J., 1817. *Observations on the Structure of the Brain, Comprising an Estimate of the Claims of Drs. Gall and Spurzheim to Discovery in the Anatomy of that Organ* (Edinburgh: William Blackwood)
— Grimm, M., Kleine-Tebbe, C. and Stijnman, A., 2011. *Lichtspiel und Farbenpracht: Entwicklungen des Farbdrucks 1500–1800; aus den Beständen der Herzog-August-Bibliothek; [Ausstellung der Herzog-August-Bibiothek Wolfenbüttel … vom 11. März bis 28. August 2011]* (Wiesbaden: Harrassowitz)
— Hunter, J. 1841. 'On the changes in the colour of the iris produced by inflammation', *Edinburgh Monthly Journal of Medical Science*, February, 79–84
— Karliczek, A., 2013a. 'Die Bemessung des Himmels: Das Cyanometer des Horace-Bénédicte de Saussure', in Breidbach, O. (ed.), *Über die Natur des Lichts* (Wiederstedt: Novalis Museum), 49–60
— Karliczek, A., 2013b. 'Vom Phänomen zum Merkmal: Farben in der Natur-geschichte um 1800', in Vogt, M. and Karliczek, A. (eds), *Erkenntniswert Farbe* (Jena: Ernst-Haeckel-Haus), 83–111
— Karliczek, A., 2014. *Modelle des Lebendigen: Interaktionen von Physiologie, Biologie und Pathologie von Boerhaave bis Meckel* (Jena: SALANA)
— Karliczek, A., 2016. 'Natur der Farben – Farben der Natur: Die Eigenschaft Farbe zwischen natürlicher Ordnung, Naturbeschreibung und Natur-erkenntnis um 1800', in Dönike, M., Müller-Tamm, J. and Steinle, F. (eds), *Die Farben der Klassik* (Göttingen: Wallstein Verlag), 173–204
— Karliczek, A., 2018. 'Zur Herausbildung von Farbstandards in den frühen Wissenschaften des 18. Jahrhunderts', *Ferrum. Nachrichten aus der Eisenbibliothek* 90, 36–49
— Karliczek, A. and Schwarz, A., (eds), 2016. *Farre. Farbstandards in den frühen Wissenschaften* (Jena: SALANA)
— Kuehni, R. G. and Schwarz, A., 2008. *Color Ordered. A Survey of Color Order Systems from Antiquity to the Present* (Oxford and New York: Oxford University Press)
— Kusukawa, S., 2015. 'Richard Waller's Table of Colours (1686)', in Bushart, M. and Steinle, F. (eds), *Colour Histories: Science, Art, and Technology in the 17th and 18th Centuries* (Berlin and Boston: De Gruyter), 3–21
— Linnaeus, C., 1735. *See Introduction*
— Prange, C. F., 1782. *Farbenlexicon: Worinn die möglichsten Farben der Natur nicht nur nach ihren Eigen-schaften, Benennungen, Verhältnissen und Zusammensetzungen sondern auch durch die wirkliche Ausmahlung enthalten sind; Zum Gebrauch für Naturforscher, Mahler, Fabrikanten, Künstler und übrigen Handwerker, welche mit Farben umgehen* (Halle: Hendel)
— Prout, W., 1819. 'Description of a urinary calculus, composed of the lithate or urate of Ammonia', *Medico-chirurgical Transactions* 10, 389–95
— Radde, O., 1877. *Raddes Internationale Farbenskala: 42 Gammen mit circa 900 Tönen* (Hamburg: Verlag der Stenochromatischen)
— Schäffer, J. C., 1769. *See Introduction*
— Simonini, G., 2018. *See Introduction*
— Spillmann, W. (ed.), 2009. *Farb-Systeme 1611–2007. Farb-Dokumente in der Sammlung Werner Spillmann* (Basel: Schwabe)
— Waller, R., 1686. 'A Catalogue of Simple and Mixt Colours, with a Specimen of each Colour prefixt to its proper Name', *Philosophical Transactions of the Royal Society* 16, 24–32

SOURCES OF ILLUSTRATIONS.

2 © The Trustees of The Natural History Museum, London; **6–7** *Werner's Nomenclature of Colours*, Patrick Syme, 1821; **8–9** Geoscientific collections, TU Berg-akademie Freiberg; **10–11** MS Typ 55.9 (43). Houghton Library, Harvard University; **12–13** Tennants Auctioneers, North Yorkshire; **14–15** © The Trustees of the Natural History Museum, London **17** Wellcome Library, London; **18al, 18ar** © The Trustees of the Natural History Museum, London; **18bl, 18br** *Entwurf einer allgemeinen Farbenverein*, Jacob Christian Schäffer, 1769; **21al** By permission of the Royal Irish Academy © RIA; **21ar** Geoscientific collections, TU Bergakademie Freiberg; **21b** The Picture Art Collection/Alamy Stock Photo; **22al** *Handbuch des oryktognostischen Theils der Mineralogie*, Johann Friedrich Wilhelm Widenmann, 1794; **22ar** *Versuch einer Mineralogie*, Franz Joseph Anton Estner, 1794; **22b** *Méthode analytique des fossiles, fondée sur leurs caractères extérieurs*, Henri Struve, 1797; **25al, 25ar** *Versuch eines Farbensystems*, Ignaz Schiffermüller, 1772; **25bl, 25br** *A Treatise on Diamonds*, John Mawe, 1823; **26al** *A Treatise on the External Characters of Minerals*, Robert Jameson, 1805; **26ar** © National Gallery of Scotland; **26b** David Rumsey Map Collection, David Rumsey Map Center, Stanford Libraries; **29al** VTR/Alamy Stock Photo; **29ar** agefotostock/Alamy Stock Photo; **29bl, 29br** *Werner's Nomenclature of Colours*, Patrick Syme, 1821; **30al** *On Colour, and on the Necessity for a General Diffusion of Taste Among all Classes*, John Gardner Wilkinson, 1858; **30ar** *Chromotaxia seu nomenclator colorum polyglottus additis speciminibus coloratis ad usum botanicorum et zoologorum*, Pier Andrea Saccardo, 1894; **30bl, 30br** *A Nomenclature of Colors for Naturalists*, Robert Ridgway, 1886; **36** *Birds of America*, Vols. I–IV, John James Audubon, 1827–1838; **38–40** *Werner's Nomenclature of Colours*, Patrick Syme, 1821; **41** Private Collection; **44a** *Birds of Europe*, Vol. 5, John Gould, 1832–37; **44bl** *Neerland's Plantentuin*, Cornelis Antoon Jan Abraham Oudemans, 1865; **44br** *The Mineral Kingdom*, Vol. 2, Reinhard Brauns, 1912; **45a** *British Oology*, William Chapman Hewitson, 1833; **45bl** © The Trustees of the British Museum; **45br** *British Mineralogy*, James Sowerby, 1802–17; **46a** *Birds of Europe*, Vol. 5, John Gould, 1832–37; **46bl** *Billeder af Nordens Flora*, A. Mentz, C.H. Ostenfeld, 1917; **46br** *Naturgeschichte des Tier- Pflanzen- und Mineralreichs*, Gotthilf Heinrich von Schubert, 1886; **47a** *Birds of Europe*, Vol. 4, John Gould, 1832–37; **47bl** Leemage/Universal Images Group via Getty Images; **47br** *The Mineral Kingdom*, Johann Gottlob Kurr, 1859; **48a** *Birds of America*, Vols. I–IV, John James Audubon, 1827–38; **48bl** *Billeder af Nordens Flora*, A. Mentz, C. H. Ostenfeld, 1917; **48br** *Premier mémoire sur les kaolins ou argiles à porcelaine*, Alexandre Brongniart, 1839; **49a** *Birds of Great Britain*, Vol. 2, John Gould, 1862–73; **49bl** Art Collection/Alamy Stock Photo; **49br** *The World's Minerals*, Leonard Spencer, 1916; **50a** Wellcome Library, London; **50bl** *Billeder af Nordens Flora*, A. Mentz, C. H. Ostenfeld, 1917; **50br** *The Mineral Kingdom*, Vol. 2, Reinhard Brauns, 1912; **51a** *Birds of Great Britain*, Vol. 5, John Gould, 1862–73; **51bl** 'Grapes – White Hamburg', George Brookshaw, 1812; **51br** *The Mineral Kingdom*, Vol. 2, Reinhard Brauns, 1912; **54al** *Birds of Europe*, Vol. 3, John Gould, 1832–37; **54ar** Dorling Kindersley/UIG/Bridgeman Images; **54b** *Specimens of British Minerals*, Philip Rashleigh, 1797; **55al** *Birds of Great Britain*, Vol. 2, John Gould, 1862–73; **55ar** *British Phaenogamous Botany*, William Baxter, 1832–43; **55b** *The Mineral Kingdom*, Johann Gottlob Kurr, 1859; **56a** *Birds of Europe*, Vol. 2, John Gould, 1832–37; **56bl** *Deutschlands Flora in Abbildungen nach der Natur mit Beschreibungen*, Jacob Sturm, 1798; **56br** *A Treatise on Diamonds*, John Mawe, 1823; **57a** *Birds of Europe*, Vol. 5, John Gould, 1832–37; **57bl** Florilegius/Alamy Stock Photo; **57br** *British Mineralogy*, James Sowerby, 1802–17; **58a** *Birds of Great Britain*, Vol. 1, John Gould, 1862–73; **58bl** DEA/G. Cigolini/De Agostini via Getty Images; **58br** *Specimens of British Minerals*, Philip Rashleigh, 1797; **59al** *Birds of Europe*, Vol. 4, John Gould, 1832–37; **59ar** *Deutschlands Flora in Abbildungen nach der Natur mit Beschreibungen*, Jacob Sturm, 1798; **59b** *The Mineral Kingdom*, Vol. 2, Reinhard Brauns, 1912; **60al** *A Treatise on British Song-birds*, Patrick Syme, 1823; **60ar** Florilegius/Alamy Stock Photo; **60b** *The Mineral Kingdom*, Vol. 1, Reinhard Brauns, 1912; **61al** *Birds of Europe*, Vol. 3, John Gould, 1832–37; **61ar** *British Mineralogy*, James Sowerby, 1802–17; **61b** *Illustrationes florae Hispaniae insularumque Balearium*, Vol. 1 t.47, Heinrich Moritz Willkomm, 1886–92; **64a** *Birds of Great Britain*, John Gould, 1862–73; **64b** *The Mineral Kingdom*, Vol. 1, Reinhard Brauns, 1912; **65** *Neerland's Plantentuin*, Cornelis Antoon Jan Abraham Oudemans, 1865; **66a** *The Naturalist's Miscellany*, George Shaw, Frederick P. Nodder, 1789–1813; **66bl** Florilegius/Alamy Stock Photo; **66br** *The Mineral Kingdom*, Vol. 1, Reinhard Brauns, 1912; **67a** *Birds of Europe*, Vol. 4, John Gould, 1832–37; **67bl** *Phytanthoza iconographia*, Johann Wilhelm Weinmann, 1737; **67br** *The World's Minerals*, Leonard Spencer, 1816; **68** *Birds of Europe*, Vol. 5, John Gould, 1832–37; **69a** *Neerland's Plantentuin*, Cornelis Antoon Jan Abraham Oudemans, 1865; **69b** *The Mineral Kingdom*, Vol. 2, Reinhard Brauns, 1912; **70al** *The Book of Butterflies, Sphinxes and Moths*, Thomas Brown, 1832; **70ar** *Choix des plus belles fleurs*, Pierre-Joseph Redouté, 1833; **70b** *Specimens of British Minerals*, Philip Rashleigh, 1797; **71al** *British Butterflies*, James Duncan, 1840; **71ar** Florilegius/Alamy Stock Photo; **71b** *The Mineral Kingdom*, Johann Gottlob Kurr, 1859; **72a** *British Quadrupeds*, William MacGillivray, 1849; **72b** Wellcome Library, London; **73** Florilegius/Alamy Stock Photo; **75** *Encyclopédie, ou dictionnaire raisonné des sciences, des arts et des métiers*, Denis Diderot, Jean le Rond d'Alembert, 1751–1777; **77al, 77ar** *De re metallica libri XII*, Georgius Agricola, 1621; **77bl** *Physica subterranea profundam subterraneorum genesin*, Johann Joachim Becher, 1669; **77br** *Systema naturae*, Vol. 3, Carl Linneaus, 1735; **78–79** Reproduced by kind permission of the President and Fellows of Queens' College, Cambridge; **81a** *Versuch einer Geschichte von Flötz-Gebürgen*, Johann Gottlob Lehmann, 1756; **81bl, 81br** *Von den äusserlichen Kennzeichen der Fossilien*, Abraham Gottlob Werner, Leipzig, 1774; **82** Klassik Stiftung Weimar, HAAB, Ruppert 4789; **85al, 85ar** *Deliciae naturae selectae*, Georg Wolfgang Knorr, 1766; **85bl** *Familiar Lessons on Mineralogy and Geology*, John Mawe, 1826; **85br** *A Treatise on Diamonds*, John Mawe, 1823; **86al** David M Beach; **86ar** *Memoirs of the Wernerian Natural History Society*, Vol. 4, Wernerian Natural History Society, 1822; **86bl** Collector's cabinet drawer (Anonymous Dutch) © Centraal Museum, Utrecht; **86br** Private Collection; **88** *Birds of America*, Vols. I–IV, John James Audubon, 1827–1838; **90–91** *Werner's Nomenclature of Colours*, Patrick Syme, Edinburgh, 1821; **94a** Florilegius/Alamy Stock Photo; **94b** *Underground Life*, Louis Simonin, 1869; **95** Florilegius/Alamy Stock Photo; **96a** *Birds of Europe*, Vol. 5, John Gould, 1832–37; **96b** Florilegius/Alamy Stock Photo; **97** *Exotic Mineralogy*, James Sowerby, 1811; **98al** *Birds of New Guinea and the Adjacent Papuan Islands*, Vol. 2, John Gould, 1875–88; **98ar** *Deutschlands Flora in Abbildungen nach der Natur*, Jacob Sturm, 1798; **98b** *Exotic Mineralogy*, James Sowerby, 1811; **99al** *The Coleoptera of the British Islands*, Vol. 5, W.W. Fowler, 1891; **99ar** *Choix des plus belles fleurs*, Pierre-Joseph Redouté, 1833; **99b** *Specimens of British Minerals*, Philip Rashleigh, 1797; **100al** *A Selection of the Birds of Brazil and Mexico*, William Swainson, 1841; **100ar** *The natural history of Carolina, Florida, and the Bahama Islands*, Mark Catesby, 1754; **100b** *British Mineralogy*, James Sowerby, 1802–17; **101al** *British Butterflies*, James Duncan, 1840; **101ar** The Natural History Museum/Alamy Stock Photo; **101b** *The World's Minerals*, Leonard Spencer, 1916; **102al** 510 Collection/Alamy Stock Photo; **102ar** bauhaus1000; **102b** *Naturgeschichte des Tier- Pflanzen- und Mineralreichs*, Gotthilf Heinrich von Schubert, 1886; **103al** *Birds of Great Britain*, Vol. 3, John Gould, 1862–73; **103ar** *Favourite Flowers of Garden and Greenhouse*, Edward Step, 1896; **103b** *Gems and Precious Stones of North America*, George Frederick Kunz, 1890; **104al** *Gleanings of Natural History*, George Edwards, 1758; **104ar** *Phytanthoza iconographia*, Vol. 2, Johann Wilhelm Weinmann, 1737; **104b** *Specimens of British Minerals*, Philip Rashleigh, 1797; **105al** *British Butterflies*, James Duncan, 1840; **105ar** *The Botanical Magazine*, Vols. 1–2, 1787–89; **105b** *Gems and Precious Stones of North America*, George Frederick Kunz, 1890; **106** *Birds of Europe*, Vol. 3, John Gould, 1832–37; **107a** *Flora graeca*, Vol. 6, John Sibthorp, James Smith, 1828; **107b** *The Mineral Kingdom*, Johann Gottlob Kurr, 1859; **110al** Album/Alamy Stock Photo; **110ar** *Flora parisiensis*, Pierre Bulliard, 1776–1783; **110b** *The Mineral Kingdom*, Vol. 2, Reinhard Brauns, 1912; **111a** *De Uitlandsche Kapellen: Voorkomende in de Drie Waereld-deelen Asia, Africa en America*, Vol. 3, Pieter Cramer, Caspar Stoll, 1782; **111bl** *Edwards's Botanical Register*, Vol. 23, John Lindley, 1829–47; **111br** *The Mineral Kingdom*, Vol. 2, Reinhard Brauns, 1912; **112al** *Birds of New Guinea and the Adjacent Papuan Islands*, Vol. 2, John Gould, 1875–88; **112ar** *Choix des plus belles fleurs*, Pierre-Joseph Redouté, 1833; **112b** *Gems and precious stones of North America*, George Frederick Kunz, 1890; **113a** *The Coleoptera of the British Islands*, W. W. Fowler, Vol. 4, 1891; **113bl** *Medical Botany*, Vol. 2, William Woodville, 1832; **113br** *The Mineral Kingdom*, Johann Gottlob Kurr, 1859; **114al** *British Butterflies*, James Duncan, 1840; **114ar** *The Ladies' Flower-Garden of Ornamental Perennials*, Vol. 2, Jane Loudon, 1849; **114b** *The Mineral Kingdom*, Johann Gottlob Kurr, 1859; **115al** *Birds of New Guinea and the Adjacent Papuan Islands*, Vol. 2, John Gould, 1875–88; **115ar** © Florilegius/Mary Evans; **115b** *British Mineralogy*, Vol. 1, James Sowerby, 1802–17; **116al** ilbusca; **116ar** *Choix des plus belles fleurs*, Pierre-Joseph Redouté, 1833; **116b** *The Mineral Kingdom*, Vol. 1, Reinhard Brauns, 1912; **117al** *The Zoology of the Voyage of HMS Sulphur*, Richard Brinsley Hinds, Vol. 1, 1843; **117ar** *Belgique horticole*, Vol. 6, Charles Morren, 1856; **117b** *Specimens of British Minerals*, Philip Rashleigh, 1797; **118al** Florilegius/Alamy Stock Photo; **118ar** *Choix des plus belles fleurs*, Pierre-Joseph Redouté, 1833; **118b** *The World's Minerals*, Leonard Spencer, 1916; **119al** Florilegius/Alamy Stock Photo; **119ar** *Icones plantarum medicinalium*, Vol. 5, J. Zorn, 1779; **119b** *Familiar Lessons on Mineralogy and Geology*, John Mawe, 1826; **120** *British Butterflies*, James Duncan, 1840; **121a** *Neerland's Plantentuin*, Cornelis Antoon Jan Abraham Oudemans, 1865; **121b** *A Popular Treatise on Gems*, Lewis Feuchtwanger, 1859; **123al** *The Natural History of British Birds*, Vol. 1, Edward Donovan, 1794; **123ar** *The Natural History of British Birds*, Vol. 4, Edward Donovan, 1794; **123bl, 123br** Florilegius/Alamy Stock Photo; 124–125 Tennants Auctioneers; **126** CUL DAR 44: 13, Reproduced by kind permission of the Syndics of Cambridge University Library; **128–129** © The Trustees of The Natural History Museum, London; **131a** © The Trustees of The Natural History Museum, London; **131bl, 131br** Historic England Archive; **132–133** © The Trustees of The Natural History Museum, London; **134a** Album/Alamy Stock Photo; **134bl, 134br** *Journal of a Second Voyage for the Discovery of a North-west Passage from the Atlantic to the Pacific*, William Edward Parry, 1825; **136–137** *British Oology*, William Chapman Hewitson, 1833; **139al** *Zoology of New Holland*, Vol. 1, George Shaw, 1794; **139ar** *A new elucidation of colours, original prismatic, and material*, James Sowerby, 1809; **139bl, 139br** *An Exposition of English Insects*, Moses Harris, 1776; **140–141** © The Trustees of The Natural History Museum, London; **142al, 142ar** *A History of North American Birds*, Vol. 2, Spencer Fullerton Baird, Robert Ridgway, Thomas Mayo Brewer, 1905; **142bl, 142br** *Color Standards and Color Nomenclature*, Robert Ridgway, 1912; **144** *Birds of America*, Vols. I–IV, John James Audubon, 1827–38; **146–147** *Werner's Nomenclature of Colours*, Patrick Syme, 1821; **150al** Florilegius/Alamy Stock Photo; **150ar** *Flora Batava*, Vol. 1, J. Kops, 1800; **150b** Historical Images Archive/Alamy Stock Photo; **151a** *De Uitlandsche Kapellen: Voorkomende in de Drie Waereld-deelen Asia, Africa en America*,

Vol. 4, Pieter Cramer, Caspar Stoll, 1782; **151bl** *Illustrations of the Flowering Plants and Ferns of the Falkland Islands*, E. M. Cotton, E. F. Vallentin-Bertrand, 1921; **151br** *British Mineralogy*, Vol. 3, James Sowerby, 1802–17; **152al** *British Butterflies*, James Duncan, 1840; **152ar** *Les Liliacées*, Vol. 7, Pierre-Joseph Redouté, 1805; **152b** Nastasic; **153al** The Reading Room/Alamy Stock Photo; **153ar** *The Flora Homoeopathica*, Edward Hamilton, 1852; **153b** *The World's Minerals*, Leonard Spencer, 1916; **154** *Birds of Asia*, Vol. 6, John Gould, 1850; **155a** Florilegius/Alamy Stock Photo; **155b** *Underground Life*, Louis Simonin, 1869; **156al** *Birds of America*, Vols. I–IV, John James Audubon, 1827–38; **156ar** *Medical Botany*, Vol. 3, William Woodville, 1832; **156b** *The Mineral Kingdom*, Johann Gottlob Kurr, 1859; **157al** *The Moths of the British Isles*, Richard South, 1920; **157ar** PhotoStock-Israel/Alamy Stock Photo; **157b** The Palmer; **158a** *Birds of Europe*, Vol. 5, John Gould, 1832–37; **158b** *Gems and Precious Stones of North America*, George Frederick Kunz, 1890; **159** *Neerland's Plantentuin*, Cornelis Antoon Jan Abraham Oudemans, 1865; **162al** *Beetles in Russia and Western Europe*, Georgiy Jacobson, 1905; **162ar** *Billeder af Nordens Flora*, A. Mentz, C. H. Ostenfeld, 1917; **162b** Private Collection; **163a** *Birds of Europe*, Vol. 5, John Gould, 1832–37; **163bl** © Florilegius/Mary Evans; **163br** *The Mineral Kingdom*, Vol. 2, Reinhard Brauns, 1912; **164al** *British Butterflies*, James Duncan, 1840; **164ar** *American Medical Botany*, Jacob Bigelow, 1817; **164b** *Exotic Mineralogy*, James Sowerby, 1811; **165a** *Birds of Great Britain*, Vol. 5, John Gould, 1862–73; **165bl** Florilegius/Alamy Stock Photo; **165br** *The Mineral Kingdom*, Johann Gottlob Kurr, 1859; **166a** *De Uitlandsche Kapellen: Voorkomende in de Drie Waereld-deelen Asia, Africa en America*, Pieter Cramer, Caspar Stoll, 1782; **166bl** © Florilegius/Mary Evans; **166br** *The World's Minerals*, Leonard Spencer, 1916; **167a** *The Zoology of the Voyage of HMS Sulphur*, Vol. 2, Richard Brinsley Hinds, 1843; **167bl** *Edwards's Botanical Register*, Vol. 25, John Lindley, 1829–47; **167br** *The World's Minerals*, Leonard Spencer, 1916; **168** The Picture Art Collection/Alamy Stock Photo; **169a** Pictures Now/Alamy Stock Photo; **169b** Bilwissedition Ltd. & Co. KG/Alamy Stock Photo; **170** *Birds of Great Britain*, Vol. 3, John Gould, 1862–73; **171a** © Florilegius/Mary Evans; **171b** *The Mineral Kingdom*, Vol. 1, Reinhard Brauns, 1912; **173al, 173ar** © National Gallery of Scotland; **173bl, 173br** *A Botanical Drawing-book*, James Sowerby, 1788; **174al** *A New Treatise on Flower Painting*, George Brookshaw, 1818; **174ar** *A Series of Progressive Lessons Intended to Elucidate the Art of Flower Painting in Water Colours*, 1824; **174bl** *Lessons in Flower Painting*, James Andrews, 1836; **174br** *A New Elucidation of Colours, Original Prismatic, and Material*, James Sowerby, 1809; **176–177** MS Am 1118.11. Houghton Library, Harvard University; **179al** The Natural History Museum/Alamy Stock Photo; **179ar** *Systema naturae*, Vol. 10, Carl Linnaeus, 1758; **179bl** *Grundriss der Kräuterkunde zu Vorlesungen entworfen*, Carl Ludwig Willdenow, 1792; **179br** *The Principles of Botany, and of Vegetable Physiology*, Carl Ludwig Willdenow, 1805; **180–181** *The Botanical Register*, Vol. 5, James Ridgway, Sydenham Edwards, 1819; **182a** Ronald M. Bodoh; **182b** © National Gallery of Scotland; **184–185** © The Trustees of The Natural History Museum, London; **187a** © bpk/Staatsbibliothek zu Berlin; **187bl** *Termini botanici iconibus illustrati*, Friedrich Gottlob Hayne, 1807; **187br** © bpk/Staatsbibliothek zu Berlin; **188al** *Zur Geschichte, Cultur und Classification der Georginen oder Dahlien*, Wilhelm Gerhard, Leipzig, 1836; **188ar** *Traité sur la culture des oeillets*, Ragonot-Godefroy, 1842; **188bl** *Chromotaxia*, Pier Andrea Saccardo, 1894; **188br** *Répertoire de couleurs pour aider à la détermination des couleurs des fleurs, des feuillages et des fruits*, René Oberthür, Henri Dauthenay, 1905; **190** *Birds of America*, Vols. I–IV, John James Audubon, 1827–38; **192–194** *Werner's Nomenclature of Colours*, Patrick Syme, 1821; **195** Private Collection; 198al Florilegius/Alamy Stock Photo; **198ar** © Florilegius/Mary Evans; **198b** *The World's Minerals*, Leonard Spencer, 1916; **199al** *A Treatise on British Song-birds*, Patrick Syme, 1823; **199ar** *Billeder af Nordens Flora*, Vol. 1, A. Mentz, C.H. Ostenfeld, 1917; **199b** *Specimens of British Minerals*, Philip Rashleigh, 1797; **200a** Album/Alamy Stock Photo; **200bl** U.S. Department of Agriculture Pomological Watercolor Collection. Rare and Special; Collections, National Agricultural Library, Beltsville, MD 20705; **200br** *The World's Minerals*, Leonard Spencer, 1916; **201a** Florilegius/Alamy Stock Photo; **201bl** © The Robin Symington Collection/Mary Evans Picture Library; **201br** *Underground Life*, Louis Simonin, 1869; **202al** *Birds of Great Britain*, Vol. 3, John Gould, 1862–73; **202ar** © Florilegius/Mary Evans; **202b** *The Mineral Kingdom*, Vol. 1, Reinhard Brauns, 1912; **203a** *Birds of Australia*, Vol. 7, John Gould, 1840–48; **203bl** *Edwards's Botanical Register*, Vol. 23, John Lindley, 1829–47; **203br** *British Mineralogy*, Vol. 2, James Sowerby, 1802–17; **204** Florilegius/Alamy Stock Photo; **205a** *Choix des plus belles fleurs*, Pierre-Joseph Redouté, 1833; **205b** *Exotic Mineralogy*, Vol. 2, James Sowerby, 1811; **208al** Dittrick Medical History Center, Case Western Reserve University; **208ar** Album/Alamy Stock Photo; **208b** *British Mineralogy*, Vol. 1, James Sowerby, 1802–17; **209al** *Birds of New Guinea and the Adjacent Papuan Islands*, Vol. 1, John Gould, 1875–88; **209ar** Historic Images/Alamy Stock Photo; **209b** *The Mineral Kingdom*, Vol. 2, Reinhard Brauns, 1912; **210a** *The Quadrupeds of North America*, Vol. 3, John James Audubon, 1849; **210bl** *Herbarium Blackwellianum*, Vol. 2, E. Blackwell, 1754; **210br** *Specimens of British Minerals*, Philip Rashleigh, 1797; **211al** *The Book of Butterflies, Sphinxes and Moths*, Vol. 2, Thomas Brown, 1832; **211ar** *Billeder af Nordens Flora*, Vol. 2, A. Mentz, C.H. Ostenfeld, 1917; **211b** *British Mineralogy*, Vol. 4, James Sowerby, 1802–17; **212al** *Birds of New Guinea and the Adjacent Papuan Islands*, Vol. 1, John Gould, 1875–88; **212ar** *Flore Médicale*, Vol. 2, François-Pierre Chaumeton, 1833; **212b** *The Mineral Kingdom*, Vol. 2, Reinhard Brauns, 1912; **213a** *Birds of Great Britain*, Vol. 2, John Gould, 1862–73; **213bl** *Phytanthoza iconographia*, Vol. 1, Johann Wilhelm Weinmann, 1737; **213br** *Die Mineralien: in 64 Colorirten Abbildungen Nach der Natur*, Johann Carl Weber, 1871; **214a** *Birds of Europe*, Vol. 5, John Gould, 1837; **214b** ZU_09; **215** Florilegius/Alamy Stock Photo; **218al** *Birds of Europe*, Vol. 2, John Gould, 1832–37; **218ar** *Billeder af Nordens Flora*, Vol. 2, A. Mentz, C. H. Ostenfeld, 1917; **218b** *The World's Minerals*, Leonard Spencer, 1916; **219al** *Birds of Great Britain*, Vol. 2, John Gould, 1862–73; **219ar** *Cistineae: The Natural Order of Cistus; Or Rock-rose*, Robert Sweet, 1830; **219b** *The World's Minerals*, Leonard Spencer, 1916; **220a** The Natural History Museum/Alamy Stock Photo; **220bl** *Etudes de fleurs et de fruits: peints d'après nature*, Henriette Antoinette Vincent, 1820; **220br** *British Mineralogy*, Vol. 1, James Sowerby, 1802–17; **221al** Album/Alamy Stock Photo; **221ar** *Edwards's Botanical Register*, Vol. 27, John Lindley, 1829–47; **221b** *Underground Life*, Louis Simonin, 1869; **222a** Bilderbuch für Kinder, Vol. 4, Freidrich Johann Bertuch, 1802; **222bl** *Familiar Indian Flowers*, Lena Lowis, 1878; **222br** *Exotic Mineralogy*, Vol. 2, James Sowerby, 1811; **223a, 223bl** Florilegius/Alamy Stock Photo; **223br** *Exotic Mineralogy*, Vol. 2, James Sowerby, 1811; **225**, *Traité complet de l'anatomie de l'homme*, Marc Jean Bourgery, 1831–54; **226** Geoscientific collections, TU Bergakademie Freiberg; **229, 230al, 230ar** Wellcome Library, London; **230bl** *Fasciculus Medicinae*, Johannes de Ketham, 1493; **230br** *Inquiry into the Nature and Treatment of Gravel, Calculus, and Other Diseases Connected with a Deranged Operations of the Urinary Organs*, William Prout, 1821, State Library of Victoria; **233** Wellcome Library, London; **234** *Instructions générales pour les recherches et observations anthropologiques*, Paul Broca, 1865; **236** *Birds of America*, Vols. I–IV, John James Audubon, 1827–38; **238–240** *Werner's Nomenclature of Colours*, Patrick Syme, 1821; **241** Private Collection; **244a** *Birds of Europe*, Vol. 3, John Gould, 1832–37; **244bl** *English Botany, or Coloured Figures of British Plants*, Vol. 7, J.E. Smith, 1863–99; **244br** *British Mineralogy*, Vol. 3, James Sowerby, 1802–17; **245a** *The Hemiptera Heteroptera of the British Islands*, Edward Saunders, 1892; **245bl** Mary Evans Picture Library; **245br** *The Mineral Kingdom*, Vol. 2, Reinhard Brauns, 1912; **246** *Birds of America*, Vols. I–IV, John James Audubon, 1827–38; **247a** *The Mineral Kingdom*, Johann Gottlob Kurr, 1859; **247b** *Afbeeldingen der artseny-gewassen*, Vol. 2, J. Zorn, P.L. Oskamp, 1796; **248** *Deliciae naturae selectae*, Vol. 1, Georg Wolfgang Knorr, 1766; **249a** *Herbarium Blackwellianum*, Vol. 2, E. Blackwell, 1754; **249b** *The World's Minerals*, Leonard Spencer, 1916; **250al** *Birds of Europe*, Vol. 3, John Gould, 1832–37; **250ar** *The Mineral Kingdom*, Vol. 1, Reinhard Brauns, 1912; **250b** *Pomologie française*, A. Poiteau, 1846; **251al** *Birds of Europe*, Vol. 3, John Gould, 1832–37; **251ar** *Flora Danica*, G. C. Oeder, 1761; **251b** *British Mineralogy*, Vol. 1, James Sowerby, 1802–17; **252a** Wellcome Library, London; **252bl** *Phytanthoza iconographia*, Vol. 2, Johann Wilhelm Weinmann, 1737; **252br** *British Mineralogy*, Vol. 1, James Sowerby, 1802–17; **253a** PhotoStock-Israel/Alamy Stock Photo; **253bl** *Die Rosen nach der Natur gezeichnet und coloriert mit kurzen botanischen Bestimmungen begleitet*, Carl Gottlob Rössig, 1802–20; **253br** Private Collection; **254a** *British Butterflies*, James Duncan, 1840; **255a** *Allgemeines teutsches Garten-Magazin*, Vol. 6, 1804–11; **255b** *The Mineral Kingdom*, Johann Gottlob Kurr, 1859; **258a** *Birds of New Guinea and the Adjacent Papuan Islands*, Vol. 3, John Gould, 1875–88; **258bl** Historic Images/Alamy Stock Photo; **258br** *The Mineral Kingdom*, Vol. 2, Reinhard Brauns, 1912; **259a** *The Zoology of the Voyage of HMS Sulphur*, Vol. 1, Richard Brinsley Hinds, 1843; **259bl** *Edwards's Botanical Register*, Vol. 15, John Lindley, 1829–47; **259br** Private Collection; **260al** *Gleanings of Natural History*, Vol. 2, George Edwards, 1758; **260ar** LLP collection/Alamy Stock Photo; **260b** *The Mineral Kingdom*, Vol. 2, Reinhard Brauns, 1912; **261al** The Natural History Museum/Alamy Stock Photo; **261ar** *Bilderbuch für Kinder*, Freidrich Johann Bertuch, 1802; **261b** *Gems and Precious Stones of North America*, George Frederick Kunz, 1890; **262a** *Gleanings of Natural History*, Vol. 2, George Edwards, 1758; **262bl** *British Phaenogamous Botany*, William Baxter, 1832–43; **262br** *Underground Life*, Louis Simonin, 1869; **263al** Wellcome Library, London; **263ar** *The New Botanic Garden*, Sydenham Edwards, 1812; **263b** *The Mineral Kingdom*, Johann Gottlob Kurr, 1859; **264al** *The Zoology of the Voyage of HMS Sulphur*, Vol. 1, Richard Brinsley Hinds, 1843; **264ar** *Medical Botany*, Vol. 2, William Woodville, 1832; **264b** *Specimens of British Minerals*, Philip Rashleigh, 1797; **265al** *Histoire naturelle des oiseaux de paradis et des rolliers*, François Le Vaillant, 1806; **265ar** *Flora Parisiensis*, Vol. 1, Pierre Bulliard, 1776; **265b** *British Mineralogy*, Vol. 1, James Sowerby, 1802–17; **266a** *Birds of Great Britain*, Vol. 5, John Gould, 1862–73; **266b** *The Mineral Kingdom*, Vol. 1, Reinhard Brauns, 1912; **267** *The New Botanic Garden*, Sydenham Edwards, 1812; **270al** Album/Alamy Stock Photo; **270ar** *Svensk Botanik*, Vol. 8, J. W. Palmstruch, 1807; **270b** *British Mineralogy*, Vol. 1, James Sowerby, 1802–17; **271al** Florilegius/Alamy Stock Photo; **271ar** © Florilegius/Mary Evans; **271b** SSPL/Getty Images; **272a** *Birds of Great Britain*, Vol. 1, John Gould, 1862–73; **272bl** The History Collection/Alamy Stock Photo; **272br** *British Mineralogy*, Vol. 4, James Sowerby, 1802–17; **273al** Florilegius/Alamy Stock Photo; **273ar** *Traité des arbres et arbustes*, Vol. 2, H. L. Duhamel du Monceau, 1804; **273b** *The World's Minerals*, Leonard Spencer, 1916; **274al** *Birds of Europe*, Vol. 3, John Gould, 1832–37; **274ar** *Billeder af Nordens Flora*, A. Mentz, C.H. Ostenfeld, 1917; **274b** *The Mineral Kingdom*, Johann Gottlob Kurr, 1859; **275a** *Birds of Great Britain*, Vol. 4, John Gould, 1862–73; **275bl** *Billeder af Nordens Flora*, A. Mentz, C.H. Ostenfeld, 1917; **275br** *The Mineral Kingdom*, Vol. 2, Reinhard Brauns, 1912; **276a** *Birds of Europe*, Vol. 3, John Gould, 1832–37; **276bl** Historic Images/Alamy Stock Photo; **276br** *The Mineral Kingdom*, Vol. 2, Reinhard Brauns, 1912; **277a** *Birds of Great Britain*, Vol. 5, John Gould, 1862–73; **277bl** *Phytanthoza iconographia*, Vol. 2, Johann Wilhelm Weinmann, 1737; **277br** *Specimens of British Minerals*, Philip Rashleigh, 1797; **278a** Florilegius/Alamy Stock Photo; **278bl** LLP collection/Alamy Stock Photo; **278br** *The World's Minerals*, Leonard Spencer, 1916; **279al** *Birds of Europe*, Vol. 1, John Gould, 1832–37; **279ar** Florilegius/Alamy Stock Photo; **279b** *Gems and Precious Stones of North America*, George Frederick Kunz, 1890; **280a** *Birds of Great Britain*, Vol. 5, John Gould, 1862–73; **280b** *The Mineral Kingdom*, Johann Gottlob Kurr, 1859; **281** Album/Alamy Stock Photo

Front cover, left to right, *Birds of Europe*, John Gould, Vol. 5, 1832–37; *Exotic Mineralogy*, James Sowerby, 1811; *English Botany*, J. T. B. Syme and James Sowerby, Vol. 2, 1864; *The Botanical Magazine*, Vol. 1, 1788; *The Mineral Kingdom*, Johann Gottlob Kurr, 1859; *Birds of Australia*, John Gould, Vol. 5, 1840–48; *Neerland's Plantentuin*, Cornelis Antoon Jan Abraham Oudemans, Vol. 2, 1865; *Birds of Great Britain*, John Gould, Vol. 5, 1862–73; *Birds of Great Britain*, John Gould, Vol. 3, 1862–73; *Choix des plus belles fleurs*, Pierre-Joseph Redouté, 1833; *Deliciae naturae selectae*, Georg Wolfgang Knorr, Vol. 1, 1766; *Edwards's Botanical Register*, Vol. 15, John Lindley, 1829–47.

Back cover *Birds of America*, John James Audubon, 1827–38.

ACKNOWLEDGMENTS.

Patrick Baty: Imagine sharing a house with a non-German speaker who has set himself the task of translating large parts of an eighteenth-century technical work printed in the unfamiliar German *Fraktur* or Gothic script. Without the support of my wife, Alex, shielding me from the real world and offering words of encouragement, I would have found it quite impossible to complete the task. To her is due an enormous thank you.

Thanks also go to Tristan de Lancey, Jane Laing, Phoebe Lindsley, Isabel Jessop, Sarah Vernon-Hunt and Susanna Ingram at Thames & Hudson.

Peter Davidson: I would like to thank Mary Nemeth, Joyce Dixon, Giulia Simonini and Alison Turnbull for being instrumental in building up my knowledge of *Werner's Nomenclature of Colours*. Thanks also go to my friends and colleagues at National Museums Scotland, the National Library of Scotland, Edinburgh University Library and Technische Universität Bergakademie Freiberg. Finally, I would like to record my personal thanks to my dear friend Robin Hansen who suggested me to the publishers.

Elaine Charwat: I would like to thank the Oxford University Museum of Natural History, its people, animals and objects, for sharing their knowledge and stories, Isabelle Charmantier at the Linnean Society for her advice, and Lukas, for sharing the journey.

Giulia Simonini: I would like to thank Francesca Terzi, Hans Walter Lack, Friedrich Steinle, Peter Davidson, Joyce Dixon, Mary Nemeth and André Karliczek.

André Karliczek: I would like to thank John Vivian for providing the English translation of my essay, as well as Friedrich Steinle, Giulia Simonini and Konrad Scheurmann.

The *publisher* would like to thank Stephen Atkinson and the team at the Natural History Museum, London, for their help identifying species, and Fergus Egan, Oliver Nelmes and Alpana Sajip for their research work.

ABOUT THE CONTRIBUTORS.

Patrick Baty is the author of *The Anatomy of Colour* and the owner of specialist paint business Papers and Paints, London. He runs a consultancy that advises on the use of paint and colours in historic buildings and has worked with Dulux and Little Greene to develop ranges of traditional paint colours for English Heritage.

Peter Davidson is the Senior Curator of Minerals at National Museums Scotland. Here he manages the museum's mineral and meteorite collections, develops exhibitions for the museum and other institutions around the world, and conducts research into the history of mineralogy.

Elaine Charwat is currently conducting a doctoral research project into natural history models and casts as 'knowledge objects' at the Oxford University Museum of Natural History in collaboration with UCL; she has previously worked as Special Collections Librarian at University College Cork, and at the Linnean Society of London.

Giulia Simonini is a conservator, palaeographer and art historian, and is currently researching a Ph.D thesis on colour systems in eighteenth-century Europe at Technische Universität Berlin.

André Karliczek works on the development of colour standards, the theoretical medicine of the Enlightenment and evolutive and ecological influences on visual perception; he is a member of the German Optical Museum and part of the innovation project Cultur3D, which explores new possibilities for the 3D-modelling of cultural assets.

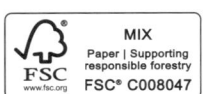

Published in North America 2021 in arrangement with Thames & Hudson Ltd., London, by Princeton University Press, 41 William Street, Princeton, New Jersey 08540

press.princeton.edu

First published in the United Kingdom in 2021 by Thames & Hudson Ltd, 181A High Holborn, London WC1V 7QX

Nature's Palette © 2021 Thames & Hudson Ltd, London

For image copyright information see pp. 286–7.

Designed by Daniel Street, Visual Fields

Library of Congress Control Number: 2020941844

ISBN 978-0-691-21704-8

Printed and bound in China by C&C Offset Printing Co. Ltd.

10 9 8 7 6 5 4

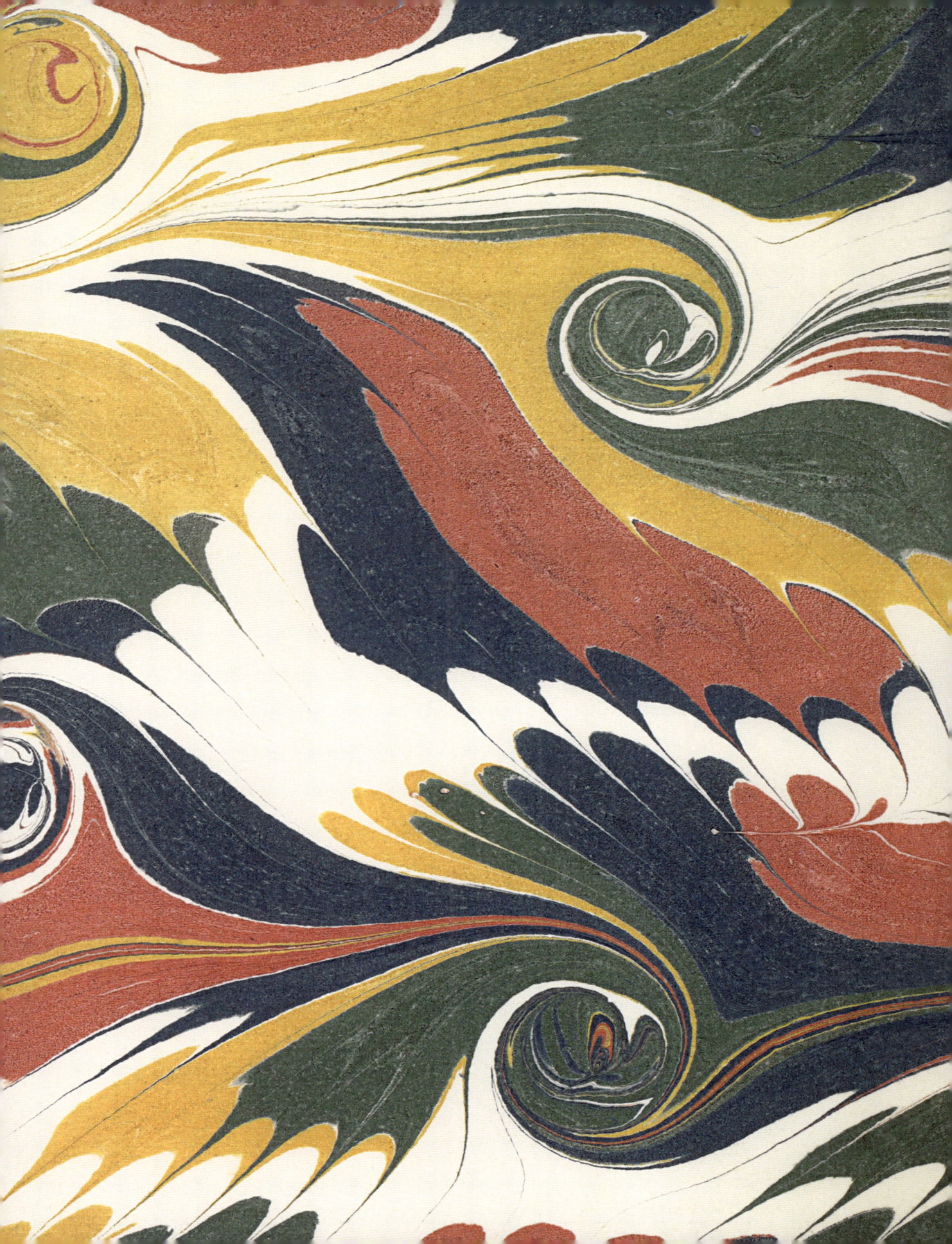

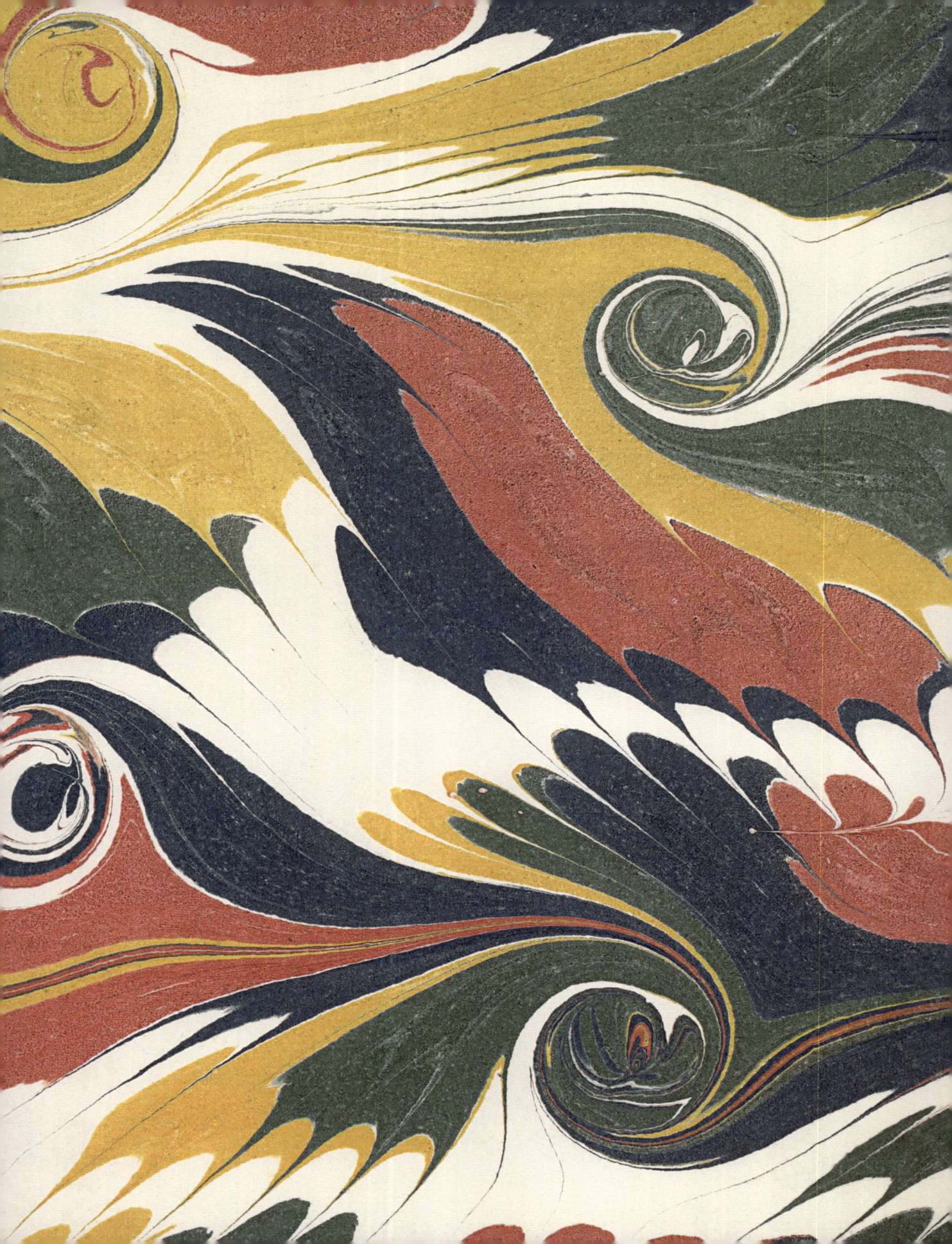